MODERN ENVIRONMENTAL DESIGN

A project primer for complex forms

ANDREW WATTS

Birkhäuser Newtecnic

CONTENTS

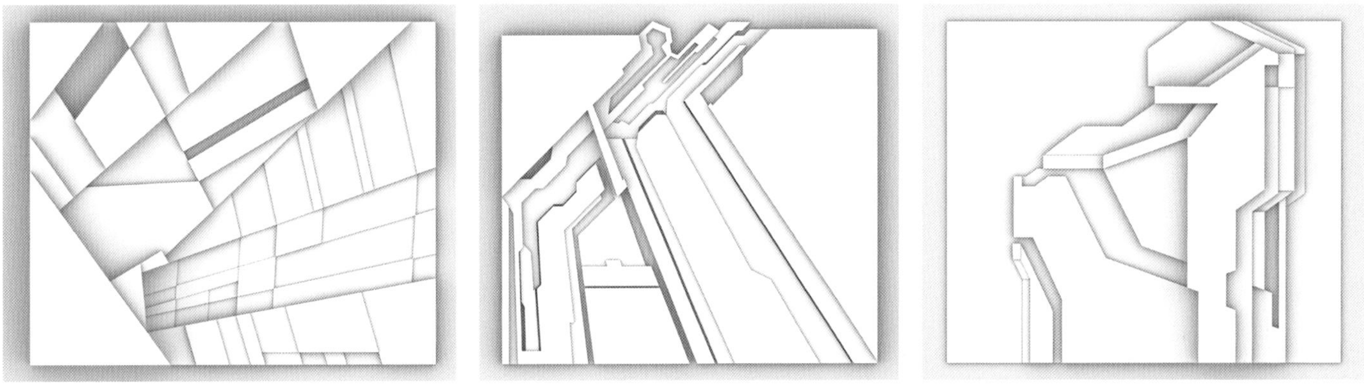

Examples of spatial and volumetric compositions used in projects, shown in low-relief. The compositions illustrate the use of overlaid volumes and spaces.

The example compositions shown here are independent of the strategies for environment, structure and spatial arrangements described for each project.

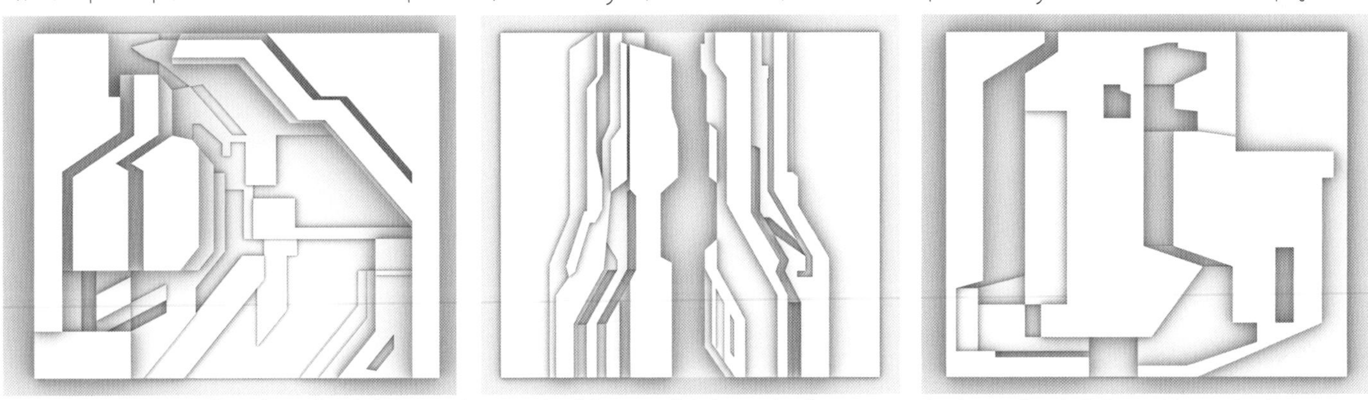

The compositions are independent of scale; being used across the full range of design tasks, from masterplanning to facade design and internal volumes.

Themes explored in this book

This book sets out 18 building design primers which explore the following themes:

- Greater levels of controlled daylight to interior spaces by reducing depth of floor plates.
- Controlled admission of sunlight to activity spaces.
- Open floor plates which suit natural cross ventilation.
- Services as active controls positioned near their point of use, including facade zones.
- Open spaces between blocks, linked by bridges.

The introductory texts to each project set out a specific theme which has been applied to the project. The principles of environments within buildings are explored through a specific text at the beginning of each project. The environmental controls described in this book are set either within the facade zone or within a specific 'support space' within each building. These controls aim to reduce energy consumption both during the construction and operation of buildings.

The projects in this book allow **greater controlled daylight into interior spaces by reducing the depth of floor plates** below that of what might be expected. This approach aims to provide a well-lit space adjacent to a window; while increasing the area of façade, the aim is to reduce the energy consumption of electrical lighting of the building in use.

Controlled admission of sunlight to activity spaces allows daylight to be drawn in through parts of the external envelope, such as at floor level. The exclusion of all direct sunlight can lead to a loss of light and shade in internal spaces.

The projects described have **open floor plates which suit natural cross ventilation**. These spaces are unobstructed by the need for services or internal circulation to occupy activity spaces. Ventilation ducts and associated equipment can be accommodated within facade zones.

Services as active controls are positioned near their point of use, including facade zones. This approach is an alternative to grouping services in areas which are remote from the main spaces. Servicing

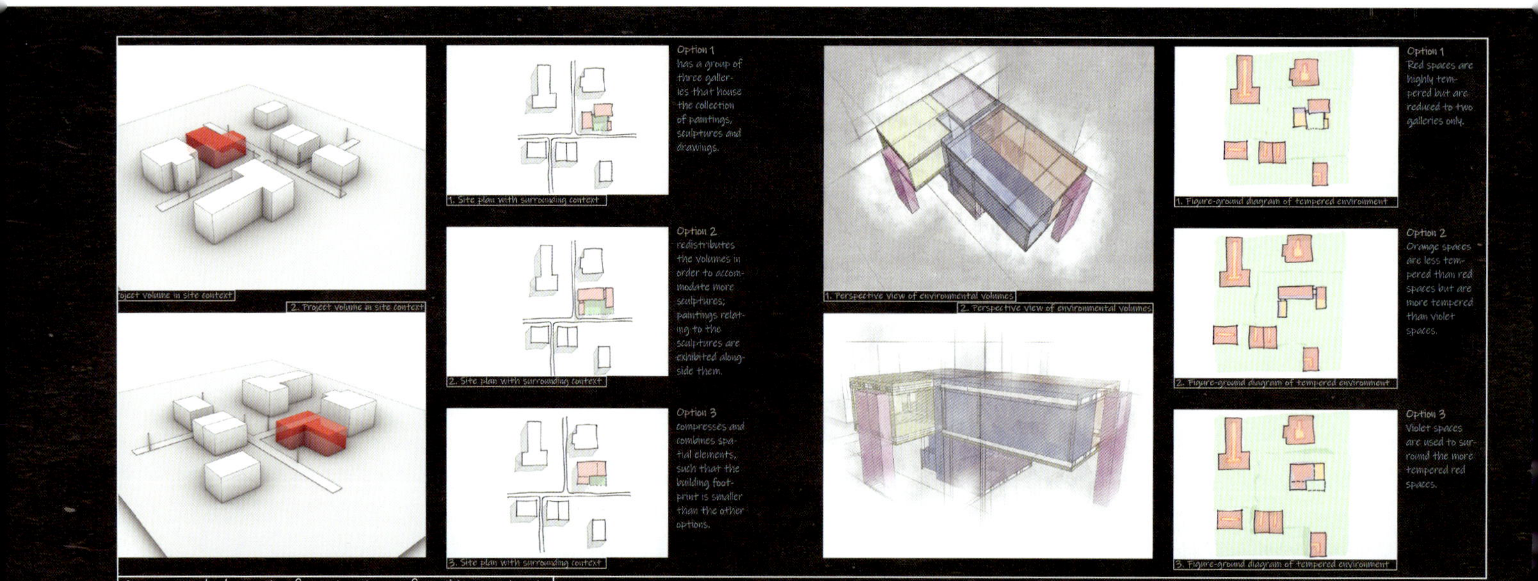

An example layout of a strategy for site context

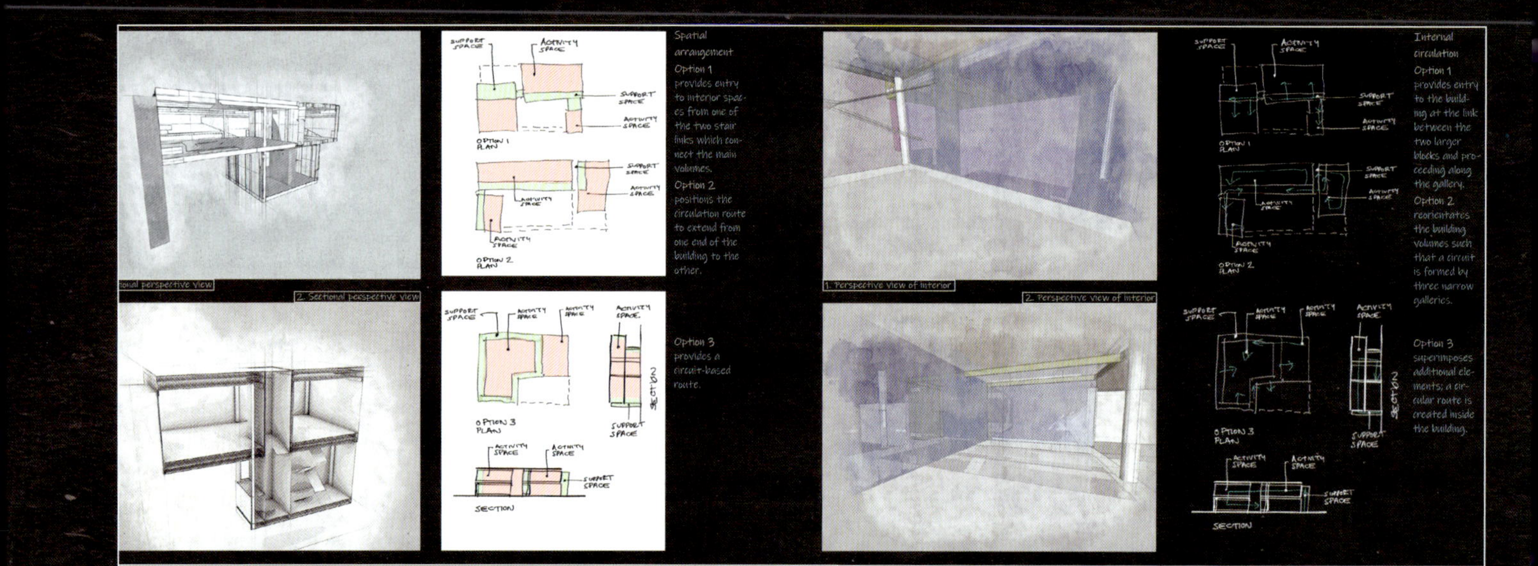

An example layout of a strategy for spatial arrangement and internal circulation

equipment is set outside the space where possible in order to enhance natural ventilation, daylight and solar control. The positioning of services equipment, set close to their point of use but within a separate space, allows clear floor plates to be created. Designs that would have required deep floor plates are divided into two or more constituent parts or 'blocks'. These buildings are set out with **open spaces between blocks**, linked by bridges which may be usable space in a building or could form circulation routes only. The spaces between adjacent blocks are external where possible in order to allow cross ventilation of the blocks.

Strategies for building design at an early stage of a project

This primer for building design projects, like its companion volume *Modern Structural Design*, sets out design strategies used in example buildings which have been designed by Newtecnic. The designs are theoretical versions, or generalised versions, of projects designed by Newtecnic. **Strategies have been used in the early stages of the designs shown in this book: site context, spatial arrangement, internal circulation, environment, structure and typical bays.** Each project demonstrates buildings of complex form which can be constructed from commercially available systems. The text for each strategy aims to illustrate themes from associated strategies for the same project; strategies are not 'siloed'. The general principles of these systems are set out in the *Modern Construction Handbook* (Birkhäuser, 2019) and *Modern Construction Envelopes* (Birkhäuser, 2019). These two books show how a technical understanding of systems can contribute to the creation of internal spaces and external forms, together with an environmental design which reduces – as much as possible – the energy consumption of buildings and well as the energy used in their construction. A reduced energy consumption includes an ability to recycle and reuse components and assemblies used in the construction of the building; this approach can result in building forms which look different from their predecessors as a result of the opportunities presented by construction technologies. This design approach does not begin from the point of view of providing technical

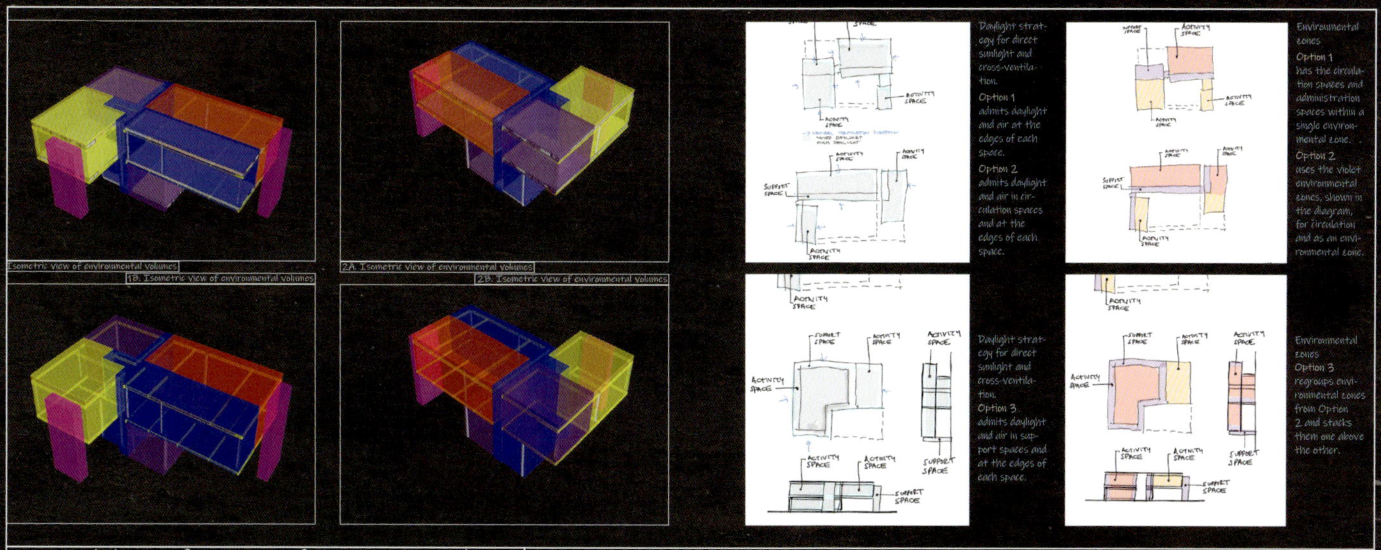

An example layout of a strategy for environmental design

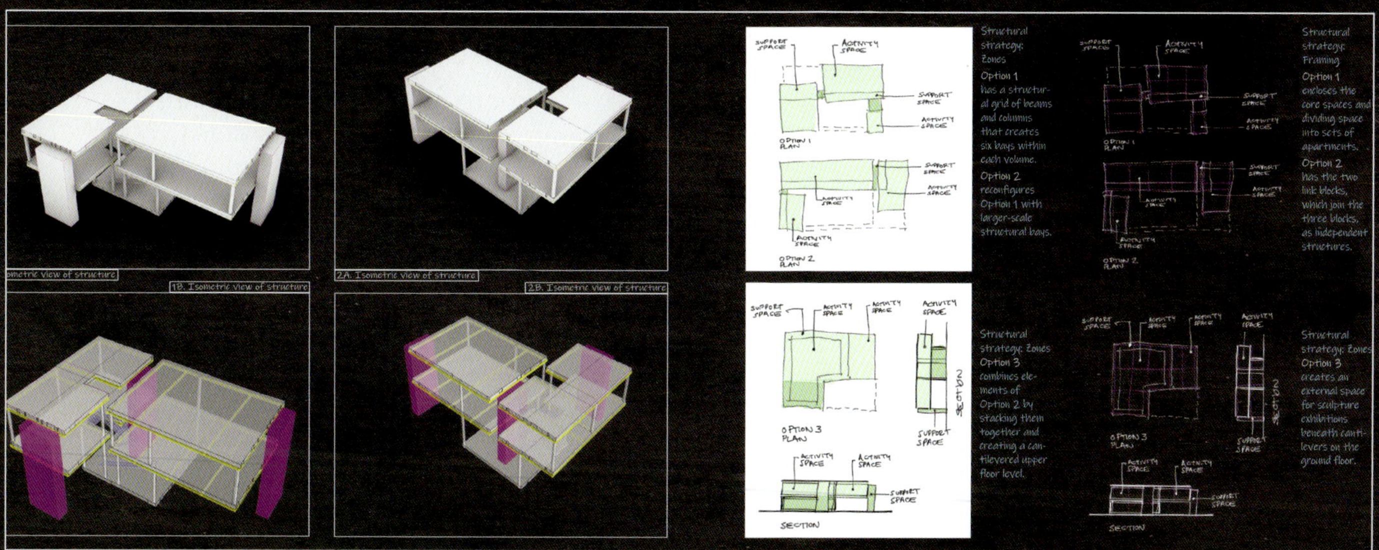

An example layout of a strategy for structural design

solutions that enable novel building forms to be realised, but instead uses technologies to create space through environment, structure, external envelopes and internal envelopes of spaces. A key aspect of this design approach is to integrate internal wall finishes with external envelopes; deploying construction technologies used for environmental design and for structural design.

The design strategies shown in this book focus on buildability, the energy consumption of the building when in use, and how well the building fits within the surrounding cityscape or landscape. The project examples illustrate outputs an **early stage** of a building design; how the environmental strategy might respond to the other strategies of spatial arrangement, internal circulation, structure and typical bay design, which are specific to the project. Each building design is explored through three options for each of the key aspects of **early stage** building design. An objective of each strategy is to optimise the materials used in the construction of a building and to optimise the energy required to operate the building when in use.

Design strategies

The environmental strategy integrates issues from the other strategies to create an early-stage design which informs the spatial and structural design. The environmental design can partly determine the approach taken to both structural and envelope design. The strategies for each of the projects draw general principles from each aspect of the building design and do not set out the specific conditions of any project, nor does the text elaborate on the specific layouts or construction systems chosen. Instead, general principles and wider issues within each design draw together information of interest to the reader.

Qualifying comments

The information set out in this book is intended to be a source of general information, not for specific application to any project. This book does not necessarily endorse or justify the strategies set out, since techniques and priorities in building design are in a continual state of change and development.

1. Perspective view of exterior

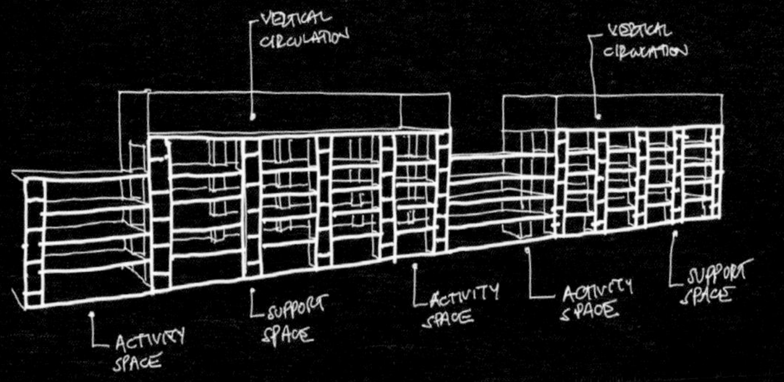

2. Perspective view of exterior

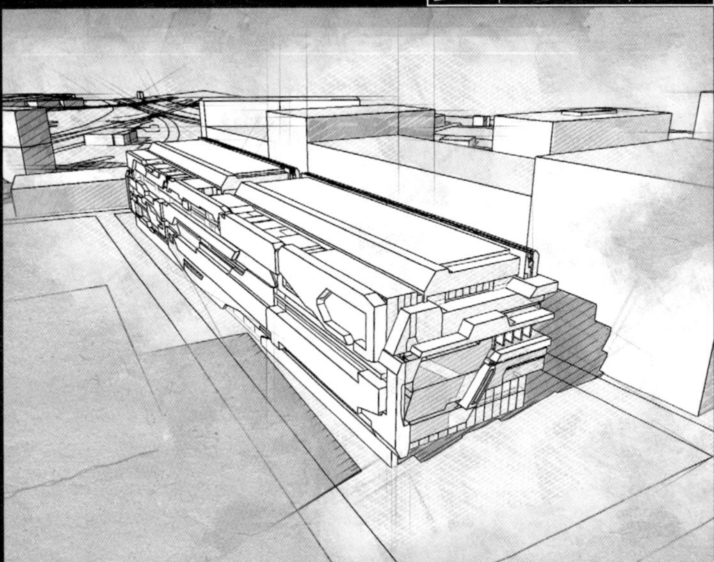

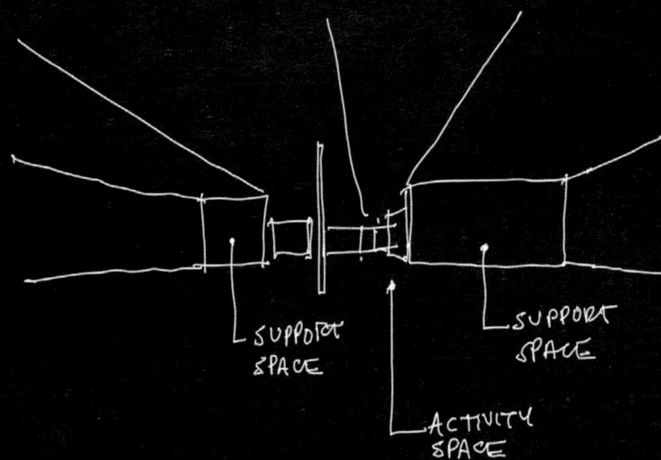

Environmental patterns of use

This building is required to be naturally ventilated for part of the time; mechanical ventilation and air conditioning are used to create a mixed-mode method of ventilation which provides the benefits of both fresh air and the benefits of a tempered environment in different spaces at the same time.

This approach is realised with the use of environmental zoning within the building. Spaces are grouped in accordance with their frequency of occupation, size and the numbers of people using those spaces. Each environmental zone, comprising either a group of spaces or a single large space, is connected by a set of mechanical and electrical services installations; arranged in grouped packages. This system is distributed around the building, such that the distance between the spaces being serviced and the equipment that services those spaces is as short as possible. A key aim is to reduce inefficiencies in the use of energy by optimising the energy requirement for individual spaces, reducing the need for ducts and electrical supply routes as much as possible. Adjacent spaces may be serviced very differently at the same times of day. The support spaces in this building are primarily rooms for air-handling units and boilers at roof level, together with washrooms, lifts/elevators and stairs set into cores. These service spaces require a level of environmental control which is not as closely controlled as that of the activity spaces; natural ventilation is used more frequently than is the case for activity spaces.

Activity spaces fulfil the functions that they are specifically created to provide, being served by equipment from adjacent support spaces. There is a clear differentiation between the geometry and arrangements of support spaces, with their pared-down simplicity, and the variety of forms used for activity space. Support spaces use the minimum arrangement required for moving around the building and for supplying mechanical and electrical services to the different geometries of activity spaces.

This approach is different from that of providing highly temperature-controlled circulation spaces and washrooms. Instead, support spac-

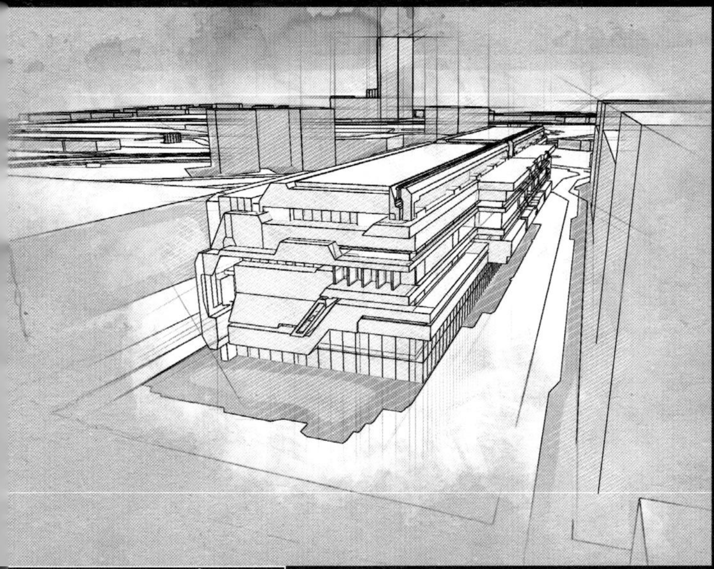

. Perspective view of exterior

4. Perspective view of exterior

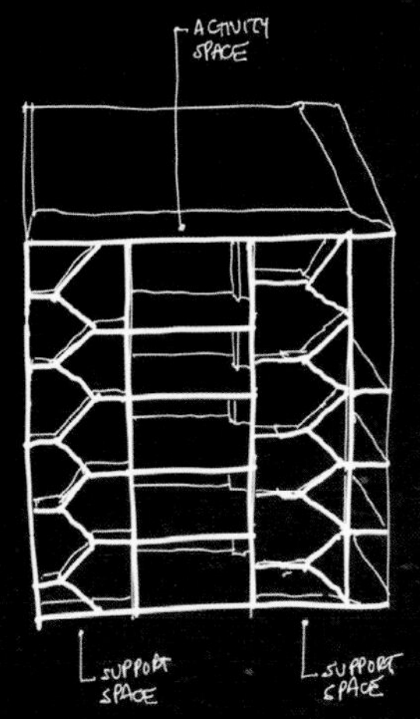

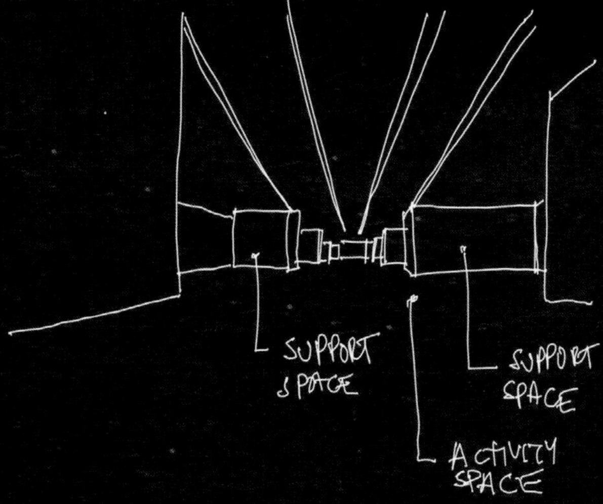

es are arranged with a geometrical simplicity that allows them to be arranged efficiently. As a result of circulation and activity space being separated, staircases, corridors and lifts/elevators form a part of support spaces rather than being set within primary spaces in order to allow activity spaces to be completely open floor plates. In support of this approach to spatial arrangement is the introduction of the 'user manual' that records 'patterns of use' of the environmental control systems. The requirements for heating, cooling, ventilation, solar control and electrical light is recorded in a manual through the use of an interactive program where building's patterns of use can be documented. The environmental control system can respond to the use and frequency of ventilation; adjusting itself to suit the way the building is used.

The building 'learns' from its own patterns of use, allowing each space to be serviced efficiently. For example, spaces can be ventilated mechanically or naturally, and be illuminated electrically or naturally in response not only to movement around the building but also to patterns of use within the building. Information is collected in the user manual through the use of the interactive program, which is essentially a program administered by each team within the building. The software program continuously updates itself through both current and historic patterns of use. This method ensures that the interiors of buildings remain both welcoming and efficient in their optimisation of temperature control and in the use of electrical light. The user manual aims to provide an evolving set of information that is connected directly to the building management system.

An approach to the environmental design of this project was to develop an integrated strategy of reducing energy consumption by following patterns of energy use, and looking at how those patterns could allow the building to reduce its own energy consumption without the need for the individual user or groups of users to determine which lights are turned on or off; which rooms are ventilated and at what times of day. Patterns of use of environmental control systems become part of a 'learning' process communicated through the user manual.

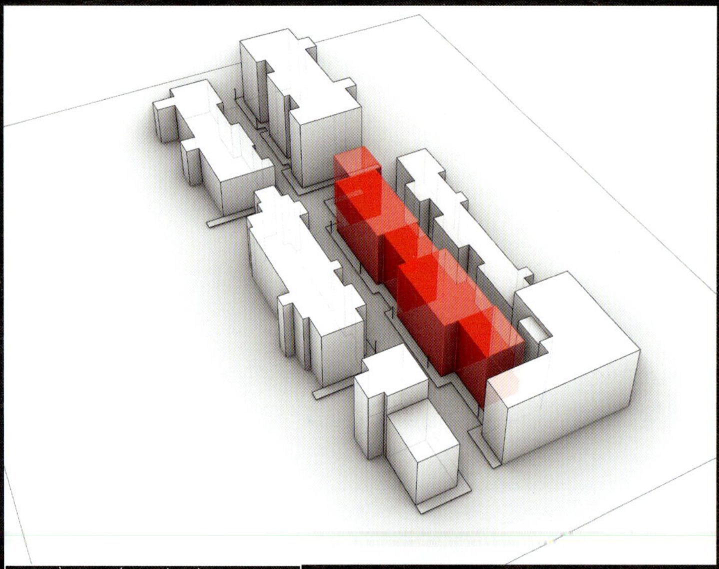

1. Project volume in site context

2. Project volume in site context

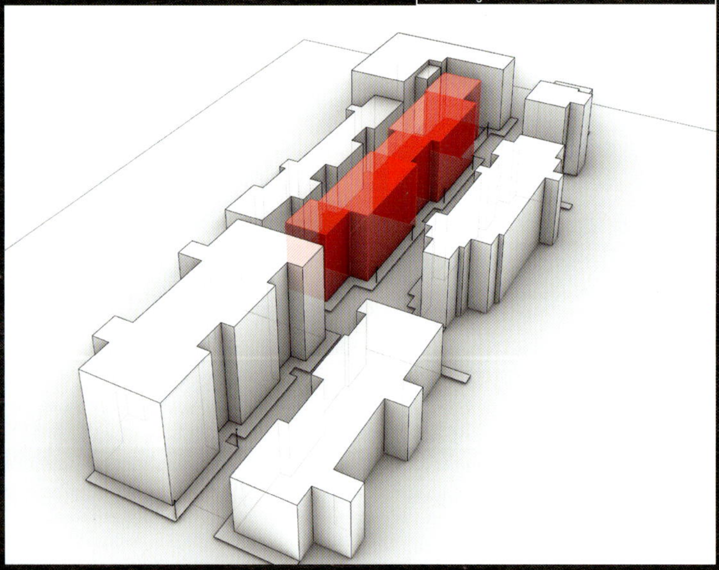

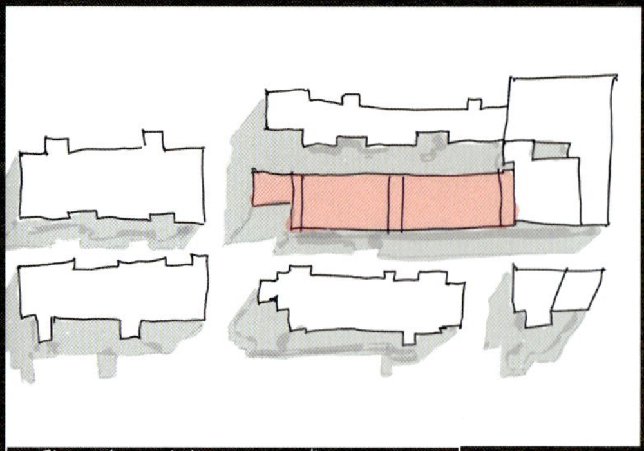

1. Site plan with surrounding context

Option 1 arranges the building as two main blocks which are separated by a service core in the middle as well as at each end.

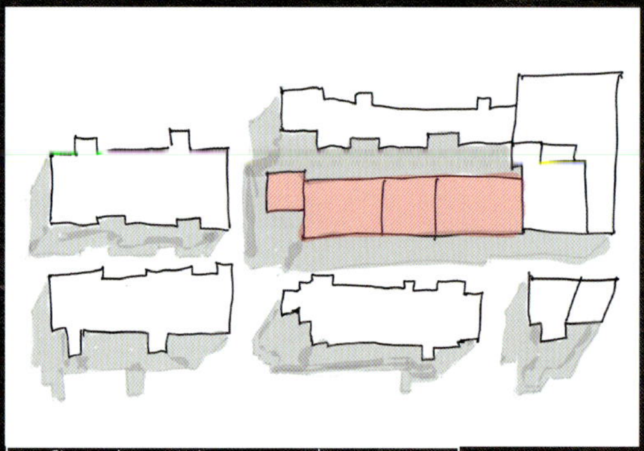

2. Site plan with surrounding context

Option 2 widens the central circulation space in order to add the functions of the main entrance to the college at ground floor level.

3. Site plan with surrounding context

Option 3 arranges the building as two larger blocks with communal spaces on the ground floor and accommodation above.

Site context

This student residence project requires a large number of students to be accommodated over three floors and comprises a library, a dining hall, an amenities space and student rooms.

The brief/program for this project is for a collegiate environment, arranged over several floors on one part of a site currently occupied by an educational building that was no longer in use. The brief/program evolved in a way that avoided the need to demolish the existing building by integrating it into the new development. This approach led to a design that avoided stacking new floors of accommodation over multiple levels in a semi-high-rise solution. Instead, the accommodation is arranged over four floors as three separate blocks, with a library and common room block arranged in a linear arrangement of connected forms that sits adjacent to the existing building, creating courtyards between the new and old buildings. A series of connected spaces is created that can be walked through, from end to end and up and down three floors. The breaking down of the accommodation into smaller units, and as apartments rather than as individual study bedrooms, provides a sense of community to these student rooms spaces that a semi-high-rise building, or a series of stacked spaces over 10 floors, might not have achieved. The approach also has the benefit of retaining existing buildings, rather than demolishing serviceable structures. Option 1 arranges the building as two main blocks which are separated by a service core in the middle as well as at each end. The main entrance is set at the corner of the site with a space in front to allow for people to gather and to meet those who are entering or leaving the building.

The two main blocks have student accommodation on the upper floors and common spaces on the ground floor. The blocks are arranged as a continuous rectilinear form with recesses in the volumetric massing. The three circulation zones also accommodate service zones; these are recessed in relation to the two main blocks in order to signal the 'linking' role of the external forms that accommodate circulation within the context of the site. The entrance 'block' sits apart from the two

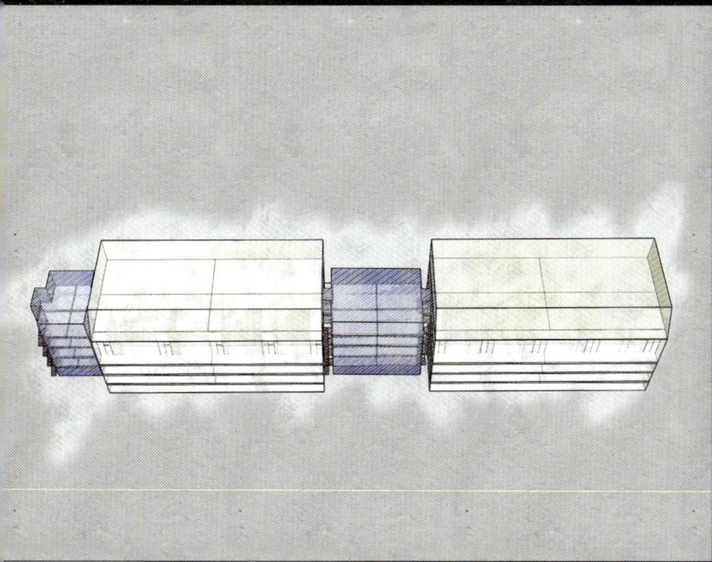

. Perspective view of environmental volumes

2. Perspective view of environmental volumes

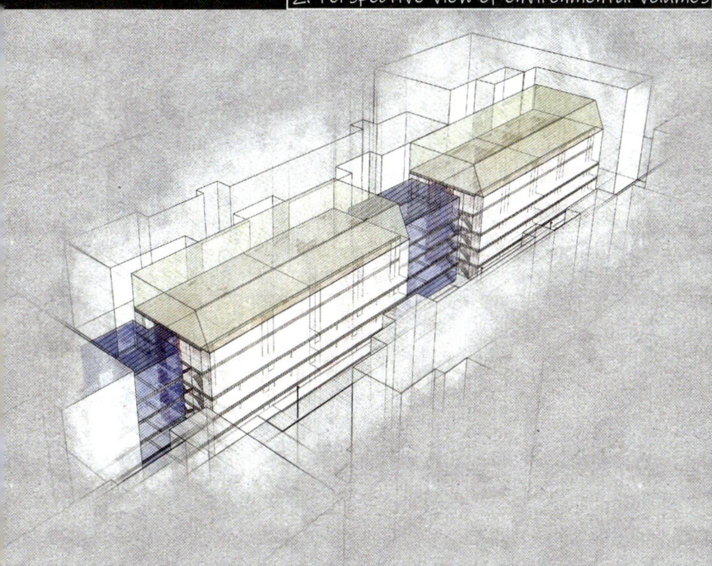

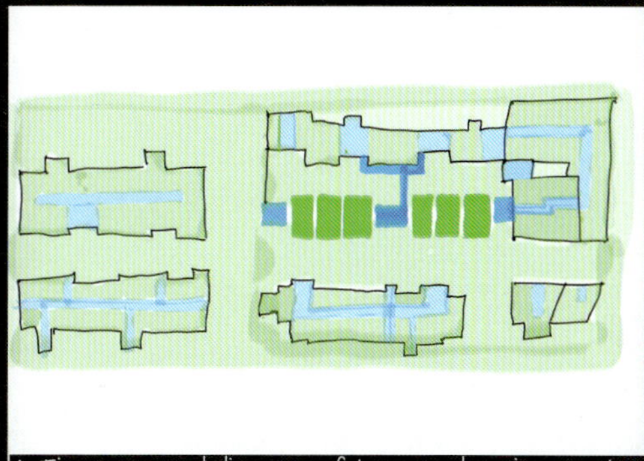

1. Figure-ground diagram of tempered environment

Option 1
Dark green spaces are highly tempered but are limited to accommodation volumes only.

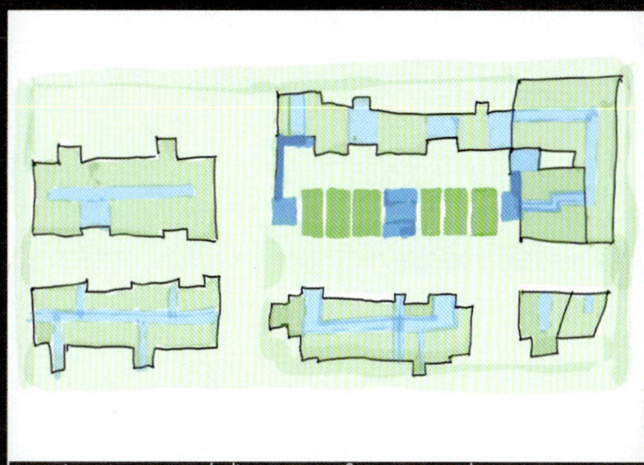

2. Figure-ground diagram of tempered environment

Option 2
Dark blue spaces are less tempered than dark green spaces but are more tempered than light blue circulation space.

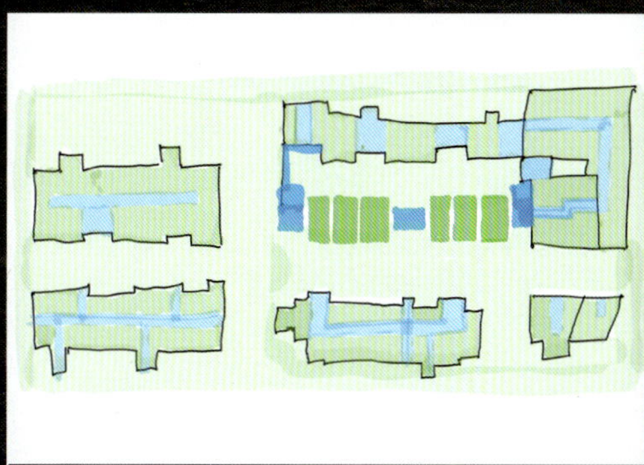

3. Figure-ground diagram of tempered environment

Option 3
Light blue spaces are the least tempered spaces, these spaces interface directly with external space.

main blocks, which provides a reception space on the ground floor, with the dining room and meeting hall and library arranged on the upper floors. Option 2 widens the central circulation space in order to add the functions of the main entrance to the college at ground floor level. The three main blocks are aligned with one another; the smaller corner block which is recessed from the street in Option 1 is now pushed back further towards the adjoining building. The main change from Option1 is of moving the entrance to the link between the two buildings, and to have a secondary entrance on the street which forms a small external space. The college has a larger reception space and corresponding larger dining room within the central space, which also contains circulation space that was previously occupied by the more slender circulation zone of Option 1. In Option 2, the smaller corner block of Option 1 and one of its service zones are integrated into the central block of this option. The smaller corner block becomes a larger library which is accessed from the enclosed 'college side' space into the library. This entrance is made visually significant as a result of the block being moved further away from the street, projecting into the space between the new building and the existing building. The parts of the building facing the existing building now create a set of three courtyards such that the external walls of the existing building that face the new part of the college become walls to a courtyard instead of being walls enclosing a light well.

Option 3 sets the primary parts of the building as two larger blocks with communal spaces on the ground floor and accommodation above. In this option the central space is recessed, both from the street side and from the adjoining side, in order to create a more comfortable link with the existing buildings behind, which can be accessed from the link. The smaller corner library block is as per Option 2.

In Option 3 the main entrance is further recessed in order to provide the space for gathering. A secondary entrance is accommodated at the corner of the site from the street into the first block. The library entrance is still from the shared space between buildings; a corner block on the street which forms a 'pivot' between adjacent streets.

1. Sectional perspective view

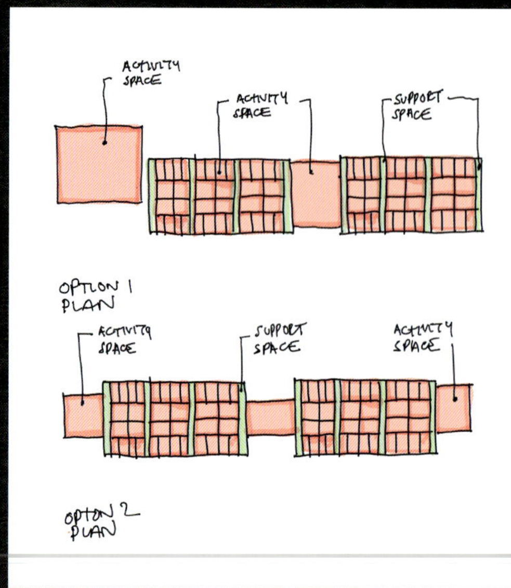

Spatial arrangement Option 1 arranges the building as two blocks separated by a service core in the middle as well as at each end. Option 2 widens the central circulation space in order to add the functions of the main entrance at ground floor level.

2. Sectional perspective view

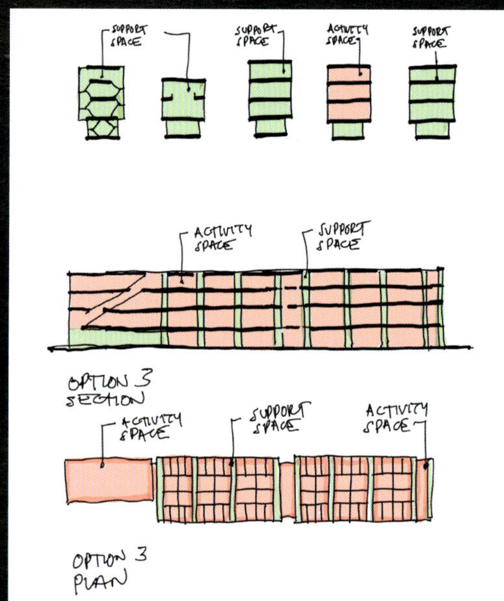

Option 3 arranges the building as two larger blocks with communal spaces on the ground floor and accommodation above.

Spatial arrangement

A primary consideration of the overall arrangement is to provide a set of courtyard spaces between the existing building and the new building. The existing building is recessed from the street and does not have a clear visual expression as a result. The new building is set on what was previously a row of small buildings; the relationship with the existing building was one of integrating the new with the existing. The existing building has two projecting bays which are used to create courtyards between them. The volumes that face these external rooms are arranged in a way that turns the space between the new and old buildings into external spaces in their own right. These external spaces form a sequence of outdoor rooms that extend the length of the building. Each constituent form of the new building is designed to geometrically address its own courtyard. The arrangement of student rooms follows this principle. Since most rooms are the same in size, the division of rooms into building forms which address the courtyard provides the ability to create a specific identity for each block, based on a close geometric integration with the outdoor spaces. The library is set at one end of the site, forming a volume which encloses the end of the courtyard spaces. The entrance to the building is set where the new building is set at its closest point to the existing external walls; existing and new building touch at this point. Staircases and lifts/elevators are set into the void between the two sets of forms. Externally, the courtyards and garden space continue beneath the staircase as part of the uninterrupted set of outdoor rooms and links between them.

The constituent forms of the building that address the courtyards are the same as those that face the street; the visual rhythm of these forms is determined by the courtyard elevations on the opposite side of the building; rooms that look both onto the street and into the courtyards. Each room is accessed from a single core and staircase without corridors; the advantage of this arrangement is that students can share a suite of rooms from a single point of access. Every set of rooms is accessed directly from a staircase. The central court has an adjacent dining hall; students are not expected to cross the campus to the main

. Perspective view of interior

2. Perspective view of interior

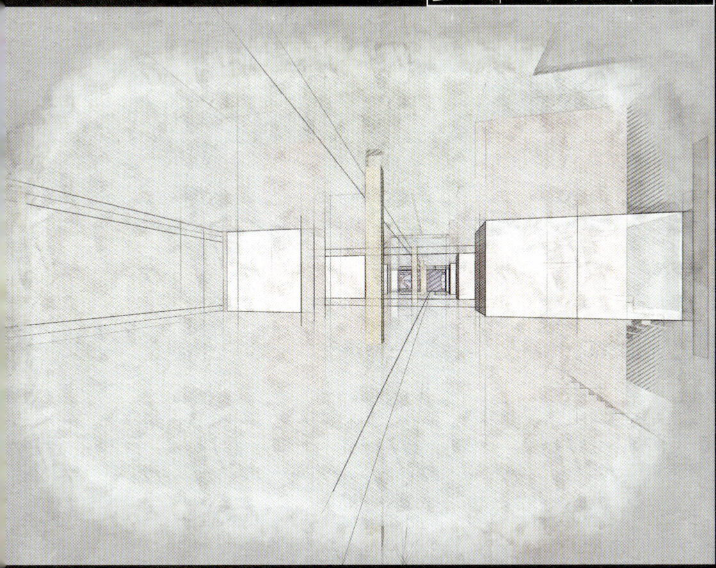

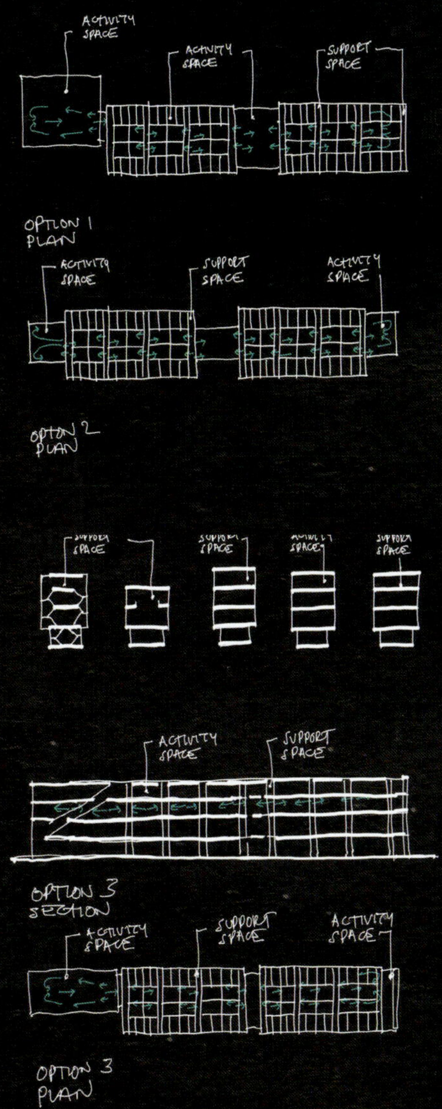

Internal circulation.

Option 1 arranges circulation from a single entrance at one end of building.

Option 2 arranges circulation from entrances at each end of the building.

Option 3 arranges circulation from a single entrance at the centre of the building.

dining hall for meals, providing a more collegiate atmosphere for students. Utility rooms for laundry, storage and boiler space are positioned within the pitched roof volume immediately above the student rooms. The top floor is separated from the floor below in order to avoid sound transmission from the utility floor to the floors with student rooms immediately below.

The spatial arrangement is one of a linear arrangement of spaces, but rooms are not accessed by corridor: they are accessed by individual service cores which can be reached from the upper ground level amenities floor. The spatial arrangement is one of taking a traditional model of a four-sided college building that encloses a central courtyard; unfolding this arrangement to form a straight line. The volumes at each end of the building house the library and student common rooms. A double-height volume for the common room and a triple-height space for the library form 'bookends' to the arrangement of spaces. Common rooms for different year groups interlock vertically in order to give a mezzanine experience in each of the double-height spaces.

Internal circulation

The stair cores provide circulation space associated with each apartment accessed directly off the core. Storage spaces are set on the landings of staircases which project outwards above the building. Clear rectangular spaces are formed for the student apartments, main court and dining hall. In Option 1, the main accommodation blocks on each side of the central court are arranged between a set of staircases, positioned between blocks of apartments, with additional stairs set at the ends of each block. Each accommodation block has a circulation zone for students on the lowest level. Information desks and office space for support staff are set between the staircases and lifts/elevators. The accommodation blocks are set either side of the central court. The main court is effectively a building within a building. A colonnade is set within the external volume. At the entrance to the rooftop building, the central court is the circulation hub, creating a sense of connection within the college accommodation. The court also provides a space which can be both inhabited and traversed.

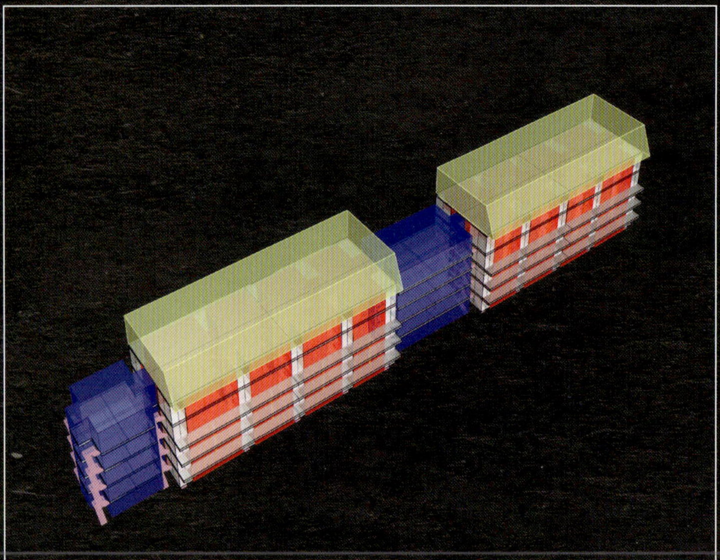

1A. Isometric view of environmental volumes

1B. Isometric view of environmental volumes

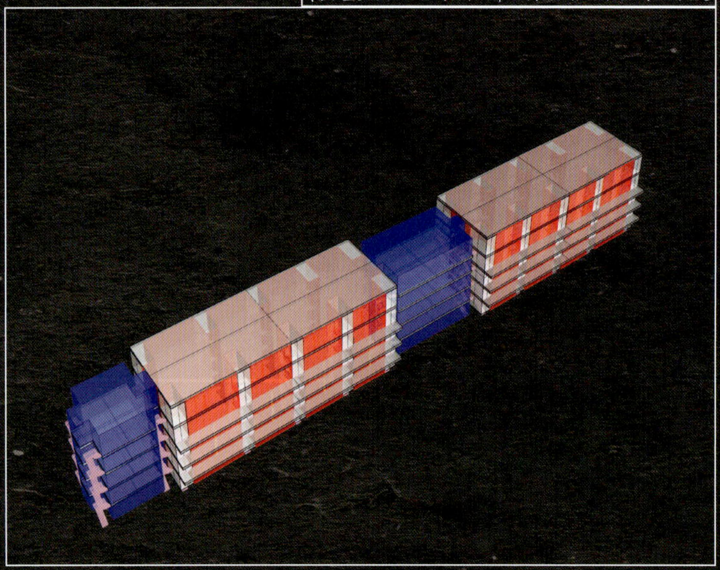

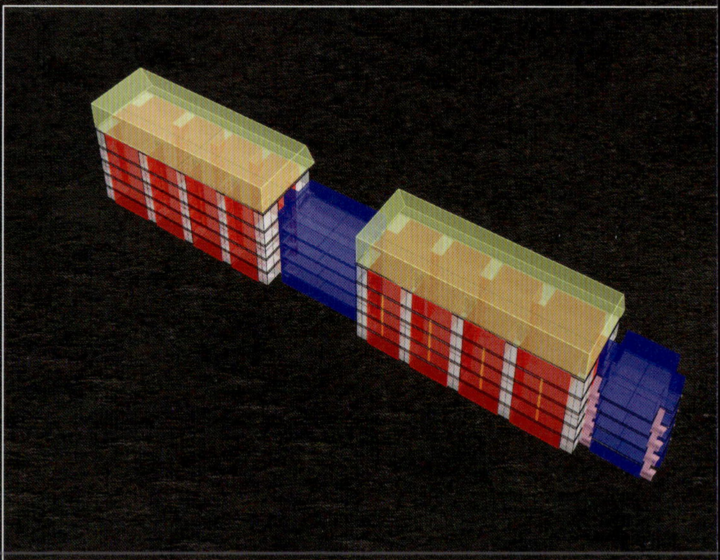

2A. Isometric view of environmental volumes

2B. Isometric view of environmental volumes

Environmental strategy

The environmental strategy benefits from the use of the mainly reinforced concrete structures by allowing them to be heated or cooled following the 24-hour cycle of changes in temperature that even out the temperature differences between night and day, permitting the building to be heated or cooled with the least amount of energy. Opening windows throughout encourages the use of night-time ventilation in this moderate climate.

A balance is struck between the levels of embodied energy in the concrete construction and the energy required to run the building in use, with the emphasis on having low levels of background heating during daylight hours and a release of heat energy through the floor slabs at night-time to assist with the cooling down assisted by natural ventilation in this cross-ventilated series of spaces. The absence of a central corridor allows all spaces to be cross-ventilated naturally, avoiding the need for mechanical ventilation in student rooms. The environmental strategy was approached with three options: Option 1 proposes natural ventilation or primary ventilation through stair cores, and underfloor heating or background heating. This was in response to Option 1 for structure, which makes use of reinforced concrete shear walls of a large surface area for night-time natural ventilation through windows, in combination with under-floor heating or background heating. This environmental design approach suits structural strategy Option 2, which is a steel frame with cross-braced cores. Option 3 makes use of fan-assisted ventilation through the cores, which suits the corresponding structural strategy of shear walls in reinforced concrete and steel columns.

A primary aim of the environmental strategy is to introduce as much natural cross ventilation as possible by benefitting from the high number of cores in public areas or shared areas. Option 3 is the preferred option for the winter months. Option 1 works well in the mid-season and Option 2 works well in the summer. In this case, all three options, although primarily intended for different structural options, respond to the opportunities presented by the structural options rather than

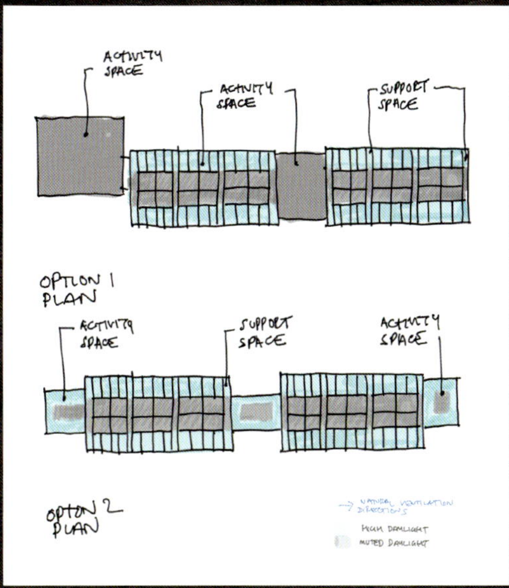

Daylight strategy for direct sunlight and cross ventilation.

Option 1 arranges the building as two blocks separated by a service by a service.

Option 2 widens the central circulation space in order to add the main entrance floor.

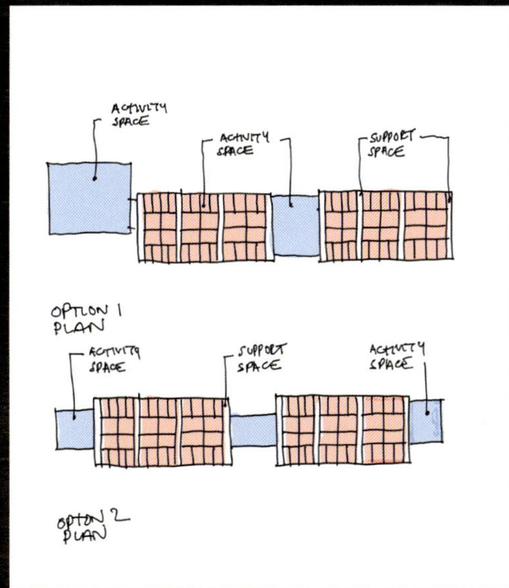

Environmental zones

Option 1 proposes natural ventilation or primary ventilation through stair cores, and underfloor heating or background heating.

Option 2 suits structural strategy Option 2.

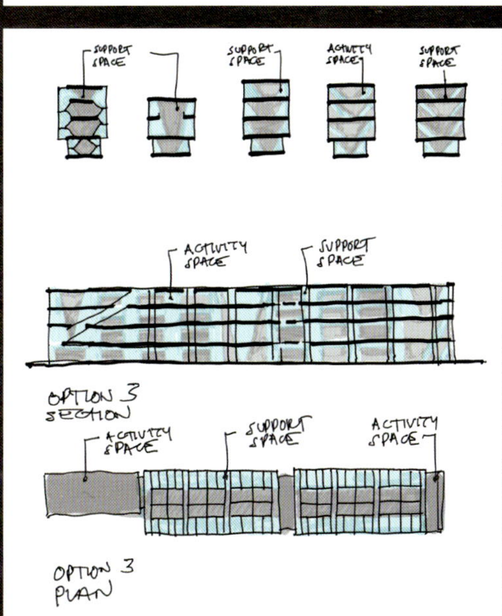

Daylight strategy for direct sunlight and cross ventilation.

Option 3 arranges the building as two larger blocks with communal spaces on the ground floor and accommodation above.

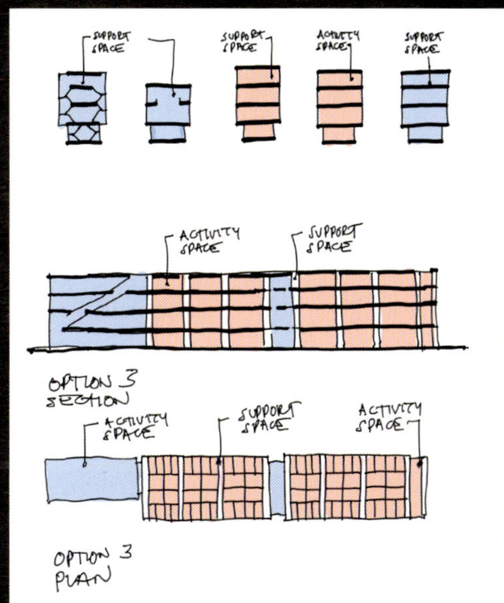

Environmental zones

Option 3 makes use of fan-assisted ventilation through the cores.

being governed by them. A provision for acoustic attenuation is used for both structure-borne sound and flanking transmission from floors and walls, both internally and adjacent to the facades. In addition, technical rooms are located at the roof level of the new building, above common spaces. At the strategic level, sound attenuation on accommodation floors is achieved by zoning; service spaces, as structural cores, provide an acoustic buffer with adjacent sets of rooms. Cores also provide a thermal buffer, such that acoustic zones and thermally controlled zones coincide.

At the lowest level of the rooftop building, activity spaces such as rooms for teaching and research, which are used during daylight hours, are separated by 'buffers' of support spaces. In addition, a phasing of use is created where spaces used primarily during the day provide an acoustic and thermal buffer for those used during evenings and weekends. For example, spaces where quiet study time is needed, typically during evenings and early mornings, are set adjacent to service-space buffers. Teaching spaces and communal spaces, when not in use, also provide buffers at the strategic level. During the day, where all floors including study bedrooms are in use, the building is used as a set of zoned communal study areas. Student apartments become shared study spaces for use during the daytime, with ease of access to the library as well as facilities for printing and associated workshop services. The zoning of acoustic separation with a corresponding structure is a primary driver for the environmental strategy.

The environmental control informs the three options for the environmental strategy. Option 1 uses ventilation through the stair cores into student rooms; heating is provided by background under-floor heating. For Option 2, the benefit from the framed construction is a provision of natural ventilation through the windows with under-floor background heating.

Options 3 makes use of the service cores, where fan-assisted ventilation through these spaces is provided where the air is pre-heated or pre-cooled. Each solution benefits from the use of the thermal mass of walls together with cross ventilation.

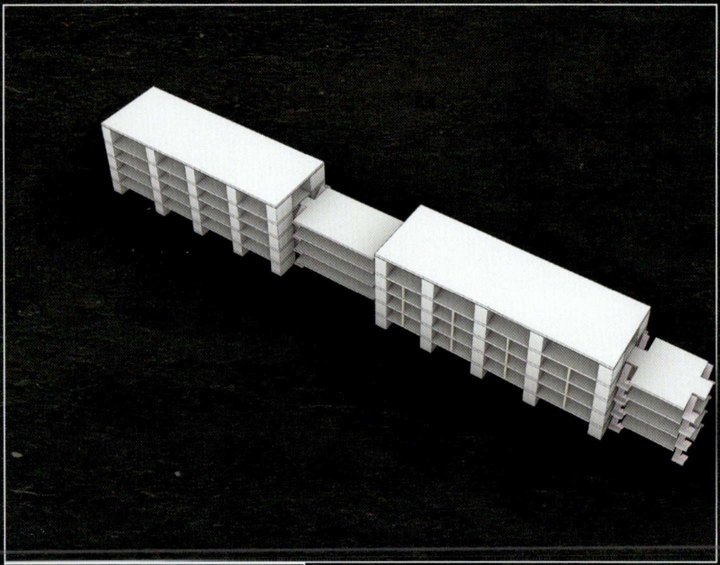

1A. Isometric view of structure

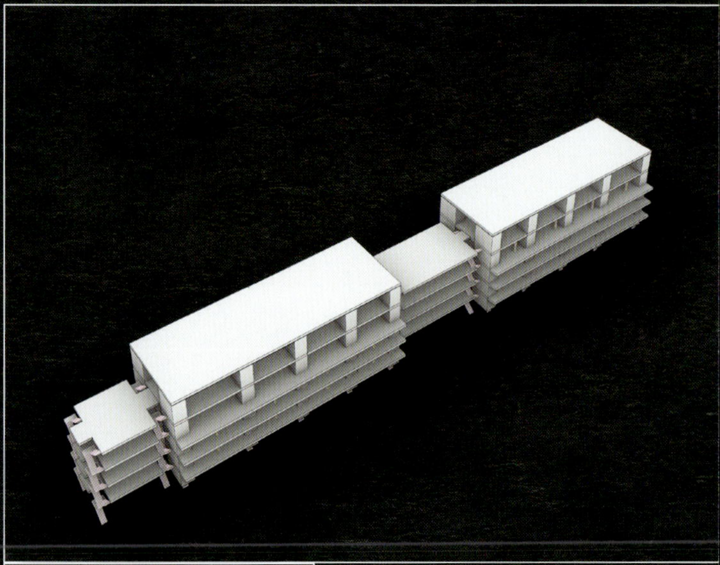

2A. Isometric view of structure

1B. Isometric view of structure

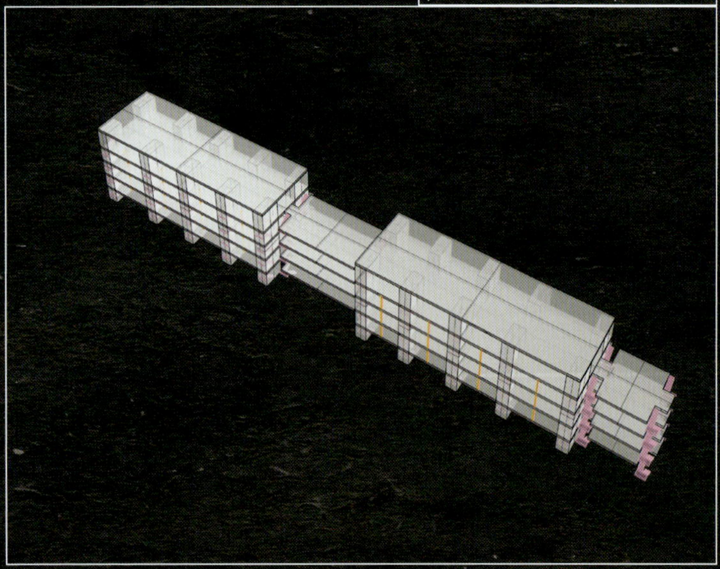

2B. Isometric view of structure

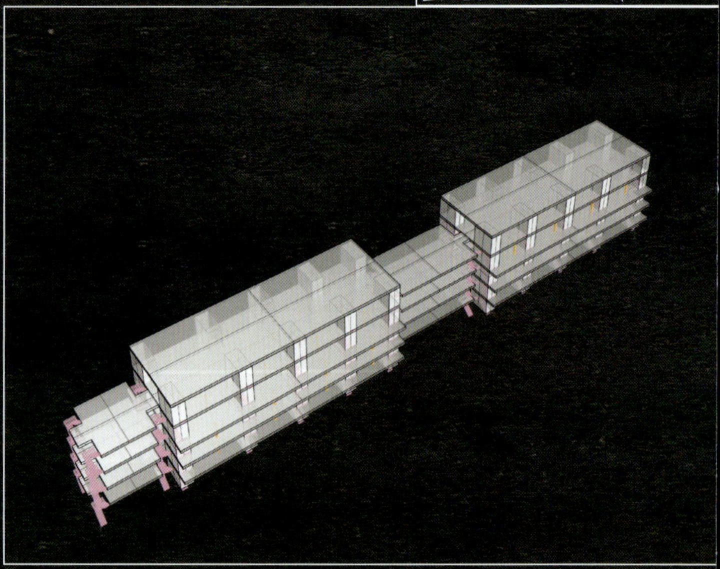

Structural strategy

The structure of the building is created as a set of reinforced concrete frames which are set out in a stepped section, such that student accommodation is arranged across half-levels with voids linking parts of the building. The breaks between floor slabs are filled with stairs and lifts/elevators to provide access to the different levels in the section. Floor slabs step up by a half level both along the length of the elevation and in the width of the building, creating the characteristic end elevations where the position of structural slabs is revealed. Slab edges are thermally insulated and clad with panels that reflect the position and the importance of the floor slabs and upstands to floor slabs. The long elevation of the building has non-load-bearing cladding panels in GFRC which reflect the organisation behind, comprising a complex arrangement of space of different volumetric sizes. The complex arrangement is reflected in an irregular column grid that follows the needs of the different student apartment layouts; rooms have an irregular layout which does not follow a module; the structural arrangement of floor slabs and columns reflects that requirement. The long facade reveals the arrangement of the student rooms, library and dining hall which are fitted together in an interlocking arrangement of spaces. The corresponding structural arrangement is based on a set of slabs set at different levels along the length of the building, with an irregular column grid. Columns are continuous through their height, with no transfer structures needed to achieve the spatial arrangement required in the brief/program, which is one of requiring a close interconnection between student rooms, common facilities, dining halls and a library.

The structural strategy of Option 1 is of structural walls which traverse the narrow width of the building, enclosing the core spaces and dividing space into sets of apartments.

Option 2 is of a frame that is assisted structurally by the concrete cores. Option 3 is of structural walls being formed as cores and mixing those with columns in the accommodation spaces. Option 3 uses the least amount of material of all options. Option 2 is largely a steel frame, while Option 3 is a mixed solution of reinforced concrete and steel in

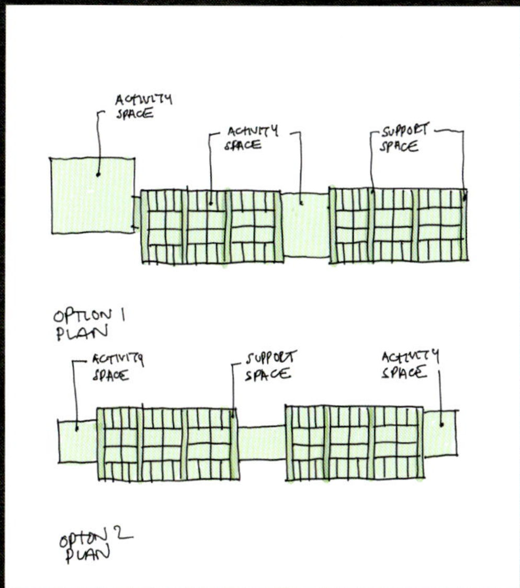

Structural strategy: Zones

Option 1 has structural walls which traverse the narrow width of the building.

Option 2 has concrete cores that assist the structural stability of the frame.

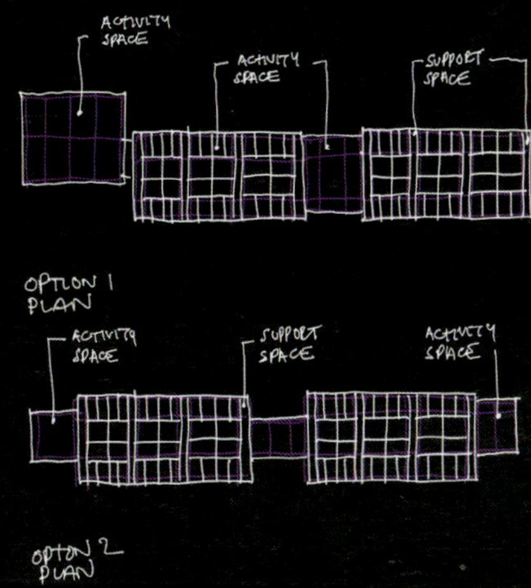

Structural strategy: Framing

Option 1 encloses the core spaces and dividing space into sets of spaces.

Option 2 is largely a steel frame.

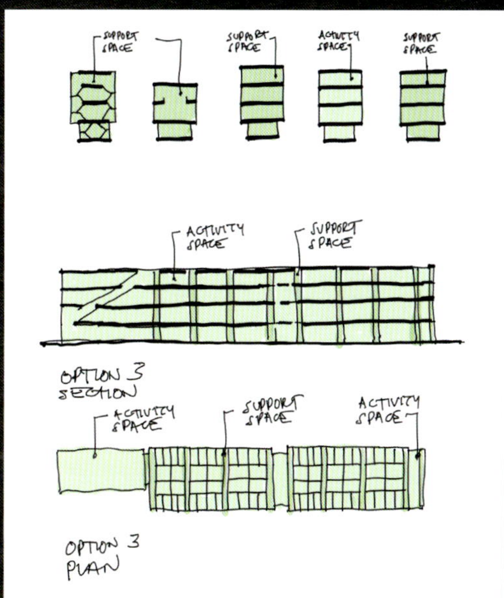

Structural strategy: Zones

Option 3 has structural walls formed as cores and mixing those with columns in the accommodation spaces.

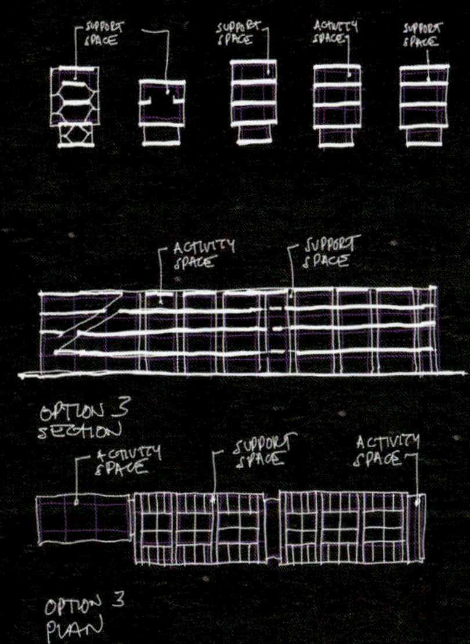

Structural strategy: Zones

Option 3 is a mixed solution of reinforced concrete and steel.

order to create the forms of the building with greater economy. Option 1 has a set of structural walls that are used to divide the apartments or student rooms, dividing the staircases to create cores for circulation between the main court and the library at one end of the building, and common rooms at the other end of the plan. Library and common rooms are single spaces with reinforced concrete walls, high-level glazing and a north-light arrangement. The main court also has a large rooflight as a benefit of its rooftop location. Reinforced concrete slabs are set between the cross walls which define the space for the main court. The structure is visible only on the narrow end facades where floor slabs are stiffened by edge beams. The facade panels are formed in GFRC (glass fibre reinforced concrete) to provide a durability to the facade materials.

Option 2 uses vertical columns, inclined columns and beams to create the structure as a fully framed reinforced concrete frame with reinforced concrete slabs. The volumes of the library and common rooms at each end of the building contribute to the overall structural stability, together with the main court structure in the centre of the arrangement; columns which are visible are formed in protected steel.

Option 3 is a hybrid solution of structural walls set within the cores in order to provide sound insulation between circulation areas and apartments, as well as providing the required durability and longevity of the building fabric. The dividing walls between student rooms are framed and infilled with non-load-bearing walls whose finishes contrast with the structural frame and walls, which are visible. The dining hall and the main court are also framed and in-filled with non-load-bearing walls. The structure has smaller forms set at high level that appear to be discontinuous with the structure below. The structural columns are continuous through the height of the building, but the floor slabs and roof forms cantilever by a modest amount in order to create the sense of different spaces being formed at high level; spaces that the visitor or the student would wish to inhabit for study. These roof-level spaces are library and study rooms, formed by a mix of columns and structural walls that support floor slabs and roof enclosures.

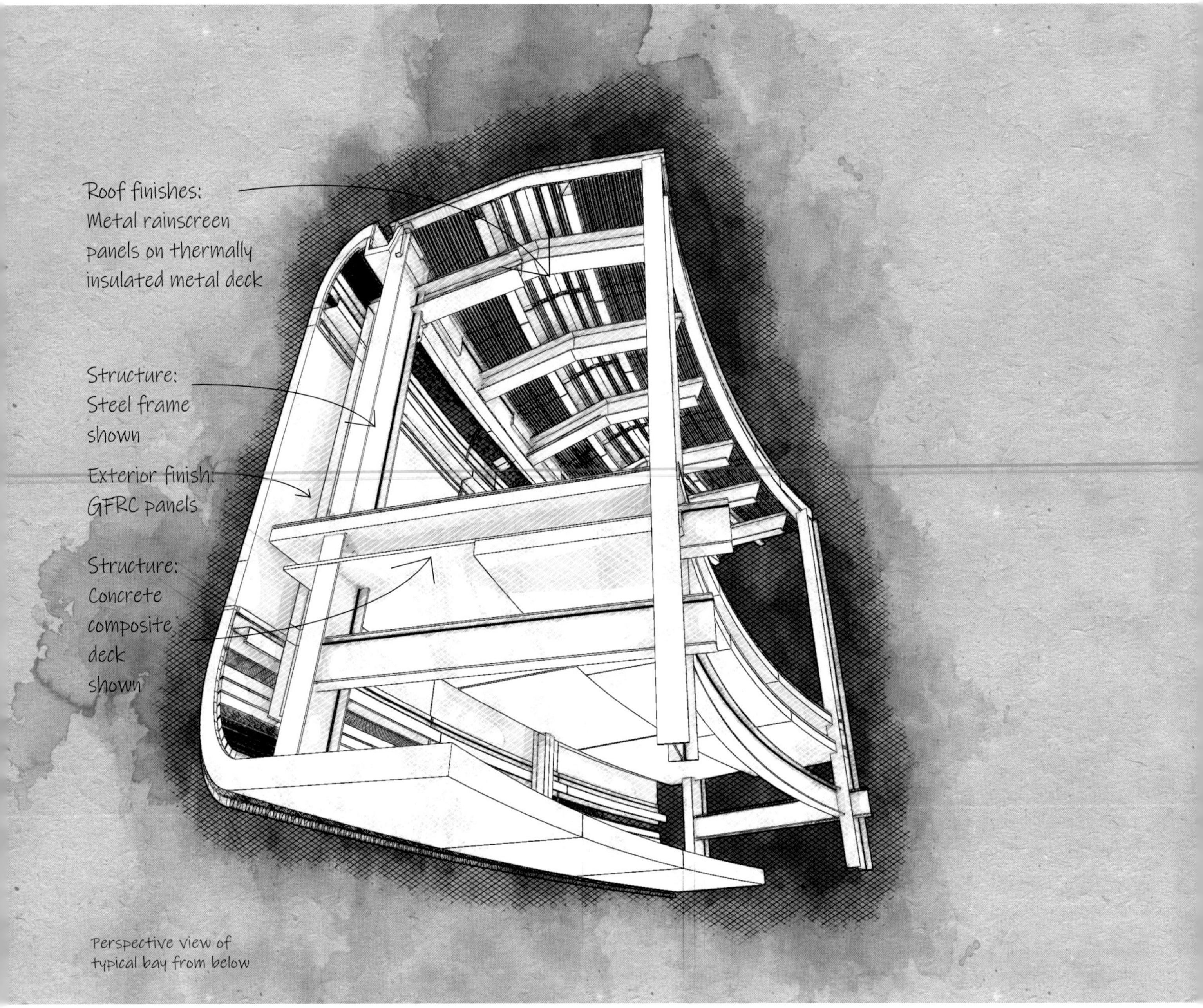

Perspective view of typical bay from below

Typical bay adjacent to facade

The long elevations generally face north and south; the south-facing elevations are designed to provide passive solar shading along the length of the facade. The north facade catches sunlight in the early morning and early evening for most of the year.

The form of the building creates a passive solar control as a result of deep reveals to windows, as well as overhanging forms which shade the study bedrooms. The form of the building is arranged such that natural ventilation can function across the width of the building. This full cross ventilation can be provided as a result of the absence of internal corridors that would divide apartments into a single aspect type. Instead, each apartment is arranged as a set of study bedrooms with a central communal study space. This arrangement avoids the need for additional mechanical ventilation.

Rooms are arranged in a continuous 'row' along the length of the facades; there is no volumetric differentiation between the staircases and the rooms in terms of the arrangement of form and of glazing; windows are used to differentiate, visually, a series of spaces behind of different occupation. However, the design has a high level of differentiation between spaces.

The expression of the external envelope is one of differentiation, but of following the larger-scale concept of the overall building form. The design provides a highly differentiated sub-division of form; this approach is taken in order to separate the forms visually both at the large scale of massing and at the small scale of individual spaces behind the facades. This expression of form follows the large-scale arrangment of adjacent buildings by harmonising with them at the level of the overall form in order to provide an independence of function and performance of the spaces which the neighbouring buildings do not possess. Facades have glazed windows made from aluminium using a visually similar language of construction to that of neighbouring buildings. Walls and roof facades are clad in GFRC (glass fibre-reinforced concrete) panels; the material is exposed, where possible, to internal spaces in order to harmonise visually with their metal -finished interior

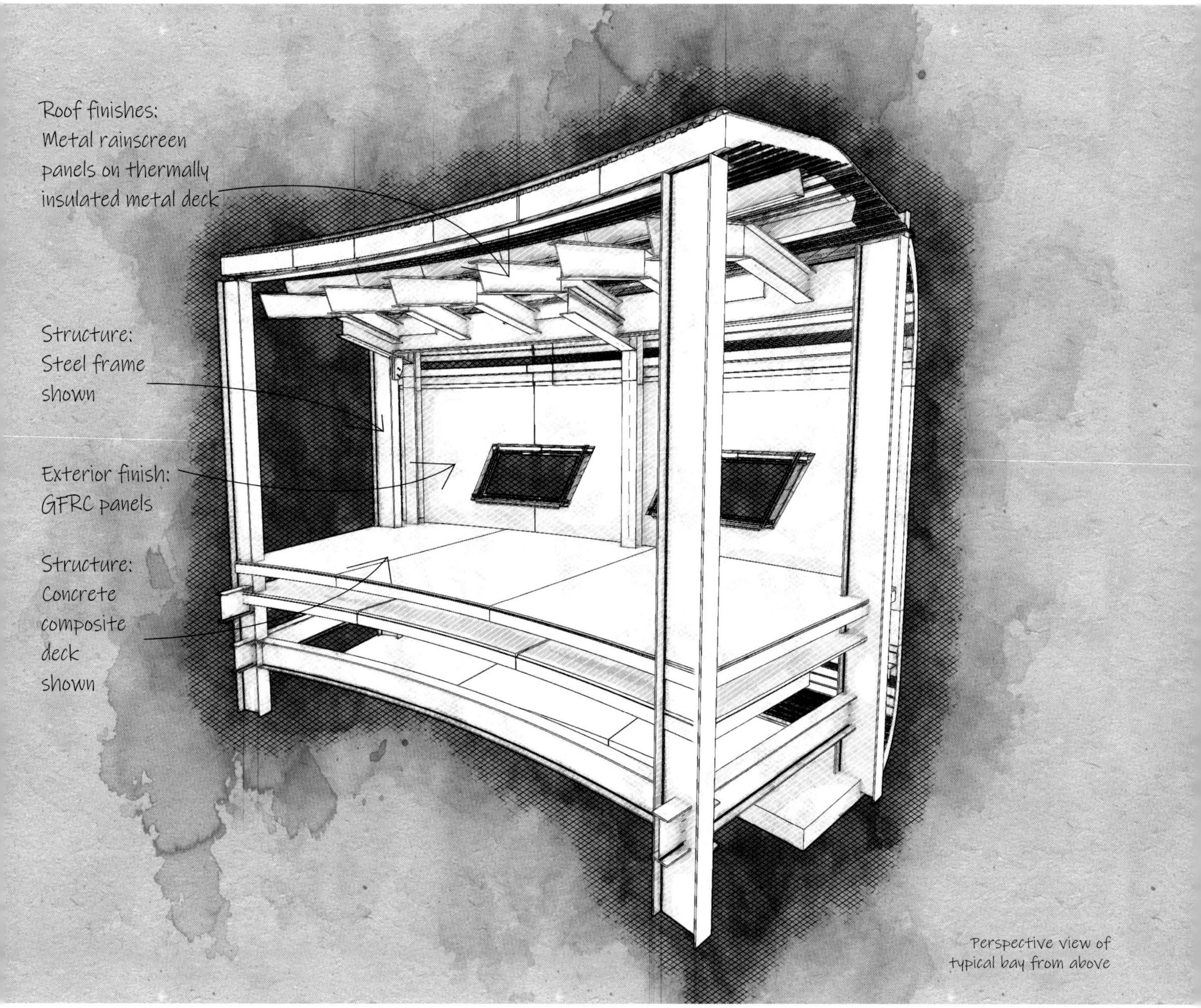

Perspective view of typical bay from above

fittings and laminate-based furniture.

The internal face of facades has built-in shelving for books and study materials inside each room; they surround the glazed openings in each room, and are formed from the same materials as the windows; a metal-based assembly of glazing and shelving with a fold-out study table and a study bench set beneath each window. Cross walls, which extend across the width of the building, are concrete based; walls are finished in plaster, with reinforced concrete beams and columns having an exposed concrete self-finish. Structural concrete walls also have a self-finish with joint lines near floor and ceiling level which coordinate visually with non-loadbearing partitions and interior walls. The built-in shelving, located on the internal face of external walls, is fixed to the backing wall which encloses the building. GFRC panels are set in rainscreen configuration. The environmental control installations are set into the facade build-up, resulting in the 'thick wall' arrangement that provides passive solar control. The rooms, visually, have a focus of the external walls being the main study zone. For this reason, light is provided at a high level such that rooms have a more inward-looking than outward-looking character; full views outside are provided in communal areas and in entrances to the libraries and common rooms.

The GFRC-clad facade panels have the textured cementitious finish associated with in-situ/cast-in-place reinforced concrete; inner walls are lined with metal-based furniture, and the joinery for doors and framing inside is all in laminates. There is a hierarchy from the robust, durable quality of the concrete externally, through to the visually more refined furniture fixed to the facades internally, to softer laminate-based joinery and furniture.

The envelope of Options 1 and 2 is reinforced concrete. The facades for Option 2 are also formed in GFRC panels or precast concrete panels. These cementitious panels benefit from the longer spans between the shear walls, such that the facade panel goes past the central beam and column which is used to divide the student rooms. The facades for Option 3 are of cladding panels in either reinforced concrete or GFRC with a panel arrangement to suit the limitations of material size.

1. Perspective view of exterior

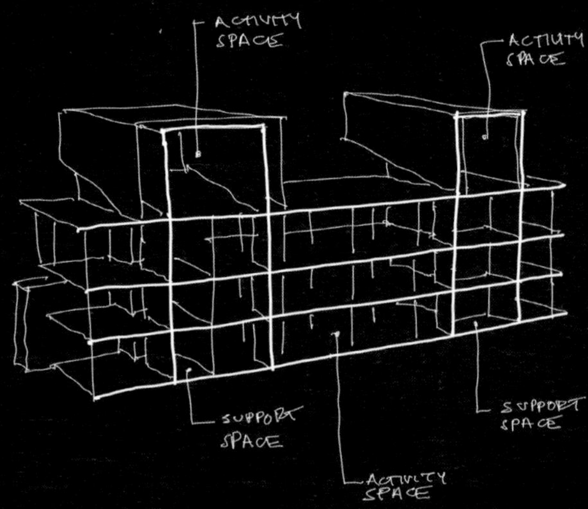

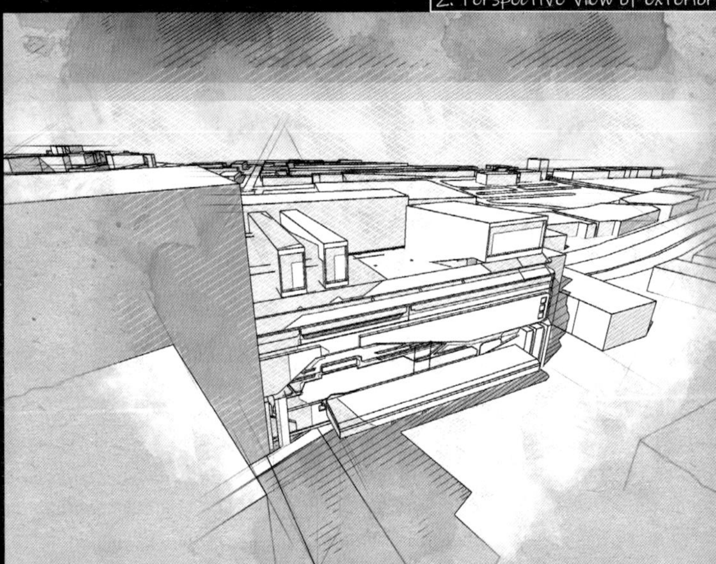

2. Perspective view of exterior

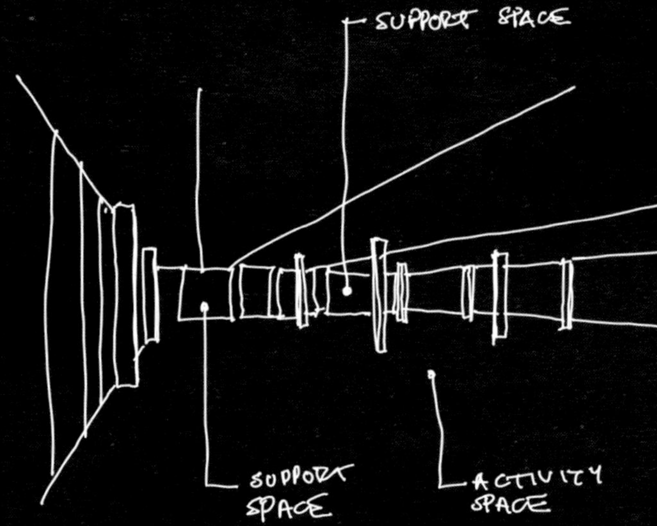

Locally based production and on-site fabrication

A key theme in this project is to encourage the participation of local contractors, fabricators and installers in the construction of this project. This building is inserted into an existing urban environment that was constructed in the recent past; an importance was placed on constructing the new building with the assistance of local fabricators and contractors. Partial prefabrication was the preferred method of construction in order to make the installation easier for building assemblies. As a result, systems for structure, envelope and environmental control are refined and simplified; enabling components to be fabricated locally. The simplified component geometries of the building form can be produced without the need for specialised fabrication equipment. This approach enables local companies to bid successfully for the construction work, providing local employment and reducing the transport emissions associated with delivering materials, components and assemblies to the project site from a long distance. Striving for increased simplicity in system assembly also provides clarity in the construction, along with advantages in structural and material efficiency. The integration of different system components for this small-scale building has resulted in multi-functional components, which increase the efficiency of the system in terms of cost. The systems for structure, envelope and environment followed a design and analysis process which involves finite element analysis, prototyping and physical testing. Full scale mock-ups and physical testing are undertaken in order to validate the performance of the systems. A key aspect of this project was that it could be constructed using locally based systems for environmental control. The approach taken was to divide the building into small-sized 'modules' of space such that the building could be constructed without the tools and equipment that would be required for larger-scale environmental systems, structures and envelopes. Consequently, the approach taken was not to use large-scale construction techniques in a relatively small building, but instead to scale up the construction methods and systems associated with small-scale buildings. This approach suited the brief which was geared towards a high level

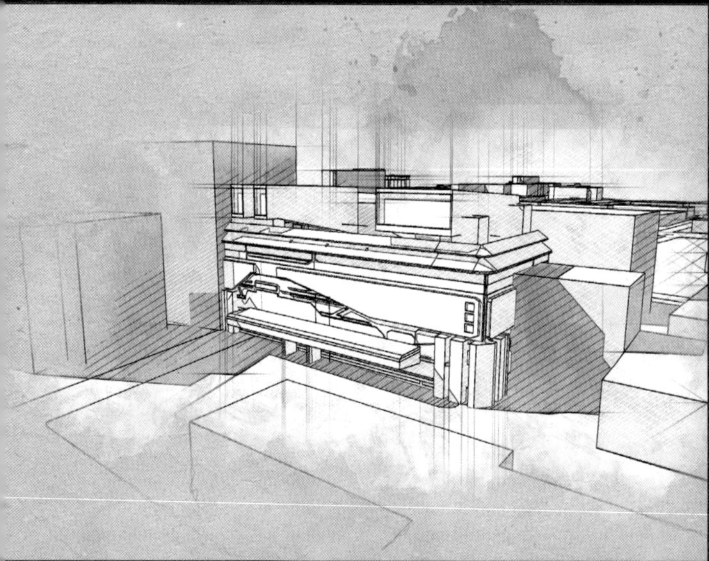

. Perspective view of exterior

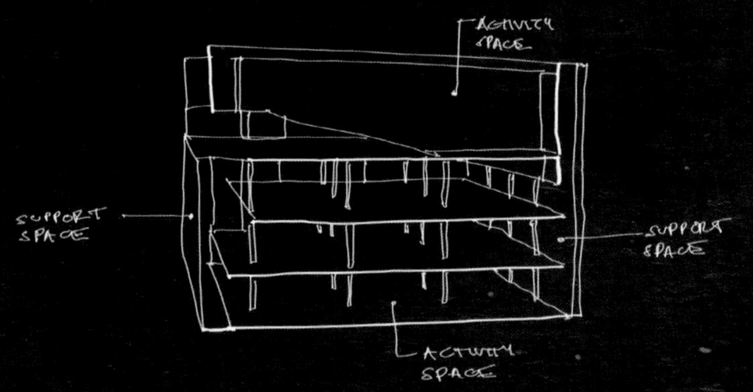

4. Perspective view of exterior

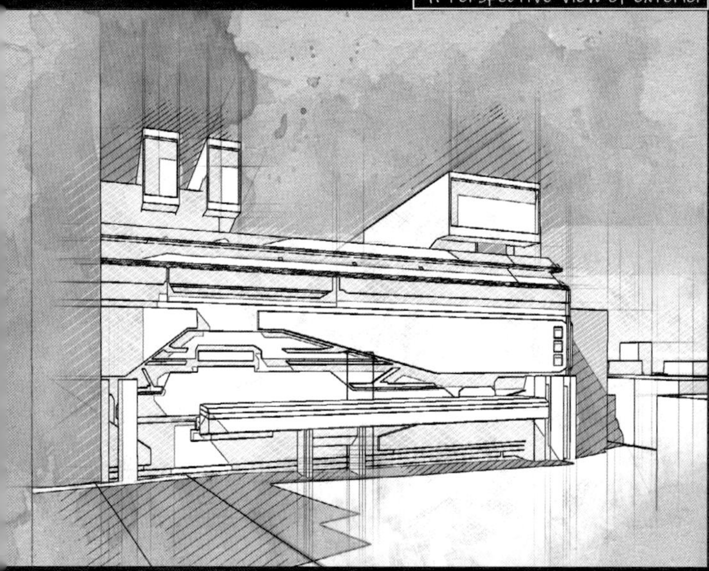

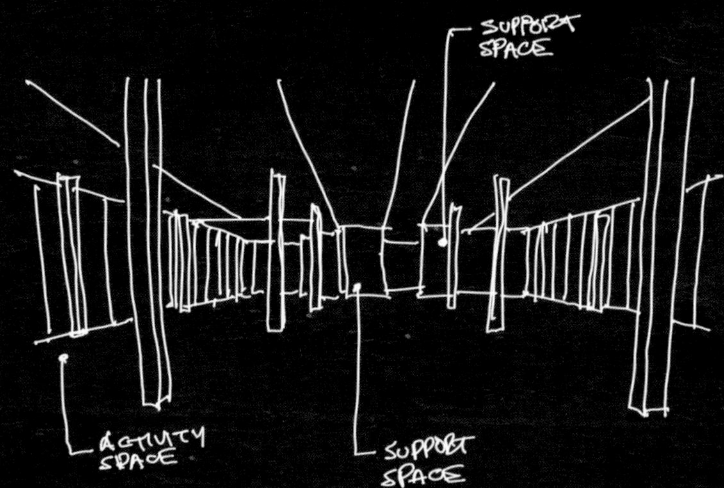

of differentiation of the volumes in the building so that the building was not a rectilinear box with smooth facades, but one which had elements that were clearly visible as linked volumes, almost as separate buildings which form part of the overall construction of this single building. This approach allowed the facades to be made as a regular small-scale system for metal panels and for glazing. The structure has columns set within a smaller column grid that would typically be associated with a building of this scale in order to create small-scale spaces around the central space, the cinema. This large single space is without internal columns, but has trusses set at roof level which enclose the space; columns beneath the cinema space support the floors and enclosing internal walls. This allows the construction to be one that could be undertaken by a local company who are adapted to smaller-scale projects. This approach reduces the energy used to construct the building as a result of materials and labour being locally sourced; systems are not required to be prefabricated, brought to site and lifted into place. Systems can be constructed from a steel frame, clad in site-based metal panel systems with a limited area of glass. This approach of using lightweight assemblies uses a smaller-scale installation method of a mobile crane which lifts panels into place which have been part-fabricated at ground level, within the site boundary, or alternatively being assembled on one of the lower floor plates. Scaffolding is used to guide panels for floor, roof and wall into place. This approach combines skills for smaller-scale construction to be applied to larger-scale projects. This method allows a high level of geometry differentiation which is required between the constituent forms that comprise this building to be achieved economically. The project brings together a set of forms which are visually independent of one another when the building is viewed from the street or from surrounding buildings. This economical form of construction allows the value of a high differentiation of form to be achieved with an economical system that is very effective when repetition of building form is not a requirement. The approach taken towards the design of this building allows each volume to achieve its performance requirements economically and independently of its neighbouring forms.

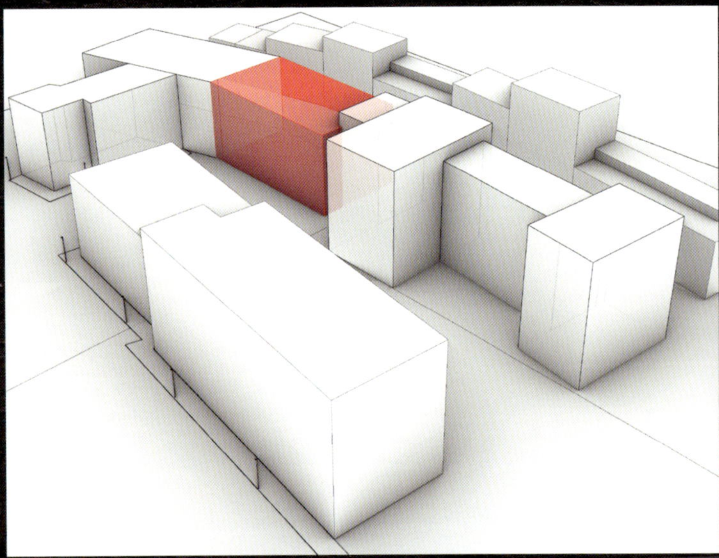

1. Project volume in site context

2. Project volume in site context

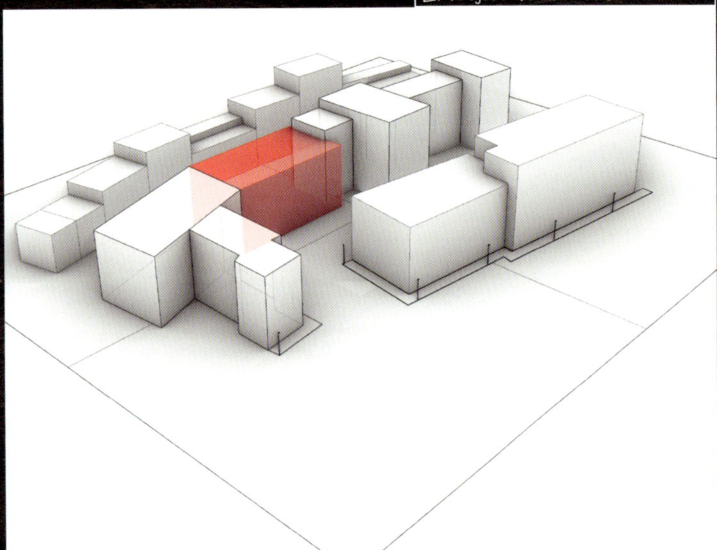

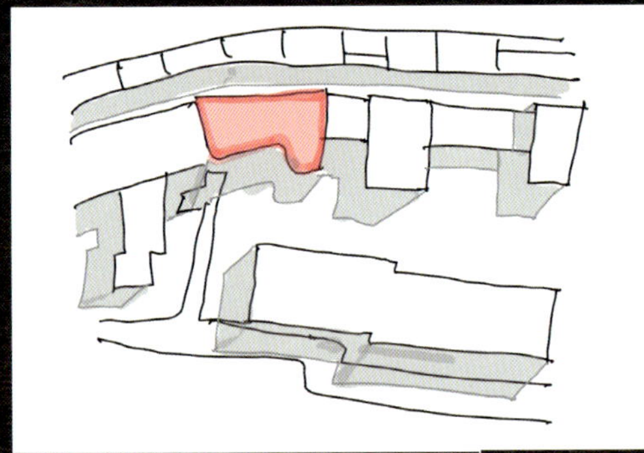

1. Site plan with surrounding context

Option 1 uses a flat facade, on the west-facing side adjacent to the street, that fits the profile of the existing buildings.

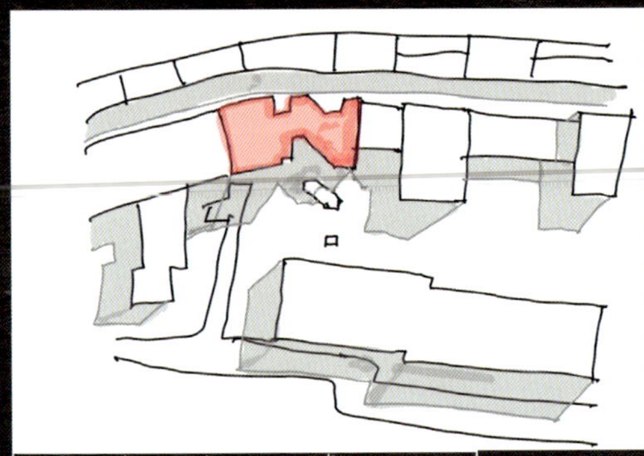

2. Site plan with surrounding context

Option 2 divides the site into much smaller segments, making deep 'cuts' into the site which are not built upon, in order to enrich the flat streetscape.

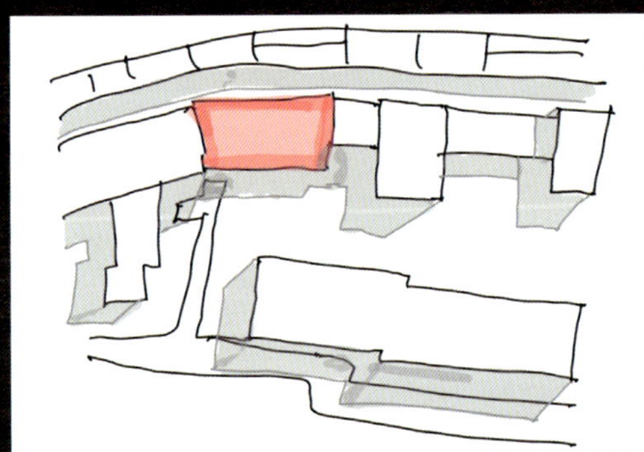

3. Site plan with surrounding context

Option 3 has flat facades both on the street and on the square, and has small place-making devices of seating and sculpture on the square.

Site context

This building is for a set of cinema theatres in a warm temperate climate. The primary cinema spaces are positioned above a large entrance space required for meeting and greeting visitors which also serves as the lobby for the food and beverage area and associated exhibition space. This entrance space is seen as a public space; an extension of the public space outside. The key theme of the theatre is its role as an arthouse cinema with an annual cinema festival and the ambience of an all-year-round festival which is not available locally. The building is one which aims to draw in passers-by from the new public space in front of the main facade.

The site context is a newly formed public square in a large town; a city square for which the publicly oriented activities of the cinema complex has an outward expression to the main space. This facade engages with that public space through its three-dimensional modelled surfaces. The elevations are arranged as individual small-scale modules in order to have the sense of the facade being highly articulated, with many different functions going on behind these walls. This approach of urban form follows in the tradition of the small-scale nature of building developments in that part of the city.

The main facade of the building has the form of the cinema volume projecting out from the building to form a deep entrance canopy. That elevation is east facing, allowing this orientation to have its signage illuminated at dusk while ensuring that the signage is visible in daylight in the public space in front of the east-facing facade. The west-facing facade is less visually articulated, but has similar projecting forms and has no illuminated signage. The two side elevations, north and south, abut adjacent existing buildings.

A rooftop terrace provides access to the roof-level enclosures which accommodate restaurants and two small cinemas. The terraces are external and open to the weather, but benefit from canopies that are used for part of the year to provide protection from wind and rain.

Three options for site context are presented here. Option 1 uses a flat facade, on the west-facing side adjacent to the street, that fits the

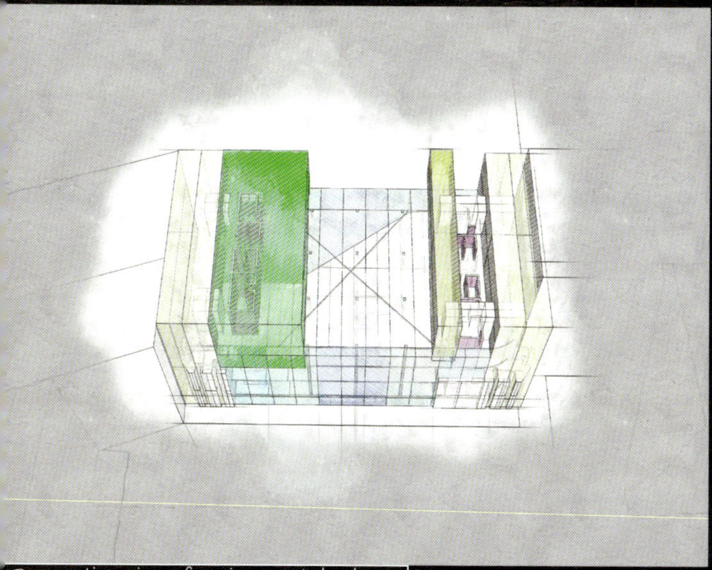

Perspective view of environmental volumes

2. Perspective view of environmental volumes

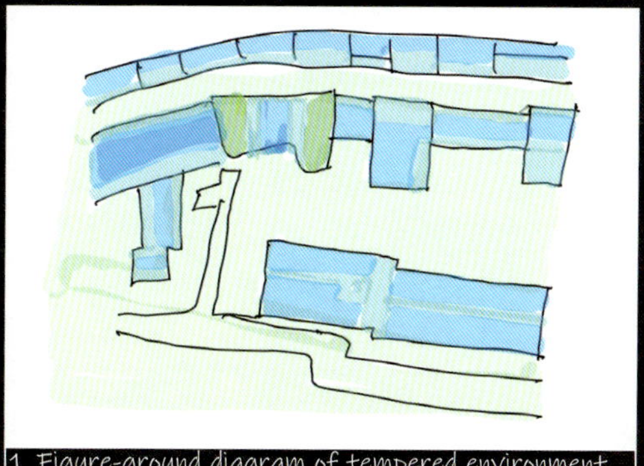

1. Figure-ground diagram of tempered environment

Option 1
Dark green spaces are highly tempered but are reduced to cinema theatre volumes only.

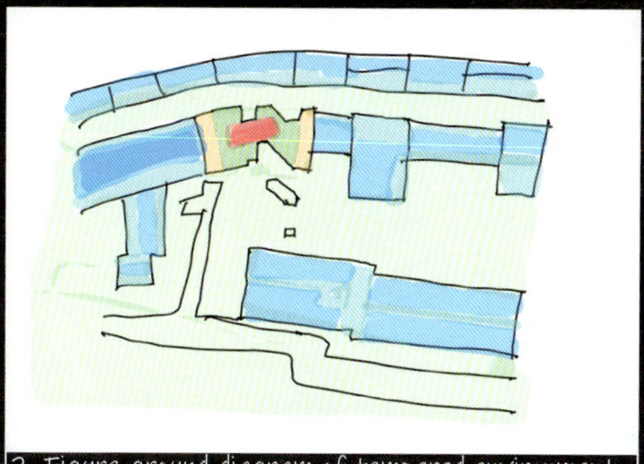

2. Figure-ground diagram of tempered environment

Option 2
Red spaces are external enclosures. Dark green spaces are tempered more highly than orange spaces. Blue spaces are less tempered than orange spaces.

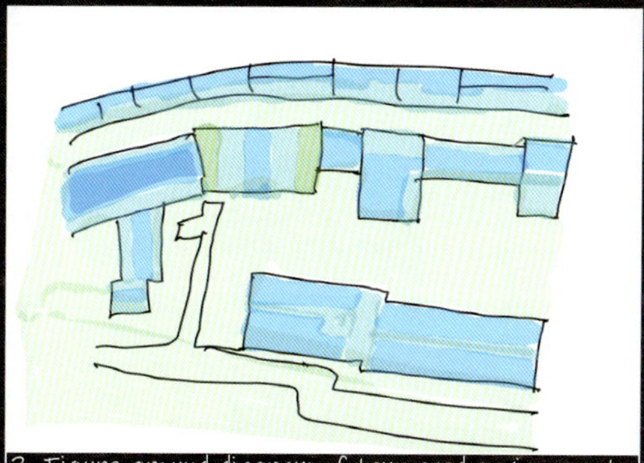

3. Figure-ground diagram of tempered environment

Option 3
Dark blue spaces are more tempered than light blue spaces; both are the least tempered spaces.

profile of the existing buildings. A geometrically sculpted and openly expressive facade is set onto the east-facing side that faces the square. This east-facing facade makes use of 3D decorative sculptural forms and seating, and a semi-enclosure on the square to create a space for visitors to congregate and listen to music; creating a space to visit rather than to pass through. Option 2 divides the site into much smaller segments, making deep 'cuts' into the site which are not built upon, in order to enrich the flat streetscape. This approach is used on both sides of the building in order to create internal spaces which separate the functions into individual volumes that can be clearly seen, and are expressed on the facades. This expression continues out into the public square, where there are spaces for listening to music, for sitting and enjoying the space, for which fragments of seating and low walls for sitting are provided. Option 3 has flat facades both on the street and on the square, and has small place-making devices of seating and sculpture on the square; creating a space that suits both walking and sitting; a space for music activities, which was encouraged as part of the brief/program. In this option, the second phase of the development, in a Phase 2 building design project, would increase the size of the public space to twice the size of this design, creating a second space for public gatherings. Option 3 is preferred, as it provides the greatest amount of flexibility for both the owner and for the city, moving the direction of the expression of the function's spatial organisations behind the facades through the visual differentiation of the flat facades, rather than through a volumetric carving or sculpting of the facades themselves.

A key approach to the design is one of differentiated forms that create a dynamic sense of activity within this commercial district, using volumes that do not exceed the size of the forms of adjacent buildings. In most cases the constituent parts of the building are smaller than those of neighbouring forms: The design reduces the scale of building volumes by basing the design on a set of juxtaposed volumes formed from the varied spaces in the building, which are economical to construct without the need to simplify the arrangement of forms.

1. Sectional perspective view

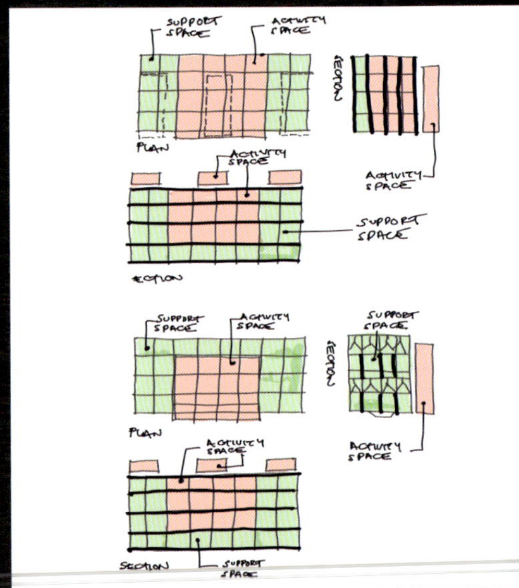

Spatial arrangement

Option 1 arranges the building as an 'egg in a box'. Smaller cinema spaces are arranged at roof level.

Option 2 wraps secondary spaces around the inner cinema theatre.

2. Sectional perspective view

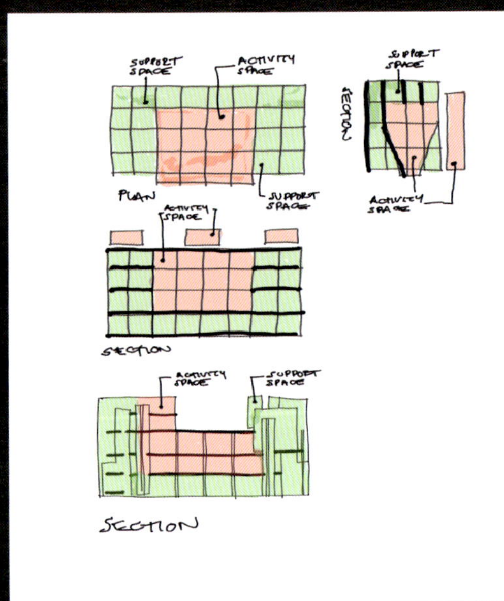

Option 3 models the cinema theatre as an inclined volume which forms sculpted spaces surrounding the form.

Spatial arrangement

The project aims to bring the atmosphere of a film festival to a smaller scale; a venue where film themes change weekly. Consequently, the cinema provides a mixture of spaces for circulating, for seating discussion groups and for informal meetings and seating, in the manner of a traditional theatre.

The spatial arrangement is based on the needs of smaller self-contained spaces which are visible on the facade. This spatial arrangement suits the need for a high level of visual articulation on the facade in order to break down the large-scale volume into a smaller streetscape-scale facade. The facade is more about place-making than imposing a large-scale identity of the form of the building.

For this reason, a large glazed facade at the front is not used; instead, a visual articulation is expressed of each volume and function that lies behind the facade. The arrangement of the facade reflects the different functions and activities that operate within this cinema complex. The spatial arrangement is based on having stairs, lifts and washrooms on the sides of the building where they abut the neighbouring buildings. These are 'support' spaces, or service spaces. In the centre of the spatial composition is a large cinema; facing the street is a circulation space and cafe for the cinema space, used as a meeting area before visitors enter the cinema and where they gather after the show.

The cinema is surrounded by both secondary exhibition spaces and circulation spaces which extend up to roof level. The two projecting volumes have the smaller art-house-based performances, with their more informal atmosphere of arrangements of armchair seating. For the visitor to the building, the spatial arrangement is revealed primarily through the two long facades, and the secondary reading is seen at roof level where the terraces give visual clues to what activities are taking place within, and around, one side of the building. Flexibility of future use was a primary consideration in the arrangement of spaces; the large inner space can be used for functions other than as a cinema. For this reason, the inner sloping floor of the main cinema can be removed to reveal a flat floor surface beneath.

1. Perspective view of interior

2. Perspective view of interior

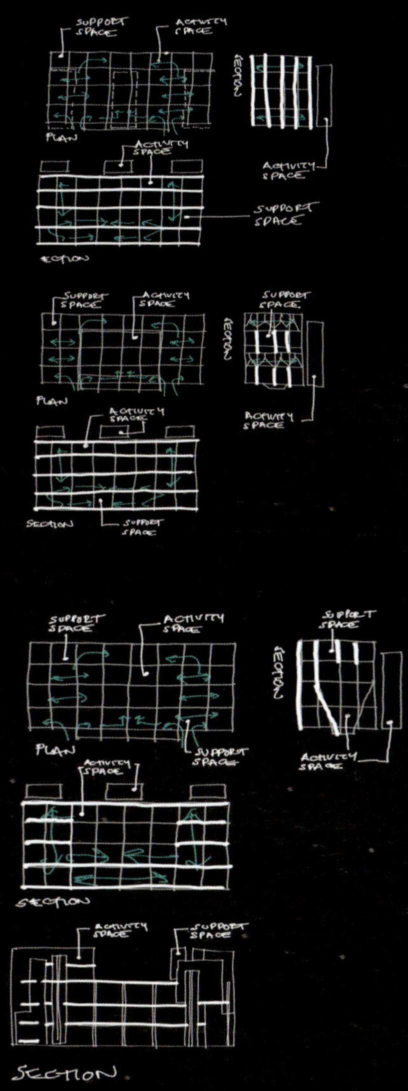

Internal circulation

Option 1 arranges circulation within the two end spaces of the building.

Option 2 arranges circulation spaces on three sides of the building, in plan.

Option 3 arranges circulation spaces on four sides of the building, in plan.

Internal circulation

Visitors enter the reception area on the ground floor, below the projecting volume of the cinema. Staircases direct visitors up to the cafe areas and the projecting volume of the cinema lobby; an area providing views down through glass screens. This projecting volume creates an interaction between inside and outside. From the upper lobby, cinemagoers can pass on up to a roof terrace level; to the projecting volumes of the arthouse cinemas and restaurants. The two arthouse cinema volumes have glazed areas that allow them to be used for meeting and conference space.

When the cinemas are in use, a full-height panel drops down in the manner of a lifting door down over the glass walls to create the cinema screen onto which films are projected. There are three options for the circulation around the building, which are reflected in the three options for the environmental zones, since each environmental zone encloses a set of spaces which are grouped by function. Circulation Zone 1 contains the support spaces of vertical movement: washrooms and storage spaces. Circulation Zone 2 accommodates semi-enclosed spaces for exhibitions and meeting areas which are essentially open spaces. Zone 3 is an enclosed cinema space. In Option 2, the size of the spaces is arranged with support spaces on the edges and the cinema in the centre, which is surrounded by circulation spaces. In Option 2 the circulation forms a circuit, surrounding the central cinema space. In Option 1 the zone for circulation is a linear volume with movement going from front to back and up and down each of the spaces, where each of the zones is linked by small openings that provide a link from one zone to another.

In Option 3 the inhabited facade zone around the perimeter of the building is a development of Option 1, where there are zones which 'penetrate' into the building through the facade; like a series of rectilinear shapes which are stacked together to form zones of space and circulation which are revealed on the facade. This is the preferred opposite solution for both environmental control and internal circulation, as movement occurs within each function and within each zone.

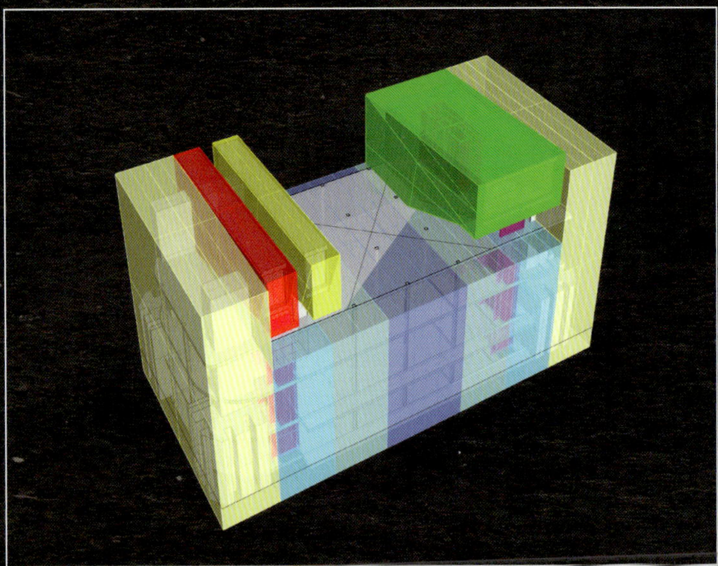

1A. Isometric view of environmental volumes

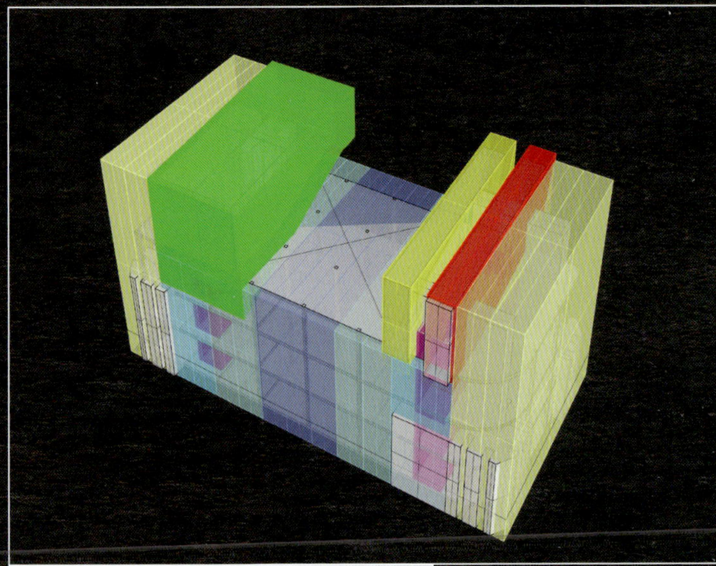

2A. Isometric view of environmental volumes

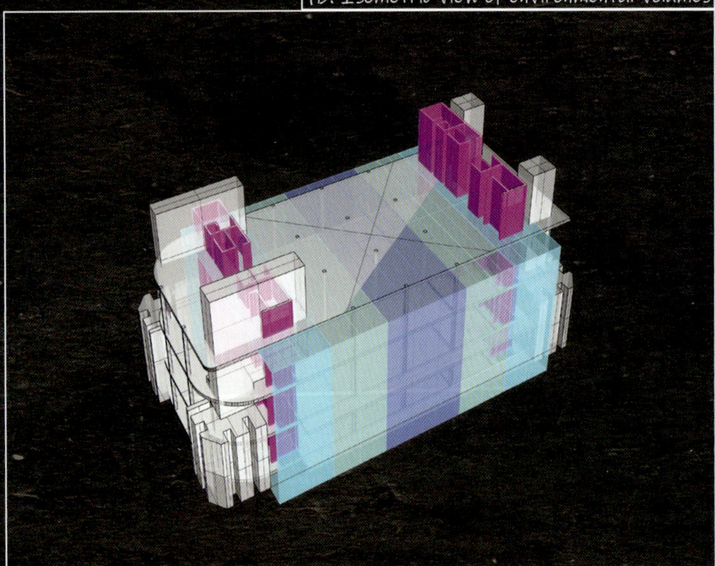

1B. Isometric view of environmental volumes

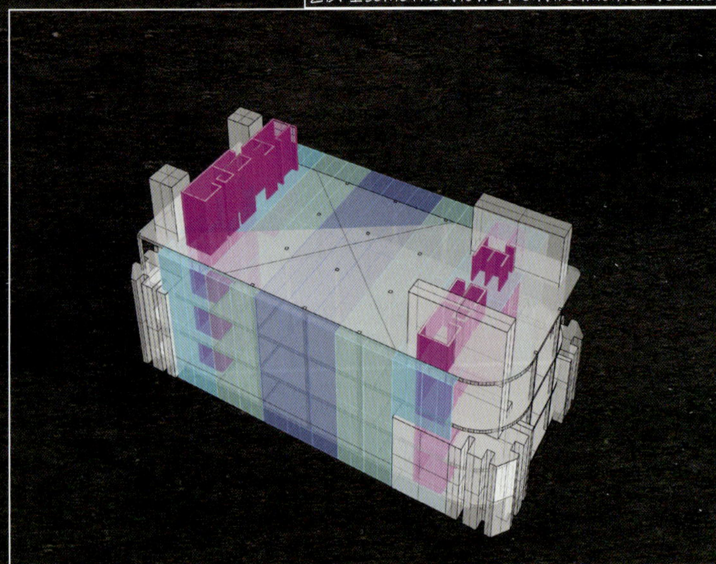

2B. Isometric view of environmental volumes

Environmental strategy

Environmental zones are built around the primary space of the cinema theatre where the primary requirement is for cooling. In addition, high air changes per hour are required by the support spaces surrounding the theatre. One key consideration in the design is to have a continuous circulation space around the theatre, the cinema volume being like an 'egg in a box' or a 'building in a building'; an enclosed volume with ancillary spaces around it. The surrounding spaces host new exhibitions each month, allowing the spaces surrounding the theatre to have changing functions, with fewer air changes per hour required than within the central volume. Cool air supplied to the theatre is filtered, recirculated and partially replaced in the support areas around the cinema theatre space.

The environmental strategy is one of encouraging natural ventilation in spaces that surround the main cinema. Enclosed spaces within the building are mechanically ventilated to extract heat, which is used to supply the surrounding spaces in the winter and mid-season.

The environmental strategy comprises three options. Option 1 has Environmental Zone 1 both in plan and in section on the edges of the building adjacent to the adjoining buildings. Zone 2 is set on either side of Zone 1. Zone 3 is set in the centre, with Zone 2 on either side at roof level. The three cinema halls comprise a Zone 4, which is externally mounted. Option 1 provides flexibility of use within the building, and addresses the main functions of having the cinema in the centre of the building with the service zones on the edges of the building. Option 2 is an 'egg in a box'. It has all support functions and secondary spaces set either side of the central volume of the cinema as a large self-contained, environmental space in the middle. This is surrounded by the circulation and activity spaces, directly following the functions in a simplified form, as an 'inhabited facade'. This provides a separate environmental zone in each of the 32 square-shaped areas of the facade, projecting them back into the building as a series of boxes extruded out into the facade. This is the environmental strategy selected for the building, as it fits well with the structural Option 3 which drives the environmental

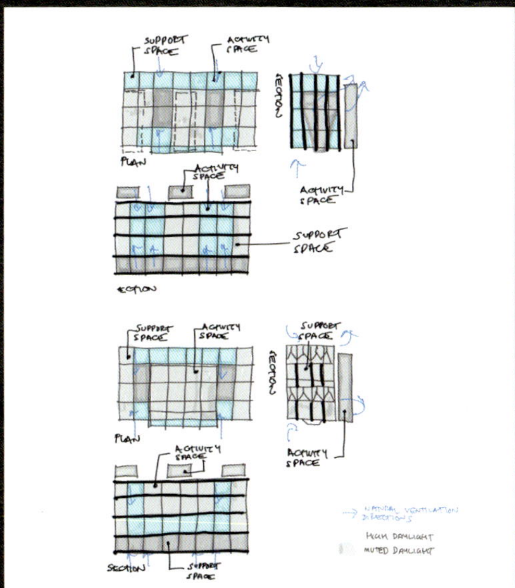

Daylight strategy for direct sunlight and cross ventilation.
Option 1 admits daylight on two sides of the building, through the full depth of the circulation spaces.
Option 2 widens the central circulation space in order to add the main entrance floor.

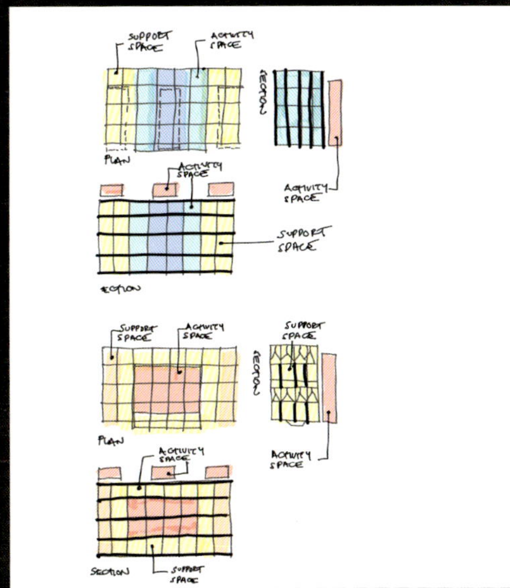

Environmental zones
Option 1 has the main functions of having the cinema in the centre of the building.
Option 2 has all support functions and secondary spaces set either side of the central volume of the cinema.

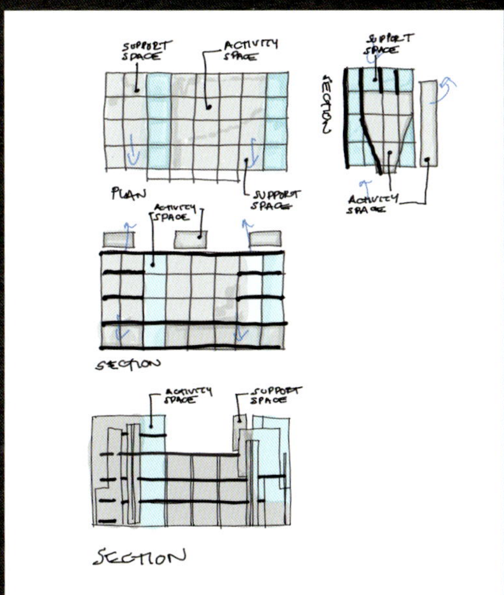

Daylight strategy for direct sunlight and cross ventilation.
Option 3 admits daylight and natural ventilaton in narrow bands extending the full depth of the building.

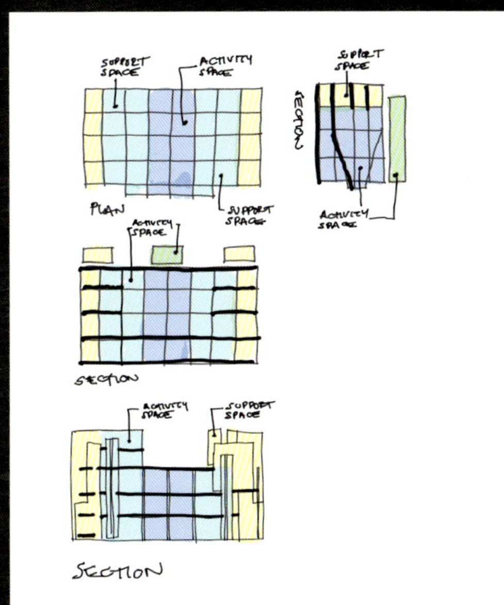

Environmental zones
Option 3 has spaces serviced individually and independently from one another at roof level.

zones. Although the environmental zones correspond to the current functions, they can be combined to form larger rectilinear zones from the cube-like structural modules.

The building is to be constructed by a local building contracting company, as part of the construction method of using systems which are adapted to the smaller-scale services. Installation of the mechanical ventilation is one of a set of package units which are mounted at roof level and which serve each of the spaces, or each of the zones. Ducting is simplified such that there is a vertical supply and extract for the main cinema space, and packaged self-contained installations for the supporting spaces in the building. A limitation of this method is that air cannot be redistributed easily from space to space, but each system can be controlled independently in order to minimise the use of energy in the building for spaces which are not occupied.

This system works for Option 3 but is less suited to Options 1 and 2, which have larger-scale systems for each group of spaces. In Option 3, which is the preferred option, spaces are serviced individually and independently from one another at roof level. This provides a system which can be installed economically and which suits modest-scale construction methods.

This approach to design increases the possibility of using natural ventilation and daylight as a result of the forms being separated out into forms which avoid the deep plan arrangement of buildings where natural light and air cannot penetrate far into the building. The use of narrower floor plates with light and air being able to reach into the building reduces energy consumption for mechanical ventilation and electrical lighting. This approach results in the volume of the building increasing upwards, but this requirement brings the possibility of open spaces at roof level and the ability to introduce terraces at different levels within a building; terraces that might be set internally, externally or may form thermal buffer zones when used as winter gardens or semi-external spaces. The use of a structure which is integrated with these semi-external spaces, and not separate from them, allows the form of construction to remain economical.

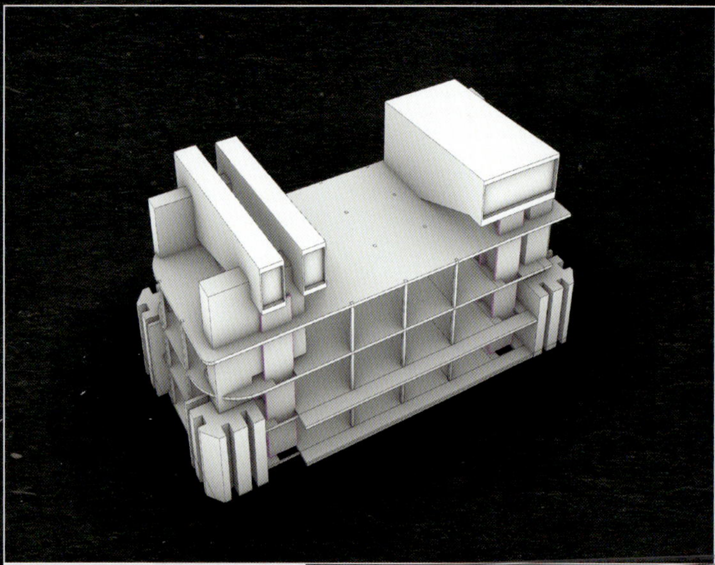

1A. Isometric view of structure

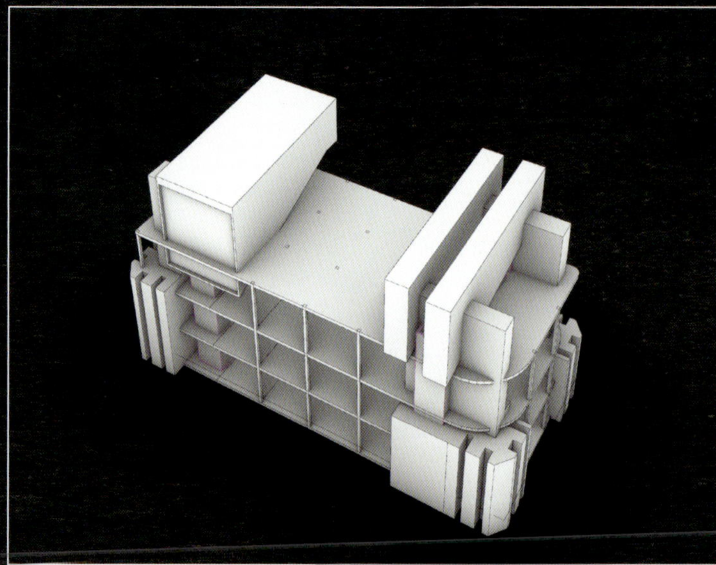

2A. Isometric view of structure

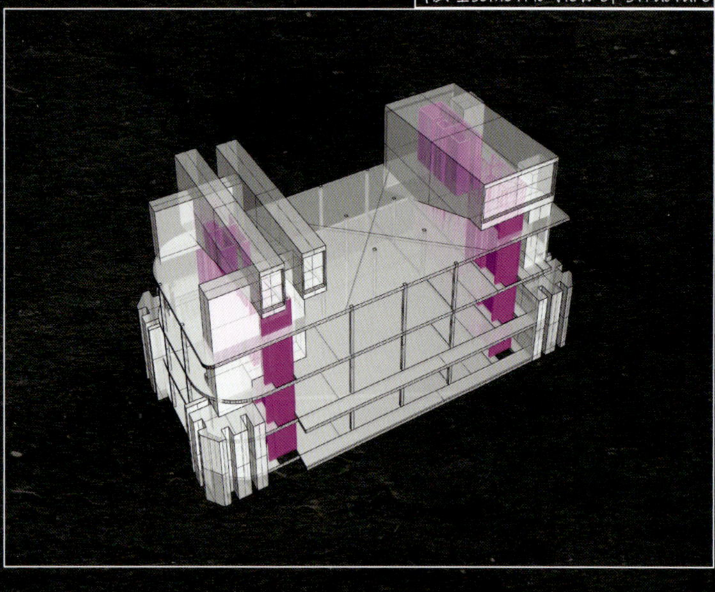

1B. Isometric view of structure

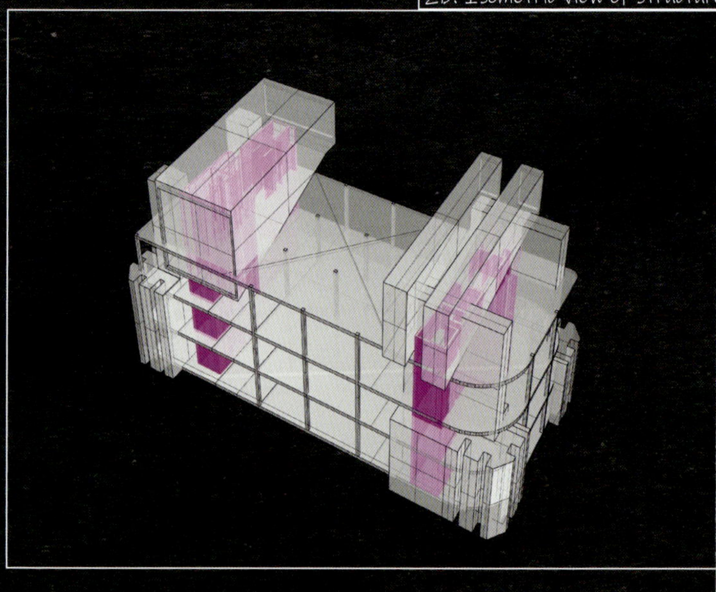

2B. Isometric view of structure

Structural strategy

The structural design strategy comprises a set of 6.0 metre by 6.0 metre by 6.0 metre cubes set together to provide modules for the set of cinemas that comprise this building. The 6.0 metre-based module is fabricated as a series of steel frames that are fixed together to form a continuous steel frame; some of the elements are prefabricated at corners and as roof volumes. Other elements are mainly site assembled and are fixed to the modular steel frames; site-assembled elements are mainly on the side of the building that faces the square. The structural arrangements inside the building use different unit sizes, 3.0 metres wide x 4.5 metres long, that consider the need for smaller spaces which cannot have structural members crossing through internal walls. This modular arrangement allows components to be delivered by road in a semi-prefabricated form that reduces significantly the time required for installation on site, which is a key requirement of the brief/program. The steel frame makes use of canvas textile-based sheets which are stretched from the steel frames to create canopies for external breakout spaces at terrace level.

The structural strategy has three options. Option 1 has peripheral steel columns and steel frames in a two-way spanning grid. The central area of the cinema is enclosed with structural walls in concrete. Alternatively, those walls could be made from triangulated steel framing. Option 2 has structural walls which enclose the edges of the central cinema, extending the full width of the building between support spaces. The remainder of the structure is a two-way spanning set of trusses over the central cinema space. Option 3 is a steel-framed solution, where the main beams are spanning across the full width of the centre, extending out to the two facades, such that the same structural solution seen on the two long facades extends all the way through the building; nothing is concealed structurally inside the building. Option 3 is preferred as this provides a single structural solution for the building that extends through its full width, providing a simplified structural solution and avoiding having a different structural arrangement internally, which would provide less flexibility should the configuration of the build-

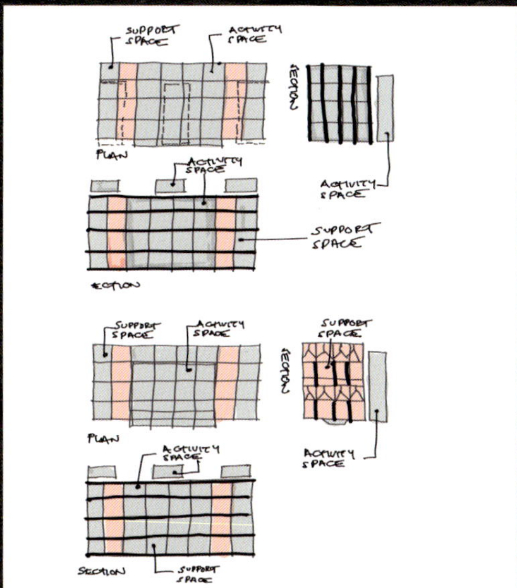

Structural strategy: Zones

Option 1 has peripheral steel columns and steel frames in a two-way spanning grid.

Option 2 has structural walls which enclose the edges of the cinema.

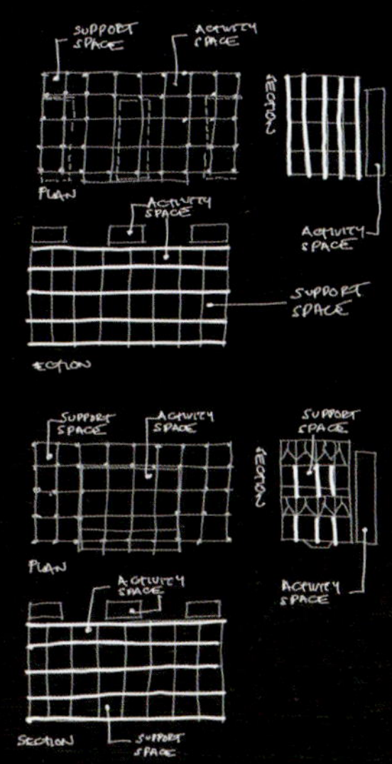

Structural strategy: Framing

Option 1 has a central area of the cinema enclosed with structural walls in concrete.

Option 2 has structural walls extending the full width of the building between support spaces.

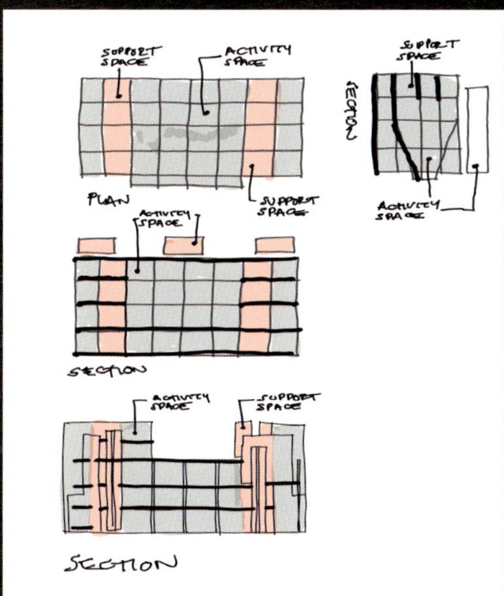

Structural strategy: Zones Option 3 is a steel-framed solution, where the main beams are spanning across the full width of the centre.

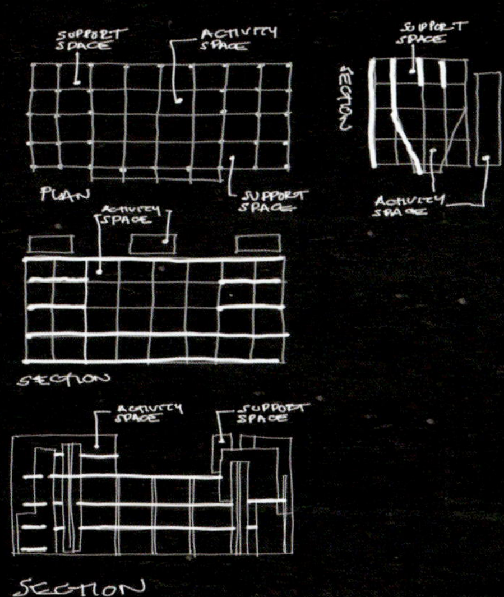

Structural strategy: Zones Option 3 provides a single structural solution for the building that extends through its full width.

ing need to change in the near future.

The primary structure comprises a grid-like structural frame which is modular and which is consistent in size throughout the floors that comprise the central structural form. Secondary structural elements are added to this frame, comprising 'blocks' which enclose primary spaces within the building, including the cinema volumes set on the roof and the overhanging box-like forms. The projecting canopy structure at the mid-height of the building encloses a part of the reception area positioned in front of the cinemas. This cantilevered form is structurally continuous with the inner structural frame. The use of a modular inner frame allows the secondary structural elements to be added with relative ease as they follow the same dimensional arrangement as the primary form. The secondary structures effectively surround the inner rectilinear frame, as well as setting forms at roof level to create a rich geometric structural form that makes use of an economical form of a steel frame with additional secondary structures. The approach allows forms to be created which are at the same scale as the surrounding buildings, and allow large-scale openings to be formed within each bay for the passage of natural ventilation and daylight through the depth of the building. The relatively shallow depth of the floor plan adds further economy to the structure, which uses a regular structural grid. The centre of the rectilinear structure is effectively hollow at the upper levels in order to create the space for a cinema. The roof of the cinema is enclosed with trusses which provide an economic covering to the central space. The smaller cinema enclosures are set on the sides of the cinema structure so that the trusses form an economical enclosure; they are not required to carry the loads of any additional forms above. The structures are of different scales and sizes in order to provide the richness of form associated with this part of the city, without reducing the massing of the building to a single rectilinear form. The richness of the volumetric composition is partly achieved with an economical form of steel construction. The frame is clad in lightweight panels which avoid large areas of glass and which are considerably lighter, making fewer demands of the supporting structure.

Project 02. Arthouse cinema
Typical bay adjacent to facade

Perspective view of
typical bay from below

Typical bay adjacent to facade

The facades are based on a 6.0-metre x 6.0-metre cube that forms the structural bay for the complete building. There is a subdivision into a 2.5-metre, cube-shaped facade bay with a 500-millimetre module on each end of the panel, providing a module that is dimensionally compatible with the 6.0-metre-wide and 6.0-metre-high panel for the facades. This module is continued around the full extent of the building, allowing a high degree of variation both in the ability to project out balconies as well as provide inclined elements that respond to the specific spatial needs inside the building. The module also creates an outer zone of the building that is highly differentiated in its volumes in relation to the central space. The 6.0-metre grid of the inner building surrounds that of the outer building, which follows the same grid but has some smaller components that fit within it to create the high level of spatial differentiation in response to the brief/program, which requires that spaces are environmentally independent of each other around the building. This was achieved by using the same construction system but reducing the member size to fit a 2.5-metre and 500-millimetre facade grid, using a light-gauge steel carrier frame to which the cladding panels are added. The modular nature of the facade panels allows them to be swapped out and replaced in response to changes of use within the spatial arrangement without an associated high cost of doing so. This approach allows secondary and tertiary items to be added to the facade structure, such as balconies supported on lightweight steel frames, rather than using a solution of cantilevered slabs, for example. The outer areas of the building use the same structural components for small-scale assemblies around the site for washrooms that form part of the building. The finishes are all robust and durable, allowing the facades to weather well and form part of the aesthetic, which is one of a robust, visible structure.

The external envelope takes the different facade treatments of Option 3, which is the preferred option, and provides a single facade system across both long elevations, but with different materials applied to each. This approach of a single system with a variation between functions

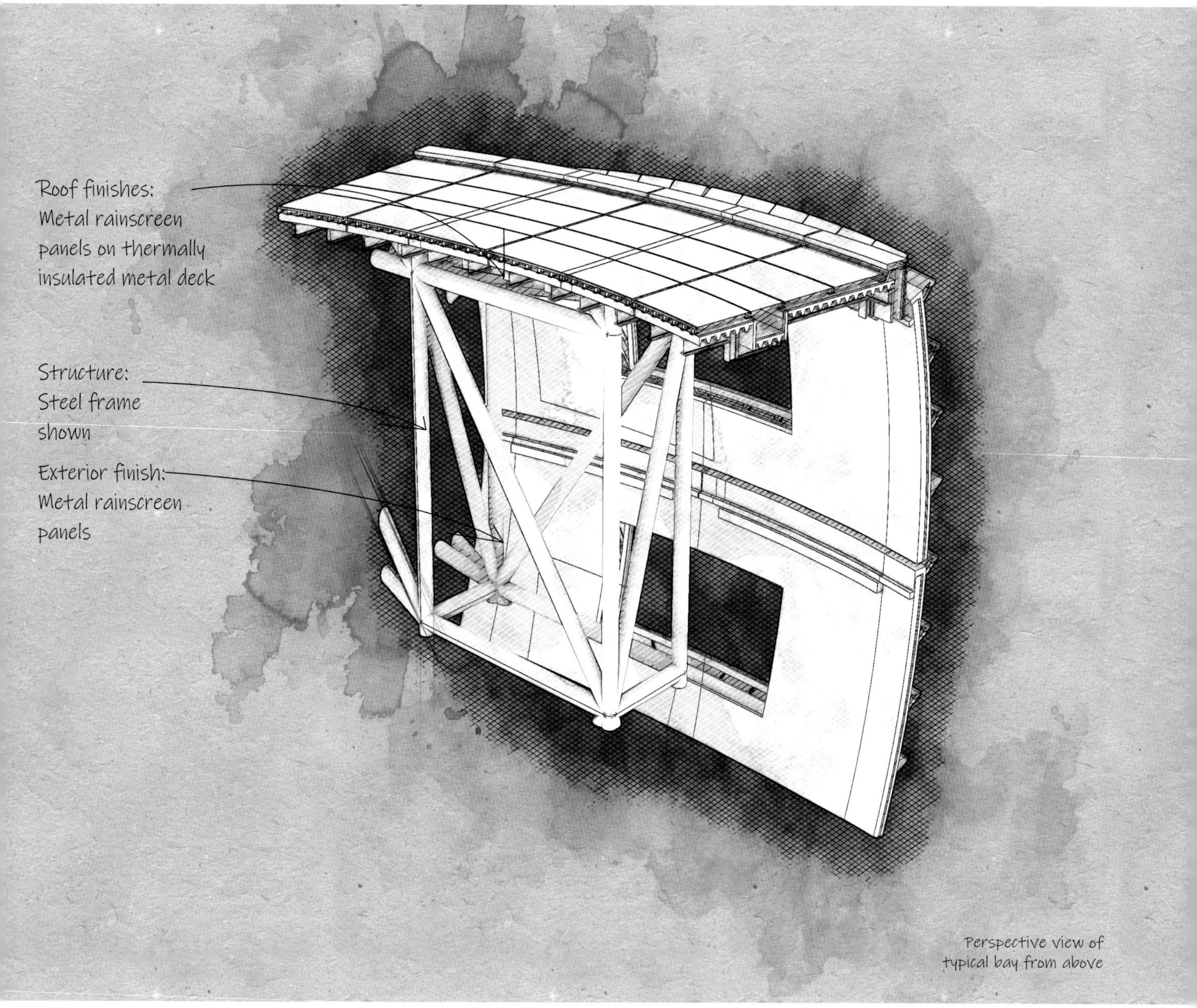

Perspective view of typical bay from above

avoids the need for interfaces between different facade treatments that would otherwise create a set of very different building forms. The variation in the breaking down of the facade into small volumes is achieved economically with a single facade system, as would have been the case with a historic built example in the city.

The frame allows for facade panels to be removed and swapped out. Most facade panels are on a 2.5-metre by 2.5-metre module fitting with edge panels into a 6.0-metre by 6.0 metre frame, which allows them to arrive by road for their installation on site.

Design of the cinema does not rely on having only billboard advertising of films or even having large-scale media wall projections for advertising, but instead has a set of interacting volumes that have small screens set into them to provide information for the public, which can be viewed both internally and externally.

Glazing is small scale with windows opening out onto the street in specific locations to create views in and out of the building. This approach is used instead of large glazed panels which would have been unsuitable for site installation. The facade makes use of a mixture of metal framing and metal rainscreen panels with windows inserted into them. The scale of the framing of the facades suits site-assembled facade construction with pre-assembled panels fabricated off site. Light gauge steel framing is used, similar to that used for the internal spaces. This approach is an alternative to an all site-based construction, both in order to reduce cost and to add value to a complex form, which brings the advantage of reduced energy consumption as a result of the potential for greater use of natural ventilation and daylight in circulation areas. The use of semi-prefabrication allows different facade panel sizes to be used to enclose the different secondary structures and spaces while remaining within the economical grid of the supporting structure. The use of small-scale panels contrasting with larger panels creates an arrangement which adds a visual complexity that might have been missing in a simplified, large scale building form in this location, while also meeting the performance requirements of the different spaces which are enclosed by the envelope.

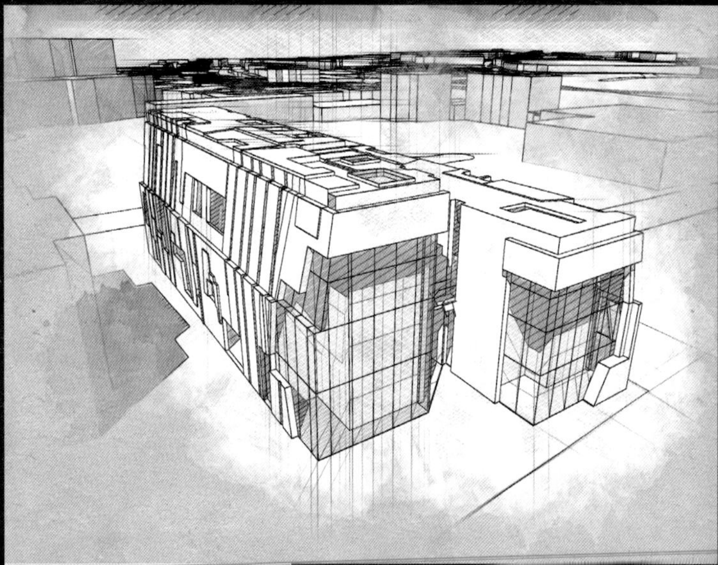

1. Perspective view of exterior

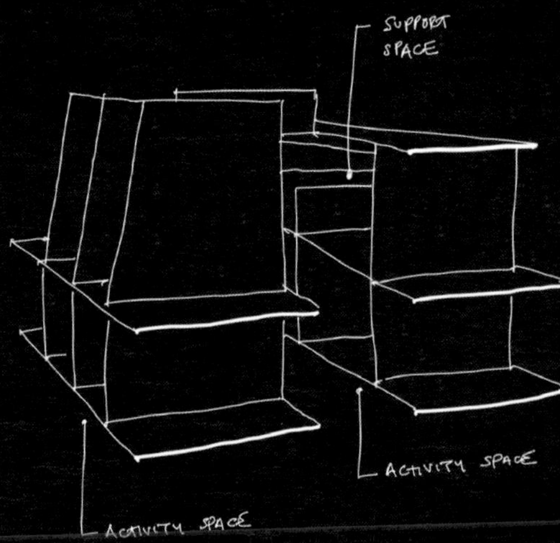

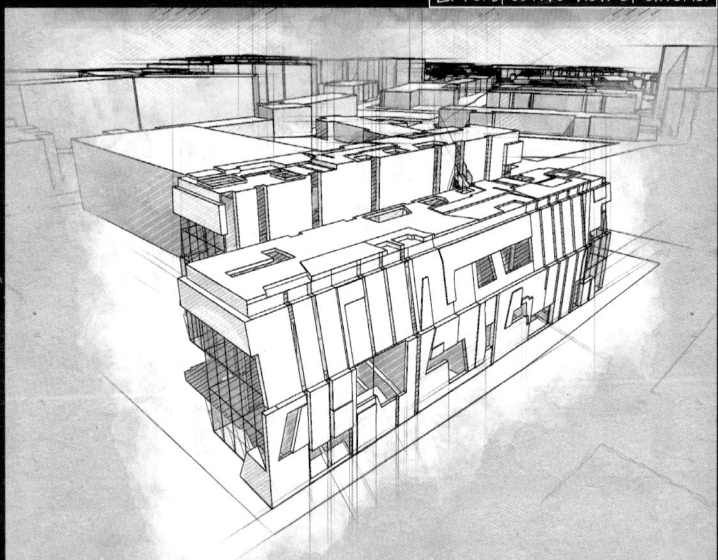

2. Perspective view of exterior

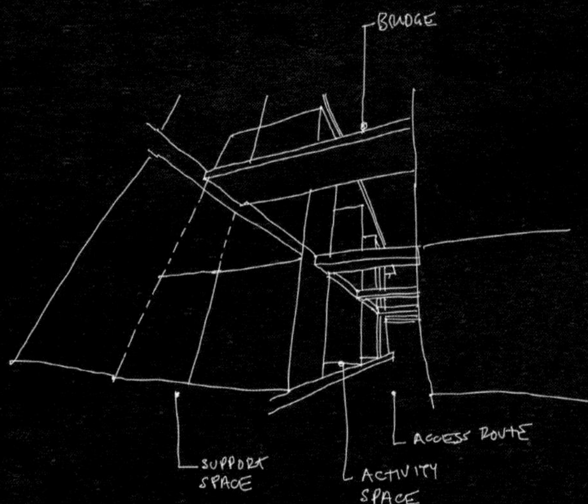

Services-free internal space

The environmental approach to this project is based on the need to have geometrically clearly defined spaces that are free of visual obstructions, to allow internal spaces to be as flexible as possible in their use and that avoid the potentially high environmental cost of the need for extensive refurbishment. As part of this strategy, groups of different-sized spaces are juxtaposed and linked within the podium in order to allow them to be combined differently in the near future; a set of linked spaces defined by the environmental treatment of the facades that are adjacent to these spaces, as well as the circulation cores set within, and between, the sets of spaces. The corresponding environmental concept is based on having facades which address the specific requirements for natural daylight and natural ventilation in each space. As a result, support spaces for services are positioned at the ends of the building as cores; the required stability of the building structure is provided by the cores accordingly. Option 3 is the preferred option for each of the six strategy categories; the corresponding structural configuration of columns set within the central circulation cores, instead of structural walls, allows the core to be repositioned laterally. 'Breakout' areas of floor slab allow sections of structural floor slab to be lifted out to allow new stairs and a lift/elevator to be inserted. Option 1 has central cores that already occupy the full length of each building, forming a continuous service spine of mechanical and electrical services. Option 2 sets the services and circulation zones both at the ends of the building and alongside an external wall in the centre of the building. Option 3 has both 'activity' spaces and 'support' spaces in the centre of the building.

In order to achieve clear and open spaces in all three buildings, the floor slabs are supported by downstand beams in order to allow the central part of the floor to be removed in the near future for circulation cores or services cores to be relocated. The use of downstand beams creates the basis of environmental zones for each of the five sets of spaces created in Option 3. The floor slabs in each environmental zone have a set of cast-in channels in the slab soffit (underside of slab) to facilitate

Perspective view of exterior

4. Perspective view of exterior

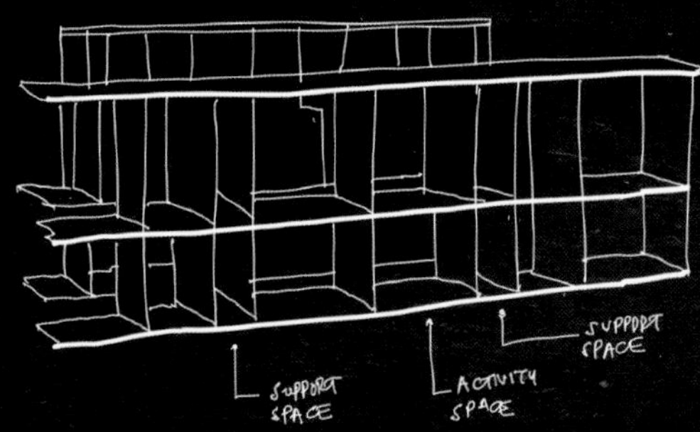

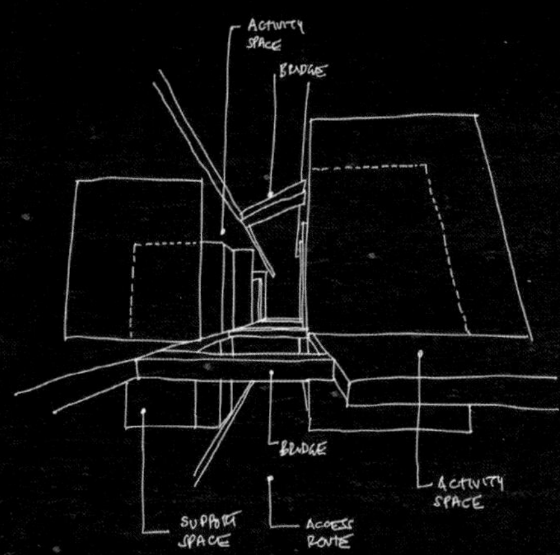

the fixing of a suspended ceiling and wall partitions below. The edges of the floor slabs, adjacent to the facades, will have cast-in inserts on their vertical faces to fix secondary facade devices, such as solar shading devices, to be added or modified at a later date. The ability of the structure to allow for future additions to the ceilings and facades is a key part of the environmental strategy; avoiding the structure being unable to meet the changing requirements of the use of internal spaces and the environmental strategy required for their implementation.

Services-free space is introduced as roof-mounted service modules which are fixed to the roof of the inclined facades, with services being distributed across the adjacent glazed roof and downwards into the internal spaces. An alternative system in place allows services to pass down through the opaque roof into the opaque wall areas internally, so that air is distributed at levels within the large internal spaces as well as within the adjacent fully glazed volumes. The glazed parts of the building have solar shading at roof level in the form of solar baffles, which control daylight but also enable two-storey internal display areas to be daylit without the associated glare. The service modules have a visual identity of their own and are arranged across the roof, such that the functioning of the services and the supply is straightforward to modify and adjust to suit changing patterns of use. This approach requires openings to be formed in floor slabs in order for air-handling ducts, for example, to be modified to pass downwards vertically from the roof, should modifications to air supply be required.

The spatially complex arrangement of volumes does not suit services being distributed vertically in cores and horizontally on the ceilings of each floor; cores do not serve individual spaces. Instead, cores are arranged for circulation and washrooms; services are distributed from roof level to suit the spatial arrangement. The juxtaposition of spaces occurs only horizontally, in the sense that spaces of the same shape are stacked vertically from a single floor plan. The approach of stacking spaces vertically provides a high level of differentiation in plan, which assists in the generation of an economical structural arrangement which suits the vertical distribution of services.

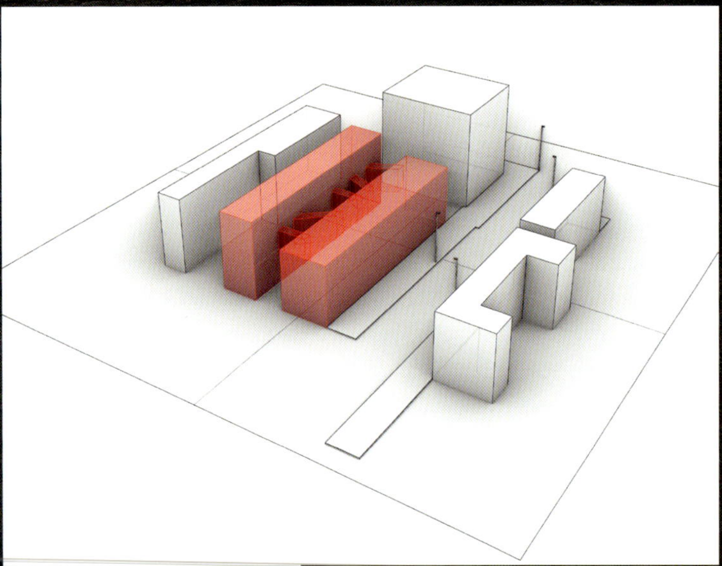

1. Project volume in site context

2. Project volume in site context

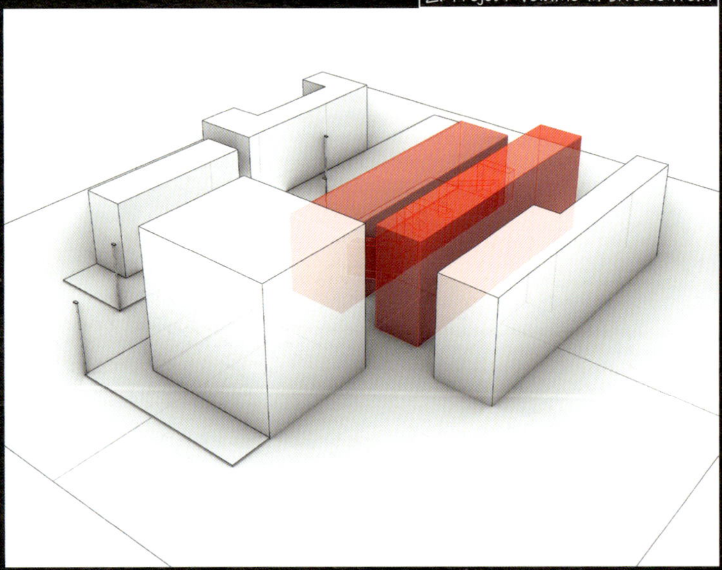

1. Site plan with surrounding context

Option 1 comprises a single rectilinear box, positioned within the site boundary, with gaps between the new building and the surrounding buildings.

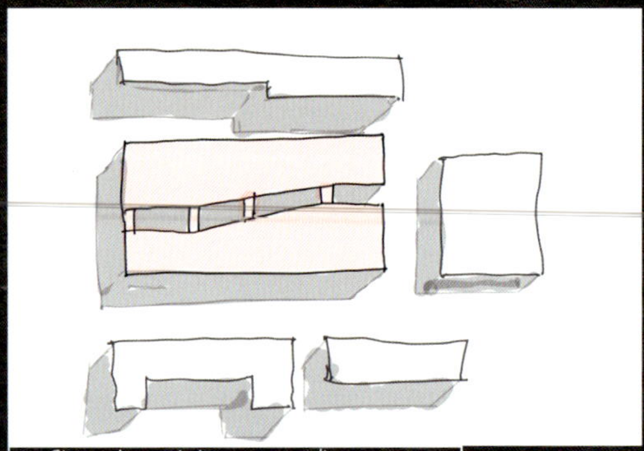

2. Site plan with surrounding context

Option 2 occupies the full extent of the site and pushes the building to the edges, up against its neighbouring buildings.

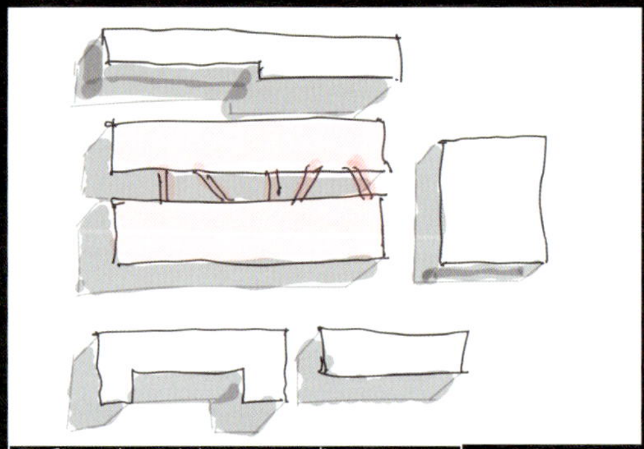

3. Site plan with surrounding context

Option 3 is a 'kit of parts' of different facade elements; large-scale lifting doors, services equipment on the roof and large-sized floor plates.

Site context

The building is set within a semi-urban context; an area undergoing revitalisation and redevelopment, with a mixed set of uses in the immediate area. New projects for light industry, leisure and residential projects surround the site; the context is one of a complete semi-urban block, with buildings of different size set adjacent to the rectangular plot that is occupied by the building. The overall forms that comprise the building are arranged to be similar in size to the massing of its neighbours. This research and development facility for a car manufacturer has large-scale dedicated spaces with a large amount of mechanical and electrical equipment. This makes the spaces much less flexible in the long term, as 'strong floors' are required; these are floors with fixing points for testing and lifting equipment cast into strengthened reinforced concrete floor slabs. The different volumes of the building are set into a 'terrace' arrangement; positioned side by side, with service modules set within the terrace but extending a full floor height above adjacent spaces in order to accommodate rooftop technical equipment, including air-handling units and chillers for mechanical ventilation of the spaces beneath. This makes the spatial arrangement of the building something resembling a ground-scraper where the 'activity' spaces and the' support' spaces of the services design are set out and made visible across the roof; similar to that of a service riser in a tall building, but appearing to have been laid on its side for this project. The site context for Option 1 is one of the single rectilinear box, positioned within the site boundary, with gaps between the new building and the surrounding buildings. The facility is located in an industrial area where neighbouring buildings have regular vehicle deliveries, both in the access yard side of the building and on the side of the building facing the road; pedestrian access is set on the roadside. This arrangement of box-like forms, at the urban design scale of the project, allows manufacturing and fabrication to take place at the rear of the building, facing the service yards with access for arrival and departure of vehicle assemblies. The front of the building is divided into two parts for offices and for meetings and reception space.

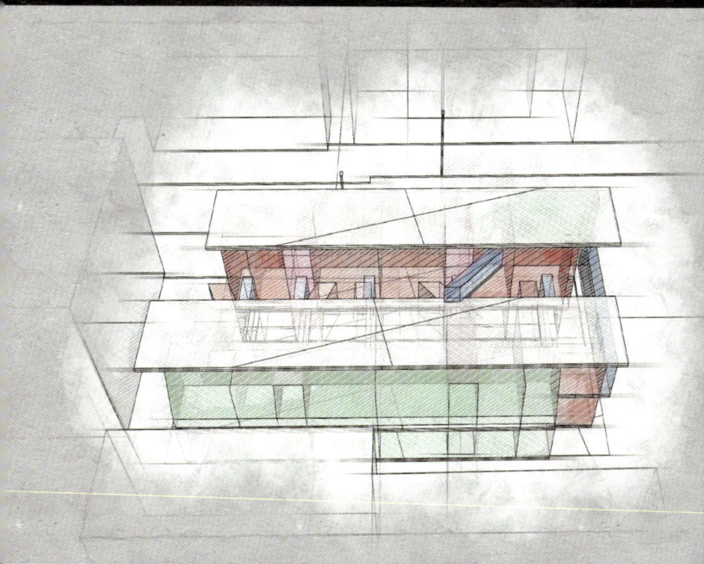

Perspective view of environmental volumes

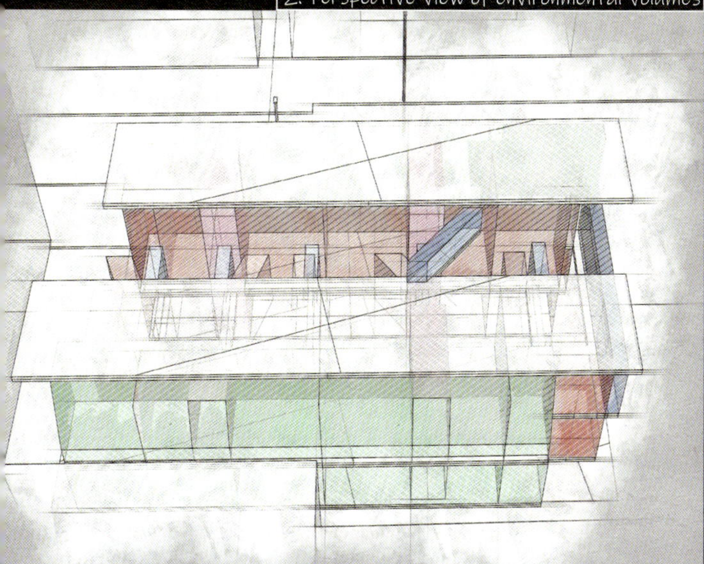

2. Perspective view of environmental volumes

1. Figure-ground diagram of tempered environment

Option 1
Red spaces are highly tempered. Green spaces are less tempered; these are internal circulation spaces.

2. Figure-ground diagram of tempered environment

Option 2
The blue spaces are less tempered than the red spaces, but more tempered than the green circulation spaces.

3. Figure-ground diagram of tempered environment

Option 3
The red spaces are more subdivided than Options 1 and 2; providing opportunities for greater energy saving in their use.

Option 2 occupies the full extent of the site and pushes the building to the edges up against its neighbouring buildings; the form of the building is dived into two separate forms that create a service yard, or route. The two parts of the building are linked by enclosed bridges at the upper level. This service route also ensures the provision of sufficient daylight to enter the building, and meets the required distance between each block. This option allows for vehicle access for arrival and departure of assemblies by way of the side wall of each block, a manufacturing fabrication facility which can extend from the front to the back of the site with the offices set up in their space adjacent to it. Option 2 is essentially two cranked boxes linked by brdges; one for offices and one for fabrication.

Option 3 provides a more granular approach of being able to make the building from a 'kit of parts' where more flexibility is provided than is the case in Options 1 and 2, by using the full width of the site but not cranking the building forms. This configuration makes access for components and vehicle assemblies easier to manage than is the case with the previous options, and provides flexibility for vehicle and pedestrian access along the whole of the courtyard. The vehicle yard access side of the building, office facilities and technical facilities for manufacturing are located on top of the building and arranged such that they create meeting spaces at a low level with services equipment at roof level. These modules can be repositioned during the life of the building: by lifting crane, in order for future rooflights to be introduced above office spaces, or alternatively as a result of roof-mounted modules being repositioned. Option 3 is a 'kit of parts' of different facade elements: large-scale lifting doors, services equipment on the roof and a glazed area on the facades and large-sized floor plates that provide the high level of flexibility that is anticipated to be required during the life of the building. The modules project out from the building in order to align with projections of the adjacent existing buildings, tying them together visually while aligning the yard facade with that of the adjacent building. This arrangement allows all building volumes to be fitted together neatly within the urban design context.

1. Sectional perspective view

2. Sectional perspective view

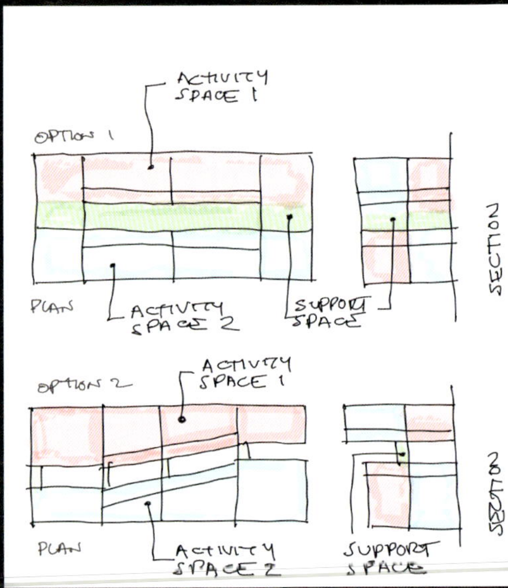

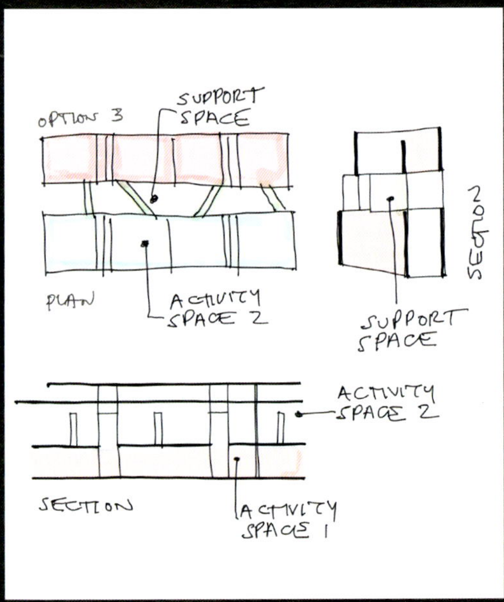

Spatial arrangement

Option 1 configures the building as a rectilinear box, independent of the buildings next to it.

Option 2 uses the full width of the site over a single storey with the flexibility of being able to change the studio space into fabrication space.

Option 3 has the building's width reduced in order to avoid clashing with windows and openings in one of the adjacent buildings.

Spatial arrangement

The project comprises two superimposed elements of space: ground floor garages for the physical testing of vehicles and an assembly workshop for vehicles set on the floor above. A third component comprises a design studio, set in various configurations. Roof-mounted services equipment supplies heating and cooling energy to the two floors beneath the roof.

The spatial arrangement of Option 1 configures the building as a rectilinear box, independent of the buildings next to it. This approach allows a straightforward subdivision of space between fabrication, which is at the rear of the side facing the delivery yard, and studio spaces at the front, facing the street and support spaces for vertical circulation and washrooms. Storage space is provided at the intersection of the studio and fabrication space, with associated entrance and stairs at the far corners of the building.

Option 2 forms a continuous external space down the centre of the buildingwith the flexibility of being able to change the studio space into fabrication space, and vice versa. The fabrication space is extended out into the yard, but does not use as much space as Option 1; forming a different shape from Option 1. The support spaces are a single spine, which extends the length of the building at the yard side of the studios and divides the fabrication space. Support spaces are roof mounted in order to allow the fabrication space to become a single combined volume.

In Option 3, the footprint of the building forms a wider service and access yard. The width of the building is reduced in order to avoid clashing visually with windows and openings in one of the adjacent buildings. The studio space is arranged over two storeys; the fabrication space is over a single storey. The support spaces required for the fabrication area that would have been inside the area footprint are now roof-mounted. This approach still allows for studio space to be used on the ground floor for fabrication, but with a lower floor-to-ceiling height than the current fabrication space. This arrangement provides some flexibility, but more importantly provides a compact arrangement of spaces.

Perspective view of interior

2. Perspective view of interior

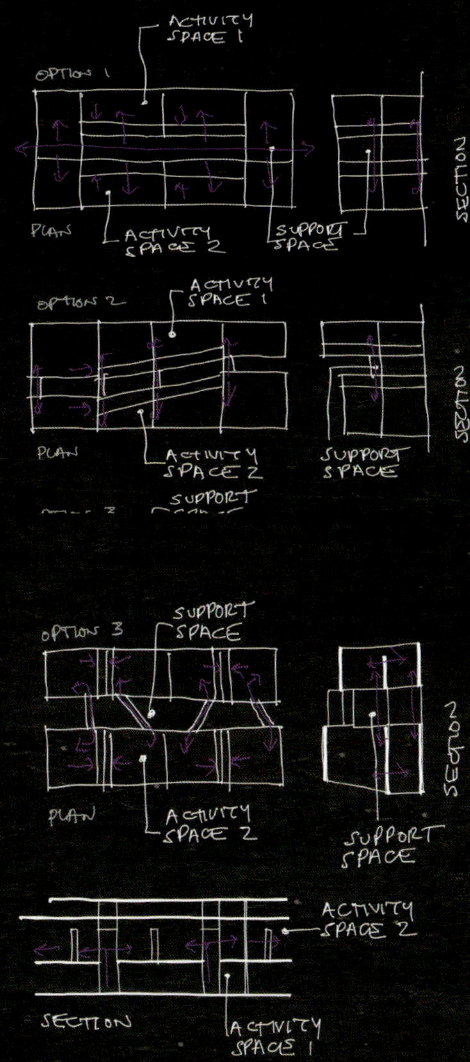

Internal circulation

Option 1 is based on having separate entrances for the studio spaces and access for the arrival and departure of assemblies.

Option 2 has the access for the studios on the roadside facade.

Option 3 provides access to circulation from the junction of the studio and the fabrication space on the street side.

Internal circulation

This is a building where components are assembled, trialled and tested, and are implemented in different versions of rapid prototype car assemblies, which can then be lowered to the garage below for bench testing which is followed by track testing nearby. Modifications are carried out within the workshop; these are often large-scale modifications required to overcome unexpected limitations in vehicle design. The aim of the building is to enable prototypes to be optimised for road-based vehicle performance, in an environment which enables all skills and expertise to be accommodated together in a single, compact building. The facility carries out two types of testing:

On-track testing and on-road performance testing, monitored by electronic equipment accommodated in the interstitial zones between the garages. The second type of testing of prototypes is to establish their smooth-running performance on the road. These test laboratory facilities require a taller space, which is accommodated in the volumes which form the upper level space for the fabrication of automotive assemblies. The internal circulation for Option 1 is based on having separate entrances, for the studio spaces and access for the arrival and departure of assemblies, located at the rear of the fabrication space within the enclosed service yard. The entrance to the building is also within the service yard. This arrangement of circulation allows easy access to both studio and fabrication. In Option 2 the access for the studios is on the roadside facades. There is an additional possibility of the fabrication also being accessed from the roadside, though this access is intended primarily as a means of escape during fire. Access to the fabrication space for deliveries is provided by the service road, or yard, and access to the studios and fabrication space takes place along the full extent of the back of the studio space. Option 3 provides access to circulation from the junction of the studio and the fabrication space on the street side. Access can be given through to protecting modules which take visitors directly up two floors to the top floor level, where they can go to meeting rooms with views down into the studio and workshops below.

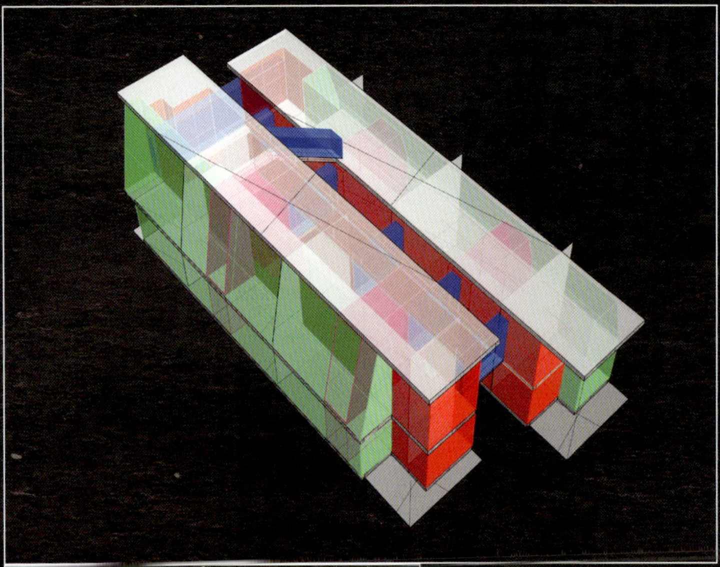

1A. Isometric view of environmental volumes

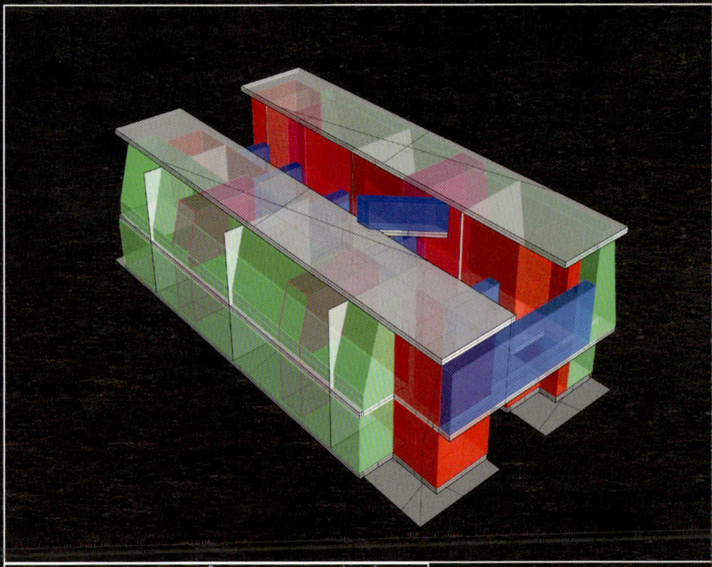

2A. Isometric view of environmental volumes

1B. Isometric view of environmental volumes

2B. Isometric view of environmental volume

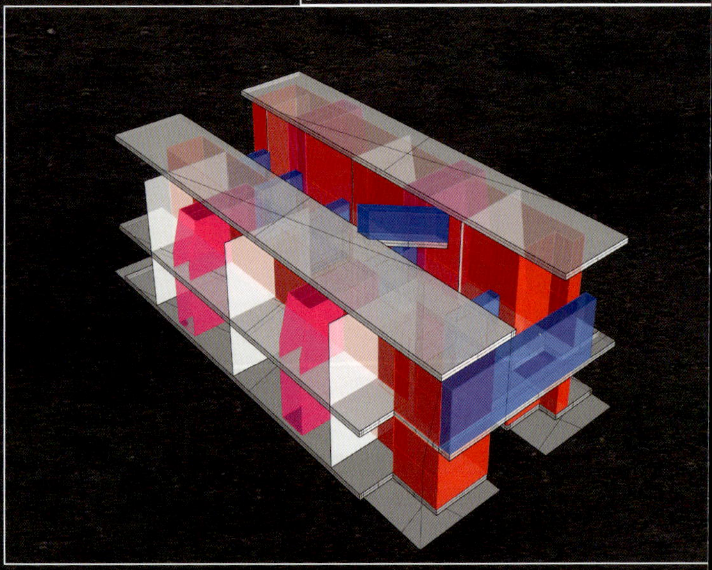

Environmental strategy

The environmental strategy is based on the excess heat generated in the fabrication shop being recycled by a heat exchanger to the spaces below, which often need to have the doors open to provide access for vehicles. This provides warmth in winter and cooling energy in the summer months. The building comprises four environmental zones: the garages, the fabrication workshops, the mechanical testing laboratories and the design studio. The roof of the garages, accommodating the services installation, is laid out in the manner of a 'circuit board diagram' of the electrical and mechanical functions of services equipment. This approach is used in order for the building to be maintained and serviced with ease. Below the roof level the fabrication space has largely opaque external walls following the customary layout, specific lighting conditions and inward focus required in manufacturing buildings for car prototypes. In this case, the manufacturing is miniaturised into a compact set of workshops. The roof also provides the 'support' spaces, or service spaces, for the volumes beneath. The roof level is the entrance deck to the building, enclosed in glass; the services equipment is set above this level. Access to spaces is downward into each of these spaces; the top-down approach to access provides access to meeting rooms and design studios, with views down to workshops and the garage set beneath.

The project is set in a temperate climate, providing the contrasting areas of enclosure and glazing required to have high levels of thermal insulation to maintain constant temperature and humidity. Glazed areas have deployable blinds to control daylight. Breakout spaces, meeting rooms and offices have night-time natural ventilation, with mixed natural ventilation and mechanical ventilation during the day. The environmental options are all based on a separation of the environmental zones for fabrication and for studio space. Studio spaces are well lit with natural daylight; fabrication spaces have much less daylight, with north light introduced at roof level and high-level horizontal bands of windows for reducing the amount of light that enters the space but which is evenly distributed across the space. Studio spaces use much

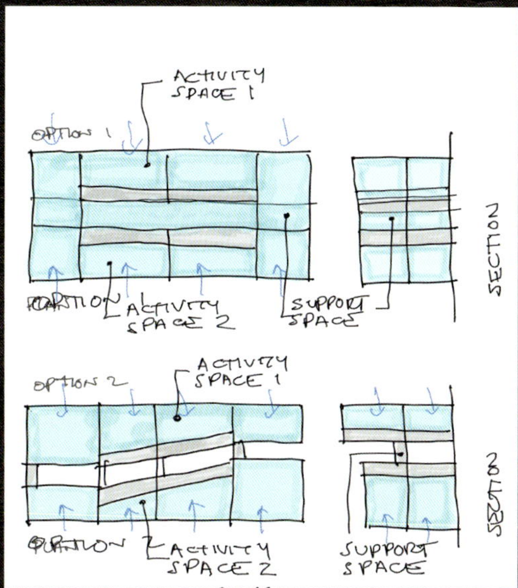

Daylight strategy for direct sunlight and cross ventilation.

Option 1 has well-lit spaces throughout the building.

Option 2 has well-lit spaces on the sides and spaces with reduced daylight adjacent to circulation areas.

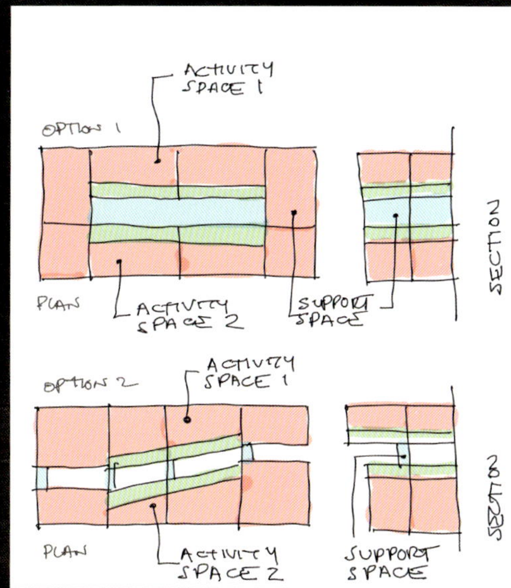

Environmental zones

Option 1 has a fabrication space serviced from a support space which is set on one side of the fabrication shop.

Option 2 has a separate environmental system for each set of spaces.

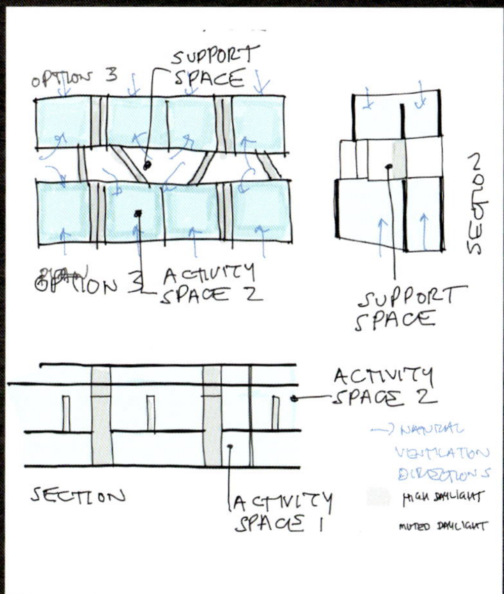

Daylight strategy for direct sunlight and cross ventilation.

Option 3 has well-lit edges of the building and reduced daylight in the centre of the floor plates.

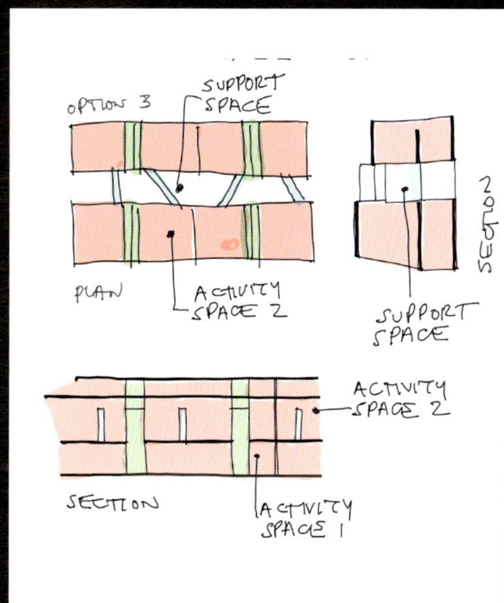

Environmental zones

Option 3 has service space located at roof level above the fabrication space in order to provide tall, open spaces.

more desk-oriented lighting during daylight hours.

In Option 1, the fabrication space is arranged such that the volume is serviced from a support space which is set on one side of the fabrication shop and extends the full width of that space in order to provide a clear space for fabrication within the workshop. Separate spaces for meeting rooms, washrooms and stairs are set on the floor plate immediately above. Design studios have a single environmental support unit in each space. A double-height studio space allows for an additional floor to be introduced into the void; space that is expected to be required in the near future.

Option 2 uses a single spine of support spaces set down the centre of the building; set to the back of the studio spaces and which traverse the fabrication space. The arrangement of units for supplying ducted air and electrical services to each studio space and fabrication space is to have mechanical ventilation supplied from the roof level of this support spine, with ducted air being supplied and returned by separate systems into both the studio spaces and the fabrication and garage spaces. In Option 2, the environmental system for each set of spaces is separate in order to allow each to change its functioning in response to expected changes in the way the spaces are used; allowing greater or lesser capacity for each of the environment zones; either studio or fabrication/garage space. In Option 3, the studio spaces are arranged over two floors, with naturally well-lit floor plates and a support space arranged down one side of the building, including enclosed meeting rooms for the fabrication support spaces. Service space is located at roof level above the fabrication space in order to provide tall, open spaces with mechanical and electrical equipment that is roof-mounted; facilitating maintenance and routine adjustment of equipment to be carried out independently of operations within the building. In Option 3, the studio and fabrication space are closely linked with a 'porous' divide between the two activities.

The flexibility of use of these spaces is made possible by openings formed within floor slabs, which allow services to be re-routed to meet changing requirements in the use of spaces.

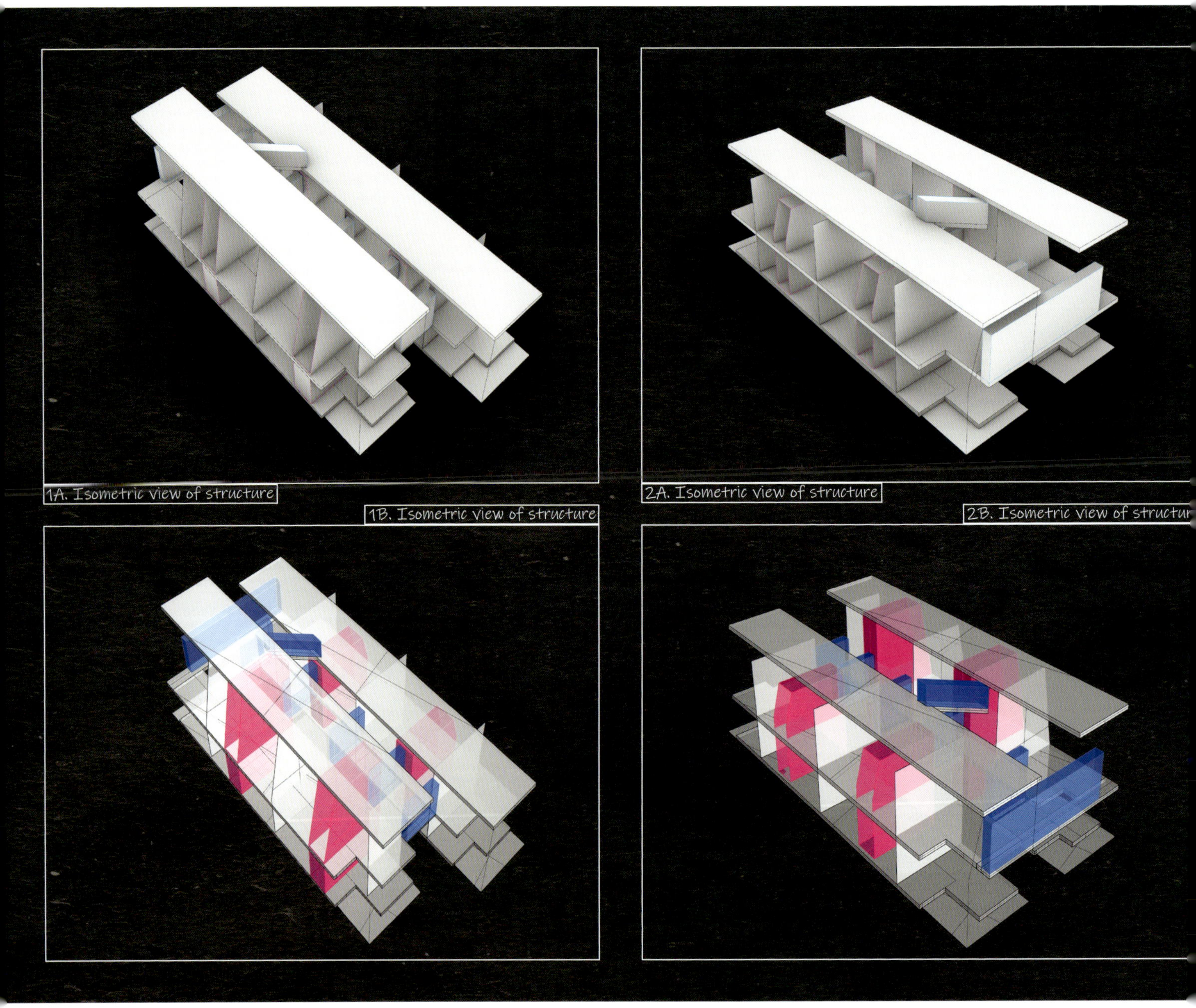

1A. Isometric view of structure

1B. Isometric view of structure

2A. Isometric view of structure

2B. Isometric view of structur

Structural strategy

The ground floor garages have 9.0 metre spans in elevation, and they are set out in bays 6.0 metres deep to create workshop modules of 9.0 x 12.0 metres or 9.0 x 18.0 metres. The space in the building to service the equipment is provided in the void between the ground floor garages and the upper storey production of fabrication shops. The building is constructed as prefabricated components of wall and floor units: delivered to site for rapid assembly in order to minimise interference with activities within adjacent buildings, which are owned by the same company.

The structural strategy for Option 1 is to have steel columns with composite metal decks, providing a single-storey enclosure. A steel-framed roof is set on top in order to provide flexibility of changing arrangements of mechanical and electrical services; the metal roof can be modified with much greater ease than a composite metal deck. The steel roof allows a wide range of mechanical electrical equipment to be mounted on it and moved around. Access across the roof is provided by steel deck walkways fixed to the profiled metal deck roof. Option 2 has a steel frame set over two floors; cross-braced with steel framing to provide the required additional support. Option 3 takes the geometry of the different forms and allows them to be self-supporting using steel box sections, arranged as frames that support the loads of the walls as well as the reinforced concrete framing supporting floor slabs with intermediary columns. The modular and prefabricated nature of Option 3 allows the elements to be de-mounted and moved around the site as required, in response to anticipated changes in the design and production of prototypes in the near future, with a view to them becoming a permanent production facility rather than a research-based facility.

The structural concept is one of using strengthened light-gauge steel framing for both walls and floors. The framing is used either as non-loadbearing infill panels or as structural wall panels for both external and internal walls. Framing for both walls and internal floors is formed as prefabricated cassettes; additional structural steel columns and beams are needed in areas where longer spans are needed. This is

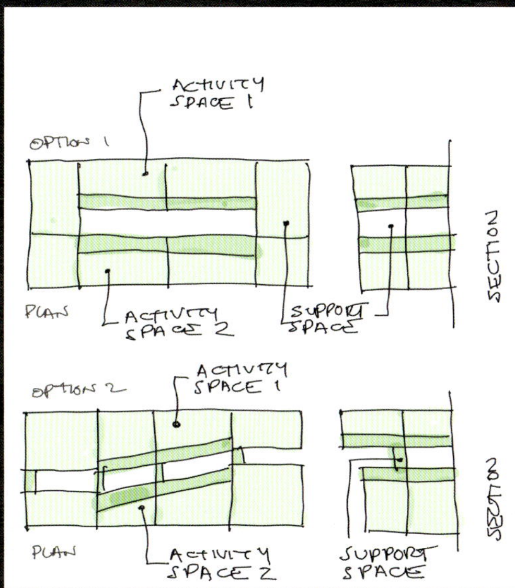

Structural strategy: Zones
Option 1 has a steel-framed roof set on top in order to provide flexibility of changing arrangements of services.
Option 2 has a steel frame set over two floors.

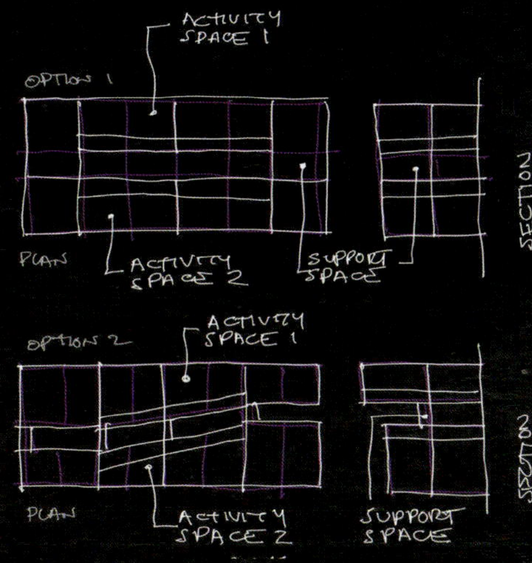

Structural strategy: Framing
Option 1 has steel columns with composite metal decks, providing a single-storey enclosure.
Option 2 is cross-braced with steel framing to provide lateral stability.

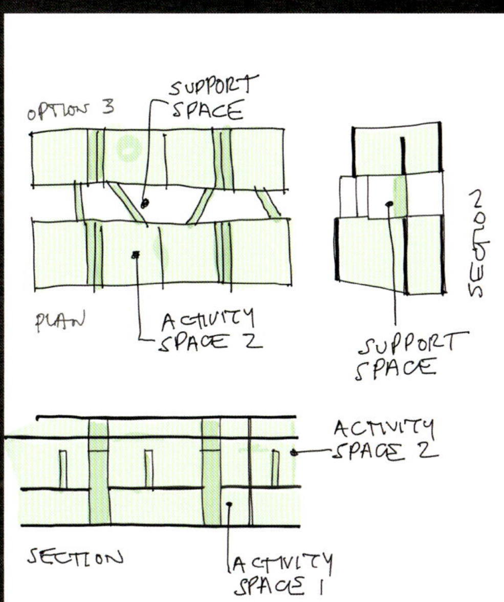

Structural strategy: Zones
Option 3 allows the elements to be demounted and moved around the site as required.

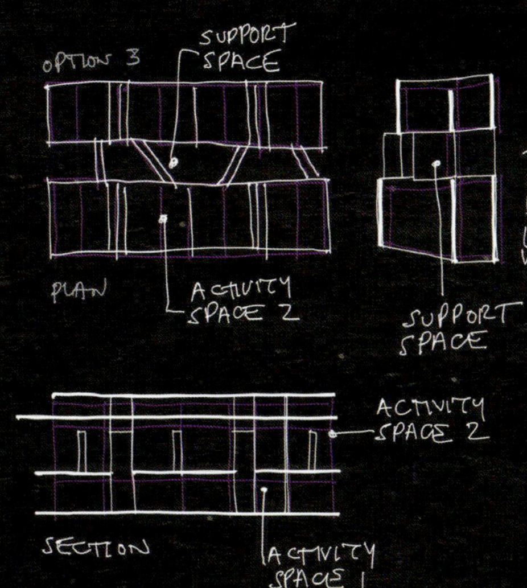

Structural strategy: Zones
Option 3 uses strengthened light-gauge steel framing for both walls and floors.

partly a site-based method of construction and is partly prefabricated; wall panels and floor panels are assembled off site and are lifted into place on site. The use of this strengthened lightweight construction is followed in the glazed areas, without wide and deep framing for windows formed from the light-gauge steel frame, not from regular glazing sections. As a result, the two-storey framing is made from rectangular hollow sections which are set into a frame that forms walls, floors and roof. Rectangular hollow steel sections are used as beams across the width of the glazed spaces, in order to provide support where it is uneconomical to integrate within the window frame. In these areas, bands of glass are inserted as tall narrow windows with framing at their edges, avoiding the need for any additional steel structure. Narrow roof lights are supported by rectangular hollow section framing, with double-glazed units set onto an aluminium frame and silicone seals between them in order to provide the thermal break that allows this structural system to be used. An advantage of light-gauge steel framing is that the framing can respond to the geometries of internal spaces; partial fabrication of wall and floor assemblies also suits this small-scale construction method. In some places the use of light-gauge steel framing avoids the need for a large-scale primary steel frame with infill walls. In this project, light-gauge steel frame panels are used in three different applications; as infill to a large-scale steel frame, as infill to a small-scale steel frame comprising rectangular hollow sections, and as self-supporting panels.

Where the panels are used as infills to a large-scale steel frame, panels are supported on the edges of floors; panels are supported directly on the floor at the base of each panel. Facade cladding is fixed to these panels. Where panels are fixed within a lighter steel frame of rectangular hollow sections, light-gauge steel panels are fixed within the depth of the frame, supported on beams that form part of the structural frame. Floors are supported by the steel frame.; cladding is fixed to the panels. Where panels are used as structural components, without a supporting steel frame, wall panels and floor panels are connected such that vertical framing and floor framing are structurally continuous.

Perspective view of typical bay from below

Typical bay adjacent to facade

The roof of the fabrication space has rooflights with retractable covers which are thermally insulated. These 'pop out' screens allow daylight to enter production spaces when needed in response to a requirement for flexibility in directing and controlling the admission of daylight. Opaque panels can move across the roof; operated electrically.

The external envelope for Option 1 is based on metal cladding which can be arranged either horizontally or vertically. The cladding can extend across the facades and over the roof; the main facade in this building is the roof. As a result, in Option 2 the roof is clad in open-jointed GRC (glass-fibre reinforced concrete) paving slabs, which can be walked upon.

In Option 3 the walls and roofs are made as prefabricated wall and roof panels using a single type for both wall and roof, which are partly in rainscreen configuration for the roof, and in sealed panel configuration for the walls. The same principle applies to the roof of Option 3, which is a set of lightweight sandwich panels which can be walked upon for access, held in place by the structural steel frame beneath.

The external envelope, with its prefabricated panels and rainscreen panels, responds to the structural as well as environmental design. Panels are non-load-bearing cladding panels. For the different spaces with a single envelope system, greater thermal insulation is provided in the office and studio spaces, and in the production spaces, and a higher level of thermal insulation is provided in the glazing for the office spaces. The production spaces have doors which are open for part of the day, and which need to be heated and cooled rapidly with a minimum loss of efficiency from the heating or cooling supply in the fabrication shop.

The facades of this building are formed as brick panels set on a light-gauge steel framing with a board on top on both sides to create a fire-resistant construction. Brick walls are arranged with joints that form straight vertical panels, set at different depths to form a low relief for panels across the roof and facades. This approach is taken in order to allow services to be installed on the outer face of the building, incorporating gas and water supply boxes which would otherwise be exposed

Perspective view of typical bay from above

if a deep facade zone were not used. Glazing is fabricated as silicone-sealed, double-glazed units to provide a showcase for products within the building. The opaque walls also contain lifting doors to allow access and egress of materials and products into and out of the building. The glazing joints follow those of the adjacent brick panels in a departure from a rectilinear geometry; fixed back on the steel frame which is formed to support this irregular-shaped glazing set within different depths of the adjacent opaque walls.

Brick was the preferred material as it was used for the existing buildings around the site which have been refurbished. In most cases only the brick facades remain of those buildings; the interior structures and floor plates have been constructed within those brick facade forms.

The brick walls make use of regular bricks; this is not brick slip construction with panels which are mechanically fixed to a supporting frame of extruded aluminium sections. Bricks are supported at each floor level on stainless steel shelf angles. A cavity tray that drains the void between the brick outer wall and the backing wall is drained immediately above the stainless steel angles. The brick course that is supported by a stainless steel angle makes use of specially shaped bricks in order to reveal the thickness of the brick where possible, such as around window openings. Notched bricks are needed where the brick wall continues through the height of the building. Bricks are arranged in panels such that there is a continuous vertical joint near the corners in external walls.

Setting joints away from corners allows the expression of a notional 'thickness' to these brick walls, which are expressed visually as vertical panels that extend continuously from ground to roof. Corners of facades are not formed as a visual 'fold' from one vertical plane to another; instead, the vertical joint set near the corner allows the brick wall that forms the corner to have a brick return which is perpendicular to the wall. The change in angle from one wall to another occurs at the continuous vertical joint, which forms a visual 'pivot' from one wall to another. The use of recessed joints between vertical planes of brick provides a sense of walls as panels rather than as a continuous 'wrap'.

1. Perspective view of exterior

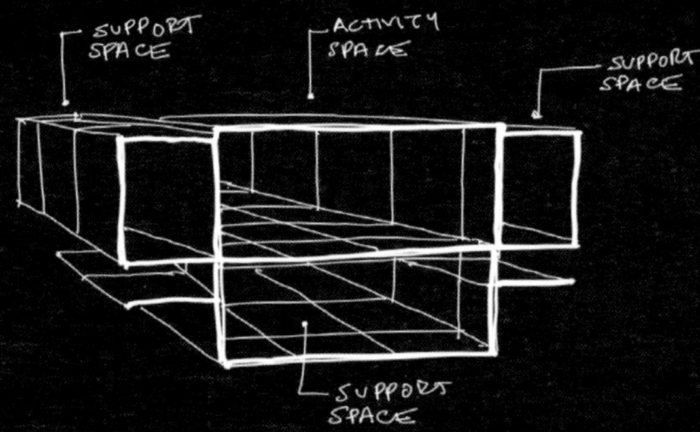

2. Perspective view of exterior

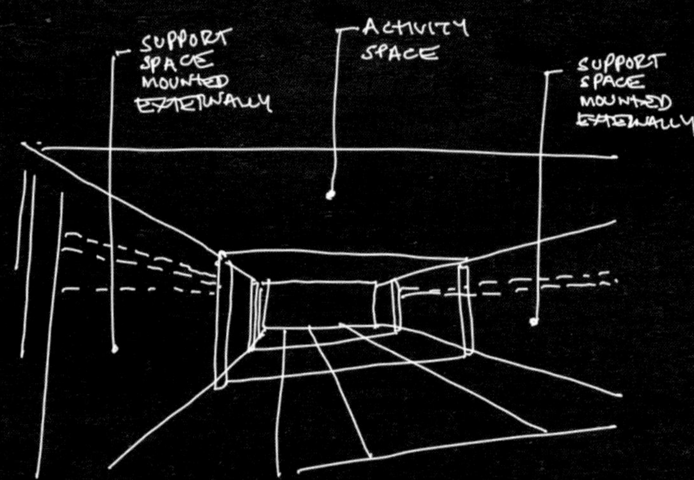

Adapting and moderating the building in use

An aim of this project is to provide design documentation that embodies a 'set of instructions' to demonstrate the means to 'adapt' the main spaces in the building for specific tasks, as well as how to 'moderate' the environment created within the building. 'Adapting' the building is based on the possibilities for adaptation and changes in the use of internal and external spaces made possible as a result of the 'loose-fit' between the systems used to construct the structure, the external envelope and the environmental control systems.

A loose fit between these systems is a relationship between components and assemblies which are interdependent rather than independent of one another, but which allow for structure, facades and environmental control systems to be changed with relative ease while still benefitting from their limited interdependence. The building has been designed to be relatively easy to disassemble for reuse or the recycling of components and assemblies. 'Moderating' the building is about optimising performance requirements at a given point in time, without making that optimisation a permanent change in the overall performance of the building systems for structure, envelope and environmental control. Changes in performance requirements are often the result of an evolution of environmental control requirements, such as the ventilation or solar control within interior spaces. This process of the optimisation of the environmental performance of spaces within the building can be solved through a modified relationship between structure, envelope and environmental controls instead of a single change to one of these systems.

An approach of seeking the continued interdependence of systems, rather than a partial replacement of one system, can be very economical. For example, fixed facade panels that have been designed for a specific performance in daylight and solar transmission can have areas of panel fitted with additional solar protection with relative ease, when coordinated with an associated adjustment of the functioning of the mechanical ventilation system immediately adjacent to that area of facade. In this project, a key part of the program/brief was to show

. Perspective view of exterior

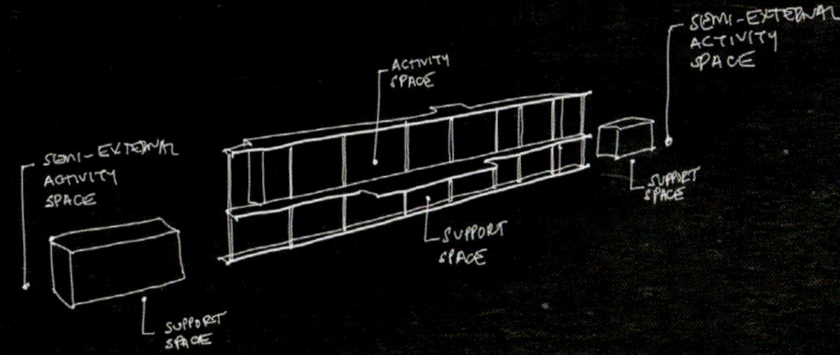

4. Perspective view of exterior

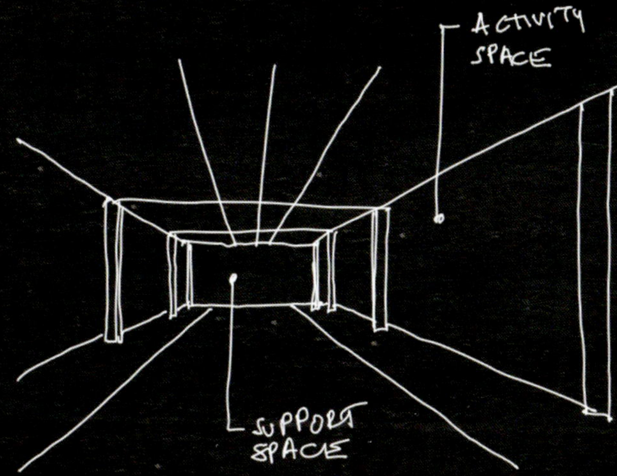

how small changes could be made to the environmental control system during the first 24 months of use. This request was made in response to anticipated changes in the patterns of use of both the 'activity spaces' – or main spaces – in the building, and the 'support spaces' – or service spaces – such as washrooms, stairs, lifts and storage. This ability to recalibrate the environmental controls would save the building owner the potential cost and waste of over-providing levels of environmental control which were not required by the building users.

This approach of 'adapting' and 'moderating' will allow the building users to move from being 'passive' participants in the control of their environment within the building, to becoming 'active' participants without the need to make significant changes to systems installed within the building, including solar control panels on facades.

Information about optimised performance can be recorded in a 'user manual' which develops as a set of instructions for the day-to-day use of the building. This evolving document will become a companion to the maintenance manual for the building. The user manual sets out an evolving understanding from the point of view of the building user: the relationship between the built assemblies as experienced by the user. In terms of adapting the building to take into account changing patterns of use, systems that comprise the spaces and fabric of the building may be removed and replaced during the lifespan of the building. This requirement that activities within the building may change within a few years, and that a design strategy is required to be put in place in response to that requirement, formed a part of the brief/program. The aim of the 'user manual' part of the design documentation is to avoid the situation of disposal and replacement of parts of the building which will not appear to be needed in the near future; the suggested maintenance, recycling and re-use of components and assemblies is set out in the user manual.

The manual is adapted and moderated from the technical specifications that form part of the maintenance manual for facade, roof, mechanical and electrical systems. This evolving body of information informs the operation of the building management system.

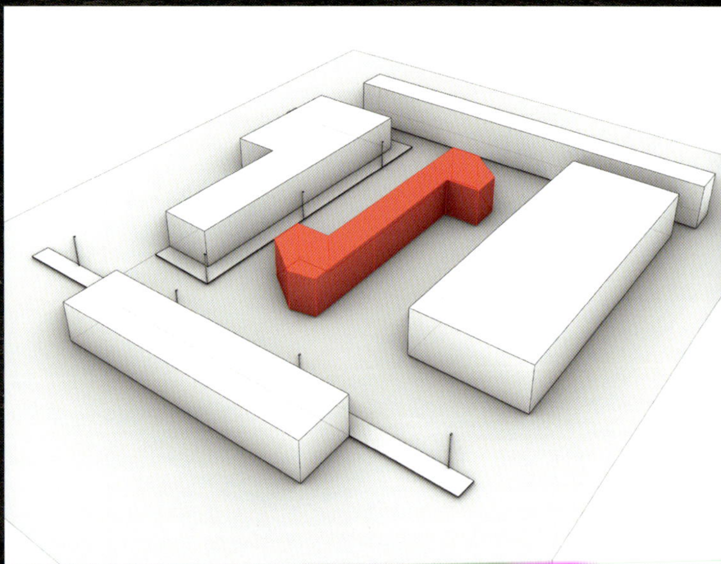

1. Project volume in site context

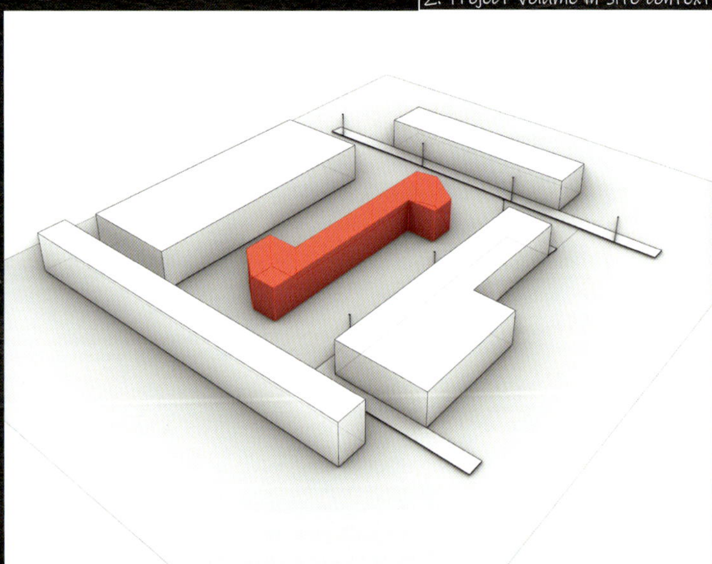

2. Project volume in site context

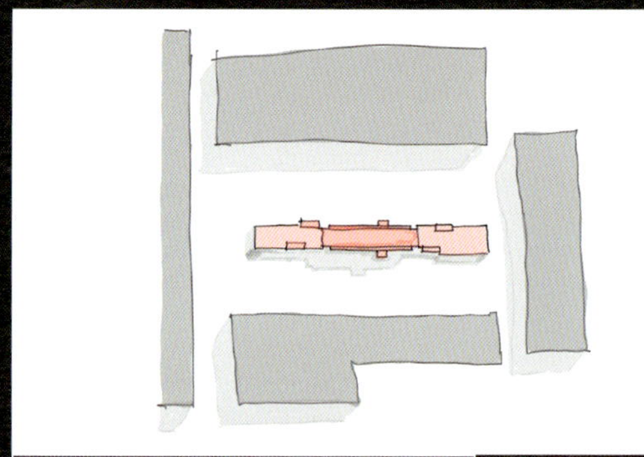

1. Site plan with surrounding context

Option 1 sets the building across two floors in order to fill the site and join the two buildings on both sides.

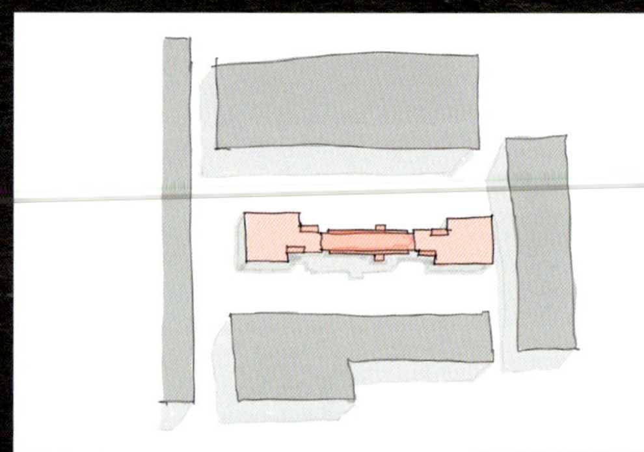

2. Site plan with surrounding context

Option 2 the building stands alone, with a small gap between adjacent buildings; arranged in a square shape over a single storey.

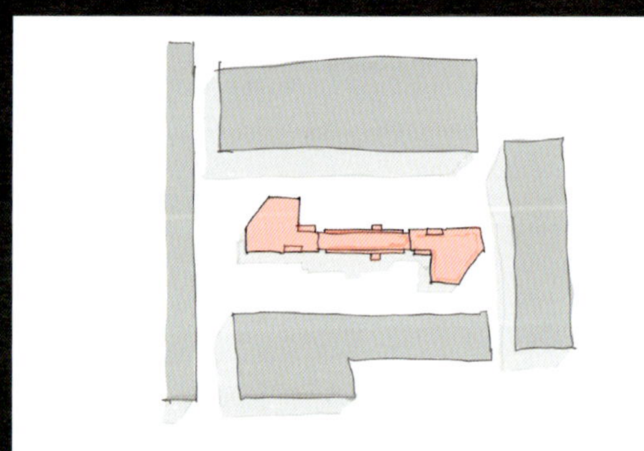

3. Site plan with surrounding context

Option 3 allows for the building to be accessed both on foot and from small vehicles from the side of the building.

Site context

This light industrial building is characterised by its location within an existing factory environment, with a single road at one end of the site; an island site with little access for road vehicles. The site has open space on three sides, the boundary being enclosed by chain link fences that enclose adjacent outdoor storage yards for materials. The site has no buildings surrounding it; nearby buildings are single-storey, metal-clad industrial buildings for both the manufacture and storage of materials. Despite the proximity of open storage space, the site is restricted in size, making it necessary to arrange spaces over two floors.

The building is located in a warm temperate climate. The design studios and prototyping areas are located on the upper two floors with storage of equipment and materials located at ground floor level. The design space is set out on the first of the upper floors, which has an open deck. The air-handling units are set on the first-floor level attached to the sides of the building; this avoids the need for equipment to be mounted within the building spaces, which are very limited; every space already has a double function assigned. Service equipment is fixed to the sides of the building rather than at roof level, for ease of maintenance access, allowing the top floor activities in the building to use this space for research and development activities.

The site context for Option 1 is to set the building across two floors in order to fill the site and join the two buildings on both sides of the building. The continuation of the urban streetscape was considered with Option 1, but the approach was considered not to be sufficiently robust if adjacent buildings are demolished; an event which is being considered for the near future. In Option 2 the building stands alone, with a small gap between adjacent buildings; arranged in a square shape over a single storey. This option has difficulties in the servicing of the building, which has to be from the street as the space behind is not easily accessible. Option 1 would also be accessed only from the street. Option 3 allows for the building to be accessed both on foot and from small vehicles from the side of the building, where an access road is introduced for both pedestrians and vehicles. This is a light industrial building with

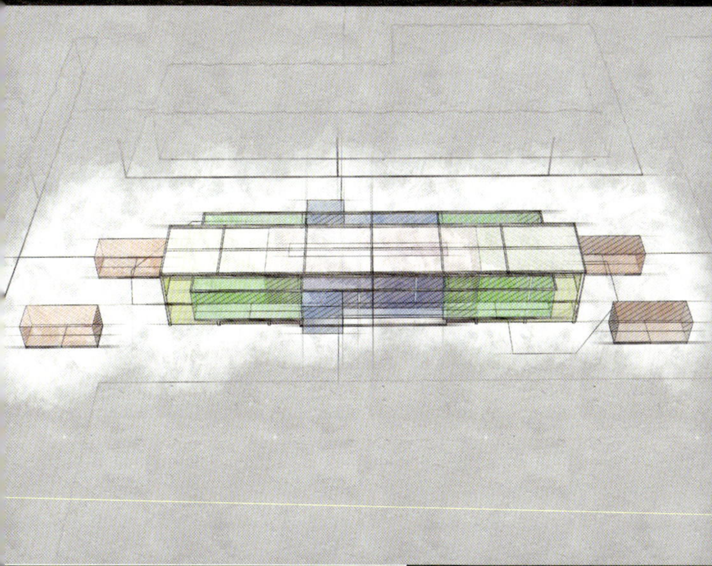

Perspective view of environmental volumes

2. Perspective view of environmental volumes

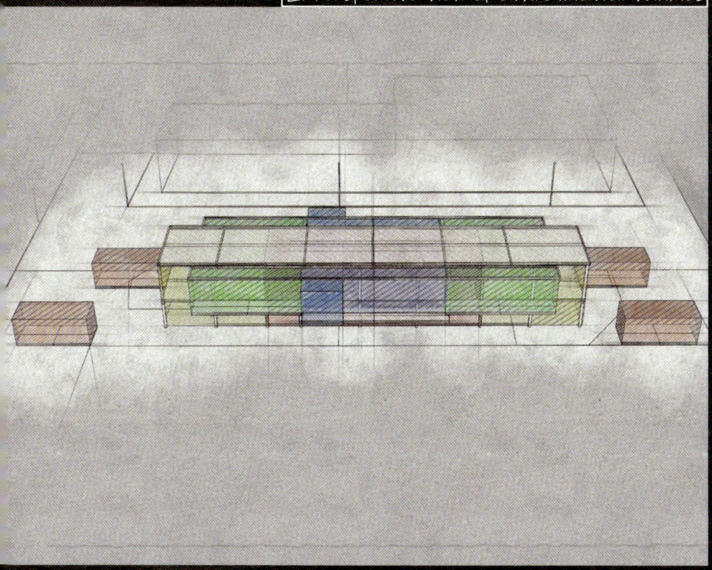

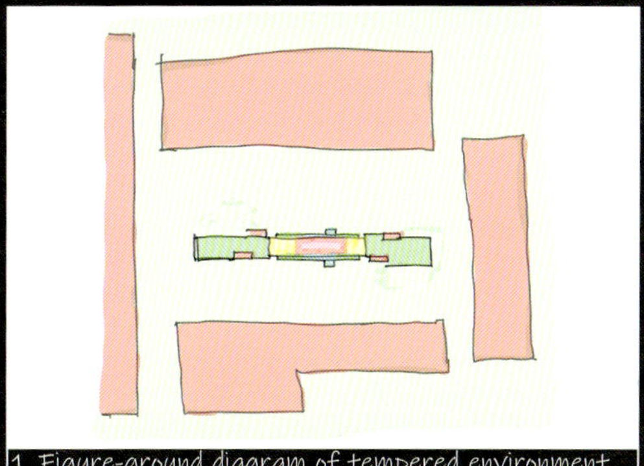

1. Figure-ground diagram of tempered environment

Option 1
The areas of red space consume a similar amount of heating and cooling energy.

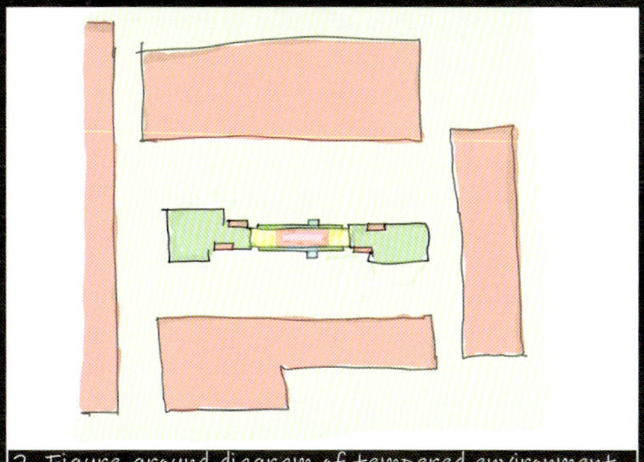

2. Figure-ground diagram of tempered environment

Option 2
Dark blue spaces are less tempered than red spaces, but are more tempered than yellow spaces.

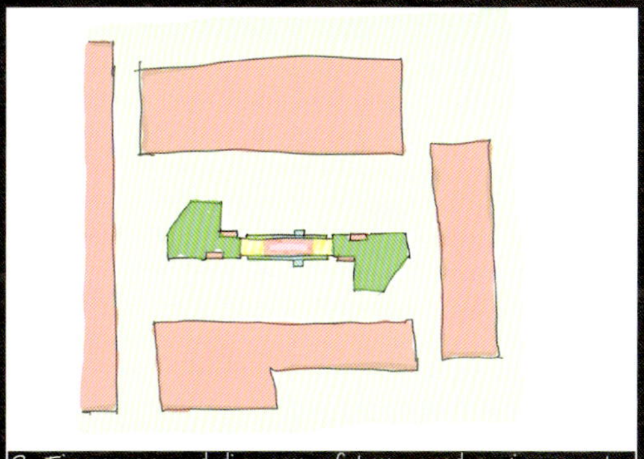

3. Figure-ground diagram of tempered environment

Option 3
Dark green spaces are less tempered than yellow spaces and blue spaces.

a functional mixture of making things and designing products; it is standalone, an autonomous object 'parked' on the site that is engaging with its neighbours but is not attempting to fit into its built environment, which will change significantly over the next 10 years.

This standalone research and development building is characterised by a need for self sufficiency for most of the activities carried out within. Consequently, spaces are designed to be capable of being adapted for multiple tasks. The building comprises a ground floor with exhibition space, which can be enclosed or deployed as an external canopied space. This canopied space can be adapted with additional electrical lighting as well as packaged pieces of equipment for its short term environmental control. There is little need for it to be made secure as this is part of an access-controlled site. The building has other elements in it which can be deployed, such as additional ground floor rooms. The upper level has an open deck that can also be enclosed with panels on both sides. Panels can be raised and owered in the manner of a sash window. The overhanging services area which is hanging from the top of the building creates an additional services support area which also provides points of support for a deployable space for small-scale conferences, exhibitions and large-scale presentations, with the benefit of having a deployable roof canopy. The wall panels used to make these temporary enclosures are stored in a ground floor storage space. Panels are joined together to create temporary rooms and larger enclosures; the permanent spaces in the building are too small for these activities and the ground floor area is needed for specific activities which would not be compatible with a permanent arrangement of conference and presentation spaces. The geometry of the conference spaces is required to vary between events, so do not suit permanently closed spaces on the ground floor. This is a building which is self-contained but has extra elements that can be deployed by being assembled quickly: an approach which suits this temperate climate which can be hot in the summer, but is ideal for presentations, conferences and exhibitions to be accommodated in temporary pavilions which are attached to the sides of this agile building.

1. Sectional perspective view

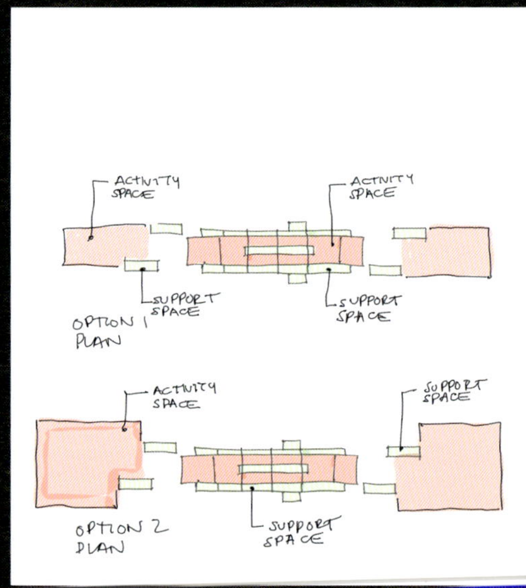

Spatial arrangement

Option 1 arranges the building as a single block enclosing a service core in the middle.

Option 2 makes a semi-closed link with deployable pavilions at each end of the building.

2. Sectional perspective view

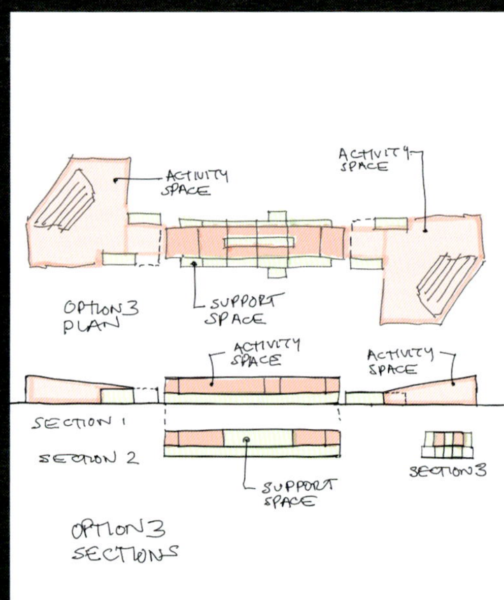

Option 3 makes a fully-closed link with deployable pavilions at each end of the building.

Spatial arrangement

Conceptually, this building is a shed, allowing occupants to inhabit a creative environment which is independent of the activities being carried out in other areas of the factory; requiring only electrical power, water supply and drainage. The requirements for limited electrical and mechanical servicing, supplied by the adjacent factory environment, is intentional; a largely self-sufficient, independent environment is a key requirement for this building. This concept is carried through in the building construction, which is that of a 'kit of parts' where the building can be partly demounted and put together in different ways; panels can be moved around and rearranged during the lifespan of the building, to suit the changes to the activities carried out in this 'skunkworks'. Self-sufficiency is very much part of the thinking and everything has a double use. Internal walls are also intended to be whiteboard presentation boards that can be demounted and used as part of a large-scale furniture arrangement; the space under the cantilevered end can be inhabited with a lightweight frame to cladding panels attached for purposes of creating an external presentation space. A characteristic of the existing factory is that it is constantly changing; buildings are periodically demolished and rebuilt. This building is designed to respond to that changing environment by allowing its relationship with the surrounding buildings to inform how it will be developed and sustain continuous development, rather than remaining a small building that would become 'victim' to the changes in the buildings that surround it.

This building seizes the opportunities offered by its neighbours; solar shading provided by an adjacent building, becoming a 'limpet' and eventually attaching itself to the side of the adjacent building, or 'parking' itself alongside that building. Its very mobility is key to its endeavour to remain an independent institution within its factory environment. The spirit of independence of the team that inhabits the building is very much at the centre of its design. The building up to the low-level roof space is used as an additional design studio; an opaque form that extends across the roof, lit naturally at its ends only in order to provide controlled daylight.

Perspective view of interior

2. Perspective view of interior

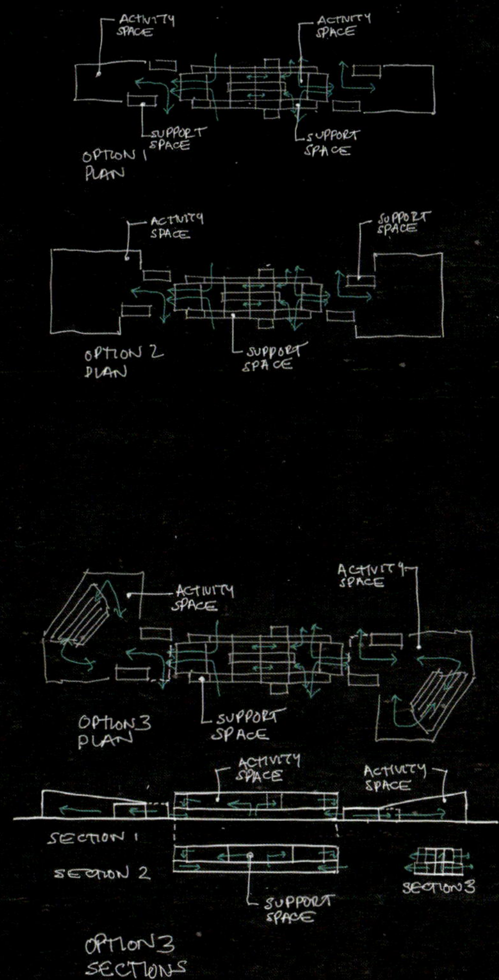

Internal circulation

Option 1 arranges circulation from a single entrance at the centre of the building.

Option 2 arranges circulation from either end of the building.

Option 3 arranges circulation from sets of stairs located within the ground floor central enclosure.

Internal circulation

The circulation within the building is organised around the need to connect the service cores rather than provide short links between spaces. Stairs are mounted externally in order to provide space within the facility that is as clear as possible; spaces are accessed from the ends of the building. Circulation for building users proceeds through the linked spaces which are all open within the inner 'core' of the building with a notional corridor down its centre, extending from one end of the stair access down to the outer open deck.

Although this is a relatively simple building, the circulation within it is required to be sufficiently flexible for a range of functions to be carried out with changing requirements; the building has to reconfigure itself by the sliding and repositioning of screens in order for the spatial arrangement to function in different configurations. The primary circulation is through a central core that extends up the centre of the building with vertical circulation at each end. Set in the centre, alongside washrooms, the circulation route – with a stair at each end – allows the building to be divided into self-contained sections. The middle portion of the building provides access to both halves of the building.

The second essential part of the circulation is the 1.5-metre-wide space which is the interstitial zone between the outside of the building and its inner wall, allowing the interstitial space to be inhabited. This interstitial space is also a space to walk through, open from end to end, and is enclosed with both semi-opaque facades and with glazed windows. This space is also an interstitial environmental zone, between outside and inside, to deal with the harsh climate, addressing a need to balance the thermal insulation of the external walls with lightweight wall panels and structures that can be demounted and moved in this harsh climate. The buffer zone around the perimeter of the building provides its own circulation zone, a deck around the building which forms a transition zone between outside and inside. The inner part of the building is fully tempered and is divided into separate functions. The internal circulation can be increased by adding a stair in order to divide the spaces further.

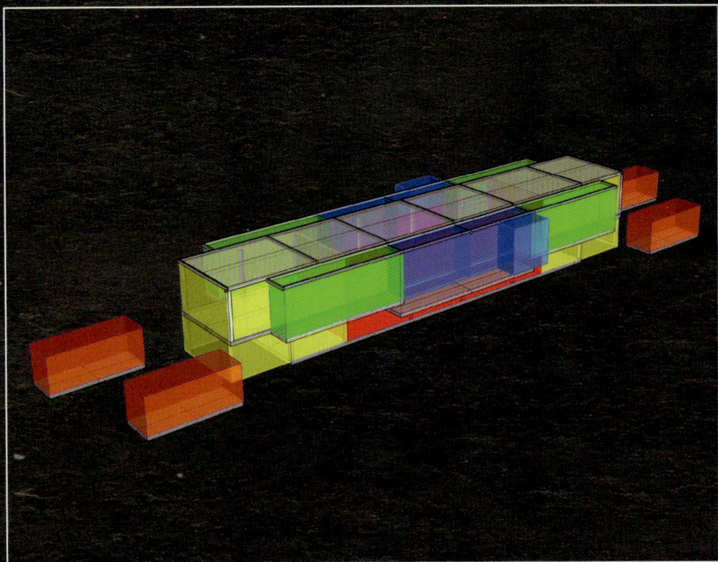

1A. Isometric view of environmental volumes

1B. Isometric view of environmental volumes

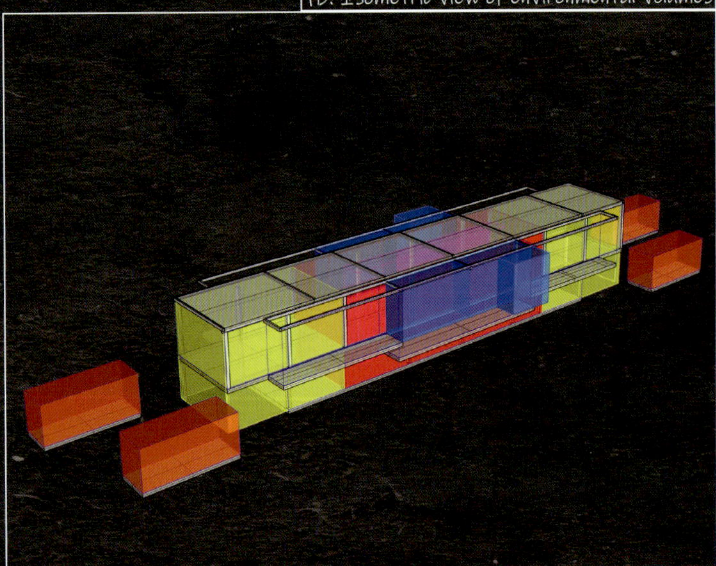

2A. Isometric view of environmental volumes

2B. Isometric view of environmental volume

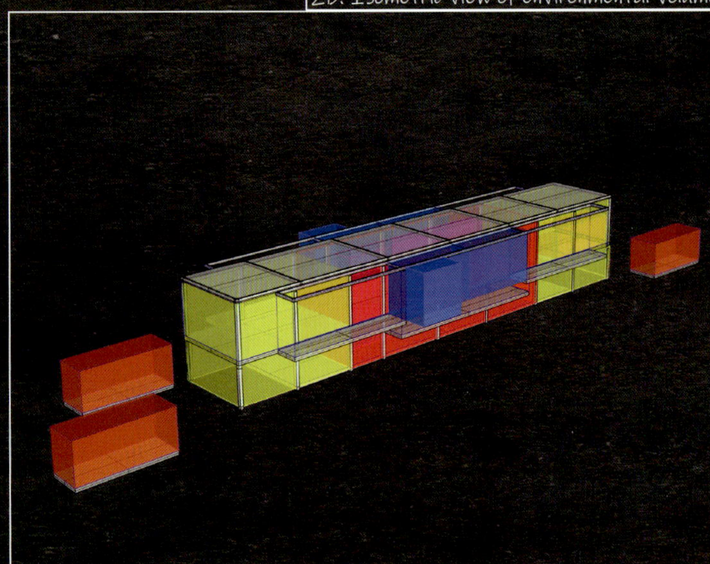

Environmental strategy

The environmental strategy for Options 1 and 2 is to have warm or cool air passing through the building, using an energy recovery system which is roof-mounted. This straightforward use of a single environmental zone works well for the simplified volumes where a single function is being carried out. The environmental strategy and design for Option 3 is more complex as a result of the design being both demountable and having a more complex spatial arrangement due to it being arranged within a smaller range of spaces. Option 3 has three versions within it: one version provides three environmental zones on the upper floors, with a slow heating and slow cooling zone in the centre of the building and its core support spaces immediately adjacent. A space at each end of the building is naturally ventilated and is less thermally controlled, in order to allow windows to open to the outside air. A closer link is provided between inside and outside in the use of the spaces; end spaces are less tightly controlled from an environmental point of view than the inner spaces. A second version is to move through the floor zones such that the air is distributed more dynamically with a similar arrangement to Option 1. The third version of Option 3 is to have a double wall construction where the outer wall, the void between the outer wall and the inner wall has air drawn through it in order to supply highly thermally insulated inner spaces over three floors with heat recovery at roof level. The environmental strategy is one of using the service modules, which are fixed to the sides of the building, to provide active environmental controls to serve spaces within the building, as well as to provide additional temporary services such as lighting equipment. Additional items such as electrical fans can be attached to the framing, which projects from the ends of the building to create two sets of external conference spaces as a result of the use of deployable screens and a canopy. The framing supporting the services equipment for the temporary external spaces is deployed on sliding rails which are supported on fixed trussed beams, in order for the equipment to project out into the spaces at each end of the building. The ends of these beams are propped onto the trussed columns which provide support at each end of the build-

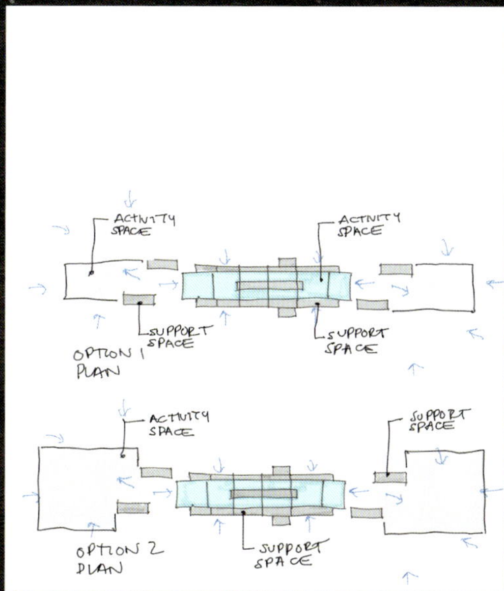

Daylight strategy for direct sunlight and cross ventilation.

Option 1 admits daylight and ventilation to the central parts of the building.

Option 2 admits daylight and ventilation to the end spaces of the building.

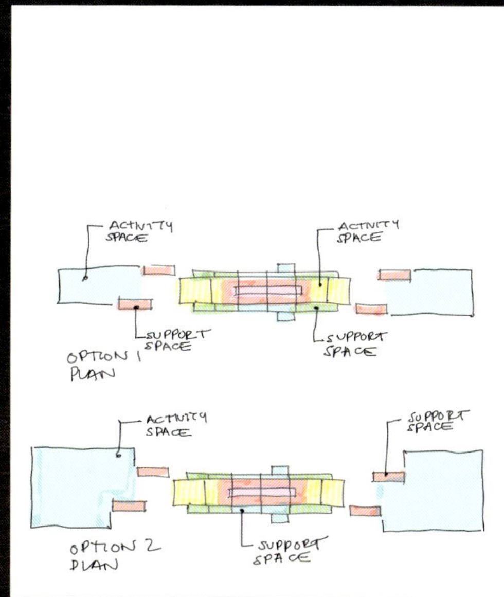

Environmental zones

Option 1 and Option 2 have warm or cool air passing through the building, using an energy recovery system which is roof mounted.

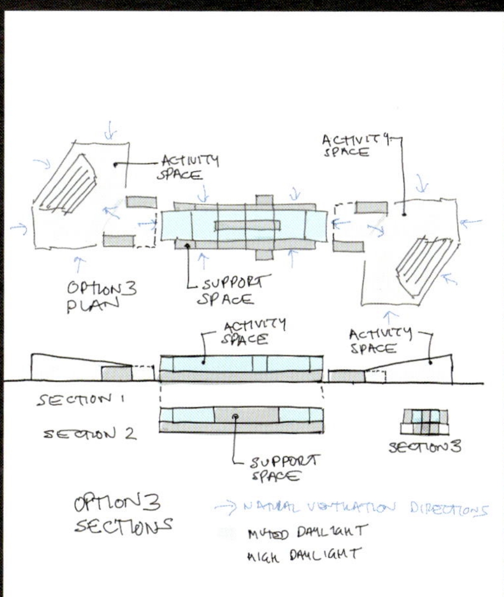

Daylight strategy for direct sunlight and cross ventilation.

Option 3 admits daylight and ventilation from top-light admitted in the centre of the building. Spaces at the sides of the building are not daylit.

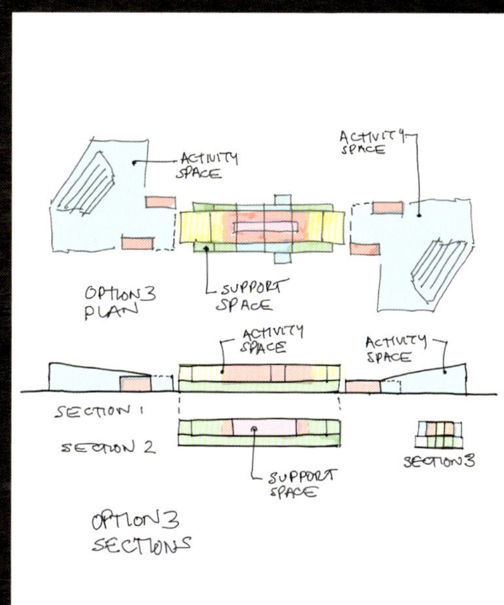

Environmental zones

Option 3 is both demountable and has a more complex spatial arrangement due to it being arranged within a smaller range of spaces.

ing. The enclosed volume of the building increases by a factor of four when the temporary enclosures are deployed. The equipment creates temporary environments with sufficient thermal comfort and fresh air across these enclosed spaces both in mid-season and during summer months. The temporary enclosures are serviced directly from equipment mounted on the supporting structure, with electrical fans projecting fresh air through these spaces during winter months.

Tempered air is provided to both the permanent space and temporary enclosures, from packaged units fixed to the deployable hinged trusses. When not in use, these units are stored in the ground floor enclosure which forms the permanent part of the storage space. Much of the services equipment is stored within wheeled packages which can be taken out of the permanent storage area and mounted on the framing when deployed. The temporary conference spaces are created as a result of them being deployed from the external structure, made practical by the deployment of environmental equipment and controls. These environmental controls are also not only capable of being deployed in support of the temporary enclosures, but are key to making those spaces practical to use, from the point of view of climate control.

The climate control equipment can have additional functionality installed within the system; alternatively, it can be partially replaced, such that it serves only the environmental zones externally; being deployed to become part of temporary environmental zones. The equipment can be increased in scope and complexity in order for audio-visual presentations to be made; associated computer equipment can be deployed as a semi-permanent part of the building. Electronic equipment, such as that used for audio visual displays is stored in the ground floor permanent enclosure.

Access for the cleaning and maintenance of equipment can be undertaken at ground level from the outside of the building; upper floors can be reached from a scissor lift which moves around the building to clean windows and to do routine maintenance, including the replacement of light fittings. This approach ensures that cleaning is carried out regardless of whether the mobile ends of the building are deployed or stored.

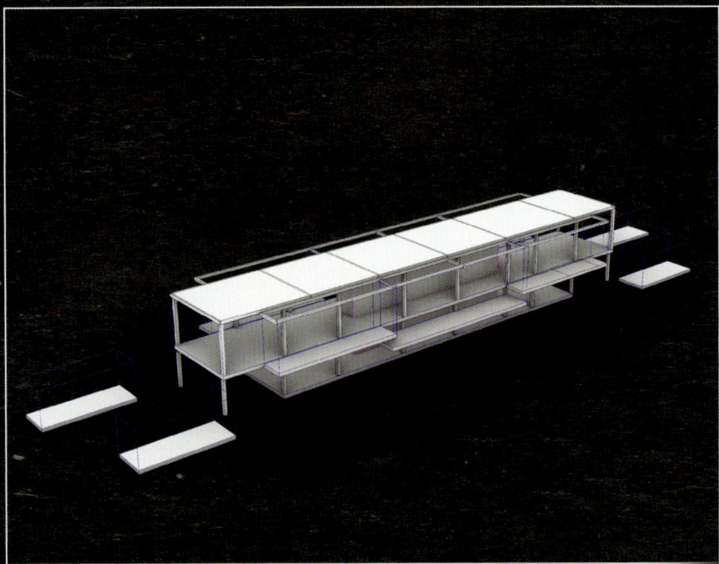
1A. Isometric view of structure

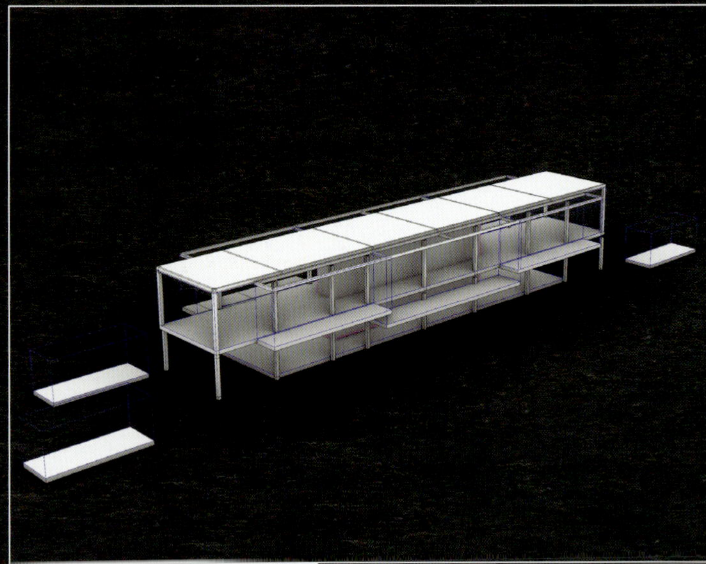
2A. Isometric view of structure

1B. Isometric view of structure
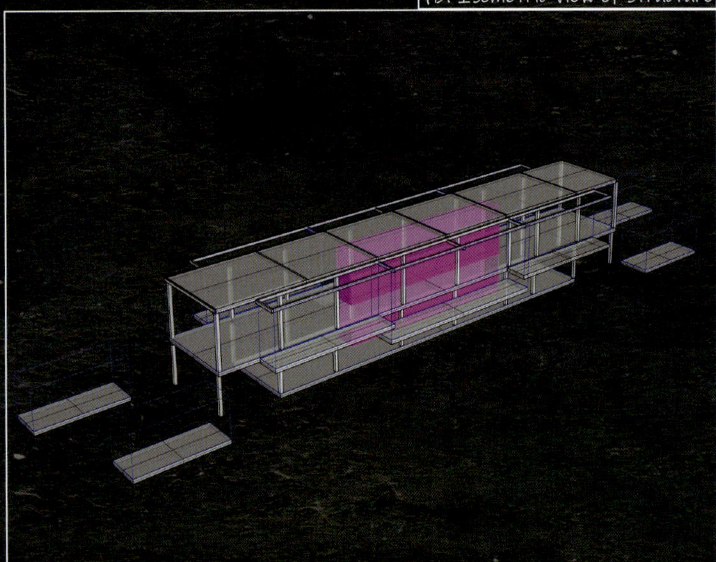

2B. Isometric view of structur
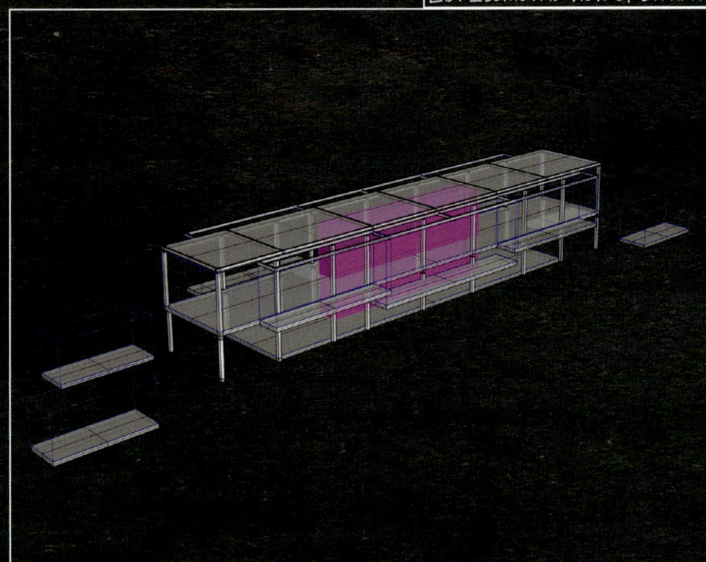

Structural strategy

The building is constructed as a steel frame; the cantilever is created in a semi-monocoque construction and uses a mixture of steel and aluminium framing. The primary frame is in steel; the secondary frame is in aluminium. The semi-monocoque approach is used in order to provide a long cantilever at one end of the building; avoiding the need for trussed framing in the cantilevered balcony space.

The structure comprises two parts: an inner steel frame and an outer set of trussed beams and columns which are folded when not in use, and are unfolded and deployed when providing support for the temporary wall panels and roof canopy. The deployable elements of structure have packaged services equipment fixed to the beams. The packaged units can be dismantled and reattached to the beams and columns when these components are either deployed or folded back into their stored position. The temporary wall panels and roof canopies can be deployed either before or after the packaged units are fixed; the two sets of components are separate.

The structure of this project is of a set of steel and aluminium frames which extend both vertically and horizontally to form a stiff box-like enclosure, set at 1.5-metre centres and based on a 6.0-metre structural grid; this frame supports the floor plates as well as the outer cladding panels which have an additional role of supporting mechanical and electrical services. The role of the external envelope supporting the services equipment led to the choice of a semi-monocoque frame, with its inherent strength and flexibility in its structural layout; avoiding the need for 3D steel trusses in a triangulated form, which would have been far more difficult to use given the need for structural members to be arranged regularly in a truss when compared with a semi-monocoque frame. This semi-monocoque framework provides an opportunity to fix air-handling ventilation louvres on the inner side of the external envelope in order to provide both mechanical and natural ventilation throughout the building. The facade is clad in both metal panels and GRP (glass-fibre reinforced polyester) panels in order to create a wrap around the mechanical and electrical equipment and allow interior spaces, created

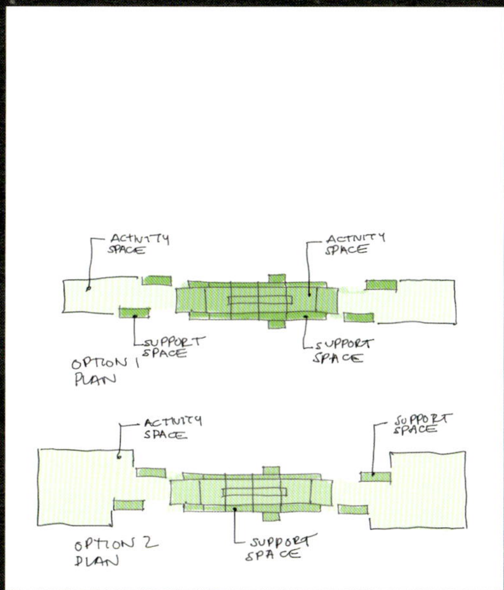

Structural strategy: Zones

Option 1 is based on a steel frame – which extends over two floors in part of the building.

Option 2 has roof trusses spanning from side to side, with columns around the edges.

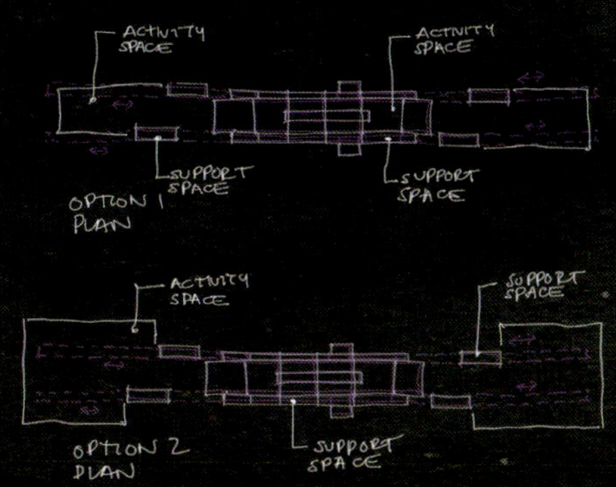

Structural strategy: Framing

Option 1 has a steel frame with steel bracing around the edges of the building.

Option 2 has no intermediary columns, as the roof trusses span the full width of the building to create a steel-framed enclosure.

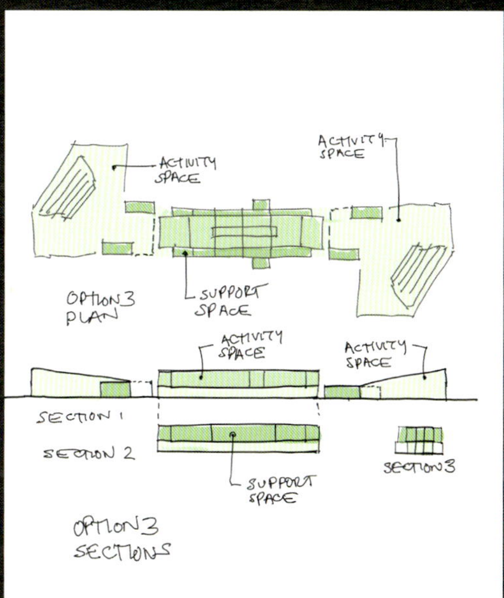

Structural strategy: Zones

Option 3 has structural walls formed as cores and mixing those with columns in the accommodation spaces.

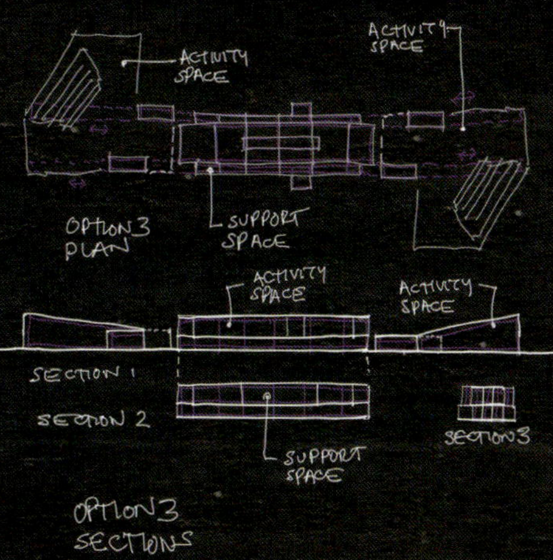

Structural strategy: Zones

Option 3 has a steel frame as its structure with a composite steel and concrete deck.

by the semi-monocoque enclosure, to be sculpted and revealed both externally and internally. The envelope moulds itself around the forms of the building, which allow it to depart from the expectation of a regular rectangular box-like form to a series of six linked spaces.

Spaces are joined horizontally at the upper level, with a large external deck area at one end of the building. Daylight is allowed to enter from visually slot-shaped openings formed in the facade at the mid-length of the building.

The structural strategy for Option 1 is based on a steel frame – which extends over two floors in part of the building – and one floor in one area, to create a roof terrace at the second floor level. The steel frame has steel bracing around the edges of the building to provide the required structural stability.

Option 2 is of a similar design but, with roof trusses spanning from side to side, has columns around the edges. There are no intermediary columns as the roof trusses span the full width of the building to create a steel-framed enclosure. As with Option 1, structural stability is provided by steel bracing around the perimeter of the building.

Option 3 has a steel frame as its structure with composite steel and concrete deck. Hot rolled sections, spanning from one side of the building to the other, create a relatively narrow space which is fully demountable, with the steel floors, constructed in deep aluminium sections, making them more lightweight and easier to move without the use of a large mobile crane. A small mobile crane would manage the demounting and relocation of this building.

Demountability is a primary consideration of the structural design, as the building is required to be able to be relocated in another part of this factory. For that reason, all three options are suitable; Options 1 and 2 may require intermediary steel columns to be introduced in order to reduce the spans between the trusses for Option 1's roof and Option 2's roof. In Option 3, the narrower scale size of the building makes it well suited for demountability in modules, and the envelope has been designed as a modular prefabricated large-scale panel that can be removed quickly.

Project 04. Research and development building
Typical bay adjacent to facade

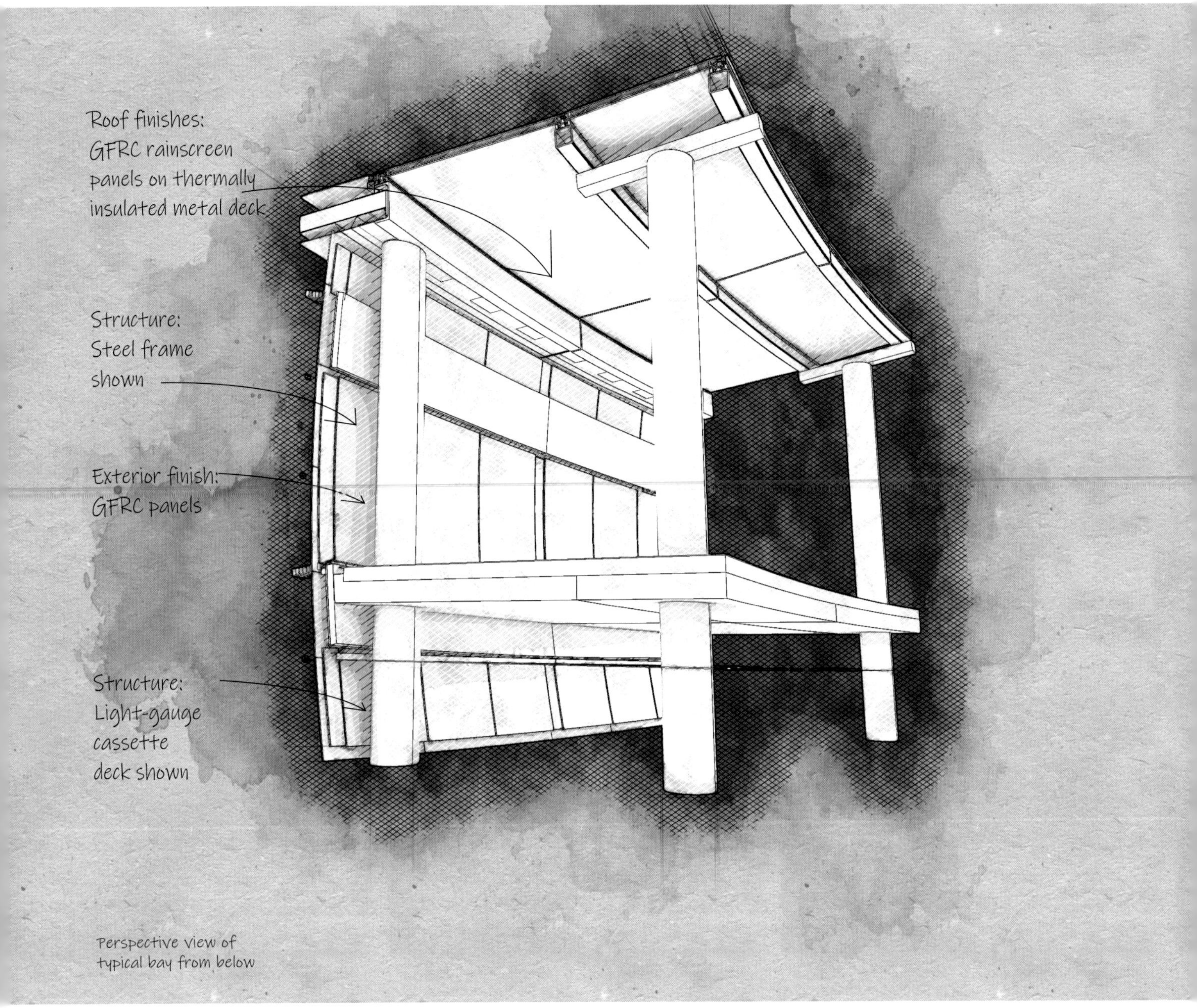

Perspective view of typical bay from below

Typical bay adjacent to facade

The use of GFRC (glass-fibre reinforced concrete) panels and GFRP (glass-fibre reinforced polymer) panels provides the different levels of durability required in the external envelope. GFRC panels are used at the ground level, and GFRP panels are used for the two floors above that level. The GFRP panels have the benefit of reducing the weight of GFRC panels on the primary structure; being moulded allows for a high degree of differentiation between the five spaces or between floor levels needed to create the different types of spaces inside, going from opaque-facade open space to glazed-facade studio space, to storage space at the far end of the building. The panels on the outside of the building can be moved; they are a mixture of vertical facade panels and mechanical and electrical equipment integrated into the facades. The mechanical and electrical equipment has facade panels which are moulded around them. The equipment itself allows the space inside to be as large and as clear as possible. The external envelope of the building comprises two layers, an outer layer of thermal insulated panels with a double-glazed unit providing high levels of daylight for work being undertaken in the two-metre-wide zone of this building. The inner zone is highly thermally insulated, with translucent or transparent GFRP panels which are light in weight. All facade elements are light in weight; the double-glazed units can be replaced with a polymer-based clear sheet in order to enhance this quality.

Glazing is aluminium framed, and highly thermally insulated. Opaque panels are prefabricated at 3.0 metres to 4.5 metres wide, spanning between members of the structural frame, which is also lightweight, set at 3.0 metre centres. The envelope has an expression which is more reminiscent of transport devices than of traditional buildings, and is expressive of its relocatable nature. This visual expression of moving from place to place fulfils part of its role of generating new technologies within this factory setting.

The external envelope of the building is formed as a set of panels which are light in weight; a mixture of cladding panels which are supported by a steel frame of mostly trussed construction. The enclosure for much

Perspective view of typical bay from above

of the building conceals the trussed steel frame in order to provide fire protection while benefiting from the lightness of the system.

Visually, the design is one of having highly thermally insulated spaces with rooflights that draw daylight down into the building as required. Internal spaces have electrical light fittings to provide deployable task lighting. Rooflights allow most of the daylight into these spaces as the walls are required internally for areas of whiteboard and for the visual projection of sketches and documents. As a result, there are no windows visible on the facades; rooflights provide daylight within the building.

The cantilevered balcony at the upper level can be enclosed during winter months with translucent screens that can be deployed in order for the space to be tempered. The screens are deployed by sliding them onto fixed frames; panels are lowered and raised in the manner of sash windows. Deployable screens for the external conference and exhibition spaces are also formed in a lightweight durable fabric, which provides screens which are of a single layer only. Alternatively, a set of thermally insulated translucent panels can be used instead to suit the time of year and associated weather conditions. These screens are formed as framed aluminium panels with translucent thermal insulation added as a further layer; the weathertight envelope is provided by the fabric screens. Entrances to these temporary pavilions are provided by doors which form part of the permanent building such that temporary doors are not required. Part of the ground floor storage space serves as lobby space for entry into the each of the deployable conference spaces.

The temporary wall panels can be used as internal partitions in the permanent enclosure on the upper floor, as well as being used as an alternative set of panels for enclosure of the open space formed by the cantilevered deck at one end of the building. The external envelope can accommodate the storage of fabric sheets in containers which are fixed to the deployable trussed beams. The use of temporary panels allows their eventual replacement to be straightforward.

1. Perspective view of exterior

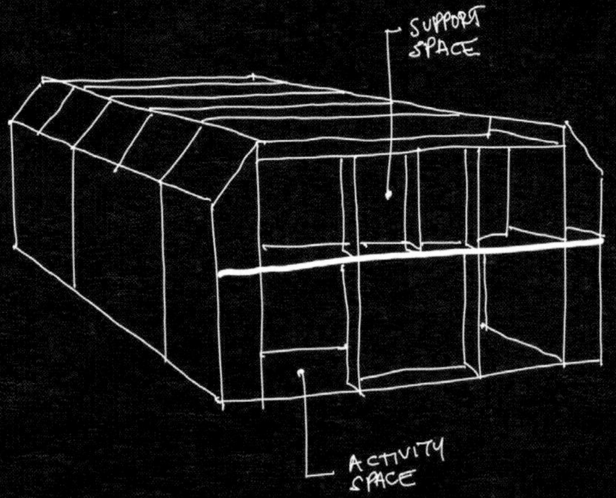

2. Perspective view of exterior

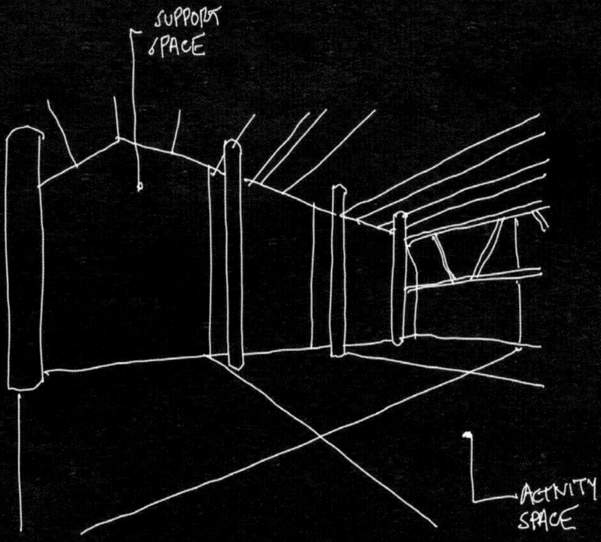

The relationship between support space and activity space

A key part of the approach to the environmental design of this industrial start-up building is the relationship between 'support' spaces, or service spaces, and 'activity' space, or floor plates. This clear division of useable space and service space allows the environmental design to serve internal spaces efficiently in their use of energy when used in combination with filtered natural daylight, filtered natural ventilation and solar shading. As a result, the services installation responds – locally within spaces – to daylight and natural ventilation; spaces in the building are set out for cross ventilation and filtered daylight. Support spaces are positioned adjacent to where they need to supply services to the main areas; located in separate areas so as not to interfere with the spatial clarity and functionality of the floor plates. Mechanical and electrical equipment is set out with its own functional clarity in supplying services to main spaces, using the shortest routes and shortest distances between the point of supply and the point of use. Support cores for lifts/elevators, stairs and vertical service runs are accommodated in a volume which is clearly separate from the main floor plates. This approach allows units to occupy spaces that are maximised in size while creating a clear relationship between internal spaces and the outside; admitting required levels of daylight and natural ventilation. This approach to air movement allows air to pass from one end of the work spaces to the other in a controlled manner that reduces the need for air conditioning. This need for ventilated facades results in cores being put into a separate zone and each work space having its own environmental zone. This approach results in the characteristic setup of units. As a result, the voids through the building, required for stairs and lifts/elevators, provide an element that contributes to the structural stability of the cores. The need for separation between core and adjacent floor plate was necessary for acoustic insulation from flanking sound and sound transmitted between the support spaces and the workshops. Acoustic separation is also required between support space and workshop; sound transmission is reduced by the use of lightweight structural walls with additional dry-wall buildup on each side of the wall.

. Perspective view of exterior

4. Perspective view of exterior

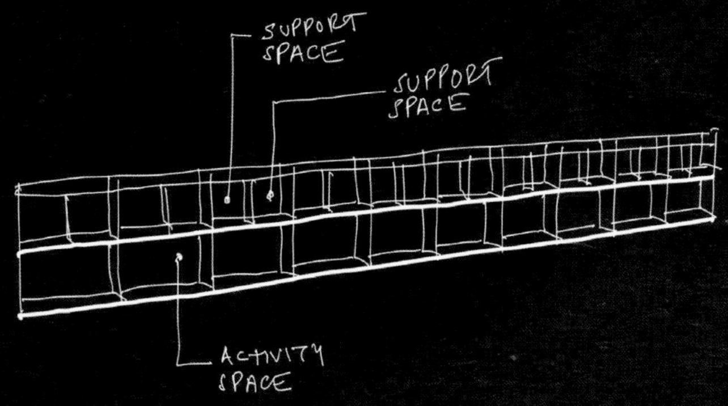

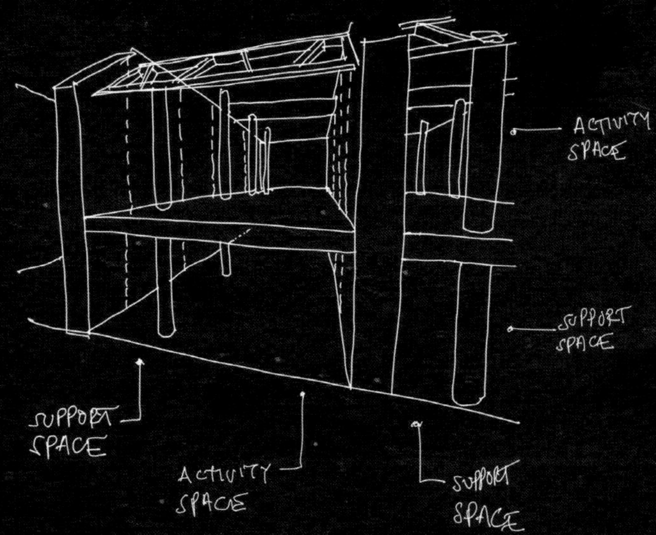

Each of the three options sets out a different approach to the relationship of support space to activity space. All options use prefabricated elements of staircase, washroom and space for ventilation equipment in order for each element to be used in different configurations without the need for variations in their design to suit each specific combination of stairs, washrooms and environmental control assemblies. This approach allows a high number of different spatial combinations so that staircases, washrooms and service rooms are constructed to a common module in order for them to be configured differently across the site. Option 1 assumes that the staircases will be set on one side the main space, with washrooms being positioned on the other side of the building. Option 2 groups them together at the ends, providing banks of washroom and staircase, while Option 3 groups support space in the centre, with four activity spaces arranged around them. The approach of the prefabrication of support space is efficient where it does not form part of the floor plate that is used in the activity space; either in its construction or in its regular functioning. The three options set those service spaces apart from the floor plates, but Option 3 integrates them to form L-shaped floor plates arranged as two sets of working spaces. Alternatively, in Option 3, floors can be used as clear rectangular activity space to accommodate equipment which is unencumbered by the L-shape of the plan. This approach could be developed further as two cores that extend outwards to the external walls of units; the other two units being larger or of different shape, allowing all spaces to be unimpeded rectangular spaces.

In this project, activity space and support space are structurally independent of one another, such that either set of spaces can be dismantled and reconfigured to suit the needs of any volume. The relatively long-term nature of the use of these spaces over the next 10 years, in different possible configurations, has been considered through the different scenarios of the use of internal space.

The approach to this project is based on the repurposing of this building over the next 25 years in order to avoid waste; to allow the buildings to respond to change and to constantly renew their vitality.

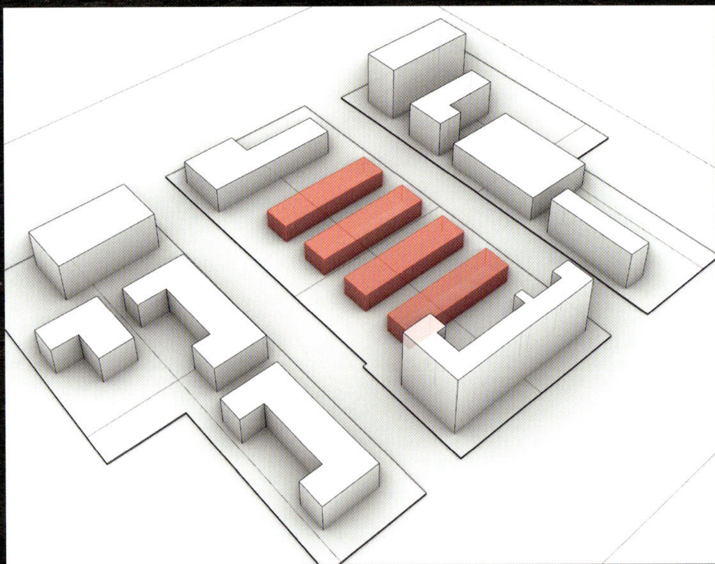

1. Project volume in site context

2. Project volume in site context

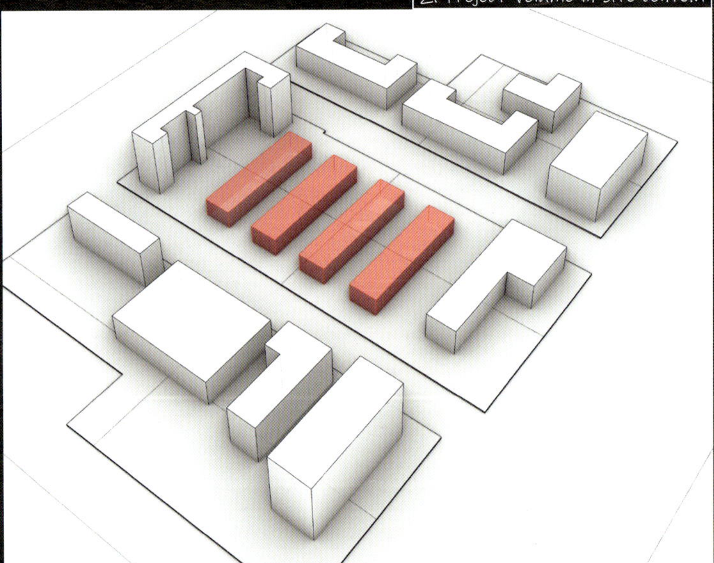

1. Site plan with surrounding context

Option 1 comprises blocks of eight workshop units with further subdivisions possible.

2. Site plan with surrounding context

Option 2 increases the possible floor plate by dividing the units into two groups instead of four.

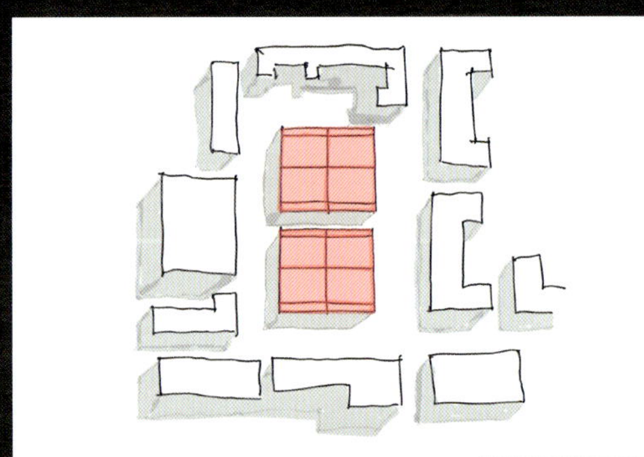

3. Site plan with surrounding context

Option 3 groups units together, such that the arrangement becomes one of two groups of four.

Site context

This project is an automotive design and research centre. The research and development work is to be carried out in a series of workshop garages, resembling the environment of a pit-lane garage in a car racing circuit. Different components and assemblies are developed in adjacent workshop spaces, allowing partial assemblies to be brought together. Components and car assemblies move from workshop to workshop as well as in and out of each workshop to the adjacent road circuit; primarily for the performance testing of prototype vehicles.

The site context is one of an open space in a large factory environment which had previously been used for car parking, which has now been moved to the edge of the site, to an area on which buildings cannot currently be constructed. The three options are developed as a result of the repeated use of one module type. This type is arranged either in rows of enclosed buildings or set out as back-to-back modules, or alternatively in groups of four. In each case the service spaces are arranged at the ends of a row, between units or in the centre of a group of four units. The site context suits a mixture of those solutions; a single solution would not provide the flexibility of space. The group of four units occupies half the available space of the site; the other half of the plot accommodates a second block, comprising a part of Option 2 and part of Option 1. This arrangement is made possible as a result of the service spaces being set between these activity spaces. The use of lifting doors around the full extent of both sides of the building provides the possibility of vehicles being able to bring materials and components at one end of a unit, and for goods to be despatched from the other side of the unit.

This approach of delivery in and despatch out allows a linear workflow of tasks to be carried out. This approach is a key aspect of site context. providing greater safety for those working there as a result of maintaining a one-way flow of materials, components and assemblies. In a car vehicle-dominated environment, the context of a factory is one in which this building wants to display itself as a machine with which staff members interact in their work; a visually dynamic environment where

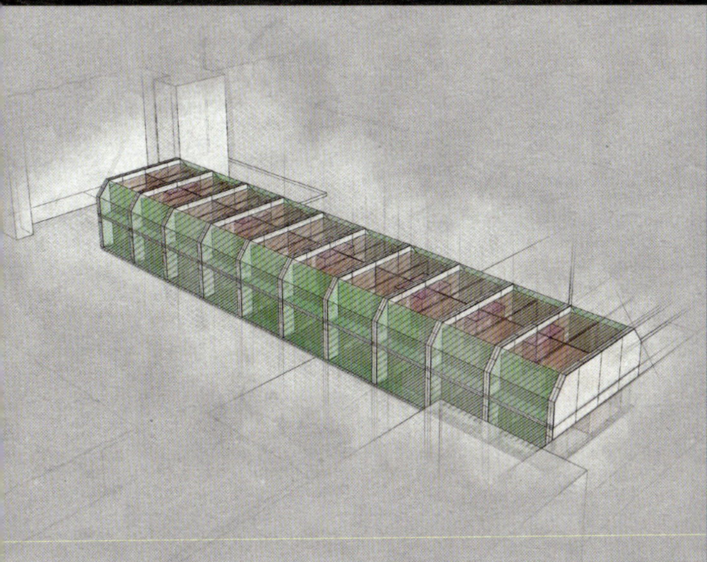

. Perspective view of environmental volumes

2. Perspective view of environmental volumes

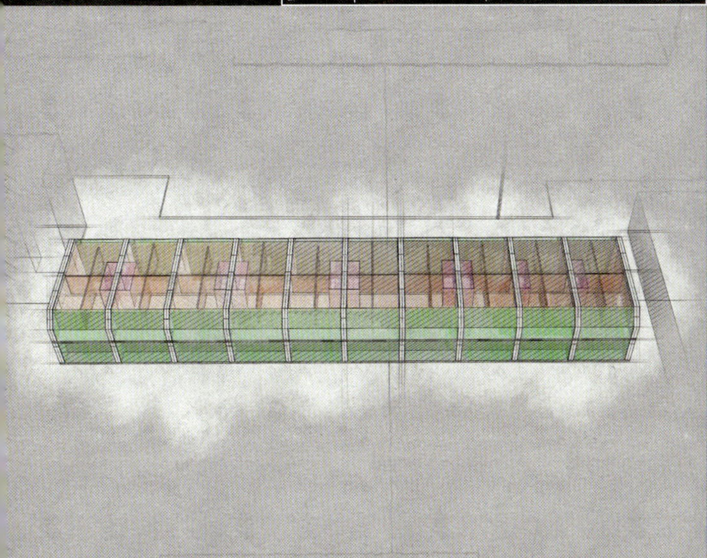

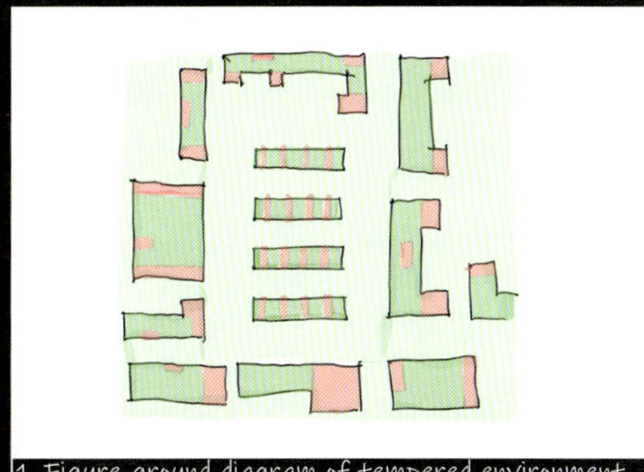

1. Figure-ground diagram of tempered environment

Option 1
Dark green spaces are highly tempered but occupy only 60 per cent of the total floor area. Support spaces shown in red are less tempered.

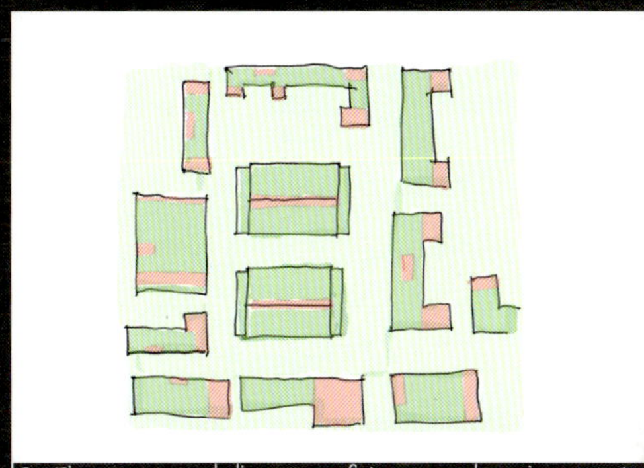

2. Figure-ground diagram of tempered environment

Option 2
Dark green spaces are highly tempered; occupying 75 per cent of the total floor area.

3. Figure-ground diagram of tempered environment

Option 3
Dark green spaces are highly tempered; occupying 80 per cent of the total floor area.

people can see in and can see what is going on as well as being able to have views out to other parts of the factory. The sense of enclosure and the sense of not being able to see people within this factory complex is alleviated by the translucency of areas of the factory, where other buildings surrounding this project have been constructed as opaque enclosures. The arrangement of buildings follows the orientation of surrounding buildings; not breaking with that geometry at any point to create a specific 'entrance', for example. All units have equal importance; the buildings occupy a position as a new 'component' within an existing factory.

The site context for Option 1 comprises blocks of eight workshop units with further subdivisions possible. Blocks of units are distributed across the full extent of the site in a way that provides access from both sides, while having the possibility of building across the gap between the buildings to create a single envelope. The units can be subdivided further into a total of 16 units from the eight units required. They can also be joined together into double-sized units, as four larger units, by joining adjacent workshops. Option 2 increases the possible floor plate by dividing the units into two groups instead of four. This provides the ability to extend sideways into the units and is based on the access for each unit being from each end of the building. Like Option 1, Option 2 uses the full extent of the site footprint.

Option 3 groups these units together, such that the arrangement becomes one of two groups of four, arranged in a square, where each unit can extend into the unit immediately behind it, or adjacent to it. This creates four units which can be subdivided either as Option 2 or by extending or subdividing them as shown on the diagram, where the access is what is on the opposite side from Option 1. Option 3 functions as a result of being able to have a means of escape from the main axis, and from the side of each of the units. This configuration would not function if a third set of units were joined on the side, but this arrangement uses the full extent of the site boundary, providing flexibility both as bigger square units and as bigger L-shaped units.

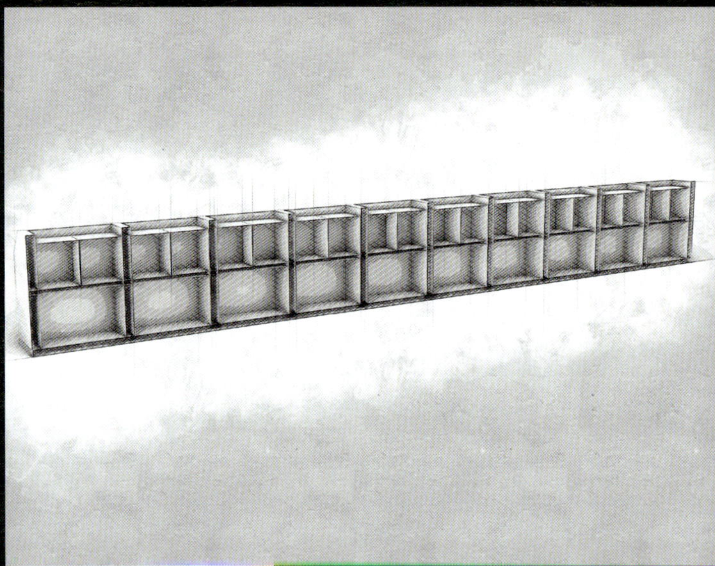

1. Sectional perspective view

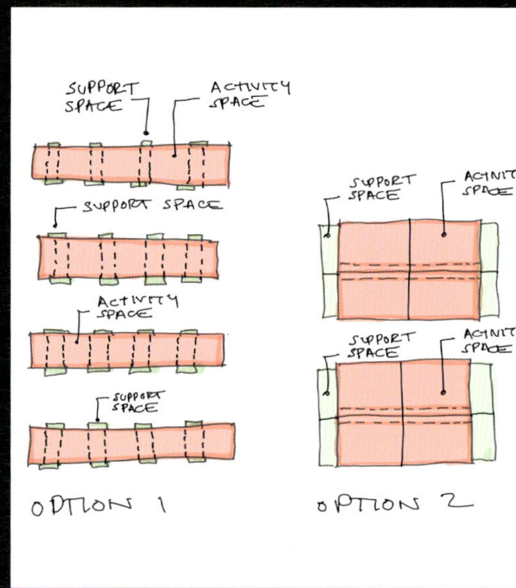

Spatial arrangement

Option 1 is based on having four separate buildings that provide between one and four subdivided building units.

Option 2 sets the services, installations and equipment on the roof.

2. Sectional perspective view

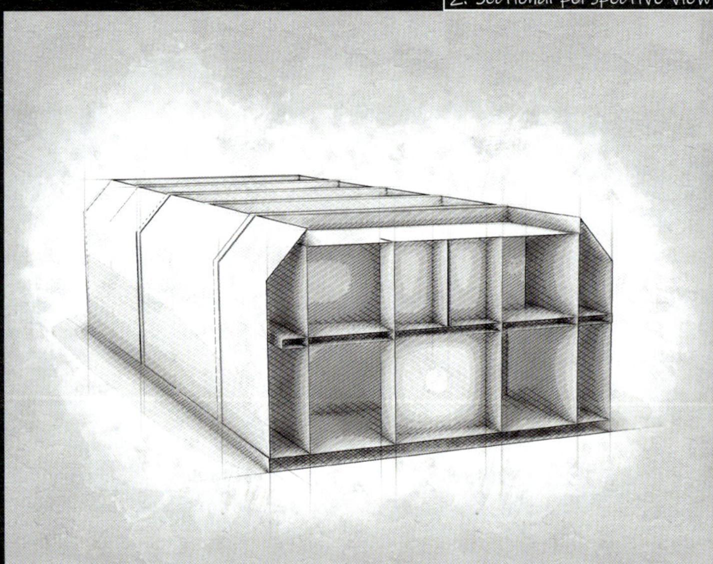

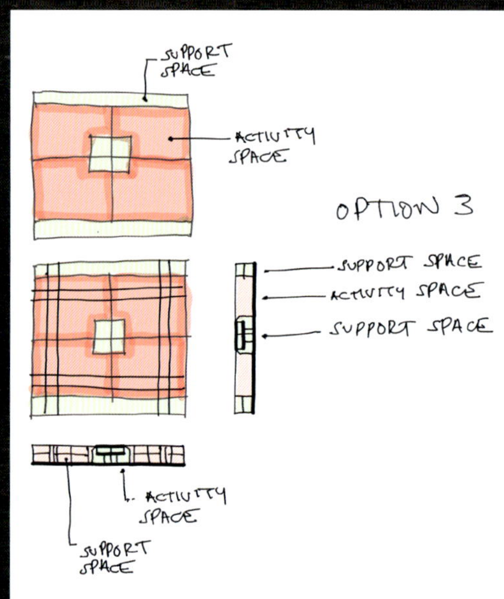

Option 3 divides each building into four units; this configuration being possible because access can be made from the front of each unit.

Spatial arrangement

The choice of adjacent garages and workshops is used deliberately in place of implementing a long and continuous production line. A key concept is that at every stage of the design, research and development of each car model requires only small teams that need to have their own equipment and independent storage spaces. This approach is very different from a regular car factory; the aim is to provide smaller and more focussed spaces for small teams working on ambitious car design and prototyping projects.

The spatial organisation of the units in Option 1 is based on having four separate buildings that provide between one and four subdivided building units. The space between the units can be constructed to create a single large volume or, alternatively, a combination of volumes. The servicing of these spaces is provided by the external walls that accommodate washrooms and meeting rooms, set on both sides of the large opening doors at each end. Deliveries of vehicle components and assemblies can be brought in at one end and despatched from the other end; there is a throughput across the complete width of the building. These spaces are double-height volumes with no mezzanines within them. Option 2 sets the services, installations and equipment on the roof. Entry points to the building units are positioned above the dividing walls between adjacent units such that dividing walls are permanent; the subdivision of spaces on both sides of that dividing wall can be adjusted, moved or removed, but the service of equipment takes place entirely at roof level.

In Option 3 each building is divided into four units; this configuration being possible because access can be made from the front of each unit, with means of escape being provided from the side of each of each unit to provide an alternative means of escape. This configuration of alternative escape routes directly to the outside cannot be provided for units greater than four units arranged in a square. The service space is set at the junction of the four units such that the dividing walls can be removed or moved around while the service space in the middle remains unchanged.

. Perspective view of interior

2. Perspective view of interior

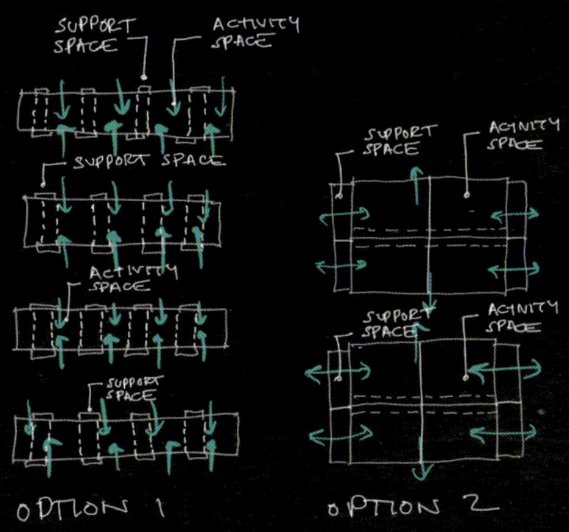

Internal circulation

Option 1 is based on entering through side doors between the main lifting doors of each unit.

Option 2 has access doors for pedes-trians open into the middle of the unit.

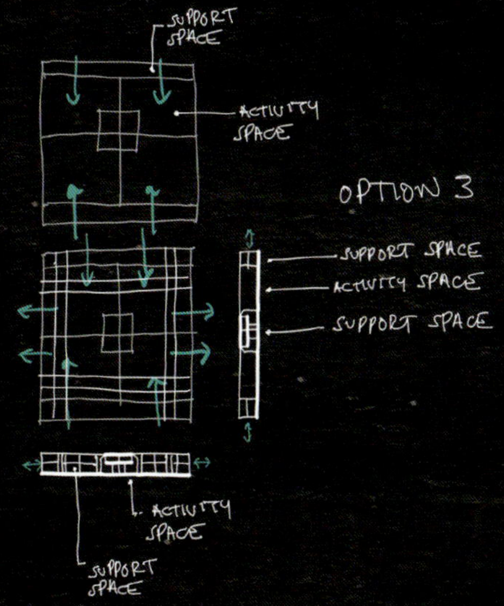

Option 3 is the safest from the point of view of the separation of vehicles and pedestrians.

Internal circulation

Groups of buildings are set opposite one another, with space between them for the manoeuvring of vehicle prototypes which are taken out for testing and for despatch to other parts of the company. Vehicles parts are stored in small containers near the entry doors to each unit, at the opposite end from those items that leave the unit.

The internal circulation of Option 1 is based on entering through side doors between the main lifting doors of each unit. Access takes place through the service 'boxes', which are attached to the front of the facade. The service space includes access to stairs; a prefabricated module that essentially provides access into the zone between the main spaces of the building.

Option 2 provides access from each end of the units, and has doors as a means of escape in the centre of each unit. Those doors can be increased in number by cutting away the openings in the profiled metal sheet panels arranged on the facades.

Option 3 has primary access for vehicles in the same orientation as Option 1; pedestrian access is through the sides of the units. Option 3 has the advantage of separating out the directions of access for vehicles and for pedestrians. Option 2 has this benefit but to a lesser degree, as the access doors for pedestrians open into the middle of the unit. Option 1 has the benefit of having access which is separate from the vehicles but is still adjacent to those vehicles; close user coordination between pedestrian and vehicle use is required. Option 3 is the safest from the point of view of the separation of vehicles and pedestrians.

The arrangement of circulation between buildings is laid out in order to avoid awkward junctions and unexpected corners which would create points of danger for those walking between buildings; all junctions and corners are predictable both for the pedestrian and the road vehicle. A key approach to the circulation between buildings is one of safety for all users. Safety is achieved through visibility, straight lines of movement and the avoidance of blind spots, either at corners or between units.

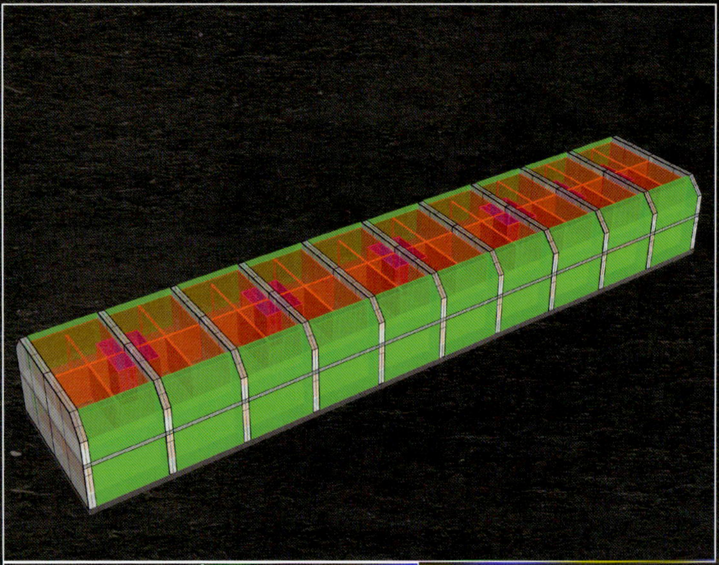

1A. Isometric view of environmental volumes

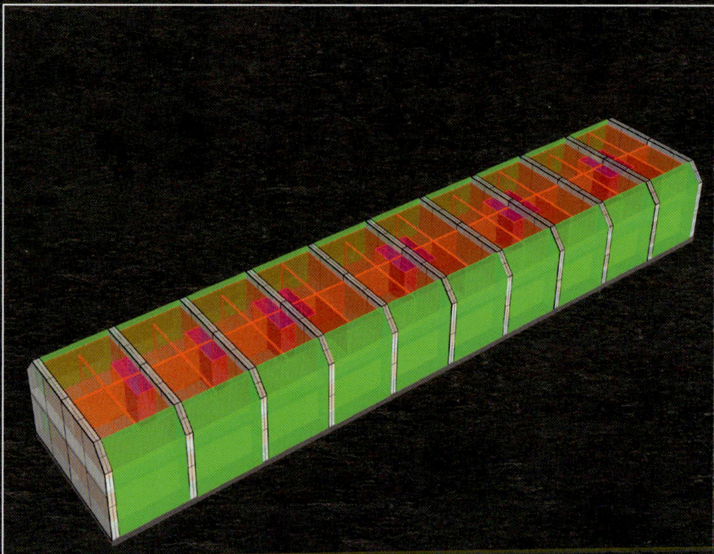

2A. Isometric view of environmental volumes

1B. Isometric view of environmental volumes

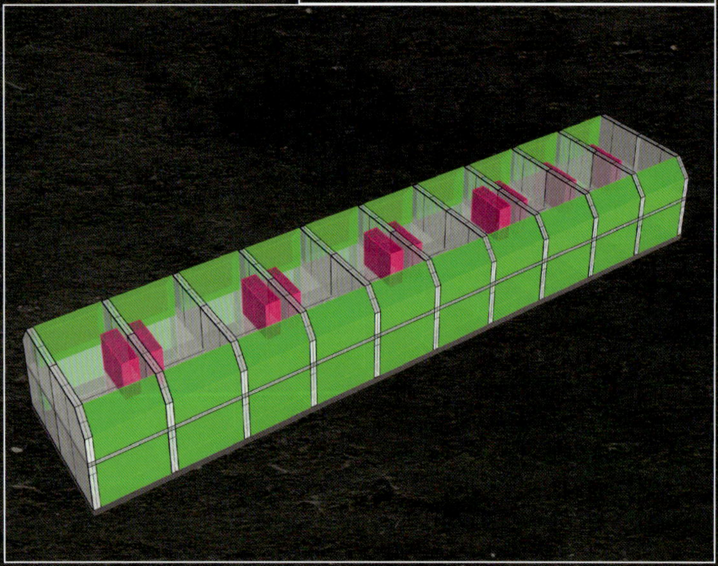

2B. Isometric view of environmental volume

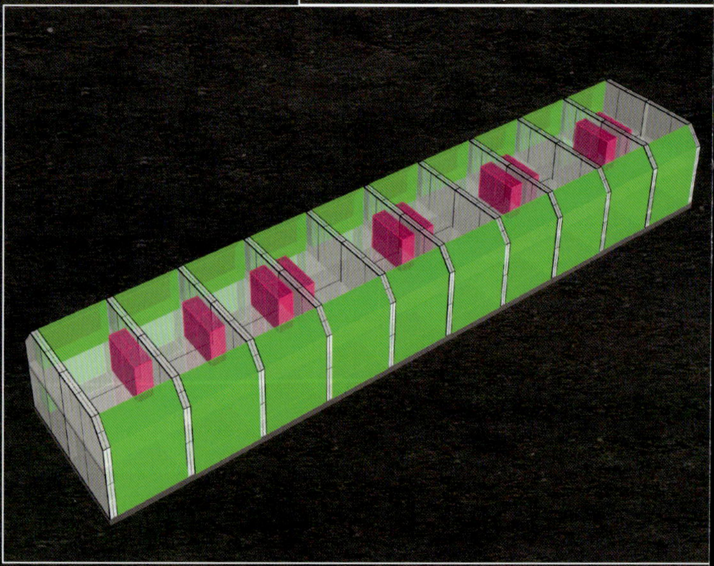

Environmental zones

The environmental strategy is informed by having different amounts of transparency and associated thermal insulation in each of the units. The default arrangement for each unit is to have glazed doors which can open vertically inwards as large-sized lifting doors; doors are operated for either the arrival or despatch of goods, or alternatively to benefit from the mid-season climate. These doors lift upward to the ceiling level inside each unit. A separate opaque panel, positioned in front of the service area, slides in front of that glazed door if required; the sliding opaque wall panel is highly thermally insulated. The unit can be enclosed visually and thermally by sliding the wall panel in front of the glazed panel; this panel has a relatively low level of thermal insulation as a result of its construction. The panel slides in front of the glazed door if an enclosed environment is required. This arrangement provides a hybrid solution of 20% of the wall becoming opaque and 80% of the wall becoming glazed, with daylight being admitted on one side. Alternatively, 80% of the wall area can become opaque, with 20% being glazed; different arrangements can be used to suit specific tasks being carried out within each unit.

For example, panels can slide to the centre to provide 10% daylight adjacent to the sides of each unit, providing entry to these units through the service area and circulation space between units. This avoids the need to have doors fitted into the glazed or opaque wall panels. The panels are also set out on the inclined roof area such that the glazing can be covered with insulated panels. The strategy for environmental control is one of changing the levels of thermal insulation and daylight provision within each workshop; service zones are used for access and circulation through units in addition to their accommodation of services equipment.

Support zones have high levels of thermal insulation as they are largely environmentally passive in their ventilation requirements. Background heating is provided, with natural ventilation being used in summer months in order to optimise their energy consumption. Activity spaces have glazed walls, including rooflights that allow top light to enter

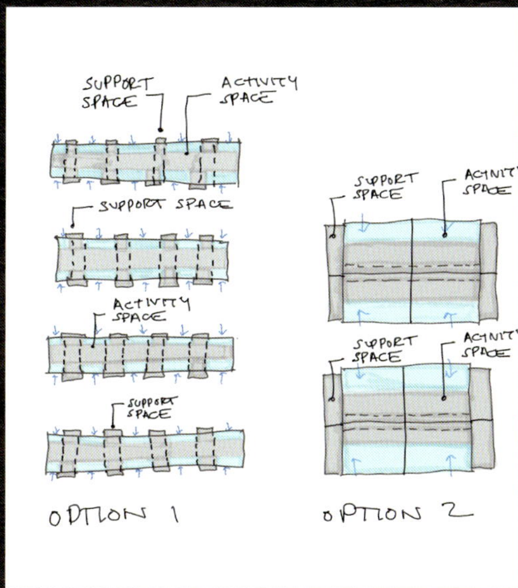

Daylight strategy for direct sunlight and cross ventilation.

Option 1 admits daylight only near the external walls that are adjacent to doors.

Option 2 continuously admits daylight adjacent to the facades.

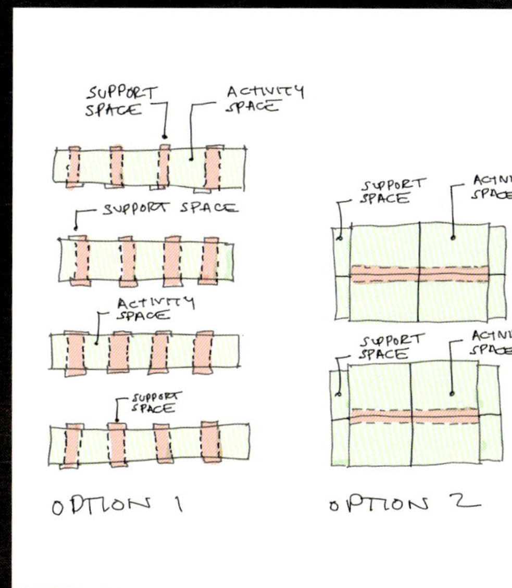

Environmental zones

Option 1 is based on having separate units for air conditioning for each workshop and for the zones between workshops.

Option 2 creates an environmental zone at roof level which extends down into the unit itself.

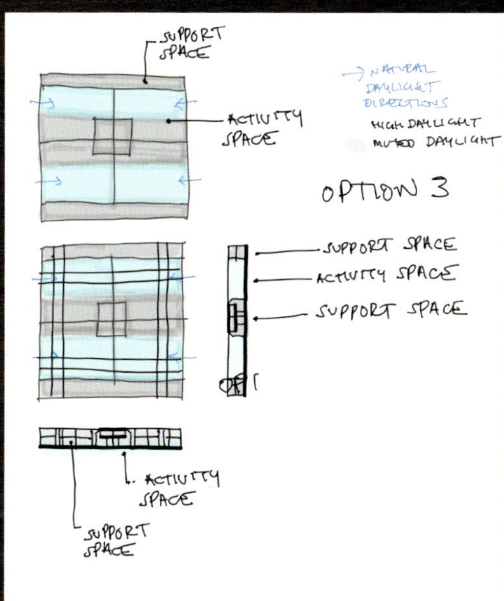

Daylight strategy for direct sunlight and cross ventilation.

Option 3 admits toplight in the centre of the spaces. Support zones have subdued daylight.

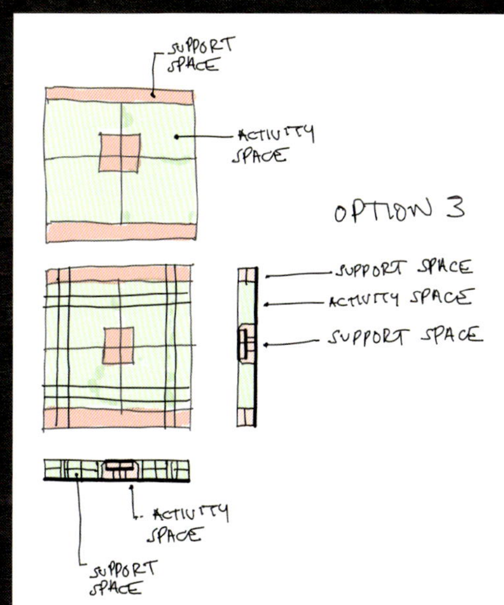

Environmental zones

Option 3 has the environmental zones positioned in the centre of the building, and on its two edges.

spaces to suit different lighting and natural lighting conditions for the assembly works being carried out inside the spaces below. The glazed doors and inclined rooflights provide three different directions from which light can enter the internal spaces. The louvres on the roof provide the ability to exclude daylight or to direct sunlight into the building.

The environmental strategy for Option 1 is based on having separate units for air conditioning for each workshop and for the zones between workshops. The workshop zone can have meeting rooms inserted in order to integrate washrooms and services.

Spaces for full air-handling ducts and plumbing are provided accordingly for modules to be plugged in and moved as required within that red zone. The green zone is less tightly controlled, environmentally, and has a quick-response heating and cooling system in order to temper the space quickly for relatively short periods. Doors are open for part of the day, set at each end of the unit.

Option 2 creates an environmental zone at roof level which extends down into the unit itself, as shown in the red zone in the diagram. The zone immediately beneath the red zone is tempered; it has prefabricated units attached to it with air-handling sockets ready for additional flexible ducting to be added to this more controlled environmental zone. The area shown in green is like Option 1; semi-tempered with a quick-response heating and cooling system that activates with the opening and closing of the doors during working hours.

Option 3 has the environmental zones positioned in the centre of the building, and on its two edges; environmental zones are smaller than in Options 1 and 2. The more closely controlled red zone extends the full width of the buildings at the edges, but only occurs at the centre in order to provide maximum flexibility for use of the space. The central core is fixed, whereas at the edge, the cores along the edges can be extended up through the full width of the building.

Spatial layouts of the services equipment spine comprise access stairs at the end of the building, chillers and air-handling units. All are accessed by perforated metal decks which provide the required level of safety for maintenance staff.

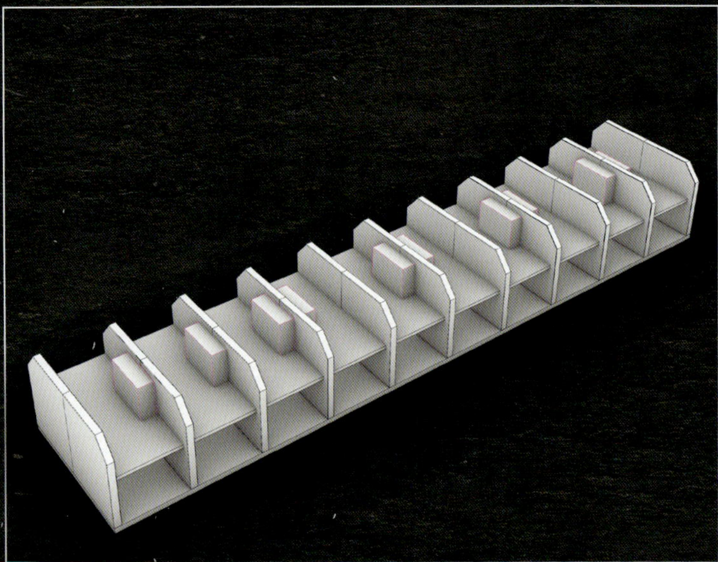

1A. Isometric view of structure

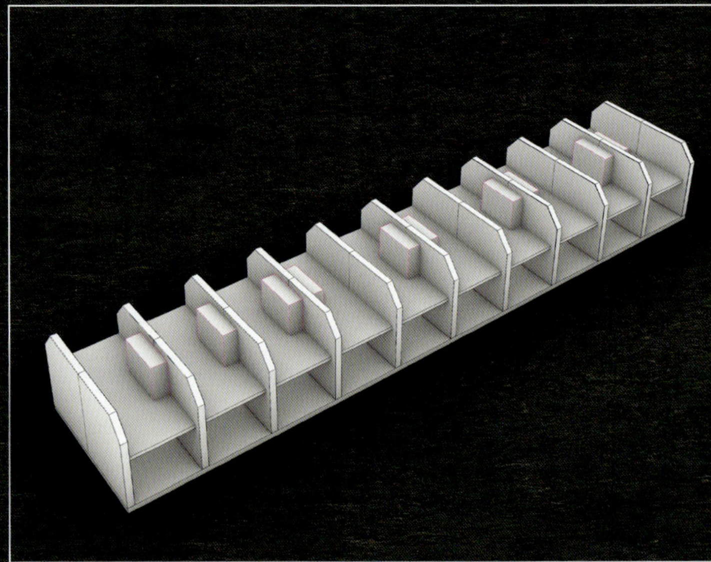

2A. Isometric view of structure

1B. Isometric view of structure

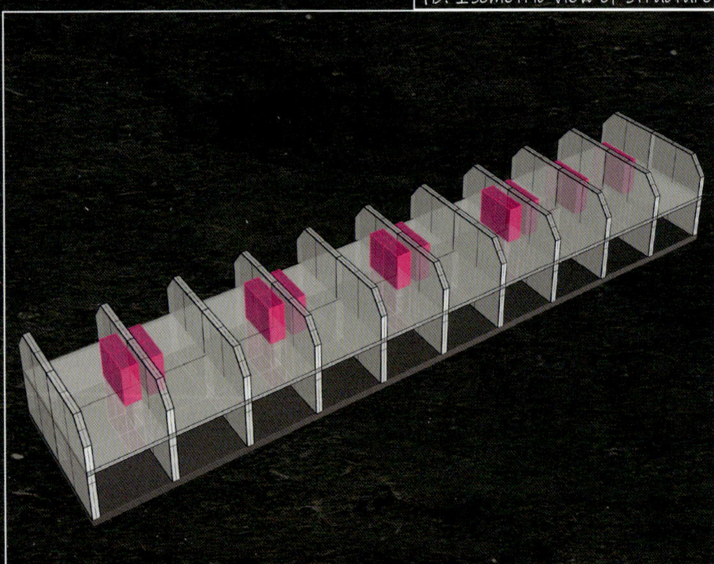

2B. Isometric view of structur

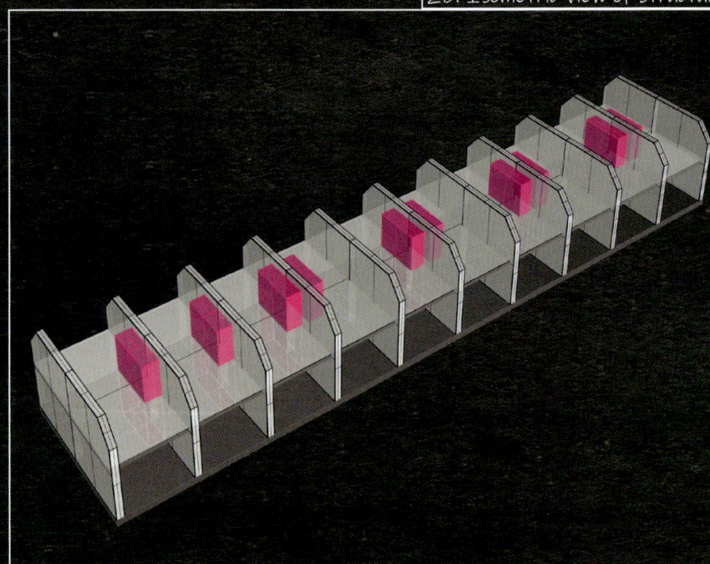

Structural strategy

The structural design is based on a series of 'inhabited' walls; a series of lightweight 'pods' that divide the workshops into a series of frames which are light in weight, arranged as 'pods'. The lightweight stacked pods are joined together with roof trusses which provide a separate roof to each of the environmentally separate workshop spaces. The rooftop spine, an externally mounted service core for the installation of mechanical ventilation, is positioned so that the building can be serviced and maintained without interrupting the work going on in the design studios. Service spaces are located completely externally, with a separate team of engineers and maintenance staff looking after the performance of all those spaces without having to interface with the commercially sensitive operations inside each garage workshop. The structural concept is of a structure which is partially steel framed and partially reinforced concrete framed. The use of reinforced concrete brings to this project the durable surface finish required for the dividing walls between units, used instead of a drywall solution.

The disadvantage here of metal panels is that its use cannot provide the level of sound insulation required from the noise generated by vehicles undergoing testing; not from inside to outside but between adjacent workshops. The reinforced concrete walls also have a function of reducing flanking sounds between adjacent workshops; projecting fin walls are provided for this purpose. The reinforced concrete walls are constructed as diaphragm walls, with a thermal insulated core which is positioned to provide a continuity of thermal insulation with adjacent facades. Lifting doors are made from insulated metal panels.

The structural strategy for Option 1 is based on using the externally-fixed support spaces of washrooms, storage and services equipment as the primary structural component. This component comprises portal frames set on either side of the service zone. These portal frames support the roof and form a table-like frame, of which there are four set along the length of each of the buildings. These portal frames are linked by roof trusses which span between these portal frames; onto which the external envelope of roof panels is attached.

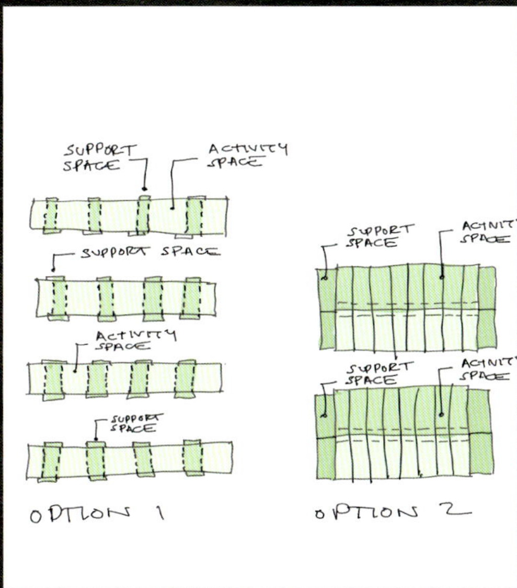

Structural strategy: Zones
Option 1 uses the externally fixed support spaces as the primary structural component.
Option 2 uses portal frames as single frames, joined together by roof trusses.

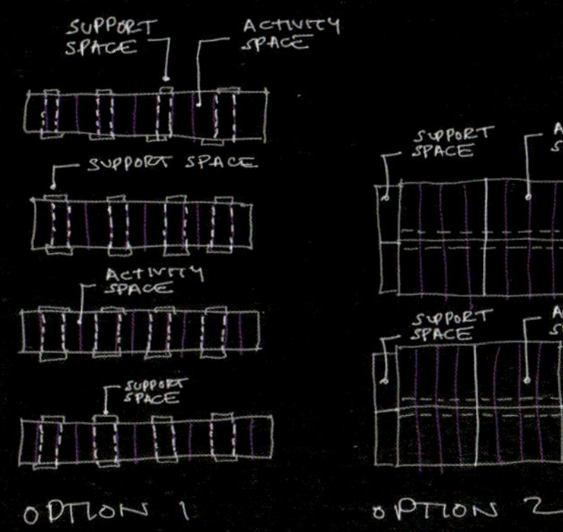

Structural strategy: Framing
Option 1 has a primary structural component comprising portal frames set on either side of the service zone.
Option 2 uses portal frames as single frames joined together by roof trusses.

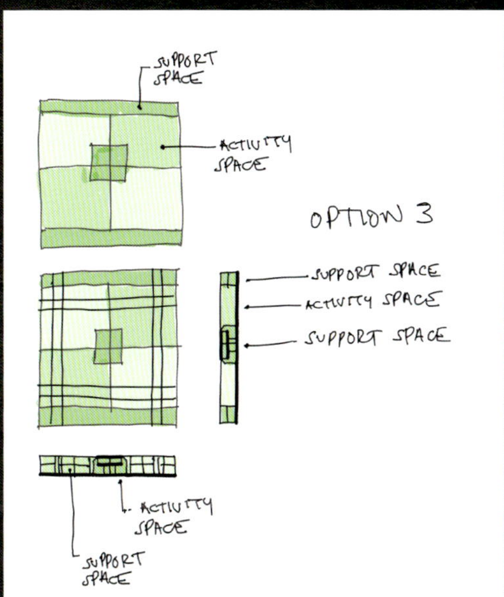

Structural strategy: Zones
Option 3 uses portal frames which span from side to side of each unit, supported at the mid-span by the service spaces in the middle of the building.

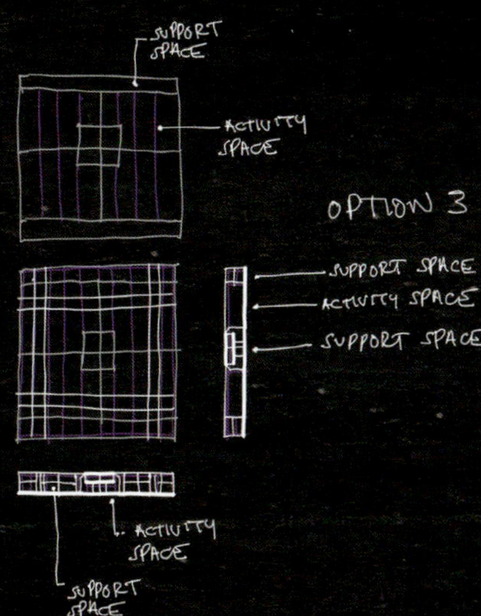

Structural strategy: Zones
Option 3 uses a wider portal-frame structure set in the middle; trusses are set at roof level, spanning between these frames.

Option 2 uses the supports to roof-mounted services equipment, as the primary structural components to which cranked columns are added to form a portal frame arrangement. This arrangement is different from that of Option 1. The portal frames are single frames, joined together by roof trusses. Structural stability is provided by bracing at roof level, in the plane of the roof, to provide the overall stiffness for the roof with equivalent bracing being provided in the dividing wall between the units in the vertical plane. Stiffness in the vertical plane is also provided by trusses set above the opening doors, as well as between doors.

Option 3 uses portal frames which span from side to side of each unit, supported at the mid-span by the service spaces in the middle of the building, as well as by smaller service spaces on the side of the building; both are framed at their perimeter. A wider portal-frame structure is set in the middle; trusses are set at roof level, spanning between these frames. Service equipment on the roofs of each of the long buildings is supported by distributing the loads across four separate steel beams, rather than supporting them directly onto the structural wall below. The aim of distributing loads, making them as even as possible across the roof of the facades, allows the structure to become more economical by avoiding a hierarchy of primary and secondary members.

Columns are placed outside the zone of the service space. Structural support within service spaces is provided by walls constructed from a light gauge steel frame, which also forms the enclosure. This area has staircases that are light in weight, set within a fire-resistant enclosure created by the walls of the service space. Activity spaces have their own columns such that floors can be demounted to suit operational changes. Mezzanine floors are made as prefabricated units so that they can be removed and changed to suit the evolving needs of this facility. The three structural options are all based on the principle of the support spaces being structurally independent of the activity spaces that accommodate design and workshop facilities. This approach allows the 'pods' to be relocated or changed more easily.

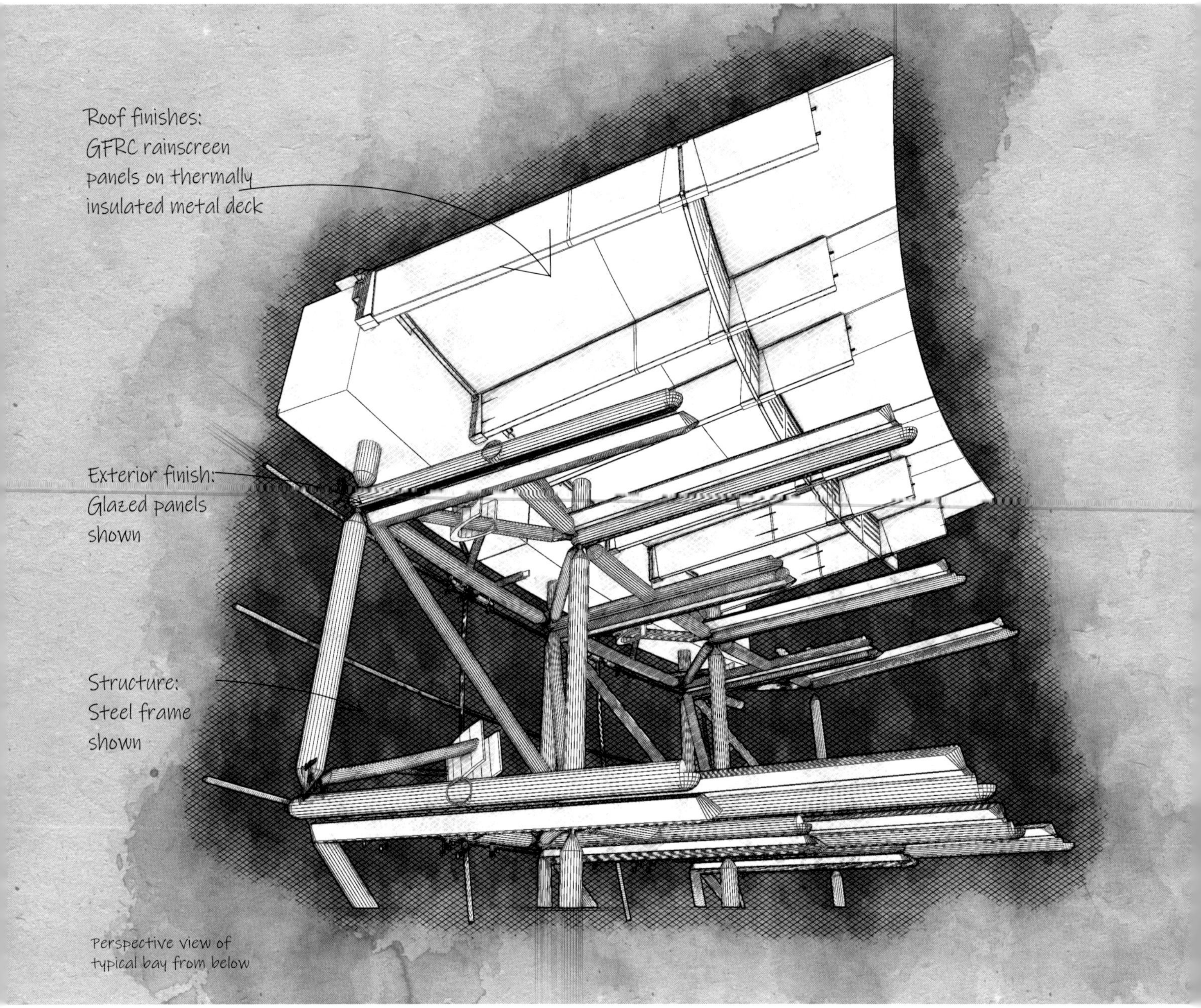

Perspective view of typical bay from below

Typical bay adjacent to facade

A typical bay is formed by a set of opaque panels, a lifting door and an inclined glazed roof; all of which are supported by a steel frame. The opaque panels can slide horizontally to enclose the glazed door; the door can be raised to provide access for vehicles on both facades. The roof has environmental control equipment installed beneath a solar shading canopy and between rooflights, which can be moved to suit operational requirements in the units beneath. The solar shading canopy comprises a set of louvres which can change orientation to suit functional requirements. All four assemblies – opaque panels, lifting doors, rooflights, solar shading and environmental control equipment – can be moved in order to respond to changing requirements in the workshops and studios below. The ability to move parts of the walls and roofs is achieved economically.

The need for increasing the mass of a wall, to reduce the sound transmission, results in the outer lifting doors being made as horizontally folding doors clad in GFRC (glass fibre reinforced concrete) to match the concrete facades. The concrete facades are also clad in GFRC and are panelised to achieve the sound attenuation levels required. The advantage of GFRC is that panels can be removed if damaged and replaced from the outside of the building; panels can also be cleaned easily. Inner concrete walls, with their outer surface of mineral-fibre insulation allow the inner wall of concrete to be made continuous with a steel structure of box-section steel beams which are bolted and made structurally continuous with the concrete. This provides a rigid outer layer to the building, allowing the doors or lifting panels and glazing to be openable while remaining large-scale components. Their weight is accommodated easily by the composite steel and concrete structure. The use of the reinforced concrete outer walls with the steel framing reduces the need for stiffening in the inner cores, which are required to be flexible for changes of use, where the individual garages may need to be linked by removing the cladding that separates them with stairs, washrooms and control rooms situated within. Stairs are also made from aluminium; they are prefabricated, to be demounted and moved

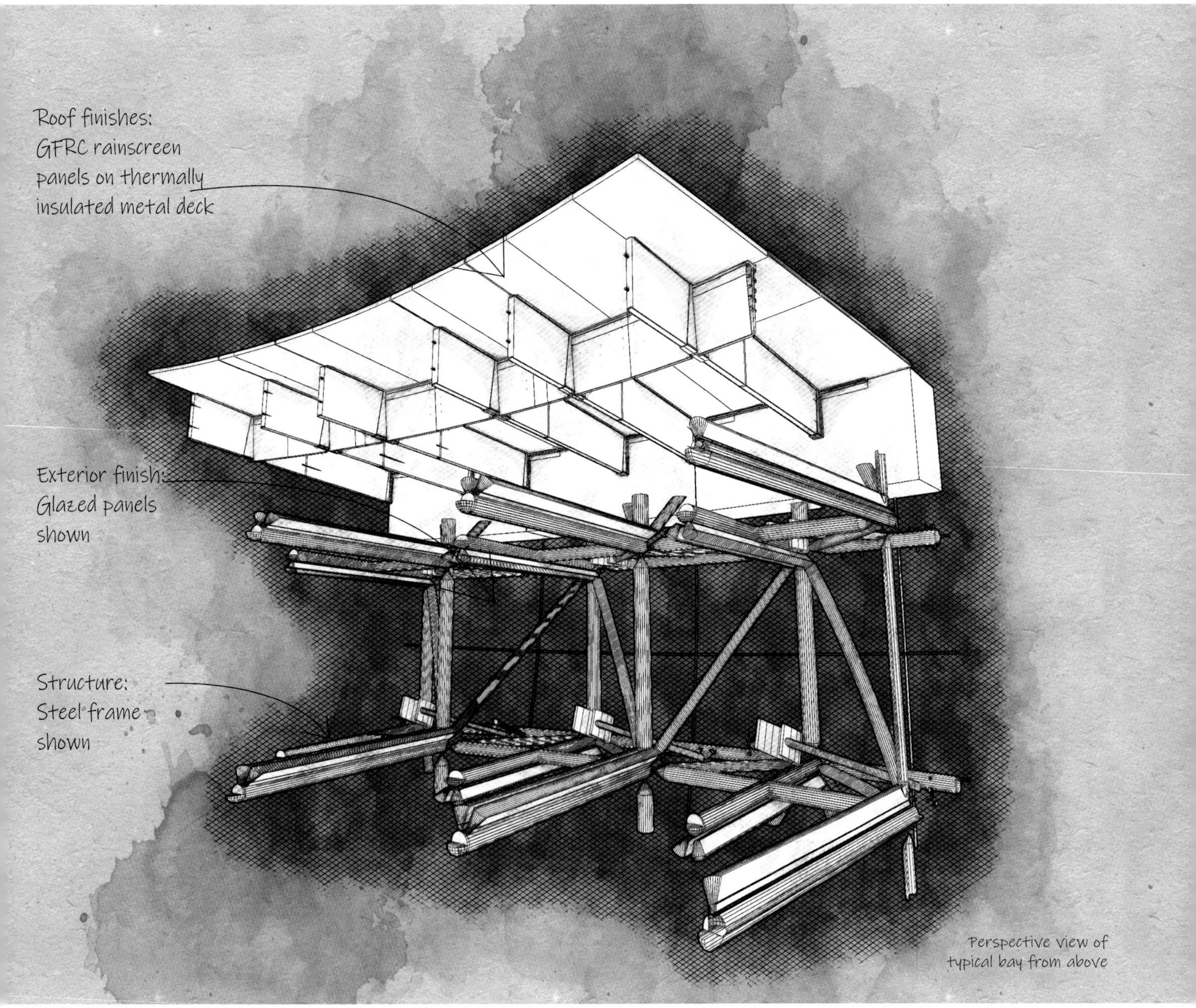

Perspective view of typical bay from above

around the building as required. Fire protection to the staircase enclosures is provided by fire-rated lightweight panels, rather than by heavyweight concrete panels. The buildings are required to have a high level of sound insulation and the flexibility of being able to open and close the spaces to be linked, as the car design projects vary in size and scope. Thermal insulation between units is provided by the whole width of the core. This building uses the principle of using a mix of material thicknesses to reduce high frequency and low frequency sounds around the perimeter and uses the full width of the inner spine cores to provide the same performance by using a 3.0-metre-deep space, but with its central void and thermal insulation set on both faces.The external envelope strategy for Option 1 is to have full-height opening doors with trusses set immediately above the doors for their support, as well as to provide structural stability for the building. The service modules are set as part of the facade. A metal rainscreen, with a lightweight metal-framed insulated backing wall, provides the flexibility needed to create openings for services equipment or for windows, for example. The flexibility of approach that is provided by the metal rainscreen meets the requirements of flexibility that is introduced in the structural strategy. Option 2 has full-width doors that cover the full width of the facade; side panels are made as metal rainscreens, as in Option 1. The rainscreen panel system allows for flexibility of use and the introduction of large-scale elements such as glazed panels. This aim is achieved by removing complete rainscreen panels, and replacing them with glazed panels that can be glazed into the same framing type. The larger scale of these side walls makes it less compelling to use a metal-framed backing ball with rainscreen panels, but suggests that prefabricated wall panels spanning from floor to ceiling are more efficient, as changes on the larger scale of this facade can be achieved more easily using removable or demountable faced metal panels. Option 3 uses metal doors in the same way on opposite sides of the building with metal panels arranged as per Option 2. The difference between Options 2 and 3 is essentially within the roof; the service zone projects above the level of the roof in Option 3.

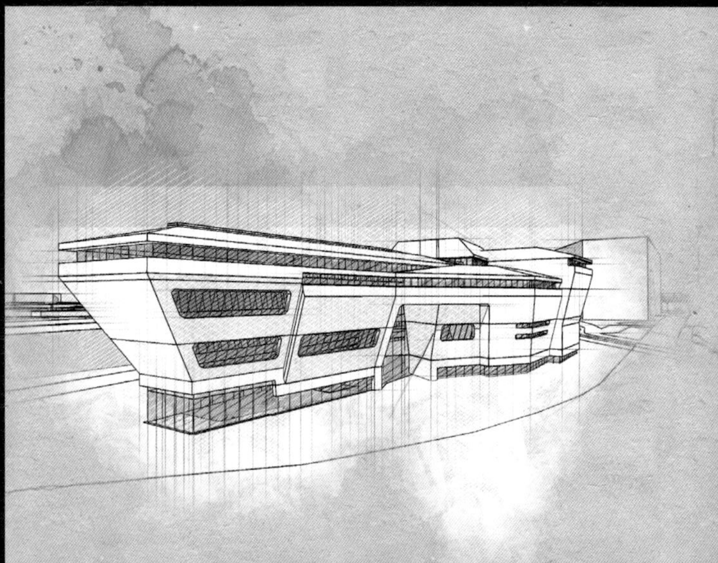

1. Perspective view of exterior

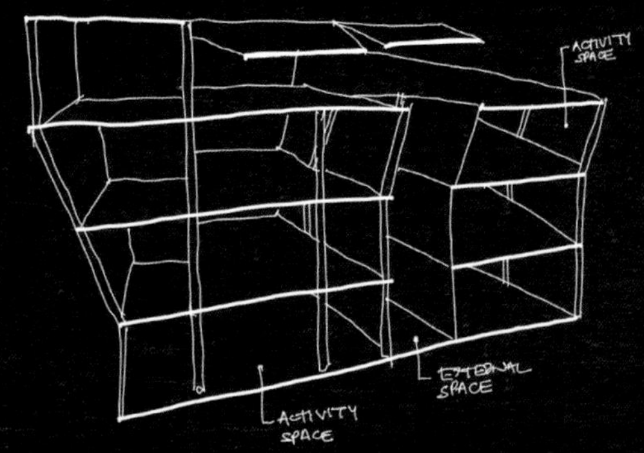

2. Perspective view of exterior

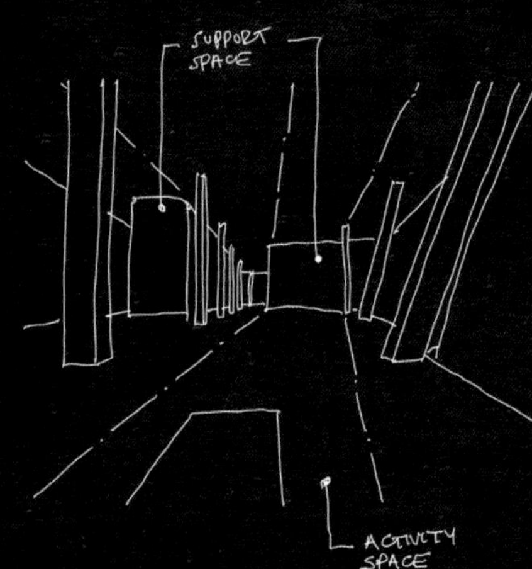

Zoning in environmental design

A key consideration in the design of this project is the provision of environmental zones in the building. These are zones that are formed by grouping all spaces within the building which share a common set of 'active' systems of mechanical, electrical and plumbing systems as well as 'passive' systems of controlled natural ventilation – including night-time thermal mass cooling as well as daylight control.

A key driver in the provision of mechanical ventilation in this project is to provide an 'active' control to minimise the energy needed during periods of necessary use in creating comfort conditions within each space, which is balanced with the use of natural ventilation provided by 'passive' devices set into the facade system. The opening of windows is not considered to be a controlled method of introducing air into the internal spaces of this building. Trickle ventilation is provided for some service spaces, but passive devices set into the facades are used to supplement mechanical ventilation in 'activity' spaces, or main floor plates, in supplying the required air changes and thermal comfort conditions.

In this project, environmental zones are divided by identifying spaces in the building and grouping them by function and by their expected frequency of use. These groups of spaces are compared initially with the external environmental conditions of the range of the sun's path, air temperature, relative humidity and wind at different times of year. The orientation of spaces requires a response in its environmental design. Groups of spaces that have similar requirements for environmental control, and similar exposure to external conditions, are grouped as environmental zones.

Some environmental zones which are set adjacent to one another have 'buffer' zones set between them, mostly created by internal circulation spaces. In addition to 'buffer' zones which are set between some 'environmental' zones, additional 'semi-internal' and 'external' zones are created within the spatial arrangement of this building in order to provide naturally ventilated and passively solar-controlled spaces which can be regarded as being outside the building envelope, and which require limited active controls. Winter gardens are considered to be 'semi-exter-

Perspective view of exterior

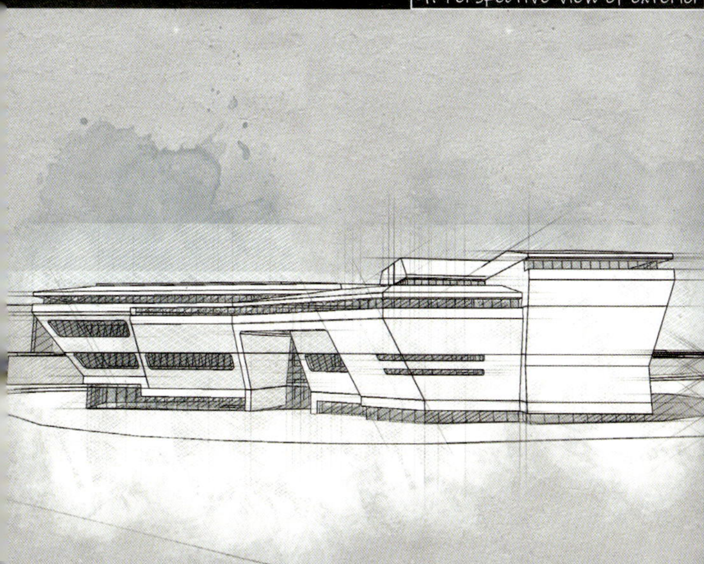

4. Perspective view of exterior

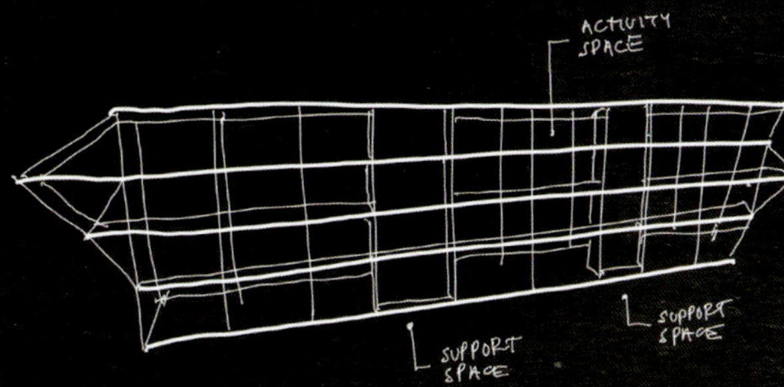

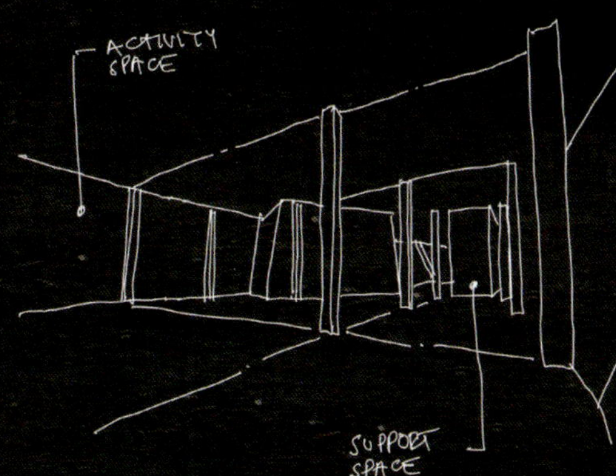

nal', while terraces are considered to be 'external', even when passive partial protection from wind and sun is provided. A double-skin facade creates a further buffer zone of winter gardens such that the environmental zoning is not concerned only with the grouping of spaces, but also with the zoning of associated mechanical equipment such that spaces and ducts are serviced by a common system. For this reason, the creation of environmental zones is also determined by the means of distributing air and services mechanically around the building using routes that are efficient for use of space, for thermal efficiency and for electrical efficiency in their operation.

The environmental zones in this building are defined principally by three sets of criteria: mechanical ventilation and natural ventilation, daylight and electrical lighting, solar shading and solar control glass. The arrangement of these zones is also informed by the use of those spaces: hours of occupation, numbers of people and frequency of use. Natural ventilation suits a range of outside temperatures and relative humidity, including night-time ventilation for cooling the building. The control of daylight is based on different daylight conditions and hours of daylight, with an associated requirement for electrical lighting. Solar control is based on fixed devices which will reduce solar gain at different times of day for different times of year.

Daylight has a relatively modest influence over the environmental control of spaces, as light shelves on facades redirect sunlight and daylight into the rooms by reflecting them off ceilings. Floor plates are considered to be 'parcelled up' as environmental zones as a result of the functions that are undertaken in each of the spaces of the building. The effects of solar gain are small as a result of the use of light shelves and horizontal louvres in glazed areas. The environmental zones are divided up as a result of the use of space; when and which spaces are populated, the time and the equipment is used to provide the level of heating or cooling required for those work groups.

This project addressed these issues through the use of geometry in order to enhance natural ventilation, daylight and solar shading through the geometry of the external envelope.

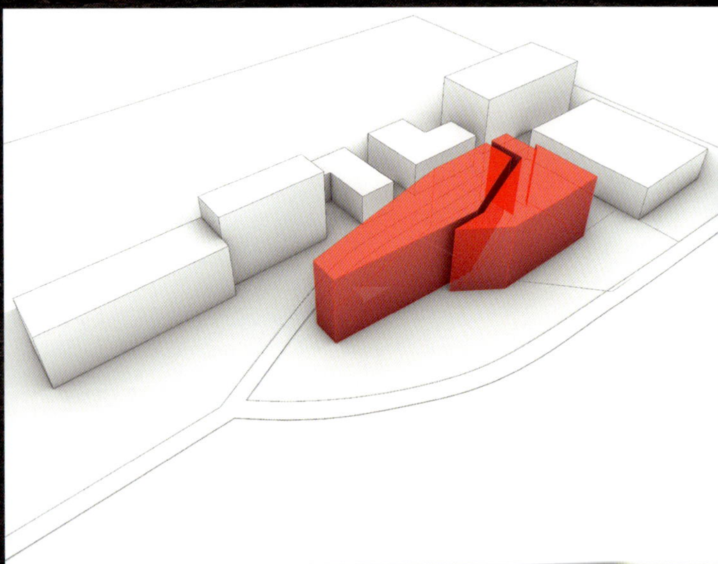

1. Project volume in site context

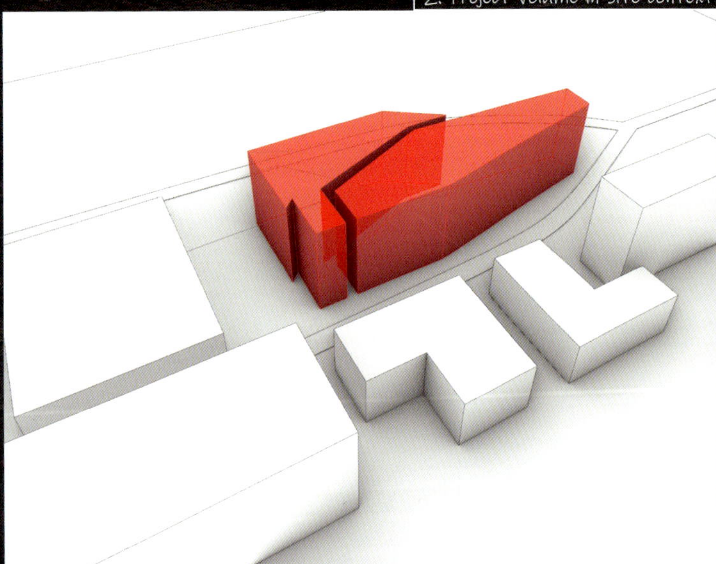

2. Project volume in site context

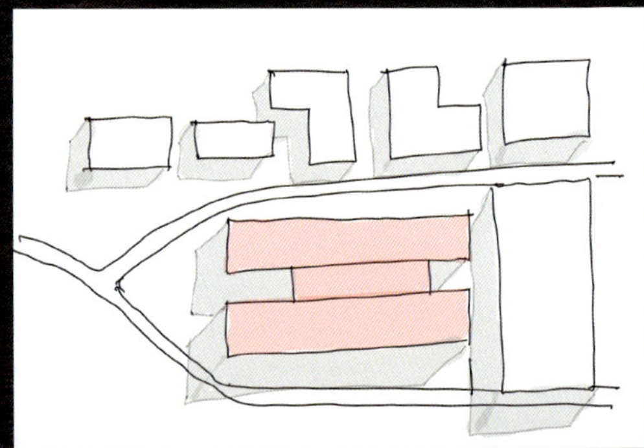

1. Site plan with surrounding context

Option 1 divides into two blocks to allow daylight to be admitted to all internal spaces through a link block that joins the two parts of the building.

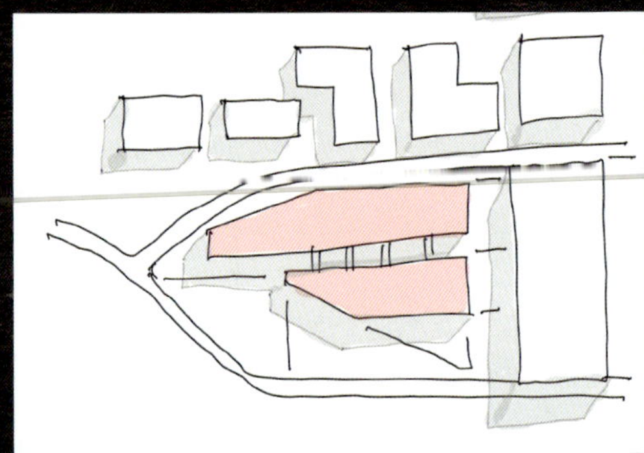

2. Site plan with surrounding context

Option 2 uses a geometry of two blocks which are inflected in order to respond to the road pattern around the building.

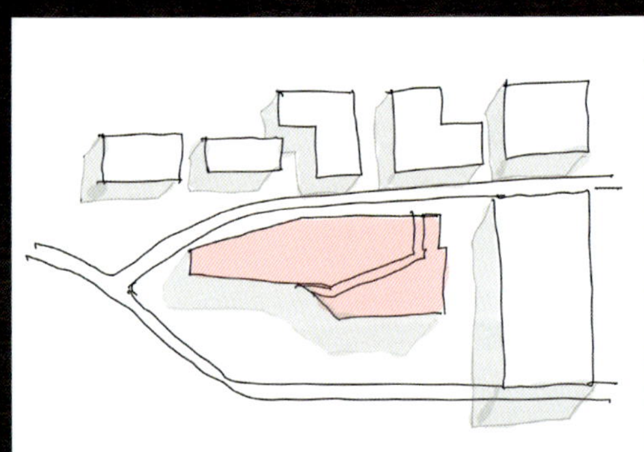

3. Site plan with surrounding context

Option 3 eliminates the link between the two buildings as a result of the two wings being smaller in size than other options.

Site context

This project is a university campus building for the teaching of sciences, with associated research laboratories. Lower floors contain teaching rooms and lecture theatres; upper floors accommodate post-doctorate research spaces. These spaces are nested together in a structure that comprises a set of closely spaced steel members forming a steel frame. This allows the structure to transition from forming a large enclosed space, such as a lecture theatre, to adjacent smaller teaching rooms and laboratories.

The site context for Option 1 comprises a distribution of space over three floors. Spaces are divided into two blocks to allow daylight to be admitted to all internal spaces through the introduction of a link block that joins the two parts of the building. The link block is largely glazed in order to admit light to the edges inside the building. This option does not respond specifically to the context or form of the site but is consistent with the geometry of the surrounding buildings. The residual space between the roads and the building is filled with hard landscaping that includes planted trees and seating clusters that follow the structural grid from inside to outside the building; the structural grid is extended across most of the site externally as a way of the building visually 'taking possession' of the site. This approach creates a usable external space along the long axis of the central link space; the building can be accessed from either end of the glazed link volume. In Option 2, the geometry of the two blocks is inflected in order to respond to the road pattern around the building, providing the opportunity to create external spaces which are framed by a continuation of the main walls and the lines of the geometry of the building, which extend out into the landscape. This creates three external spaces which are semi-enclosed, and which have an identity which is linked to the building geometry. An additional floor level is added to the building in order to maintain the required floor area. Option 3 takes Option 2 and develops it further in order to eliminate the link between the two buildings as a result of the two wings being smaller in size and therefore being able to be joined without the need for a link space between the two blocks. The external

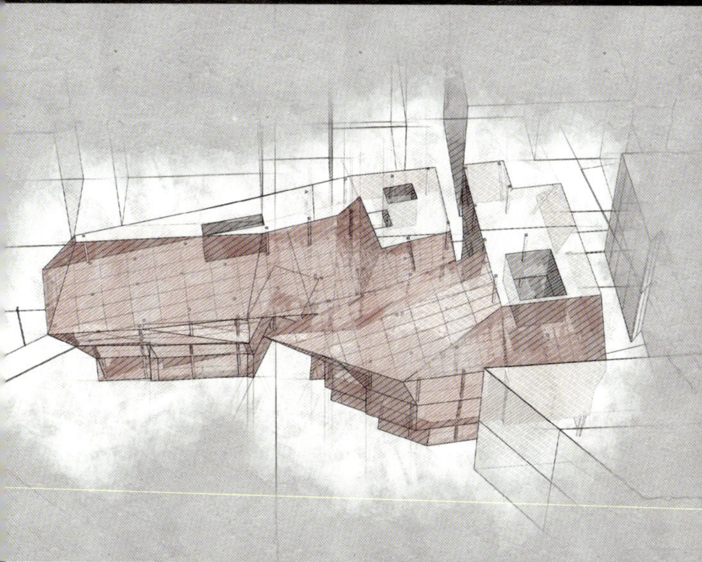

Perspective view of environmental volumes

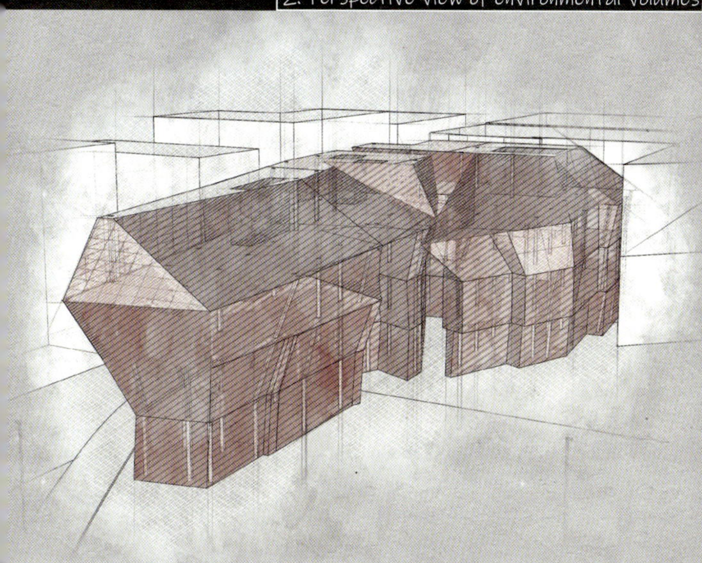

2. Perspective view of environmental volumes

1. Figure-ground diagram of tempered environment

Option 1 has red spaces which are highly tempered but are reduced to small volumes only.

2. Figure-ground diagram of tempered environment

Option 2 has dark green spaces which are less tempered than red spaces; occupying different blocks. Light blue spaces are less tempered than green spaces.

3. Figure-ground diagram of tempered environment

Option 3 does not have light blue spaces as the two blocks are divided. External bridge walkways, with canopies, link the two blocks.

spaces created around the building can now be created as three linked spaces that occupy most of the unbuilt part of the site as a result of the facades providing a primary backdrop to each space.

The site context is one of the buildings of similar height that surround the new building; the new bulding does not exceed the height of its neighbours. The general appearance of surrounding buildings is one of concrete walls with windows set into them. The facades of existing buildings are characterised by both long strips of window and punched hole windows set within concrete-faced facades. These buildings date from various periods within the past 40 years. This project uses the visual vocabulary of ribbon windows for the middle floors. The floor-to-ceiling glazing on the ground floor is also used in parts of the surrounding buildings. An overhanging eaves at roof level provides some shading and higher levels of daylight at the top floor level than is required on lower floors. On the middle floors, a mixture of windows and opaque wall were required to suit the anticipated use of those spaces; these spaces are not all outward facing activities that require daylight. Some spaces are for presentations and exhibitions that require the lighting to be controlled. Although the language of the existing campus was followed, the use of opaque spaces was not found on neighbouring buildings; spaces without windows were positioned at the ends of each floor plate in order to provide a visual harmony with existing buildings. The construction systems used were effectively an 'update' of the same systems used on neighbouring buildings. Opaque walls are given a surface texture which is more varied and more responsive to the geometry of the building than was generally used in earlier years; the windows in the new building have curved corners in response to the idea of the windows being 'punched holes' in a large-scale opaque wall. Curtain walling was not used as it does not feature in neighbouring buildings and would have brought no advantages to the overall design. The only area of full-height glazing is on the ground floor, where the glazing responds to the need to have transparency from outside to inside, as well as have the option of introducing more opaque panels with ease, by replacing the clear glass with opaque glass.

1. Sectional perspective view

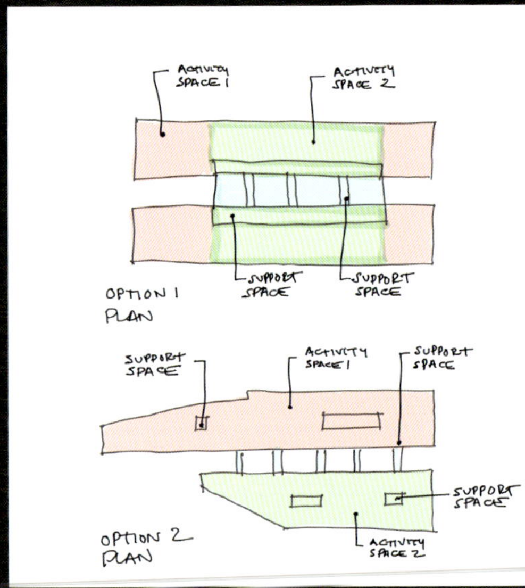

Spatial arrangement Option 1 arranges the building as two blocks separated by a service core in the middle as well as at each end. Option 2 widens the central circulation space in order to add the functions of the main entrance.

2. Sectional perspective view

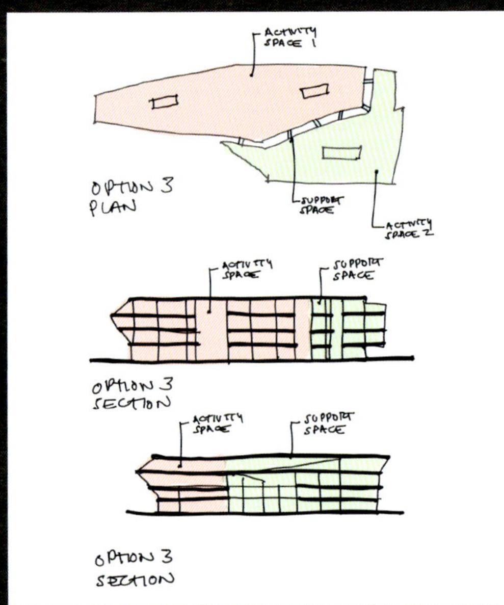

Option 3 arranges the building as two larger blocks with communal spaces on the ground floor and accommodation above.

Spatial arrangement

The need for flexibility of use for the research buildings, and the associated flexibility requirements for mechanical ventilation, led to these spaces being separate from other functions within the building. In this approach, environmental zones within each space are set within the floor and ceiling zone of each space, rather than considering each complete set of spaces to comprise an environmental zone. This strategy allows research spaces to be accessed from both the raised floor void and the ceiling void.

Option 1 for the spatial arrangement takes Option 1 from the site context and adds internal service spaces of washrooms, stairs, lifts/elevators and storage space, which are set adjacent to the link spaces at the entrance to each wing. Each wing is serviced by a core which is positioned in the area where there is the least amount of usable daylight and which is the least private and has the least differentiated of spaces. This arrangement creates a set of 'end' spaces, highlighted in red in Option 1, with a second set of spaces, highlighted in green, adjacent to the service cores. The central spaces have a different quality of light from the ends; space in the centre is daylit from one side only, whereas the end spaces are naturally lit on three sides.

Option 2 uses the opportunity of the site's shape to widen the floor plates in the centre, but narrow them down at their ends, following the geometry of the site boundary. This approach allows service cores to be located in the centre of each block rather than adjacent to the edges of the link space. This repositioning of the service cores creates new internal spaces which are set between the enclosed cores for stairs, lifts/elevators and washrooms; glass-enclosed meeting spaces in the centre of the building.

Option 3 takes this 'deep-plan' approach of creating a very wide floor plate with more internal space than is typical, and uses the geometry of the building to respond, not just to the geometry of the site, but to the preference set out in the brief/program for the minimum space allocation for service cores. This arrangement of service cores in the centre of each floor plate allows the link space to be removed; floor

Perspective view of interior

2. Perspective view of interior

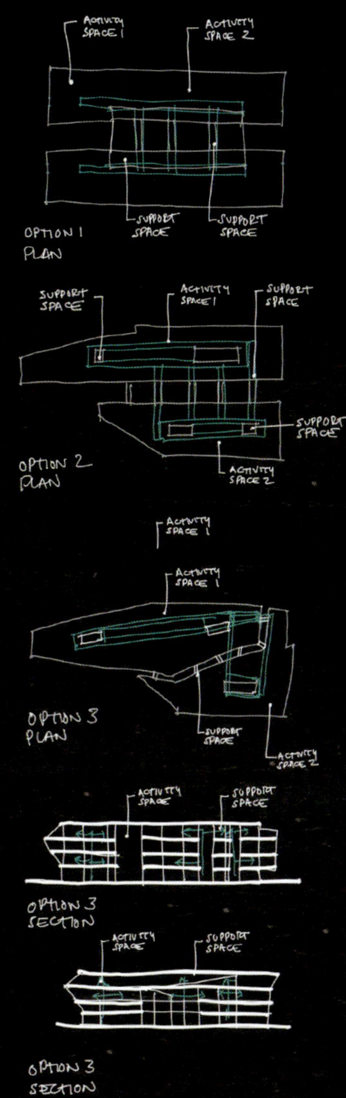

Internal circulation

Option 1 is based on adding corridor spaces to access the floor plates set near the centre of each of the floor plates.

Option 2 has a circulation arrangement which is increased to two sets of corridors in each block.

Option 3 combines the floor plates of each block, linking the circulation routes around each service core.

plates become more efficient as a result of moving vertical service riser space into floors and ceilings, serviced from a smaller set of cores than that shown in Options 1 and 2.

Internal circulation

Each of the three sub-divided blocks has its own vertical core arrangement to provide facilities for stairs, washrooms and the vertical risers for the services. The arrangement is such that two of the sub-divided blocks have enclosed lecture theatre space without columns, and large spaces each have a column-free 10.0-metre-wide space. This is a result of the use of linear 'spine' service cores in all options.

The internal circulation for Option 1 is based on adding corridor spaces to access the floor plates which are set near the centre of each of the floor plates. Each bridge in the shared link space creates a circulation route from one block to the other, passing through the core to the circulation space shown in the illustration. This 'ladder' arrangement of routes provides an efficient distribution of circulation routes through the building. Option 2 has a circulation arrangement which is increased to two sets of corridors in each block as a result of the introduction of wider floor plates; circulation routes pass around the edges of the cores, creating those two circulation circuits in each block being linked by four bridges. This arrangement provides a higher percentage of the floor area being allocated to internal circulation than Option 1. This arrangement is simplified in Option 3 by combining the floor plates of each block and linking the circulation routes around each service core; resulting in a simplified layout with fewer circulation corridors.

An advantage of using bridges to link the spaces across the central space is that an enclosed bridge is a space in itself, and can be widened in order to become an inhabited space rather than a route through a building from one space to another. The design developed arrangements of bridges; superimposed sets of inhabited spaces; staggered sets of spaces and bridges in a further staggered arrangement of alternating inhabited bridges and open circulation routes. This building could be developed as a set of bridges only, with no continuous floors.

1A. Isometric view of environmental volumes

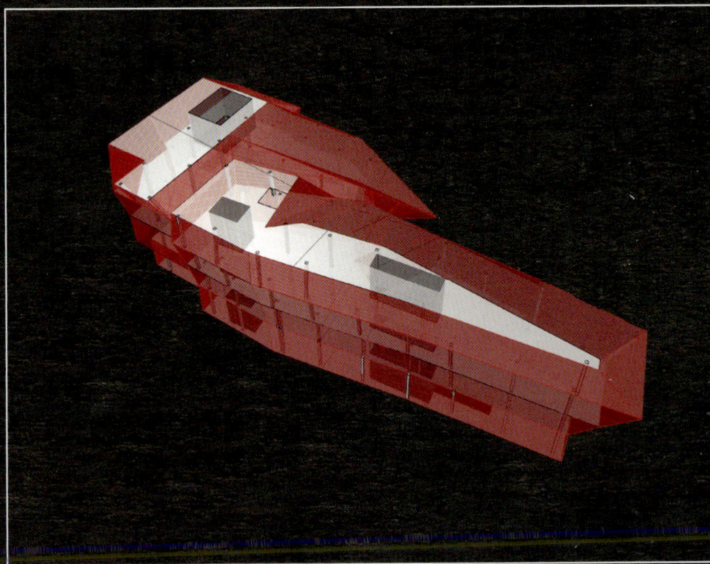

2A. Isometric view of environmental volumes

1B. Isometric view of environmental volumes

2B. Isometric view of environmental volume

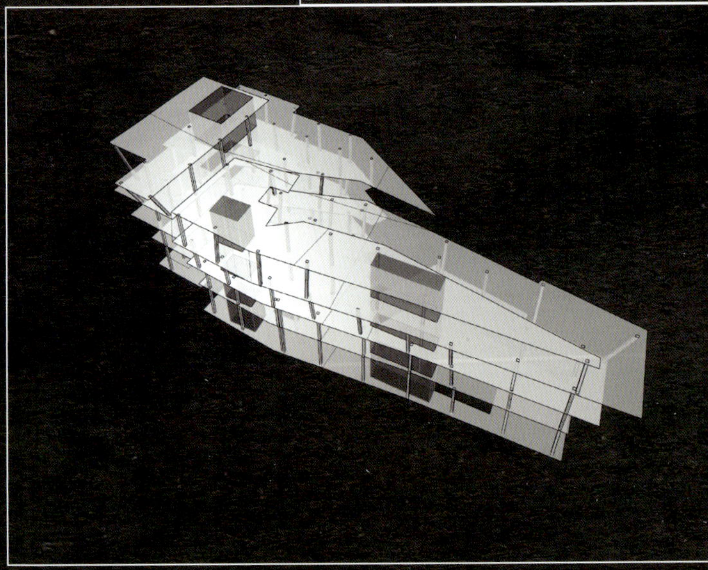

Environmental strategy

A central requirement of this project is to bring fresh air from outside to provide natural ventilation through the building as well as to introduce as much natural daylight as possible to the communal spaces. For that reason, the solution was to form 'crevices' and openings deep in the plan, to allow windows to be positioned where needed and to have volumes separated from one another in order to allow daylight to penetrate between the blocks and ensure that daylight was distributed to where it is needed specifically. For this reason, the building is not a glass box with a narrow plan which would allow large amounts of daylight to enter the building, as might be the case with a regular office building arrangement. In this building there is a need for a compact volume on a compact site within a university campus, which provides as much natural daylight and natural ventilation as possible. Daylight is introduced into teaching areas with long 'slot'-style windows.

The environmental strategy is based on separate service provisions for the 'activity' spaces or main spaces in each of the two blocks; this approach ensures that cross ventilation of fresh air can be provided and controlled. The aim of natural ventilation is achieved as a result of the arrangement of windows and ventilation panels; opening up more of the facade than would be achievable with 'trickle' ventilators. A flow of natural air from outside to inside, in the mid-season, is supported periodically by electrically-operated fans that form part of the mechanical ventilation system for the building. The two volumes of the building are configured to allow each building to have a modified set of environmental zones.

Option 1 of the environmental strategy makes use of the Option 1 site context layout and applies an environmental zone to the shared space in the centre of the glazed atrium, using the same environmental volume extending into the cores from the sides of the building; a result of the spaces being daylit on one side of the building only. A second environmental zone is created as a result of the environmental conditions in the end zones of the building being different, as shown in red in the illustration for Option 1. A third environmental zone occupies the

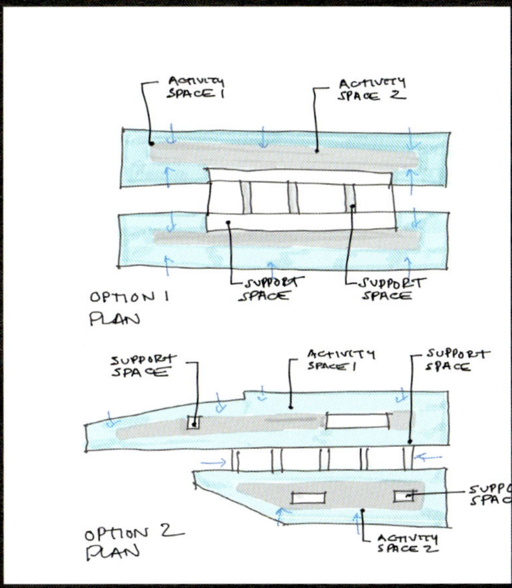

Daylight strategy for direct sunlight and cross ventilation.

Option 1 arranges the building as two blocks separated by a central void.

Option 2 widens the central circulation space in order to add the main entrance floor.

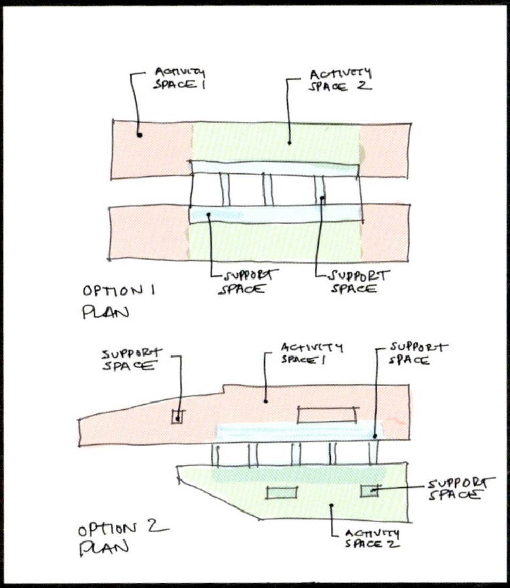

Environmental zones

Option 1 applies an environmental zone to the shared space in the centre of the glazed atrium.

Option 2 takes its characteristic form from the site context.

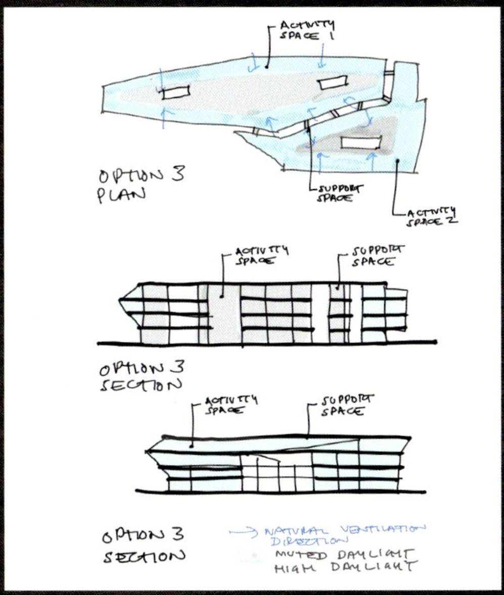

Daylight strategy for direct sunlight and cross ventilation.

Option 3 arranges the building as two larger blocks with communal spaces on the ground floor and accommodation above.

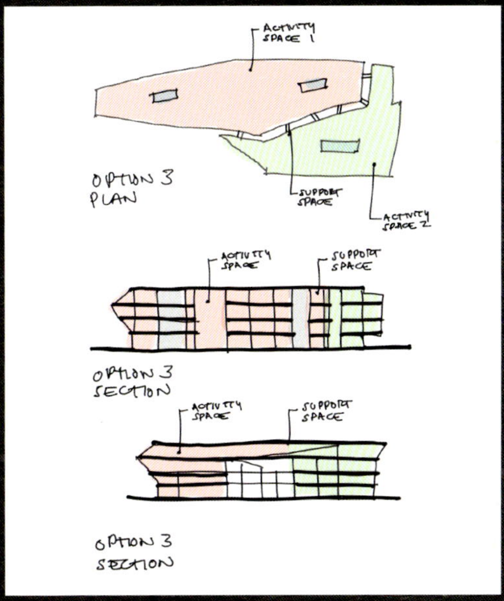

Environmental zones

Option 3 creates a link space; the associated cores now have separate environmental controls.

glazed link space. Option 2 takes its characteristic form from the site context; extending out the environmental zone from the link space into the cores. The widening of the floor plates in response to the geometry of the site boundary allows each of the two blocks to be considered as being two environmental zones. Option 3 simplifies the idea of the environmental concept of Option 2, and combines the two zones. The link space and the associated cores now have separate environmental controls, but these are essentially supplied by the main floor plates, shown in red and green.

In addition to the use of environmental zones to provide different levels of daylight, mechanical ventilation and solar control, an environmental zone is formed at each end of the building, where exposure to the effects of the sun is at its highest. Solar protection is provided from east- and west-facing sun; where there is an increased need for solar shading rather than temperature control. They are positioned in order to provide clear floor plates within and have the advantage of being able to have services distribution of air and light following direct lines between those cores. Those lines follow the structural grid, which is rotated in order to correspond to the environmental grid, which is one of ducts and task lighting set at ceiling level in order to ventilate the spaces mechanically. Natural ventilation follows those same lines but air is drawn in from outside directly with fans and distributed through the building using the same ducts and outlets as well as extracts because opened windows would not provide the regular flow of air that is required in these spaces, but the ventilation does not require cooling or heating for several months of the year when this system of natural ventilation can be used.

The bridges of Options 1 and 2 are also considered to be environmental zones; their position in plan changes the amount of solar gain they experience, both from high-angle sun and from sun in the late afternoon. The roofs of the bridges are opaque and thermally insulated; their edges overhang the glass below in order to provide passive solar shading from the rooflight at the top of the building. Option 3 was developed to form a set of bridges across a void between the two blocks.

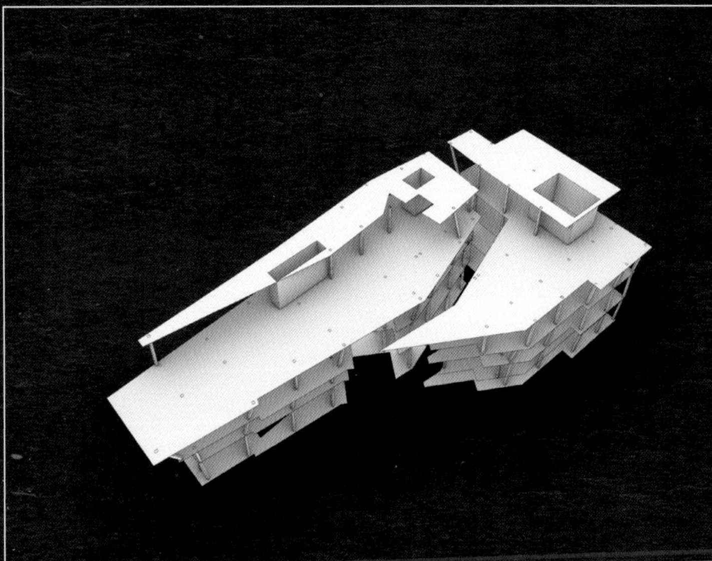

1A. Isometric view of structure

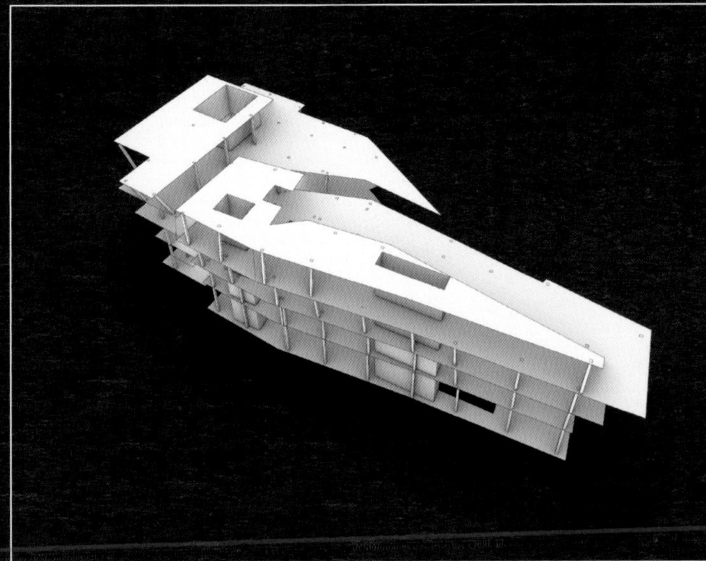

2A. Isometric view of structure

1B. Isometric view of structure

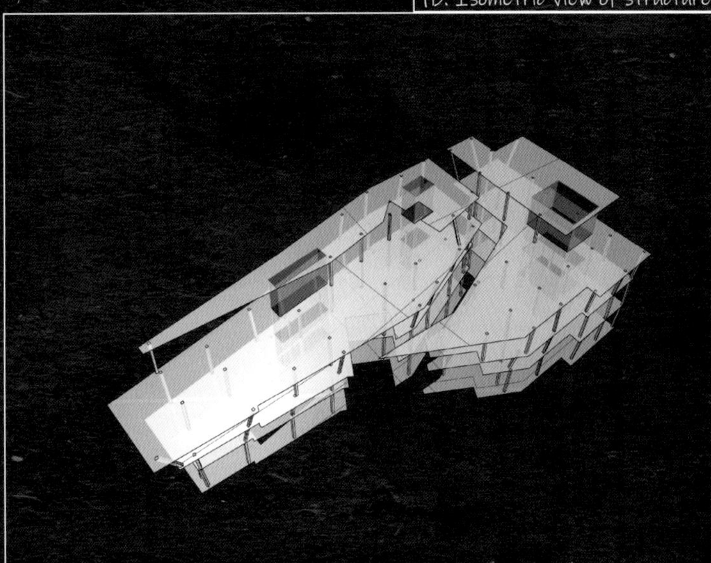

2B. Isometric view of structur

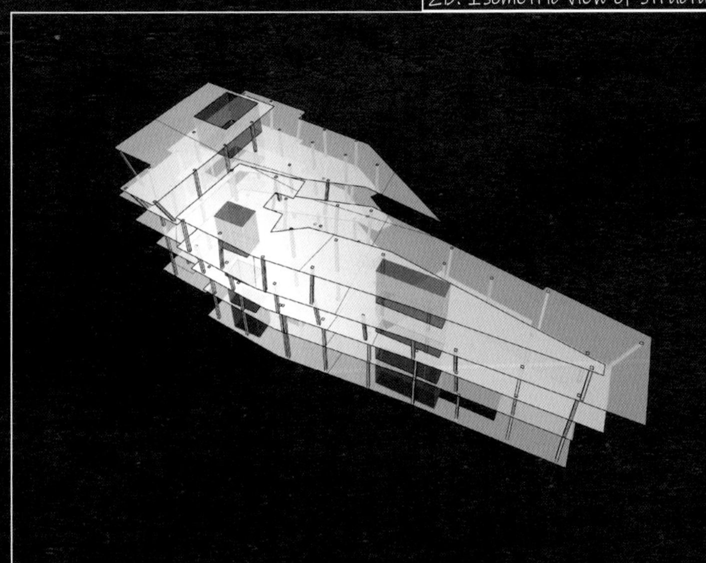

Structural strategy

All structural strategy options are of steel-framed design as a result of the flexibility required to make changes to the structure quickly in the near future. The steel frame also allows the different cladding systems to be coordinated using prefabricated methods instead of the casting-in of facade fixings into a concrete slab or beam set adjacent to the facades. The extensive use of prefabrication to increase the speed of construction on site is a key part of the brief/program.

The building has two independent structures which are constructed as steel frames. The steel frame uses a mixture of beams and trusses to provide the deep-plan floor plates required in all the structural options presented here. The structural concept is one of a set of structures which are supported independently but which are linked. The structural design for all three options allows smaller-scale structural components and assemblies to be added on as the building is extended, as is expected in future years. Additions to the building can be created by either adding to one of the two individual structures or by creating a separate structure, separated with a 'link' circulation space between the new and existing blocks; typically with stairs, lifts/elevators and a service riser between the two buildings.

The structural strategy for Option 1 is based on using a regular grid of columns with irregular-shaped beams. The two blocks are constructed as separate structures with link bridges across the entrance volume such that the voids between the bridges allow light to pass through from the top to the bottom of the building.

Option 2 widens and inflects the floor plate in response to the form of the site, with an advantage of being able to use the cores as elements for creating stiffness in the centre of each of the floor plates. The bridges remain as Option 2, linking the two separate structures.

Option 3 unifies the form by creating a more condensed and more compact floor plate by shifting the level of the rectilinear column grid at the line between the two building volumes, where they intersect. This allows the link space to be removed to form, partially, a single structure where the floor plates within that structure are stabilised by the cores,

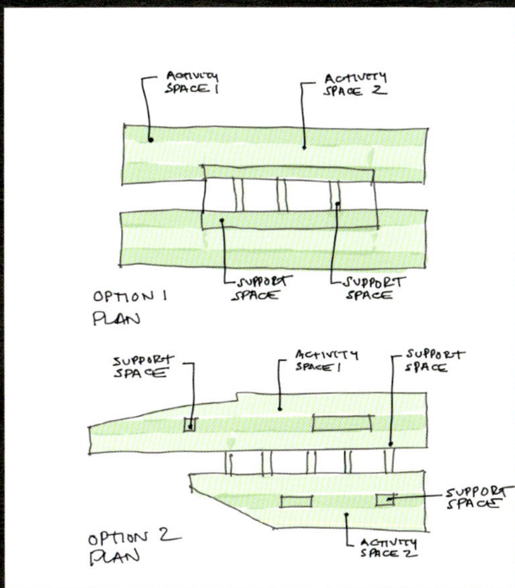

Structural strategy: Zones
Option 1 is based on using a regular grid of columns with irregular-shaped beams.
Option 2 has concrete cores that provide structural stability to the frame.

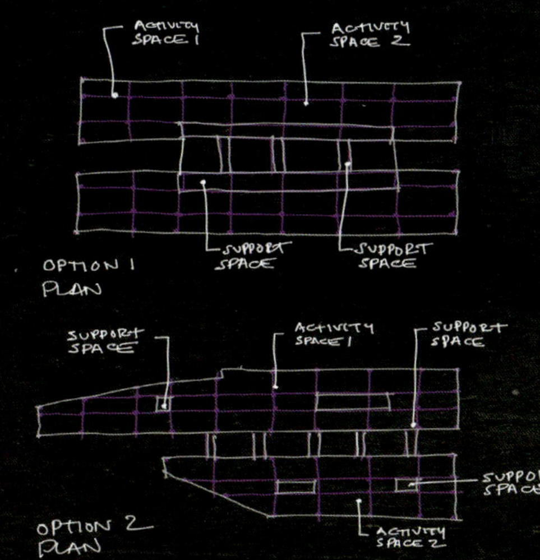

Structural strategy: Framing
Option 1 has two blocks which are constructed as separate structures, with link bridges across the entrance volume.
Option 2 is largely a steel frame.

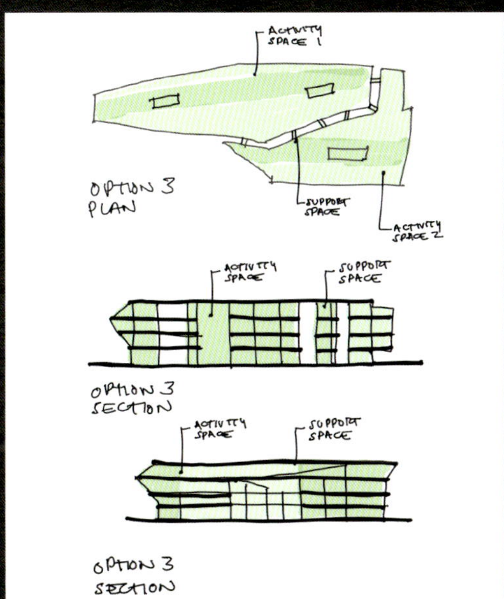

Structural strategy: Zones
Option 3 unifies the form by creating a more condensed and more compact floor plate by shifting the level of the rectilinear column grid.

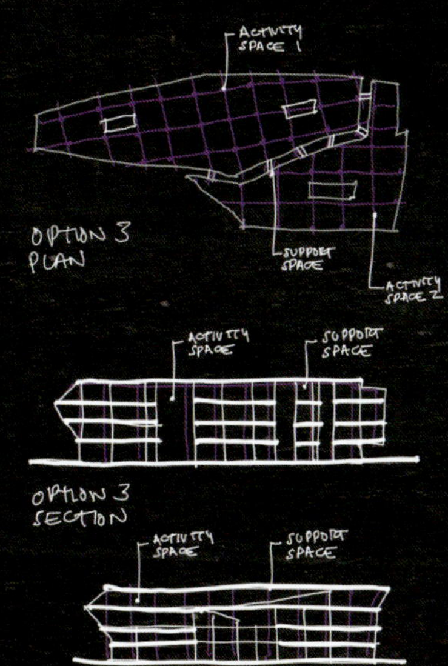

Structural strategy: Zones
Option 3 widens and inflects the floor plate in response to the form of the site.

which are now inserted inboard from the edges of each floor plate.

The structural strategy for Options 1 and 2 is to consider the two blocks as separate structures which are linked by bridges. The bridges are formed as separate structures which are supported on the edges of floor plates. This approach allows the bridges to be aligned with the environmental grid rather than the structural grid. In Option 3, the building is joined as a single floorplate, but could be pulled apart again at the line that joins the two half blocks, to form a V-shaped void between the two blocks.

Bridges could be set parallel to the edges of one side of the void in order for the bridges to be set at different angles to one another. In all options the bridges form either inhabited spaces, used as meeting rooms, or are used as covered passages for the circulation of occupants from one block to another. The inhabited bridges are used as work spaces and meeting rooms and are of different width to suit different work environments. Narrower bridges serve as passages; traversing the building from one block to the other. A further development of these three options is to consider the building as a set of bridges that are linked by narrow areas of floor plates, one bay wide. The spatial arrangment for this option is based on a 7.5-metre x 7.5-metre grid, forming a single bay. The next bay is occupied by bridges; the following bay is a narrow floor plate, forming alternating bays of narrow floor plate and bridges. This approach creates interstitial space that is external, and which can be protected from the effects of the sun, but where each part of the building is enclosed. Every bridge is enclosed; the arrangement of bridges is staggered such that there is a mixed rhythm of enclosed workspaces and passages, which are bridges.

The occupied or 'inhabited' workspace bridges do not serve as passages. The pedestrian bridges and the inhabited bridges are separate and are offset from one another in order to create a rhythm of bridges, which are all supported on a structural grid of columns and beams. A large amount of internal space becomes external, encouraging the use of natural ventilation and daylight into small spaces; a small space at the scale of a team, not a large floor plate.

Perspective view of typical bay from below

Typical bay adjacent to facade

The facades accommodate full-height walls, terraces and individual long balconies. The walls are inclined to reduce the amount of solar gain incident on the facades. The two blocks that comprise the building have long glazed slots set just below the roof level of each block. This solution provides a visual sense of a cluster of buildings formed by 'gaps' and 'cuts' formed within the facades; a visual expression of the blocks being juxtaposed to make visible the different functions within the building, rather than forming a continuous building form. Volumes link together, visually, at a high level; a move required to ensure an ease of circulation within a part of the building that accommodates a single function of research; lecture rooms, seminar rooms and laboratory-based research is carried out in these roof-level spaces. This upper level has garden terrace spaces set into it, densely planted; providing a contrast with the closely integrated spaces arranged within the building volumes. The external walls make use of a glazed wall which extends from floor to ceiling at ground floor level; upper floor levels have a continuous opaque facade system formed in mechanically fixed terracotta tiles and long slot windows. This arrangement provides the required level of daylight into the deep-plan floor plates used in all three design options. Some areas within the building require only low levels of daylighting; for enclosed workspaces and laboratory-based tasks. These areas of facade have cementitious panels, arranged on a floor-to-ceiling grid arrangement. These panels are formed as large-scale GFRC panels. The monolithic nature of these large GFRC panels is in contrast with the small-scale slot glazing, which is inserted into the facade as long and continuous 'ribbons' set along the length of these spaces. The facades are a mixture of 'unitised', or prefabricated, curtain wall and site-assembled curtain wall.

A key aspect of the facade design is to provide solar shading whose geometry responds to the path of the sun, in excluding the effects of solar gain through glazed parts of the facades; mainly the two long facades. The two short ends of the building have opaque facades with service areas behind them. The solar shading on the long facades is of

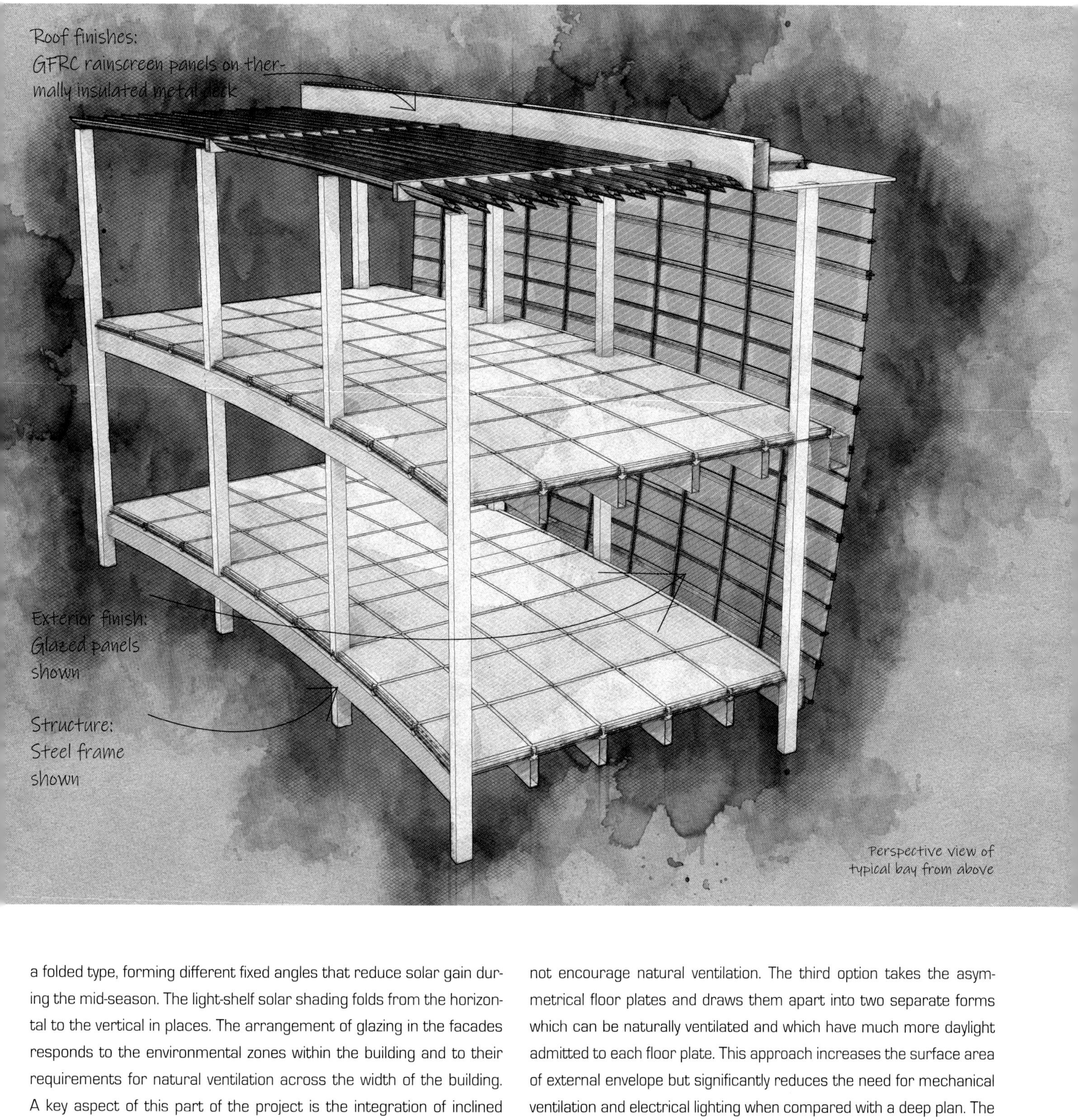

Perspective view of typical bay from above

a folded type, forming different fixed angles that reduce solar gain during the mid-season. The light-shelf solar shading folds from the horizontal to the vertical in places. The arrangement of glazing in the facades responds to the environmental zones within the building and to their requirements for natural ventilation across the width of the building. A key aspect of this part of the project is the integration of inclined facades within the spatial arrangement in order to provide passive shading. The facades incline inwards, allowing regular facade systems to be used as the basis of the design.

The facade forms are adjusted from the straightforward rectilinear design of Option 1 in order to respond to sun angles and to increase the amount of natural ventilation across the building. Option 1 provides natural ventilation across two blocks; Option 2 pushes the two blocks together, resulting in a deep floor plate. The increased depth of floor area generates the need to introduce internal circulation through this space in order to access subdivided space; the circulation route follows the line of division between the two blocks. However, this form does not encourage natural ventilation. The third option takes the asymmetrical floor plates and draws them apart into two separate forms which can be naturally ventilated and which have much more daylight admitted to each floor plate. This approach increases the surface area of external envelope but significantly reduces the need for mechanical ventilation and electrical lighting when compared with a deep plan. The overall form of the building responds to the need to have groups of workspaces in the building which were not achieved with the rectilinear form. The spatial arrangement requires spaces of different size which gave rise to the characteristic plan arrangement of the building in Option 3. The solution to have asymmetrical spatial arrangements for the two blocks provides a reduced energy requirement that results in a typical bay with shading on the facades. The arrangement of the shading panels is directed by the path of the sun. A full-height slot that divides the building into two volumes is linked by bridges that are mostly self-shading while still providing natural ventilation.

1. Perspective view of exterior

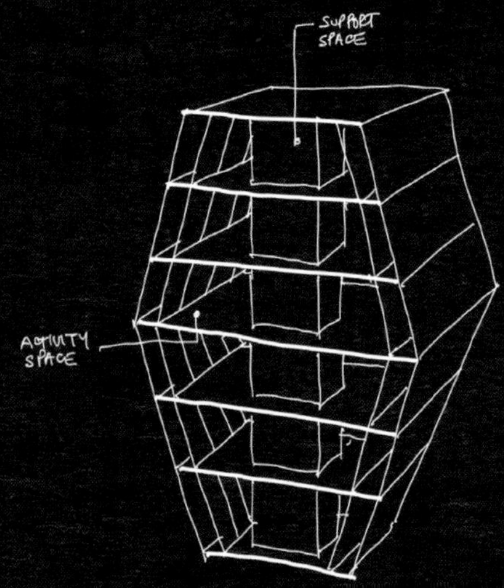

2. Perspective view of exterior

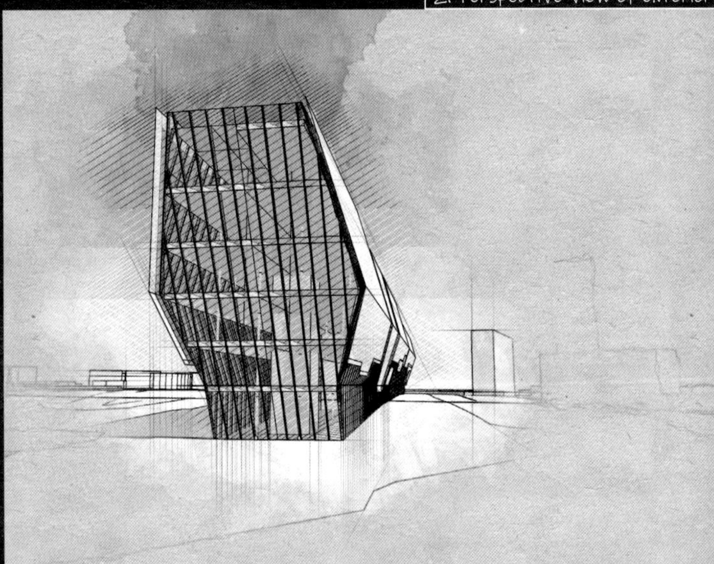

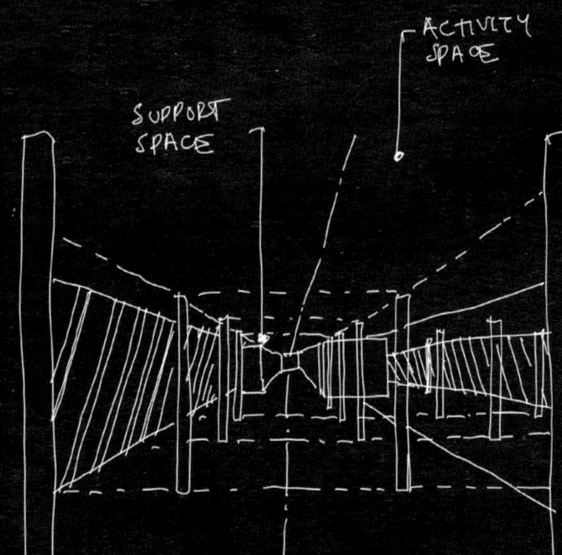

Envelope as environmental support space and weather barrier

A key method of implementing this approach is to have a componentised installation of both the building-wide mechanical ventilation installation and assemblies for natural ventilation set within the facade system. This approach allows the supply of mechanical ventilation and that of natural ventilation to be changed from one to the other as a 'hybrid' approach to ventilation, using assemblies that are fixed within the facades as prefabricated elements. The envelope for this building is both a zone for the support of environmental control equipment and support for manufacturing machinery as well as providing a weather barrier and solar-shading layer. This envelope zone is formed in a twin wall configuration comprising an outer layer of solar protection panels, an inner facade and deck set between these layers for the support of services equipment and associated distribution. The external envelope accommodates these environmental support systems within a deep facade volume which is naturally ventilated and which provides a controlled provision of daylight and natural ventilation into the different spaces within the building. The size of the facade grid is determined as much by the equipment that it accommodates as by optimised sizes of wall panels. The specific dimensions of the grid are also determined by the spaces within the building that are served by the technical equipment and technical performance of the facades. The arrangement of volumes within the facade zones are determined by the needs of the environmental zones within the factory, all of which have different requirements as each zone has a different function as being either part of a manufacturing process or part of a design or management process. The building is also seen as part of the marketing process used by the company. Each of these work zones is subdivided into module-sized volumes for equipment that will service those spaces. The supporting structural grid for the facades is sufficiently refined in its arrangement to accommodate an external envelope which is largely glazed, with an additional perforated metal outer screen. This is a factory which is open to views from outside to inside, and vice versa. The ground floor is where manufacturing is carried out; these areas do not have views

Perspective view of exterior

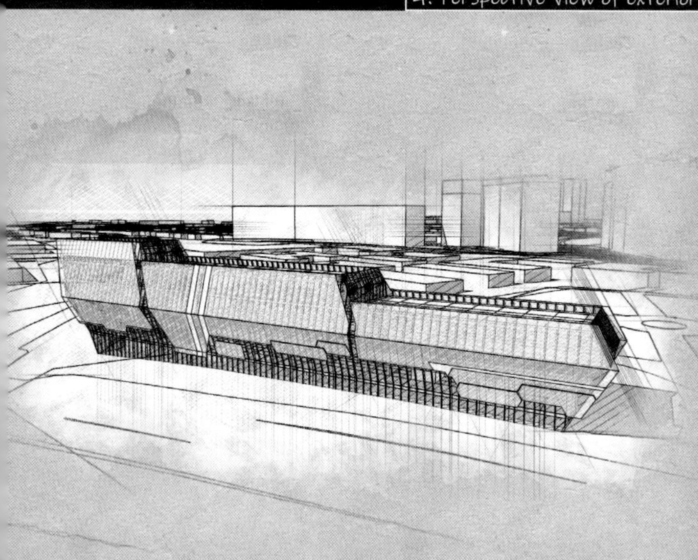

4. Perspective view of exterior

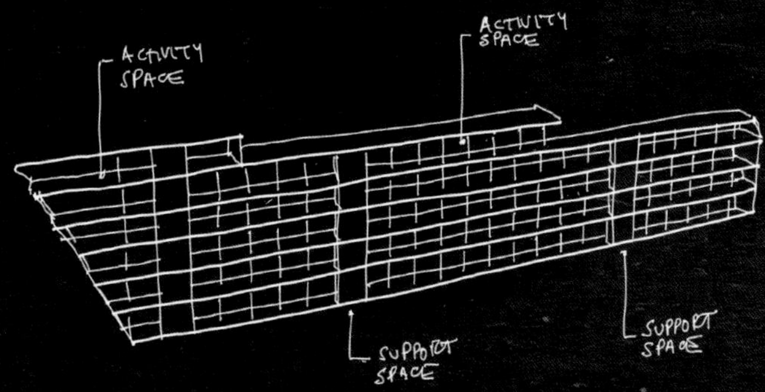

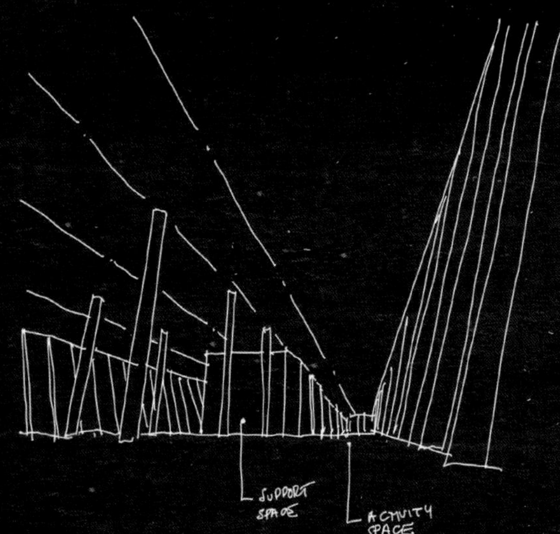

directly in or out; the upper floors fulfil that role. The environmental grid also accommodates the lighting layout; based on a module of the internal lighting arrangement, which is common to both manufacture and office space. All floors have a tall floor-to-ceiling height in order that a future expansion of manufacturing might extend to assembly being carried out on an upper floor; assemblies would be carried on overhead rails which would descend to the ground floor. Services and support systems have been enclosed within the facade zone in order to have spaces within the building which are entirely clear, forming open rectilinear spaces that provide as much flexibility as possible for the evolution of processes of design, manufacturing and management. This approach includes having a reduced number of columns within internal spaces. This method of organising space allows the building to be formed as a set of modules: manufacturing hall, design studio, management offices and meeting rooms; support spaces and associated equipment are set within the facade zone. The service space within the environmental zone, that envelops the perimeter of the building, changes in depth throughout the height of the building, giving rise to the characteristic form. The ground floor does not require a deep facade zone; its associated environmental controls and equipment are accommodated in the facade zone set above ground floor level. The facade zone provides both a weather barrier, in the form of glazed facades, and a solar control provided by an outer screen wall of louvres. The supporting frames for the facade layers and the decks which carry the equipment are supported by a structure which forms an integral part of the primary structure. This approach of having a double row of columns at the perimeter of the building avoids the need to have a structure which is lighter in weight and independent of the primary structure. The double row of structure allows the facade zone to be a part of the spaces provided within the building, while also forming a semi-external interstitial zone between outside and inside. The double row of structure continues across the roof of the building; the basis of a structure for which fewer columns are required inside the design studios and offices set immediately beneath the roof.

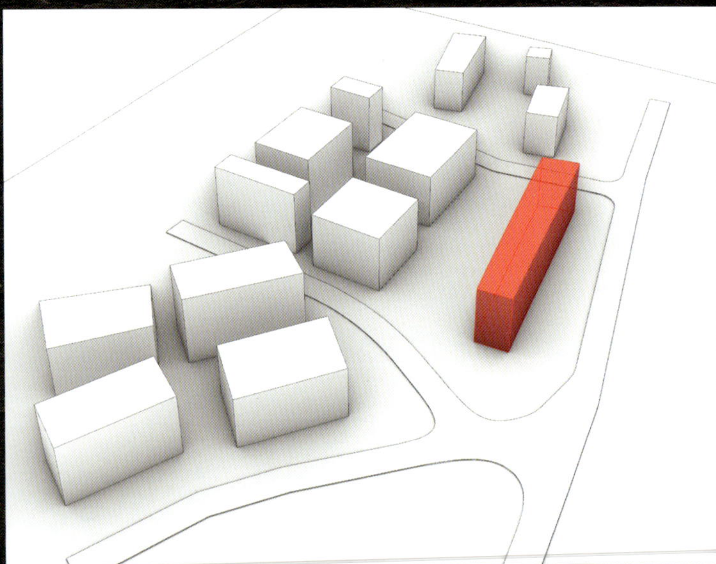

1. Project volume in site context

2. Project volume in site context

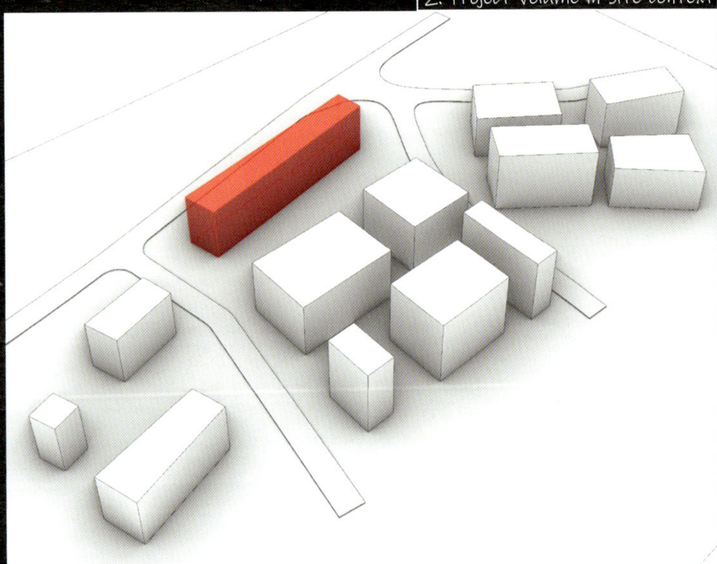

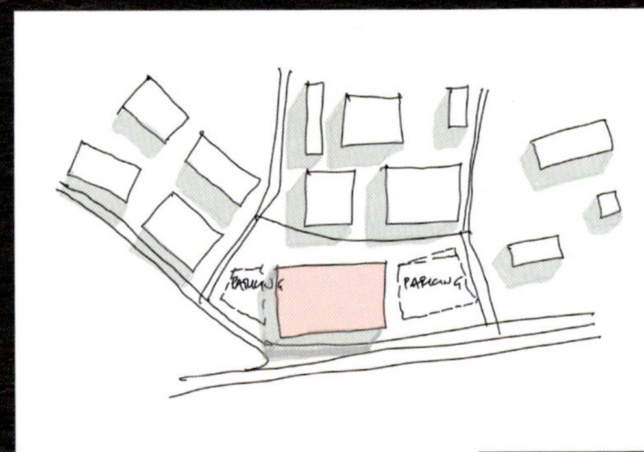

1. Site plan with surrounding context

Option 1 sets out the factory as a single form in order to reduce the external envelope and the built volume to the smallest possible size.

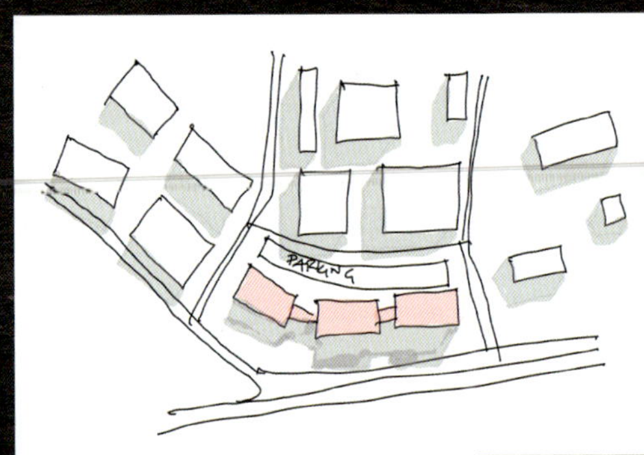

2. Site plan with surrounding context

Option 2 divides the building into three separate volumes in order to benefit from the curve of the site.

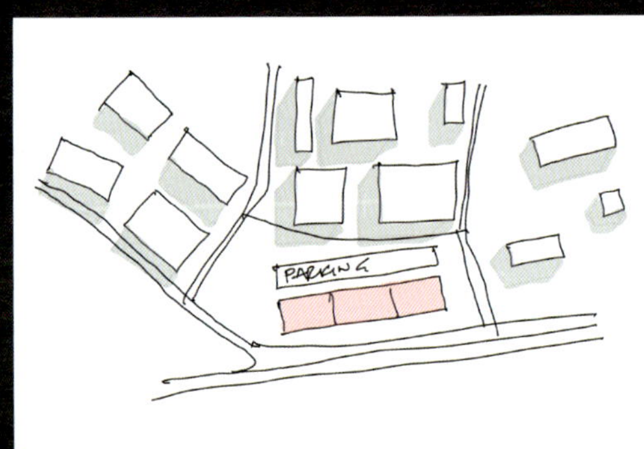

3. Site plan with surrounding context

Option 3 groups the three blocks, taken from Option 2, into an aligned set of volumes that are set parallel with the main road.

Site context

The site context is at the edge of a city that has grown considerably in recent years; its form can be seen at a distance from a highway nearby. The building inhabits an isolated plot of land, such that the form is visible from all sides; taller than surrounding buildings by a factor of two as a result of the need to accommodate a large number of spaces on different levels. The characteristic forms are a 'map of functions'; the internal spaces are revealed as external forms. The silhouette of the long elevations reveal both the presence of roof terraces and steps in the form of the building that provide views within the building which create a sense of community within the organisation.

The site context is an unbuilt part of the city, at its edge. The building is arranged onto a possible arrangement of future buildings set out on a non-rectilinear grid. The grid is formed of a mixture of diagonal and orthogonal lines that create pockets of non-rectilinear space that are occupied by parking spaces for employees. Car spaces are arranged to follow the non-orthogonal grid, leaving pockets of space that that can be inhabited by small pavilions to provide social space for those working in the building, as well as providing a future possibility for the urbanisation of this site with surrounding buildings of smaller scale. Buildings would replace the car parking spaces, as transportation to and from the factory will inevitably undergo many changes in the near future, away from the use of the single-occupant private car.

This project is for a modular high-tech manufacturing research and development (R&D) and manufacturing facility for an international company. The basis of the design is a single large space that accommodates both small-scale R&D tasks and the simulated assembly tasks required for individual prototype vehicles. Spaces are arranged over four floors, with a passive cooling system on the ground floor that supplements the mechanical ventilation installation. This approach ensures that the use of energy is minimised as a result of some tasks being conducted immediately outside the large doors which enclose each space. This approach is possible as a result of the site context being away from main roads, where little dust and noise is experienced

Perspective view of environmental volumes

2. Perspective view of environmental volumes

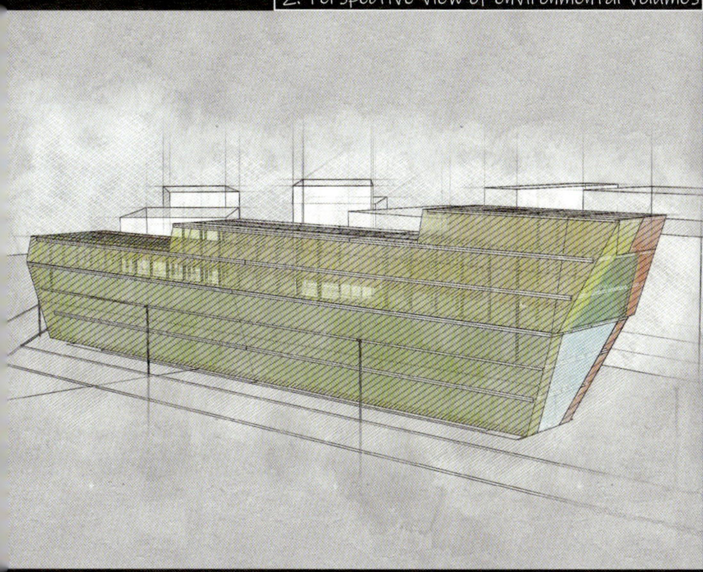

1. Figure-ground diagram of tempered environment

Option 1
Red spaces are highly tempered but are limited to service spaces that contain specific sets of equipment.

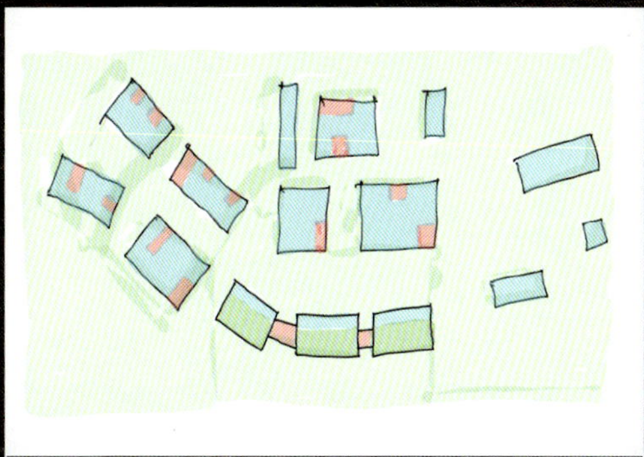

2. Figure-ground diagram of tempered environment

Option 2
Dark blue spaces are less tempered than red spaces but are more tempered than dark green spaces.

3. Figure-ground diagram of tempered environment

Option 3
Dark green spaces are the least tempered but provide significant control over dust particles enetering these spaces.

in this edge-of-town environment. The spatial arrangement of the design comprises three 'stacked' or superimposed volumes which vary in height in response to interpretations of the brief/program. Office spaces and service spaces for circulation, washrooms and electrical and mechanical equipment can be located and repositioned during the lifespan of the building, at specific points along the length of the building. These points are provided with electricity, water supply and drainage, but are left vacant for the future installation of enclosures and specific equipment. A specific feature of this design is that service spaces at roof level can be moved on rails to allow technical equipment to be relocated along the length of the assembly hall in response to expected reconfigurations of the factory layout in the near future.

Option 1 for the site context sets out the factory as a single form in order to reduce the external envelope and the built volume to the smallest possible size. Space requirements of the brief/program are approximated in order to fit this simplified form. Car parking is arranged on either side of the building in order to fit the residual spaces formed by imposing the building form on the geometry of the site; the building is set parallel with the adjacent main road. The building addresses the geometry with the road and with neighbouring buildings that are also aligned with the same road, but it is not aligned with the other industrial buildings nearby which follow completely different sets of orientation.

Option 2 divides the building into three separate volumes in order to benefit from the curve of the site and to create three separate sets of activities; the production process is divided into three approximately equal parts with a link block between each, as production passes from one hall to the next. The link also contains office space at a higher level that introduces natural light and natural ventilation to as much of this space as possible, while avoiding glare from contrasting light levels within the same space.

Option 3 groups the three blocks, taken from Option 2, into an aligned set of volumes that are set parallel with the main road. The car-parking arrangement is aligned with the building; occupying roughly the same footprint as that of the building.

1. Sectional perspective view

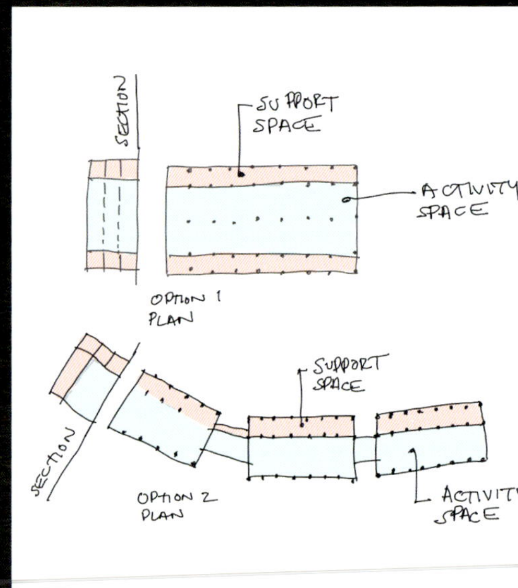

Spatial arrangement
Option 1 has incoming goods and materials being brought into the building at one end; production starts at this end of the building.
Option 2 has production arranged along a single curved line.

2. Sectional perspective view

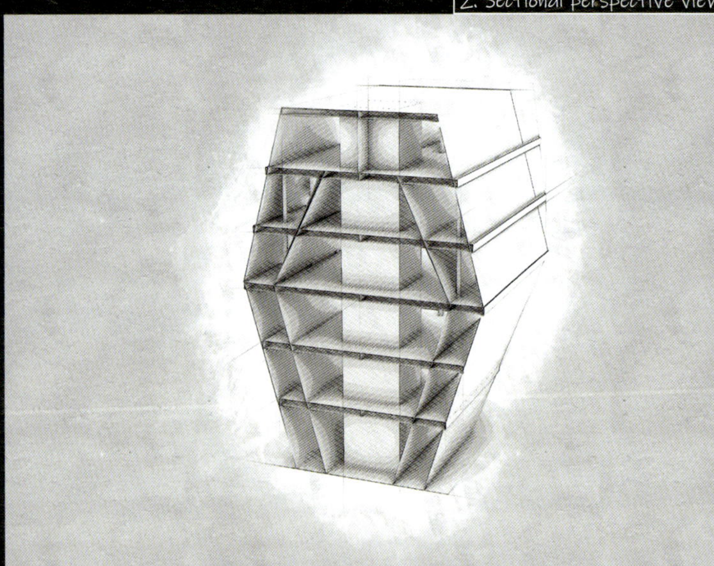

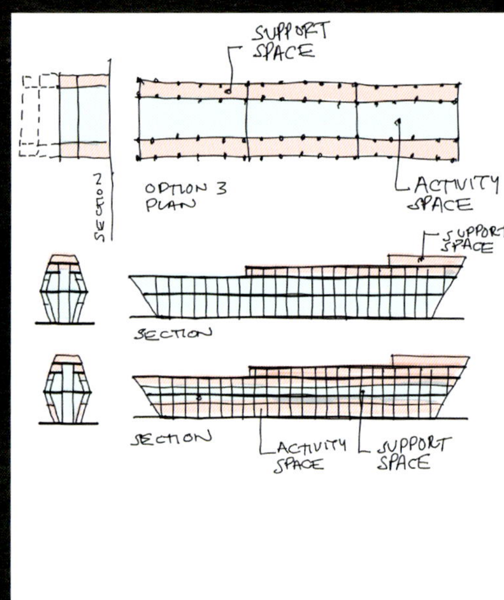

Option 3 has offices arranged on both sides of the assembly halls, linked to form a single unified space.

Spatial arrangement

The building is divided into three sections which reflect the three parts of the production process, each having very different requirements; all accommodated within a single facility. The manufacturing, research and development and commercial aspects are accommodated side by side and on different floor levels. The ground floor forms a continuous product assembly area divided into three halls. Support activities and services for each production hall are accommodated within the volumes which flank the assembly halls, and are attached to the sides of the building.

The design allows for additional smaller volumes to be added in the near future without disrupting the current spatial arrangement. In the current design, additional volumes are attached to the roof and to upper floors, from the first upper floor level upwards. This arrangement results in the use of opacified glazing at ground level; areas of clear glazing are created by removing the opacifying area locally, resulting in distinctive but discontinuous bands of glazing.

The spatial arrangement of Option 1 is of incoming goods and materials being brought into the building at one end; production starts at this end of the building; successive processes add more components and assemblies which either pivot at some point and return in the opposite direction or continue in the same direction, where completed goods exit the building at the end of the manufacturing process. At upper levels, office space is set out on either side of the production space over several floors.

Option 2 uses a layout which accommodates the offices on one side of the production space only, with the production being arranged along a single curved line, following the same production line process of moving from one end of the factory to the other end. The link blocks between production halls separate the different functions of pre-assembly, assembly and painting. The link blocks contain service space and checking space to allow assemblies to be monitored before continuing to the following stage. Option 3 has offices arranged on both sides of the assembly halls, linked to form a single unified space. The link pieces

Perspective view of interior

2. Perspective view of interior

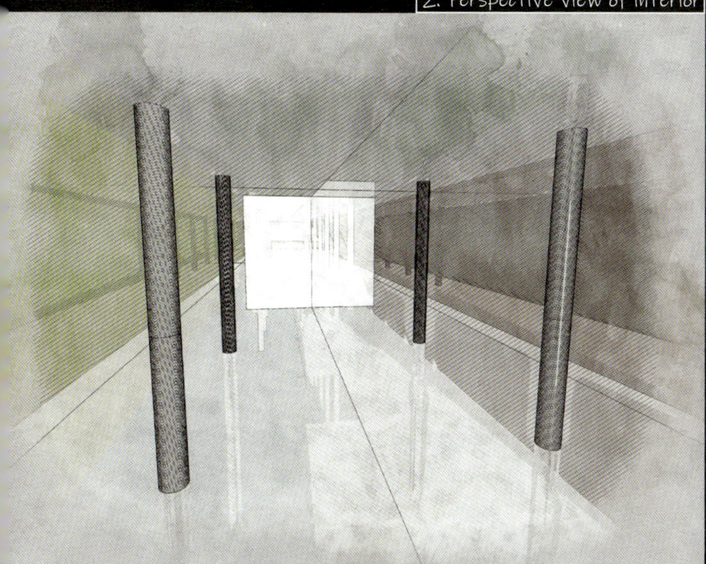

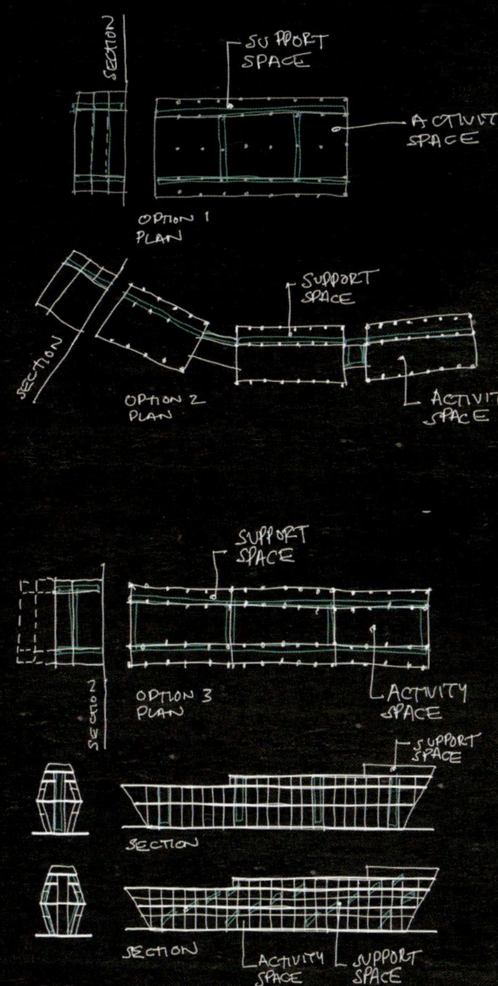

from Option 2 are omitted in order to address issues of difficulties for future optimisation of production processes; each production hall and link block is clearly defined in Option 2. This issue of near future change is addressed by the introduction of a single production hall. The office space on either side corresponds approximately to each of the production processes.

Internal circulation

The canyon-like effect, created by the sequence of manufacturing spaces creates a sense of visual connection through the different parts of the building, while maintaining views in and out of the main production facility. The internal circulation of Option 1 is based on corridors which extend along both sides of the production halls. Corridors are linked by bridges on the upper level immediately above the production halls. At the level above the bridges, circulation routes in the full floor plates accommodating the office space follow those of the bridges beneath.

In Option 2 the main support spaces for the factory production floor are based in the 'nodes' within the link blocks between the assembly halls. The link blocks contain spaces for washrooms, canteens and storage. The offices, which are set on one side of the building, extend over three floors to provide accommodation for design studios, marketing and sales suites, together with office space for management teams that support production tasks on the ground floor.

Option 3 brings together all parts of the activities in the building by locating the common facilities for food and beverage, for all staff, on the top floor: positioning space for design studios, engineering, production, marketing and sales beneath, in cascading floors of offices. All company activities can be seen from this vantage point across the different floors below, with a glimpse of the factory floor. The circulation is set out along both sides of the support spaces, extending up into the floors which span the full width of the building.

The small pavilions set within the car park form part of the circulation outside the building, serving as hubs for communication with the factory. Pavilions are linked by pedestrian routes set between rows of cars.

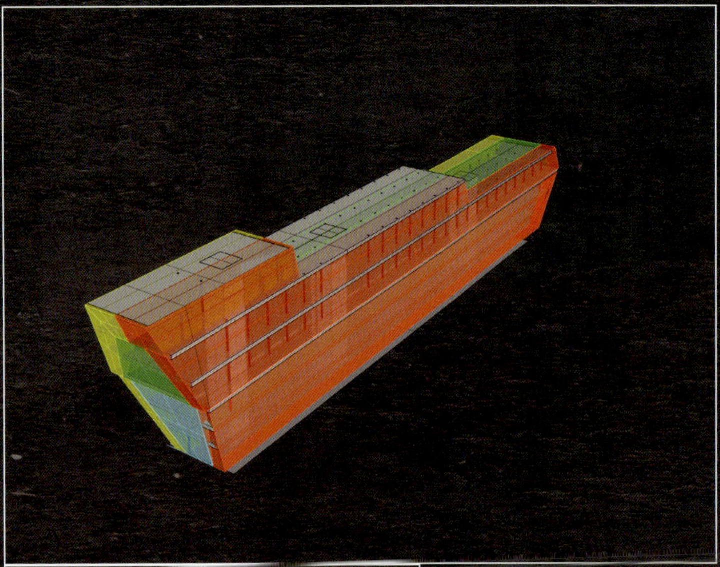

1A. Isometric view of environmental volumes

1B. Isometric view of environmental volumes

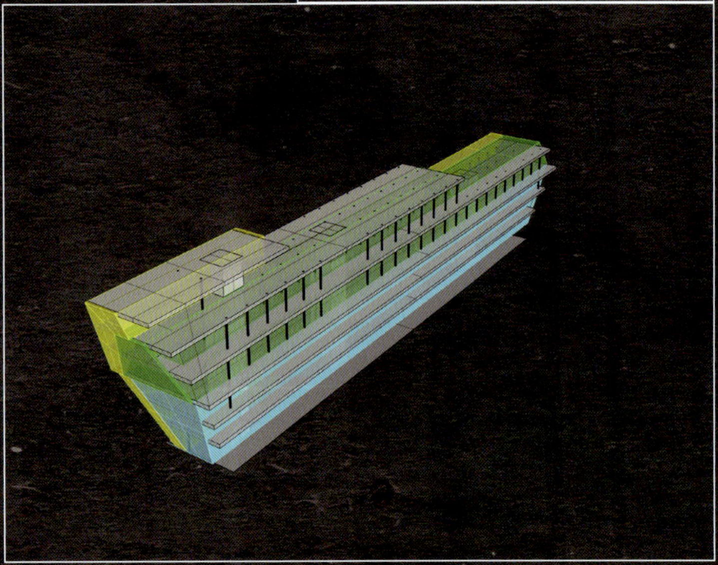

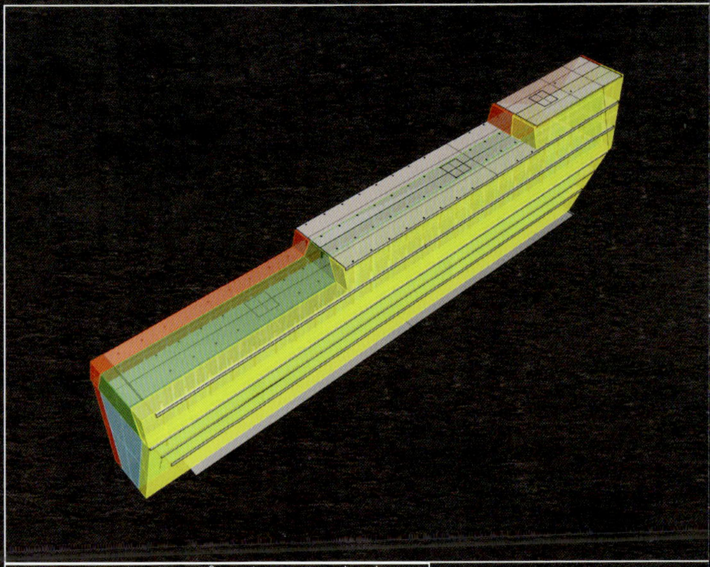

2A. Isometric view of environmental volumes

2B. Isometric view of environmental volume

Environmental strategy

The environmental strategy is one of ensuring that all parts of the building which are serviced, are accommodated within an environmental zone at the edge of the building which is formed as a deep external envelope. Inside the building, the environmental controls are such that all ground floor spaces are mechanically ventilated in order to avoid dust in the factory area. Upper floors can be naturally ventilated at different times of year; ducted and filtered fresh air, directly from outside, serves office space and design studios. Natural ventilation occurs through cross ventilation; assisted by a fan-assisted mechanical system. A key aim is to reduce the energy needed to heat, cool and ventilate the interior spaces; filtered air is supplied from outside and is directed across the building. In response to the different numbers of people occupying any office space at any given time, the factory is arranged as three environmental zones that suit all three of the options developed for this project. The arrangement of these zones also responds to the different industrial manufacturing processes undertaken in the building.

The environmental strategy encourages the use of natural daylight as much as possible in order to avoid the need for electrical lighting during hours of daylight. This aim is achieved by twin wall facades. The solar shading on the outer facade layer comprises louvres which are adjusted to suit the time of year and are manually operated in winter, mid-season and summer. The louvres create different visual effects through the year in response to the changing levels of daylight and sunlight. The orientation of louvres, grouped in panels, can be changed to suit the needs of individual spaces immediately behind the facades. Areas of glazed roof have a very similar arrangement of louvres that provide bands of controlled natural light to the top floors of the building. The top floor spaces accommodate exhibition spaces as well as the communal volumes for the canteen and rest areas, all of which require top light that is muted, that illuminates this floor evenly throughout its depth.

The building is solar shaded on its long sides as a result of the local climate, which has hot summers and cold, dry winters. Behind the solar shading the facades are either fully opaque to accommodate technical

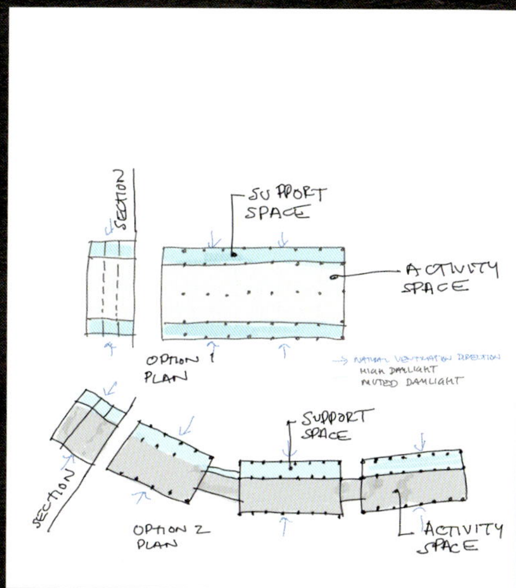

Daylight strategy for direct sunlight and cross ventilation.
Option 1 admits daylight and fresh air on the two long sides of the single building.
Option 2 admits daylight and fresh air on one side of the single building.

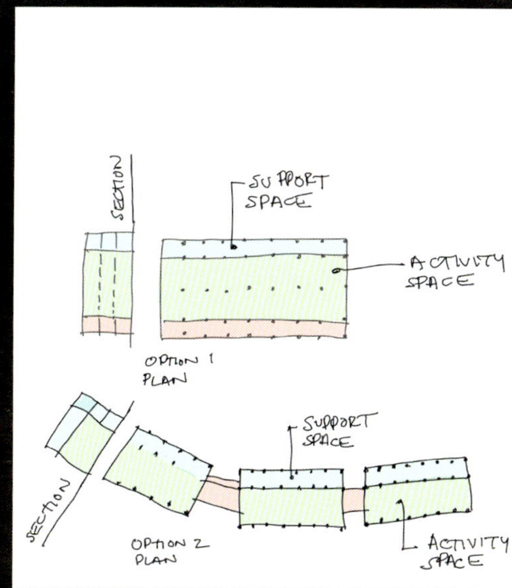

Environmental zones
Option 1 has an environmental zone on one side of the production hall which extends across the offices located at high level.
Option 2 has the areas for canteen, washrooms and rest areas in the connecting zones between the three blocks.

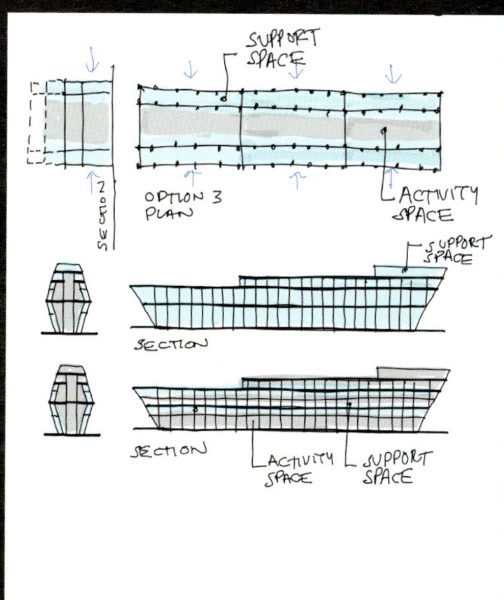

Daylight strategy for direct sunlight and cross ventilation.
Option 3 admits daylight and fresh air deep into the building on both of the long sides.

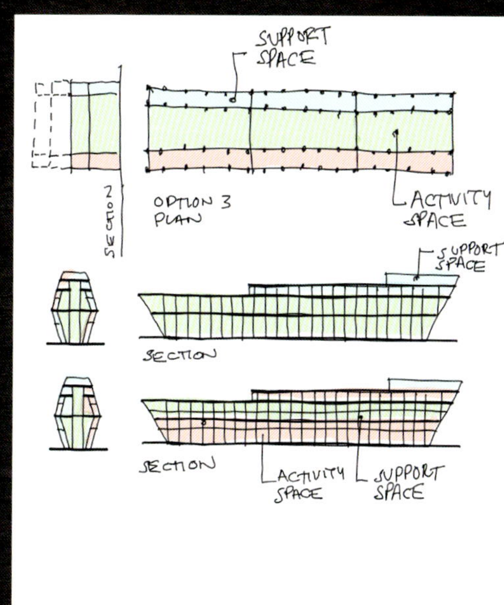

Environmental zones
Option 3 has a continuous band of support spaces for the factory, for canteens and washrooms on three floors.

and services equipment, or are fully glazed in order to allow as much daylight as possible. For summer months, the facades have additional deployable shading which is lowered from the roof level and is set on the outer face of the glazed facades. Solar shading panels are set on rails which can slide the full length of the building to suit the changing needs of daylight control within.

The environmental strategy uses the 'spine' core spaces that extend down the sides of the building as conduits for fresh air, brought in from the top of the building and circulated down through the interstitial spaces, through to the main production spaces. This is done in order to encourage natural ventilation during the mid-season. Circulation routes around the building form canyon-like spaces where people interact and where communal canteen facilities are provided. These spaces are the primary sources of natural ventilation. The canyons are set out in streets set on each side of the building.

The environmental strategy for Option 1 has an environmental zone on one side of the production hall which extends across the offices located at high-level in response to the functions of offices within it. The other side of the production hall has an environmental zone shown in red in the diagram, which is based around the needs of factory-based work in support functions of cafe and canteen facilities with associated washrooms and rest areas.

The strategy for Option 2 is to have the areas for canteen, washrooms and rest areas in the connecting zones between the three blocks, all located at a high level above the production halls which reduce in height along the full length of the assembly. Office space, which is occupied for fewer hours than the production area as highlighted in blue, are set on one side of the building and are extended above the production hall. Option 3 takes Option 2 and simplifies the layout, with a continuous band of support spaces for the factory for canteens and washrooms on three floors, and the equivalent spaces set out on the other side of the production hall. Upper floors are set out to form a set of terraced spaces linked by open stairs. The open terraces have canopy structures to provide solar shading for rest areas.

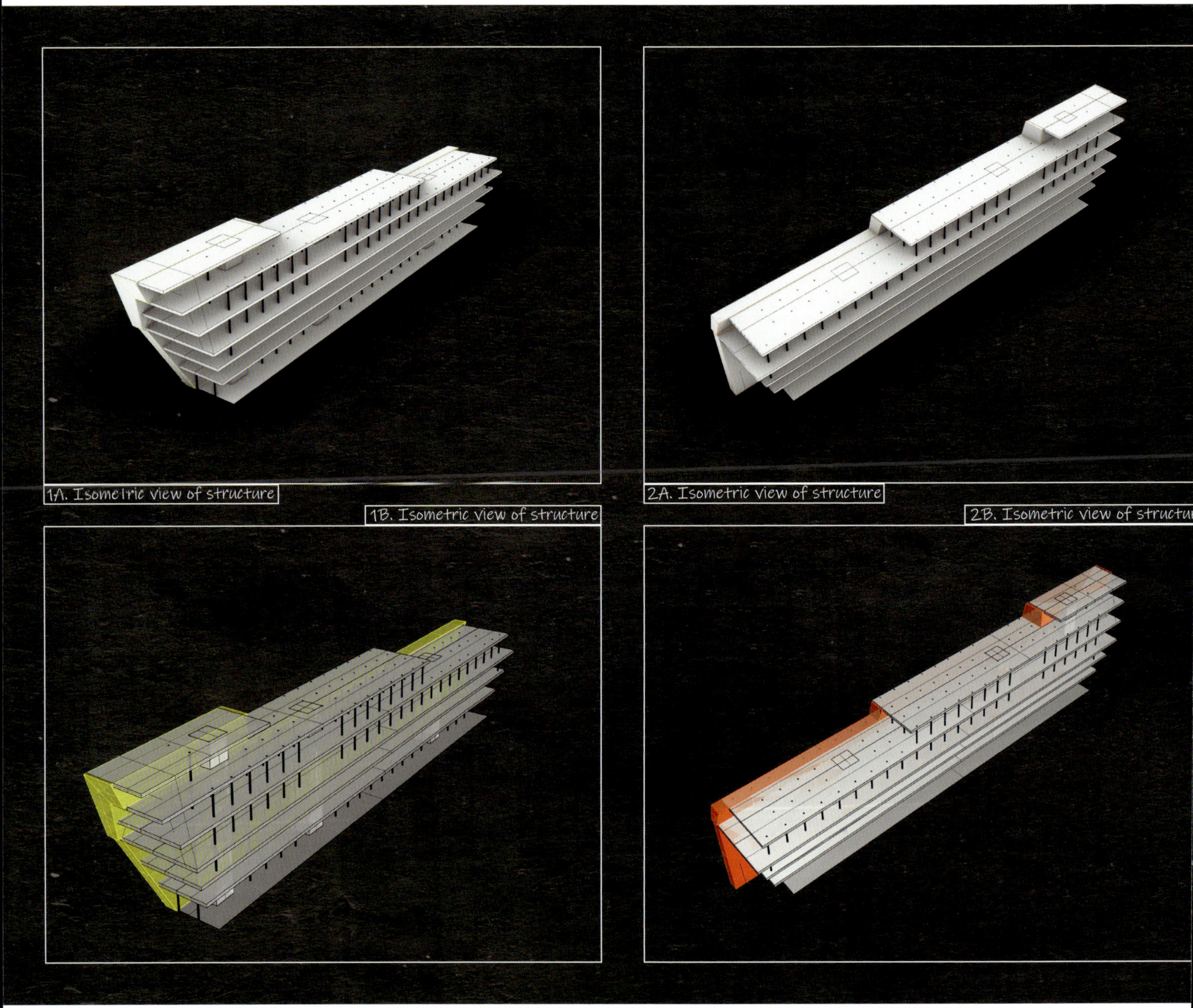

Structural strategy

The structural design of the building volumes is based on the use of a steel frame comprising a mix of hot rolled structural members and pressed steel members, spanning from between 3.0 metres and 10.0 metres. Members are fixed together by horizontal rails to form a gridded system. At the perimeter of floor slabs where they meet the facades, the structure is part-assembled as modules which are both demountable and portable for use in a reconfigured building structure. The service cores in the 'spines' set on both sides of the building volume are also ready for relocation within the building in order to suit expected changes of configuration for manufacturing tasks. The spine cores which provide external equipment for the support of robotic tools that fix components into assemblies can be pre-fabricated in sizes suitable for road transport. The assembly of the structure is such that the building comprises six separate structures set side by side which are structurally discontinuous, but linked. This project requires them to be as light in weight as possible in order to be demounted and reassembled with as much ease as possible, given the need to keep the test modules in place and allow the workshop to be reconfigured. This requirement led to the use of 'service modules' which are set on rails. The approach of a single volume on the ground floor, and three sets of spaces above, enables a robust approach to the structural design to be taken for this large-scale, and operationally complex, facility without the need for more than a single structural system of steel frames, columns and trusses spanning from one side of the building to the other. A different solution of a combinations of structural systems, with associated interfaces and connections, was avoided as a result of this economical design. The facade layer of the building avoids the need for an additional row of columns immediately behind the facade; a second layer of structural columns is added where a double-skin facade configuration is used, in locations where most technical support spaces are accommodated. As a result of the three different compartments being arranged along the sides of the assembly building, the costs of construction are redistributed between support spaces and open central spaces,

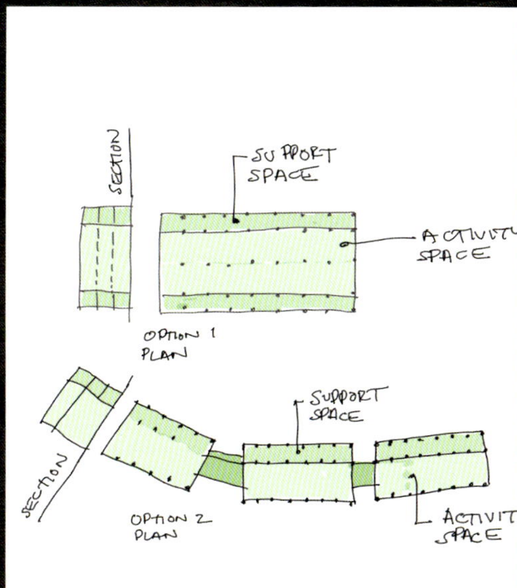

Structural strategy: Zones

Option 1 has a central row of columns to divide the production halls into two parts.

Option 2 has a column-free production space.

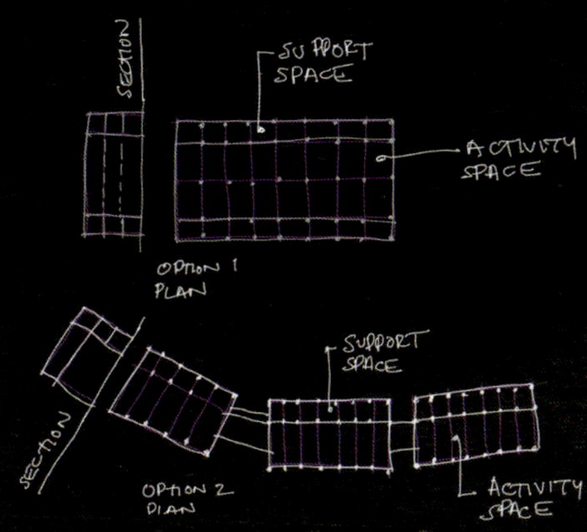

Structural strategy: Framing

Option 1 has side parts of the building with mezzanine floors inserted together, with bridges at a higher level.

Option 2 has long-spanning beams formed as trusses to span from side to side to create a high-level office space above the production halls.

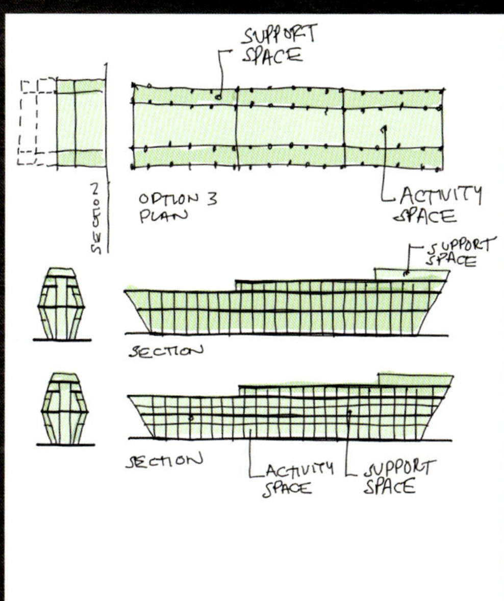

Structural strategy: Zones

Option 3 has support spaces arranged on one side of the main volume which are supported by steel frames with floor slabs set in between.

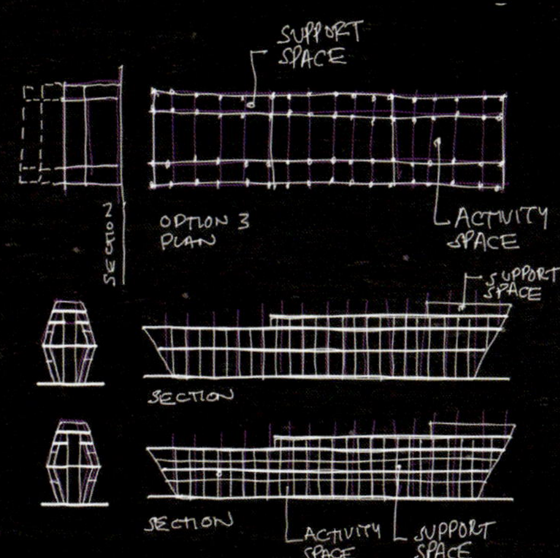

Structural strategy: Zones

Option 3 has floor levels that step down when viewed in section.

when compared with a regular structural frame of floors, beams and columns. The assembly hall is triple height in order to accommodate overhead cranes and gantries. The two 'spine' cores are discontinuous; they do not extend from one end of the building to the other. As a result, some of the stairs and service spaces are fixed to the outside of the assembly spaces, maintaining clear floor plates within the building for production. The flexibility in this approach to the structure avoids the need to rebuild parts of the building; anticipated changes can be carried out without affecting the functioning of the main spaces already in place. Additional space can be added as separate structures or as secondary structures to the existing primary structures; the building can be enclosed in a second and third layer of structure. This requirement can be achieved by either extending the roof upwards or extending the cranked walls outwards.

The structural strategy for Option 1 is one of having a central row of columns to divide the production halls into two parts, as each is arranged in two workflows, with one production part flowing in one direction before it returns back down the other half of the production. There is no need for a single-spanning structure going all the way through. The side parts of the building have mezzanine floors inserted together, with bridges at higher level which connect the office space on the sides at ground floor level. The side volumes contain support spaces for the production facilities including storage, washrooms, and air conditioning equipment. Option 2 has a structure with offices set above the production hall. There are long-spanning beams formed as trusses to span from side to side to create a high-level office space above the production halls. In Option 3, support spaces are arranged on one side of the main volume and these are supported by steel frames with floor slabs set in between. This option has floor levels that step down, when viewed in section, and follow the requirements of supporting and servicing production activities on the ground floor. Office space for design studios, production, marketing and sales also continue along the length of the building. A further development for the upper levels is to set support spaces down the length of the floor plan along its centre line.

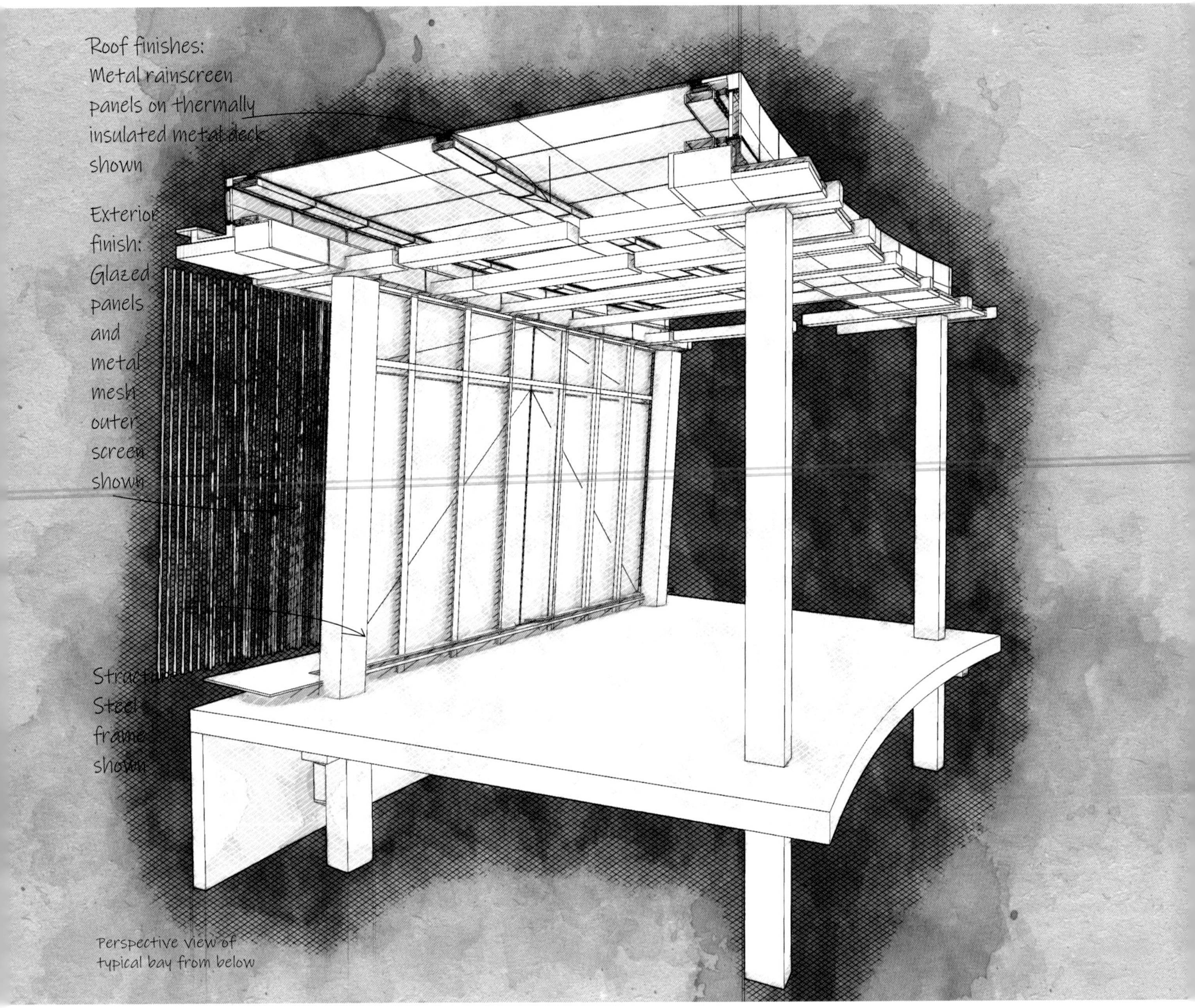

Typical bay adjacent to facade

The external envelope of the building comprises a double-skin facade, which extends from the first upper level to the top of the building. The ground floor of the building and the link pieces are glazed in regular curtain wall. The offices and canteen spaces above are largely shielded from the effects of the sun with a translucent outer facade layer. Some areas of the building have a completely opaque facade; this is where the mechanical and electrical equipment is accommodated – in locations where views are created down the length of the building, not out through the sides of the building – for reasons of functionality and security.

The opaque panels in these facade locations are rainscreen panels set into prefabricated cassettes that provide a completely prefabricated wall buildup. The double-skin facade zone is occupied by equipment that passes between maintenance access gantries; the gantries also provide access to outdoor space within the workplace. All parts of the facades can be 'stacked' vertically as modules, with services modules being fitted onto facade modules. In order to be relocated with ease, modules are set onto rails at each level; they can be moved along the length of the facades in order to provide a rapid response to changing operational needs within the facility.

The external envelope is part of a typical bay which extends the full width of the building. A typical bay comprises two layers; an internal space that extends the full width of the building, and the semi-external spaces set at the perimeter of the building that comprise the facade zone. The typical bay varies in height in response to the different floor heights, but otherwise forms a repeated bay that extends the length of the building. The inclined walls have areas of both opaque facade and translucent facade.

Office spaces have transparent glazed facades which are solar protected by the perforated metal screens set on the outer layer of the facades. The concept for the envelope is one of having a single visual expression for the building, using a single facade system that works for both manufacturing space and offices. The office spaces accommo-

Perspective view of typical bay from above

date a mix of functions: meeting rooms, conference spaces and management suites, as well as the canteen. The use of a single facade system allows the facades of the manufacturing spaces, with their varied requirements for daylight, to sit alongside the facades of office space while still maintaining a single visual expression of the overall form of the building.

Different functions accommodated within the building are not expressed visually on the facades, but the single visual expression of metal louvre panels and perforated metal panels convey a sense of unity across all tasks in the building. The physical environment within the factory is experienced as being very similar between factory and offices. Office spaces and manufacturing halls have similar sets of fittings and environmental controls for daylight, solar control and ventilation. Office spaces have generous floor-to-ceiling heights in order to be able to accommodate future manufacturing space should this be required. The external envelope is to provide a set of louvres across the facades at large scale which are operated manually to suit the changing position of the sun during winter, mid-season and summer. Louvres are deep and have different depths to suit the different spaces and functions within the building. When they are all closed, the louvres create a visual arrangement which reflects the varied requirements for daylight within the building. The larger louvres can also function as reflectors to reflect daylight across the ceilings of spaces within the building. The louvres are also used to block sunlight and admit daylight by reflecting light using the top surface of these shading devices.

The typical bays on the two short elevations have a thinner double layer facade; accommodating a narrower zone for maintenance access between the two layers of inner facade and outer screen. The glazing is opaque in response to the spaces immediately behind. Their outer screens are formed in perforated metal as the adjustability of the louvres is not a functional requirement. The pavilion hubs in the car park area are also clad in perforated metal; all service spaces are enclosed in this material.

1. Perspective view of exterior

2. Perspective view of exterior

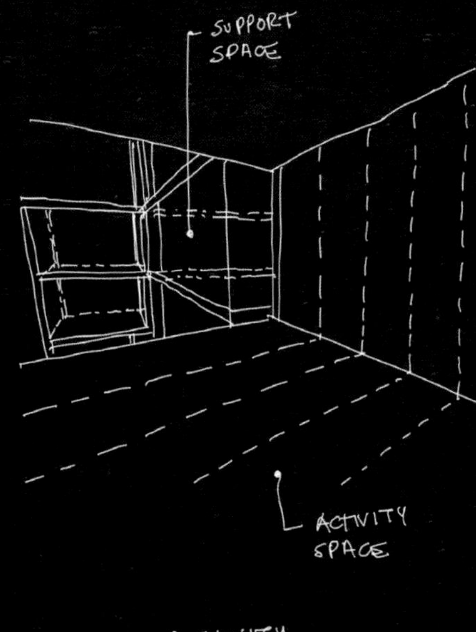

Mass customisation for environmental design

The relationship between structure and external envelope has developed in recent years as a result of the introduction of 'mass customisation' as an alternative to the production of a very limited set of components and assemblies for facade systems. The approach of greater flexibility in the design and manufacture of environmental control assemblies has come about as a result of advances in computer-driven design tools and manufacturing tools. The change to mass customisation has introduced two developments into environmental design: Increased complexity and interdependence between environmental control assemblies. In addition, both facade assemblies and structural assemblies are becoming more complex in order to meet specific performance requirements that were previously difficult to achieve. The combining of structural assemblies for primary structure, facades and roofs creates an interdependence between assemblies that can provide economies. Complexity of environmental design also originates from the geometry of the external envelope and the resulting external forms and internal spaces. In response to these trends of complexity and interdependence, there has been a reduction in the number of different components and assemblies used as a result of greater standardisation used within a reduced number of systems for structure and envelope. This reduction in the number of different types of component and assembly provides greater opportunity for their integration in a manner that is economic both in time for fabrication and for construction. The increased integration of building environment, facade and roof requires a corresponding integrated workflow which considers the complete network of design aspects and principles to ensure a high-performance, efficiently constructed building.

Computer-controlled tools have removed the imperative of mass production, offering instead possibilities of 'mass customisation' where many components of different size can be produced quickly to a high quality. At the construction stage, the geometry of parts can be output directly from a 3D model, then input to the digital manufacturing machine, allowing the efficient production of many different parts. This

. Perspective view of exterior

4. Perspective view of exterior

digital network of information can be expanded by incorporating a live project program, such that parts can be manufactured digitally when required. This approach reduces both the waste produced on site and the area required for material storage on site.

Environmental components of complex geometry can be manufactured economically by translating a digital 3D model, describing the components through a grid of points. This form of data can be input directly to a flexible moulding jig that fabricates components using this method of mass customisation. The use of a flexible jig removes the need to create temporary scaffolding which is usually costly, labour intensive and time consuming. By reducing the need for temporary scaffolding, the associated waste material on site is reduced; components and assemblies are fabricated in a controlled working environment rather than using the building site as a workshop environment. This approach is more controlled and potentially more economical. The flexible jig method also allows unique complex geometry components to be fabricated while reducing the time required for manufacture.

Solar analysis provides insight into how the environment of the internal space varies with the daily solar paths, allowing the environmental assemblies for solar shading systems fixed to facades to be customised and optimised for comfort and energy consumption. This mass customisation of fabrication of solar shading assemblies is a result of a combination of solar analysis and parametric structural analysis and design, allowing a shading system to meet specific performance requirements. Solar shading is configured in angle, frequency and orientation to control levels of solar radiation and levels of daylight within the building's environmental performance. Control of the combination of glare, solar gain and thermal insulation in specific internal spaces can be adjusted accordingly at the later stages of the design process.

A detailed environmental analysis can be conducted at the later design stages of a project to inform the environmental strategy; the aim is to reduce the number and fabrication complexity of components and assemblies in order to reduce the corresponding complexity of assembly and its associated costs.

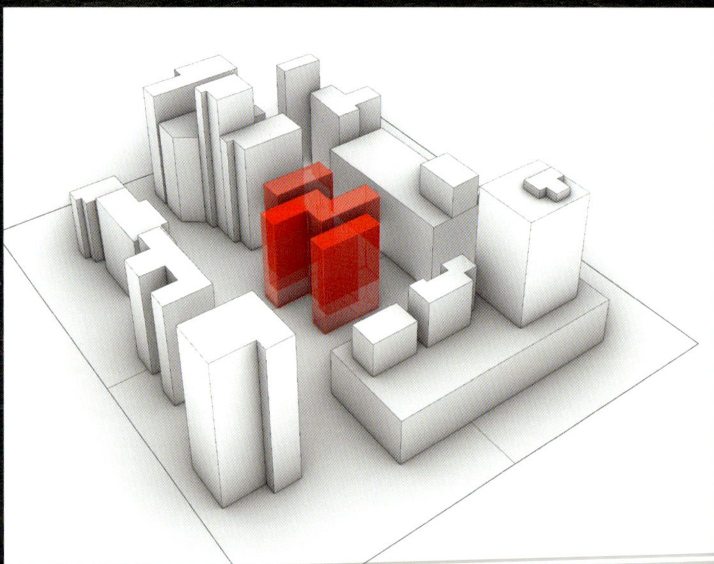

1. Project volume in site context

2. Project volume in site context

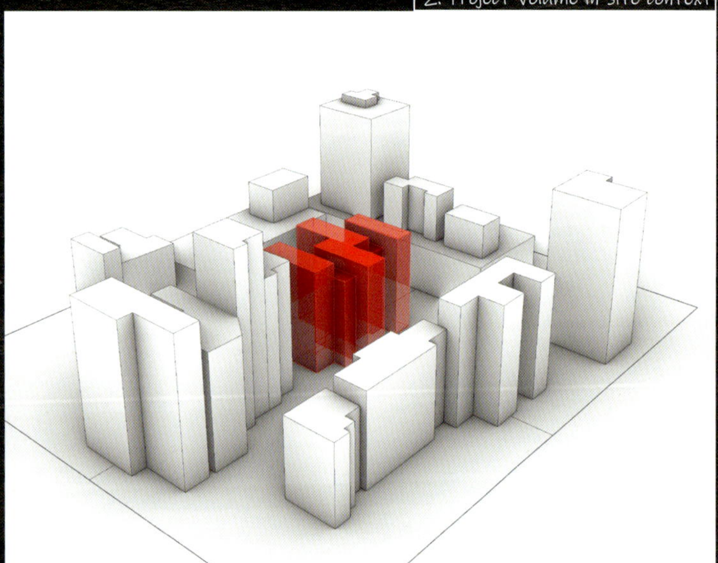

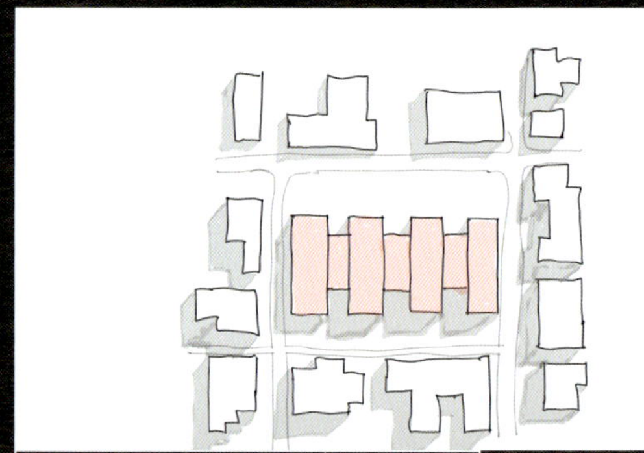

1. Site plan with surrounding context

Option 1 sets out two blocks of hotel accommodation which are parallel to one another.

2. Site plan with surrounding context

Option 2 forms a larger-sized block, which is bigger than the blocks in the city around it and then differentiates that single form.

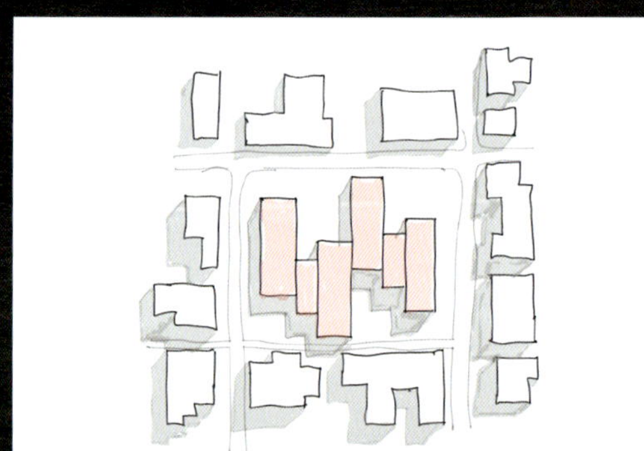

3. Site plan with surrounding context

Option 3 reduces the block sizes to those of the size of the surrounding cityscape.

Site context

Option 1 for the site context sets out two blocks of hotel accommodation which are parallel to one another, with a podium that occupies the full extent of the site. The podium spaces accommodate the hotel reception area and associated street-level commercial space. This arrangement allows each block that comprises the building to have apartment-style suites with natural daylight and natural ventilation, while omitting the need for internal corridors needed to access the apartments. This arrangement also avoids the need for significantly larger building forms than those of other blocks in the immediate vicinity. With Option 1 there is a single corridor that serves each block.

Option 2 forms a larger-sized block, which is bigger than the blocks in the city around it and then differentiates that single form in order to bring the scale of the constituent parts back to that of its immediate neighbours. Differentiation is created by stepping the apartment suites to different sizes, arranged in groups around the central corridor that forms a straight line. This approach creates a higher efficiency and clarity of layout in the apartment suites than is the case in Option 1, such that apartment-style suites are served by two cores with short corridors that lead to each apartment entrance.

Option 3 takes the idea of the building forms of Option 2 and reduces the block sizes to those of the size of the surrounding cityscape, while using the advantage of a central core, which is supplemented by a services installation set on the outside of the building. This approach avoids the need for having clusters of cores inside the building while still providing adequate light levels within apartment suites.

This is a 10-storey residential hotel building where visitors are accommodated for between three months and a year, where they essentially have a corporate home, a place to live and a place to entertain business clients. These are apartments which nestle into a business quarter, but which are not required to have a uniquely domestic identity. This is a relatively small building in relation to its bigger office building neighbours, but is of a similar height to the buildings which surround it. The site context is one of large blocks of building which have a mixture of office

Perspective view of environmental volumes

2. Perspective view of environmental volumes

1. Figure-ground diagram of tempered environment

Option 1
Dark blue spaces are highly tempered but are limited to living and kitchen spaces.

2. Figure-ground diagram of tempered environment

Option 2
Green spaces for study and small bedroom are less tempered than light blue bedroom spaces.

3. Figure-ground diagram of tempered environment

Option 3
Red circulation spaces are less tempered than green spaces for small bedroom and study.

space and apartments. The apartments in the surrounding buildings are all single storey and there is little open space nearby. The building occupies almost all the footprint of the site and faces a regular wide city street on one side, with narrower side streets; the street at the rear of the site is another small-scale street. The primary views of the building, as seen from the street, are of two blocks of similar appearance which are set side by side and are offset from one another in order to provide more light into internal spaces. The general arrangement of buildings and massing of buildings that surround the site are of buildings of different height that are monolithic, in the sense that none have lightwells set at their centre. This building follows that monolithic form, which suits the shape of the site. Apartments are each arranged over two floors; the lower floor is for entertaining and the upper floors for living and bedrooms for the occupants; private rooms on an upper floor and public rooms on the lower floor. The scale of each of the apartments is twice that of its neighbours, but floor slabs follow through at the approximate height of those of the neighbours; a choice was made to express those two-storey apartments on the elevation which forms a visual link between the surrounding buildings on one side of the street and the taller blocks of office buildings on the other side of the street.

The facades are divided into two-storey bays in order to suit the vertical emphasis and large scale of neighbouring buildings; avoiding the potentially awkward appearance of small-scale forms set adjacent to tall buildings.

The building occupies the full extent of its site, leaving one corner for entry into the building. Interaction of the building with its site location begins at the lower level, with sculpted forms that are set into the depths of the opaque facades as indented, sculpted figures which are abstracted and which mirror the activity of the street immediately adjacent. These low-relief forms are introduced into both the ground floor facades and the two floor levels above; with gradually more deeply modelled forms as they rise through the height of the building; suggesting the lives of those behind those opaque facades and suggesting the life of those passing by on the street.

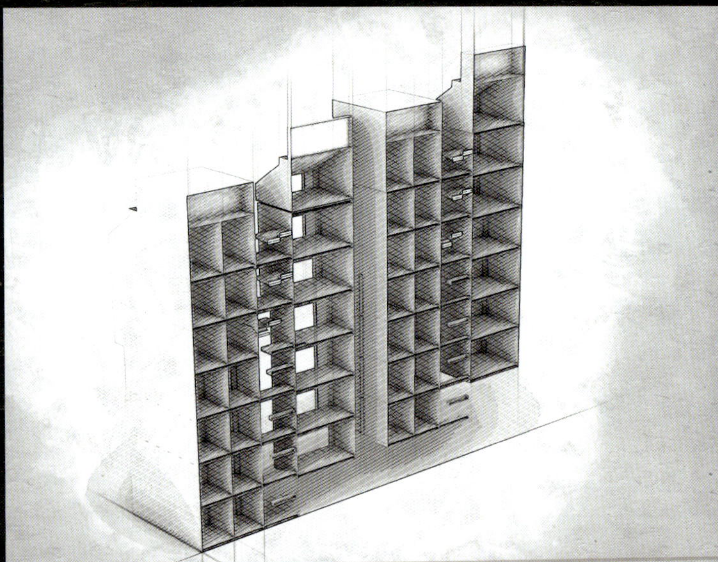

1. Sectional perspective view

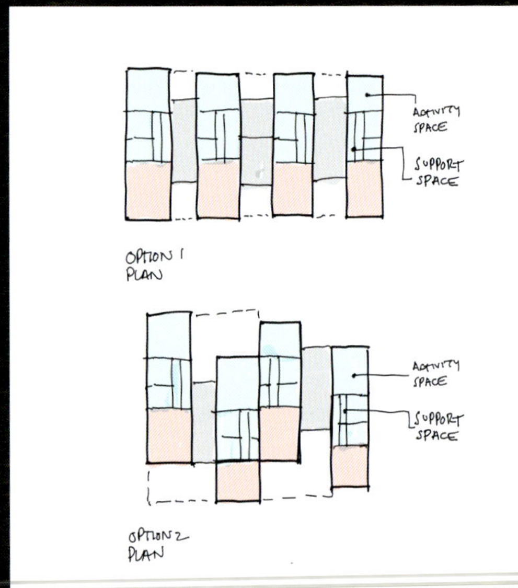

Spatial arrangement
Option 1 comprises apartments set on both sides of a central corridor for all three blocks.
Option 2 has a spatial arrangement of two blocks set on both sides of a central corridor.

2. Sectional perspective view

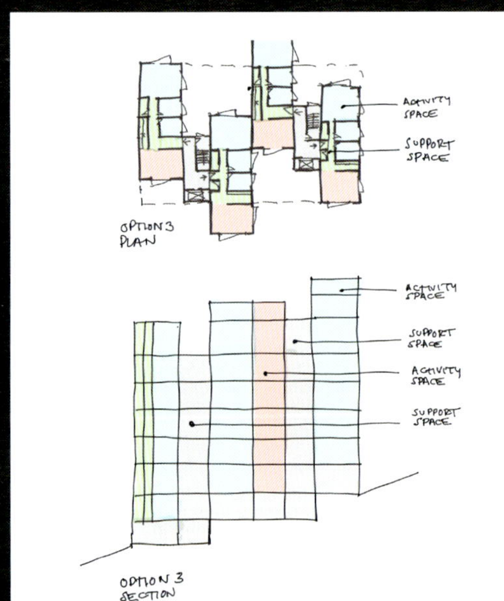

Option 3 has apartments sharing service spaces which are either integrated into apartment suites or form part of the external walls.

Spatial arrangement

The spatial arrangement of Option 1 comprises apartments set on both sides of a central corridor for all three blocks. The blocks can be varied slightly in width to suit the specific sizes of the apartments needed; every habitable room has natural ventilation. Option 2 has a spatial arrangement of two blocks set on both sides of a central corridor. The corridor is subdivided into two parts; each served by a separate core. Apartments are arranged in different sizes that create the characteristic steps in the external building form that allow subdivision into individual smaller-scale forms. Option 3 uses staggered service space such that the entrances into the building are also accessed by way of the cores and a connecting corridor that extends from end to end of the building at ground floor level; some apartments share service spaces which are either integrated into apartment suites or form part of the external walls. The spatial arrangement for the building is based on three options that organise square-shaped apartment plans to suit different external forms; arranged to allow as much light as possible into each apartment. The arrangements aim to give a sense of identity to each apartment by assembling a building form that has a similar overall massing to its neighbours.

The three options provide a separation between apartment forms in order for daylight and fresh air to be admitted into all spaces while not grouping apartments together into a large block with a central lightwell, which would not have provided the quality of space, light and ventilation that each apartment requires.

The spatial organisation of the three options is based on arrangements which allow the rooms to be well daylit and have cross ventilation where possible. A decision was taken at an early stage of the project not to have half the rooms, or the inner rooms, facing into a courtyard or lightwell, as the quality of light and fresh air was considered to be poor as well as there being a loss of amenity as a result of apartments overlooking each other in close proximity. The three options provide gaps and space between adjacent apartments, while also being arranged in a composition that works at the scale of the

Perspective view of interior

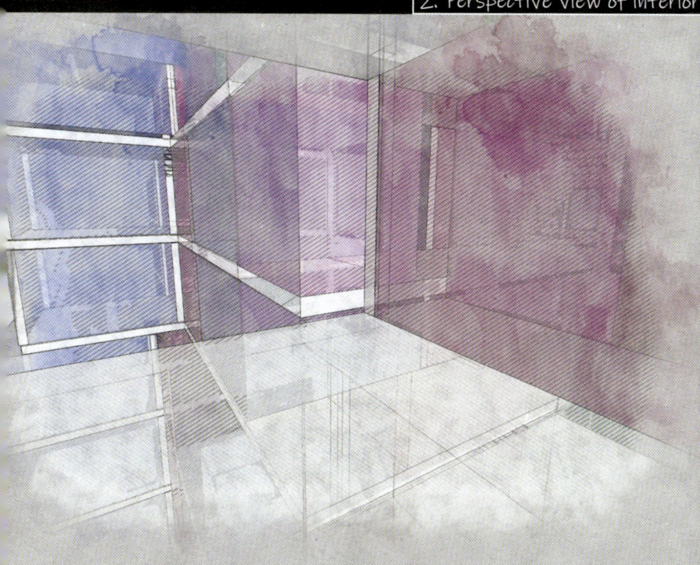

2. Perspective view of interior

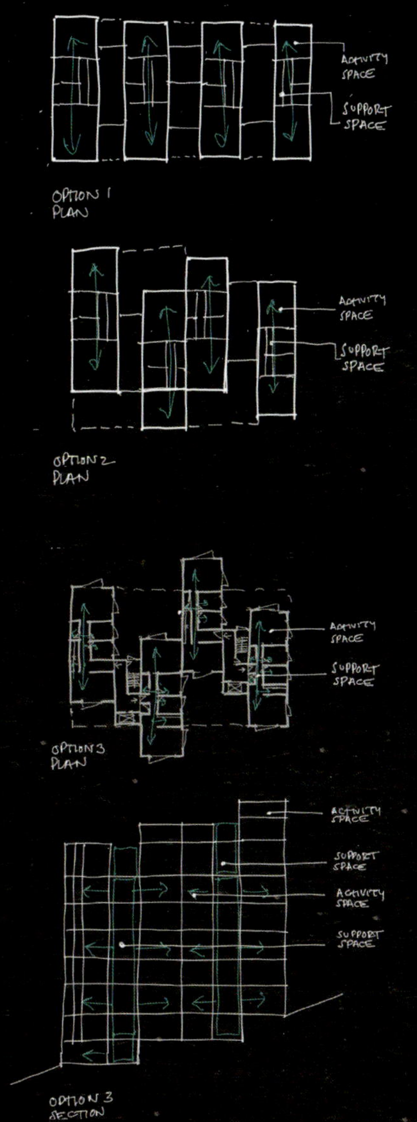

Internal circulation

Option 1 provides access to each apartment from a single corridor.

Option 2 introduces circulation cores that create separate corridor zones.

Option 3 reduces the length of corridor required to reach all of the apartments.

neighbourhood and of the city block in which it is located. The options vary from those with very high external wall areas resulting from the buildings being separated as much as possible, to blocks which more closely resemble the edges of a city block. This building uses the extent of this non-rectangular city site while providing sufficient daylight and fresh air to enter as many rooms as possible. A mini-tower was not considered for this project as the costs would have been uneconomical; the expectations of the project were of a city block compricing apartments that look out onto the surrounding streets, with both glazing and opaque walls being of a similar scale to surrounding buildings.

Internal circulation

The concepts for internal circulation are of setting access to apartments within central cores that are set between the two blocks. Rather than separate the two blocks, the cores are set within the depth of the building so that all external walls can be used to enclose habitable rooms. This approach creates internal circulation spaces which are minimised in size, with the opportunity to have apartments at different levels rather than creating a central corridor between cores. The building contains two sets of staircases which wrap around enclosures for lifts/elevators; staircases are illuminated and ventilated by rooflights.

The internal circulation of Option 1 has access given to each apartment from a single corridor. Option 2 uses the same strategy but introduces circulation cores that create separate corridor zones. Option 3 develops that access arrangement further by reducing the length of the corridor required to reach all of the apartments.

In Options. 1, 2 and 3, the ground floorl corridor forms a zone for fan-assisted natural ventilation from one end of each block to the other. This approach allows each apartment to be naturally cross ventilated. Option 3 has two configurations: An arrangement with ground floor corridor circulation zones penetrating the length of the building, while a second configuration of four separate zones for natural ventilation and access which traverses the full length of the building, and is similar to the ground floor circulation proposed in Option 1.

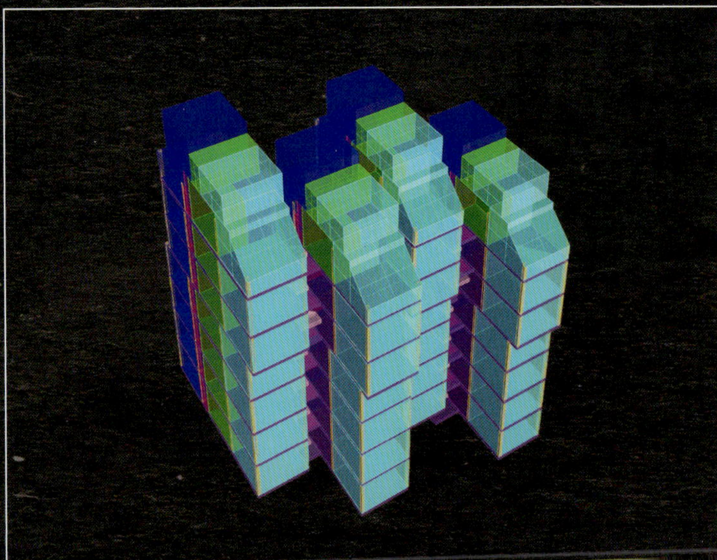

1A. Isometric view of environmental volumes

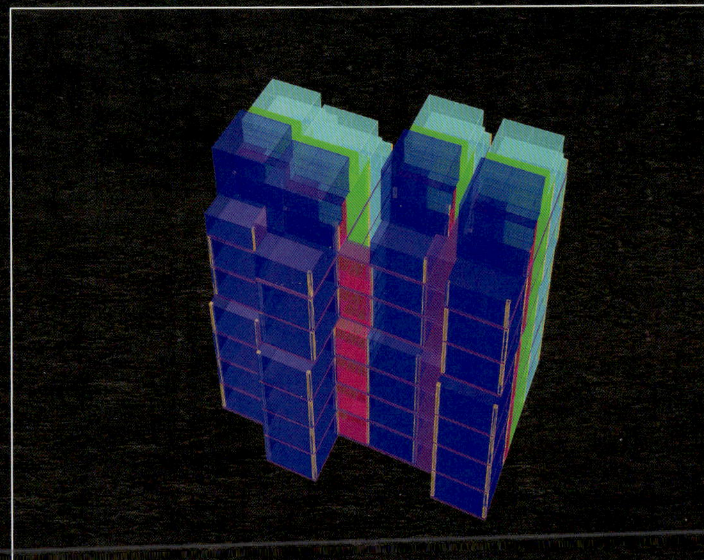

2A. Isometric view of environmental volumes

1B. Isometric view of environmental volumes

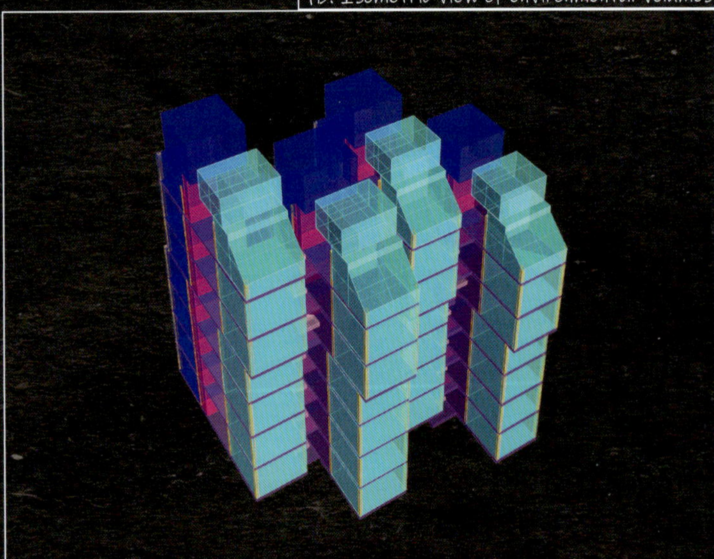

2B. Isometric view of environmental volume

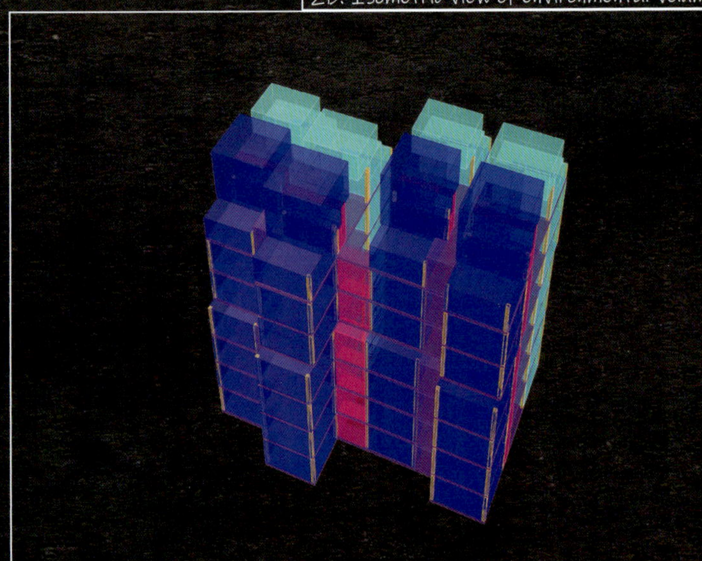

Environmental strategy

The approach to the environmental design is based on three options which separate the apartments to form different zones. The three options have gaps between apartments to allow fresh air to enter while also providing oblique views onto the surrounding streets. All options make use of an indented facade rather than a rectilinear box-like outer facade and lightwell in the centre. The lightwell approach was considered not to provide sufficient daylight and fresh air from the street. The indented facades provide side walls to apartments in order to increase the levels of daylight within spaces and ensure that natural cross ventilation can function successfully in most of the habitable rooms. The use of indented external walls ensures that the large-scale forms are juxtaposed by offsetting them against each other to create a characteristic form. The floor plans were set out on an environmental grid in order to ensure that daylight entered the building in all habitable rooms, while addressing the issues of privacy between apartments and the ability to have ventilation panels separated from glazed areas in order to enhance acoustic performance. Equipment for mechanical and electrical services is designed to be prefabricated; arriving at the site in partially assembled 'packages' where they are lifted into place with their external enclosures already in place. Larger assemblies for these services are set along the edges of the buildings in order to allow smaller technical assemblies to be bolted to them; added to the supporting structure during the early stages of occupation of the building in order to provide the high level of flexibility required in the brief/program. This aim is achieved by moving service packages with a mobile crane from outside the building; increasing the performance of the services installation by moving modules and fixing additional sub-assemblies.

Specifically, the mechanical ventilation equipment is moved locally in order to respond to changes in the internal layout of each apartment. This approach allows the system of partial natural ventilation to continue to be used effectively, instead of relying on full air conditioning in the event of changes to apartment layout. Each core and each facade-based building is constructed from hot rolled steel sections, assembled

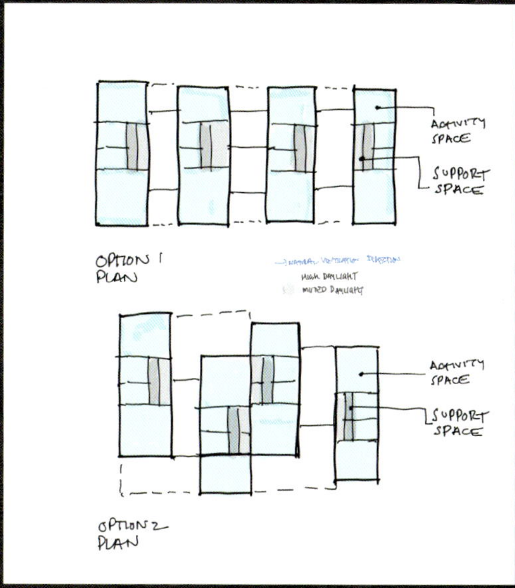

Daylight strategy for direct sunlight and cross ventilation.

Option 1 arranges the building as two blocks separated by a service core.

Option 2 widens the central circulation space in order to add the main entrance floor.

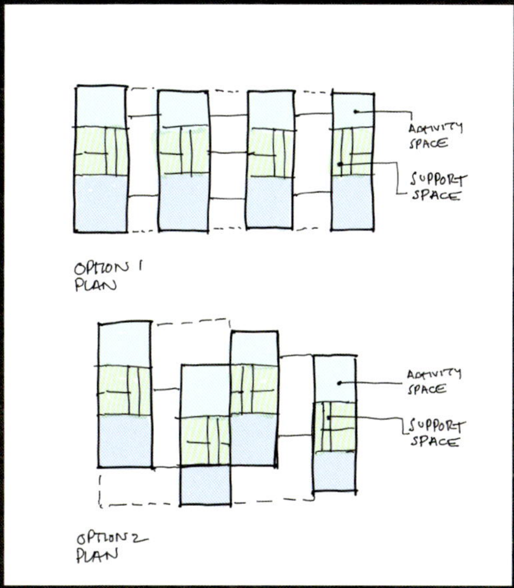

Environmental zones

Option 1 is based on treating each of the three blocks as a separate environmental zone.

Option 2 has the requirement for natural ventilation met by fresh air being introduced on one side of each apartment.

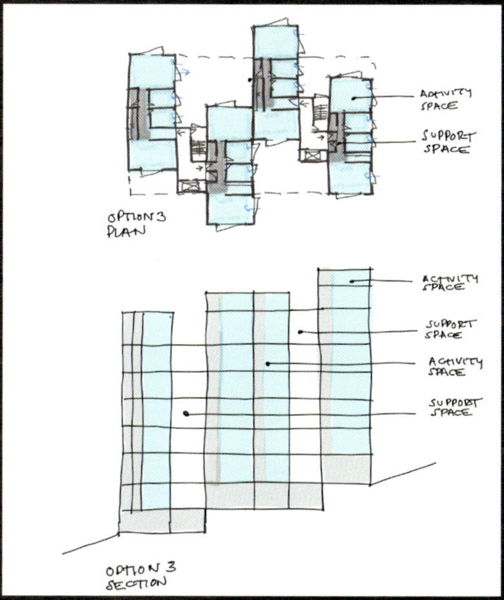

Daylight strategy for direct sunlight and cross ventilation.

Option 3 arranges the building as two larger blocks with communal spaces on the ground floor and accommodation above.

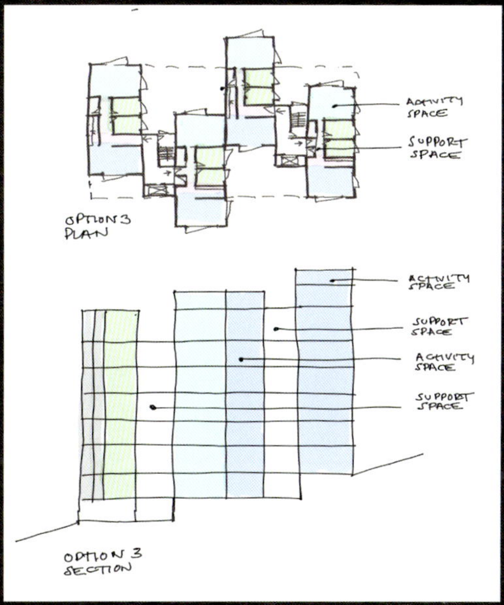

Environmental zones

Option 3 has zones for natural ventilation that are introduced into kitchens and bathrooms.

with members set at close fixing centres in order to integrate the construction of the facade and the structure which supports the external walls. The external walls are effectively a series of 'platform frames' that are put together to provide the high level of differentiation required between the internal spaces and external forms required in the brief/program. Glazed elements of the facades are formed as 'infill' panels to surrounding opaque walls; they are inserted after the adjacent opaque walls have been installed. This approach provides the basis of the environmental strategy: opening windows and facade-fixed and fan-assisted natural ventilation.

The environmental strategy provides each block with a group of environmental zones where each apartment is an environmental zone in its own right. The exception to this principle is the set of open areas located between blocks, where the larger floor plates are serviced from the adjacent cores; air is drawn down from the ceiling voids in access corridors and within each apartment. The environmental strategy for Option 1 is based on treating each of the three blocks as a separate environmental zone where each building will have similar requirements; those needs being adjusted to suit the exposure to direct sunlight and to shaded daylight. In addition, the effects of overshadowing from one block to another, and the effects of noise from traffic surrounding the site, form part of the environmental strategy. The yellow block, shown in the diagram, requires more acoustic attenuation in the external envelope than that required of the other two blocks.

Option 2 has three environmental zones, corresponding to the grey block, green block and the blue space shown in the illustrations. As a result, the requirement for natural ventilation is met by fresh air being introduced on one side of each apartment, into all rooms. Option 3 develops the arrangement of Option 2: Zones for natural ventilation are introduced into kitchens and bathrooms which are set on the external walls in order to provide larger internal spaces; protected from the surrounding traffic noise, while natural daylight and natural ventilation is introduced deep into the apartments.

1A. Isometric view of structure

1B. Isometric view of structure

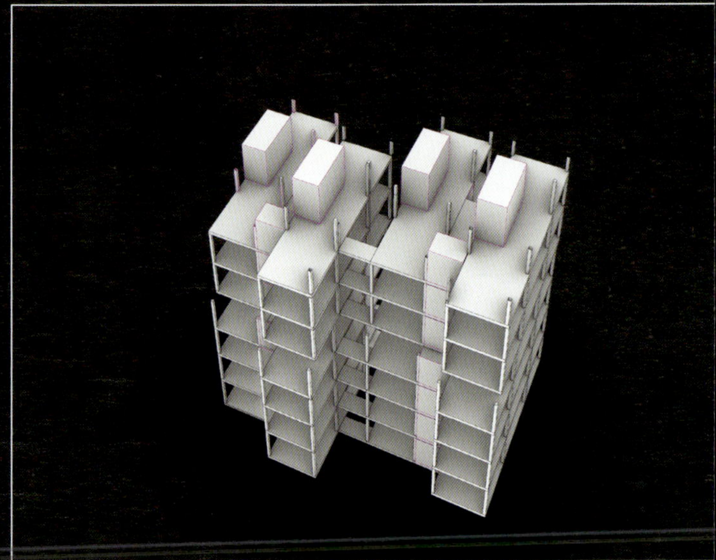

2A. Isometric view of structure

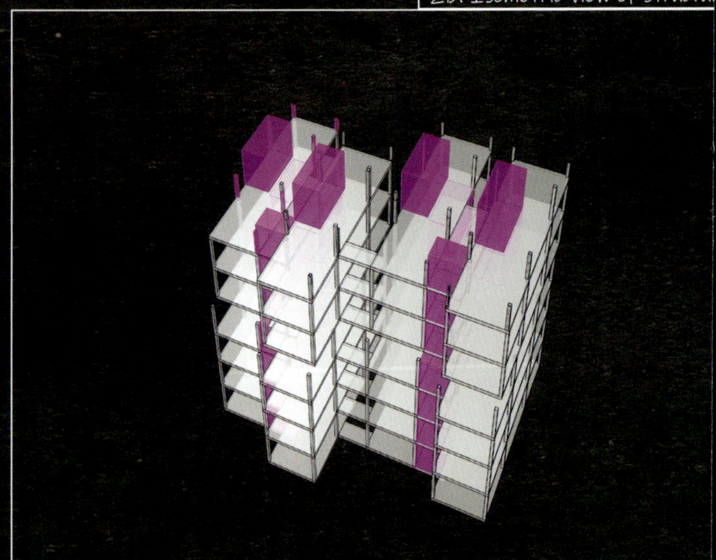

2B. Isometric view of structu

Structural strategy

The structural solution is of a hierarchy of steel-framed structures which provide long-span beams and trusses, with secondary smaller-scale steel structures nested into those primary structures. In addition to enclosing more compact spaces within the spatial arrangement, these smaller-scale structures provide part of the required stability for the primary structure. As a result, there is an interdependency between primary and secondary structure. This approach has been taken in order to have different spatial enclosures on a single floor plate and so that building users can enjoy views from space to space, within each apartment, in a characteristic staggered arrangement through the height of the building.

The overall structural design comprises four separate structures which can be joined together in different combinations. This building is very much a 'kit of parts' that creates a cluster of blocks that comprise the building. The structure uses, in part, the language of inclined steel frames which are joined together as modules. The design is aimed at prefabrication and delivery to site of completed structural sub-assemblies and structural facade modules. These sub-assemblies and modules are self supporting and are arranged to form the primary components of the building facades. The primary structure is then inserted between these primary components, taking a different approach from that taken on some typical larger-scale projects of this type in that the cores and facade structures are positioned first on site; the longer spans between core and facade are inserted as infill pieces. The cores comprise a series of parallel forms which are prefabricated. The open floor spaces are constructed on site with infill steel frames and profiled metal composite decks as floor plates, in order to provide the level of flexibility required for near future changes to the apartment layout in response to market needs. The brief/program requires early occupation of the apartments, before other parts of the project are complete. As a result, the prefabricated elements which provide 'primary' structural stability are constructed first, with elements that provide 'secondary' stability constructed afterwards, followed by the infill frames. The

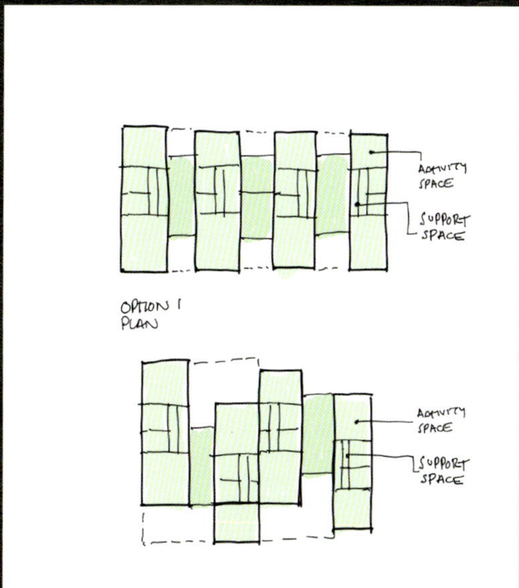

Structural strategy: Zones

Option 1 has a regular grid of columns and beams across all apartments.

Option 2 allows for more complexity of spatial arrangement by introducing a central circulation spine.

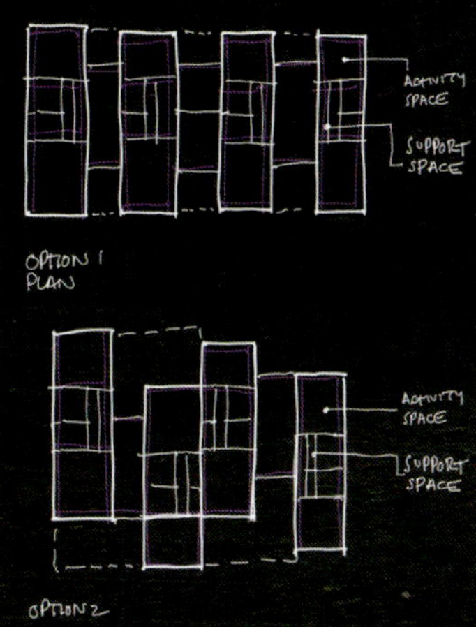

Structural strategy: Framing

Option 1 creates variation in the size of apartments by increasing the width of each block.

Option 2 allows different structural arrangements of beams, columns and dividing walls.

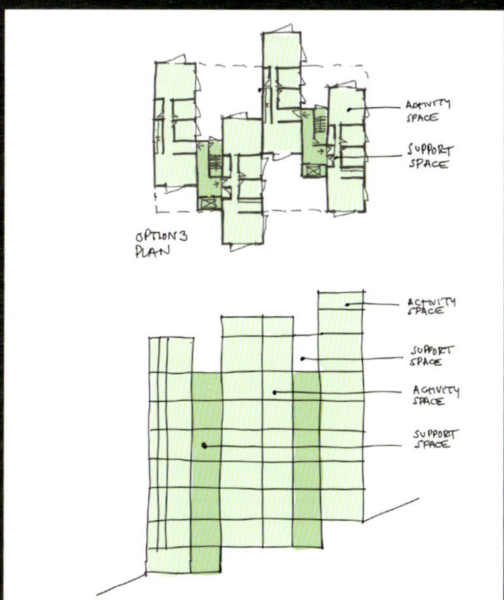

Structural strategy: Zones

Option 3 has columns set on both sides of the circulation spine.

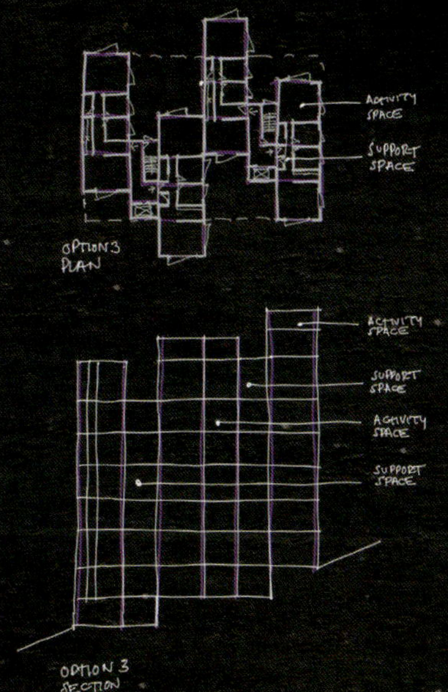

Structural strategy: Zones

Option 3 has variations in the form of the building, created by the mirrored apartment layouts.

buildings also accommodate smaller-scale modules of single-storey facade elements that are completely prefabricated offsite, and installed directly into place on site.

The structural strategy for Option 1 is of a regular grid of columns and beams across all apartments, extending down through the podium below. This economical solution creates variation in the size of the apartments by increasing the width of each block to form the slight irregularity in the structural grid in one direction only. The dividing walls between apartments all line through from block to block.

Option 2 allows for more complexity of spatial arrangement by introducing a central circulation spine at ground level, with cores that have columns set on both sides of the service 'links'. This approach allows different structural arrangements of beams, columns and dividing walls to be formed on each side of the spine. This creates, effectively, two different arrangements on each side of the corridor, and allows for a wide variation in apartment suite size within each block. Option 3 develops that theme further with columns set on both sides of the circulation spine, but with service modules set on the perimeter walls; creating spaces which engage with the externally located service spaces such as kitchens. Variations in the form of the building, created by the mirrored apartment layouts, reflect urban forms in the size and shape of surrounding buildings, allowing the building to sit comfortably within its urban environment.

The structural strategy is one of providing the economical solution of a structural frame to different arrangements of apartment spaces in various configurations which were based on a single type of apartment. Dwellings have large-scale open spaces arranged over two floors, with large spaces on the lower floor and smaller bedroom spaces on the upper floors of each apartment. No structural walls were set within the habitable spaces in order to provide the large-scale apartment spaces; columns were provided in their place. Structural walls were used between apartments for all three options. External walls can also accommodate supporting walls, but these were not needed in any of the three options shown.

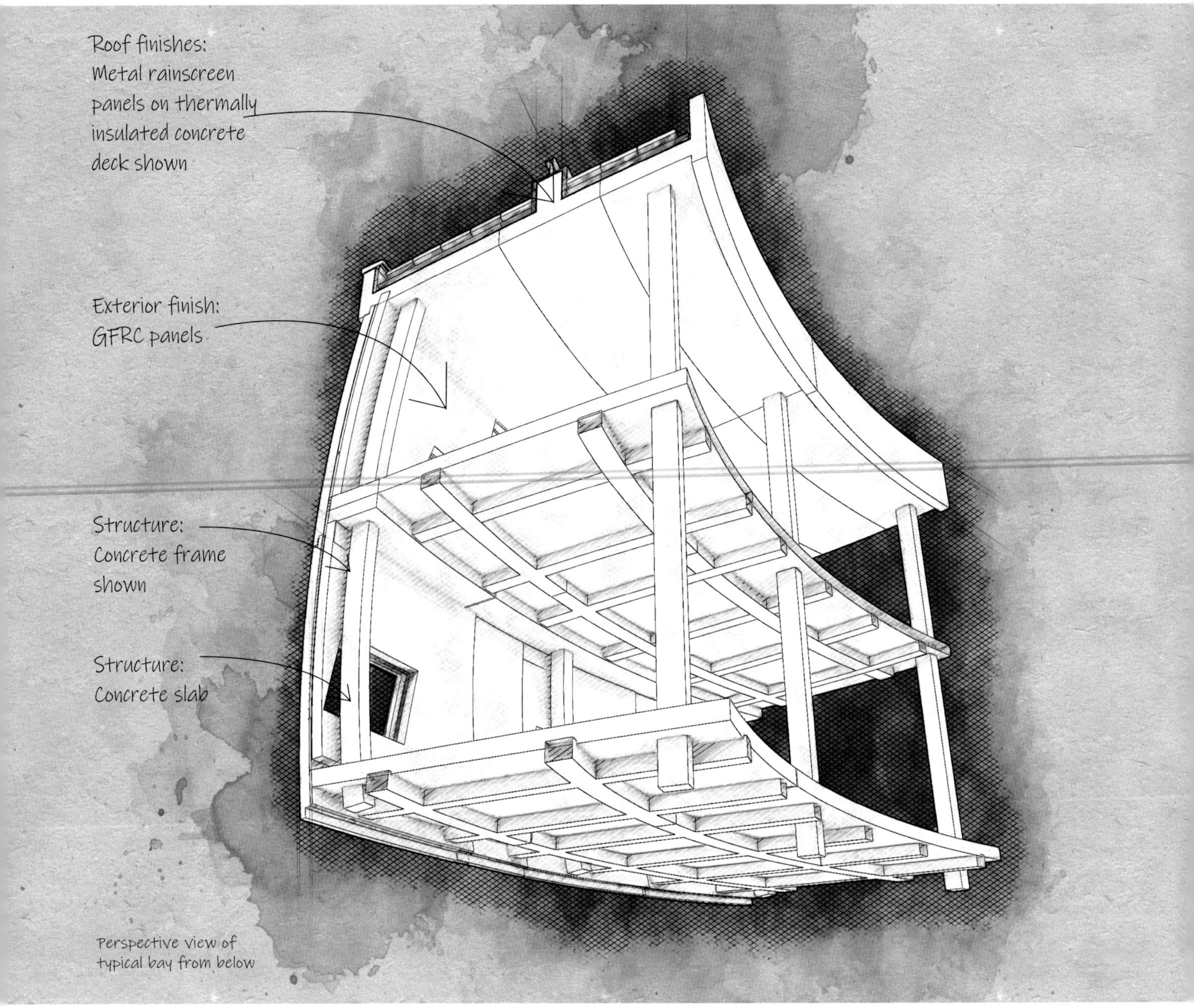

Perspective view of typical bay from below

Typical bay adjacent to facade

The external envelope brings together a highly differentiated building structure with glazed walls that allow high levels of daylight and fresh air to enter each apartment. Dwellings are all of a similar size, but apartments at the top of the building extend over two floors with arrangements such that the upper floor of one apartment is sitting above the lower floor of the apartment beneath, but over a double-height space. A stepped section was created as a result of the need to have large-scale spaces on one elevation and to have smaller-scale spaces of corresponding bedrooms on the other side of the plan. Other apartments at the top of each block are arranged where the bedrooms are positioned directly above the living rooms, such that each apartment is self-contained within a rectangular form that extends over two floors. The need to have apartments of different size with terraces led to the adoption of a solution of two blocks of building forms which are offset from each other, and which create a clarity of composition where two juxtaposed buildings are offset from each other. This provided a certain repetition and a sense of the building envelope being a recognisable form in the cityscape. The repetition of the form over two or three juxtaposed blocks was important in order to fit into the cityscape by providing a repeated rhythm. Within each of those blocks there is a high level of differentiation which occurs at the scale of the city blocks which surround it. The brief/program allowed the envelope to respond to the need for terraces in some apartments and double height spaces in other apartments, while providing external space without the need to conform to a rectilinear, vertically arranged block. The facade steps in and out with a lot of exterior space, and daylight entering apartments which are given the sense of being 'houses in the sky' and not apartments with balconies. The balconies are essentially outdoor rooms; some with winter garden glazing to create a space warmed by the sun at cooler times of the year. Bathrooms and kitchens are not stacked vertically: instead, a high level of differentiation of apartment types is provided.

The structure is a driver for the opaque external walls. Glazing is the driver in the main spaces, creating a high level of contrast between

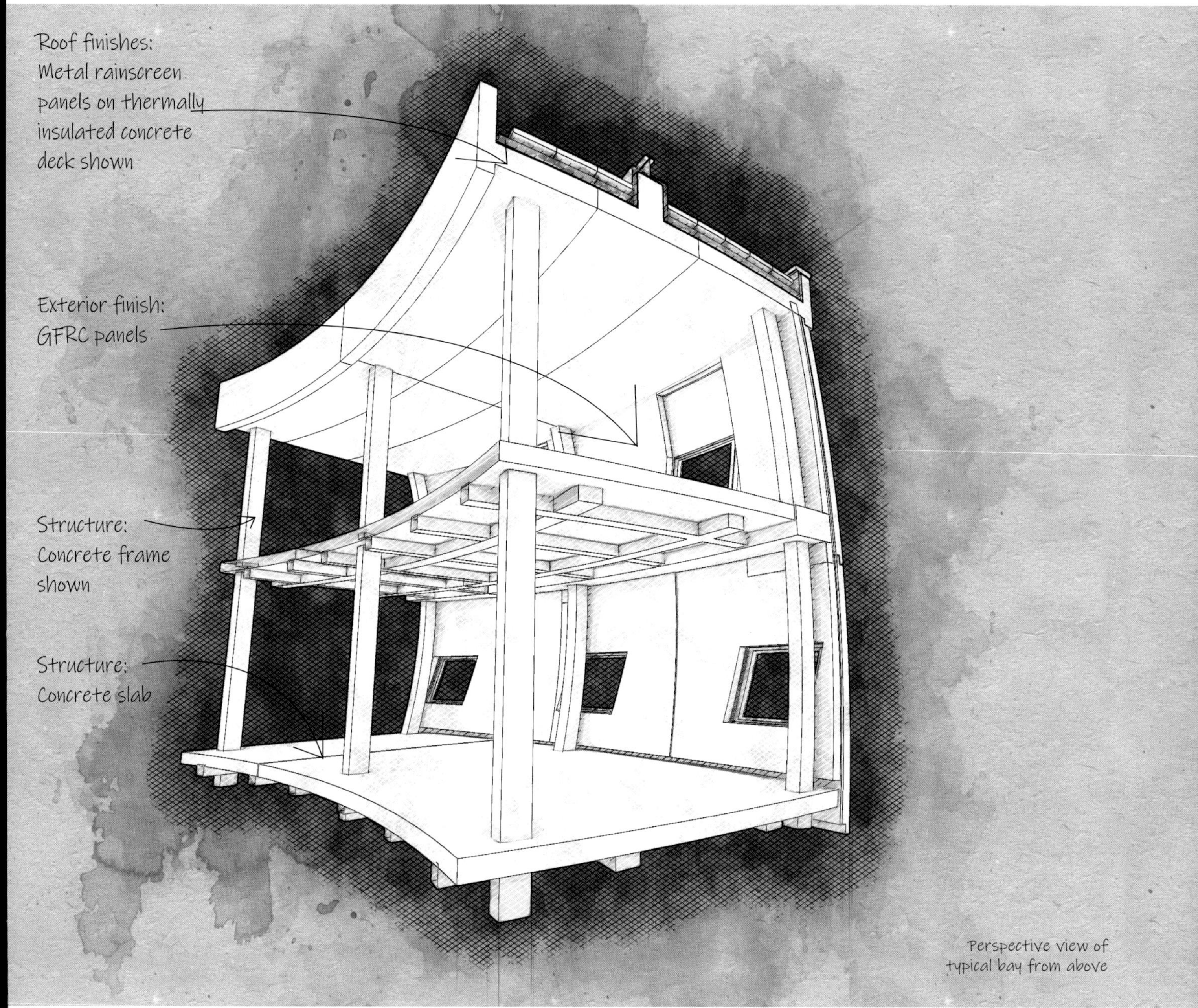

Perspective view of typical bay from above

highly glazed habitable rooms and opaque service rooms while providing privacy and a sufficient level of primary structure; an area of opaque walls in rooms where views out are not required and where a degree of enclosure is preferred. The proportion of opaque wall to glass wall was a high consideration in this design in order to avoid the sense of residents having the perception that they are living in an office environment. Areas of the facade which provide vertical access and which also house service facilities are modelled on the outside of the building The facades express a mixture of the structure and services needed to provide daylight.

A key part of the external envelope design is the opaque facades which have low-relief sculptures set into them of figures who appear to be passing each other in the street. The levels above that have more three dimensional, deeper forms, and above those levels the low relief becomes one of the geometries of the skyline. The low relief facade panels are rendered economical as a result of the use of digital moulding techniques which permit a high level of modelling that turns the opaque facades into an art form; a muted expression of life in the surrounding streets. Forms are created in low relief in order to allow them to be appreciated during the lifetime of the building. The low relief sculptures are a key benefit of the approach of mass customisation in this project; the differentiated forms of the building that result from this method are used to communicate visual ideas rather than what might otherwise become a grid-like aesthetic.

The non-rectilinear forms within the facades provide a means of adding both structural members and services equipment without them becoming visually incongruent with the other parts of the facades. All facades are enclosed in concrete-based panels which are set into thin metal frames; the overall impression of the typical bay is one of narrow framed windows and opaque panels; thin frames around the edges of all internal walls, doors and screens and trims set into floor finishes that define the perimeter of rooms – providing a space to walk around, providing a definition of space into which furniture is arranged. Light fittings are fixed to these rails at ceiling level.

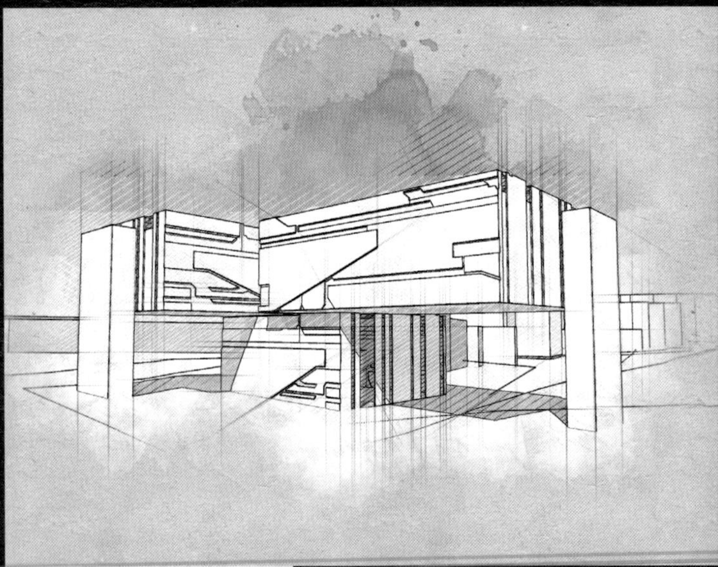

1. Perspective view of exterior

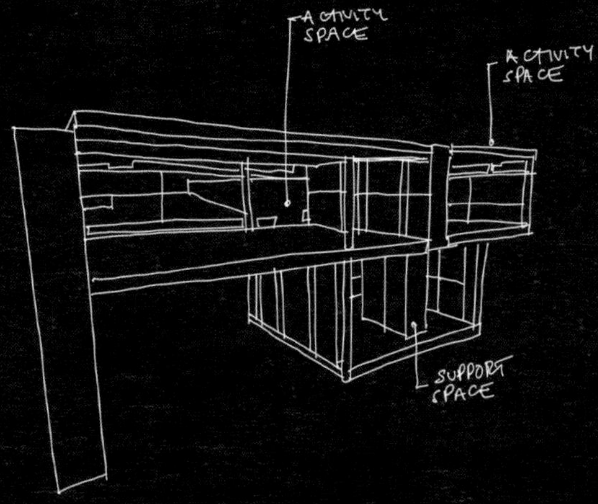

2. Perspective view of exterior

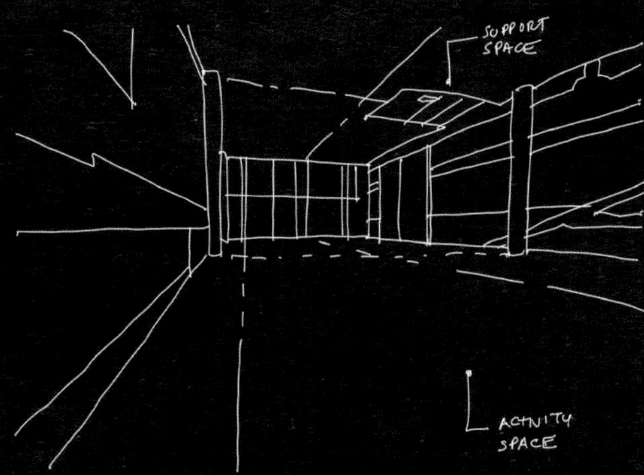

Daylighting and natural ventilation in gallery spaces

This project looks at how light can enter gallery space along lines of structure instead of from the roof, lines which might correspond with joint lines between facade panels. These joint lines could admit daylight through flaps which open and close to admit daylight, fresh air or both. Top light might be better controlled by providing both daylight and top light from varied light sources within a gallery.

The three major volumes of this gallery have different characteristics of daylight, achieved as a result of placing them at different orientations. Two of the blocks are set at a higher level; they are lit from the edges of their enclosing walls. The lower block at ground floor level has daylight entering from the sides only. The projecting volumes of the upper floors serve as canopies to create semi-external areas at ground floor level. These semi-external spaces are for the exhibition of sculptures; daylight which is both shaded and reflected illuminates their forms. In addition, this building is essentially for the exhibition of sculpture, which provides more opportunities for natural ventilation than is the case for groups of paintings or installations, where the control of temperature and relative humidity is an essential requirement. As a result, this building has a mixed system of natural and mechanical ventilation. In natural ventilation mode, fresh air is introduced from outside using a fan-assisted system which circulates air from space to space; rooms are linked in an open sequence of galleries. Staircases and support spaces also have a mixed mode ventilation system which is separate from that of the galleries. Movement through the building reveals differences between spatial experiences; the building creates a route through a sequence of linked spaces of different orientation; the visitor is reoriented from volume to volume.

This project also seeks to provide thermal insulation and solar protection, where required, in order to optimise spaces specifically for the display of artworks; optimising environmental performance while addressing the need for a dynamic relationship between daylight and electrical light, as well as mechanical ventilation and natural ventilation. However, this project does not, as a result, take the selection of environmental

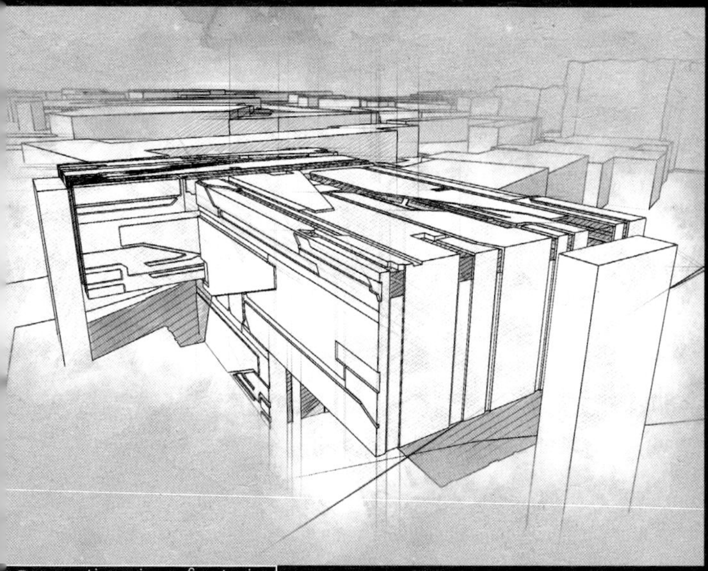

Perspective view of exterior

4. Perspective view of exterior

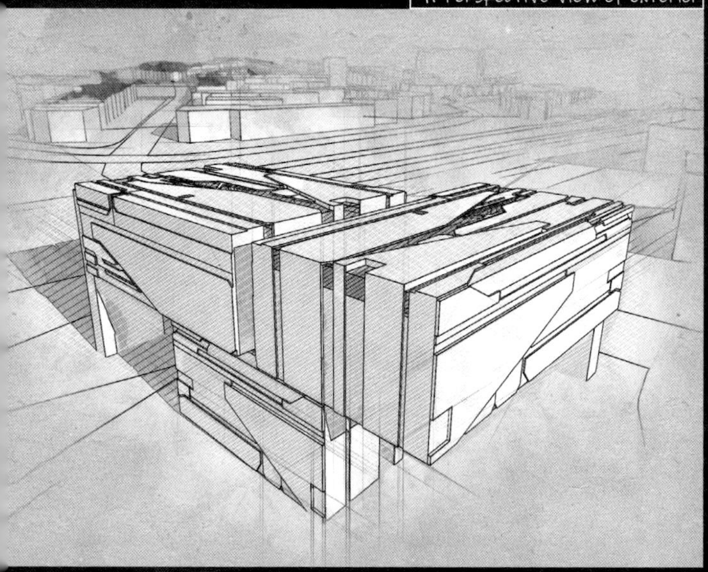

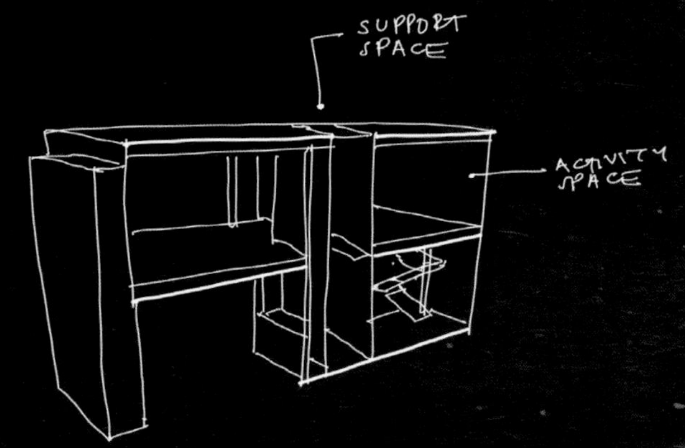

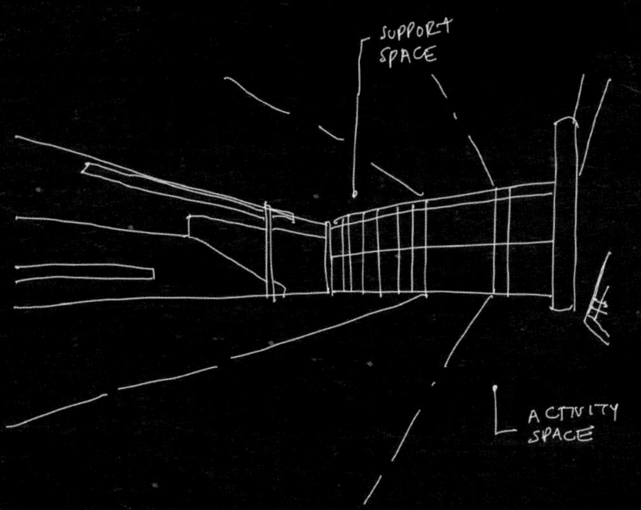

control systems, or the performance of facade systems, as possible points of departure for the environmental design. Instead, the process started with the concept of primary spaces being open spaces; then enclosing those spaces to suit the needs of function and environmental performance. The project also aims to ensure that spaces provide some level of opportunity for being adapted immediately for different effects of light and air; as a result, a range of performances has been established through modification of the design without the need to modify parts of the 'core' of its construction. Spaces are designed with this flexible approach in mind, rather than from a set of fixed and predetermined combinations of systems. This approach to environmental design avoids the need to 'optimise' performance for a range of requirements whose comparative importance will change over the first 10 years of the life of the building. For example, mechanical ventilation systems aim to vary the supply of fresh air to where it is needed in the building, supplemented by natural ventilation where possible. A key consideration in the environmental design of this building is also to provide close control of the tempered environments in each of the galleries when needed, by regulating temperature and relative humidity; there is a corresponding need to reduce the energy used to maintain these environments. This aim is achieved by accommodating the service zones into different areas which are ventilated, heated and cooled with more passive and natural ventilation; separating those areas from the core of each exhibition space – reception areas and cafes are tempered accordingly. In addition, there is a requirement for the mechanical ventilation equipment to be concealed, from the visual point of view. This requirement helps to create a clearly defined 'container' for the building and not to have the mechanical and electrical equipment visible as 'backpacks' on the sides of the building or on the roofs as something obviously masked. As a result, the environmental controls are integrated into the passive controls for roof glazing and external shading; controlling the daylight entering the spaces beneath. Temperature and humidity controls are provided by small-sized, concealed units which are fixed to facades, accessible within the building.

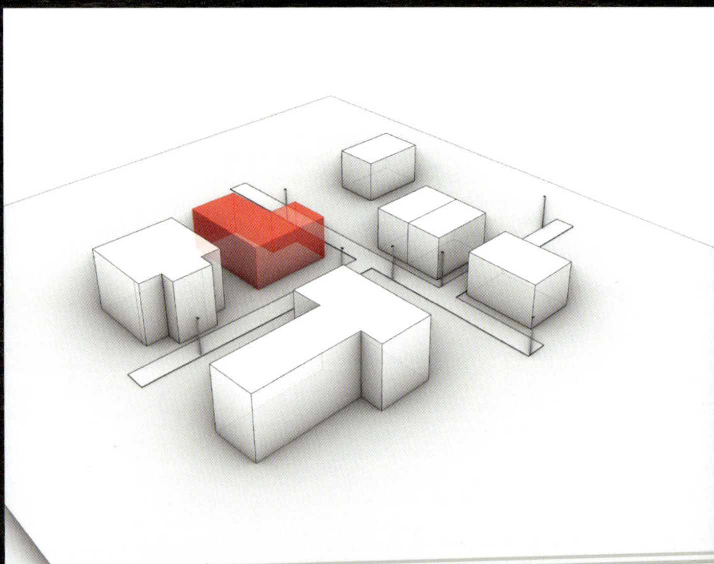

1. Project volume in site context

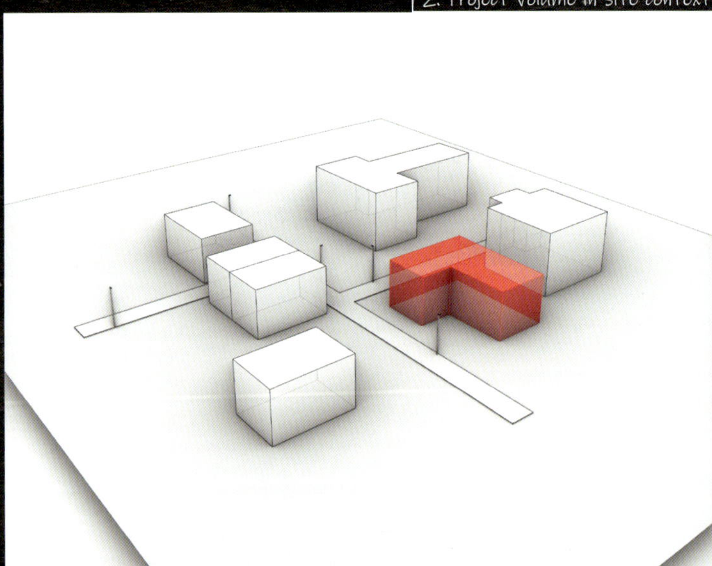

2. Project volume in site context

1. Site plan with surrounding context

Option 1 has a group of three galleries that house the collection of paintings, sculptures and drawings.

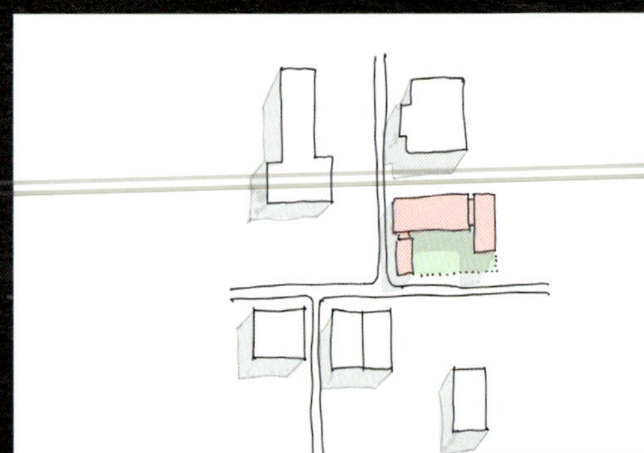

2. Site plan with surrounding context

Option 2 redistributes the volumes in order to accommodate more sculptures; paintings relating to the sculptures are exhibited alongside them.

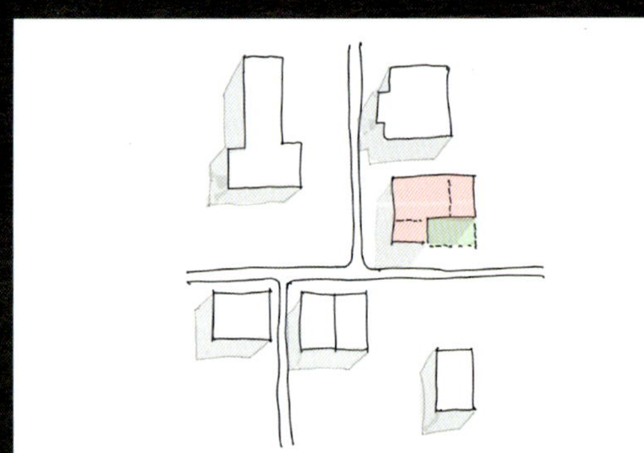

3. Site plan with surrounding context

Option 3 compresses and combines spatial elements, such that the building footprint is smaller than the other options.

Site context

This project is for an art gallery and art exhibition building which focuses on the display of large-scale sculptures. Exhibits can be viewed from outside the building by day, and during hours of darkness from below, through a glass deck set at the projecting upper floor level. The upper level provides views onto sculptures beneath, which are set externally. The upper level accommodates additional exhibition areas to form a link with those exhibited externally at ground level. The brief/program requires the internal exhibition spaces to be mechanically ventilated at the upper level and naturally ventilated at the lower level.

The site context for Option 1 is of a group of three galleries that house the collection of paintings, sculptures and drawings. The three galleries are grouped in a way that creates a route through the building as a circuit around the art gallery. Option 2 redistributes the volumes in order to accommodate more sculptures; paintings relating to the sculptures are exhibited alongside them. Elsewhere, the drawing collection is accommodated in the smaller block; larger sculptures are exhibited externally. For both Options 1 and 2, an external space is created by external walls on its three sides; a link is formed between all three internal spaces and the outside space such that, for exhibition, sculptures can be linked visually from inside to outside as part of the same set of artworks exhibited. Option 3 compresses and combines these elements, such that the building footprint is smaller and the external exhibition spaces are accommodated underneath cantilevered volumes from the upper floors, leaving a small sculpture court on the ground floor. This arrangement completes the rectangular form created by the L-shaped cantilevered volumes, which extend over two tall floors. A primary advantage of Option 3 is that taller spaces can be provided; spaces for exhibitions are arranged in a more compact and economical manner than is the case with the first two options.

The building is located in a mostly residential area within a dense urban environment; the building sits among commercial buildings at the edge of that residential area. Buildings that surround this gallery are of a similar height. The context of the site is a corner plot set adjacent to

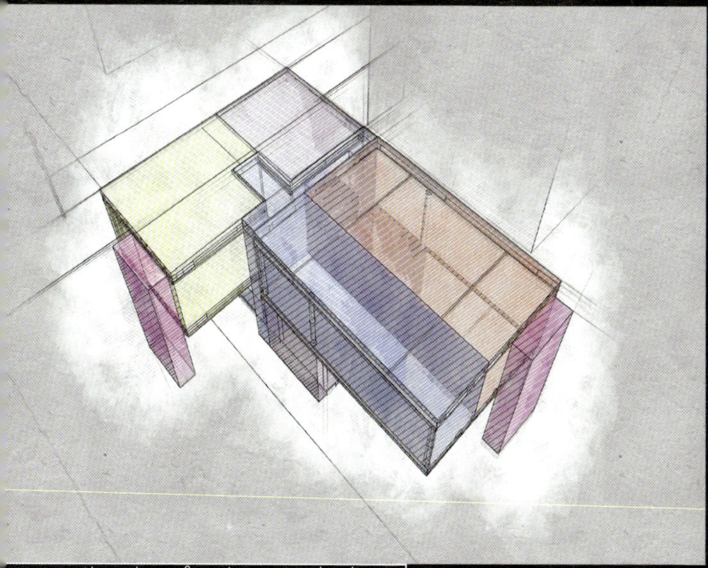

Perspective view of environmental volumes

2. Perspective view of environmental volumes

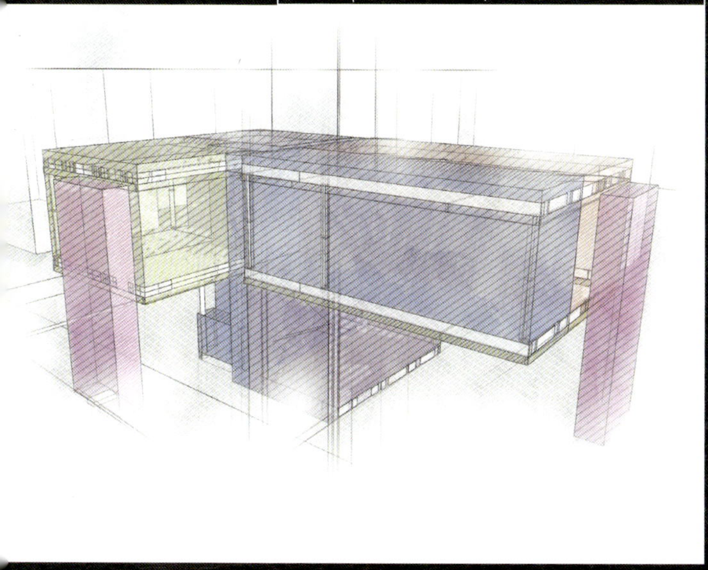

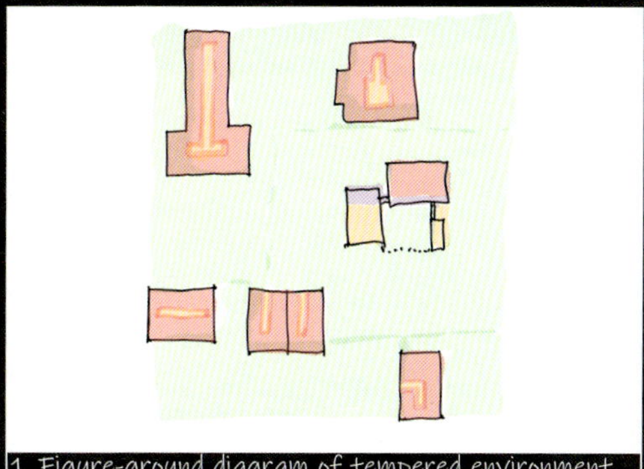

1. Figure-ground diagram of tempered environment

Option 1
Red spaces are highly tempered but are reduced to two galleries only.

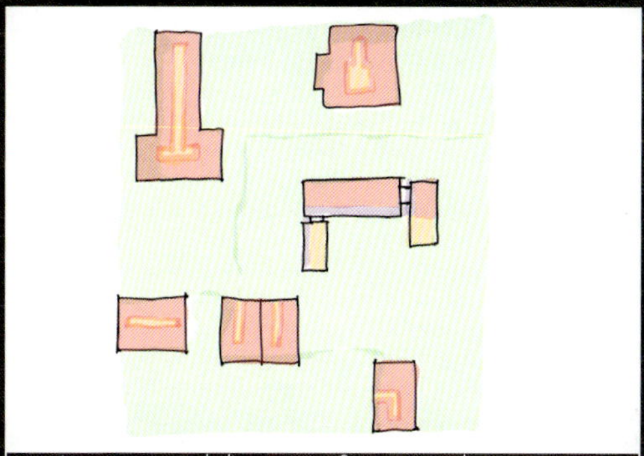

2. Figure-ground diagram of tempered environment

Option 2
Orange spaces are less tempered than red spaces but are more tempered than violet spaces.

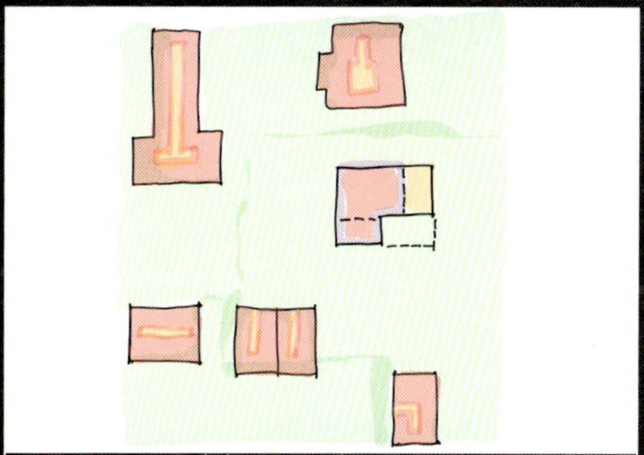

3. Figure-ground diagram of tempered environment

Option 3
Violet spaces are used to surround the more tempered red spaces.

two open park spaces that provide a well-used public amenity. The addition of external space around the building is one that strengthens this local amenity by linking the two adjacent parks visually, so that visitors can look through the open spaces at ground floor level. Views through the building allow the outdoor spaces to be seen together. The volumes of the building are mostly set at an upper level in order to create those views which were closed off by the previous small-scale buildings that inhabited the site. The new gallery forms correspond to the scale of adjacent buildings, but create visual drama as a result of these volumes being partially cantilevered and partly supported on staircases. Each of the three gallery forms has horizontal glazed slots introduced into the top edges of the facades to introduce both daylight and electrical light into the interior spaces.

The juxtaposed forms that comprise the art gallery are given visual refinements in order to make the volumes appear visually lighter; chamfers are introduced at the edges in order to reduce the perception of their mass. The staircase enclosure that provides the prop for the partially cantilevered ends of the galleries are visually disengaged from the building in order to add to the sense of visual lightness while also creating views through the building, from park to park. The visual lightness of the complete composition is achieved by both the separation of the constituent spatial forms and their juxtaposition. Each gallery volume is articulated visually within an overall form to suggest that while the urban forms appear to have been constructed as a single form, they are lightly separated but not separated to the point where each volume might appear to be disengaged from its neighbouring form, which would have made the building appear to be a temporary addition. The articulation of each of the three galleries is countered by a sense of the permanence of linking volumes closely.

The design has a high level of opaque facades, which is unusual in this neighbourhood. The building compensates for its lack of visual openness by creating open spaces at ground floor level that appear to be within the envelope of the building. The propped cantilevered spaces form a continuity with the spaces above.

1. Sectional perspective view

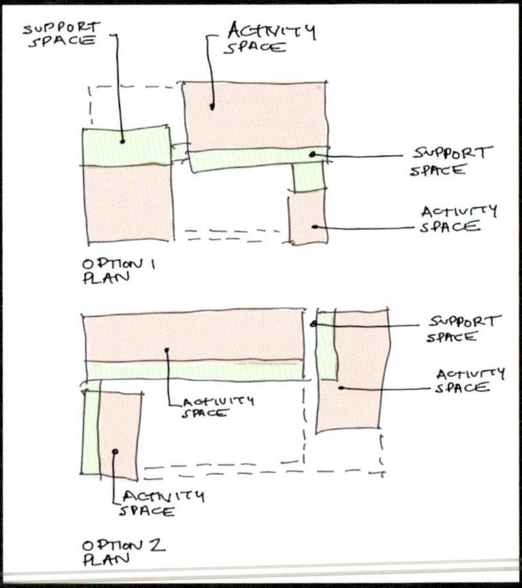

Spatial arrangement
Option 1 provides entry to interior spaces from one of the two stair links which connect the main volumes.
Option 2 positions the circulation route to extend from one end of the building to the other.

2. Sectional perspective view

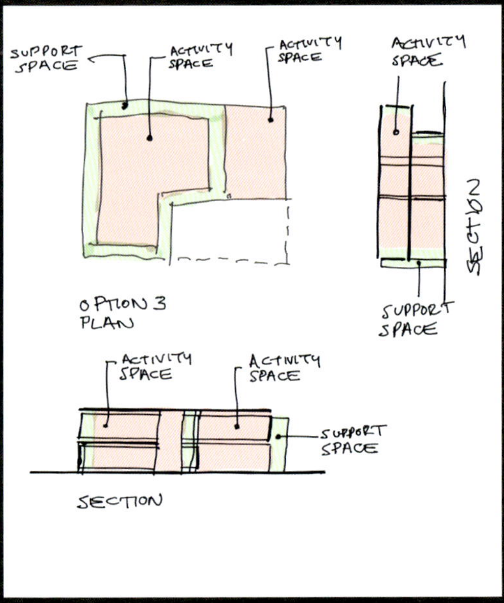

Option 3 provides a circuit-based route.

Spatial arrangement

The general spatial arrangement is to have two propped cantilevered blocks extending out from the main body of the building. Staircase structures provide additional support down to the ground level.

The main frame is formed in reinforced concrete, and accommodates intermediary floors inserted into it. Long slot vents admit daylight and air into the galleries above the ground floor exhibition spaces. The level above that of the roof is an entirely enclosed space with portal frames expanding the full width of the building. There is a spine core going down the centre of the arrangement, adjacent to the cantilever overhangs: the cantilever extends out to the other end of the building where it drops down to the ground to form an enclosure for a stair and lift/elevator. On one of the cantilevered ends the structural supports enclose a storage space for the yard beyond.

Access to the building is through an inclined glazed entrance facade at the first upper level; reached by taking an externally located stair or lift/elevator, in order to enter the building through the glazed opening by way of a bridge which links the stair with the entrance doors. The spatial arrangement of Option 1 is to enter the interior spaces from one of the two stair links which connect the three main volumes at the main entrance. The link between the two larger volumes is used for specific small-scale exhibitions in addition to its role as circulation space. The movement of visitors to the building is arranged as a route around the site. In Option 2, the three volumes are arranged such that the circulation route extends from one end to the building to the other; entering the green circulation space shown in the diagram, between the two larger blocks and circulating down into the smaller exhibition space containing drawings or specific exhibitions at the other end of the building. A route is arranged across the sculpture court where there is an inner exhibition court and an outer court, adjacent to the block near the entrance. Option 3 provides a circuit-based route, such that the spaces are of similar size but are set one on top of the other in order to provide a circuit route from space to space, allowing the sculpture courts to be set beneath the two cantilevered volumes.

Perspective view of interior

2. Perspective view of interior

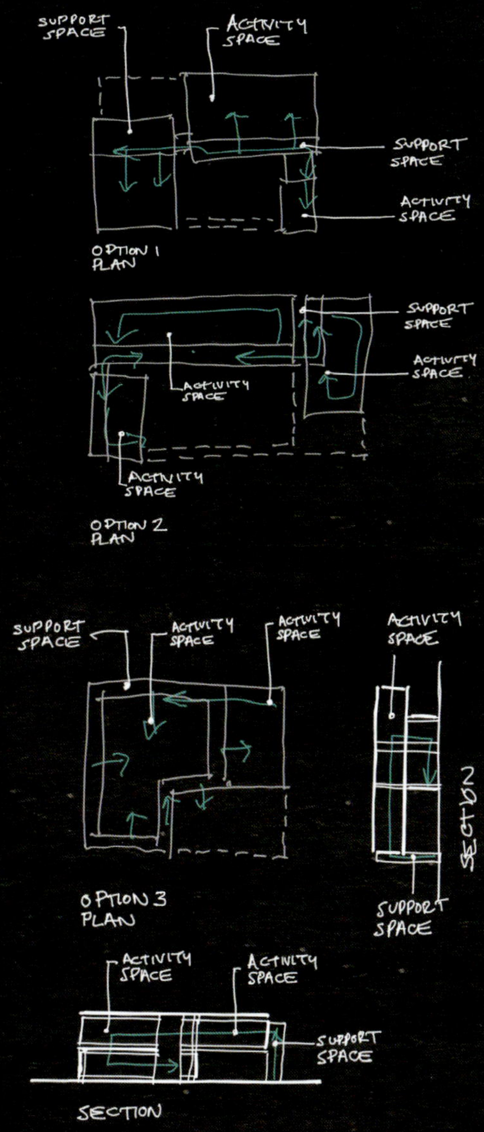

Internal circulation

Option 1 provides entry to the building at the link between the two larger blocks and proceeding along the gallery.

Option 2 reorientates the building volumes such that a circuit is formed by three narrow galleries.

Option 3 superimposes additional elements; a circular route is created inside the building.

Internal circulation

The circulation around the building is complemented by views across the site at ground level which form a triangle of lines of sight through each of the sculpture courts. These 'visual' routes through the site are complemented by the circulation routes both around and within the building.

The internal circulation for Option 1 is based on a circuit; entering the building at the link between the two larger blocks and proceeding along the gallery, into which exhibition spaces are accessed. The circuit-based circulation allows visitors to move around the building in the opposite direction, as well as providing access to secondary spaces for administration, the cloakroom and washrooms. The main gallery space can be entered from the area shown in green in the diagram for Option 1. Visitors can exit this space directly outside to the external sculpture court; re-entering the building by way of the small drawings gallery at one end of the sculpture court. From there a secondary link form takes visitors back into the corridor and into the gallery spaces. The long gallery is also an exhibition space, as shown in green. The entrance space has an adjacent landscaping area outside its more rectangular space which is also useful. The exhibition is an arrangment of sculptures outside. Option 2 takes the externally located sculpture space and provides more space in a single area by reorienting the building volumes such that a circuit is formed by three narrow galleries that provide a prominent view from the entrance; set between the two larger buildings, extending to the end of the gallery through a glazed wall to the sculpture court beyond. From this viewpoint the visitor can turn back around the sculptures towards the main entrance through a second sculpture court. This court links back into the entrance area. Option 3 comprises this same arrangement as Option 2, but superimposes additional elements; a circular route is created inside the building with views out into the external sculpture court. This court can be accessed before entering the building by stepping under the cantilevered areas and walking into the external sculpture court; a form that completes the overall rectangular footprint of the building.

1A. Isometric view of environmental volumes

2A. Isometric view of environmental volumes

1B. Isometric view of environmental volumes

2B. Isometric view of environmental volume

Environmental strategy

The environmental strategy is one of introducing an environmental grid across each of the three blocks. Each environmental grid is independent of its neighbouring grid. Unlike a structural grid, this grid is not required to form a continuity from block to block or from floor to floor. The environmental grid is based on a grid of light; an arrangement of slots for both daylight and electrical light. A key environmental theme is the slots of light introduced into the gallery spaces and small areas of glazing introduced on the facades in circulation areas to provide views down to the sculpture court at ground level.

The ground floor block is side-lit at the top of the space and at one end-office of the block in order that the three constituent parts of the building have a very different experience of daylight within them. All three spaces are designed to have natural ventilation at different times of day which are fan assisted with filtered air drawn across each volume and into the circulation spaces. Staircases and support spaces are ventilated separately.

The lighting within the building is continued outside, with an arrangement of electrical lighting fixtures that are either set into the ground to form strips of light or are supported on posts set 3.0 metres above ground level. Both sources of light illuminate sculptures during hours of darkness; the lighting also serves to indicate paths through the external display areas. The light fittings set at ground level also gently illuminate the underside of the canopy formed by the partially cantileved building forms; this lighting also illuminates the low relief of the facades in areas which do not compete visually with the sculpture display. The slots at high level that introduce daylight and fresh air are also gently illuminated; these light sources replace the need for adjacent street lighting.

The environmental strategy is based on the provision of low-energy heat sources used to control temperature in the concrete-lined spaces, and heated or cooled mechanical ventilation in spaces for circulation and support functions such as administration offices. The concrete box-like forms which cantilever out from the building use a low-speed distribution of air supplied through plenum floors; cooling or heating energy is

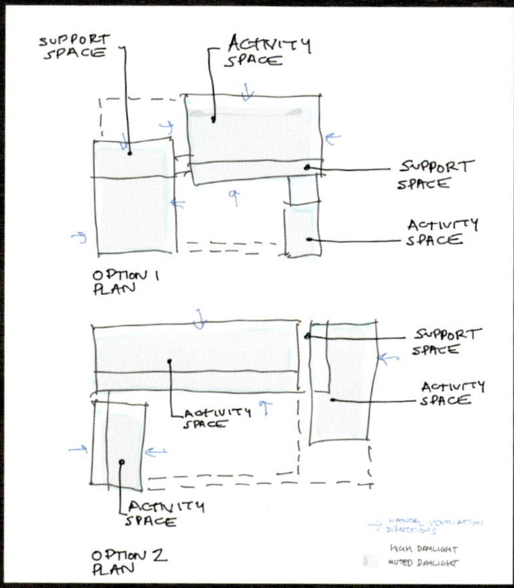

Daylight strategy for direct sunlight and cross ventilation.

Option 1 admits daylight and air at the edges of each space.

Option 2 admits daylight and air in circulation spaces and at the edges of each space.

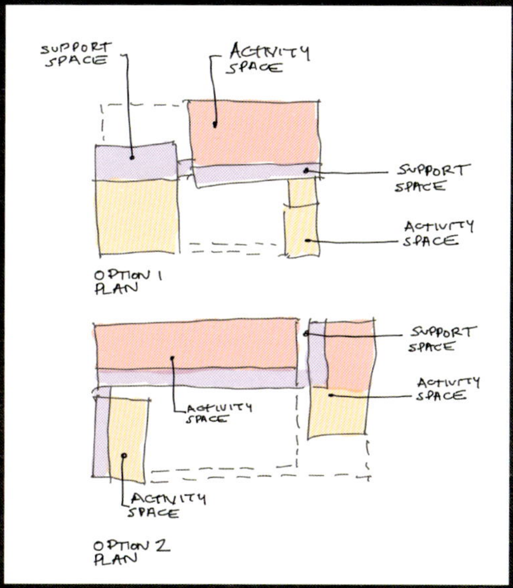

Environmental zones

Option 1 has the circulation spaces and administration spaces within a single environmental zone.

Option 2 uses the violet environmental zones, shown in the diagram, for circulation and as an environmental zone.

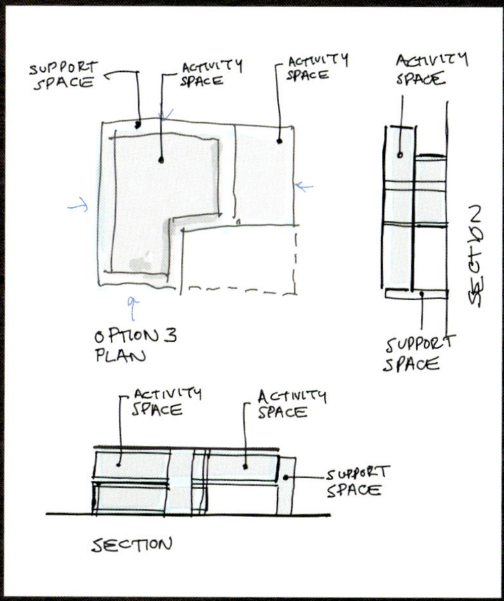

Daylight strategy for direct sunlight and cross ventilation.

Option 3 admits daylight and air in support spaces and at the edges of each space.

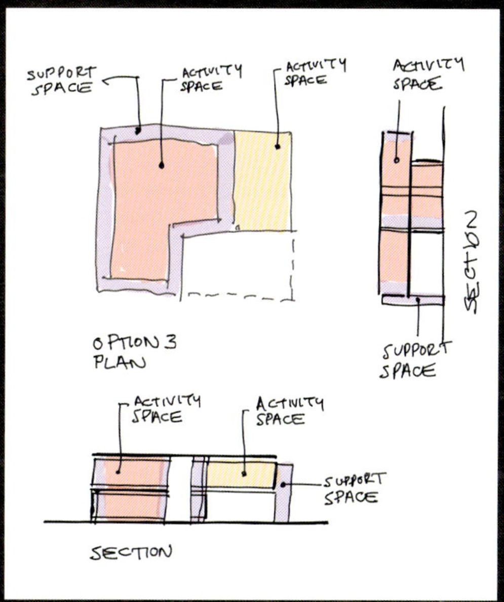

Environmental zones

Option 3 regroups environmental zones from Option 2 and stacks them one above the other.

released from floor grilles. Radiant heat is provided from the floor at the base of the cuboid space.

Heating or cooling energy is delivered to concrete spaces slowly as a result of that energy being absorbed by the structure itself, then released over a 24-hour cycle into the interior spaces. Their thermal mass makes them suitable for night-time cooling at times of year when the air temperature at night is sufficiently cool. Spaces at roof level are mechanically ventilated but also benefit from natural ventilation through the rooflights, where air can enter and leave the space freely.

A key aspect of the environmental design is to create spaces which have stable conditions of temperature and humidity for works of art such as drawings, paintings and sculptures to be exhibited.

The environmental strategy for Option 1 is to have the circulation spaces and administration spaces within a single environmental zone, where they require relatively few air changes per hour. Each large gallery space has its own environmental zone that controls the temperature and humidity of the paintings and sculptures exhibited, some of which are susceptible to moisture movement. External spaces are a key part of the environmental strategy, with shading from the effects of the sun being provided during the day; a key requirement for the display of some sculptures during summer months.

Option 2 uses the violet environmental zones, shown in the diagram, for circulation and as an environmental zone, with the two smaller volumes forming individual zones with their own environmental control systems. The large block has a single environmental control system. The next largest block has a mixed system with a high level of control on one side of the gallery (shown in orange) and an area with a reduced degree of control on the other side of the gallery, with fewer air changes per hour and more temperature fluctuations permitted.

Option 3 regroups those environmental zones from Option 2 and stacks them one above the other. The environmental zone for the circulation route circuit around the building forms part of the volumes adjacent to the facades, creating a thermal buffer zone between the main exhibition spaces and the external walls.

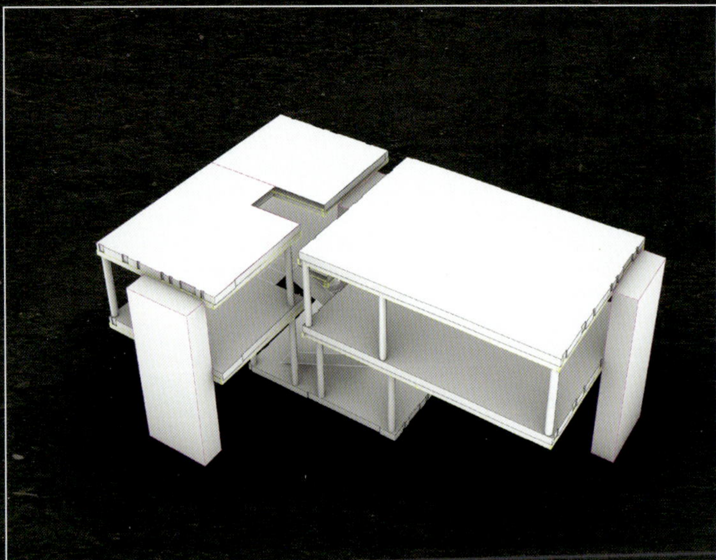

1A. Isometric view of structure

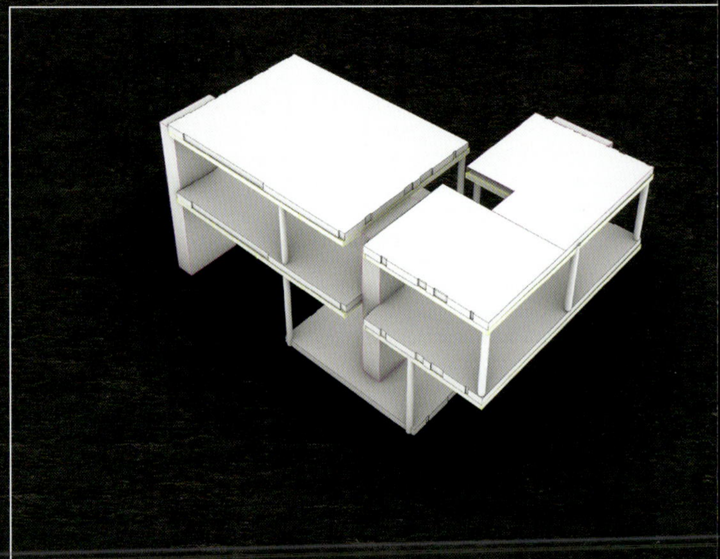

2A. Isometric view of structure

1B. Isometric view of structure

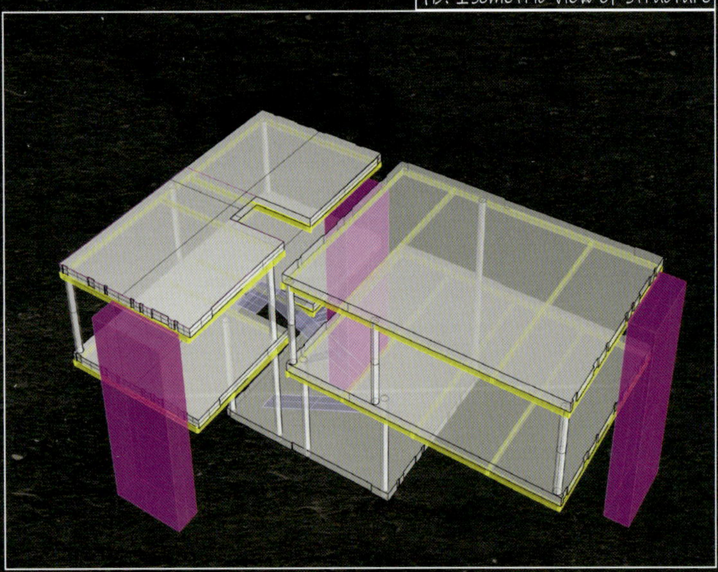

2B. Isometric view of structur

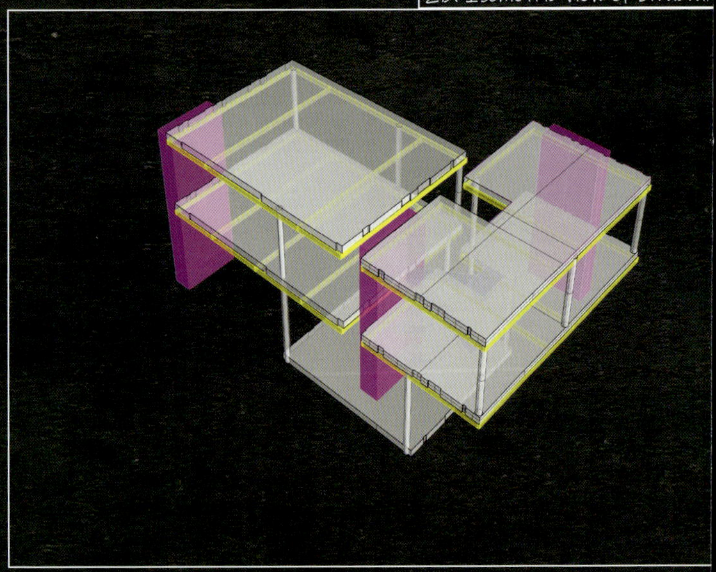

Structural strategy

The structural strategy is based on setting volumes of open gallery space at an upper level which are supported as propped cantilevers. The structure is formed as a reinforced concrete frame, providing a compatible support for large-sized external wall panels. These non-load-bearing concrete-based cladding panels reduce the weight of the structure, allowing the propped cantilever walls to remain economical. The structure forms a set of spaces within the building which are linked, but which create semi-external spaces used for the exhibition of sculptures and which create a visual lightness; the absence of concrete walls and the introduction of propped cantilevers provides views between the two adjacent parks.

As seen from outside the building, the structural frame is not visible as it is concealed behind the facade panels and thermally insulated wall. Seen from inside the building, the internal face of columns and beams of the reinforced concrete frame are visible; the internal face of the external wall is aligned with that of the columns and beams.

Structurally the building comprises a set of reinforced concrete load-bearing boxes and frames; clad externally with GFRC panels in some locations, and with reinforced concrete 'sandwich' walls in other areas. The sandwich walls have their smooth, reinforced concrete finish, exposed externally. The concrete structure is revealed on the inside; the roof structure is also formed in concrete, with a triangular grid on a space frame forming a diamond shape, providing two-way spanning beams with a concrete slab set on top of this grid. The smaller propped cantilevered element is also formed in reinforced concrete, the form of which is revealed on the facade; the structure of that form is revealed on the inside.

Internally, circulation ramps, formed as bridge structures, are set into the upper cantilevered space that sits on top of the consoles. The roof structure is supported by the reinforced concrete box beneath; extending to the edges of the reinforced concrete box. The cantilevered portion of the roof volume is constructed from the same load-bearing system as the other propped-cantilever box-like structures.

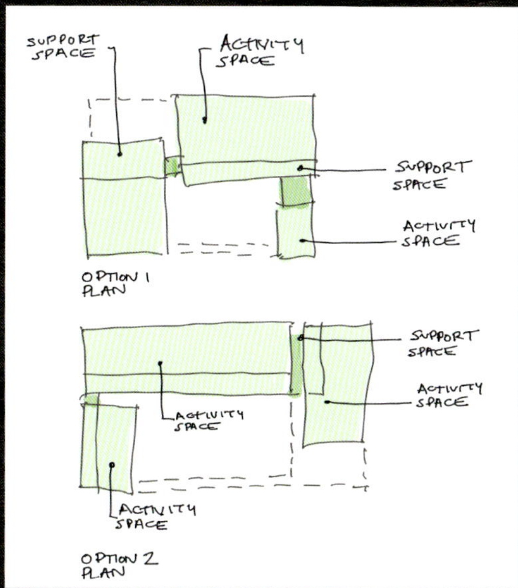

Structural strategy: Zones

Option 1 has a structural grid of beams and columns that creates six bays within each volume.

Option 2 reconfigures Option 1 with larger-scale structural bays.

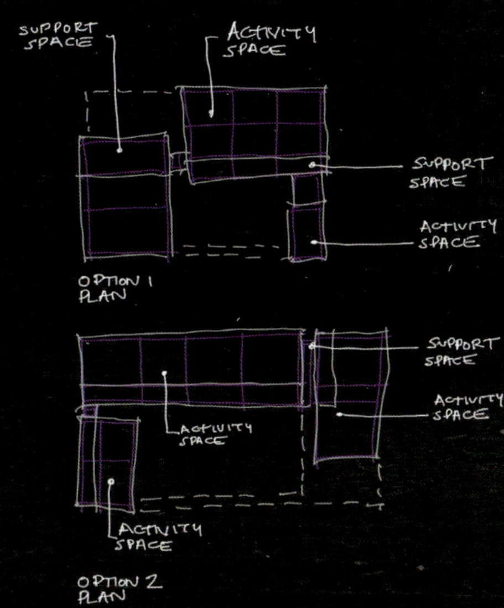

Structural strategy: Framing

Option 1 encloses the core spaces and dividing space into sets of apartments.

Option 2 has the two link blocks, which join the three blocks, as independent structures.

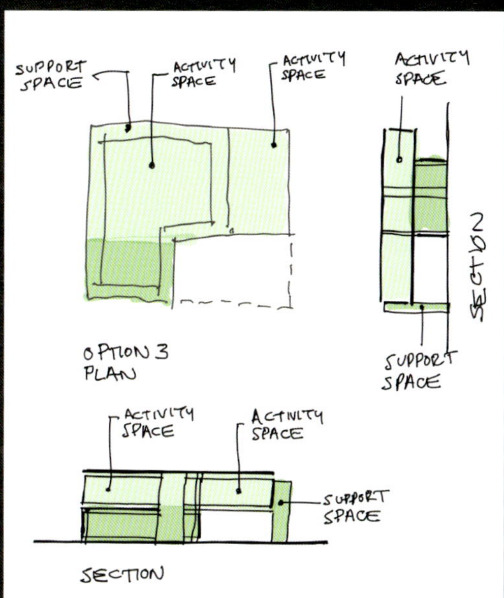

Structural strategy: Zones

Option 3 combines elements of Option 2 by stacking them together and creating a cantilevered upper floor level.

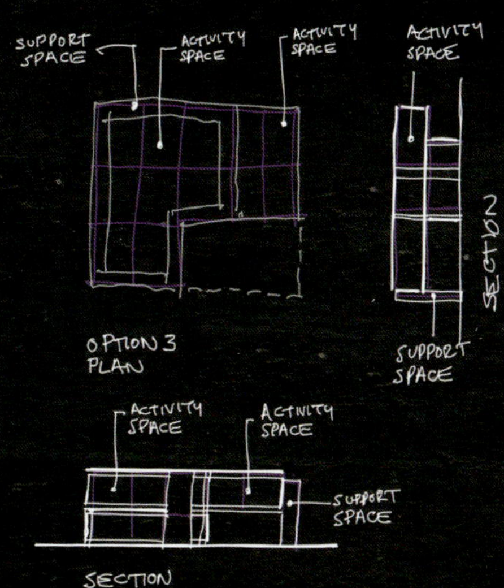

Structural strategy: Zones

Option 3 creates an external space for sculpture exhibitions beneath cantilevers on the ground floor.

The long consoles are made from reinforced concrete; openings incorporate a system of glass captured on four sides, with a large opening for the entrance doors. Visitors walk up the stairs into the mezzanine space that overlooks the main cuboid space; they are greeted at this level and then carry on up the steps to the cloakrooms at the top level. From there, the journey down the ramp within the space begins; down towards the double-height volume at ground floor level that projects out from the main body of the building. This ground floor space is constructed as a reinforced concrete frame with a non-loadbearing facade of GFRC panels. Daylight, both direct and reflected, is admitted through horizontally slotted openings in the reinforced concrete walls.

The structural strategy for Option 1 is of a structural grid of beams and columns that creates six bays within the larger volume, and six bays within smaller volume; the third volume being a box-like form without columns needed to support the roof slab. The two link buildings are independent structures which separate the three main blocks; each is a separate structure. This approach allows for the link buildings to be created as external forms in their own right, such that the two links and the three gallery blocks are articulated as urban forms; a set of smaller elements over a single storey with a tall gallery space inside each.

Option 2 reconfigures that form and has larger-scale structural bays to create two structural bays in the smaller volume, four structural bays in the larger volume and a single bay for the smallest of the three volumes. Again, the two link blocks, which join the three blocks, are independent structures, providing a set of five structures of both large scale and small scale.

Option 3 combines these elements by stacking them together and creating a cantilevered upper floor level which is supported on props, creating an external space for sculpture exhibitions on the ground floor; spaces which are sheltered from the worst effects of the sun and rain. Both cantilevered volumes are supported on structures enclosing staircases. All three options are envisaged to be formed in reinforced concrete in order for parts of the construction to be made visible; other parts are clad in GFRC, enclosing the building with a single material.

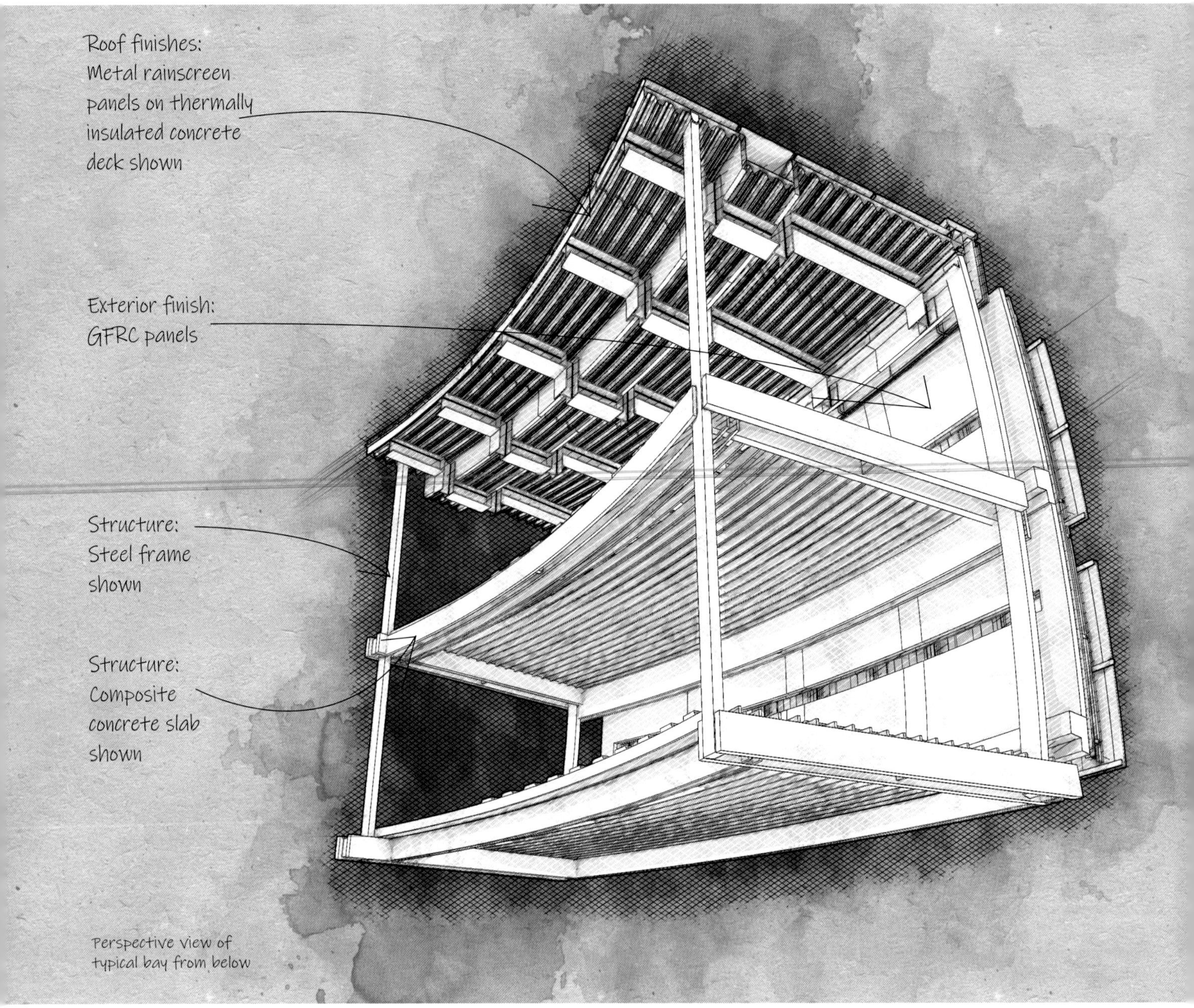

Perspective view of typical bay from below

Typical bay adjacent to facade

The external envelope of the building is formed as GFRC (glass fibre reinforced concrete) wall panels providing a visual continuity with the structural frame, which is formed as a reinforced concrete frame. The visible soffit (underside) of propped cantilevered forms has metal rainscreen panels in order to provide a visual contrast with the GFRC panels; these soffit panels reflect a softened light back to the sculptures beneath from the ground-level light sources. The soffit of each cantilevered form is a thermally insulated part of the external envelope which forms part of the canopies for the ground floor sculpture court.

The GFRC wall panels create low relief facades that visually 'map' the activities that taking place beyond; indicating the positions of staircases, ramps and the floor plates within the building. The facades have opaque glass strips introduced to illuminate the spaces with both daylight and electrical lighting. During hours of darkness the electrical lighting within these slots illuminates the sculpture garden below. The three constituent gallery blocks are formed in exposed reinforced concrete while the two service stare blocks are enclosed in metal cladding. Structurally, the staircase enclosures are formed as reinforced concrete walls which support the adjacent gallery structure. Thermal insulation is provided internally. The inner walls are formed in dry lining in order to provide a background wall that suits the different requirements of picture hanging in successive exhibitions; these interior walls follow the geometry of the outer concrete walls with their low-relief textured facades.

The external envelope as a typical bay comprises horizontal slots into the facades, using the visual language of window openings; these slots are actually opaque; drawing the eye up to the top of the building as people pass by and as they look up at the characteristic forms of the building. These slots are also not glazed, but instead introduce controlled levels of daylight into gallery spaces. The slots also introduce fresh air from outside into internal spac-es. Air is filtered before it enters the gallery spaces in order to provide a system bringing natural and mechanically ventilated air in a mixed-mode system. Light fittings

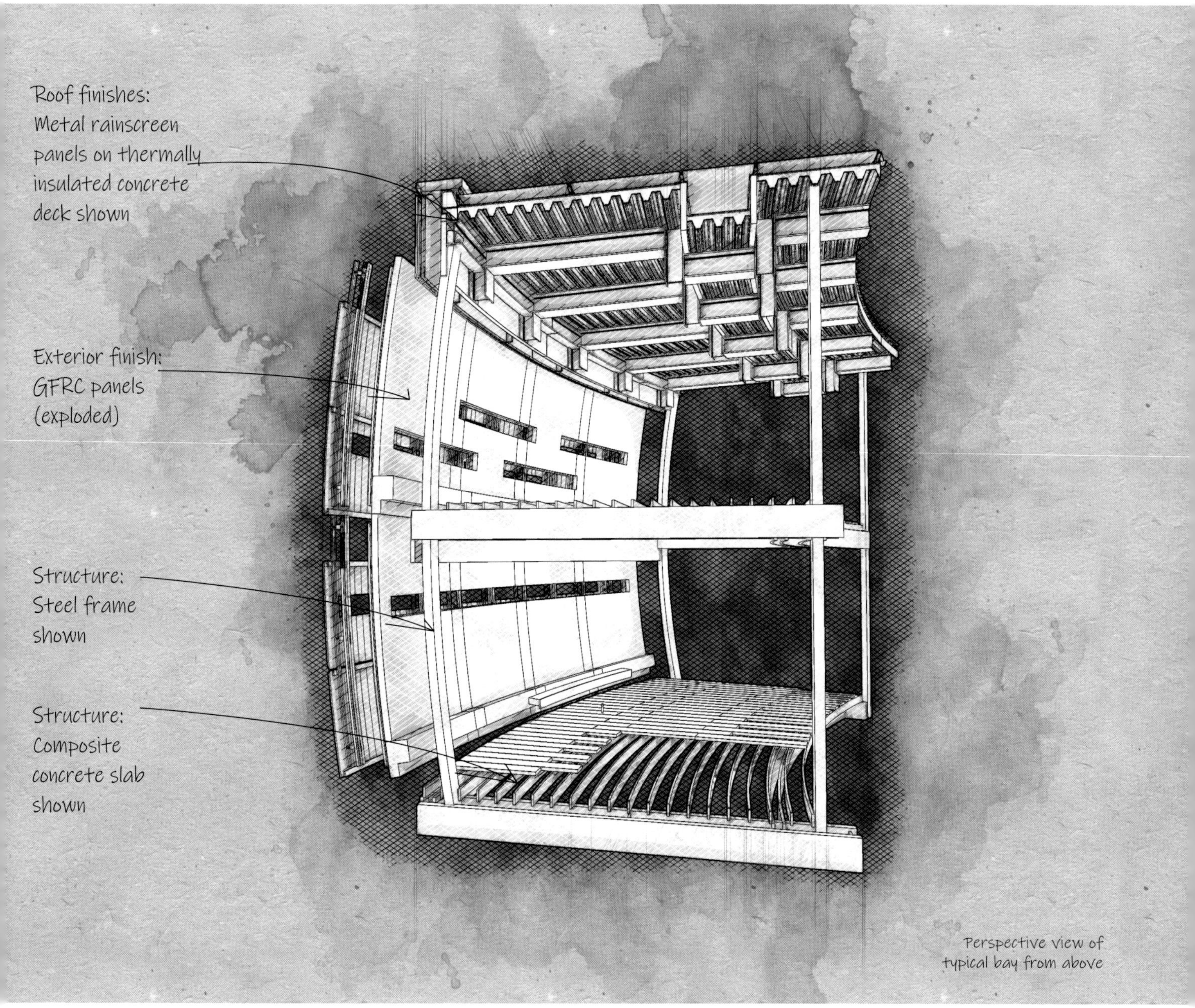

Perspective view of typical bay from above

are positioned externally, with thin glazed slots that admit daylight on the top edge of these openings. Electrical lighting is set outside the building, within these horizontal slots, in order to provide light during hours of darkness. This approach of providing internal lighting from the outside avoids the need for light fittings being visible inside the building. The glazed slots introduce light from outside by reflecting it from the ceilings rather than admitting light directly. A set of light baffles are positioned on the bottom edge of these slots in the facades in order to direct light inward from the top of each space to create the sense of an illuminated ceiling.

The external envelope aims to strike a balance between the appearance of a permanent building which fills the corner formed by the shape of the site – while fitting into its wider cityscape – and a dynamic form which suggests movement within the building and a range of internal spaces which are linked, but which provide gallery experiences of natural lighting which are different from one another. Ceilings in all galleries are formed as a visual grid of the reinforced concrete frame that forms part of the primary structure. Like the walls, the ceilings expose the inner face of the reinforced concrete beams which provide the supporting structure. Infill panels are set between the beams; these panels are set flush with the internal face of the beams, following the arrangement used on wall panels. Both electrical lighting and daylight are admitted into spaces through slots at the edges of the ceiling; light is projected across the ceilings, which have rooflights set above the internal circulation routes only.

The long strip glazing around the two cantilevered volumes is inclined and then returns back to the building. The facades comprise a mixture of reinforced concrete panels on their inside face and GFRC panels on their external face; external panels are fixed in rainscreen configuration. Floor-to-ceiling glazing which appears to be frameless is complemented by diagonally oriented pop-out slots, configured as horizontal strip windows at high level. The lift shaft is set externally, with the bridge connecting to the main building being constructed from reinforced concrete. The lift shaft is clad in steel-framed glazing.

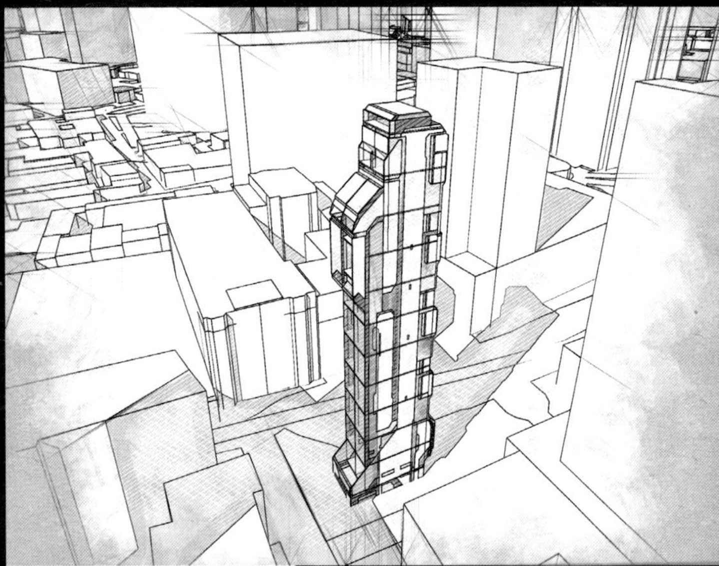

1. Perspective view of exterior

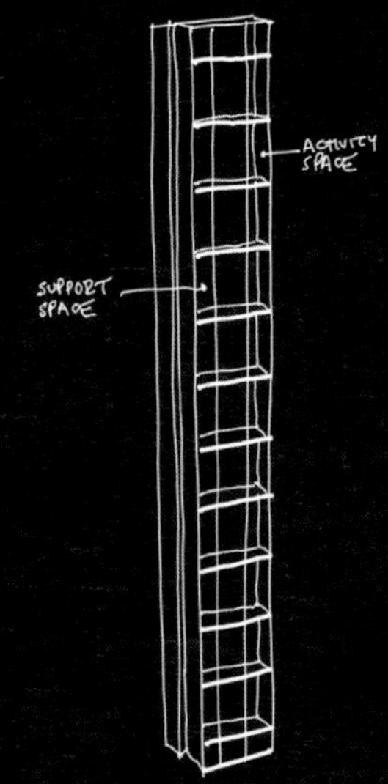

2. Perspective view of exterior

Daylight and ventilation in mini-towers

A primary benefit of using a mini-tower configuration is the ability to introduce daylight and natural ventilation into a building form which is small enough to have rooms with external views and a central circulation space; these spaces provide opportunities for fresh air and natural daylight. As a result, a primary advantage of the mini-tower is the potential for electrical lighting not to be required during daylight hours, as well as the ability to provide ventilation across the width of rooms. Kitchens and bathrooms also have the potential to be naturally ventilated through external walls, with the benefit of reducing their dependence on mechanical ventilation, allowing spaces to benefit from exposed soffits and floors. A key advantage of a mini-tower over a lower-level block, with light wells formed as external voids in the centre of the building, is being able to have clear views out of the building and not into neighbouring apartments. This building draws dwellings together around common support spaces; the more generous distance between mini-towers avoids views from one apartment into another as a result of their close proximity; views out to neighbouring buildings being more distant. The main advantages are being able to have natural cross ventilation and high levels of daylight in all spaces, which provided as a result of external walls having views out beyond the site. Blocks of dwellings which are either closely arranged with a lightwell or which face an internal garden space have a high land take and suit larger-scale projects. An individual project of modest scale on a relatively small plot of land can be configured as a mini-tower form in order to provide greater levels of daylight and natural ventilation, without the need for mechanical ventilation or additional solar shading. In some cases, the mini-tower configuration can avoid the need for floor-to-ceiling glazing which is sometimes used to introduce higher levels of daylight into spaces where a window is provided on one wall only, and where internal spaces can become too brightly daylit and have little privacy for residents. The mini-tower also means that winter gardens can be introduced as transition spaces between inside and outside in specific parts of the building, or can be omitted as the spaces themselves have

Perspective view of exterior

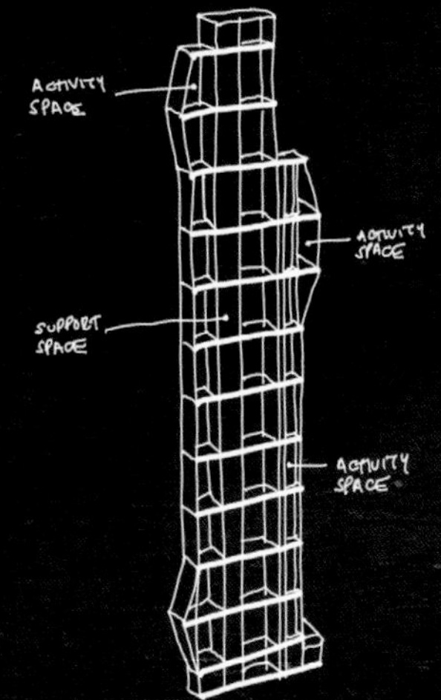

4. Perspective view of exterior

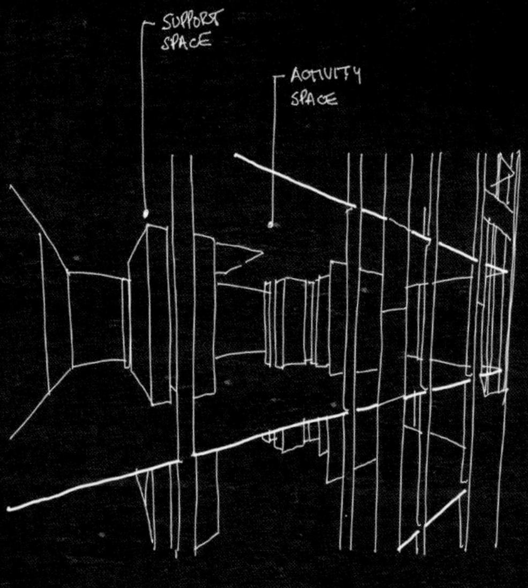

sufficient privacy at higher level to to avoid the need for a winter garden. There is a transition space from outside to inside that provides a level of semi-private space and some visual privacy from those looking into the building which can reduce daylight level significantly in the habitable spaces behind. This project uses the mini-tower concept for relatively small apartments, apartment sizes which have tall spaces of regular size where light is admitted into airy, light spaces. The apartments are arranged as duplexes with a large double height space at the front end, a single height space above the upper level with a connecting staircase within each of the two storey apartments.

The mini-tower has two forms of natural ventilation and daylight control. On one elevation there is floor-to-ceiling glass which is sealed and in which ventilation is introduced from the sides of the building through the opaque facades. This side of the building is north facing and has no solar protection. The opposite facade has solar control glass for early morning and late afternoon/evening sun. The south facade has fixed glazing; natural ventilation is provided by slots set into the sides of the glazed opening; the slots ensure that air enters from the sides rather than directly into the space, avoiding wind gusts into rooms. Slot windows in recesses are used on both glazed sides of the mini-tower. Solar shading is set on both the north and south facades. The south facade has horizontal shading set at the top of the windows. The north elevation has baffles at the sides which are formed by the returns to the windows themselves; made integral with the natural ventilation slots at the sides of the windows. These vents are formed in opaque glazing. There are no vertical projecting centre shading elements on the north facade, as this role is fulfilled by the shading set at the side of the window to create the effect of providing effective shading up to the interface of the baffles. The north and south facades have additional shading internally which unrolls from ceiling level in order to provide the reduction of glare on those glazed facades. The solar control, which is provided by the glass, has varying levels of transparency from 50% to 75% in order to provide views out from the building that are as clear as possible.

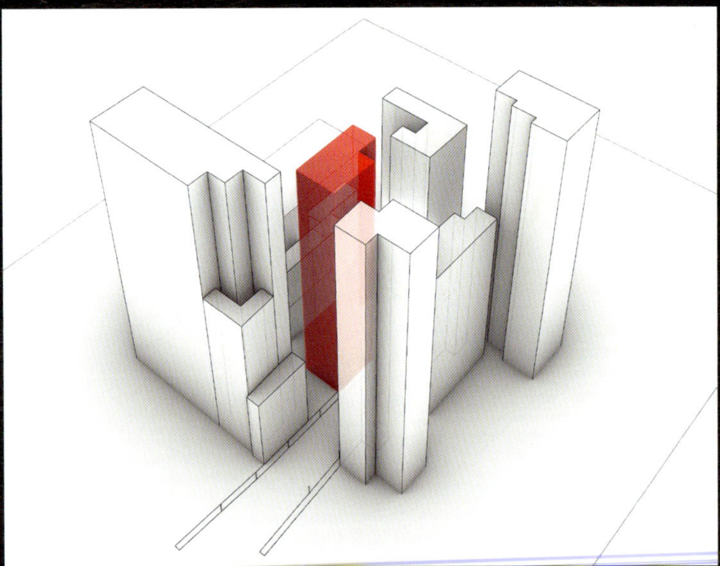

1. Project volume in site context

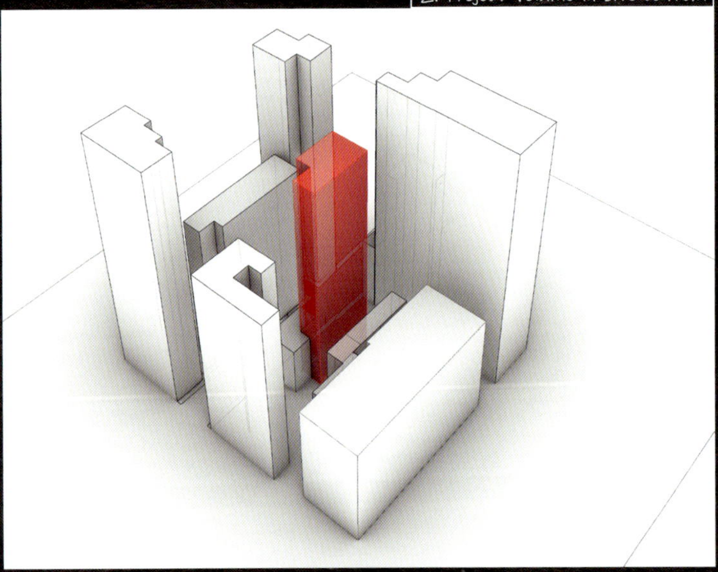

2. Project volume in site context

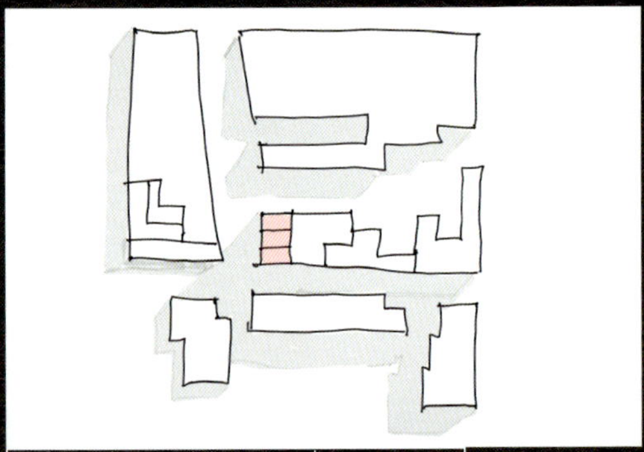

1. Site plan with surrounding context

Option 1 has two floors of duplex apartments arranged immediately above the podium level.

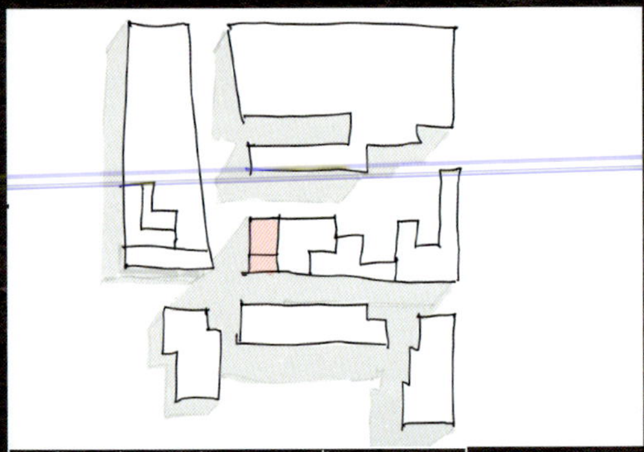

2. Site plan with surrounding context

Option 2 has the top two floors differentiated from Option 1 by the external form of the building.

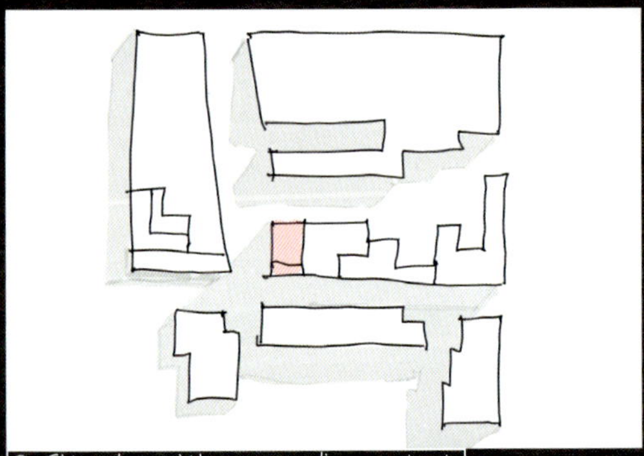

3. Site plan with surrounding context

Option 3 integrates smaller apartments at the lower level and larger-sized apartments at upper levels.

Site context

This project is for a residential building. The site context is an urban environment with a mixture of residential buildings and office buildings. The mini-tower sits at an intermediate height between neighbouring tall office buildings and four-storey commercial buildings. This building softens the edge between the two sets of building types of tall tower and regular urban blocks, creating a transition between those two scales of urban block: a transition brought about by the size of the new building, the scale of facade panels and the size of spaces within the building. The form of the building at street level is in keeping with that of surrounding buildings; this building does not have a podium in the interest of contributing to the existing streetscape. A ground-floor-level cafe and restaurant are provided for those working in buildings nearby, adding to the life of the street by installing an amenity that adds new vibrancy to it.

Natural ventilation is provided through the side facades where metal panels project forward of the main areas of an external wall. These metal panels are covers for the air-handling ducts that pass through the height of the building. The vertical joints in the panels admit fresh air from outside into each apartment through vertically-formed ventilation slots on each side wall in order to encourage cross ventilation. The vertical slots are arranged on each side of the building in order to benefit from the prevailing wind and shelter from that wind. The building management system operates the baffles as set by the occupier of the apartment. This system functions independently for each apartment.

A key characteristic of the environmental control of this mini-tower is the acoustic conditions that are experienced in urban conditions, generated at street level; a key part of the site context. For this reason, two different acoustic attenuations are provided; two sides are largely opaque and acoustically controlled. The two end facades are glazed; one facade has sliding doors with an acoustic barrier created by the Juliet balcony immediately in front of the glazed door. The other side has sealed glazing with acoustic attenuation provided by the glass. Acoustic control is provided by natural ventilation slots that can be

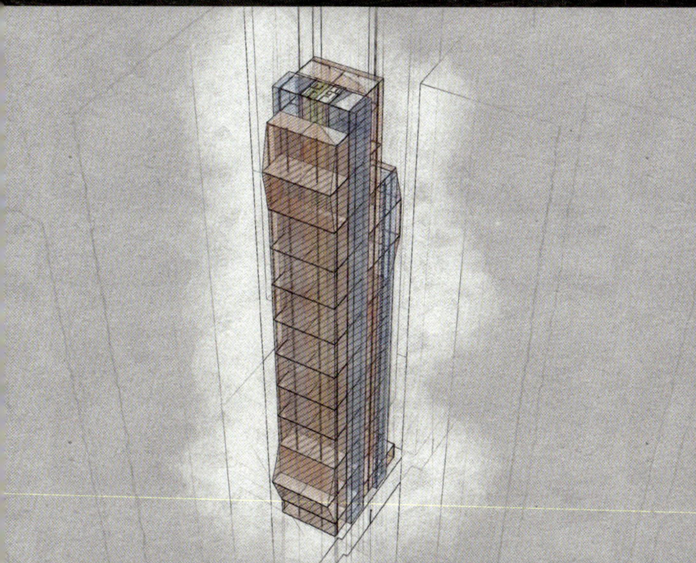

Perspective view of environmental volumes

2. Perspective view of environmental volumes

1. Figure-ground diagram of tempered environment

Option 1
Red spaces are more highly tempered than orange spaces.

2. Figure-ground diagram of tempered environment

Option 2
Orange spaces are more highly tempered than internal green spaces.

3. Figure-ground diagram of tempered environment

Option 3
Orange spaces are more highly tempered than blue spaces.

opened in the side elevations, introducing fresh air; the noise level in each room, on each side of the mini-tower, is controlled and experienced in different ways.

The facades on the building follow the types used in neighbouring buildings: full-height glazed panels and windows with Juliet balconies. Unlike nearby buildings, the windows are full width horizontally, with opaque panels providing the Juliet balcony; glazed facades have narrow bands of glazing arranged as large-scale bays which are framed with metal trim. The winter gardens have curved glass edges in order to contrast with the rectilinear geometry of the general composition of the tower; a larger-scale element in a similar language to the smaller panels added to the sides of the building. The building takes the visual language of both the neighbouring towers and four-storey residential and commercial blocks; combining them with a language of energy reduction and an openness of interior space; the building is arranged as a diagram of how it is serviced both mechanically and naturally, to create large rectilinear interiors.

The site context for Option 1 is one of a series of tall buildings in a mixed neighbourhood of office buildings and residential buildings. The urban context is one of an encouragement by city authorities to introduce more tall-building housing projects to replace low-rise buildings that are no longer in use and which offer little value to the community. Option 1 is a straightforward rectilinear block with a flat roofscape; a central core with apartments arranged around it. Two floors of duplex apartments are arranged immediately above the podium level. Option 2 has a similar-shaped building; the top two floors are differentiated from Option 1 by the external form of the building. Two-storey duplex apartments are set on the top two floors of a tower of the same height as Option 1. Option 3 integrates smaller apartments at the lower level and larger-sized apartments at upper levels; introducing four floors of duplex apartments at the top of the building without increasing its height over that of Options 1 and 2. A projecting three-storey bay is set on the glazed elevation at upper levels in order to introduce sky gardens to the project; the projecting form remains within the site boundary.

Project 10. Residential tower

Spatial arrangement and internal circulation

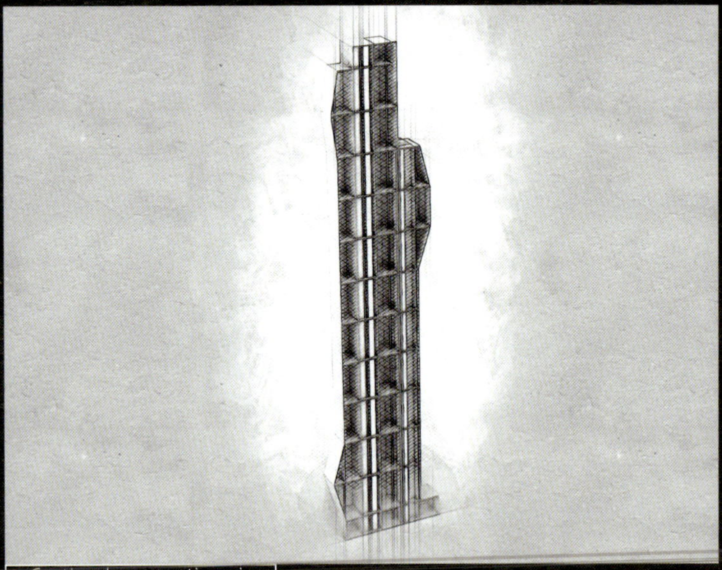

1. Sectional perspective view

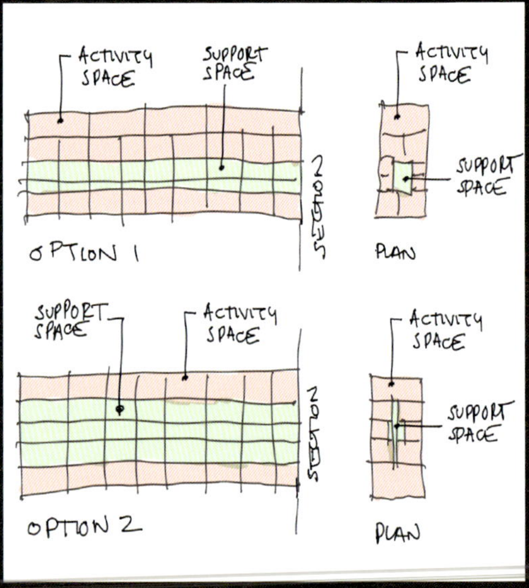

Spatial arrangement Option 1 has apartments arranged around a central core. Option 2 has a mixture of a core for support space in the centre and a corridor extending out to the apartments arranged at the ends.

2. Sectional perspective view

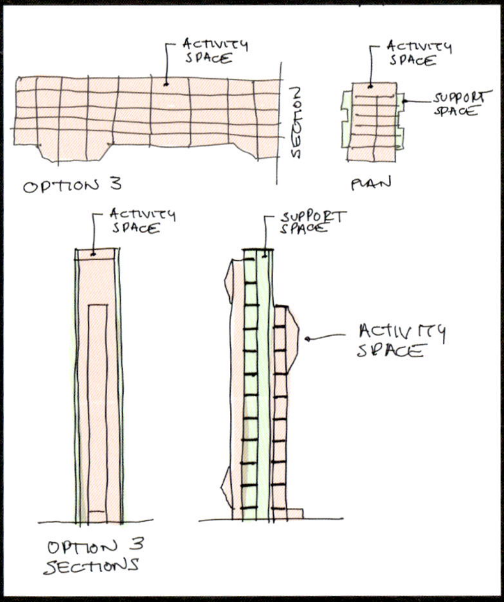

Option 3 has apartments arranged such that their access is by way of an entry block.

Spatial arrangement

This project is designed with a set of service-based 'backpacks' which are attached to the main form of the building. The backpacks contain mechanical and electrical services equipment including air-handling ducts and plumbing. This 'mini-tower' is arranged as a rectilinear form with the backpacks fixed on the sides of the building. A podium form provides an area for both the entrance and related communal facilities for residents. There is no provision for car parking, as this residence is well serviced by public transport and ride-share services.

The spatial arrangement of apartments in Option 1 is to have apartments arranged around a central core resulting in eight apartments of different sizes, with up to 10 apartments per floor. Option 2 is a mixture of a core for support space in the centre and a corridor extending out to the apartments arranged at the ends, in order to provide more flexibility in the size of the apartments. Option 3 has apartments arranged such that their access is by way of an entry block set at the base of the glazed facade. The spatial arrangement of this project is the same for all three options, which is based on a building form that has apartments on each floor with varying approaches to the internal circulation accordingly. The design has a different approach in three options for environmental controls such that provisions for internal circulation and mechanical and electrical services are grouped together as support space which is provided on both the outside and inside faces of the opaque facades, or alternatively a mixture of the two. The preferred option is to locate the service spaces on the outside with a vertically oriented provision of electrical and plumbing services enclosed in those outer wall zones. Stairs and lifts/elevators that serve each floor are arranged on the edges of the floor plates. Natural ventilation is provided in both directions along the length of the building as well as across the width of the building into habitable spaces. The resulting environmental grids are set vertically on side elevations of the building to create the characteristic arrangement of service equipment; the structural grid is linked to the environmental grid. Internal spaces are connected to benefit from the cross ventilation generated from this principle.

Perspective view of interior

2. Perspective view of interior

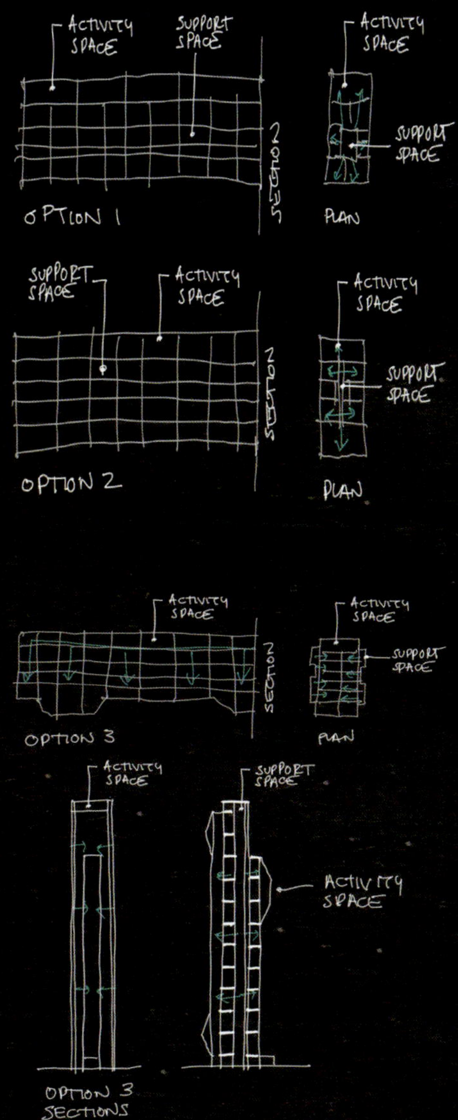

Internal circulation

Option 1 is accessed directly from a central core into apartments.

Option 2 has longer corridors and smaller cores in the centre than Option 1.

Option 3 has two separate cores providing access directly to the front doors of apartments.

Internal circulation

Apartment spaces within the towers are distributed both vertically and horizontally, with a set of 'backpack' service spines that are set onto the opaque facades on each side of the building. Vertical service cores of stairs and lifts/elevators are arranged in the centre of the building, with the service cores being arranged on the sides of the building instead of forming an integral part of the central core. This approach allows the central core to be smaller than would be the case with a combined core of services, stairs and lifts/elevators. Both core positions allow all apartments to be accessed without the need for a long corridor. A sky garden is located in the upper part of the building which is accessed from each apartment it faces. The different amounts of daylight required to be admitted to each part of the facade is controlled by an area of vertically striped glazing with narrow horizontal slot windows.

The internal circulation of Option 1 is accessed directly from a central core into apartments. Option 2 has longer corridors and smaller cores in the centre, which provides a greater reach of the access corridor into the two apartments. The internal circulation for Option 3 is to have two separate cores providing access directly to the front doors of apartments from a service area and circulation area attached to the sides of the building, such that there are two access cores and two completely separate circulation routes – both attached to each side of the building – in order to give completely clear floor plates. Circulation within apartments is based on being able to have doors opened that allow natural ventilation to function through the depth of the apartment if required. Alternatively, doors can be closed in order to provide limited natural ventilation within each room; internal circulation corresponds to paths of natural ventilation. The advantage of Option 3 is that access to the apartments is from the sides of the building and not the centre. The sides of the building provide a zone for the distribution of ducts and services through the depth of the floor decks that provides access to both apartments and service areas. The ends of these decks have glazed walls, avoiding the need for electrical lighting during the day.

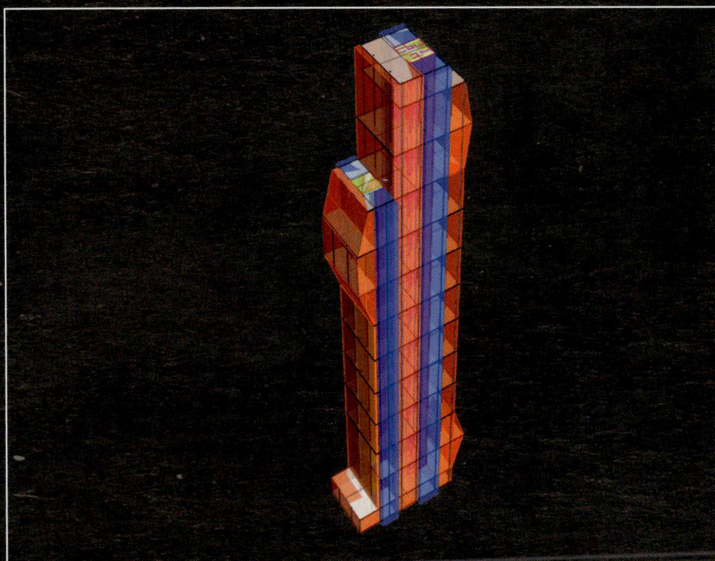

1A. Isometric view of environmental volumes

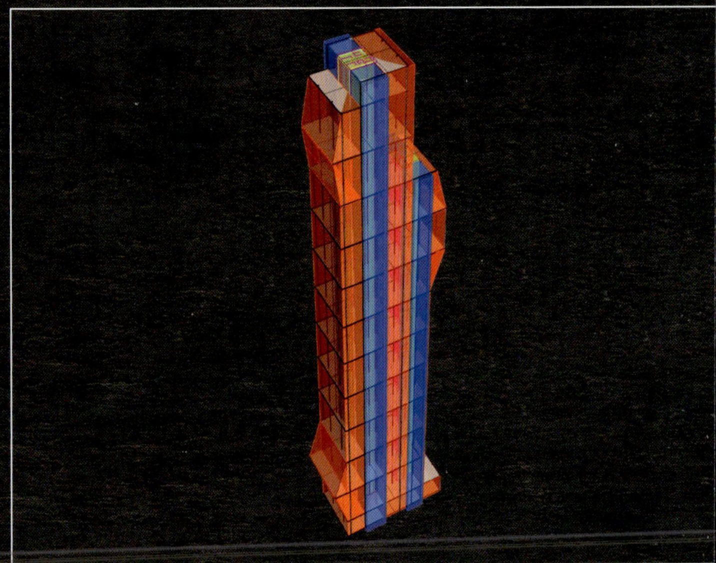

2A. Isometric view of environmental volumes

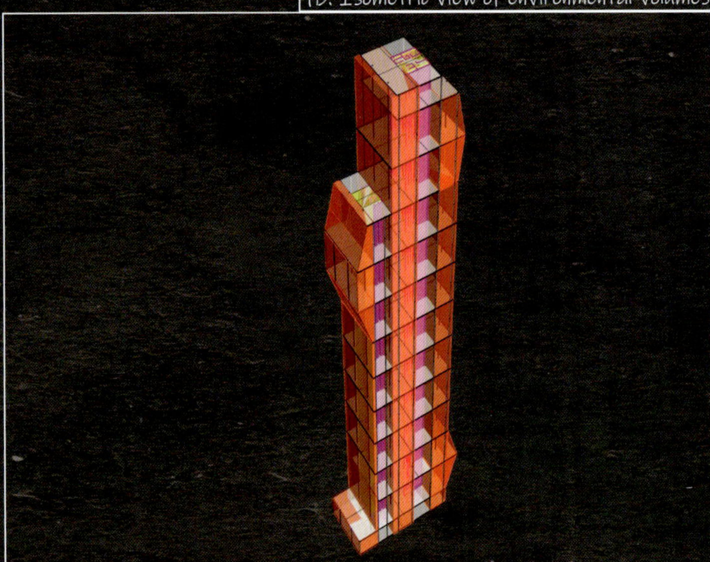

1B. Isometric view of environmental volumes

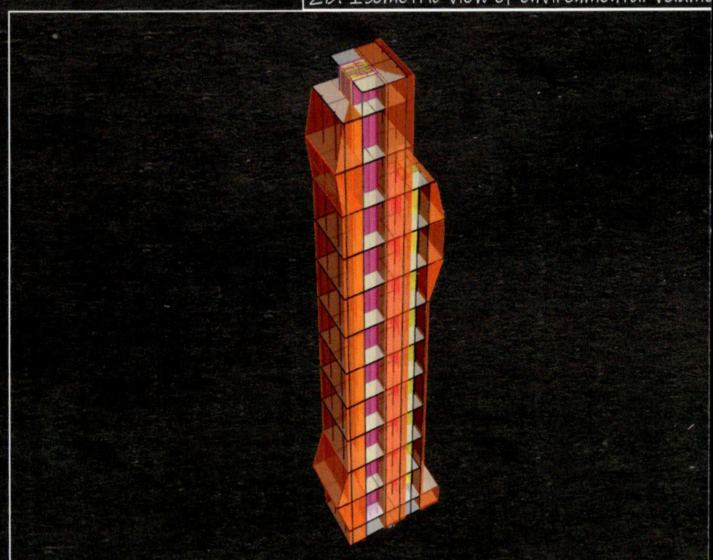

2B. Isometric view of environmental volume

Environmental strategy

The brief/program requires every habitable space to have a dual function; either as a living space or as a bedroom space. As a result, the services equipment is integrated into packed units fixed to the external walls.

The environmental strategy for Option 1 is to consider the apartments as being a single entity to be serviced equally in all spaces within the apartment. This aim is achieved with ducted air and services arriving externally from the 'backpacks' in the side walls. Electrical power is distributed internally through the vertical riser for stairs and lifts/elevators. Option 2 has a similar arrangement of apartments with stairs and lifts/elevators set in the centre of the building. Option 3 uses cores which are designed to meet the specific thermal loads in the apartments they serve; solar gain and temperature variations from direct sunlight are the primary loads.

The environmental strategy is based on creating an environmental grid of vertical service runs and horizontal floor slabs that create the characteristic grid of the three options, which range from arranging services at the edges of the side elevations to having them in the centre as well as having them in a mixed arrangement. Ducts are required to deviate from an all vertical directions in order to respond to the spatial requirements within each group of apartments, as seen on the characteristic facades.

These differences in floors are made visible; there is no concealment of the environmental functions within these surface zones, but the equipment is not revealed on the outside. The equipment is concealed and protected behind external panels which are accessible from the support spaces. Each environmental zone is accessible from the inside face of that wall in order for ducts, pipes and services to be inspected and maintained. Similarly, the staircases are set within the zone behind the external panels. The routes of these staircases vary in different parts of the tower, as revealed by the opaque panelling on the outside of the building. The service areas are wrapped and consequently revealed on the outside of the building, in the interests of economy and

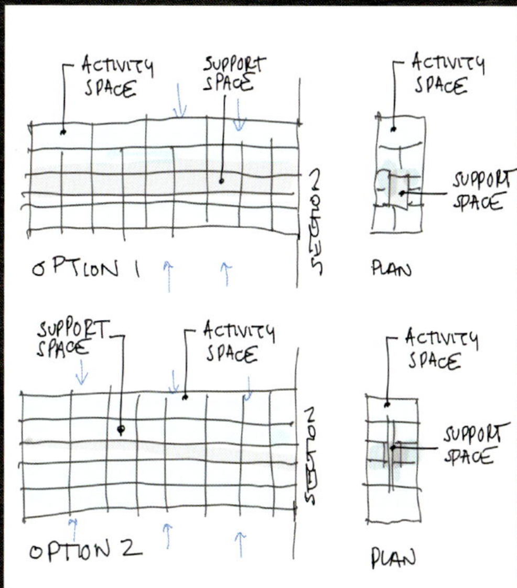

Daylight strategy for direct sunlight and cross ventilation.

Option 1 has reduced daylight and air in the central core.

Option 2 has reduced daylight and air in the circulation and support spaces.

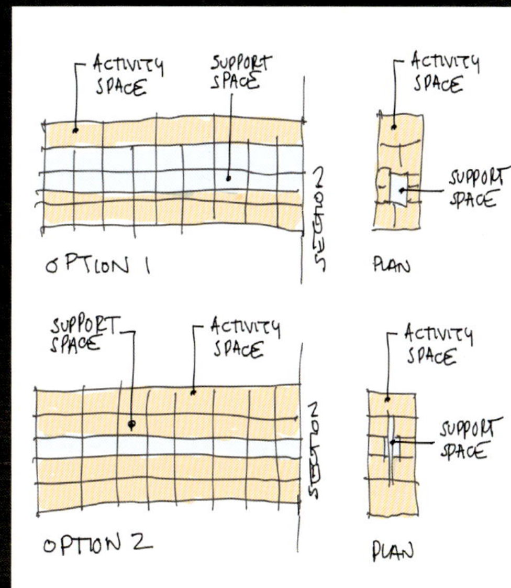

Environmental zones

Option 1 arranges the building as two blocks separated by a service void.

Option 2 has a similar arrangement of apartments to Option 1 with stairs and lifts/elevators set in the centre of the building.

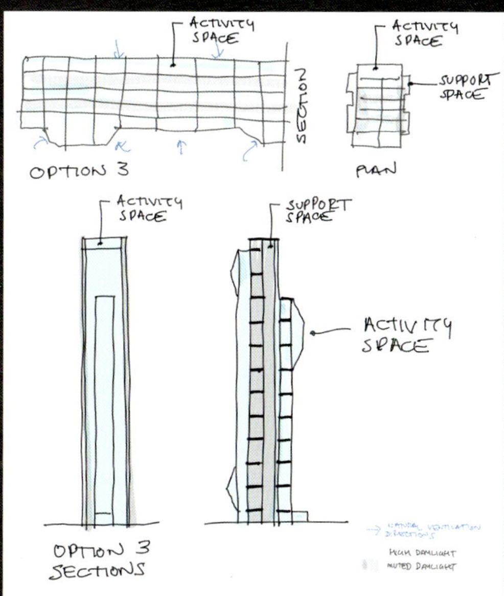

Daylight strategy for direct sunlight and cross ventilation.

Option 3 has reduced daylight and air in the circulation and side support spaces.

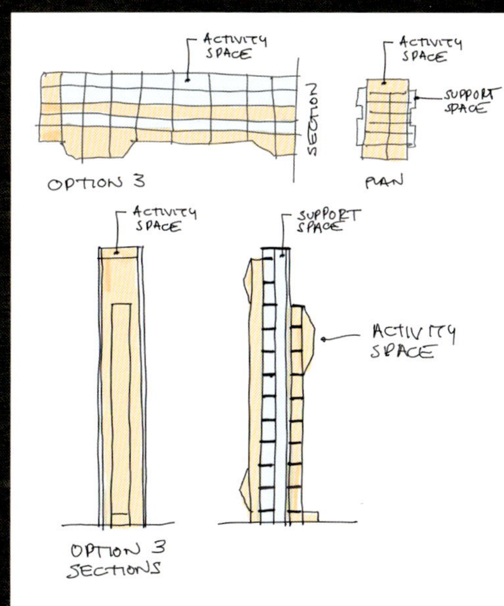

Environmental zones

Option 3 uses cores which are designed to meet the specific thermal loads in the apartments they serve.

clarity of spatial arrangement of these service areas. The structural wall is set on the inside face of the environmental zone which in each case is created on the outside of the building such that the environmental zones comprise an outer wall, an inner zone of services, staircases and a structural concrete wall which divides those service spaces from the apartments within.

The environmental strategy is based on having the same ventilation strategy for mechanical ventilation and natural ventilation, in that air is diffused from the same outlets, moving both across and down the length of the apartments. Air is introduced in the same way at the ends of each room, with natural ventilation occurring across the apartments, as well as down the length of the apartments. These routes are aligned with the internal lighting where light from hidden sources, preferred over recessed fittings, washes light across the ceilings of the apartment in an arrangement which follows the movement of air. This part of the environmental design creates accentuated lighting across the width of each of the rooms front and back and the depth of the apartment from front to back.

The solar shading on the south elevation is horizontal to exclude or control the effects of the sun, but there is still the opportunity to have shadows from the sun cast as geometric patterns on the floors.

The side walls are opaque, providing high levels of thermal insulation as well as inlet positions for both natural and mechanical ventilation, with baffles and controls set into their depth. End walls are mainly glazed, providing an emphasis in each of the main spaces of generous views outward in one direction, rather than less generous views from smaller windows in two directions.

Services that cross the circulation corridor in Option 3 are accessed from the ceiling of the deck below, where they are arranged for ease of access and replacement. This corridor accommodates all connections, from the ducts and supplies that are fixed to the facades to the interiors of apartments, where they are distributed in partition walls and ceilings. The corridor is also used to access and maintain equipment installed in adjacent service spaces.

1A. Isometric view of structure

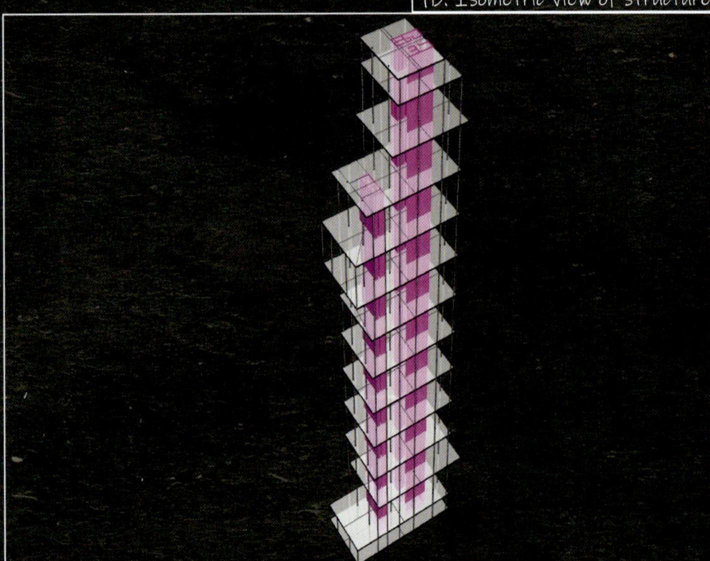

1B. Isometric view of structure

2A. Isometric view of structure

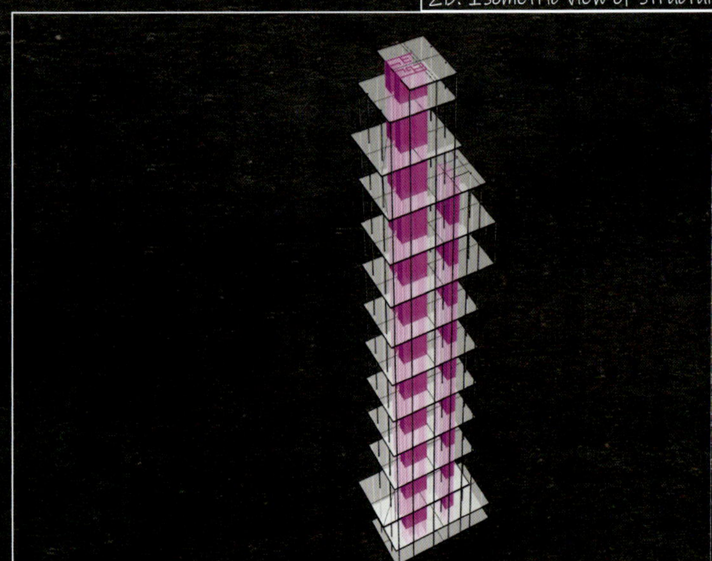

2B. Isometric view of structur

Structural strategy

The structural design of the building is of a mixed reinforced concrete and steel frame; the opaque side walls in reinforced concrete contribute to the structural stability. The use of both materials in the primary structure allows a greater flexibility in the arrangement of spaces, to provide the required spatial arrangement of apartments and winter garden terraces.

The structural design is a 6.0 metre by 6.0 metre grid of floor plates with a floor-to-floor height of 4.0 metres. The structural grid and associated column arrangement is consistent through the height of the tower. Most of the building is made from prefabricated part-assemblies which are brought to site and bolted together. The building aims to show how spaces are organised as revealed in the structural design.

The structural strategy for all three options is a mixed frame of reinforced concrete and steel, with concrete shear walls and flat slab floor decks. Option 1 forms the rectangular shape of floors and columns in reinforced concrete; the 'backpacks', balconies, projecting sky gardens and top set of floors are formed in steel. Option 2 has a similar arrangement but with the frames, comprising columns and floor slabs, arranged to suit the slightly different apartment layout. Option 3 arranges structural walls on the edges of the floor plates on opposite sides of the building to contribute to the required stability. This approach to structural stability provides clear floor plates within each apartment, regardless of the arrangement of internal partitions. Option 3 is the preferred option; providing the greatest level of flexibility of spatial arrangement on each complete floor plate.

The structural strategy is one of providing side walls which enclose the apartments as reinforced concrete structural walls. The service areas of staircases and technical equipment are accommodated outside these walls on floor slabs which project out from the building and which provide the structural support for services. Environmental control equipment is attached to the outside of those floor slabs, where staircases and lifts/elevators are positioned. In these support areas, no floor slab is provided; the building reverts to a framed construction

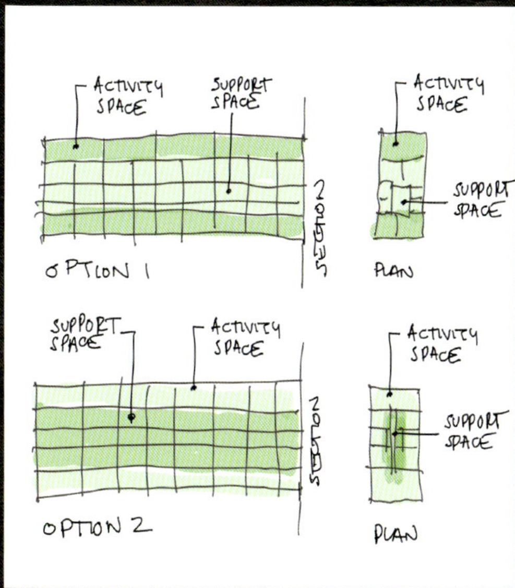

Structural strategy: Zones

Option 1 forms the rectangular shape of floors and columns in reinforced concrete.

Option 2 has a similar arrangement to Option 1 but with frames comprising columns and floor slabs.

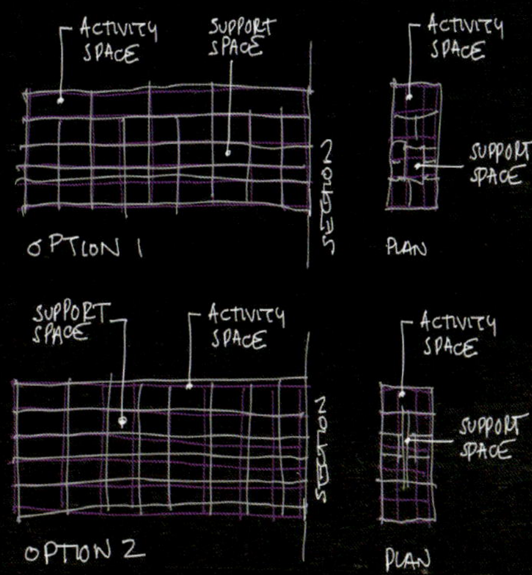

Structural strategy: Framing

Option 1 has 'backpacks', balconies, projecting sky gardens and top set of floors which are formed in steel.

Option 2 is arranged to suit the slightly different apartment layout from Option 1.

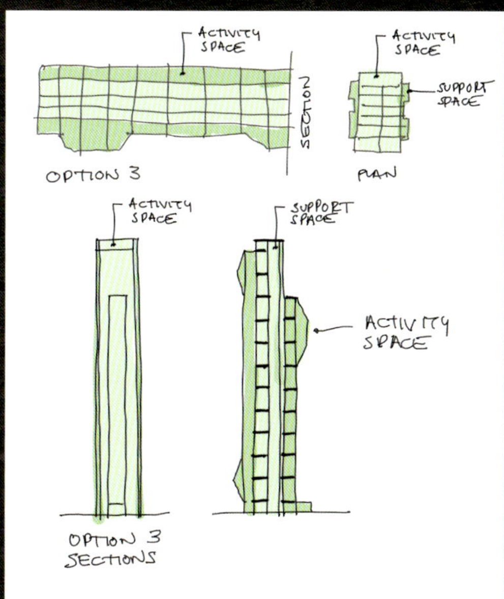

Structural strategy: Zones

Option 3 arranges structural walls on the edges of the floor plates on opposite sides of the building.

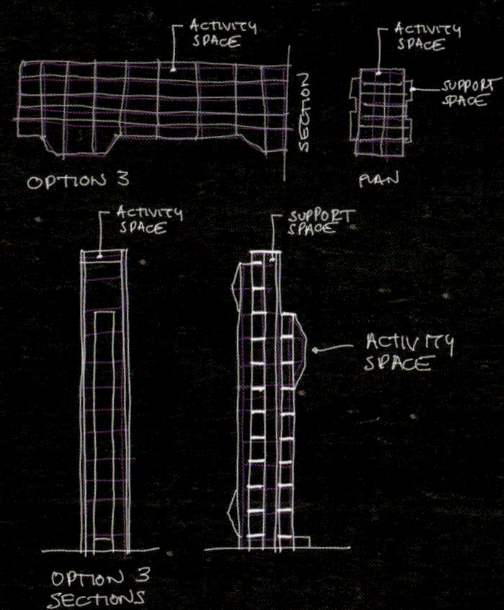

Structural strategy: Zones

Option 3 provides the greatest level of flexibility of the options for spatial arrangement on each complete floor plate.

at that point. The apartments have internal columns and no structural walls within internal spaces. The arrangement of columns allows for partitions enclosing habitable rooms, bathrooms and kitchens to be constructed independently of the requirements of structural walls, which are accommodated on the two sides of the building.

The three options for the structure respond to the requirements of the environmental design by providing additional projecting floor plates, beams and columns as a frame to support the environmental grid of environmental services, which are encapsulated within the side walls of the building.

A central aspect of the structural strategy is to match the approach to structure with an approach to building enclosure, which is a key part of the environmental strategy; one of cross ventilation through side walls. External walls are opaque and highly thermally insulated, which contrasts with the end walls which are glazed and have a balcony-style balustrade on one side of the building. Opaque elements have structural walls behind them. Glazed walls include the balcony balustrade which is formed in structural concrete; the concrete external walls are also used to support ducts for mechanically ventilated air into the apartments. Openings are cast into the concrete walls to allow the passage of ducted air from outside to inside the glazed facades, which have framing that is independent of the structure as might be expected. The concrete walls, columns and central core are designed to meet requirements for both structural design and acoustic design; an acoustic barrier is needed, as is the case with the shaft accommodating the lift/elevator and rooms that accommodate service machinery.

The structure makes use of side walls as structural elements which support and enclose elements of vertical circulation, mechanical air circulation and the distribution of electrical supplies. This approach is in contrast to the enclosure of the primary spaces used on some other projects, where the service spaces have a supporting structure which is lighter in weight to support the lighter assemblies of support spaces. All service elements are concealed within the structure; only the glazing at each end of the service corridors reveal its presence.

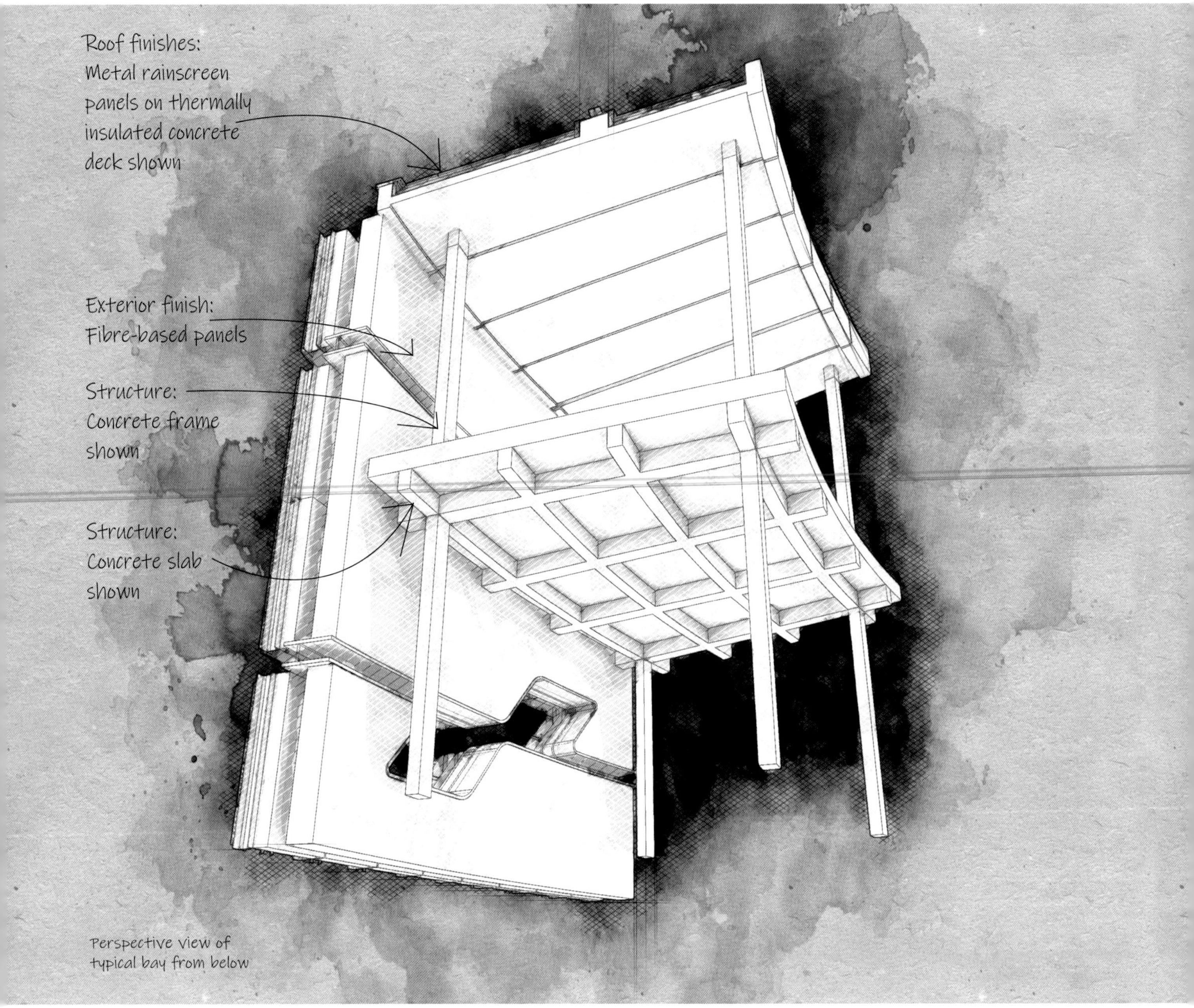

Perspective view of typical bay from below

Typical bay adjacent to facade

The external envelope is largely one of a set of opaque panels on the sides of the building, with glazed panels on the two narrower elevations. The two narrow glazed elevations are different; the north-facing wall has panels of vertical glass which extend from floor to ceiling. The opposite facade has winter gardens set within the facades with bands of glazing; a lower band accommodating a balustrade and floor slab and an upper band of windows which reach the ceiling. The winter garden elevation remains sealed for purposes of excluding wind at high level. There are no open external terraces in this relatively tall building. The side walls have concrete-based panels in a rainscreen configuration in order to provide a durable wall finish that will weather well and require little maintenance, providing shadows across the facade that emphasise the form and the panelisation at different times of day and at different times of year. For this reason, the need for light-coloured panels that excluded the use of fibre-based panels and other materials and concrete is the preferred solution due to its ability to provide large-scale panels, each of which can be installed like unitised glazed panels: that is to say without scaffolding during their installation. The bands between the concrete-based panels are formed in a mixture of glass which is clear and glass which is opaque in order to allow light to pass into service space without creating views into these utilities within the building. The upper floors have a winter garden space extending over two floors, on one side of the building, extending vertically across two sets of apartments. The ground floor has a projecting glazed rooflight and partially glazed walls enclosing it that provide a large-sized coffee shop and restaurant space.

A typical bay corresponds to an apartment module which is either a half floor or a complete floor for a larger apartment. The typical bay comprises a reinforced concrete structure of flat slab and circular columns with floor-to-ceiling glazing on two sides, which is fixed back by a steel frame in order to provide the experience of an apartment rather than a workplace. Walls that intersect with the slab edges on the glazed facade have steel trims on the outside using the same visual

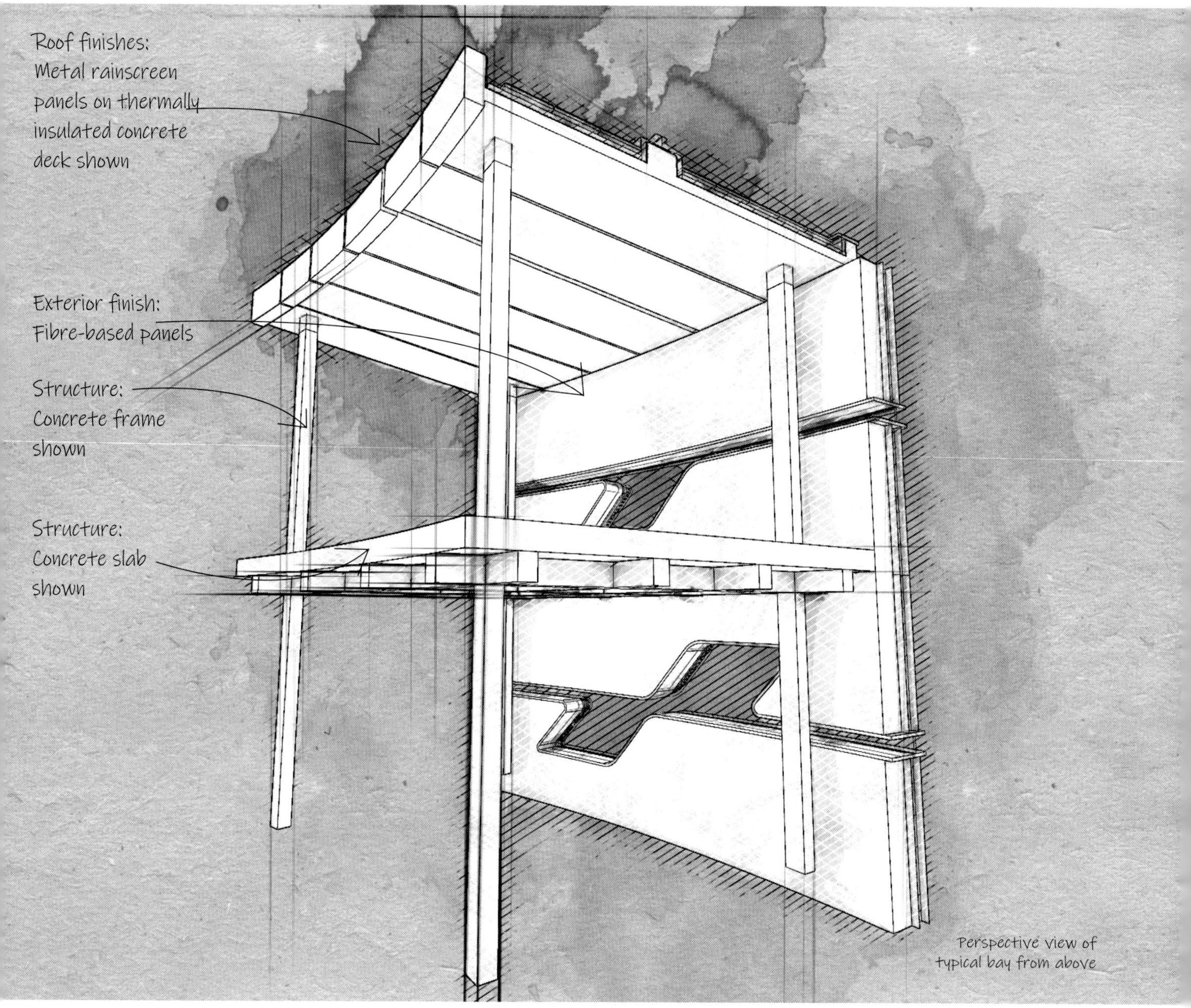

Perspective view of typical bay from above

language as the framing used for the glazing, of which the steel frame of all forms a part. This is all fixed back to the flat slabs at each floor level. The edges of the slab project slightly forward of the circular columns behind, which gives each bay the sense of being in a juxtaposed arrangement of a restrained but large-scale structure for large columns that pass through the height of the building. The industrial-style glazing contrasts visually with the structural steel frames; glazing mullions are set at 1.0-metre centres. Soffits have services fixed to the ceiling; floors are finished with a screed on structural concrete slabs. The internal walls comprise modular units for bathrooms and kitchen spaces. There is no differentiation between bedrooms and living rooms beyond the facade, which in one space is glazed full height and on the other side has a small terrace which is largely a Juliet balcony with sliding windows. The two rooms have different areas of glazing to suit the expectations of the use of each space.

Facades have metal panels on the sides, sitting alongside steel-framed glazing on the two end-glazed facades. The Juliet balcony elevation has sliding doors in order to allow the space within the room to be unimpeded by the opening of a door. The other end elevation has sealed glazing in both instances; the glazing is cleaned on the outside from a cleaning cradle that is lowered from the top of the building. Given the relatively low height of the building, the cleaning task is relatively modest. This approach of the cleaning cradle avoids the need to have opening windows where they are not required due to the height of the building. The typical bay integrates the trims used between facade panels with the trims used for the interiors of apartments; metal trims define edges to floors, skirtings and supports for lighting at ceiling level. The trims are used in narrow bands at floor and ceiling level for the supply and extraction of air within rooms. The trims for ventilation appear on one wall only in any given space.

The horizontal solar shading on the north and south facades provide light reflectors to bounce light off the top surface of the shading device, which extends from outside to inside. The top of the device has electrical lighting installed to imitate the effect of daylight.

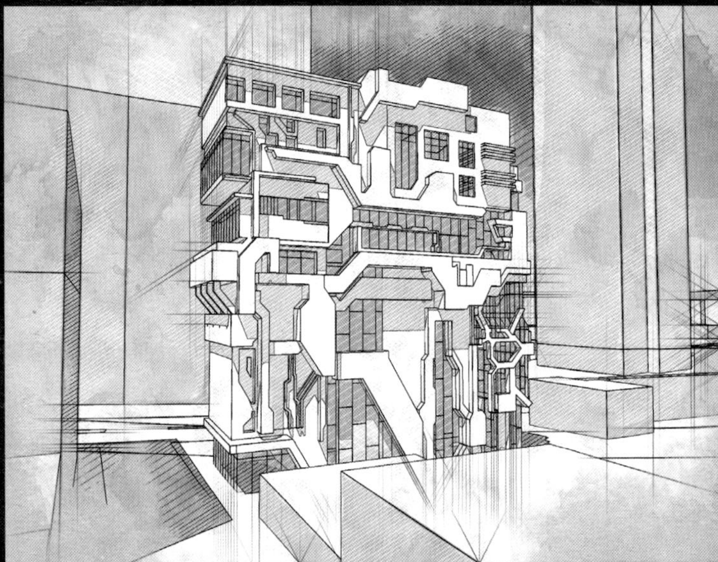

1. Perspective view of exterior

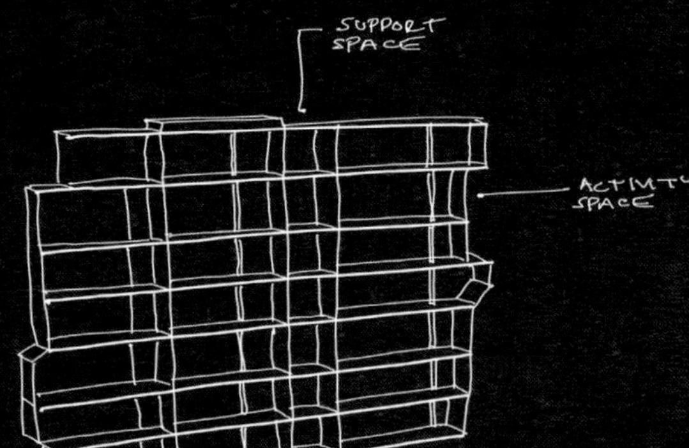

2. Perspective view of exterior

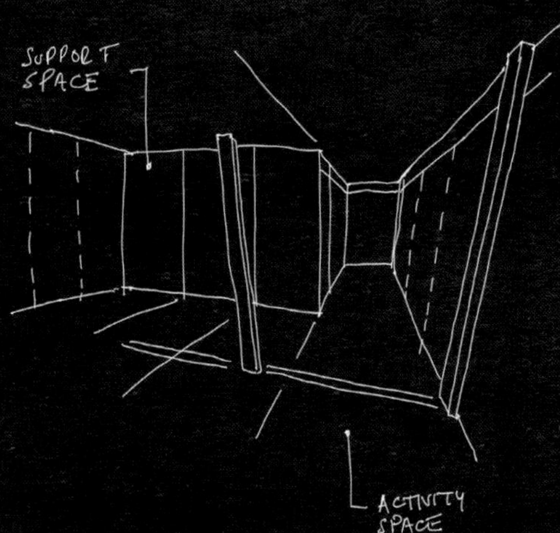

Changing environmental controls for fixed spatial arrangements

The environmental approach to this design is to address the need for flexibility of use during the lifespan of the building, such that the floor voids created can be filled in or potentially moved during the course of its life. As a result of changing patterns of habitation in the city, the brief/program requires the structure to have parts of floor slabs that can be removed and the facade to be adjustable to suit changing market conditions by changing the arrangement of the building. The owner has a long-standing presence on the site in this densely inhabited urban quarter, which has led to a preference for carrying out near-future changes to the spatial arrangement rather than demolish and reconstruct. This is also part of the company's commitment, as set out in the brief/program, to a sustainable future where building components and assemblies are reused and recycled, and not demolished; the 'kit of parts' assembly is key to providing a sustainable design. As a result, the building is made as a set of beams and columns with precast concrete slabs such that they can be removed with relative ease in the near future; voids in floors that create the communal spaces inside the building can be moved to suit changing requirements. This residential rental market is one that requires flexibility, and an ability for spatial changes to be made as a result. The use of externally mounted service equipment is a key part of the environmental design.

Internal cores are designed so that they can be dismantled relatively easily; internal columns, walls and elements of structure that form part of the facade provide the frame with elements of structural stability. The primary element for providing stability is the load-bearing facades, which form a dense frame with web-like members and structural walls added to provide the required stability. A key part of the design is to allow the building to have a flexible relationship between the enclosure and the structure in the facade. Rooms can be adjusted in layout while responding in a more flexible manner to the facades which enclose them; walls inside the apartments are not required to align with external walls. Instead, internal walls create a spatial tension between the interior space and the external frame-based forms of the load-bearing

Perspective view of exterior

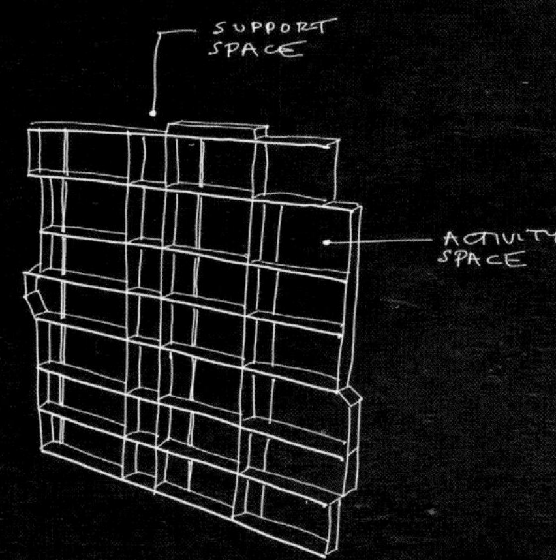

4. Perspective view of exterior

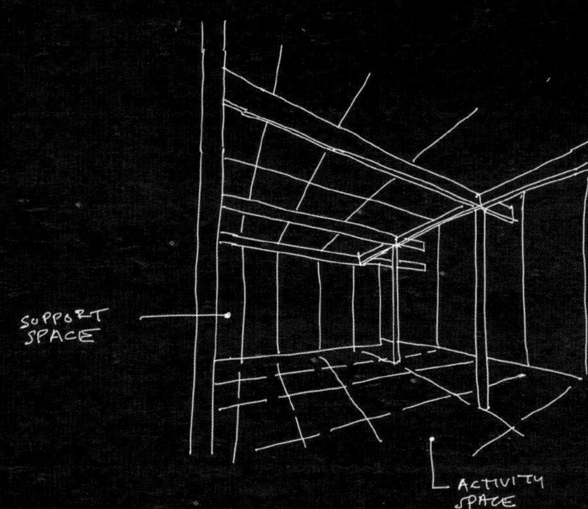

facades. The building is almost a 'refurbishment' or 'conversion' from one identity to another but within a single building design, where an interaction between what existed before and what is introduced as new is a key part of the visual tension in the design: a contrast between the design of the structure and that of the interior, instead of 'coordination by geometric alignment' between structure and interior, which is more commonly the case in comparable residential buildings.

Near-future changes in this project are provided by an exoskeleton of concrete which forms a permanent part of the design, and metal-based panels which can be replaced as required during the lifespan of the building. The exoskeleton provides a background structure for the environmental grid to be adjusted or moved in all three options in order to provide an ability for the services to be redefined within the building. Service zones are removed from each of the apartments in this residential hotel; residents are expected to stay for between only three months and a year maximum. These residences for tenants or occupants in transition allow the grouping of the services to be reconsidered as not required to be within the perimeter of the apartments, as would typically be the case with an owner-occupier or with each apartment being separately managed. In this case the building is owned by a single party who seeks flexibility in the future arrangement of the apartments with regard to their size and use, allowing the services to be grouped into cores which are set in different places within the building and which have the ability to be relocated. Services are removed and reinstalled: the aim being to allow the reconfiguring of apartments for water and electricity supply and the positions of apartments and kitchens, while maintaining natural ventilation and providing a high level of daylight control within each apartment. The approach to environmental control systems is to integrate them into facades as external wall components that can be changed independently of the interiors; partition walls and ceilings accommodate services and fittings which are difficult to replace without removing most of the internal arrangement. The facades are easier to have items of opaque wall and glazed wall changed as they interface with service items only.

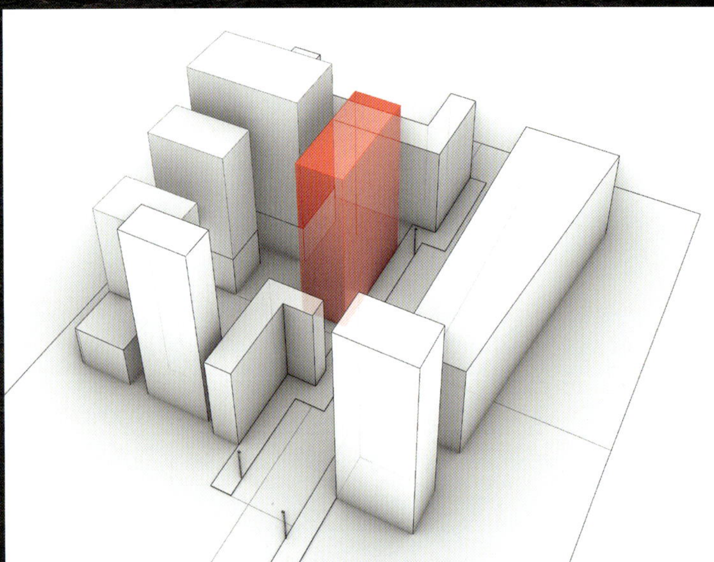

1. Project volume in site context

2. Project volume in site context

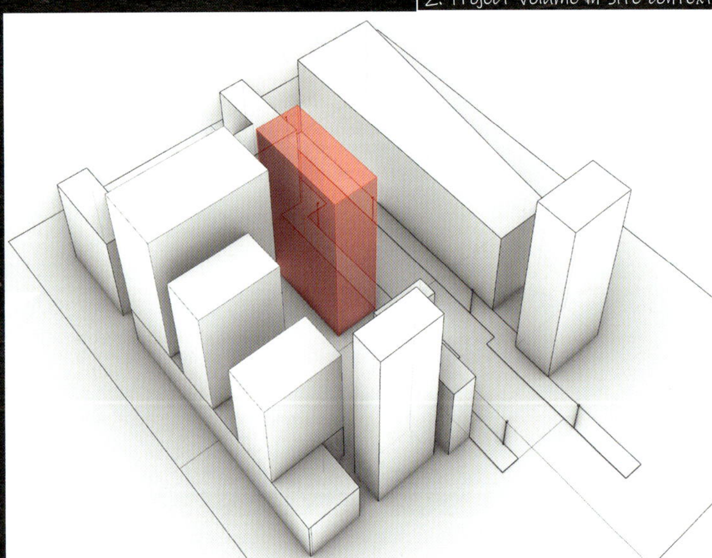

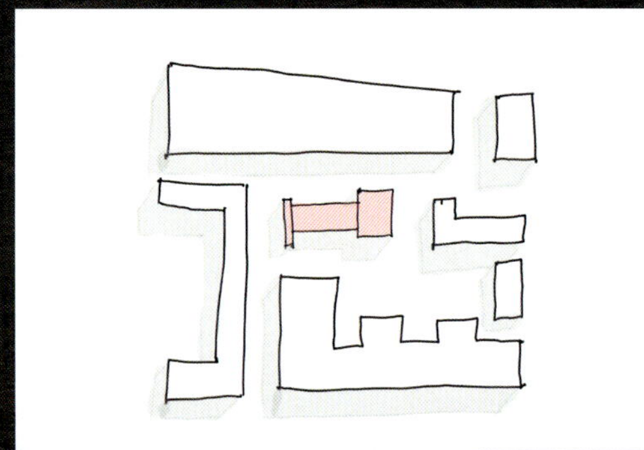

1. Site plan with surrounding context

Option 1 divides the block into three parts, one of which is apartments which face the street.

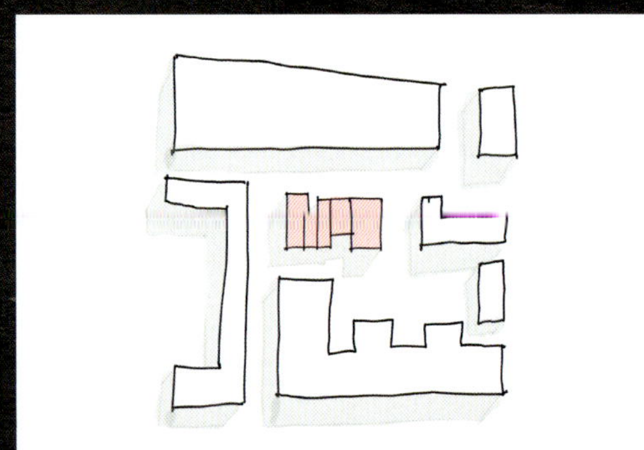

2. Site plan with surrounding context

Option 2 differentiates the block of three into larger numbers of blocks.

3. Site plan with surrounding context

Option 3 provides an alignment of the blocks, as viewed in plan, which follows the blocks adjacent to it.

Site context

This apartment building is arranged over 10 storeys, containing a mixture of apartment sizes and two-storey duplexes together with gyms. In addition, community facilities are provided for food and support services. There is a walking and running track around the perimeter at roof level, and there are shared external spaces which are relatively large-scale and replace the individual small communal areas associated with contemporary apartment buildings.

Option 1 divides the block into three parts, one of which is apartments which face the street. The second is a middle block and the end is a larger block enclosing larger apartments. The blocks are aligned with adjacent streets and follow the site footprint, filling the full extent of the site in order to align as much as possible with the adjacent buildings. Following the street layout is common to all three design options. Option 2 differentiates the block of three into larger numbers of blocks to create smaller elements which bring a level of detail and differentiation of elements of facade to this streetscape, which otherwise has large monolithic blocks of apartments and office buildings. Option 3 takes that differentiation and provides an alignment of the blocks, as viewed in plan, which follows the blocks adjacent to it, creating variation vertically in section and elevation, rather than in plan. In Option 2 the residual spaces are more difficult to use and more difficult to manage. This apartment hotel / residential hotel is set within the site context of a semi-industrial zone, and is for the use of a company that occupies a large manufacturing base facility nearby. The character of the building is one which inhabits a rugged urban environment surrounded by small workshops and light industry buildings.

The design picks up on the characteristics of some of those buildings. This apartment building is taller than its neighbours and does not suit a highly glazed set of facades, but neither does it seek to conceal itself behind solar control glass panels. At an early stage of the project, it was considered whether the building would have windows occupying 10 to 20% of the wall area, with the surrounding opaque panels having a similar glass type that would conceal a concrete frame and concrete block

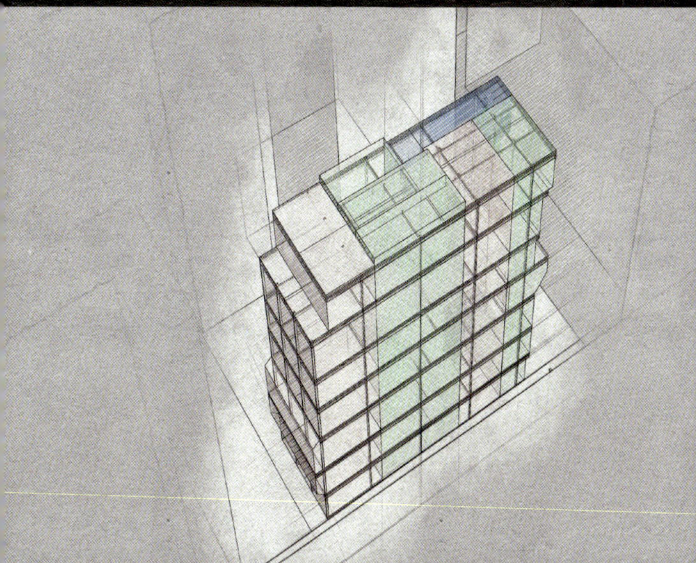

Perspective view of environmental volumes

2. Perspective view of environmental volumes

1. Figure-ground diagram of tempered environment

Option 1
Red spaces are highly tempered but are reduced to one part of the building.

2. Figure-ground diagram of tempered environment

Option 2
Dark green spaces are less tempered than red spaces.

3. Figure-ground diagram of tempered environment

Option 3
Light blue spaces are the least tempered spaces. These spaces interface directly with external space.

infill; a characteristic of other examples of this type. The building design did not seek to conceal itself behind dark glass facades to create a single rectangular form, but instead wanted to provide a high level of amenities to the residents, with large-scale spaces. High levels of daylight were required and opaque walls were specifically needed in order to provide the combination of being able to have views out as well as the privacy required in order for the apartments to neither hide away from the immediate environment nor to assert themselves above their neighbours. The building seeks to fit in with its immediate environment as a residence among light industrial buildings, asserting itself among its neighbours without changing the character of its site context.

The site context at ground floor level is of the building being surrounded by workshops and storage facilities, such that the use of the ground floor in this building has become one of sports facilities for the residents on the floors above that floor. There is no residential accommodation at ground floor level in order to be consistent with the places of work immediately adjacent to the site. The ground floor has largely opaque panels that provide views only into the ground floor, circulation spaces and reception areas. The sports facilities comprise sports courts for basketball and tennis as well as a gym and fitness training rooms. These activities are not visible from outside the building. Instead, a series of translucent walls suggest movements within the building at ground floor level to provide a dynamism and sense of activity; one of a semi-public space but which is separate from the adjacent workplace buildings.

The height of the building was a determining factor in establishing the massing of this project. The brief/program set a requirement for the number and size of each unit; this objective could be achieved only if the full extent of the site were built upon. As a result, the external walls follow the site boundary in order to ensure that the height of the building did not exceed that of its neighbours. This approach ensured that the building would be economical in cost when compared with a taller building, while still providing a range of different solutions to both the servicing and spatial arrangement of each apartment.

1. Sectional perspective view

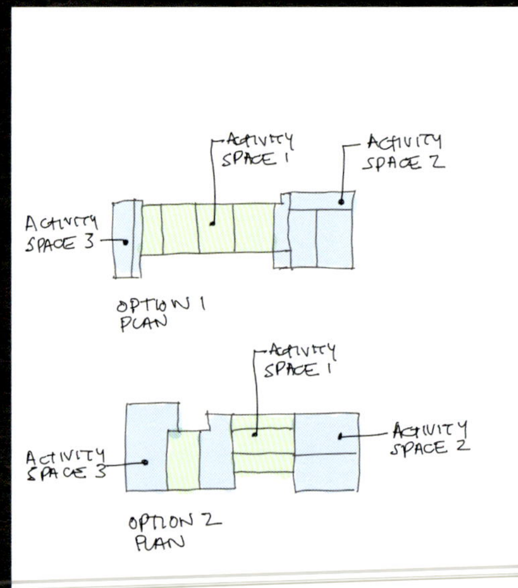

Spatial arrangement
Option 1 sets apartment access along three cores which provide entry to all apartments.
Option 2 has a varied form of apartment block created through a realignment of apartments from Option 1.

2. Sectional perspective view

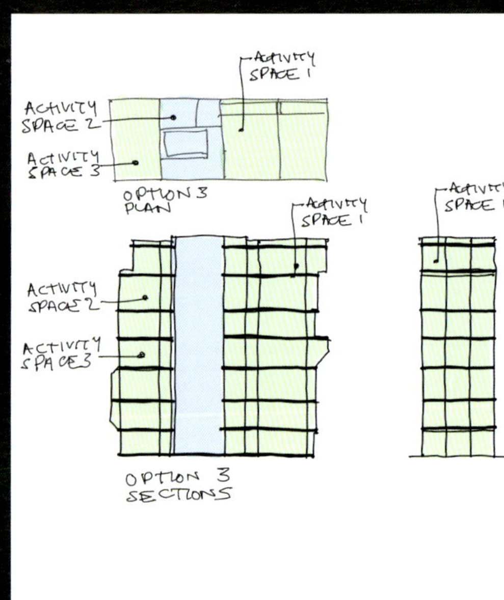

Option 3 simplifies the form back to a rectangle that aligns well with adjacent buildings.

Spatial arrangement

The apartment building looks outward to the surrounding streets as well as inwards to a courtyard; the inner courtyard is where the living spaces are located. Views across the small courtyards offer oblique views between neighbours; no two apartments directly face one another. The supporting service spaces are set between the courtyard-facing rooms and the street-facing rooms. The washrooms and utility spaces are set at the centre, with kitchens and bedrooms set on the outer facade in order to benefit from the street life surrounding the building, while living spaces are quieter and are set on the inside of the building. The spatial arrangement of Option 1 is of putting the circulation spaces in the short block at one end; another short block is set between the two larger blocks, as well as an access along one side of the end of the block. This approach provides three points of access into the three blocks; each block has its own entrance. In Option 2 the more varied form of the apartment block is created through a realignment of apartments; there is an internal void space in the larger block, forming an interlocking between volumes while having two points of access into the building; the two entrances avoid the need for corridors at upper levels, creating a sense of community around open stairwells in vertically arranged volumes of three storeys each. Option 3 simplifies the form back to a rectangle that aligns well with adjacent buildings, and the complexity in section is created by having apartments offset on different floors in relation to each other, setting more of the communal activities at the perimeter of the building, with an internal void to provide a focus between apartments, such that apartments face one another with a tree-filled internal space that is top lit. This arrangement provides an internal focus of calm, allowing the outer block to show public functions and shared facilities.

The internal focus of visual calm is reflected in the rectilinear arrangement of courtyard space that fills the shared spaces at the centre of the building. Seating spaces are set out with indented sides in order to create small pockets of floor area that accommodate shared volumes for relaxation and interaction between neighbours.

Perspective view of interior

2. Perspective view of interior

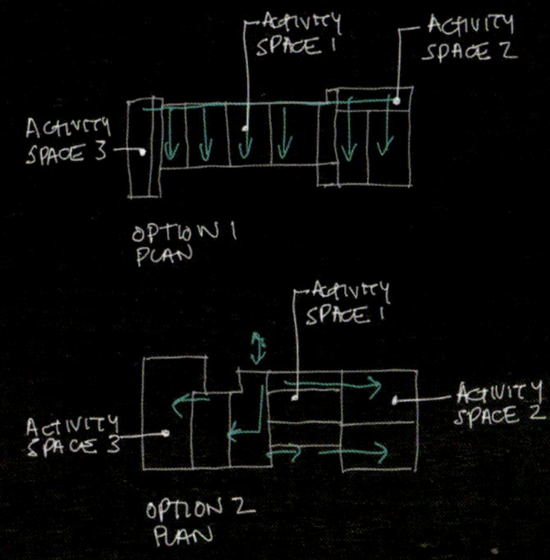

Internal circulation

Option 1 puts the circulation spaces in the short block at one end.

Option 2 sets the circulation route in the central courtyard space.

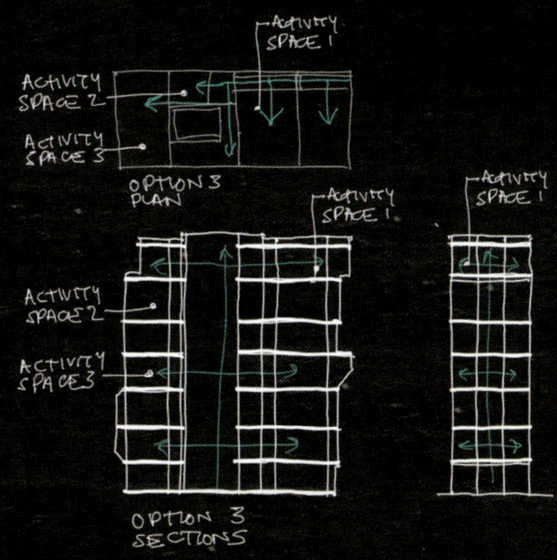

Option 3 has most internal circulation taking place along one facade.

Internal circulation

The overall spatial arrangement is one that varies from floor to floor, based on apartments being arranged in different orientations to provide an arrangement of apartments that allowed for circulation to be created either at the edges of the building, at the centre or between the apartments. These approaches to strategy were made possible by having the service elements inhabiting the external facades of the building, providing the characteristic appearance of structure and services forming opaque areas on the facade with glazed areas allowing natural light and natural ventilation into each apartment. The internal circulation is based on three approaches of having the apartments partially arranged with circulation at the edges, and with them being grouped in the centre with circulation extending from one side of the building to the other side.

The buildings are accessed from individual vertical cores of stairs and a lift/elevator, which has the benefit of avoiding the need for extensive corridors. This approach aims to create a closer sense of community and to reduce the need to construct long circulation spaces. A benefit of having stairs accessing apartments is that each apartment is then cross ventilated from the central courtyard to the street, with the possibility of being able to introduce fresh air from different sides of the building at different times of day.

The internal circulation of Option 1 sets apartment access along three cores which provide entry to all apartments and, in addition, the other side of the access corridors have shared facilities which are revealed visually on the facades. The apartments all have views on one side of the building and are protected from the effects of a noisy street on the other facade. In Option 2, apartments are much more mixed in terms of having maximised views to the outside as a result of setting the circulation route in the central courtyard space, with its easy distribution to apartments. Option 3 is a mixture of Options 1 and 2 with large groups of apartments around a small courtyard; one of the long facades is highly differentiated in form in response to its public functions; most internal circulation takes place along that facade.

1A. Isometric view of environmental volumes

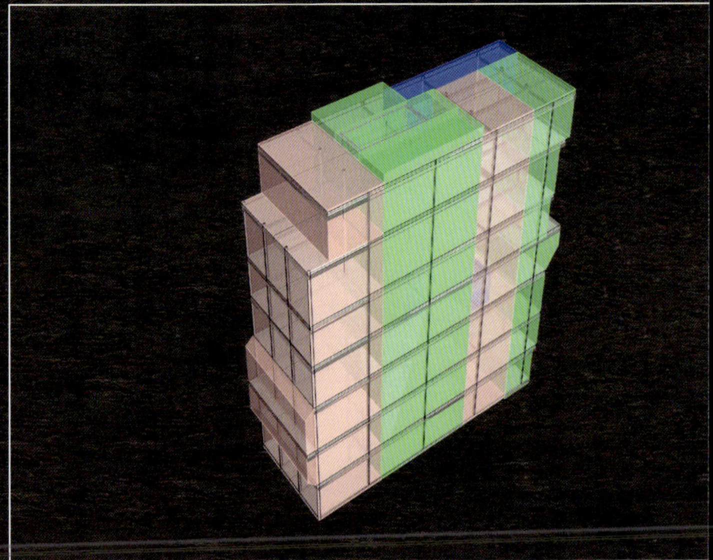

2A. Isometric view of environmental volumes

1B. Isometric view of environmental volumes

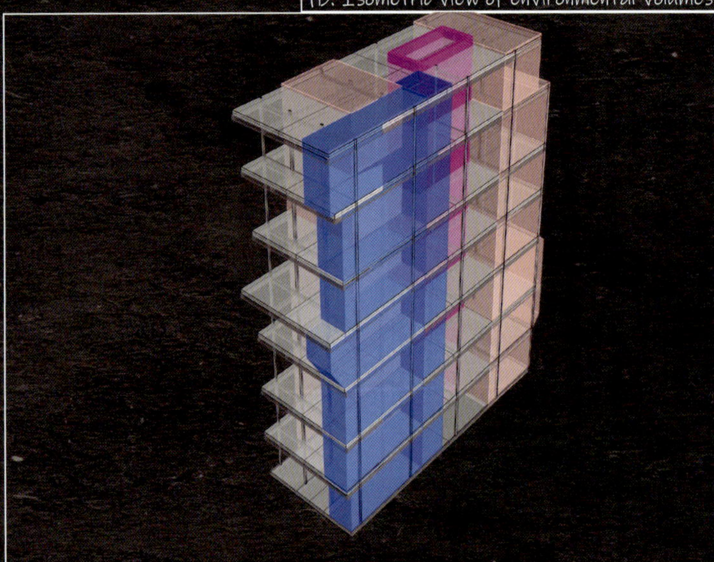

2B. Isometric view of environmental volum

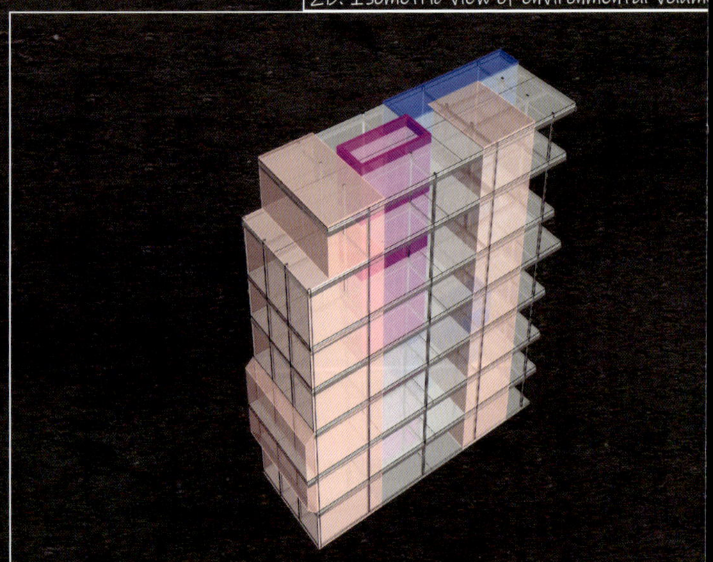

Environmental strategy

The environmental strategy is based on embodied energy considerations in the construction of the building, which are a significant feature in relation to the energy of the building in use. The apartment building benefits from the warm and dry summer temperate climate, thermally insulated for the harsher winter conditions experienced in this location. The aim here is to create a material-efficient design, as well as to encourage the use of passive ventilation, for as much of the year as possible.

The environmental strategy for Option 1 is to create three environmental zones; one for the shared access and facilities, another for the long apartment block and a third for the smaller apartment block; this block is exposed to more of the effects of the sun, whereas the long block is more protected by the access cores. Access spaces are largely naturally ventilated, except in extremes of summer and winter. In Option 2, each apartment is individually controlled. Waste heat or cooling energy that cannot be recycled is passed through the atrium space in the centre of the courtyard in order to provide seating areas in the different levels of the garden space blocks. Option 3 takes that concept further with apartments arranged around a central atrium space; as a result of higher air changes, the perimeter of the building forms another environmental zone for the communal facilities of gyms, shop and shared restaurant facilities.

Externally fixed environmental control systems and staircases are designed to provide shading to the spaces behind. This approach ensures clear views out on two sides. Most of the environmental control equipment is located on the sides facing the path of the sun; most daylight is admitted through the two side facades. Staircases are positioned on the two adjacent side facades, which are largely opaque. This approach to services distribution avoids the need for having a large rooftop service installation; the only rooftop equipment required is chillers, which are arranged in a group. Staircases are also set in the glazed double layer, as part of a set of cores which are set into a deep facade zone. Vertical duct risers are enclosed behind louvred panels

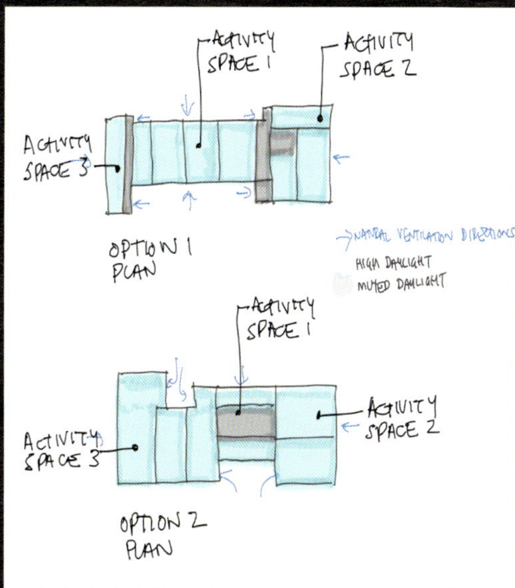

Daylight strategy for direct sunlight and cross ventilation.
Option 1 admits daylight and air to all sides of the building.
Option 2 has reduced daylight and air admitted in the courtyard space.

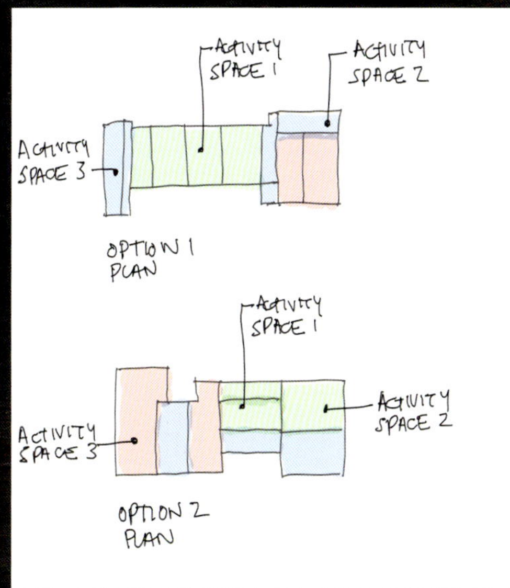

Environmental zones
Option 1 creates three environmental zones.
Option 2 has each apartment individually controlled environmentally.

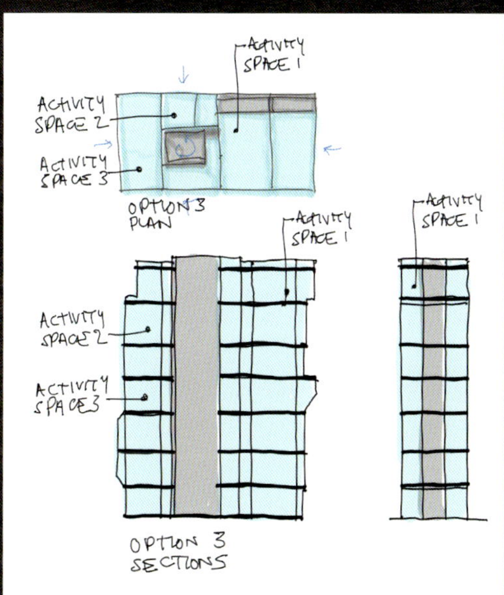

Daylight strategy for direct sunlight and cross ventilation.
Option 3 has reduced daylight and air admitted in both courtyard spaces.

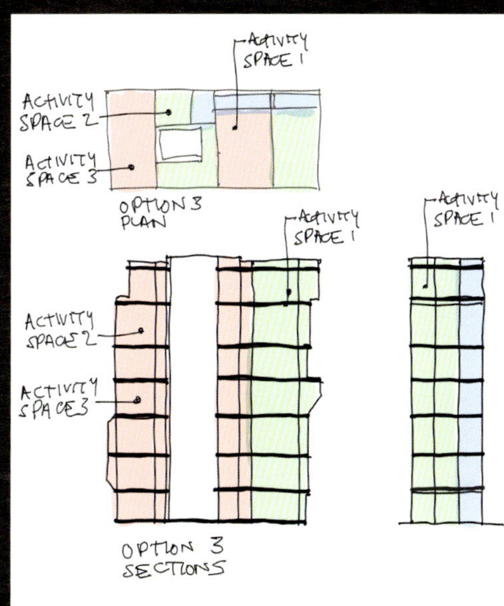

Environmental zones
Option 3- uses the perimeter of the building to form an environmental zone for the communal facilities.

which have solar protection. A storage space is located within this area behind the vertical duct risers, which are set behind the area for maintenance access. This provides both a visual shade for the spaces behind, as well as providing solar shading for the areas where maintenance staff are required to work; in order for maintenance to be carried out, equipment is taken from the glazed solar shading area into the central area, away from the direct effects of the sun.

The environmental control packages set within the facades are manufactured and assembled locally, arriving as one-storey-high panels. They are joined together on the facades to create a two-storey environmental control unit. Each unit is accessed from the floor decks immediately behind. But the decks within each environmental control module are formed as metal gratings.

The environmental strategy is based on grouping services on the outer face of the facades on all four sides. The same zone contains staircases, lifts/elevators, ducted air and electrical services that serve the apartments. This arrangement of grouped services on the outside of the building allowed the glazed facades to be arranged such that the environmental grid is a set of glazed wall panels which allow daylight and natural ventilation to enter spaces, together with requirements of structure and mechanical services, electrical supplies and plumbing. This juxtaposed arrangement suits both mechanical services and requirements for natural air, natural daylight and natural ventilation.

The proportion of opaque to areas of glazed facade is driven by a preference for natural daylight and ventilation, but with the need to provide opaque walls for privacy. Those areas have mechanical ventilation units attached to the outside, providing opportunities for air conditioning units to be attached to the facades of every apartment such that there is no central supply there from roof level.

All mechanical services are packaged, but they are grouped on different floors. The roof level accommodates some services equipment, which is then distributed down the building. Staircases and lifts/elevators are also enclosed in opaque walls, as glazing is not required to enclose them.

1A. Isometric view of structure

2A. Isometric view of structure

1B. Isometric view of structure

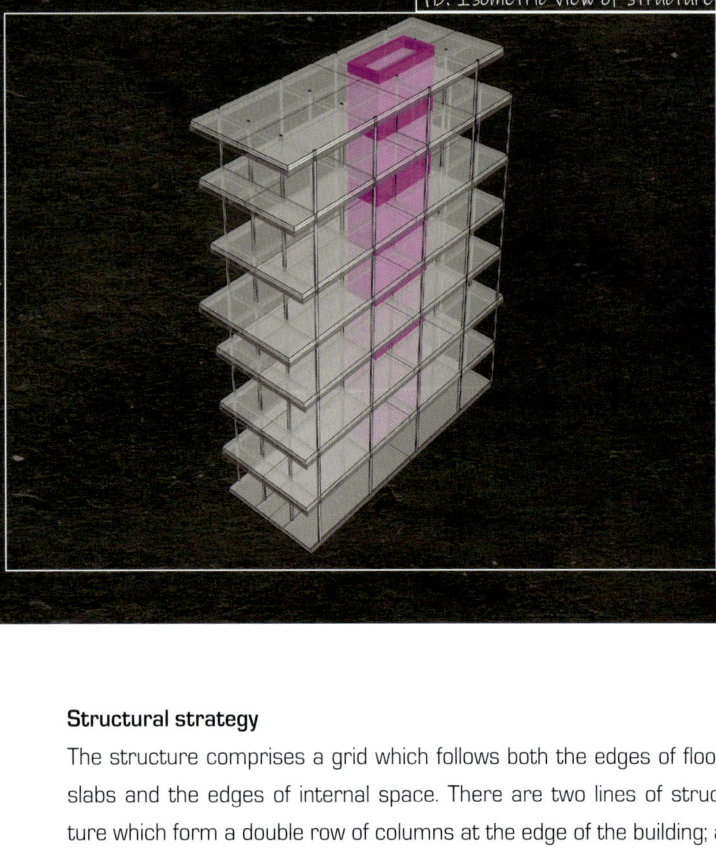

2B. Isometric view of structu

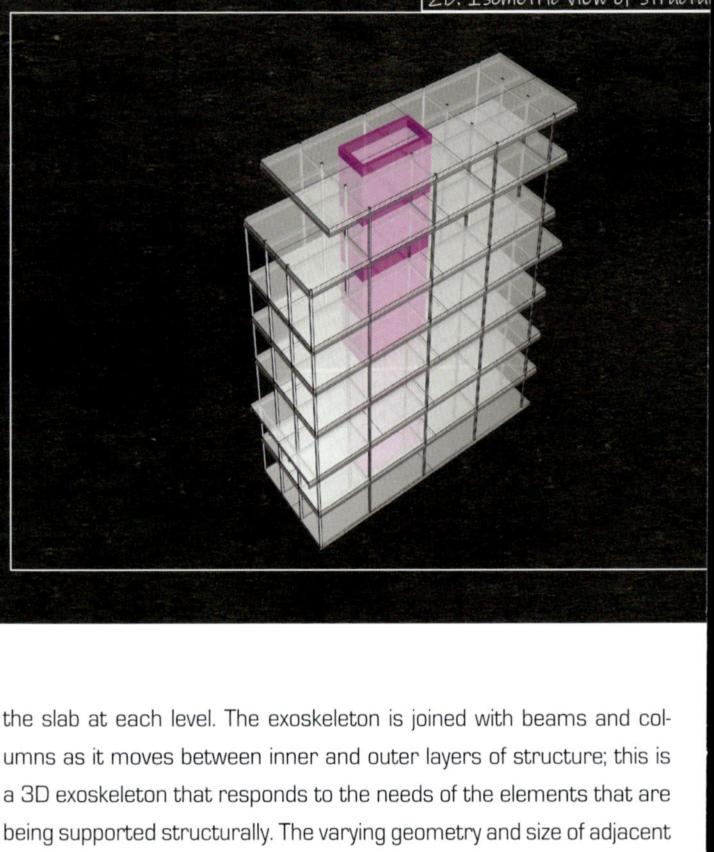

Structural strategy

The structure comprises a grid which follows both the edges of floor slabs and the edges of internal space. There are two lines of structure which form a double row of columns at the edge of the building; a second double row is set out around the inner shared courtyard. The double row adjacent to the facades supports services, staircases and lifts/elevators on the outer face of the structure; the inner double row supports indented floor slabs around the internal courtyards. In some instances, a double row of columns is not needed; the floor slab is cantilevered forward of the adjacent column in order to support mechanical ventilation equipment. Some of the seating areas are cantilevered forward of the edge of the adjacent slab; supported by beams beneath in order to create a visually calm, column-free area.

The exoskeleton varies in position; it does not occupy a single structural grid along the length of each external facade and each internal courtyard. Instead, the exoskeleton frame moves between the inner and outer gridlines adjacent to each slab edge; following the lines of the slab at each level. The exoskeleton is joined with beams and columns as it moves between inner and outer layers of structure; this is a 3D exoskeleton that responds to the needs of the elements that are being supported structurally. The varying geometry and size of adjacent structural members is a response to the different requirements.

The structural concept is one of a reinforced concrete frame with reinforced concrete slabs and a mixture of beams and precast planks, together with other areas of flat slabs and columns. The reason for a change between structural solutions is to use reinforced concrete and steel for each of the benefits they bring in order to reduce the embodied energy of the building as much as is practically possible. Structural concrete is required because of the level of acoustic insulation required between and within apartments, but has the disadvantage of having high embodied energy. The use of differentiated reinforced concrete structures is driven by the energy associated with the construction of the structure. The structural strategy for all three options is similar in having cross-wall construction in reinforced concrete and columns

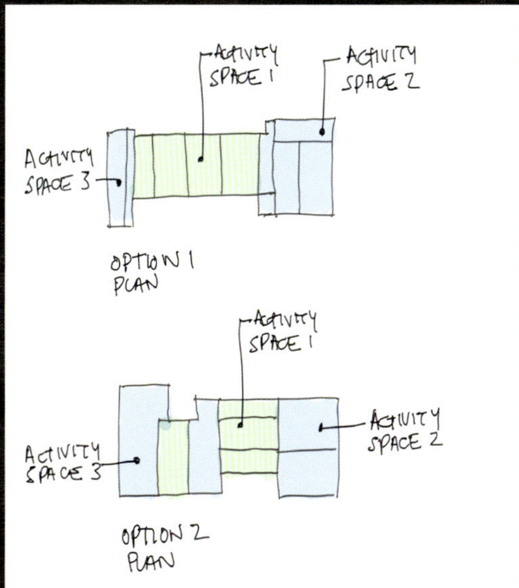

Structural strategy: Zones

Option 1 divides the structure into four zones.

Option 2 divides the structure into two zones.

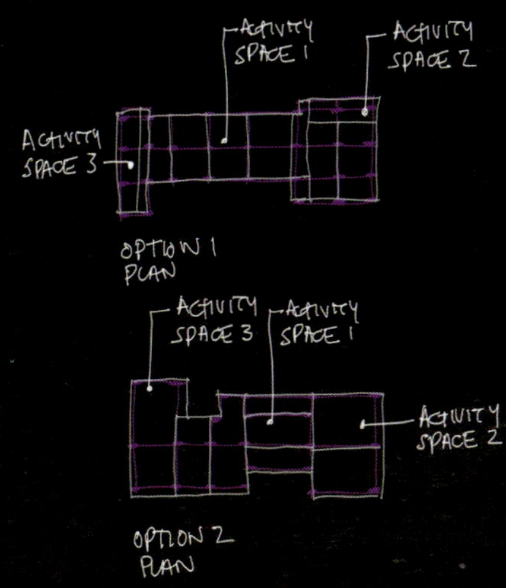

Structural strategy: Framing

Option 1 encloses the core spaces and dividing space into sets of apartments.

Option 2 is a mixed solution of reinforced concrete and steel.

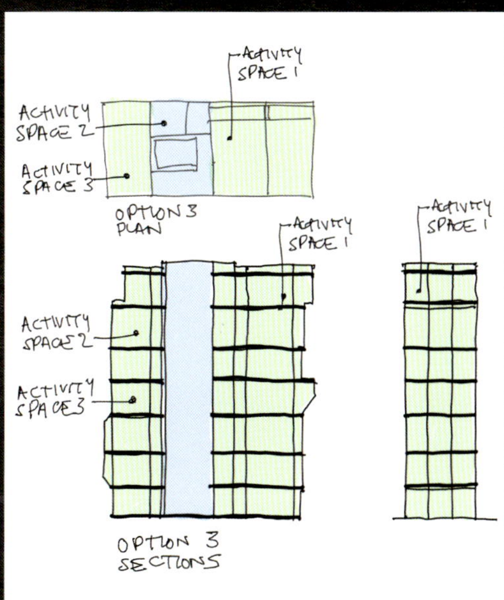

Structural strategy: Zones

Option 3 divides the structure into two zones.

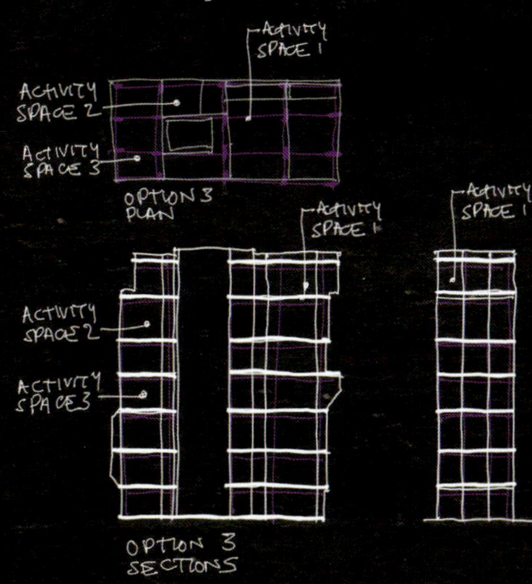

Structural strategy: Zones

Option 3 is largely a steel frame.

around the edges that provide the level of differentiation of the facades. The structural concept is of a reinforced concrete exoskeleton that is positioned externally on the corners, but elsewhere it becomes internal on the side elevations. This approach is taken in order for each of the panels to form an element that extends to the edge of the building, but which does not need to wrap around the facade. This approach will allow the environmental control assemblies to be slotted in afterwards and maintained independently of the external structure, which is thermally insulated and weather-protected independently.

The structural design is based on having an externally set arrangement of beams, columns and structural walls that support the services, staircases and lifts/elevators which inhabit the environmental zone set around the perimeter of the building. The structure has an arrangement on the facades which is different on all four sides. A key requirement was to provide support for ducts, electrical supplies and circulation so that staircases, for example, do not require glazed walls and have opaque walls as do the lifts/elevators. The internal arrangement of structure uses a regular rectilinear structural grid in order for the columns and beams to be arranged in an efficient manner, such that the structure set both on the outside of the building and its interior are different in their approach. The externally set structure is there primarily to relate to support services, whereas the internal structure creates open spaces with a rectilinear grid of columns arranged for structural efficiency.

The reinforced concrete frame providing the structure supporting the floor decks and services equipment in this building is not exposed to view. Both facades enclose the structure as services equipment is set beneath the external envelope panels. This approach avoids a difficulty in repairing and maintaining environmental control equipment in an industrial environment. This approach of enveloping the structure also serves as protection to the thermal insulation required to reduce energy consumption as a result of needing to heat or cool the structure on a seasonal basis.

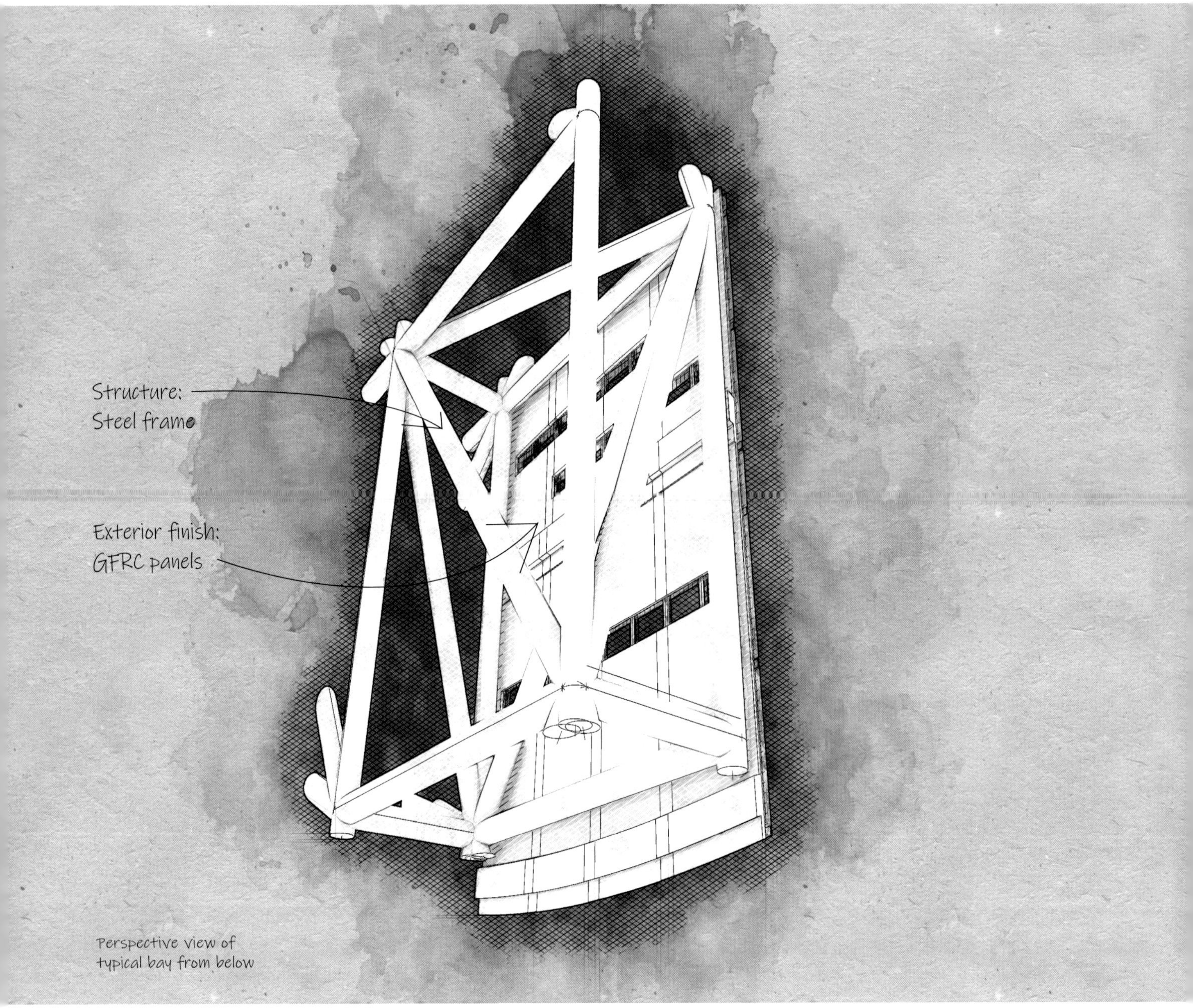

Perspective view of typical bay from below

Typical bay adjacent to facade

The envelope of the building is required to provide thermal insulation and weather protection to the load-bearing facades. Elements of structure are clad in both GFRC (glass-fibre reinforced concrete) and metal panels, which are fixed to the reinforced concrete frame of the building. GFRC is used where panels are providing long-term protection to the structure; metal panels are used where mechanical and electrical equipment, and ducts, are installed in the deep facade zone. In addition, ducted air is drawn through the facades, which have a mixture of opaque glass and metal panels in locations where ducts pass through the external envelope into ceiling voids. Mechanical and electrical services equipment is fixed to the outside of the building in order that internal spaces are as clear as possible. Equipment and air ducts that are fixed to the facades are accessed directly from the apartments for maintenance and cleaning. Part of the reinforced concrete structure has inclined beams which support elements behind them, such as reinforced concrete stairs and balconies. Clear glazed panels are used to illuminate rooms and provide views out; the level of daylight in each space is controlled both by shading devices and by projecting bays of opaque panels which enclose structure and environmental equipment. The glazing is a mixture of windows set into openings in the reinforced concrete structure, and floor-to-ceiling glazing which is supported on the top surface of floor slabs and is restrained by the underside of the floor slab forming the ceiling immediately above. A key concept of the spatial arrangement is to have apartments which look out onto a central courtyard rather than focussing on views out to the street; bathrooms and kitchens are set on the outside of the building in order for the central spaces to be opened up as much as possible. The primary spaces of living rooms and studies face the inner courtyard.

The building has 50% light transmission glass with horizontal solar shading in order to avoid the need for more heavily shaded glass that would have reduced the clear views out through the glazed walls. Instead, this project takes the different approach of putting the technical equipment for the building in the zone between the outer wall of the

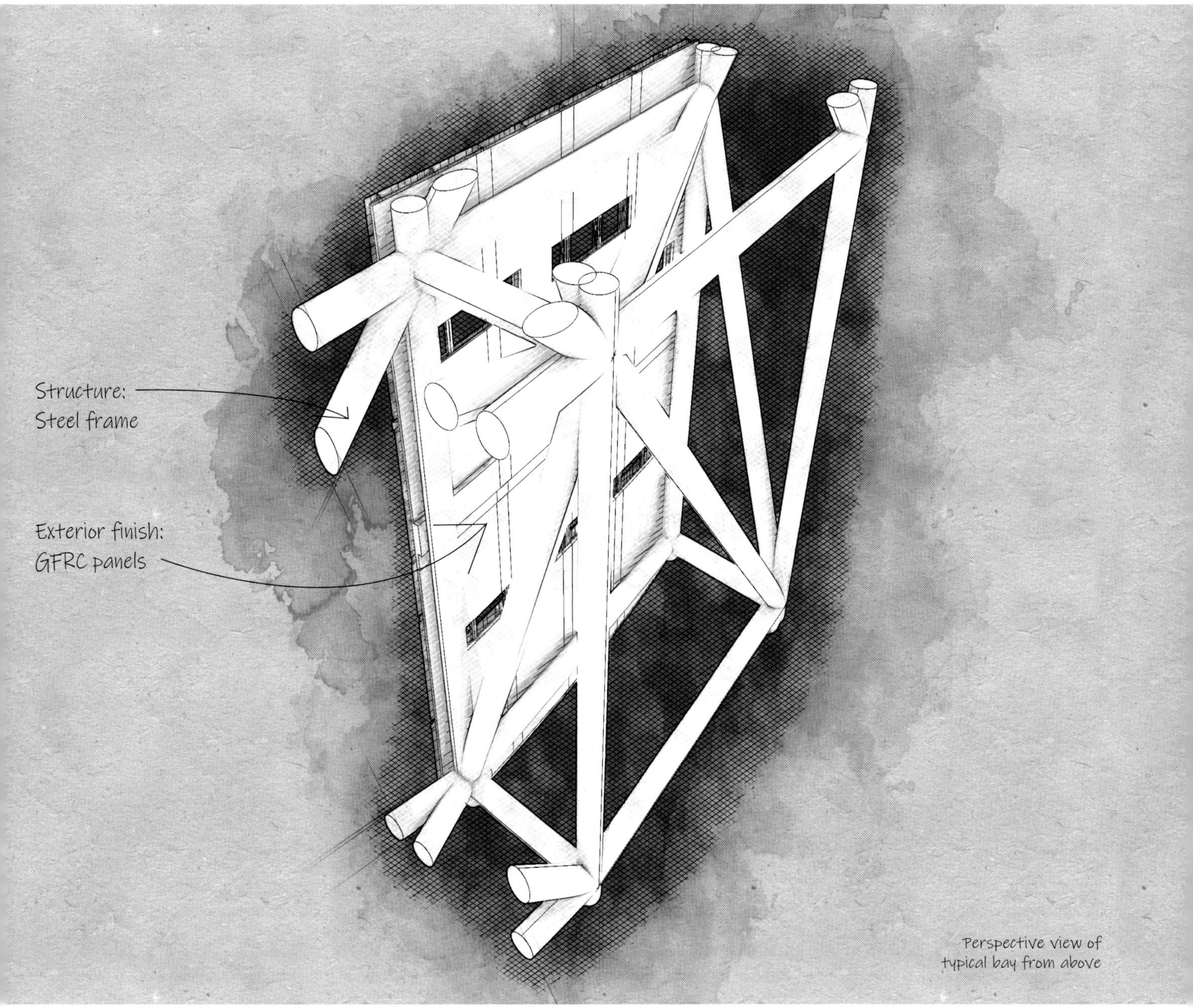

Perspective view of typical bay from above

apartments and the outer face of the facade and service zone; creating a double facade of service space which also provides natural ventilation, reflected daylight and solar control. This zone also accommodates metal staircases and environmental control equipment; packaged items of service equipment are set out across the facades. Ducted services are distributed on each floor; a deep facade of fixed solar shading devices.

The facades have a high level of differentiation that provide environmental control, mechanical and electrical services as well as daylight and natural ventilation in a passively shaded deep facade arrangement. The envelope design is based on having metal panels which wrap up the external elements of the facades. The metal panels fit in visually with the surrounding buildings, which are largely workshops and light industrial units. They provide the level of differentiation required in the general appearance of metal panels.

Metal panels are set at inclined angles in order to provide light shelves, solar shading and inlets/outlets for natural and mechanical ventilation. Panels can be adjusted to suit conditions in summer, winter and mid-season; adjustments are made manually. Some panels can be opened and closed within each apartment in order to control both natural ventilation and the entry of daylight from the floor level upwards, rather than from the windows only. Effects of daylighting can be created by the user; high levels of daylight are one of several settings.

Panels are also folded such that when opened, light is reflected into the apartment; across ceilings, walls or floors.

The approach taken to the integration of structure and services provides flexibility in the way service equipment is supported on primary structural members. The reinforced concrete frame has an exposed finish, which contrasts visually with the metal panels. No exposed or visible fixings are used, ensuring that both panels and equipment are secure and safe for maintenance access. The concrete members have chamfered edges, as do the enclosures securing the environmental control equipment; providing the visual crispness needed for both reinforced concrete construction and that of metal panel fabrication.

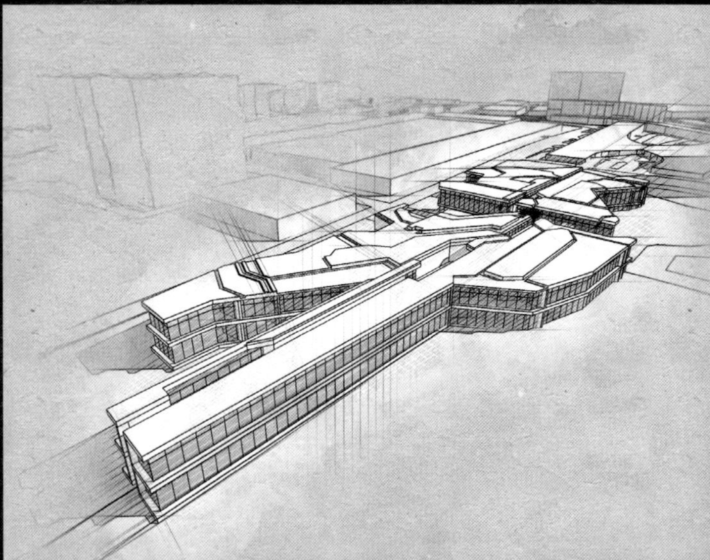

1. Perspective view of exterior

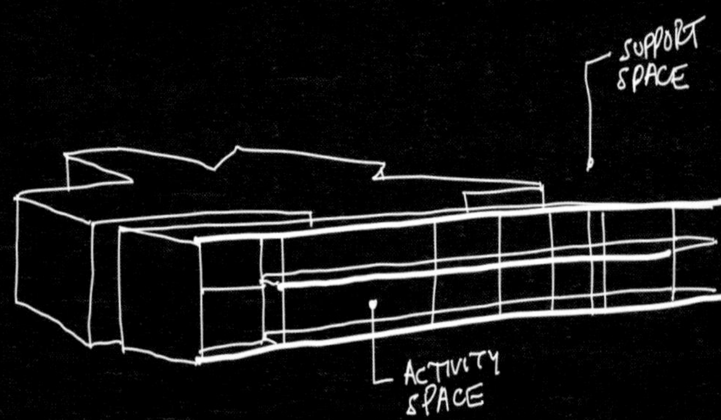

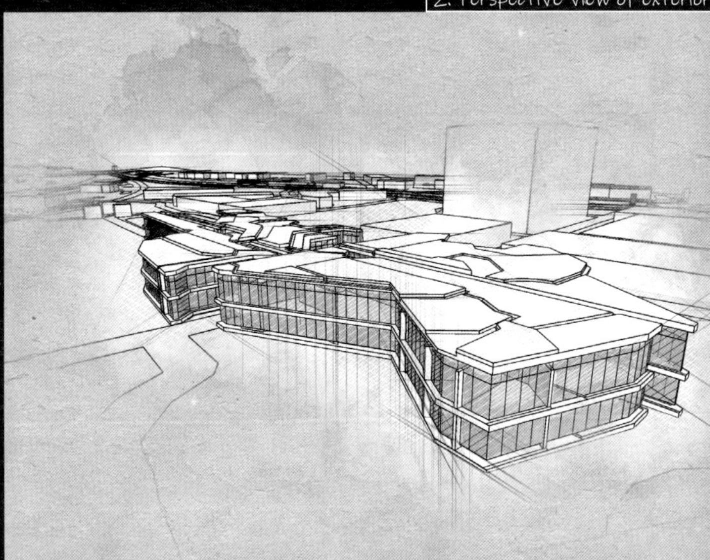

2. Perspective view of exterior

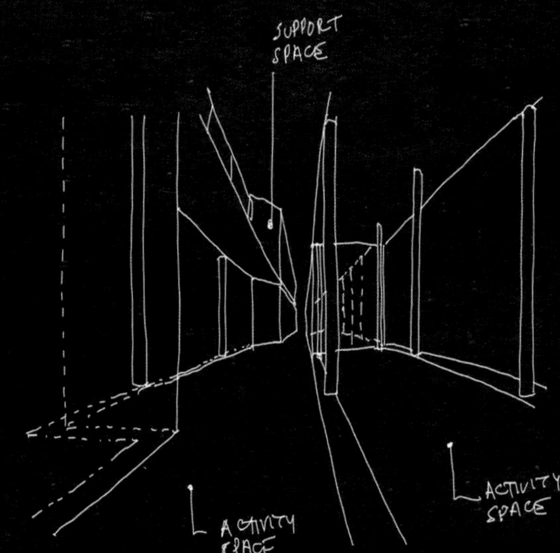

Semi-tempered spaces as environments for public art

The key environmental consideration of this project is to make a provision for the enclosed circulation spaces of this shopping mall to be open when the shop units are closed; avoiding the necessity to close public spaces outside of trading hours. The cooling and heating energy used during the day is also used after trading hours by the passive tempering of enclosed circulation areas, allowing these spaces to be publicly accessible; and without this environment becoming simply a 'display of shopfronts' which are generally illuminated at night, both in traditional open streetscapes in urban environments as well as within retail malls. A typical scenario in some retail malls is of closing public circulation areas at night; with descending shop shutters or, alternatively, shopfront lighting providing illumination and security. An alternative approach taken in this project is to provide large-scale public art installations, so that public circulation areas take on the role of providing a cultural expression as is traditionally used in urban environments: statues, fountains and seating areas. In place of that traditional arrangement, this public environment creates a complementary set of spaces which are 'public galleries' for the display of public sculptures which require protection from the effects of the weather. These are therefore well-suited to accommodation within the circulation spaces of this retail mall, for which they require a modest level of environmental control of the temperature and humidity to which they are exposed. These displays of public art can, for example, be an expression of the desire to commemorate recent events.

Public art displays are also able to bring life to the built environment during hours of darkness when the shopping mall areas are closed. Shopfronts are designed as if they were facing the street outside; there is relatively high thermal transmission from outside to inside the units and shops. This heating energy can be used in the semi-external spaces where sculptures are exhibited. The strategy is to encourage the shop owners to provide only a background heating provision within the units in order to keep temperatures high enough or low enough to suit the needs of the in-store goods. The temperature is adjusted

Perspective view of exterior

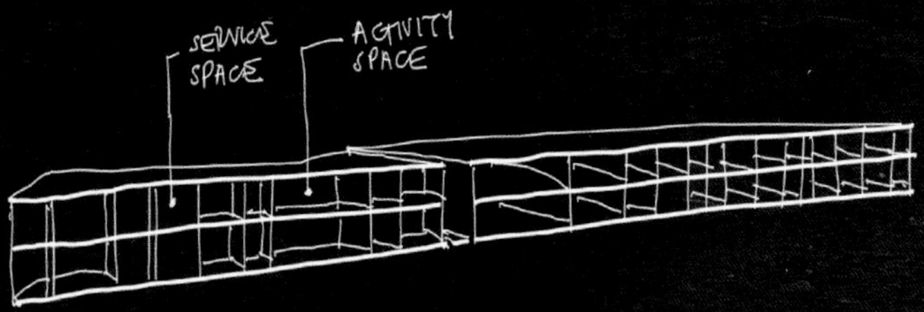

4. Perspective view of exterior

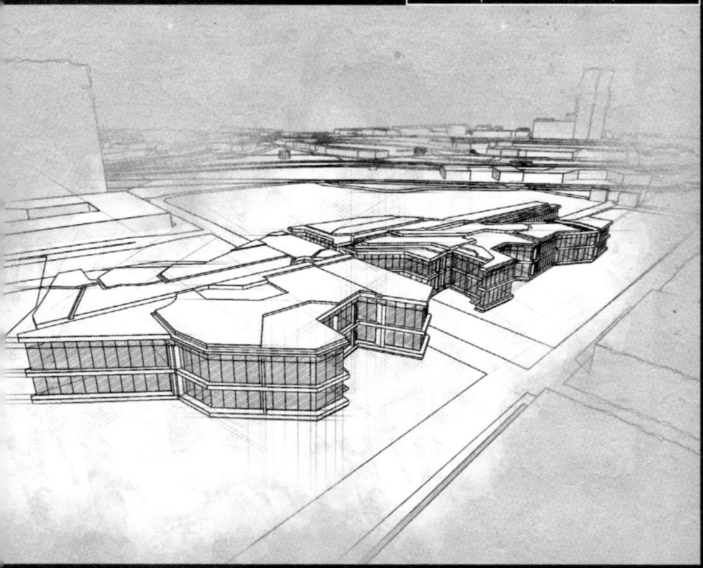

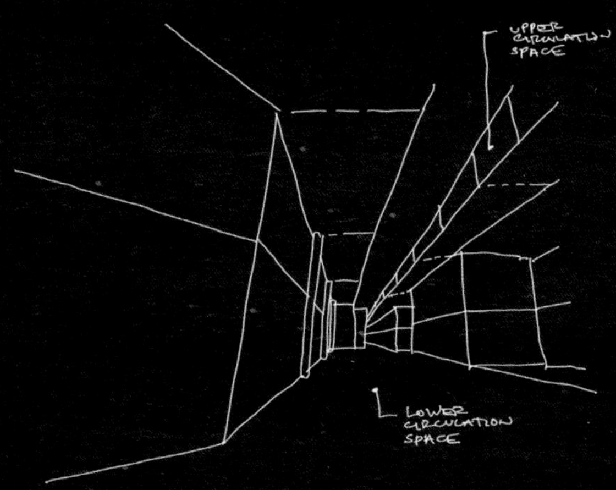

only during the 12 hours when the shops are open. This approach can provide a large energy saving while creating a clear role for the shopping mall. Public zones in this building are treated as external spaces; when the shops are closed, ventilation is provided at the ends and air is drawn through in electric fans during both summer and winter months. Background heating is provided in strategic areas where required but the experience is largely one of being outdoors, particularly during mid-season and summer months. The themes of the sculptures will encapsulate everyday life; scenes from common experiences; a commemoration of what is happening at the moment, of recent events which were considered to be positive events by the public, or events that that might be commemorated from the recent past. The interaction of public art exhibits and visitors to the retail mall provides a second level of engagement with the artworks on display.

This project aims to achieve that goal by providing seating arrangements around art work, part of which is occupied by sculpted figures. This approach helps to encourage a greater engagement with artworks and for a more extended period than a brief visit to each piece, as might be the case in an art gallery. A more extended engagement would provide a better use of the energy required to heat or cool parts of the central circulation spaces, as well as those areas which are naturally ventilated for parts of the year.

An alternative approach considered was to construct pavilions for the display of art; public art galleries that would be set within the mall. This idea competed with the need to occupy part of the mall with daytime food and beverage retail units that require circulation space within the mall for tables and chairs; not all of which are stored elsewhere when the retail outlets are closed.

The mixing of the cultural aims associated with an arts quarter was considered to be incompatible with that of a large-scale retail and leisure experience. The display of art within enclosures was seen as being a new-use category within the mall – an attraction perhaps – rather than an enrichment of a circulation space which would provide a different experience for visitors to this shopping mall.

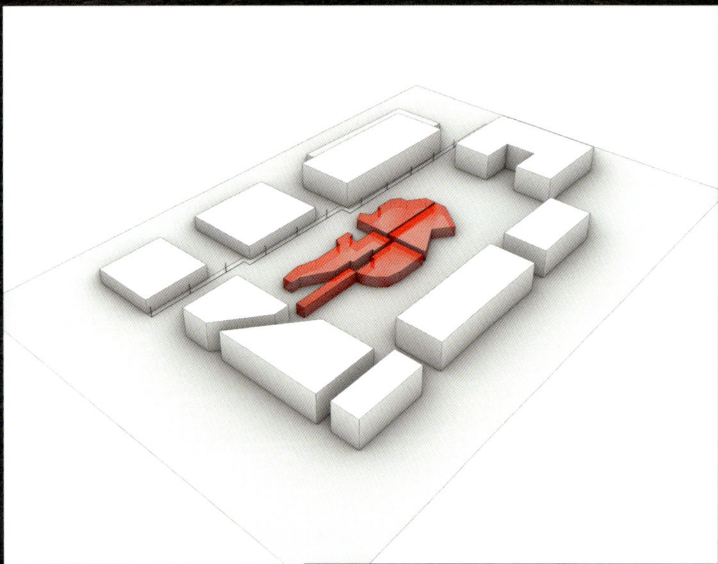

1. Project volume in site context

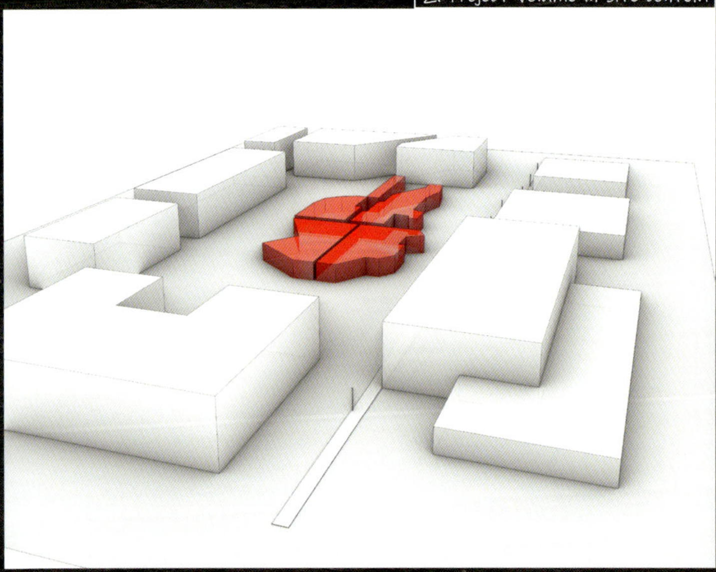

2. Project volume in site context

1. Site plan with surrounding context

Option 1 divides the building into two parts in order to respond to a central access to this large-scale retail project.

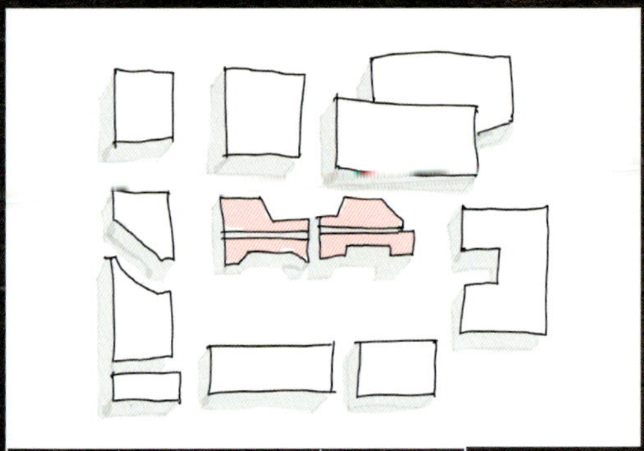

2. Site plan with surrounding context

Option 2 allows the linear nature of the forms to be explored further by using some of the geometries of existing nearby streets.

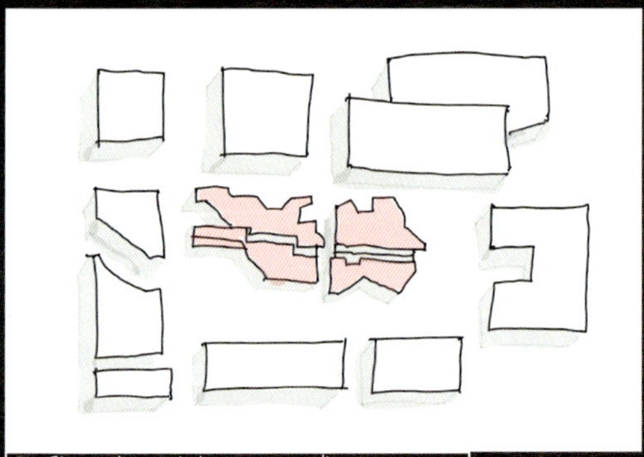

3. Site plan with surrounding context

Option 3 develops the theme of Option 2 further by responding more to the needs of the subdivision of space.

Site context

This retail centre is divided into two buildings with a central 'canyon' space that divides each of the two buildings into two parts; a cluster of buildings which comprise a set of retail units that are positioned on different levels. The canyon is not a straight street but forms a series of smaller canyon-like spaces, which are offset from one another at intervals in order to create a sequence of spaces. Each of the canyon-like spaces is part of a continuous route through the building. One end of the building comprises a long, low volume that extends outwards to provide a termination to the building, creating a large two-storey floorplate for a department store.

The site context for Option 1 is of a series of widely scattered blocks which are large-scale, two-storey buildings, interspersed with a few buildings which are up to seven storeys high. The context is of an open space where the retail centre will provide a focus for an area and a magnet for retail activity. This part of the city is used mainly during the working week; this project aims to widen that use to evenings and weekends. The design approach, from the urban design point of view, is to draw people in to give this area of the city life outside normal business hours. Option 1 divides the building into two parts in order to respond to a central access to this large-scale retail project. A central circulation route down the length of the building provides access to the retail units, arranged across two floors, with food and beverage facilities on a partial top floor. In Option 2, the linear nature of the forms is explored further by using some of the geometries of existing nearby streets, and by creating angled forms that also allow the brief/program to allow the overall building forms to respond to the needs of each tenant and of each subdivision of space, while maintaining a central straight internal canyon access. Option 3 develops this theme further by responding even more to the needs of the subdivision of space, creating opportunities for oblique views and changes of direction in the central circulation canyon in order to create a series of spaces, rather than a continuous canyon. This approach allows different areas of the retail mall to be developed; each with its own identity, linked together to create a

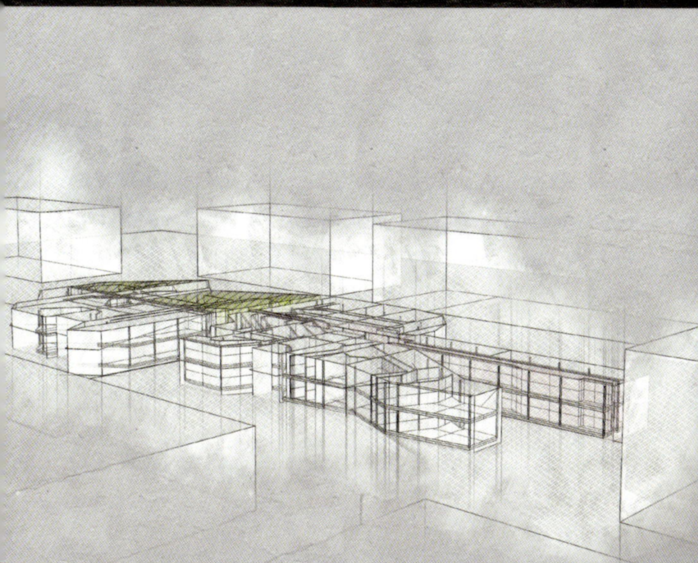

Perspective view of environmental volumes

2. Perspective view of environmental volumes

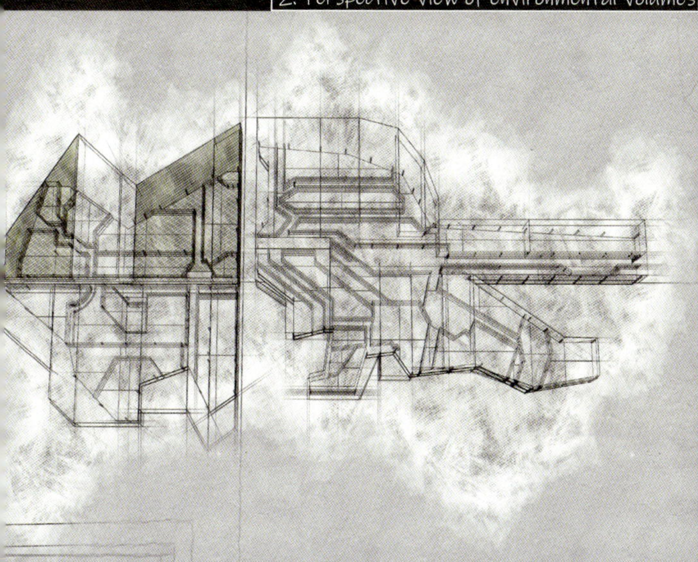

1. Figure-ground diagram of tempered environment

Option 1
Dark green spaces are highly tempered but are reduced to accommodation volumes only.

2. Figure-ground diagram of tempered environment

Option 2
Dark blue spaces are less tempered than dark green spaces but are more tempered than light blue circulation space.

3. Figure-ground diagram of tempered environment

Option 3
Light violet spaces are the least tempered spaces, these spaces interface directly with external space.

dynamic urban environment.

The approach to the site context is to provide a large number of points of entry into the building, not only at the ends of the main routes down and across the building. Shops can be accessed both from the street side and from within the building; the central streets create a temperate environment for most of the year, providing tempered air at times when it is either hot or cold outside, allowing people to enjoy a tempered environment where they can enjoy the the facilities of street food and boutiques positioned within the central mall canyon itself while still having access to the street side. Shop fronts can extend to both canyons on the internal and surrounding streets. The form of the building fills the space that would have been occupied by car parking. The building fits into a pattern of city streets and is accessed on foot from neighbouring car parking facilities; the default means of transportation to this retail mall is to use the surrounding transportation infrastructure. This is a large-scale development in a city centre area that does not have significant retail facilities available. This project is an urban insertion into a site context created by the unbuilt-upon areas that form the boundary of the site. Adjacent areas of land that were purchased for the project resulted in the unusual shape of the building. The shape of the site presented an opportunity to put building forms on the site like a jigsaw puzzle, creating an urban environment that fills the space available rather than accommodating a large area for the parking of road vehicles. The site context is one of adding pieces into an urban puzzle, and was not intended to create a form which is sealed off except for a few entrances and then a larger car parking area next to it; this is an urban-scale insertion project.

The building form inhabits an urban pattern of streets that has yet to be constructed; the three options of spatial arrangement demonstrate different ways in which the site could be developed from a large car park to a built-on piece of the city, or a set of pavilions that serve the retail mall, or alternatively how commercially run sports facilities could replace the need for the parking of private cars. In the third option, the retail mall becomes a semi-university-style centre for sport.

1. Sectional perspective view

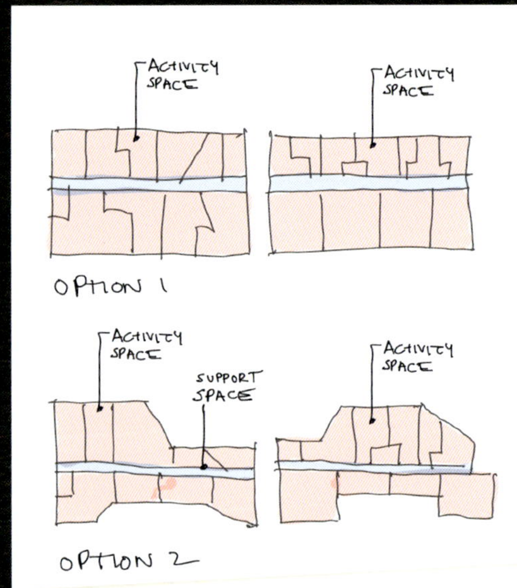

Spatial arrangement
Option 1 divides retail units into the sizes and shapes required by both the tenants and the owner.
Option 2 creates an offset between the two canyons down the full length of the retail centre.

2. Sectional perspective view

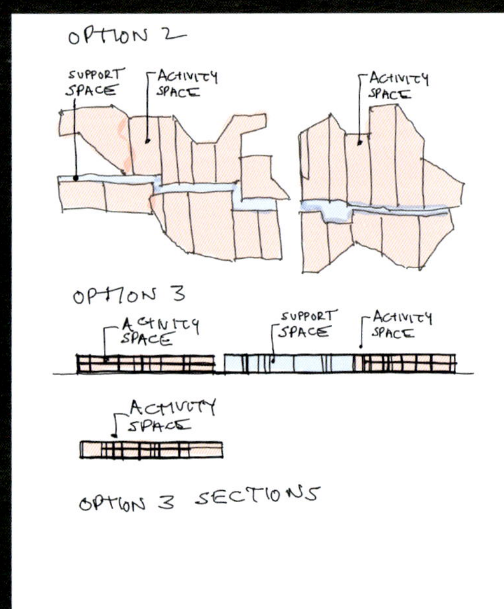

Option 3 introduces spaces which punctuate the length of the canyon as 'link' spaces.

Spatial arrangement

The spatial arrangement for Option 1 divides retail units into the sizes and shapes required by both the tenants and the owner. The shape of units varies; rectilinear, L-shaped and trapezoidal. This variation of internal form also allows for spaces of different size to be created; a retail experience of a sequence of spaces within a single shop unit. The layout also allows access to be provided to upper levels as well as some service spaces to be created for delivery and distribution of goods, separate from the movement of visitors to the building. Option 2 develops that idea further and creates an offset between the two canyons down the centre such that the full length of the retail centre, and the full length of the canyons, are not seen from any given view. As a result, the two canyons, divided at the point of the centrally positioned entrance, are each given a specific character by offsetting one from the other, as seen in the plan. The spatial arrangement of the shop units is developed further to respond more closely to the needs of each retail unit, both in size and shape. Option 3 further develops the geometry of circulation routes by introducing spaces which punctuate the length of the canyon; 'link' spaces, set perpendicular to the main direction of the canyons, create visually arresting spaces. This approach creates a set of eight different canyon experiences that are also internal spaces in their own right; they are stairs and lifts/elevators, and seating areas are not considered to be only areas of transition as a passage between floors. When compared with Options 1 and 2, this option creates greater dynamism in the relationship of the outer facades and the inner forms of shop units. There is also a more developed spatial relationship between the canyons and the retail spaces by allowing some shops to be accessed from the ends of the building rather than directly from the canyon. Regarding servicing and supply to the shop units, the topography of the site allows deliveries to be made at an undercroft level, with distribution of the goods being carried out independently of the shoppers' experience.

The spatial arrangement of the car parking areas is generated from the three options for the replacement of car parking: city quarter for

Perspective view of interior

2. Perspective view of interior

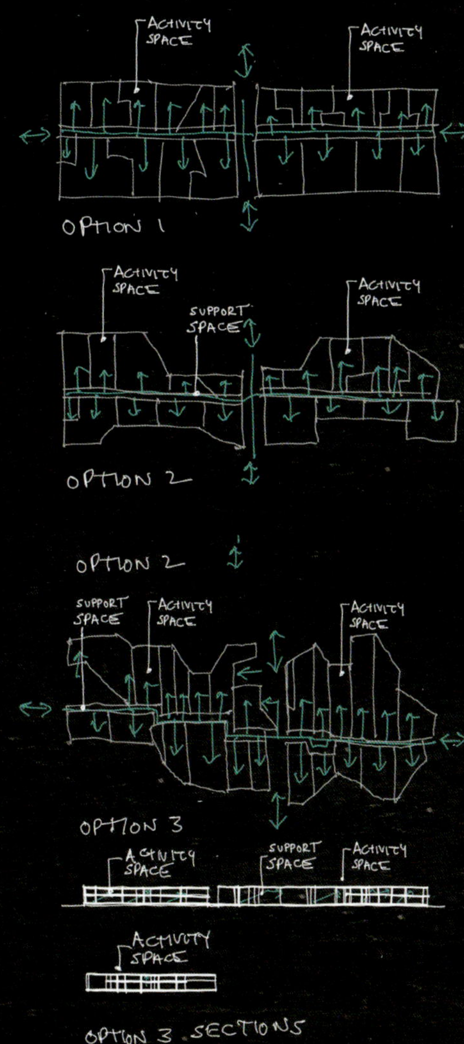

Internal circulation

Option 1 arranges circulation in a continous straight line.

Option 2 arranges circulation with indents introduced as resting places.

Option 3 arranges circulation following a stepped route throughout the length of the building.

Option 3, satellite spaces (such as cinemas and exhibition halls) for Option 2 or a commercial sports facility for Option 1. All three options are based on a reduced near future dependency on parking locally.

Internal circulation

The complexity of the forms is generated in section rather than in plan; circulation spaces allow movement on other floors, through the complexity of form. The canyon route through the complete building reveals the overall form of the centre to resemble a series of inclined terraces; walkways are not superimposed or aligned one above the other, but are stepped back from one another, on each level, to provide views up and down into smaller spaces. These secondary spaces are created by bridges spanning voids in front of shops. The bridges create voids in front of shopfronts such that they can be seen from a modest distance rather than only being visible directly in front of the shopfront glass. This allows views up and down across several floors of shopfronts. There is more of a sense of 'gaps' and 'fissures' between retail volumes. The aim here is not to replicate a traditional shopping mall with a covered roof, but instead to create greater interaction between building form, shop and street by creating voids and bridges between the retail units. Opportunities created by the geometries of these units allow people to explore the retail centre rather than follow a straight line from one end to the other, as is often characteristic of retail malls. A key requirement of this project is to create a sequence of spaces linked by a circulation route; and exploration rather than a utility of passage. Visitors move through interstitial circulation spaces between the units; circulation spaces have been grouped vertically in section to create a larger circulation area which allows shoppers to be able to discover, visually, other floors and see the retail units from below.

The internal circulation arrangements for all three options provide access through the heart of the project; drawing people that also use the surrounding urban transport infrastructure. Internal spaces are provided by the canyons that run from end to end of the building, distributing visitors from levels of the central canyon to each retail unit.

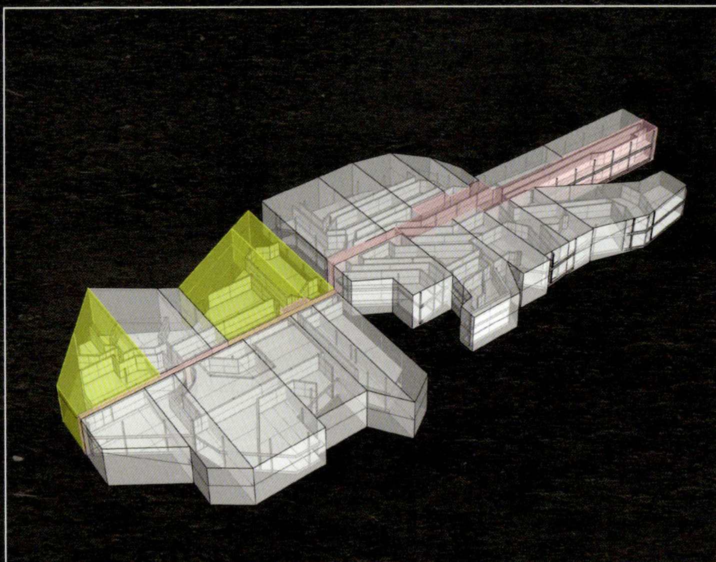

1A. Isometric view of environmental volumes

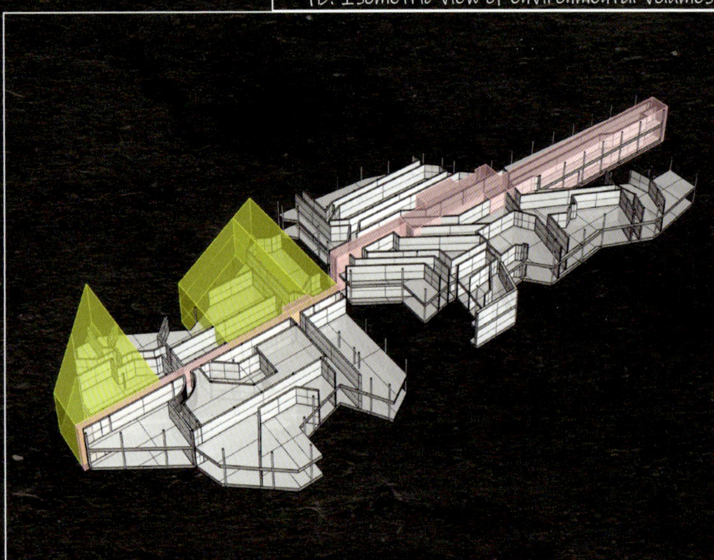

1B. Isometric view of environmental volumes

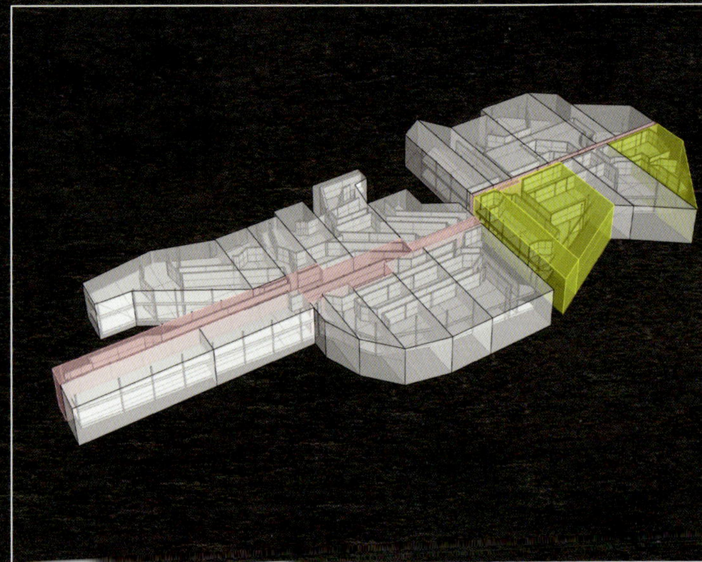

2A. Isometric view of environmental volumes

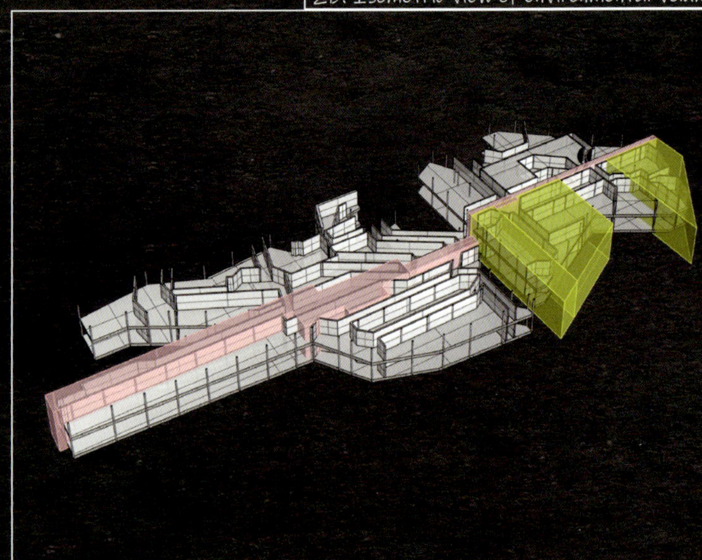

2B. Isometric view of environmental volum

Environmental strategy

The building is ventilated mechanically and serviced from the roof level; ducted air is distributed across the roof and down to all parts of the project. Some of the ducted air is provided on the outside of the building, between the inner and outer facades and between the inner partition and the outer wall, which results in some of the characteristic forms of the building. Other parts have air distribution adjacent to two column spaces, and others still leading down the interstitial spaces between the volumes that comprise the building.

The project is conceived for energy efficiency and to provide a maximum of flexibility of use by allowing the walls between retail units to be moved with relative ease, while maintaining the functioning of service cores. The environmental strategy also provides flexibility for individual tenants to expand or to relocate each unit within the centre in order to suit their changing operational requirements. This strategy is one of using a single set of mechanical and electrical equipment for the complete building. Air, water and electrical supplies are distributed at roof level in a network which distributes services vertically into the units below as a set of gridded points which are independent of service cores. Cores are used for vertical circulation only, both for visitors and for goods. This approach to the distribution of mechanical and electrical services brings the benefits of using the roofscape as a series of horizontal but linked planes to distribute services as efficiently and as flexibly as possible; providing a benefit of reducing the overall size of the air-handling units and the chillers and reducing the length of duct runs and the associated loss of heating or cooling energy. An additional benefit of the use of the roofscape for the distribution of services is that connections of air, water and electrical supplies to spaces below can be rearranged easily; moving supply from one opening in the roof for the supply of services to another.

The environmental strategy for Option 1 is of establishing three environmental zones: the canyons and the zones shown in an individual colour for each building block, in the illustration. The circulation canyons are designed as environmental 'buffer' spaces in that their controlled

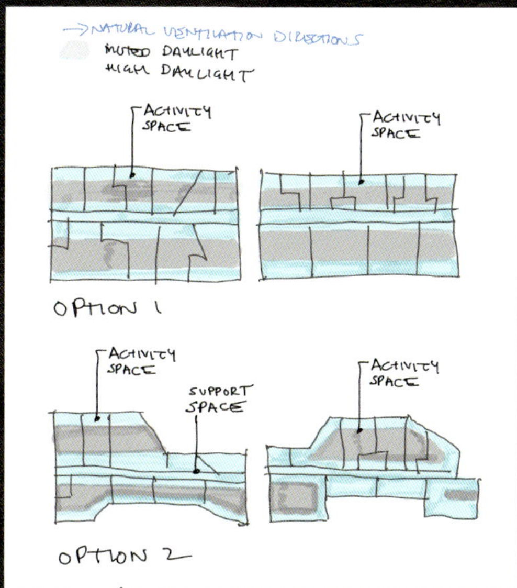

Daylight strategy for direct sunlight and cross ventilation.
Option 1 admits light and air from the long sides of the building.
Option 2 increases the proportion of spaces with subdued daylight to those which are more highly daylit.

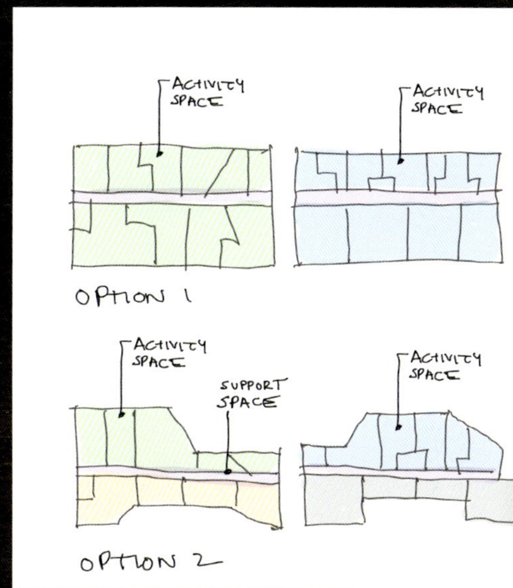

Environmental zones
Option 1 establishes three environmental zones.
Option 2 provides more environmental zones that respond to each of the four quadrants of the building.

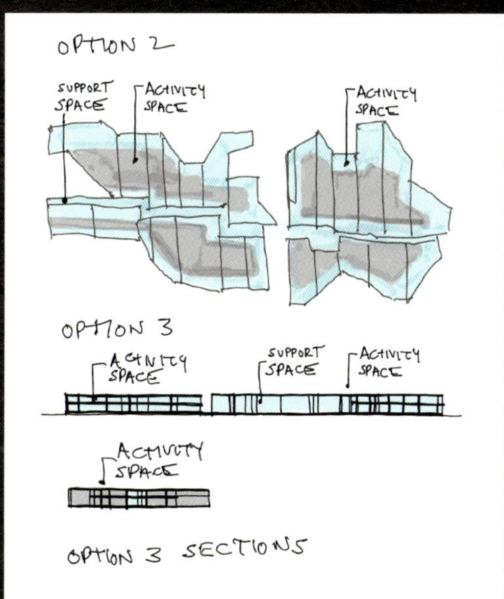

Daylight strategy for direct sunlight and cross ventilation.
Option 3 further increases the proportion of areas of subdued light to more sunlight.

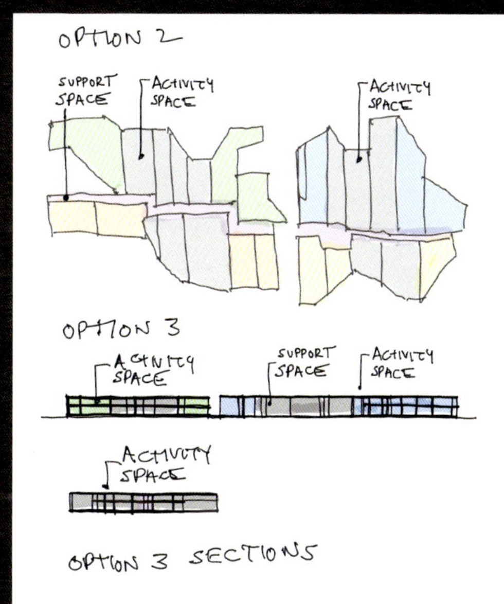

Environmental zones
Option 3 retains a single environmental zone for all circulation zones, while creating the environmental zone such that each of the spaces are further differentiated from that provided in Option 2.

level of temperature and humidity is adjusted in response to levels of air temperature and humidity in adjacent retail units. This approach allows the canyons to take up the mid-temperature between retail units set opposite one another, forming a buffer that aims to minimise the use of energy across the complete building. Each of the coloured blocks shown in the illustrations has different requirements for heating and cooling, as a result of their different orientations in relation to the path of the sun. A smaller block accommodates food and beverage areas on the top floor, which require higher air changes per hour than either the circulation routes or the shop units themselves. Option 2 provides more environmental zones that respond to each of the four quadrants of the building in response to the different temperatures and humidity controls required in spaces of different size and different activities carried out within. Option 3 develops further the differentiation of environmental zones, but retains a single environmental zone for all circulation zones, while creating the environmental zone such that each of the spaces are further differentiated from that provided in Option 2.

The environmental strategy is based on the concept for each shop unit being serviced independently of its neighbour, like a traditional street; a set of separately occupied retail premises. A high level of flexibility is introduced into the system as a result of using the roofscape as the means of distribution of ducted air, heating and cooling pipes through the retail units, including central spaces and food courts. All shops have varying requirements for ventilation and different levels of occupancy and size. The environmental strategy is to allow each unit to have its own self-contained system which is located on the roof but which can be shared with neighbouring units.

Tenants can make use of the base system provided; a high level of flexibility in environmental control is created, including the ability to draw air from the canyon spaces down the middle of the building to provide natural ventilation. This approach corresponds with a trend of seeing shops, particularly large-scale stores, having an air temperature which is cooler in winter and warmer in summer than has typically been the case in past years.

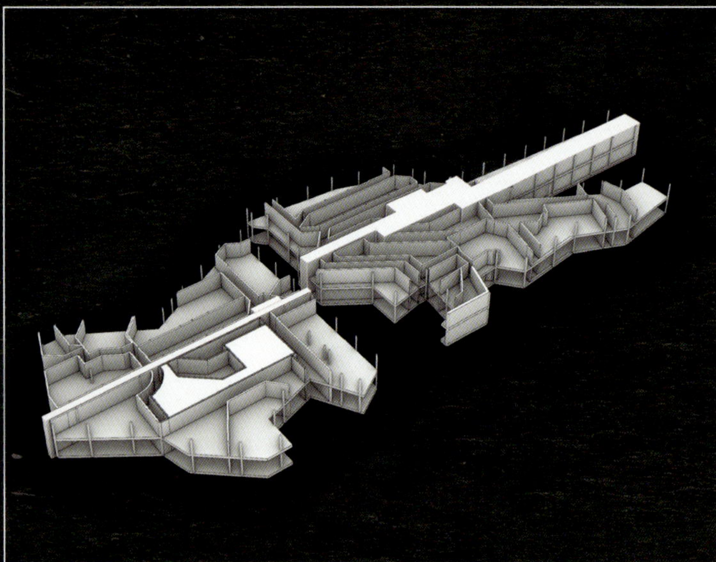

1A. Isometric view of structure

2A. Isometric view of structure

1B. Isometric view of structure

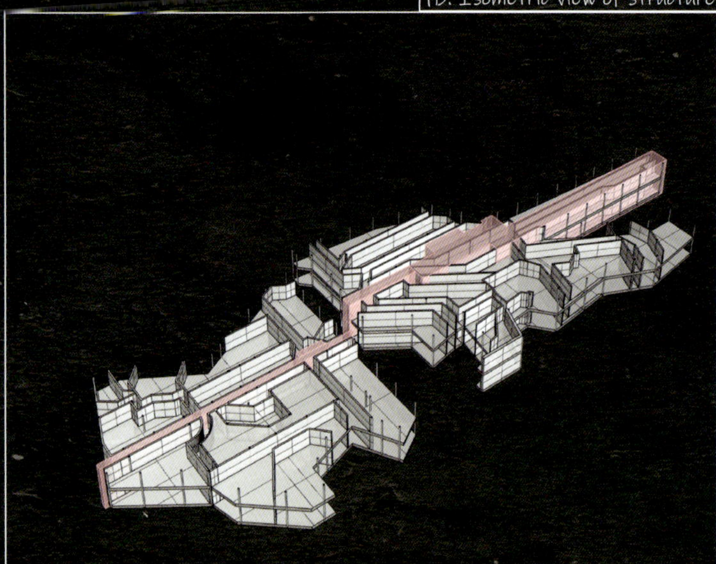

2B. Isometric view of structu

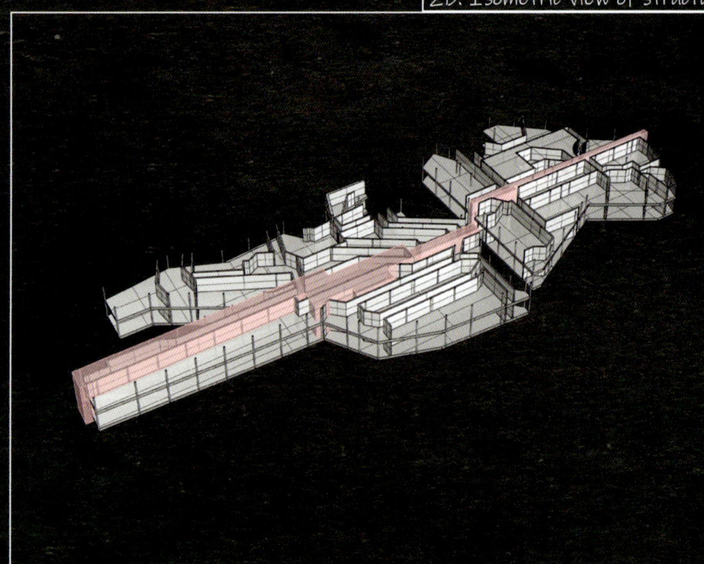

Structural strategy

The structural strategy is made in response to both the different sizes of internal space and external form, and the environmental strategy of providing a grid of openings in the floor plates and the roof deck, used for the vertical distribution of services from the roof down to the ground floor. The need for a large number of small openings in the primary structure, provided economically, has led to the use of a mixed structure of steel, with floor slabs that are a mixture of steel beams and precast concrete floor planks, and in-situ-cast concrete slabs. The building comprises a set of internal spaces and corresponding external forms that are interpreted structurally as a 'skeleton' form of frames, with a lightweight infill of non-load-bearing internal walls and external walls. The facades use the same principle of large areas of geometrically rich form as those of the interior walls. What differentiates the facades from internal walls is their additional layers of thermal insulation and weatherproofing, applied as a thin covering to the outside of the building. This structural approach allows internal spaces within it to be modified structurally to suit the changing needs of tenants, without the need for closing sections of the building while works are being undertaken. This approach suits the geometrically irregular arrangement of the structural frame, which makes use of a single grid of columns which are not rectilinear in their arrangement, but are set out on straight lines that allow the structure to be modified independently between rows of column grid.

The structural strategy for all three options is based on the use of steel frames which make use of a setting-out of column spacings which vary within groups of retail units. Each group is constructed as a set of separate structures, allowing each to be modified in the near future independently of its neighbours, as is the case with traditional arrangements of buildings of shops in an urban centre. This arrangement of columns, beam arrangements and floors avoids the need for long-spanning components which can reduce flexibility in spatial arrangements; the concept of the hangar-like space for retail units introduces difficulties of subdivision by reducing the possibility of points of structural support.

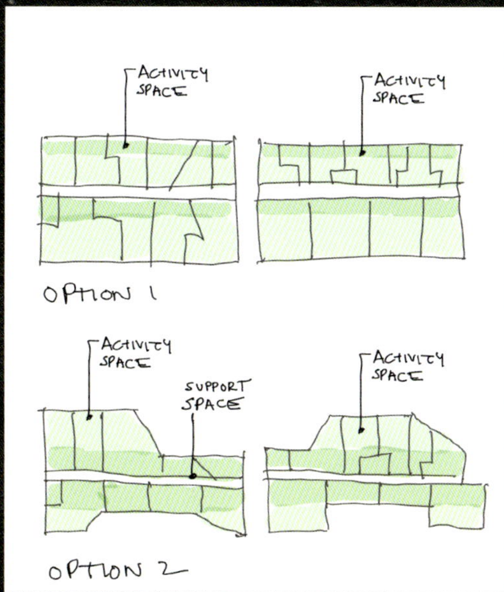

Structural strategy: Zones

Option 1 uses a structural frame with stability provided by areas of braced wall.

Option 2 uses a structural frame with stability provided by areas of cross bracing.

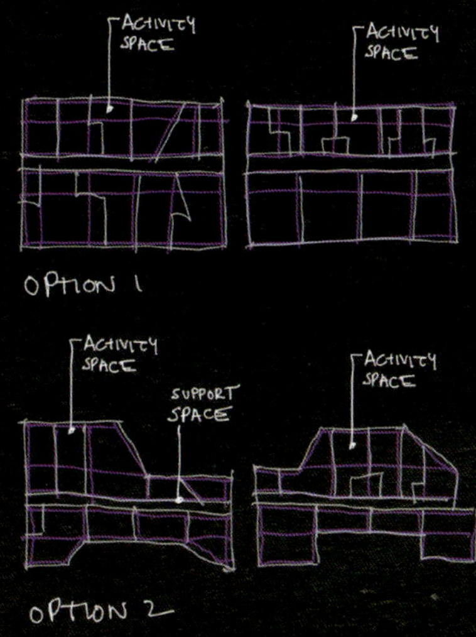

Structural strategy: Framing

Option 1 encloses a concrete frame.

Option 2 is largely a steel frame.

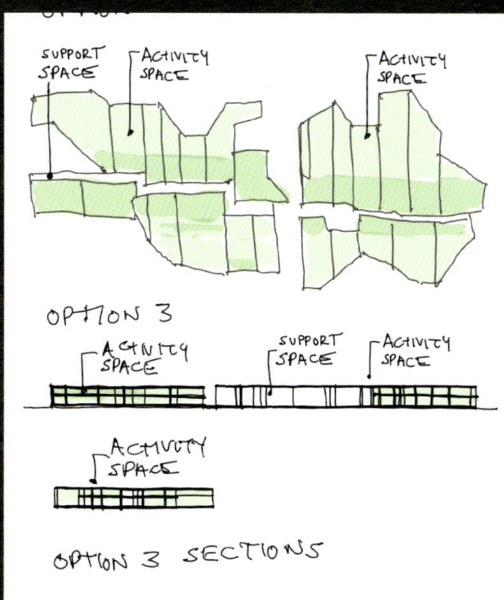

Structural strategy: Zones Option 3 uses a structural frame with stability provided by areas of braced wall and cross bracing.

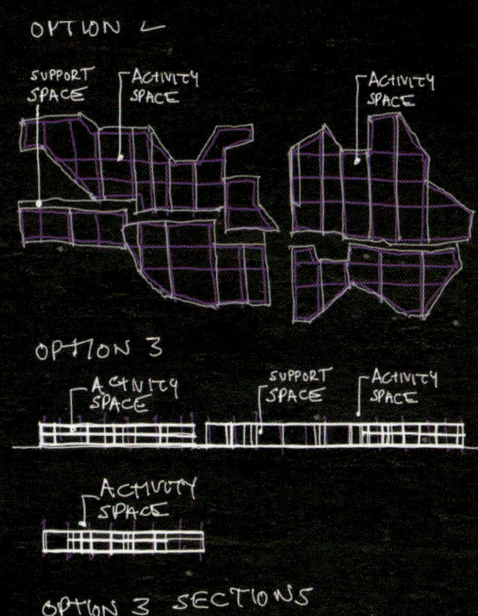

Structural strategy: Zones Option 3 is a mixed solution of reinforced concrete and steel.

This structural strategy provides those additional points of support primarily in the arrangement of columns and of small openings in floors for the distribution of services across a regular grid of vertically distributed services. The roofs and circulation spaces in all three options are treated as separate structures; the structures either form bridges between blocks and groups of retail units, or are formed as independent structures. This approach provides a greater level of flexibility in the development of the design for the near future, as well as providing a set of linked roof structures. This approach creates opportunities for the near future infill of some of the 'gaps' between spaces as well as creating new gaps; the structural strategy responds to the need for flexibility of adjustment of floor structures, within a fixed arrangement of columns, to suit the evolving needs of this set of retail spaces.

The structural design was developed with three options in response to a set of three spatial arrangements: a simplified rectilinear form, an indented form and a third option whose outline follows the edges of the street pattern. Options 1 and 2 do not develop the full extent of the site. It was established that the option of a high-density floor plan that followed the street layout was economical, but was less economical at its edges where the spatial arrangement interfaces with the facades at the perimeter of the building. Consequently, a square-shaped rectilinear structural grid was used with structural members that were arranged more closely together than the other two options, allowing them to be optimised for weight and not for the partitions between shops; such that retail units were offered on the basis of a multiple of the structural grid. This is a building where the environmental design occupies the public spaces and the retail units use a structural grid as a determining factor in the size of the units available which were still flexible in their arrangement and juxtaposition.

Structures for pavilions in the car parks are based on light-gauge steel construction, which suggests how the parking areas could be developed as an urban quarter in their own right. The structures make use of recycled metal panels which form part of the structure rather than being only a non-loadbearing cladding.

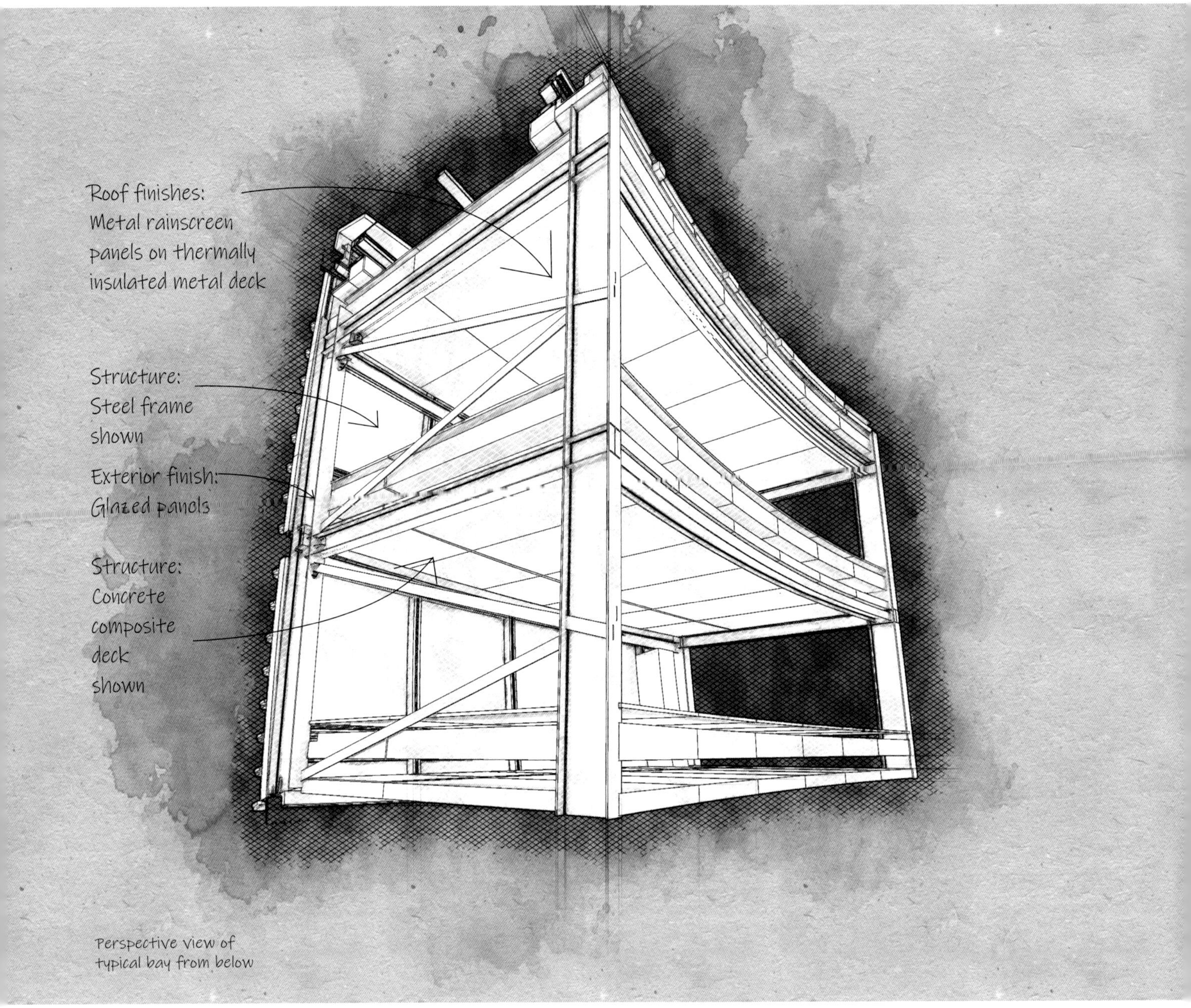

Perspective view of typical bay from below

Typical bay adjacent to facade

The strategy of the external envelope, and specifically the facades, is to reduce the amount of energy transmission from outside to inside without creating an enclosure which appears to be opaque and inward-looking. The facades, specifically, aim to create views through the complete building from one side to the other; reducing the scale of the overall building forms to create an urban design-focussed arrangement of small units. Views through the building are provided by glazed areas of facade which are linked with a corresponding area of glazed facade on the other side of the building; creating perspective views both into spaces within the building and beyond to the built environment beyond this retail mall. The creation of vistas reveals parts of the canyon spaces within the building; ensuring that internal spaces are seen as 'public space' rather than being closed-off 'private space'. This approach is taken forward by the provision of sets of large-scale sculptures as 'public art' installations which can be accessed most of the time by the public, regardless of the opening hours of retail units; much like the functioning of traditional open urban centres. The canyon spaces have a role as spaces to house public art installations rather than being only enclosed circulation spaces within a building. The external envelope is a mixture of masonry-based panels, metal panels and areas of glazing that differentiate the juxtaposed opaque forms that constitute groups of retail units.

The overall appearance of the facades is a mixture of opaque geometric forms and areas of visible structure which are enclosed as irregular-shaped glass 'slots'; the geometric arrangement of the glass slots is defined both vertically and horizontally, providing a visual 'reading' of the different spaces inside the building, as seen from the outside. This building is no enclosed 'box without windows'; this is instead a building where individual units can be seen clearly on the facade through the use of a differentiated geometry and not primarily by signage. The glazed strips provide views into the building during hours of darkness, allowing the circulation spaces to provide a gentle continuity with the adjacent urban context of streets.

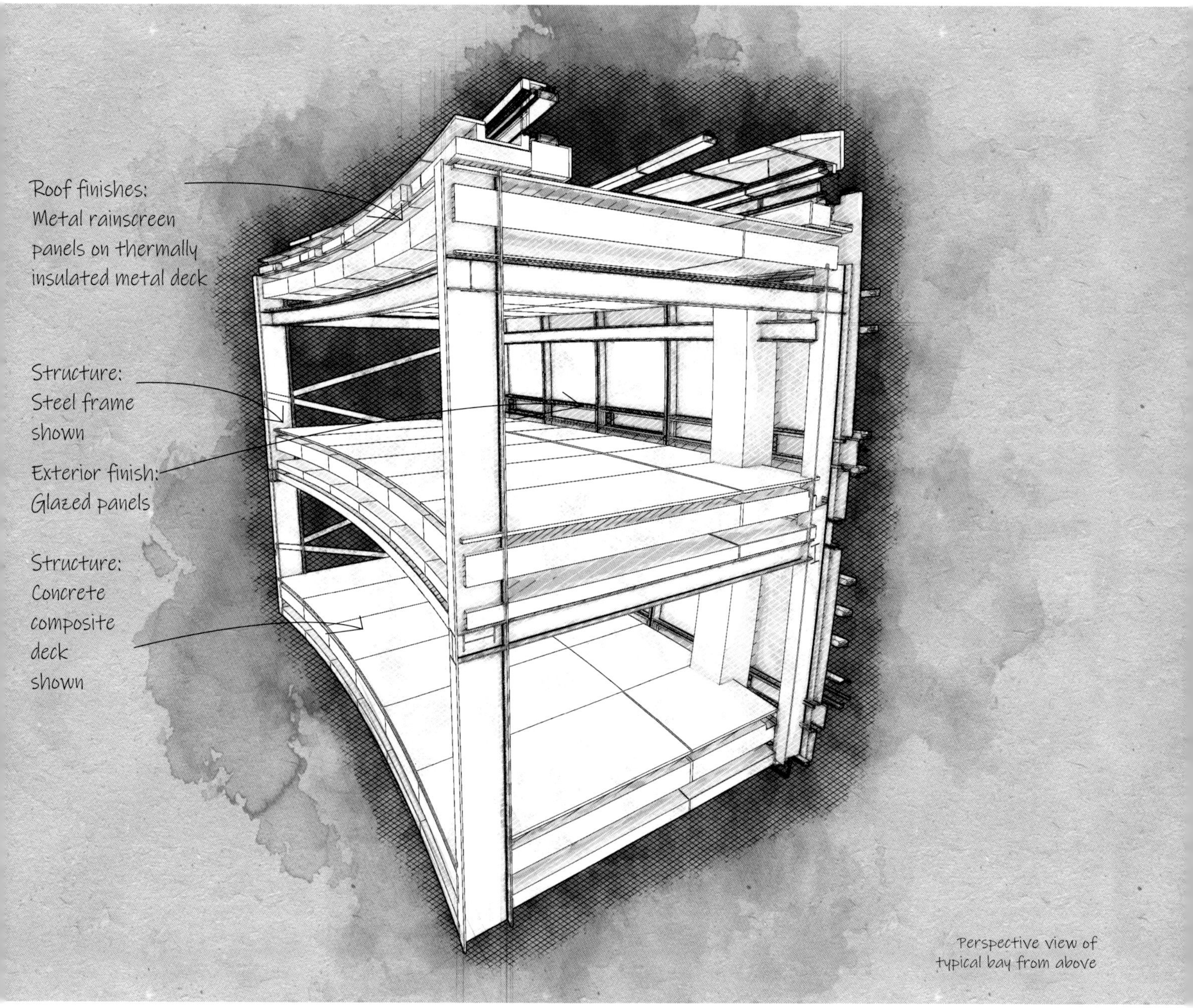

Perspective view of typical bay from above

The facades follow the lines of columns and beams which were created by the intersection of the structural grid with the edge of slab, creating bays of different length that correspond to the structural grid inside the building. The facades are enclosed with a mixture of clear glass shopfronts and opaque panels which are formed in both opaque glass and metal to create shopfronts that are visually 'barcoded', as the facades are extended through the full height of the building such that the requirements for the ground floor entrance and shopfronts are repeated on the floor above. A screen wall behind the clear shopfronts are required at ground level only, where they are accessed from the surrounding streets. The roof is the largest element of the envelope and comprises a membrane roof which is light in colour to reflect heat from the sun. An arrangement of covers over exposed ducts in the building creates the characteristic roof forms that are used as a logo for the retail centre, as seen from surrounding buildings. The solution for the roof is economical; a membrane is used continuously and the metal panels are of a similar colour to create a light-coloured continuous environmental grid, forming an irregular-shaped grid across the roofs of the building. Each quarter of the building is self-contained such that services are not required to pass over the rooflights from one side of the building to the other. This does happen in a few places and provision for a roof-level ducted enclosure has been created in a few places. The roof plan as seen from neighbouring buildings serves as a 'map of functions' for the spaces beneath. The facades for the pavilions in the car parks form part of the structure. Both structure and enclosure are loadbearing and are made from recycled materials whose performance can be considered as being safe to use for the shorter lifespan of the pavilions. The watertight structures are clad in further recycled components from other industries; washing machine panels and car body parts. The reduced durability of these assemblies is consistent with the period of leases for their commercial use; the underlying structure and enclosure remains in place for the lifespan of the shopping mall. The pavilions are expected to be a catalyst for the future development of the space occupied by car parks.

1. Perspective view of exterior

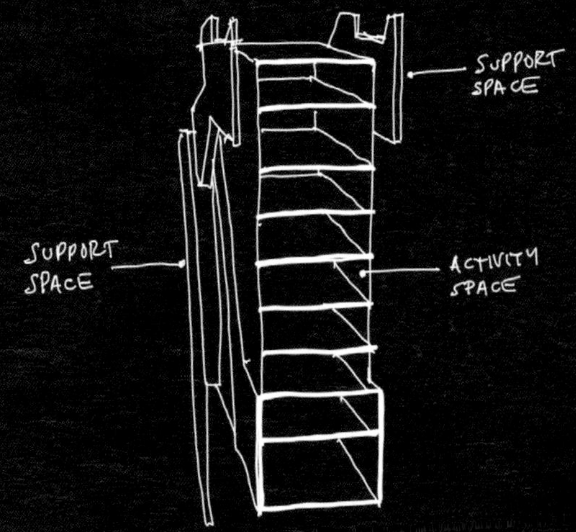

2. Perspective view of exterior

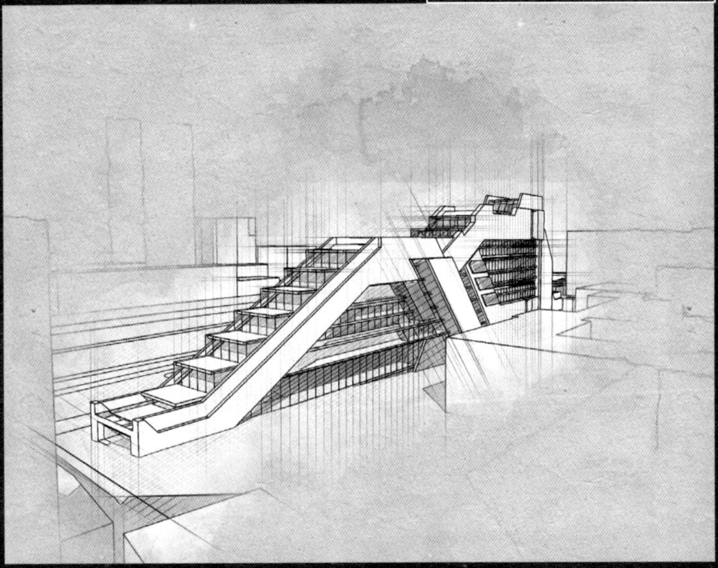

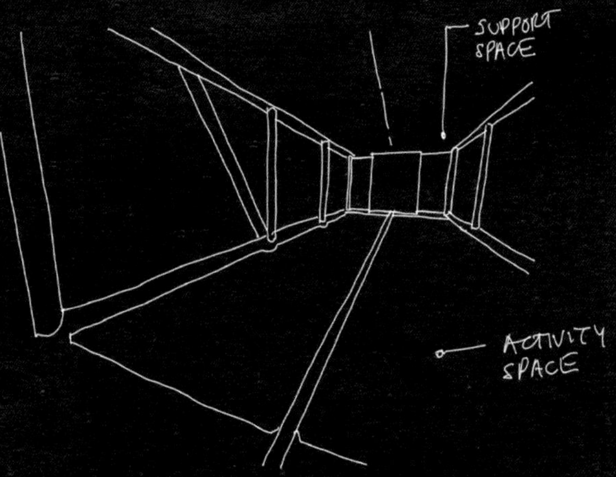

Reducing the energy expended in component replacement

A key environmental design consideration for this project is the eventual replacement and recycling of certain parts of the building. This provision is made possible by ensuring that assemblies can be cleaned and maintained easily in order to ensure that the eventual replacement is gradual; a result of removing worn/exhausted components and assemblies. In order to achieve this aim, equipment for cleaning and maintenance tasks is accommodated in the design. The strategy and equipment chosen is such that maintenance and component replacement work can be carried out safely without a high expenditure of electrical energy and without closing off parts of the building, or part of adjacent streets; no large-scale lifting equipment is needed. Most of the areas of the building which are likely to need more frequent servicing and the replacement of mechanical and electrical equipment are at a higher level. The cleaning and maintenance cycle is accommodated by equipment which is integrated into the building design. As a result, the primary structural frame of the building includes a continuous high-capacity cleaning rail. This continuous beam is used to support the high-capacity cleaning rail; positioned at the top edge of each parapet in the building added at roof level. The beam spans the full length of the building on both sides, allowing the high-capacity cleaning rail to be added with a roof-level track that supports an outboard cleaning cradle; the cradle descends to either ground level or to the next-lowest roof level. This approach of integration into the structural design, of the maintenance and component replacement equipment, reduces the need for specialist equipment to be brought to site periodically.

This approach allows spaces occupied by the opaque panels, which constitute part of the structural frame of the building, to be used as zones for circulation around the building as well as for the provision of building services. The inclined elements of structure provide an opportunity for staircases and lifts/elevators to create a visually dynamic volume as a result of the varying geometric relationship with the enclosing volume of the air-handling ducts and service conduits. The overall approach is one of creating opportunities for the vertical movement

Perspective view of exterior

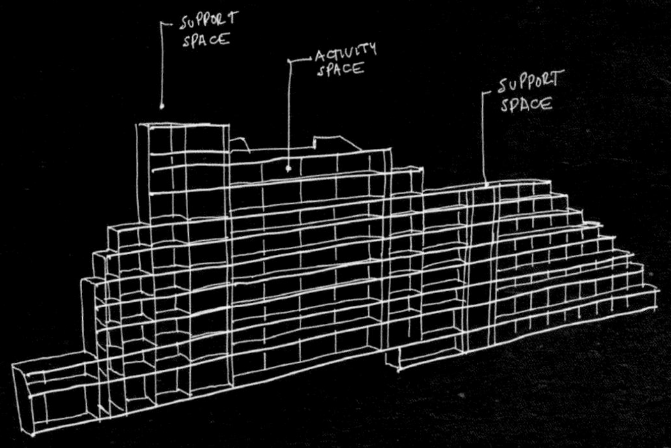

4. Perspective view of exterior

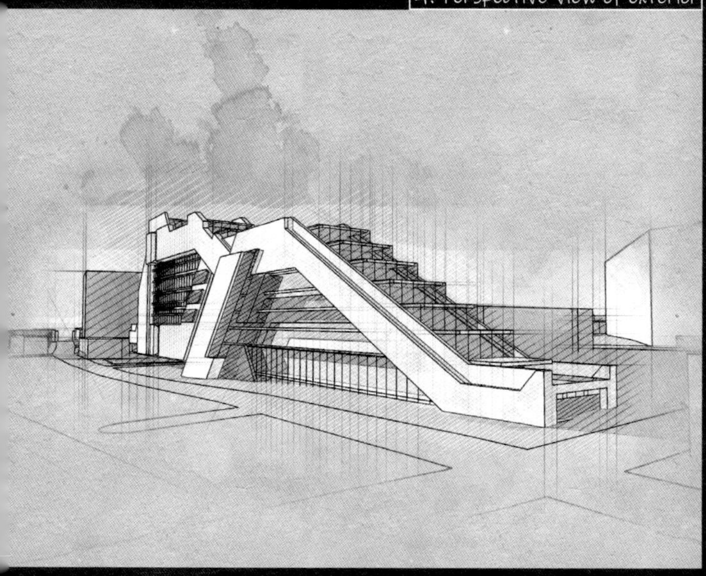

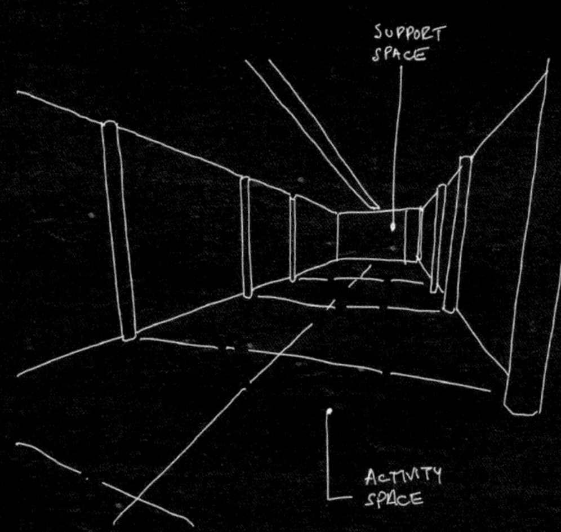

that links the commercial parts of the building with escalators that rise through parts of this resort hotel, which combines commercial facilities with hotel rooms in a single building. The dynamic form of the facades provides both views outward as well as along the length of the building for guests and visitors to the building. The arrangement of spaces ensures that views out towards the sea are provided, as well as guests being invited to feel part of a large but integrated structure of this multifunctional building.

The approach to the environmental design of this building is to be able to facilitate maintenance of services externally without the need to interrupt the resort hotel experience for guests. This building is designed so that servicing of the building from the point of view of providing mechanical and electrical services and associated access is set on one side of the building. This approach allows a building to be maintained without entering any of the hotel rooms and suites for access to ducted areas in the central corridor spaces, avoiding the need to have opening panels inside bathrooms. This approach allows part of the structural frame of the building to be integrated within spaces occupied by the zones for both circulation and for building services.

The essential idea for recycling and reuse is to provide a zone on both sides of the building which can be accessed with ease, without the need for specialist equipment for cleaning and maintenance. Maintenance access is provided by the pedestrian routes through the building; staircases and lifts/elevators line both sides of the building. Facades can be accessed by the solar shading devices which extend the full length of the building; the shading being formed as a cantilevered portion of floor slab which also serves as an access walkway. Access for maintenance staff is secured by harness and safety line. The edges and underside of access walkways are clad in GFRC-moulded panels which enhance their performance as solar shading panels. These panels also reflect low-angle sun onto the ceilings and walls to enhance the daylight provision that these devices also provide. Ease of access for the maintenance and replacement of elements of facade and environmental control systems is a key part of the design.

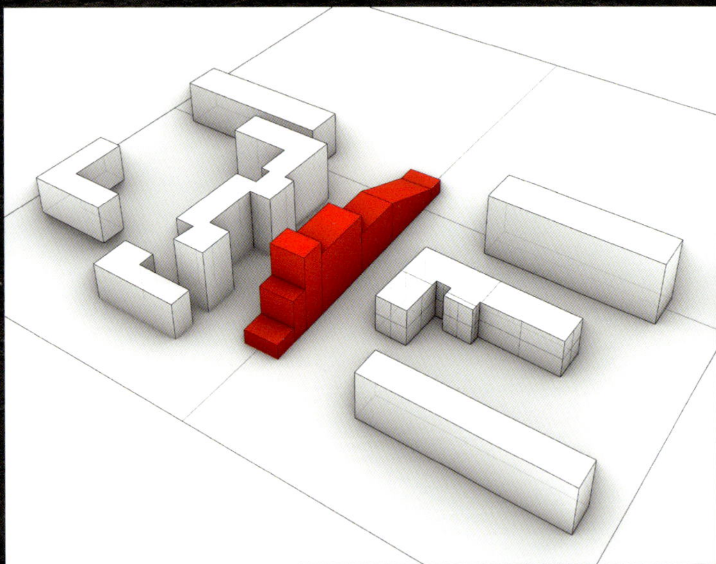

1. Project volume in site context

2. Project volume in site context

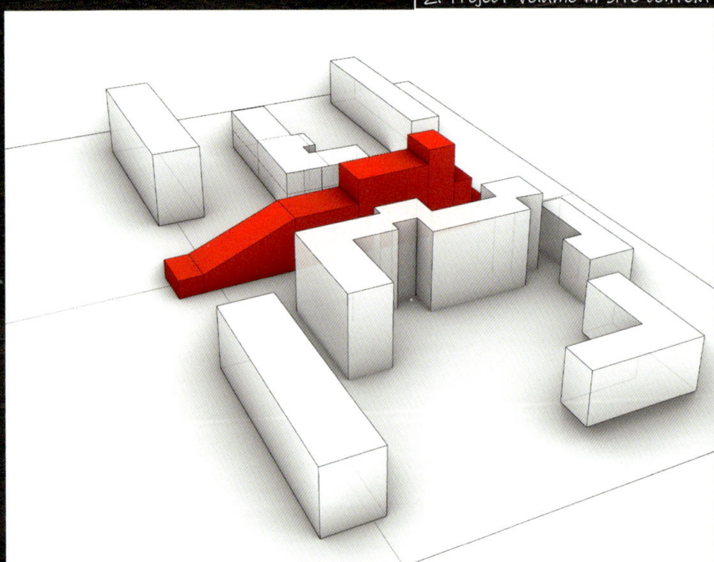

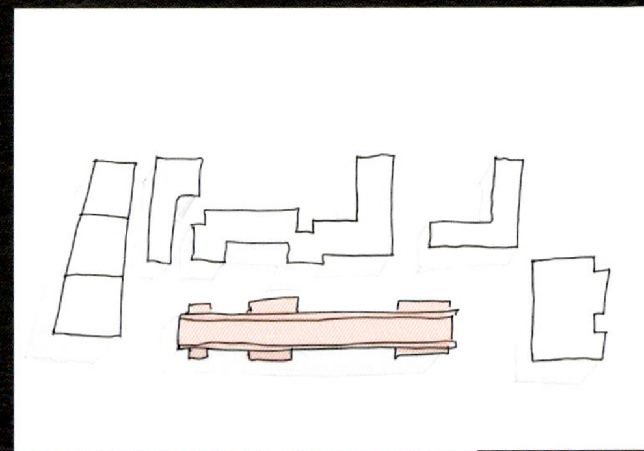

1. Site plan with surrounding context

Option 1 arranges the building as a single block with flat facades.

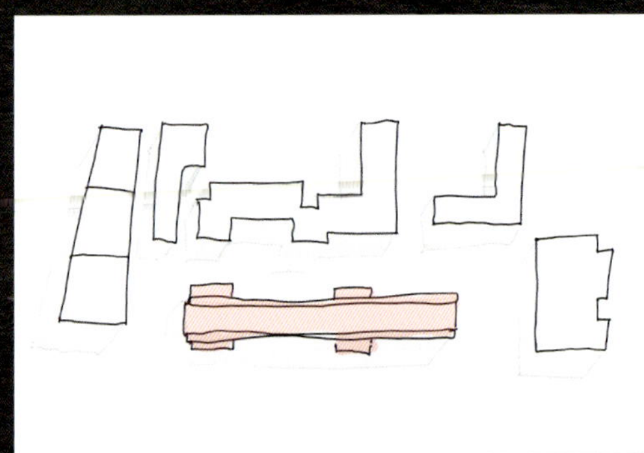

2. Site plan with surrounding context

Option 2 arranges the building as three blocks in a slightly different alignment.

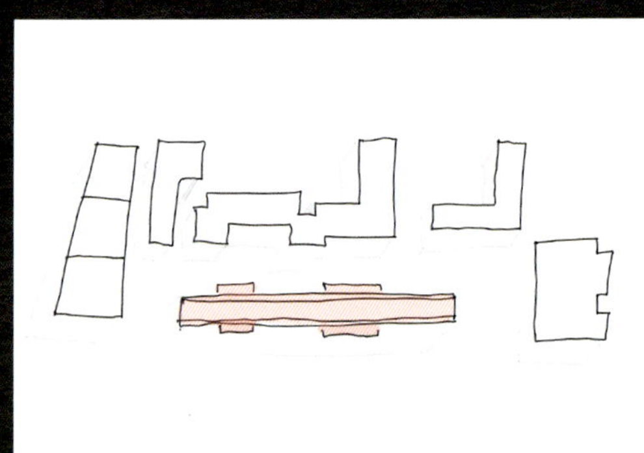

3. Site plan with surrounding context

Option 3 arranges the building as a single block with flat facades and externally set support spaces.

Site context

This project is for a resort hotel adjcent to a beach within a bay; the climate is Mediterranean. The primary requirement of the brief/program is to accommodate the key component parts of the hotel within a single environment within a site which is restricted in its width; its length is approximately 1.5 times longer than large-scale neighbouring buildings. The approach taken for this project is to provide a single building volume, as required by the brief/program, and create a high level of differentiation between constituent parts of the building without dividing these parts into separate building forms.

The spaces required in this project comprise hotel rooms, restaurants, a cinema, sports facilities and retail outlets. The guest rooms are located on the upper floors of the building and comprise small groups of between four and 10 suites. The guest rooms require the ability to exclude daylight; shutters are deployed from within the building rather than using external shading devices, which would have required electrical deployment with its associated maintenance. The lower parts of the building comprise retail units and hotel management offices; mainly on the ground floor.

The site context for all three options is one of a long, narrow site where it is considered difficult to achieve the spatial organisation required for this building. It was suggested that an adjacent site be purchased to provide additional space; this design uses the existing site only, previously used for ground-level car parking. The resulting urban design approach is to create a ribbon of spaces within 'nested', or interlocking, building forms that create a physical edge to this urban location.

The site context is a long and narrow plot, where the narrow ends face towards the sea; neighbouring hotels are arranged along the length of the beach. This hotel is set perpendicular to the other hotels. A set of terraces provide views out to the beach while other rooms are oriented into the building towards a set of 'streets' arranged on different floors in the centre of the building. Streets are arranged in vertically-arranged groups, three storeys apart, providing a visual focus of looking out into the middle zone of the building where there are res-

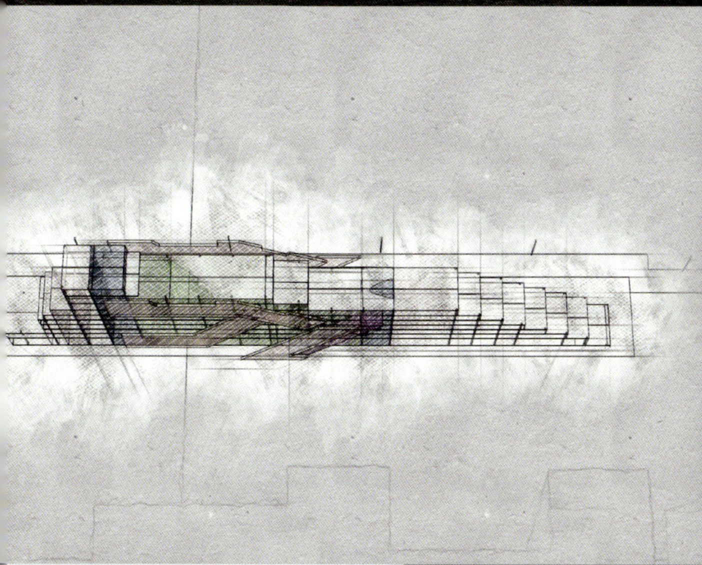

Perspective view of environmental volumes

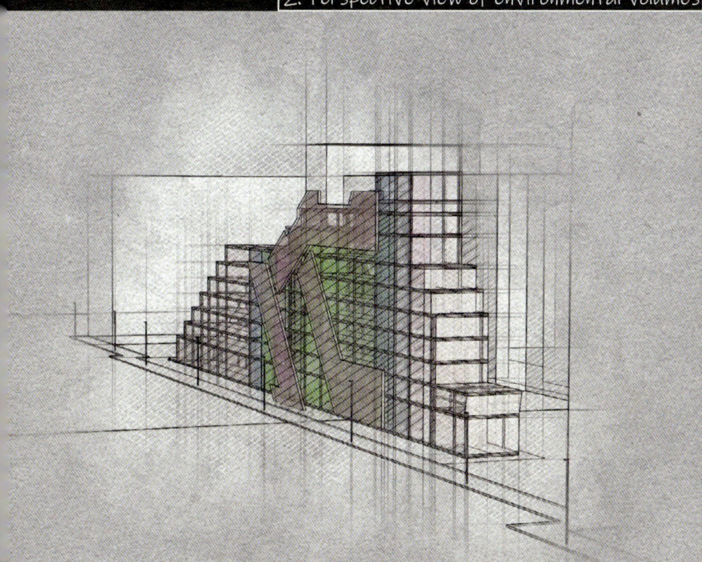

2. Perspective view of environmental volumes

1. Figure-ground diagram of tempered environment

Option 1
Dark green spaces are highly tempered but are reduced to accommodation volumes only.

2. Figure-ground diagram of tempered environment

Option 2
Dark blue spaces are less tempered than dark green spaces but are more tempered than light blue circulation spaces.

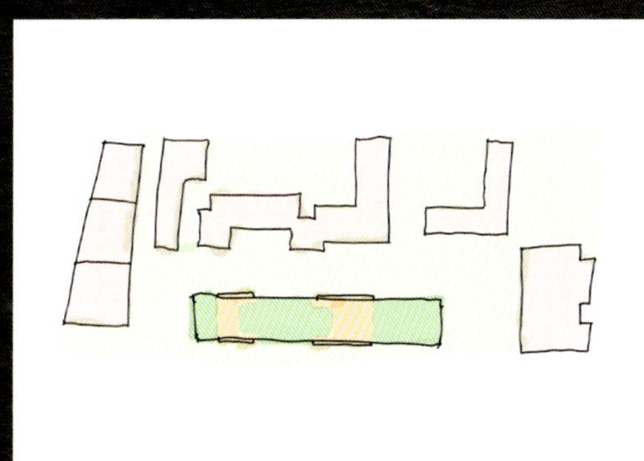

3. Figure-ground diagram of tempered environment

Option 3
Light blue spaces are the least tempered spaces. These spaces interface directly with external space.

taurants and shops on the ground floor, at mid-level and at roof terrace level. Rooms face into the central space as well as having views outwards. The rooms have an inward focus towards a glazed inner space, with borrowed light from the central space and daylight from the external wall side of each room. The structural frame is set within the circulation area away from rooms, providing views out in both directions unencumbered by either the services or by a central corridor. The site context addresses the spatial relationship with the resort hotels set on both sides of the long elevations of this building. A road immediately behind the hotel provides a point of entry to the site; the entrance addresses the road.

A set of inclined roof elevations and terraces face the sea; the inclined forms and associated visible structure provide views out to the sea from some of the hotel rooms. The building also aims to provide presence from the road such that upon arrival, guests can see a visual expression of the range of spaces within the building, provided by oblique views down the length of the facade from the entrance space onwards. These views are enhanced as a result of the facades projecting out by different amounts in order to provide a clear separation of volumes and spaces within the building, suggesting different activities within each volume inside the hotel.

The entrance stairs set on both sides of the hotel form a deep facade zone. One side of the hotel has stairs and lifts/elevators linking each floor level externally. At each floor level, through the height of the staircase, the space is inhabited by cafes and shops; forming a public space which rises to the public reception area at podium level.

The complete staircase is inhabited as a public space; providing a welcome to all visitors to this resort. The space defined by the rising staircase and lifts/elevators is part of the public realm, forming a visual continuity with the road that extends the length of the beach facing the hotel. The beach is not private: hotel and road are brought into the same public realm, avoiding a separation between the hotel and the beach community in which it is located.

Sectional perspective view

Sectional perspective view

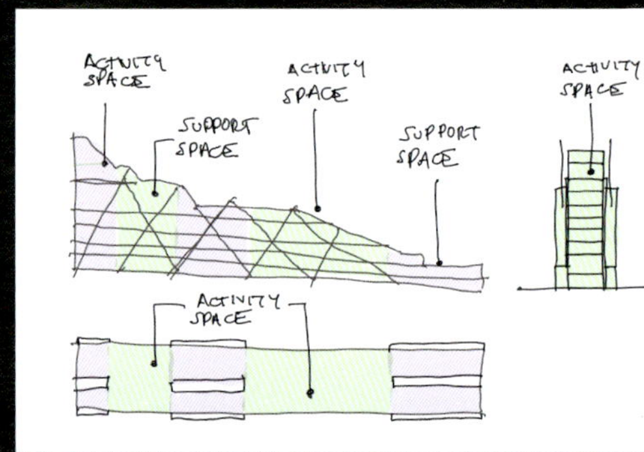

Spatial arrangement

Option 1 creates a generic set of spaces on each floor which can be organised as suites.

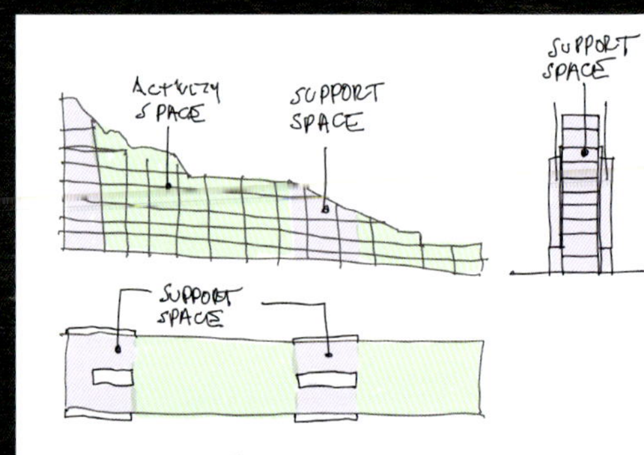

Option 2 has an additional core introduced which allows spaces to be formed as vertical clusters.

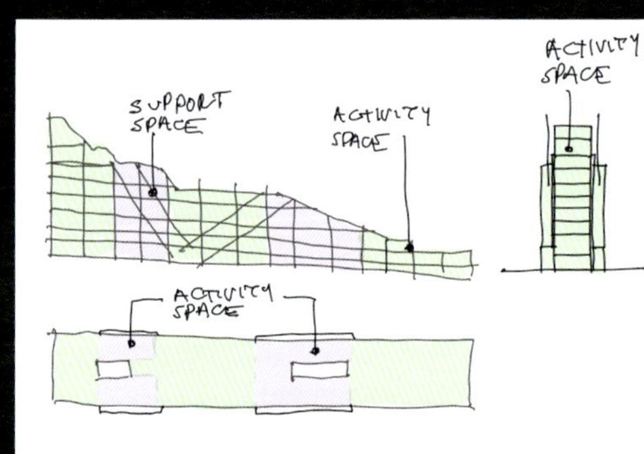

Option 3 has the central spaces in a diagonal arrangement that provides views across adjacent spaces on different floors.

Spatial arrangement

The spatial organisation focusses on bringing open space into the centre of the building by creating a sequence of smaller, linked spaces. Set above the ground floor hotel management offices and retail outlets are the guest rooms and suites. This accommodation is set across five main floor plates, linked by stairs that traverse the building diagonally as seen in the diagonal lines of the facades. The stairs also provide open links to cinema, restaurants and sports facilities on upper levels between the ground floor facilities and the upper floor activities. The building is arranged in stacks of two-storey modules of space, each with an internal stair and small lift/elevator. The lift/elevator allows items to be moved to an upper mezzanine level that provides a double-height space required for suites.

There are three different spatial arrangements for this long, thin beachside block. All arrangements follow the same basic shape in section and elevation; functions are grouped vertically in sets of spaces in order to create 'clusters' of space on the long sides of the hotel in order to avoid complete floor plates, on any level, requiring long access corridors to rooms and suites. Instead, the vertical arrangement ensures that a single cluster comprises the core facilities within the hotel on different floors set one above the other, separated from other parts of the single floor plate. This approach ensures short circulation distances between adjacent spaces occupied by the same guest group. These vertically stacked spaces are linked by stairs and lifts/elevators such that each floor plate is sufficiently small to allow horizontal circulation from one cluster to another located on the same level. Each floor accommodates three activity spaces, which are divided by two service cores which create each set of vertically stacked blocks that are set side by side; a spatial rhythm of activity space from small size to large size and back to small size.

In Option 1 that arrangement is simplified in order to create a generic set of spaces on each floor, which can be organised as suites that function in a vertical arrangement which is supported by two vertical circulation cores. In Option 2 an additional core is introduced; allowing

Perspective view of interior

2. Perspective view of interior

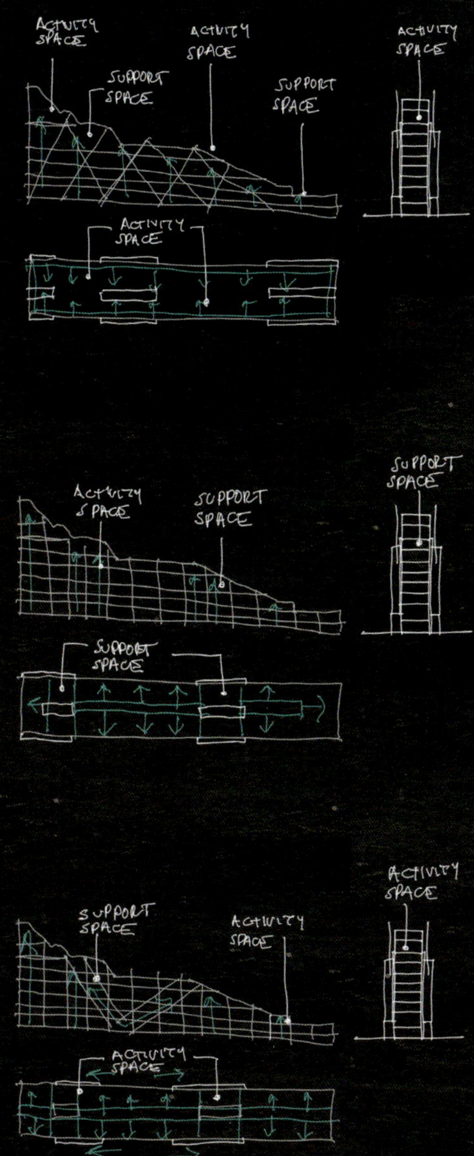

Internal circulation

Option 1 has lifts/elevators set within cores set at the edge of each open floor plate.

Option 2 corridors are positioned that provide access to adjacent suites between the corridor and the external walls.

Option 3 uses central corridors with externally mounted mechanical and electrical equipment and structure.

spaces to be formed as vertical clusters with a different hotel facility on each floor. In Option 3 the central spaces have a diagonal arrangement that provides views across adjacent spaces on different floors, as well as using those areas for circulation by stair and lift/elevator.

Internal circulation

The internal circulation for Option 1 is of lifts/elevators within cores set at the edge of each open floor plate; the floor areas are free of service space. Primary structure, circulation and mechanical and electrical equipment are provided at the edges of floor plates along the length of the long facades.

In Option 2 the two central cores introduce circulation routes. Adjacent to those cores, corridors are positioned that provide access to adjacent suites, which can either be cellular or open plan, between the corridor and the external walls. Between corridors, a zone for cafe and storage space is created. In Option 3, this concept retains the two cores in the centre of each floor plate; stairs are introduced at the ends of the building in order to have fewer stairs on the external facades. The internal circulation of Option 3 uses central corridors with externally mounted mechanical and electrical equipment and structure, but there is no circulation along the edges of the facade alone that was provided with Option 1.

The spatial arrangement is such that the volumes can be seen from the road at oblique angles from both ends of the hotel building, as guests arrive and as people pass by. The perspective view of the facades suggests that this building has a range of activities and functions within it; different from a classic resort hotel with rooms arrayed around a view of the seafront, with other activities and facilities being set within an upper-level podium.

The spatial arrangement is organised around locating some of the functions away from the facade in order to give a sense of depth to the arrangement of internal volumes. This drawing out of elements like drawers in a cabinet is an alternative to the podium solution used by the neighbouring hotels.

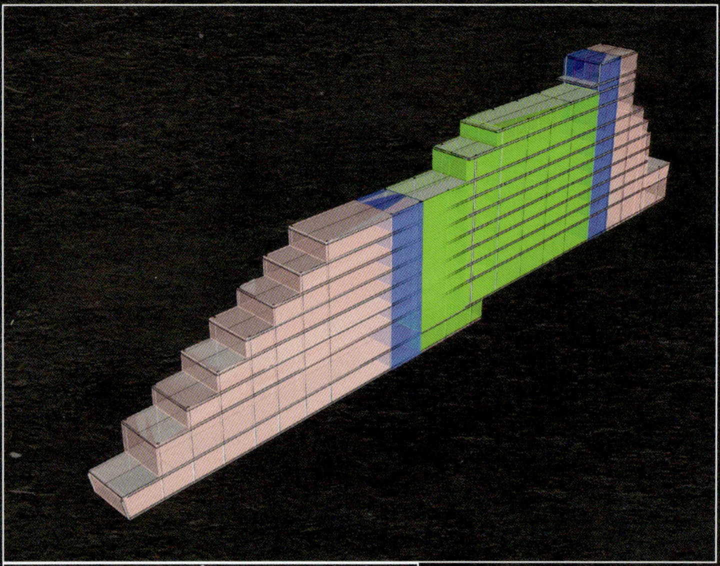

1A. Isometric view of environmental volumes

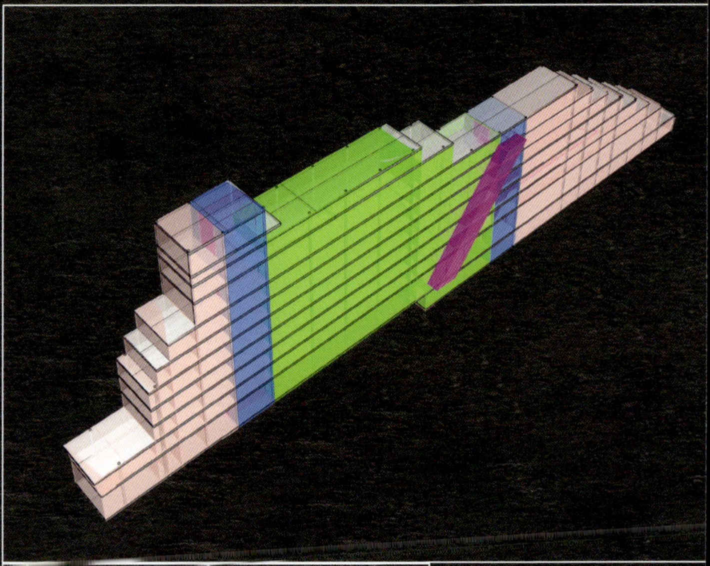

2A. Isometric view of environmental volumes

1B. Isometric view of environmental volumes

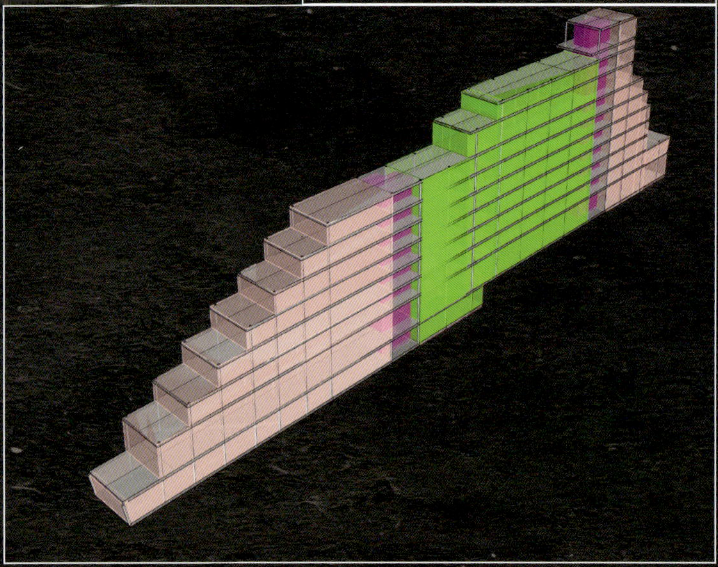

2B. Isometric view of environmental volume

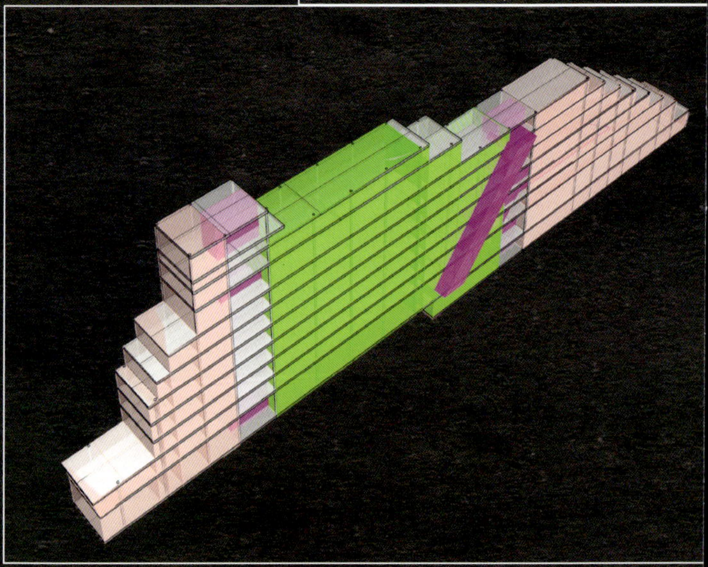

Environmental strategy

The environmental strategy focuses on the accommodation of routes for mechanical ventilation within the zone of the structural facades. The arrangement of ducts and the passage of air within the deep facade zone is set out in each of the three different options; each option arranges cores differently for the provision of vertical circulation, washrooms and service risers. All three options aim to ensure that mechanical and electrical equipment and the associated distribution of air and electrical supplies is located within the external wall zone, not at roof level and not within the cores; roofs are used as terraces for building users and floor plates are required to be clear in order to maximise the possibilities for their potential sub-division and use.

This building is arranged with service cores set along the long sides of the building; cores comprise lifts/elevators, stairs, washrooms and risers for mechanical ventilation and electrical equipment. The building is essentially one which is organised for four different groups of hotel suites to be set adjacent to one another, in a vertical arrangement; each group is contained within a single environmental zone. This arrangement is visible from the outside as a result of the arrangement of the facades.

Service cores are arranged on both sides of the building to allow the creation of hotel suites that are required to achieve flexibility of spatial use. The central 'block' of the building has an additional spine core to accommodate mechanical and electrical equipment that can provide locally ducted air, both in the ceiling plenum (void) and from the floor plenum. Air is distributed from the ceiling and is collected through the floor plenum.

The environmental strategy uses both the 45-degree inclined elements of structure and vertical columns to draw air in and around the building from a lower level; air-handling units are located at ground floor level. Air is drawn up through ducts located behind the characteristic shape of the primary structure, and that air is distributed on all floors. Behind those ducts on both sides of the building, air is distributed by way of ceiling plenums and floor plenums at each level, where air is extracted and

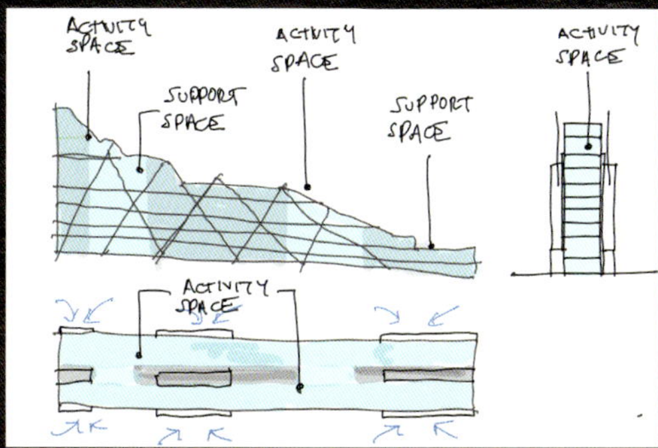

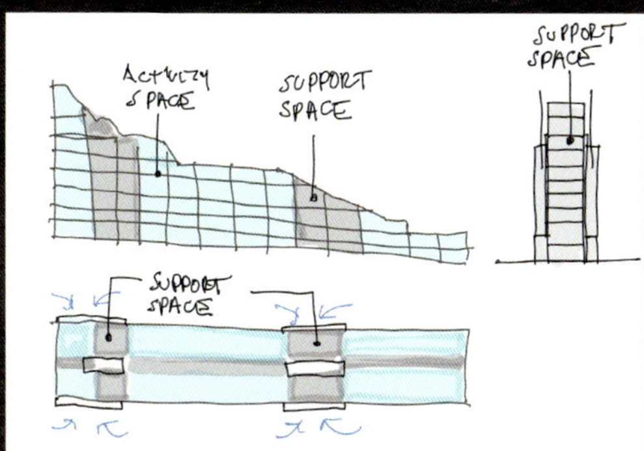

Daylight strategy for direct sunlight and cross ventilation.

Option 1
Daylight and air are introduced through the long facades of the building.

Option 2
Daylight and air are introduced both through the long facades of the building and support spaces.

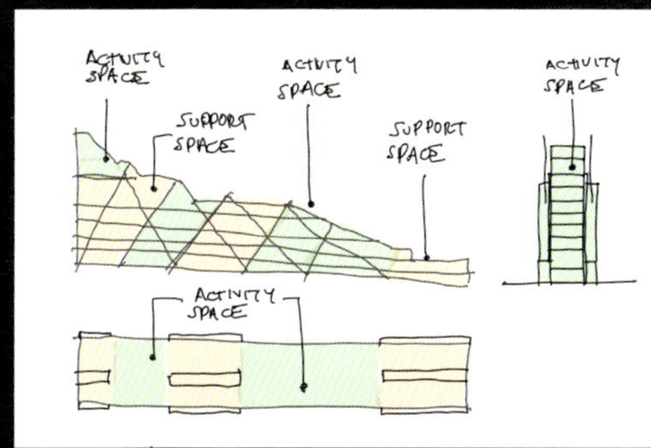

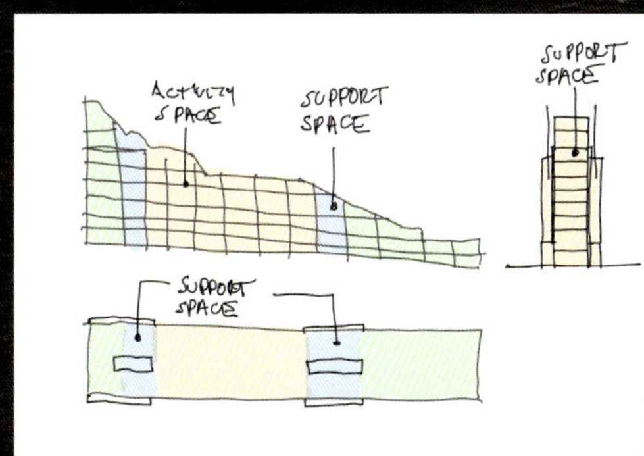

Environmental zones

Option 1
has the building banded vertically into groups of environmental zones.

Option 2
has the cores form hubs around the building.

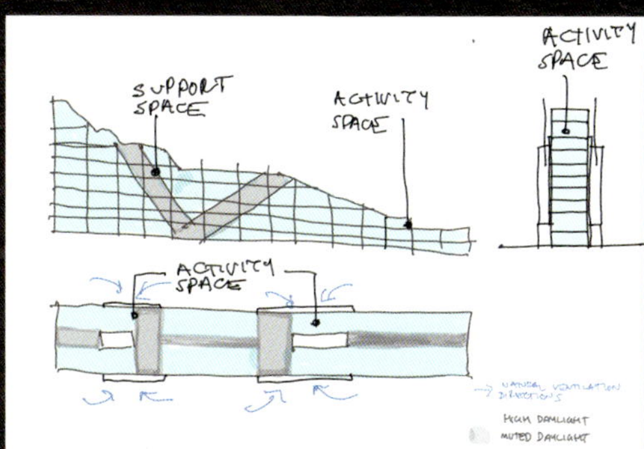

Daylight strategy for direct sunlight and cross ventilation.

Option 3
Daylight and air are introduced through both the long facades and inclined support spaces.

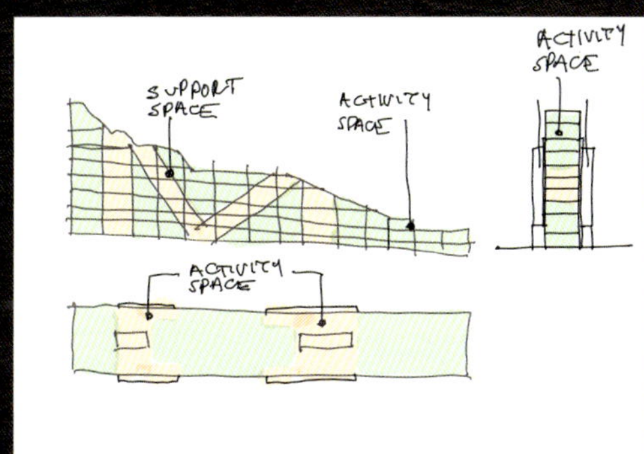

Environmental zones

Option 3
has the environmental zones follow those of the spatial arrangement.

recycled to be mixed with fresh air from outside the building.

The environmental strategies for all three options for this building follow the spatial arrangement and the internal circulation. Each option follows the functions of each space, with a zone for each of the functions within the hotel. One environmental zone for guest rooms and suites, a zone for the ground floor facilities, a zone for circulation and for the facilities at the top of the hotel. In Option 1 the building is banded vertically into groups. In Option 2 the cores form hubs around the building. The use of the ducts on the outside of the building is extended further in Option 3, where the environmental zones follow that of the spatial arrangement.

The environmental strategy is one of encouraging natural ventilation at certain times of day as a result of using cross ventilation in rooms and suites from the open areas of the internal streets to the external walls at the edges of the building. The approach is one of using passive natural ventilation where possible and to have daylight from both sides. Smaller-scale cores divide the rooms and suites such that each core has only one set of rooms on each side. This arrangement avoids the central corridor, which would have required tempering with high air changes in a very enclosed environment that would have had little daylight. This approach avoids that central corridor concept and allows daylight to enter the hotel suites on both sides of the building. The main source of cooling energy for the building is from the swimming pools, set at ground floor level adjacent to the building. These long, narrow pools store cooling energy during the day, which is released at night through heat exchangers into the hotel rooms; a part of the environmental strategy of moving cooling energy from pool to rooms and then later from rooms back to the pool. The solar shading devices set along the long walls protect spaces within the building from high angle sun on the east and west faces; the ends of the hotel are arranged in an approximately north-south direction. Solar shading for winter and mid-season conditions are provided by internal blinds which are drawn down from ceiling level; these are manually operated to suit the requirements of each guest.

1A. Isometric view of structure

2A. Isometric view of structure

1B. Isometric view of structure

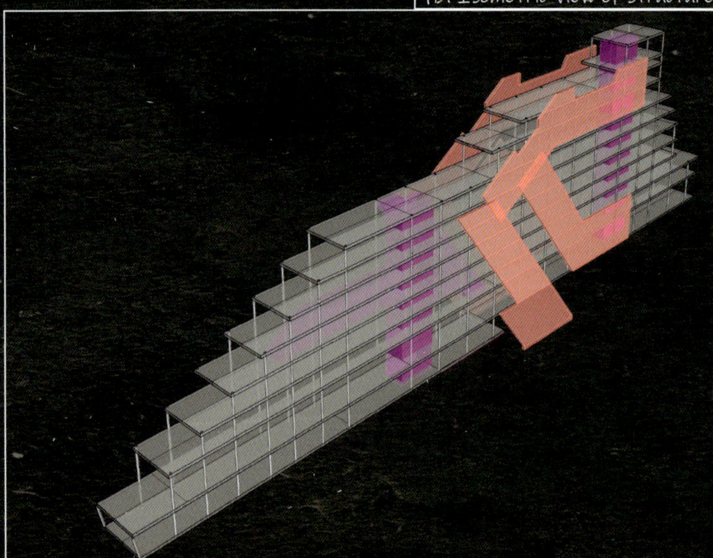

2B. Isometric view of structur

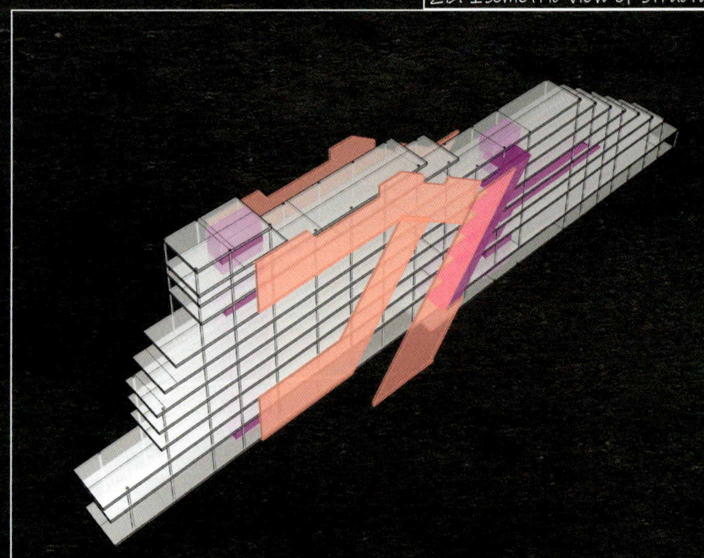

Structural strategy

The structural strategy for this building is of a primary steel frame which is set into each of the two long facades; a set of load-bearing facade frames which are connected by beams which span across the width of the relatively narrow floor plates. This structure includes, in addition to columns and beams, a large-scale diagonally based structural frame which contributes to the structural stability of the primary structure as well as providing support for inclined elements of circulation within the building.

The facade assemblies are non-load bearing and are supported on the primary structure. Consequently, the geometry of the facade panels follows that of the primary structure as well as meeting the performance requirements of the interior spaces behind the facades. The service cores are set in a different arrangement for each of the three options presented here; set either within the deep zone of the facades or, alternatively, in the centre of the floor plates to provide additional stability. The structural strategy is based on providing load-bearing structural facades that support both the floor plates within the building as well as mechanical and electrical equipment; services equipment is not roof-mounted. Services cores provide enclosures for stairs, lifts/elevators and washrooms, and risers for electrical supply, water supply and drainage. When set within the floor plates, cores provide a device to define an internal zone for meeting spaces set between those cores, so that the wide floor plates can be used to their full extent.

Option 1 uses vertical columns and floor slabs with inclined structural columns within the facade zone of the long elevations; providing both support to floor slabs and accommodation of both service cores and services distribution through the deep facade zone. The load-bearing facades are set on both of the long sides of the building; these facades support both air-handling ducts and electrical equipment. Structural stability is provided only within the zone of the external envelope; the floor plates are clear of enclosures for services. Option 2 uses a regular arrangement of columns, floor slabs and beams with the cores, positioned in the centre of the floor plates, contributing to structural stabil-

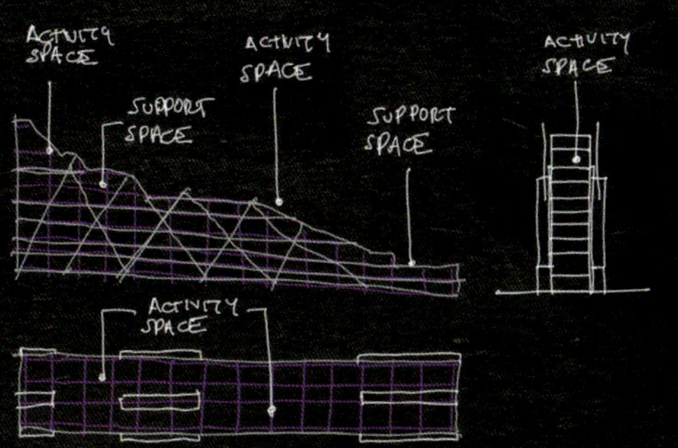

Structural strategy: Zones
Option 1 uses vertical columns and floor slabs with inclined structural columns within the facade zone of the long elevations.

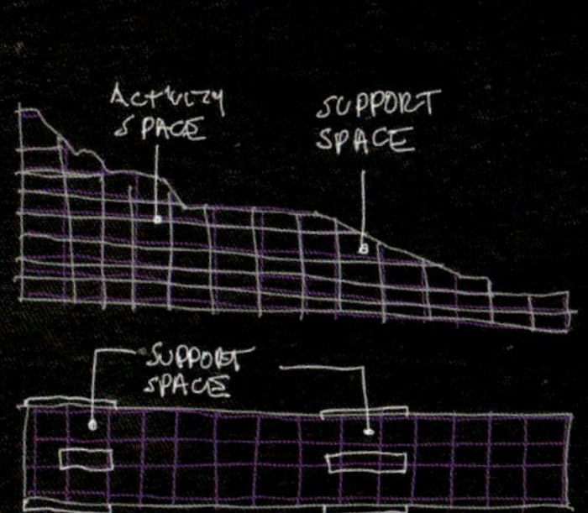

Option 2 uses a regular arrangement of columns, floor slabs and beams with the cores, positioned in the centre of the floor plates.

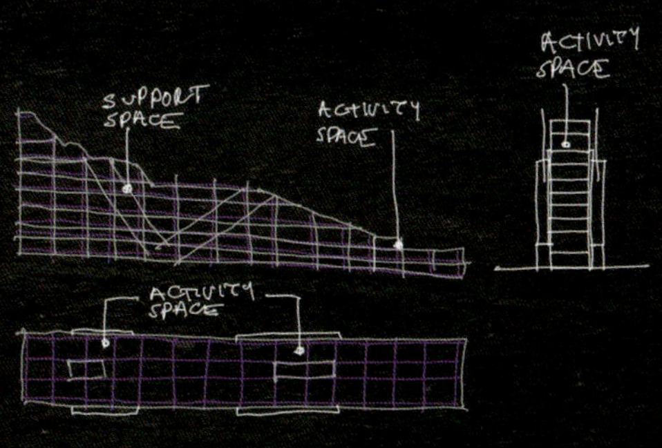

Structural strategy: Zones
Option 3 mixes the use of cores, both in the facade zones and in the centre of floor plates.

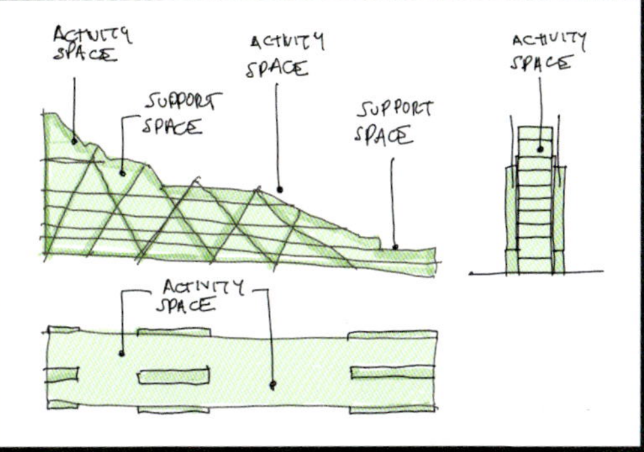

Structural strategy: Framing
Option 1 encloses the core spaces and dividing space into sets of apartments.
Option 2 is largely a steel frame.

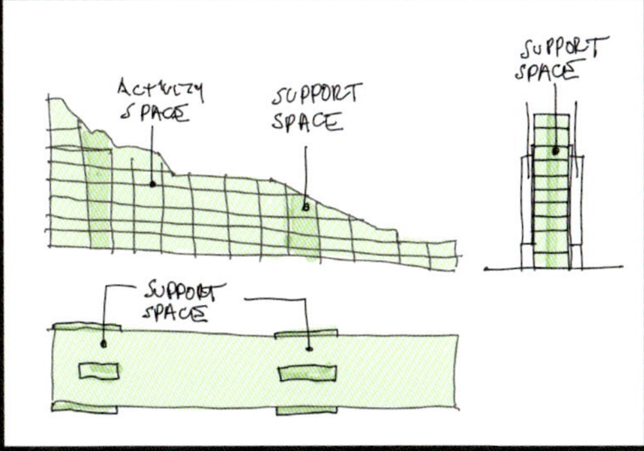

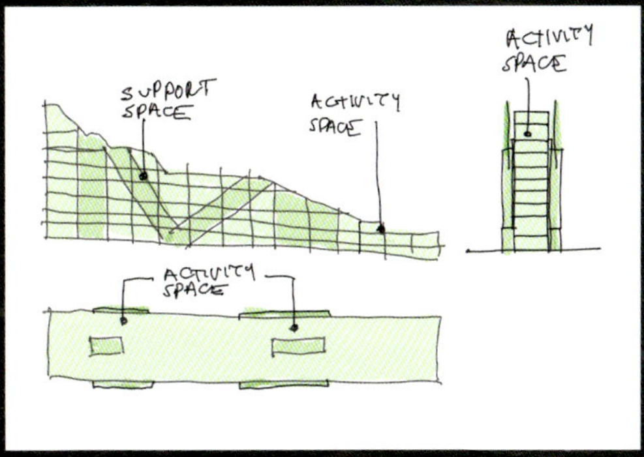

Structural strategy: Zones
Option 3 is a mixed solution of reinforced concrete and steel.

ity. In Option 3 the building mixes the use of cores, both in the facade zones and in the centre of floor plates; an arrangement that suits the need for vertically organised teamwork required in the brief/program. In this option, space for restaurants and sports facilities is provided between the cores of the central 'spine' for circulation. The open floor plates provide space for open areas of office, arranged between the central spine core and the outer stairs; and mechanical and electrical vertical service runs. Mechanical and electrical equipment is accommodated in the zones formed as both vertical and inclined 'bands' of cladding panels across the long facades.

The structure of the building is one of having an externally fixed double layer of structure which accommodates a zone for services and for vertical circulation. The double layer of structure on the outside is not continuous, but instead is located only where the characteristic forms of the exterior of the building are required to accommodate air handling ducts, staircases and lifts/elevators. Between these zones, the structure reverts to a single layer of structure with a row of internal columns. The three options explore different ways of arranging that externally oriented structure, which is defined by a requirement to support mechanical and electrical services and to form spaces for cross ventilation.

The structural strategy is one of setting loadbearing walls in the external wall zones. These elements are formed with inclined angles to suit the distribution of ducted air and services around the building, rather than being optimised for only full structural efficiency. As a result of some of the shallow angles used, some members are arranged in pairs, providing points of support for the ducted air system.

The entrance staircase, which forms a public space outside the building, is formed in reinforced concrete. The stair structure is part of the primary structure. The stair structure is set adjacent to an amphitheatre space set at the edge of the hotel; this is formed in reinforced concrete as a curved and folded slab. The open stage entered from within the hotel is formed as a timber deck in order for space beneath the stage to form part of this resort hotel.

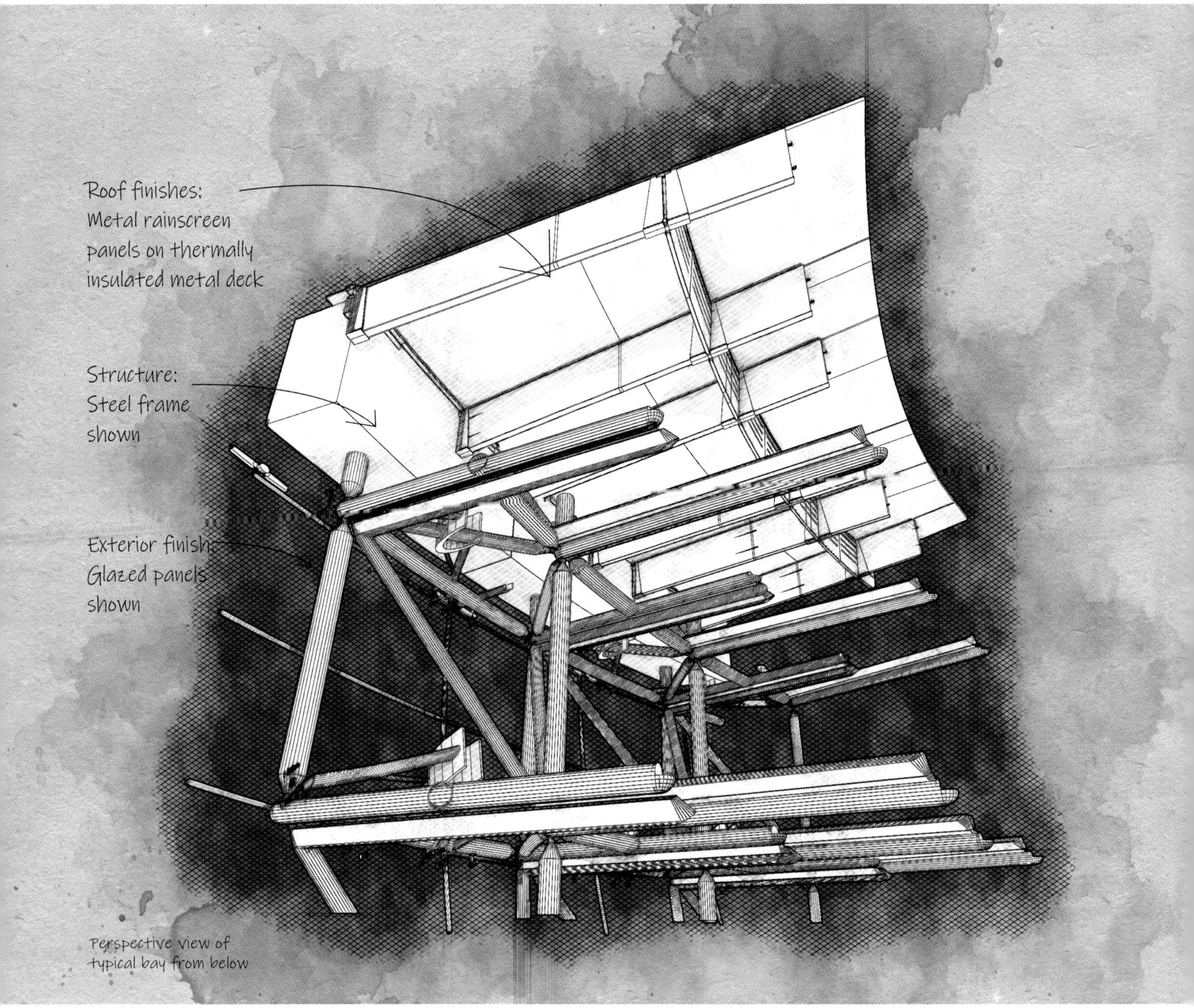

Perspective view of typical bay from below

Typical bay adjacent to facade

The building appears to be an 'extruded facade', where the facade arrangement is a visual expression of the internal spaces behind. The facades are a mixture of opaque panels and glazed panels with opaque panels being formed in GFRC (glass-fibre reinforced concrete), which are fixed to the steel primary structural frame. A steel frame is preferred over a reinforced concrete frame as facade panels are more easily fixed to steel; avoiding the need for a secondary steel frame to support the facade system.

The environmental approach to this building is to allow each of the systems used in the building to be optimised for performance, independent of the assemblies around them. Although the current method of procuring building packages for construction is one of creating different packages for the procurement of different systems in the building. Each system is selected also for its ability to interface with other packages. This building uses a different approach of optimising each element in order to demonstrate what it could do if developed independently of adjacent systems installed within the building, on its own terms, independently of the need to interface with other systems. The building is assembled as a loose-fit set of products which are optimised for their own performance with features that would otherwise not have been added to the building, but which add to the overall performance, utility and amenities within the building.

The juxtaposition of these independently designed and developed systems creates the characteristic look of juxtaposed elements, with shadow gaps set between them. The possibilities of the main products used in this building as systems have been optimised and developed on their own terms. These systems include facade panels, doors, balustrades and structural components. The inclined rooflights and energy units are independently watertight, as is the horizontal glazing, which is inclined from the top inwards. These systems are juxtaposed but are allowed to develop freely; the language of joining them together being one of the shadow gap that allows elements to come together without the need for a visual continuity between them. Interfaces are simpli-

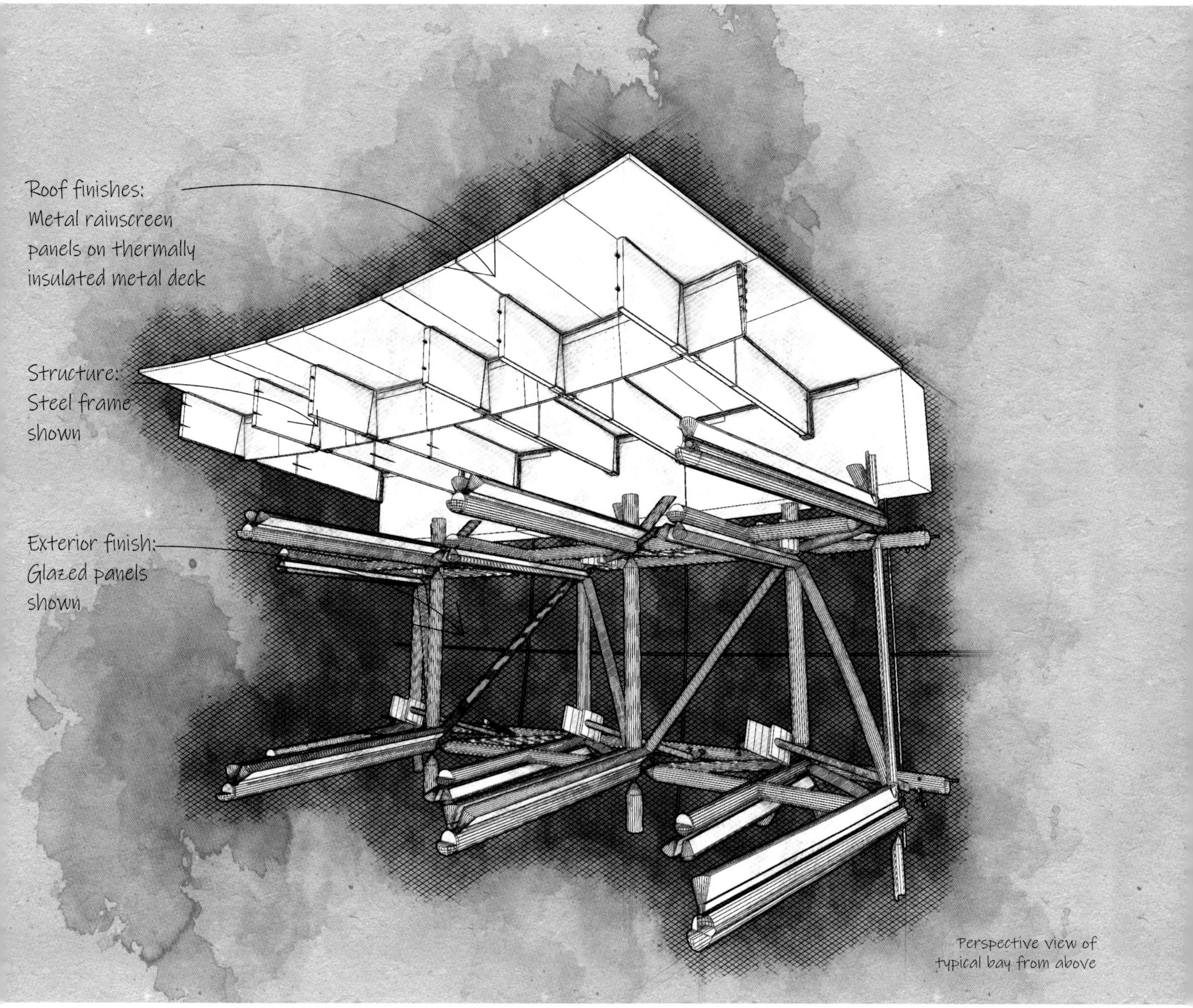

Perspective view of typical bay from above

fied by the separation of adjacent systems rather than by them being brought together in a way that suggests a visual or technical continuity between them.

The facades which are part of a typical bay are of two types: an external wall cladding of metal panels which encloses both the primary structure and the service areas, including vertical circulation and staircases. The second type is of glazed walls which enclose the hotel rooms or suites that provide a high level of daylight at both ends. Daylight is controlled by the room's occupants, who can lower blinds to control daylight levels and provide privacy. The glazing is formed as steel-framed glazed panels that provide a residential loft-like experience. This approach allows glazing to extend from floor to ceiling, with typically 1.0-metre centres between vertical steel framing members that contribute to the characteristic loft-like experience of these spaces which have exposed painted concrete floors and exposed ceilings. The glazing system has windows which are set at different heights in order for them to be opened for cross ventilation, with manually operated opening lights at low level and at high level. Opaque panels form a visual continuity with solar shading panels; both are formed in GFRC. The visual character of the building is of smooth concrete-based panels which are of a similar colour to the adjacent beach; the form of the building is one of a visual continuity with the adjacent beach, like a rocky outcrop. Glazing is recessed within the outer wall in order to enhance the appearance of the external walls as being part of that rock-like texture.

The characteristic inclined roofs are covered with foliage which extends through their height to the top-deck level of the hotel.

The overall facade composition is of a 'building within a building'. The outer shell comprises the GFRC-clad outer walls; the inner wall is comprised on hotel rooms and public facilities. The space between the two outer 'shells' is inhabited by staircases and lifts/elevators. The typical bay is in two parts; the outer GFRC shell which accommodates small retail spaces, and the inner walls, which house the main part of the resort hotel.

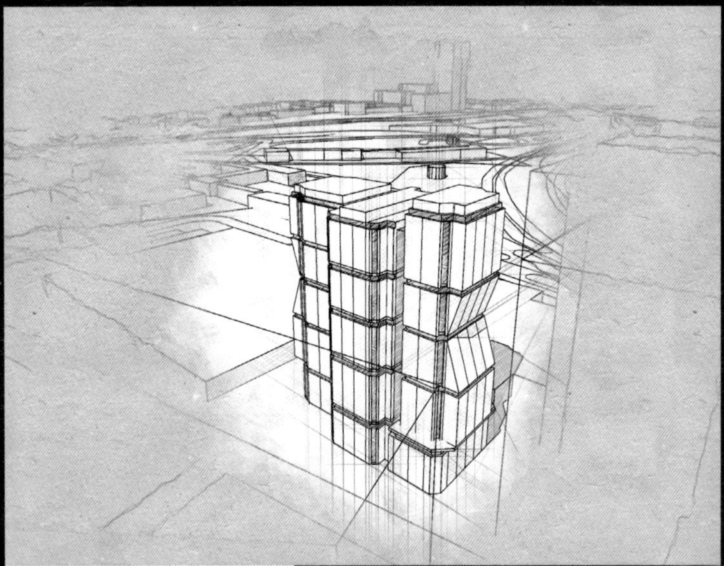

1. Perspective view of exterior

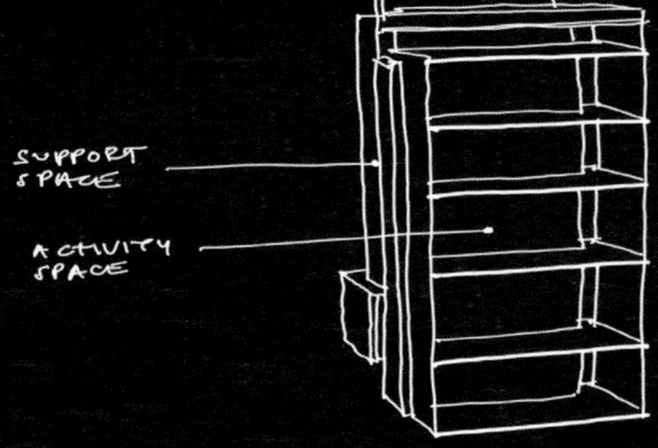

2. Perspective view of exterior

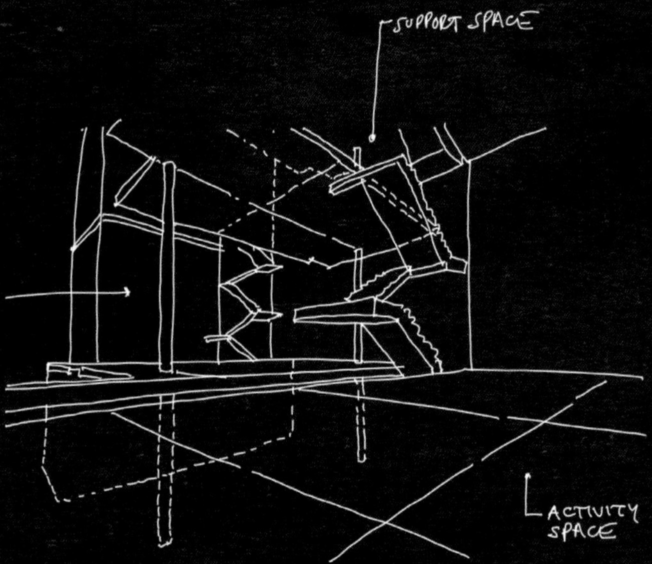

Reuse and recycling of mechanical and electrical systems

This project is based on mechanical and electrical equipment assemblies which can be added to or removed, disassembled and reused; a loose-fit arrangement of assemblies in order to respond to changes in the way the building is used. An essential approach to the environmental design is to consider the reuse and recycling of as many mechanical and electrical equipment assemblies in the building as possible, as the design life of the building in its current configuration is considered to be relatively short. The reuse and recycling of assemblies is considered to be more important than the longevity of those systems. As a result, internal space division systems and mechanical and electrical systems have been selected for their ability to be removed, replaced and recycled; to be used on other buildings within the same ownership, or even to be moved and reused on the same building. This approach has led the design to have a visually distinct set of facade panels, deck panels and mechanical and electrical equipment which is modular, self-contained and can be removed from the building. Some mechanical and electrical installations equipment is fixed as an integral part of the facade; the design approach emphasising a connection between building occupants and their use of equipment in the building – equipment which can be demounted and reassembled elsewhere in the building, rather than the equipment being considered for a one-time-only use that is much shorter than the lifespan of its internal assembly. This building is constructed largely as a kit of parts where other light manufacturing buildings in the area, owned by the same organisation, can be operated with elements swapped out between them. This building is primarily an assembly of environmental systems that serve the manufacturing tasks and air extracts associated with each of the machines used in this manufacturing facility. The envelope encloses this set of machines which are thermally insulated and protected from the effects of the weather; the structure is primarily set inside the building, but in some locations is required to be externally set in order to support pipes and ducts. The large-scale assemblies such as meeting rooms and spaces for directing operations cantilever out beyond the perim-

Perspective view of exterior

4. Perspective view of exterior

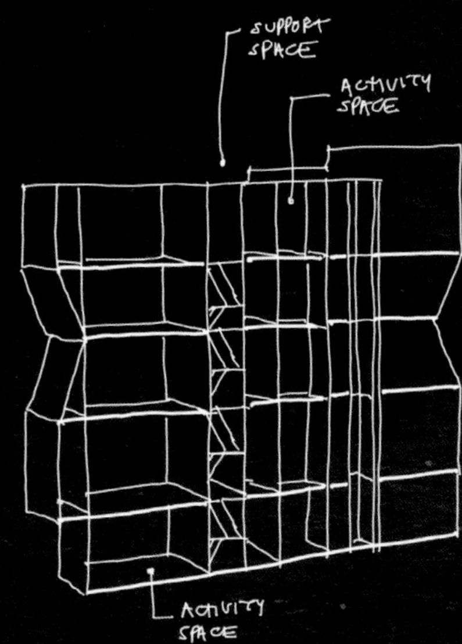

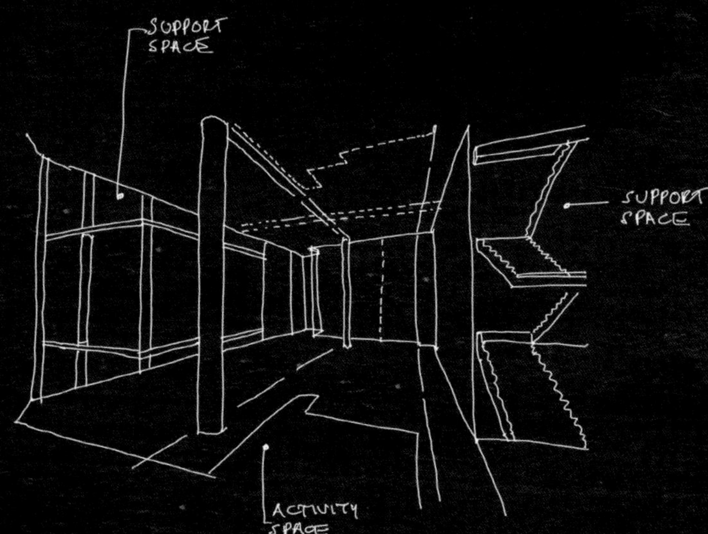

eter of the building in order to provide lines of sight for vehicles arriving and departing from the building. The remainder of the external envelope comprises lifting doors at ground level. Most of the facades and opaque thermal insulated panels on the upper floors have glazed panels in the corners only. Opportunities for glazing were presented only at the corners, which resulted in the chamfered edges to the manufacturing areas. Consequently, this building is a series of prefabricated service units which are joined together by some external wall panels. The importance of being able to reuse and recycle this equipment is a key factor in this design; the reuse, recycling and maintenance of this equipment comprises most of the building itself. An essential requirement of the structural frame was to support this equipment directly. The external wall panels which join these pieces of equipment are effectively closing panels between equipment pods. The machinery inside the building is relatively light in weight and is replaceable as small component parts. The largest components in the building are those of the compressors and fans that form part of the air-handling equipment. These components can be accessed from outside the building. The prefabricated services units have lifting panels for ease of access from the outside; from lifting platforms.

Ease of access to mechanical and electrical equipment is facilitated by access panels on external walls, both on their outside face and their inside face.

The support spaces between buildings become the 'permanent' part of the building as the three production halls can have their external wall-mounted modules, and adjacent facade panels, removed to suit near future needs. The support spaces are self-supporting, allowing parts of the floor decks in the manufacturing spaces to be changed without affecting the support spaces at roof level: environmental control equipment can be adapted and changed; the corresponding equipment for the support spaces can be changed independently of the activity spaces, but support spaces are expected to remain in place for a longer period than the manufacturing halls. The meeting rooms attached to the sides of the building can be demounted and repositioned as needed.

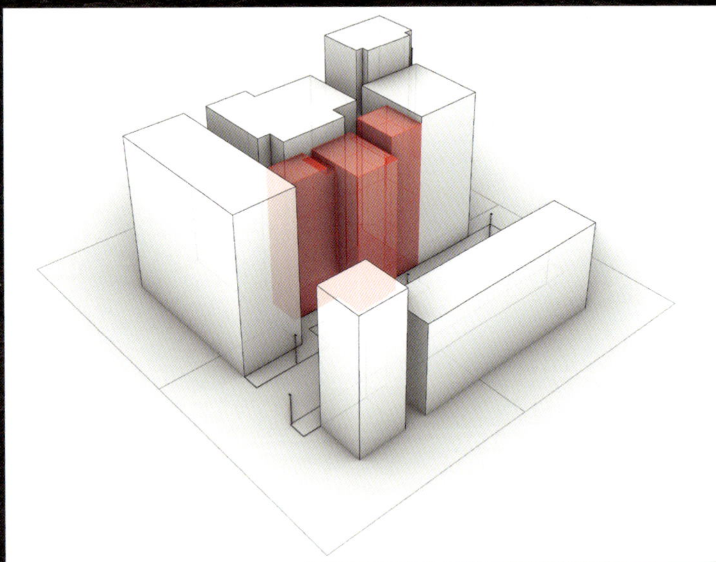

1. Project volume in site context

1. Site plan with surrounding context

Option 1 arranges the building as a series of rectilinear spaces which are linked to the two adjacent buildings.

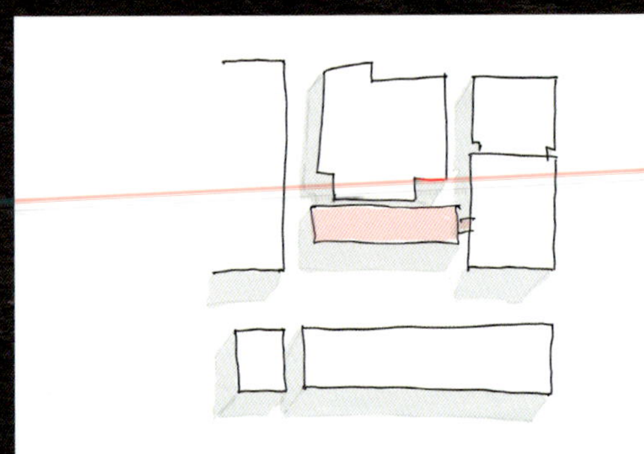

2. Site plan with surrounding context

Option 2 is positioned closer to the two adjacent existing buildings, with wider and more centrally placed links into them.

2. Project volume in site context

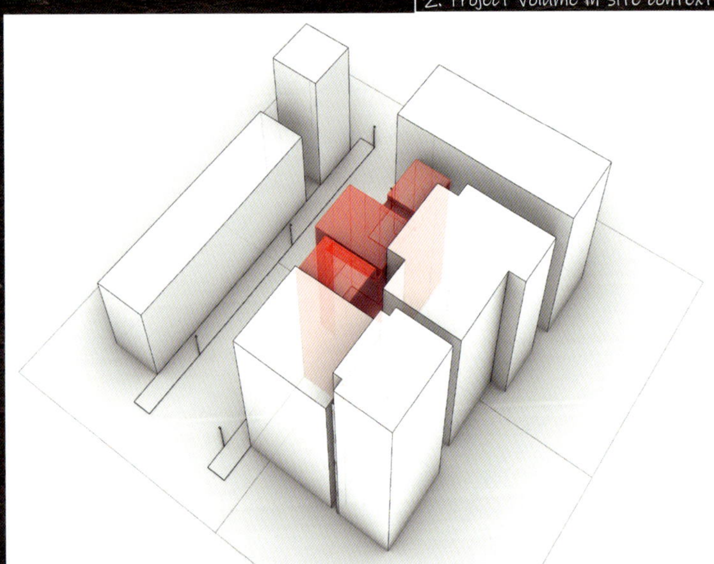

3. Site plan with surrounding context

Option 3 integrates the new building with the existing building.

Site context

This is a building whose context is at the edge of a city centre where manufacturing used to take place, and which is now being introduced by government agencies in order to stimulate the revival of manufacturing work into buildings over several storeys. The height of the building is similar to those surrounding the site, which range between eight storeys and 10 storeys.

This manufacturing facility is arranged over three floors; each floor is 10.0 metres in height. Little daylight is required to be admitted to the manufacturing areas. The building is established in 10 x 10-metre-wide modules, which are prefabricated as wall and floor sections with the primary structure being integrated with the external wall panels. The building is entirely prefabricated off site in wall and floor sections allowing the urban infrastructure location of the building to be left almost untouched, and avoiding the need for large-scale construction teams to operate on the job site. Fabrication of building structure and facade assemblies will take place at a remote distance from the building's location. The site context is of an inner-city industrial area. The harsh climate of hot, dry summers and cold, dry and partly snowy winters has resulted in the need for highly thermally insulated spaces to be provided. Neighbouring buildings comprise offices and residential buildings; as a result, sound insulation is considered a high priority; the noise of machinery and small-scale manufacturing equipment is attenuated by the external envelope. The new building connects with two adjacent industrial storage spaces.

Option 1 arranges the building as a series of rectilinear spaces which are linked to the two adjacent buildings. The new building provides a light-industrial assembly facility for the two adjacent buildings. Option 1 creates link bridges on all levels and separates the new building as an independent building form in order to fit into the existing scale of its urban location. As a result of its physical separation from adjacent buildings, this option also provides flexibility for a change in its day-to-day functioning; serving as a hub for activities which may change. The existing storage spaces retain their current arrangement and patterns

Perspective view of environmental volumes

2. Perspective view of environmental volumes

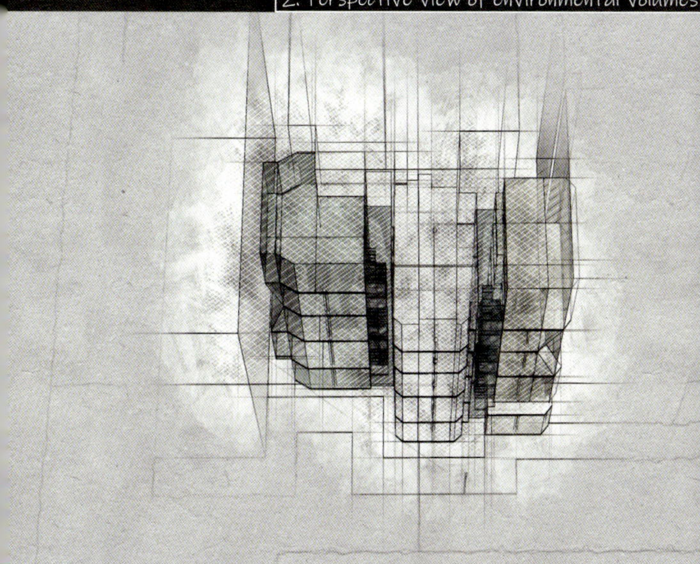

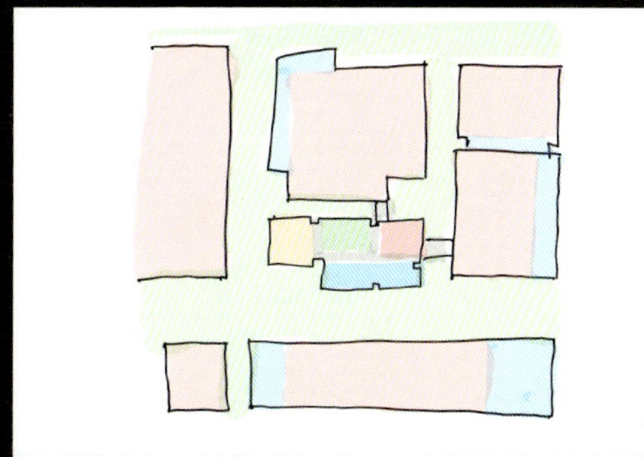

1. Figure-ground diagram of tempered environment

Option 1
Red spaces are highly tempered but are reduced to a single volume only.

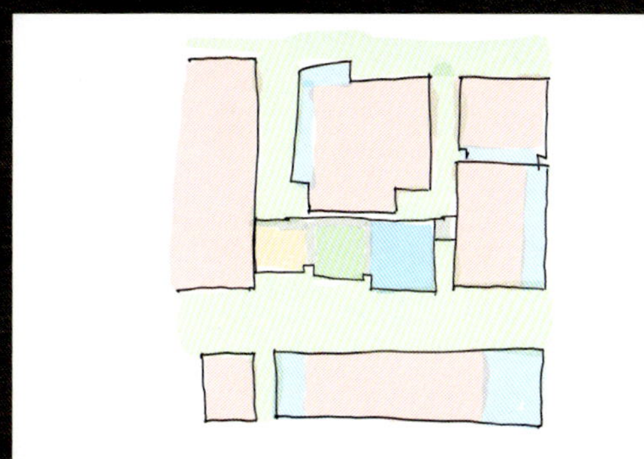

2. Figure-ground diagram of tempered environment

Option 2
Dark blue spaces are less tempered than dark green spaces but are more tempered than light blue circulation space.

3. Figure-ground diagram of tempered environment

Option 3
Light blue spaces are the least tempered spaces, these spaces interface directly with external space.

of use. Option 2 creates a different footprint from Option 1 where its external form, which has the same overall floor area as Option 1, is positioned closer to the two adjacent existing buildings, with wider and more centrally placed links into them so there is a narrow gap between the new building and the two adjacent existing buildings. Option 3 takes this idea further and integrates the new building with the existing building, on the basis that the flexibility of an independent new building is not as important as the benefits gained from integrating it directly with the existing buildings on each side.

This manufacturing building is to be shared by light industry companies; mainly startups who are renting workspace on a relatively short-term basis. A range of digitally driven manufacturing tools is provided for a range of fabrication tasks. This is not a building for large-scale manufacturing; it is for smaller-scale fabrication where there is a need for a high degree of mass customisation. The range of tasks that can be carried out in this building is specific; the facility suits those who are wanting to get products to market by fabricating working prototypes and small-volumes that can eventually be manufactured in larger scale facilities elsewhere. This allows startups to establish a minimum viable product through iterations of fabrication and associated optimisations through design development. This facility aims to welcome the return of small-scale manufacturing to this region. The building is arranged over four floors of tall spaces and occupies a small footprint. Four floors were necessary, rather than the customary single storey, due to the need to occupy a small site in order for the project to remain economical. Manufacturing equipment that is light in weight is required for product development, allowing workshops to be arranged over four floors. Access is provided by goods lifts/elevators and stairs at the edges of the building. The external walls and structure are conceived of as a kit of parts, with fixing points that are pre-positioned such that new components used for fabrication tasks can be fixed to both the floor and the vertical structure, onto which associated framing and small-scale equipment can be mounted.

1. Sectional perspective view

2. Sectional perspective view

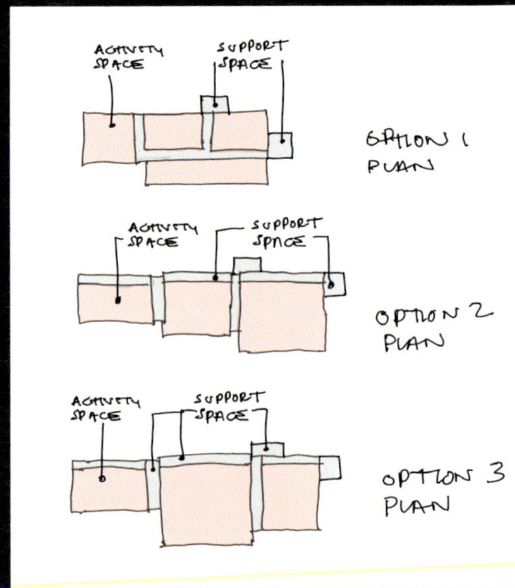

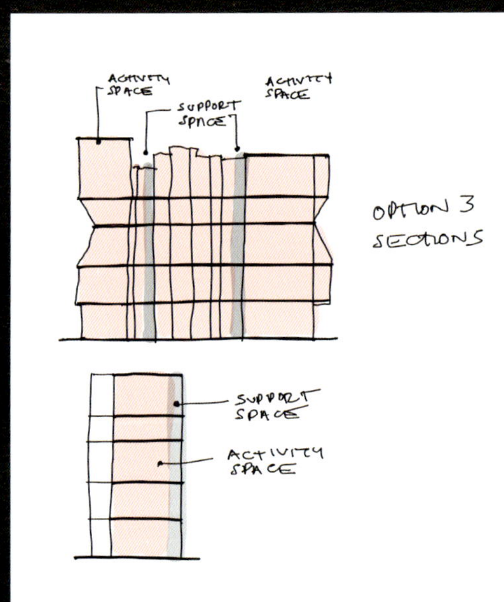

Spatial arrangement

Option 1 divides the new building into three areas.

Option 2 removes that transition space between the links to buildings, and instead has a link directly between one building with its central space and the other building.

Option 3 provides three characteristic spaces that more closely match the manufacturing requirements of the three assembly halls.

Spatial arrangement

The spatial arrangement for Option 1 is of dividing the new building into three areas. Goods are moved between the three areas of the new building and the two adjacent existing buildings by way of a link bridge. The three adjacent spaces of the new building are divided up as per the brief/program, but the corner space which links the two bridge links to adjacent existing buildings is an additional item to that required in the brief/program. Option 2 removes that transition space between the links to buildings, and instead has a link directly between one building with its central space and the other building, and the other space adjacent to it, such that three primary spaces are created following the three main processes of manufacturing used in this building. Option 3 optimises the relationship between the spaces and creates a smaller-scale series of linked blocks, which creates a volume that more harmoniously fits into the scale of buildings around it. The single block designs of neither Options 1 and 2 are in keeping with the urban scale of the blocks around it and neither do they respond sufficiently closely to the spatial requirements, which were considered to be of a fluid nature. In Options 1 and 2, some internal walls could be moved to suit the spaces required. Option 3 provides three characteristic spaces that more closely match the manufacturing requirements of the three assembly halls.

The spatial arrangement of all three options is based on taking three sets of workshops and arranging them in different sizes to suit the site which fills almost all the available footprint. All three options are accommodated within the footprint of the building, with Option 3 providing external space for access, which is expected to be for those arriving from nearby local transport links. There is no car park associated with this building. The spatial arrangement is one of three sets of relationships between buildings, independent of the planning of the internal circulation.

Buildings are arranged in a set of three forms, separated by service zones containing stairs, lifts/elevators and access corridors. The ends of each space are glazed to introduce daylight.

Perspective view of interior

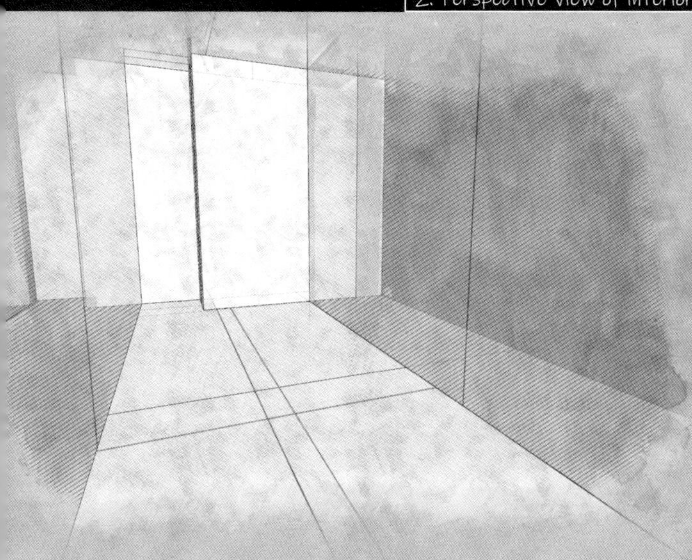

2. Perspective view of interior

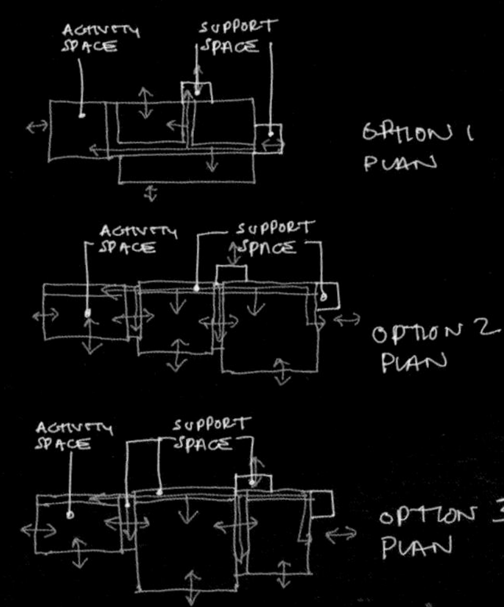

Internal circulation

Option 1 arranges circulation from a single entrance at one end of the building.

Option 2 arranges circulation from entrances at each end of the building.

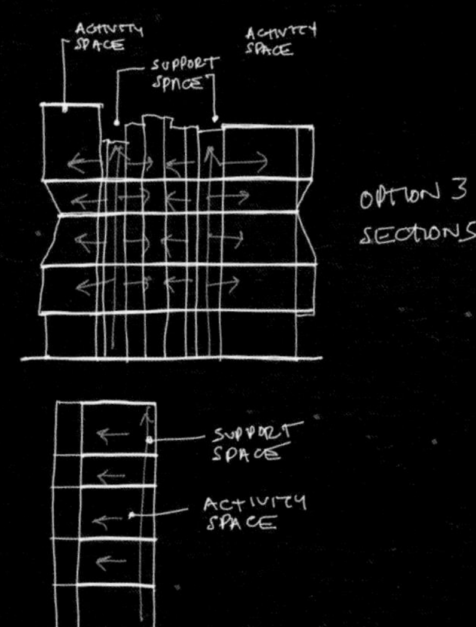

Option 3 arranges circulation from a single entrance at the centre of the building.

Internal circulation

The circulation within this building is based on providing entrances into the building and vehicle access to the building adjacent to the two links with the existing buildings, such that the new hub building can be serviced at ground floor level, at the point closest to the intersection of circulations of the two adjacent existing buildings with the new building. Pedestrian access is provided in the opposite corner, away from vehicles. Internal circulation is based on having a central corridor that provides access to the three main workspaces; this corridor links the three workshops to the 'hub' space in one corner of the building in Option 2. Because spaces are set in a continuous row, circulation is provided with a corridor positioned on one side of the building; the side adjacent to the two existing buildings which have access into the three workshops. Large-opening doors between the three workshops allow spaces to be joined for different arrangements of assembly work which is carried out inside any of the three halls. This principle of organisation applies equally to Option 3, which has additional external access decks at higher levels that provide space for additional equipment which is expected in the near future.

Internal circulation for the three configurations of workshop space is based on creating a link with an adjacent building in different configurations, whose objective is to reduce the amount of circulation space in order to reduce travel distances between spaces and between the new building and the existing building. The arrangement of options for internal circulation is dependent upon that of the adjacent building; a design requirement was that the link should be able to be made continuous with the adjoining building if required in the near future.

Front and rear walls of lifts/elevators are glazed in order to admit daylight into the service corridor. The walls enclosing stairs are glazed at the opposite end of the service corridor.

The service corridors divide the floor plates into three parts which can be naturally ventilated by admitting air through the ends of these linking spaces. Although each floor is separated, fresh air and daylight can be admitted through the service spaces.

1A. Isometric view of environmental volumes

1B. Isometric view of environmental volumes

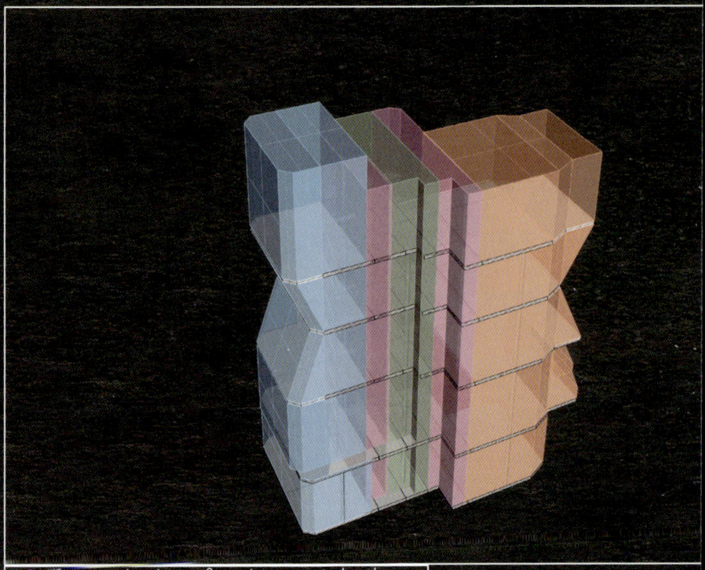

2A. Isometric view of environmental volumes

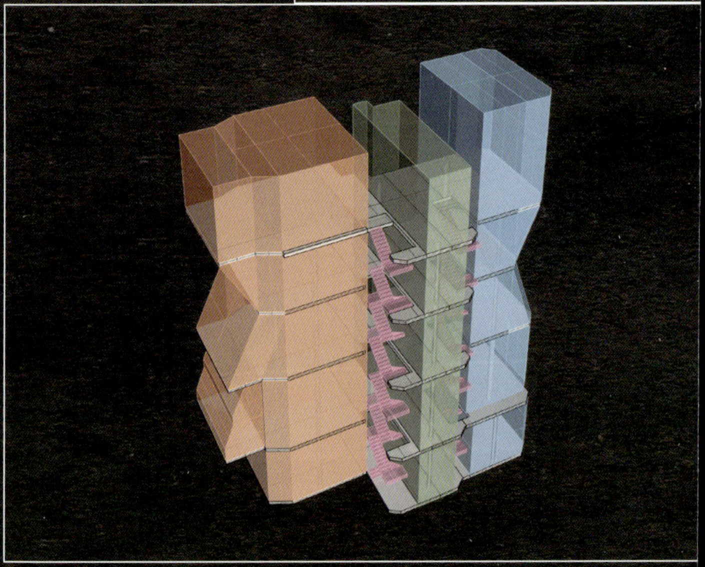

2B. Isometric view of environmental volum

Environmental strategy

Most mechanical and electrical equipment is mounted at roof level, immediately adjacent to the spaces to which they bring ducted air and an electrical supply. Unlike machinery used for assembly work within the three halls, the mechanical and electrical equipment is not required to be moved in the short term from space to space; it is anticipated that air duct routes and electrical supply within each hall will require only modest changes and updates in the near future. Mechanical and electrical equipment ducts and associated pipes are fixed on the external face of facades in order to provide as much flexibility as possible to changing functions within internal spaces. The facades have additional fixing positions in place so that mechanical and electrical equipment modules can be lifted and moved into different positions to suit changing requirements in the building; every facade panel has its own mechanical and electrical equipment docking pad which forms an integral part of the facade system. The air-handling units and associated chillers and equipment are accommodated in separate modules which are fixed at roof level. This level of flexibility required by the brief/program is made possible by the use of prefabricated mechanical and electrical equipment modules which are mainly on the roof, but are also fixed through facade panels. Full-height access doors are provided at ground floor level; retractable platforms are set at upper levels for the supply of large-scale items such as equipment parts for the machinery used in assembly tasks. The platforms are served within the building by gantry cranes; doors set around the gantry track open and close to suit operational requirements and maintain the integrity of the external envelope. Small amounts of ancillary equipment are also provided at roof level, such as generators to supply power to equipment inside the building, and associated exhaust equipment. The modular nature of the mechanical and electrical equipment provides the basis of an environmental strategy based on the reuse and redeployment of mechanical and electrical equipment modules rather than their replacement. Safety equipment and maintenance access equipment is mounted on the roof.

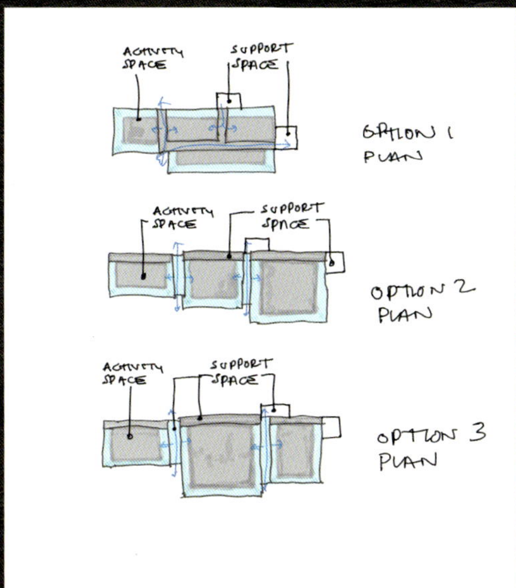

Daylight strategy for direct sunlight and cross ventilation.

Option 1 admits daylight and air in perimeter circulation spaces.

Option 2 admits daylight and air in perimeter circulation spaces and support spaces.

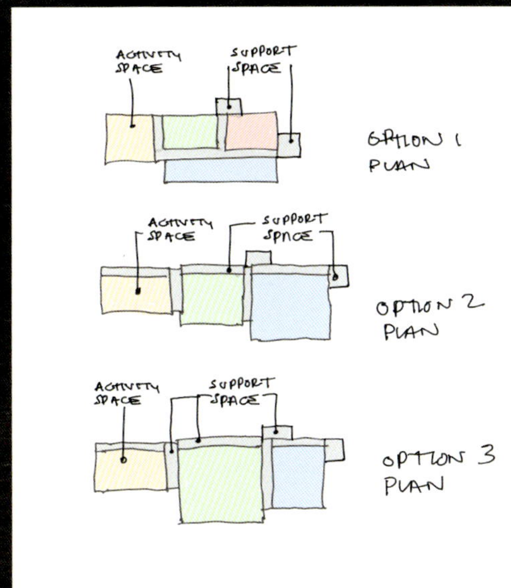

Environmental zones

Option 1 provides a link space that uses energy recovered from the adjacent spaces for either heating or cooling.

Option 2 has all three of the main spaces mechanically ventilated.

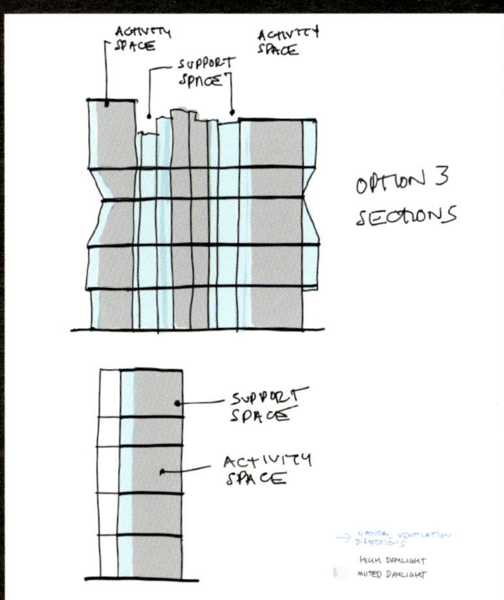

Daylight strategy for direct sunlight and cross ventilation.

Option 3 admits daylight and air in perimeter circulation spaces and support spaces throughout the height of the building.

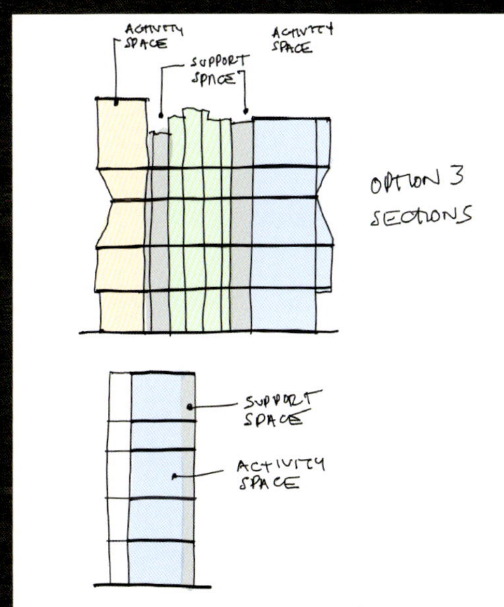

Environmental zones

Option 3 provides the ability to have natural cross ventilation from one side of the building to the other side in the mid-season.

The environmental strategy for all three options follows that of the spatial arrangement where each volume has its own environmental zone. In Option 1, a link space uses energy recovered from the adjacent spaces for either heating or cooling, and the other three spaces have different ventilation requirements, and different air changes, based on the day-to-day needs of each assembly hall. In Options 1 and 2, all three of the main spaces are mechanically ventilated. Option 3 provides, in addition to three different environmental zones, the ability to have natural cross ventilation from one side of the building to the other side in the mid-season. The environmental strategy is one of forming environmental zones for each of the three volumes established on each of the four floors; a total of 12 environmental zones. The zones on each floor are linked such that between one and three environmental zones per floor can be established; there is no connection between the environmental zones on adjacent floors as there is no link between activities carried out between adjacent floors. The air-handling equipment is fixed to the sides of the buildings, which comprises package units for air conditioning and heating equipment fixed externally, instead of being roof mounted; ducts extend down inside the building. This approach is taken in order to create completely clear volumes within the building and without the need to have services in cores that extend from floor to floor. The only connection between floors is that of the lifts/elevators and the emergency staircases; the lifts/elevators are large enough in format to be lifted up and down. The building also accommodates glazed rooflight areas which project from the building that accommodate office and meeting spaces, which are to be provided in addition to the manufacturing spaces such that these spaces have been provided without interrupting the clear rectilinear volumes of the manufacturing workshops. These meeting spaces have inclined rooflights in volumes extending out from the volume of the building, allowing vehicles beneath to circulate within the perimeter of the site. The approach of creating cantilevered volumes of workspace and services equipment at higher floor levels allows the activity space within the building to be maximised, while providing the required vehicle routes at ground floor level.

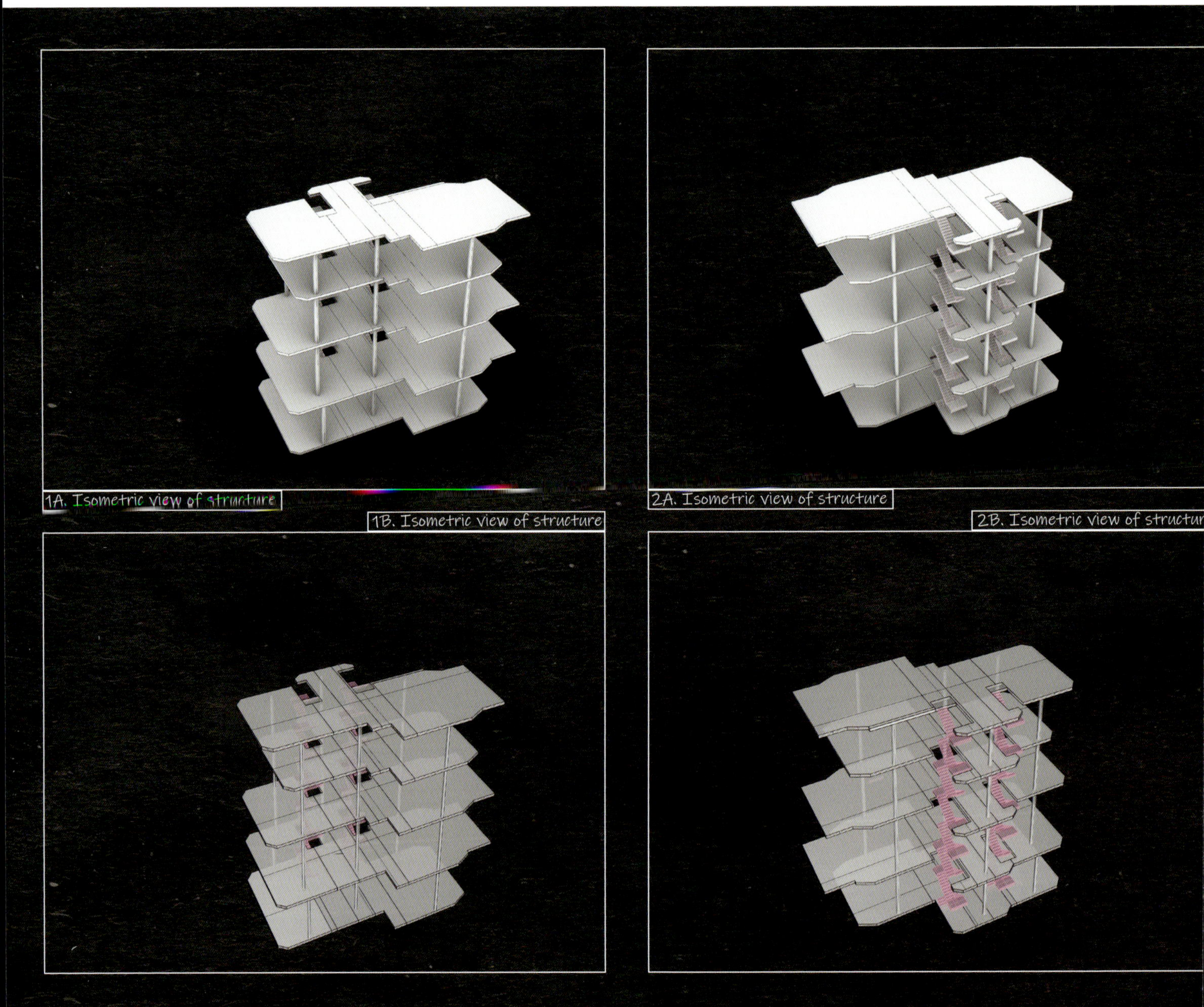

1A. Isometric view of structure

1B. Isometric view of structure

2A. Isometric view of structure

2B. Isometric view of structur

Structural strategy

The structural strategy meets a requirement of planned future phases of being able to extend the building in any direction, without the need to change the current arrangement of primary structure.

The structural design comprises a steel frame set internally, enclosed by the facades, for which stability is provided within the structural zone adjacent to that of the facades. Structural frames are positioned behind the facades; externally the form of the primary structure can be traced visually through the facade arrangement of large-size cladding panels. The facade system is entirely prefabricated; when slotted into place each panel forms part of a larger-scale panel arrangement of wider joints that follow the primary structure, to which the panels are fixed. Mechanical and electrical equipment, together with ducts, are fixed to the steel frame behind. A key requirement is to allow the steel frame to provide limited support to future secondary steel platforms set within the building; drilled holes are provided in columns accordingly. Some of the floor zones are cantilevered out of the building in order to accommodate specific functional requirements of the spaces inside; equipment is required to be moved between floors with changes in assembly processes carried out within the building. The structure is located in a specific structural zone which is independent of the functioning of the floor plates in order not to interfere with the usable floor area. The structural system is a 'stack-based' system of structural connection components that allow flexibility of the future repositioning of access decks and changes in the positions of mechanical and electrical equipment.

The building accommodates internal platforms in the form of secondary steel frames; floor decks are constructed as 'strong floors', with fixing points for secondary structure which is moved around the building like a scaled-up version of an engineering test laboratory. The secondary structure is required to support mechanical and electrical equipment, together with secondary manufacturing equipment. The repositioning of secondary structure is assisted by ceiling-mounted sliding gantries. The structural strategy for all three options is based on a steel frame

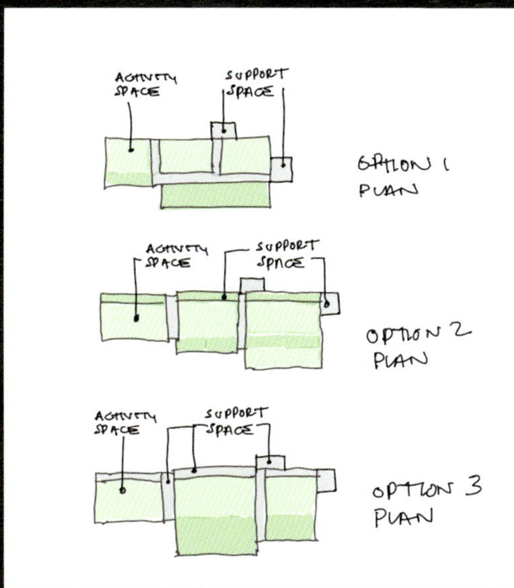

Structural strategy: Zones
Option 1 has structural walls which traverse the narrow width of the building.
Option 2 has concrete cores that provides structural stability to the frame.

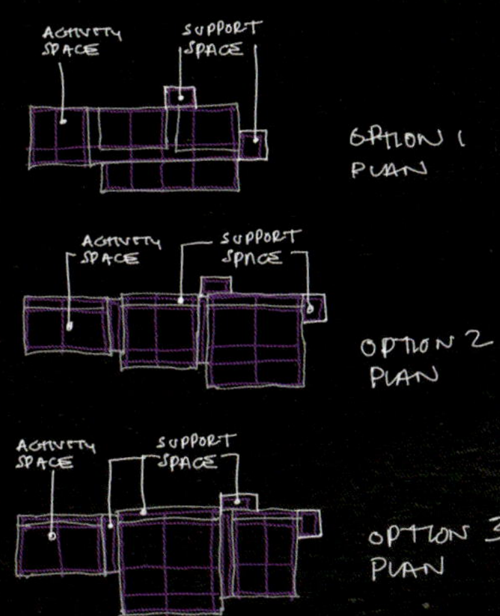

Structural strategy: Framing
Option 1 encloses the core spaces and dividing space into sets of apartments.
Option 2 is largely a steel frame.

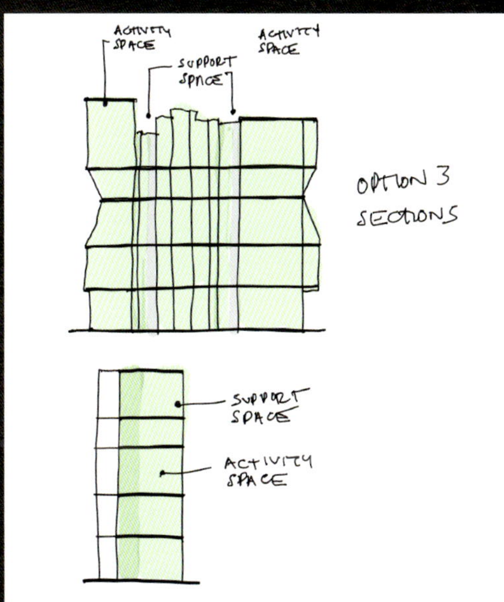

Structural strategy: Zones
Option 3 has structural walls formed as cores and mixing those with columns in the accommodation spaces.

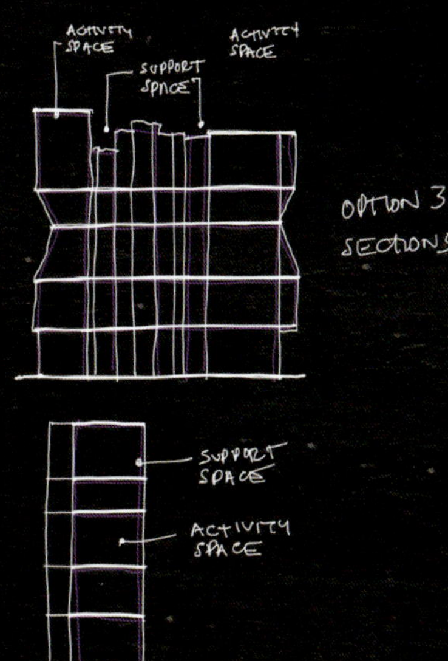

Structural strategy: Zones
Option 3 is a mixed solution of reinforced concrete and steel.

which creates large-scale, long-spanning spaces. Option 1 has a centrally arranged set of columns within the smaller spaces. Option 2 avoids centrally positioned columns by having narrower spaces, resulting in a longer and narrower building form. Option 3 can also accommodate a central column within the larger central space. Both Options 2 and 3 suit the planned future phases of extending the building in any direction without the need to adapt the building structure.

The structural strategy is one of a reinforced concrete frame with floor slabs which span between floor-supporting beams. This approach provides a set of high capacity decks for equipment to be installed; additional structural walls are provided within areas of external walls, which are aligned with the reinforced concrete columns and the perimeter of the floor slabs. The structure accommodates chamfered edges at the corners of the building where glazed slots are introduced. However in all cases, a single column is provided at the corners of the building, as a set of two adjacent columns is not required to create the chamfer. Columns positioned at corners can be seen from outside of the building where a vertical strip of glazing is introduced. At ground floor level the building extends outwards to fill part of the site to the boundary; its supporting structure of reinforced beams and columns forms part of the frame that supports the main parts of the building.

Each of the three sets of manufacturing halls is structurally independent of its neighbour, and is structurally independent of the support spaces that are set between each manufacturing hall. The service spaces comprise a grid of beams and columns which support stairs, a lift/elevator and the deck at each level that links them. Where access is provided directly to each space from the stairs and lifts/elevators, the void between them has bridges to link the adjacent manufacturing halls in each block. Some bridges are used as work space; others are offset from each other such that they do not align vertically one above the other, providing the functionality required of each space.

The link buildings form the permanent part of the building; their cross-braced framing and structural connections that reach out to the manufacturing halls make a visual statement of that permanence.

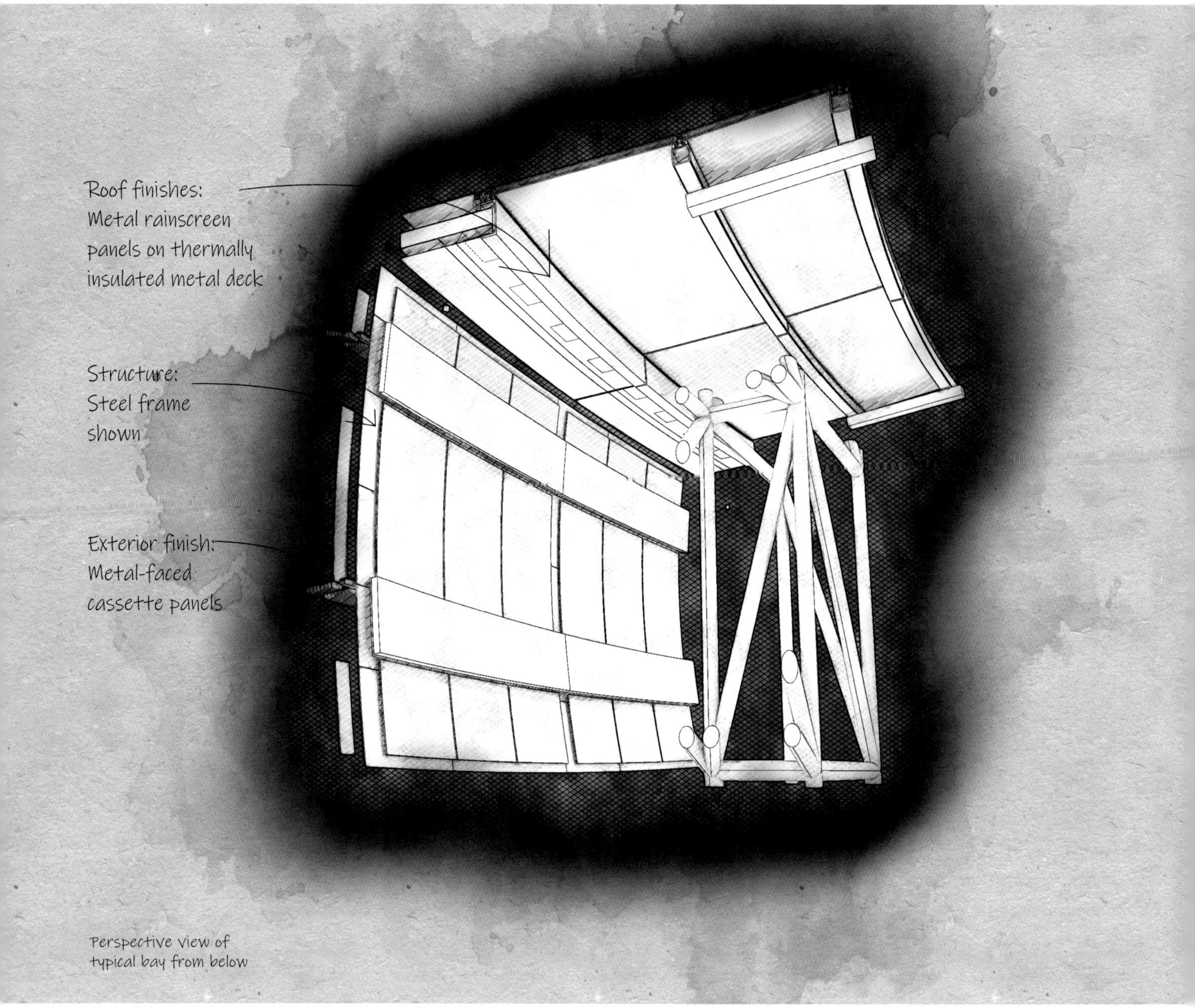

Perspective view of typical bay from below

Typical bay adjacent to facade

This building is highly thermally insulated, with bands of horizontally oriented glazing; the glass units are inclined away from the vertical plane so that clear views out can be provided while reducing reflections back into the building during hours of darkness. Corners of the building have smaller vertical glazed panels set within the prefabricated staircase cores; vertically oriented metal panels are used as solar shading devices. Mechanical and electrical equipment units, which are attached to the side of the building, allow for air to enter on one side and be exhausted on the other side; part of a system of recycling of both heat and cooling energy required at different times of the year.

Additional bracing for the structure is provided by ties that combine both horizontal and triangular forms which are a key part of the characteristic facades; this arrangement is reflected in the joints between facade cladding panels. Fixing brackets are set horizontally between adjacent blocks. The building also has deployable solar shading; individual panels that are deployed from an enclosing set of covers that protects the shading from the effects of weather when not in use. These protective covers also serve as a light reflector to bring daylight and sunlight into parts of the building when specifically required.

Facade panels are fabricated as cassette units which accommodate thermal insulation and a provision for the fixing of mechanical and electrical equipment duct runs and pipe routes, which cross the facades on their outside face. In order to reduce the effects of expected wind turbulence at corners of the building, which would cause pedestrian discomfort, corner panels are chamfered, as are coping panels at roof level.

A typical bay in this building is formed by the space enclosing a single workshop that extends over one floor level. The bay comprises deep concrete beams which are long-spanning in order to provide an economy in the span of the floor slabs in one direction, allowing large-scale openings to be formed in the facades at ground floor level for the movement of goods and materials to and from the building. The environmental design makes use of packaged units for air conditioning,

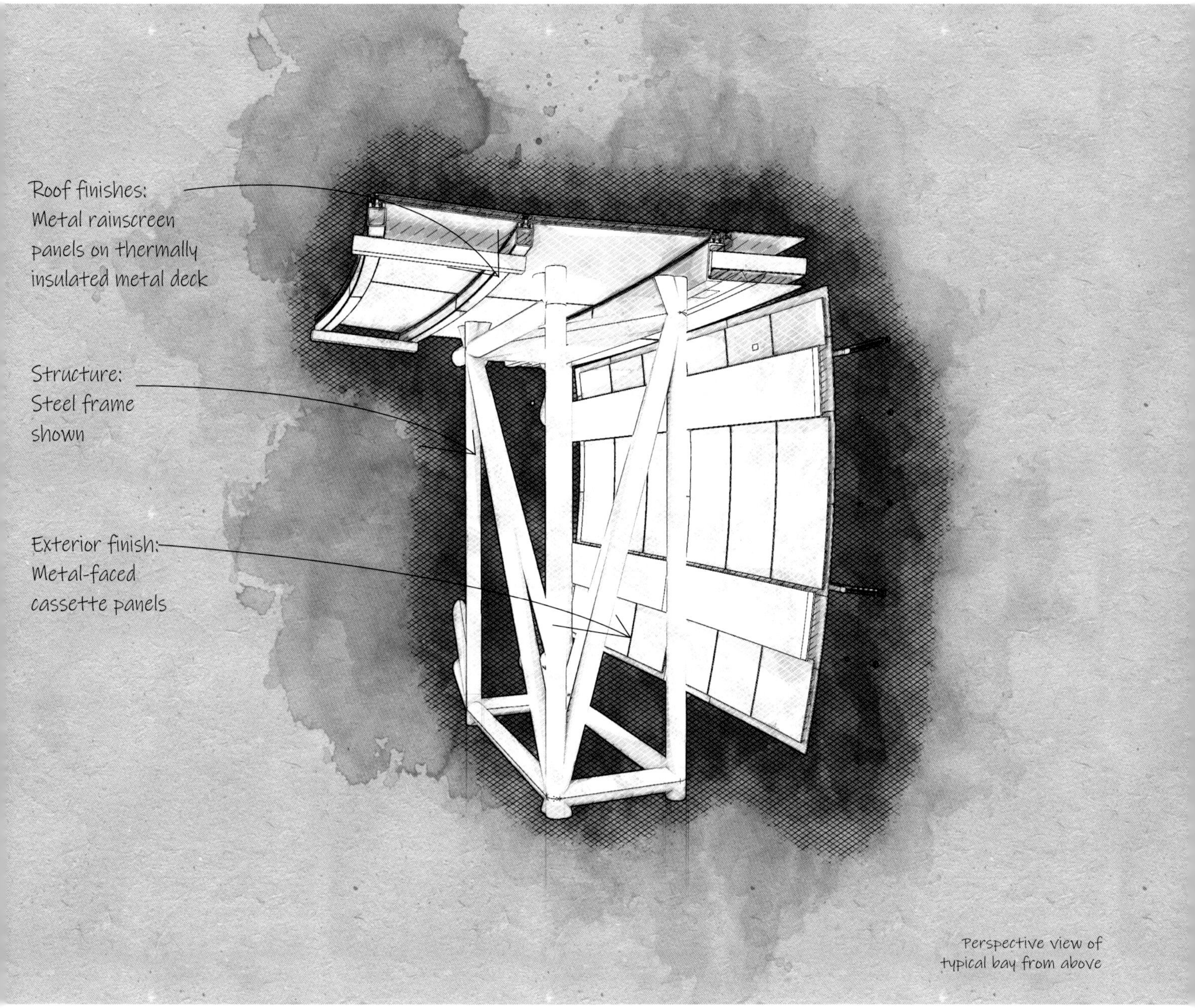

Perspective view of typical bay from above

air-handling and electrical services which are fixed to the sides of the building, most of which are integrated within the zone of the external envelope. The facade panels are manufactured as part of the equipment of the building, but are given a different visual appearance to adjacent panels which provide enclosure for the facades only. Panels for facade enclosure are formed as highly insulated, with a metal outer skin in a sandwich-cassette configuration that spans from floor to floor. Panels are 1.0 metres wide and six metres high, restrained at their mid-height by a rail which is fixed back to the primary structure. These highly insulated panels are independent of the panels enclosing the air-handling equipment and services equipment, which is fixed on the outside of the building and which is supported on the primary structural frame and walls.

Some of the services fixed to the facades are supplied from roof level; others are self-contained. The services equipment has a weather barrier of panels provided around these assemblies. Where the facade panels do not continue behind these services, prefabricated services pods are attached to the primary structure.

There are two typical bays in this project: the link buildings, which have glazed ends, and the manufacturing halls, which are largely opaque. The facades of the link buildings are enclosed in glazed panels which are smaller in size than the adjacent panels of the manufacturing halls. The link buildings are taller than the halls they serve; the space at the top of the link buildings accommodates service equipment. The sides of the link buildings have structural walls in reinforced concrete instead of bracing, which was an alternative considered at an early stage of the design. The link buildings have alternating panels of concrete and glass; the concrete forms part of the columns of this structure.

The facades of the manufacturing halls are primarily metal panels, with glass slots set into them; the reinforced concrete structure is visible in places where the structure is thermally insulated on its internal face. The glass appears only in thin slots that form windows at different heights, to create a set of four spaces with different daylight provisions in each of the manufacturing halls.

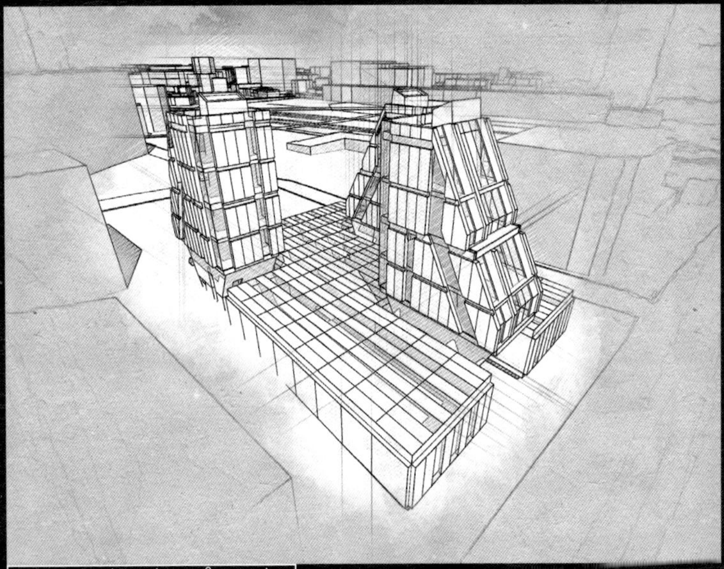

1. Perspective view of exterior

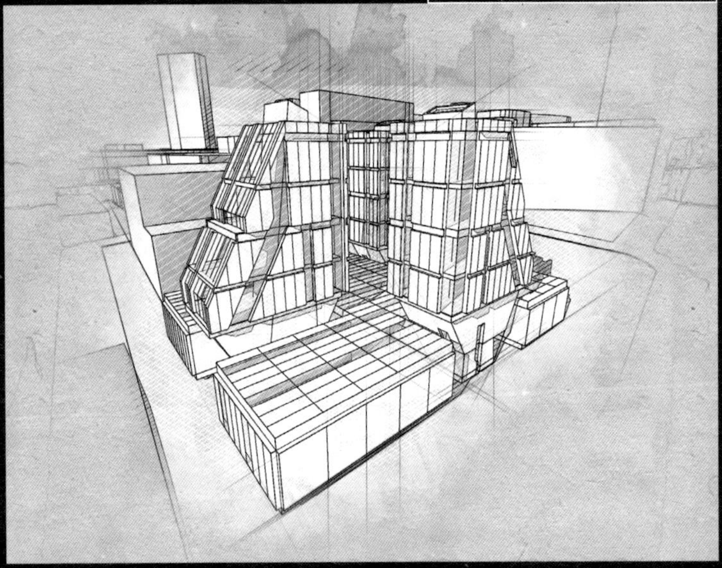

2. Perspective view of exterior

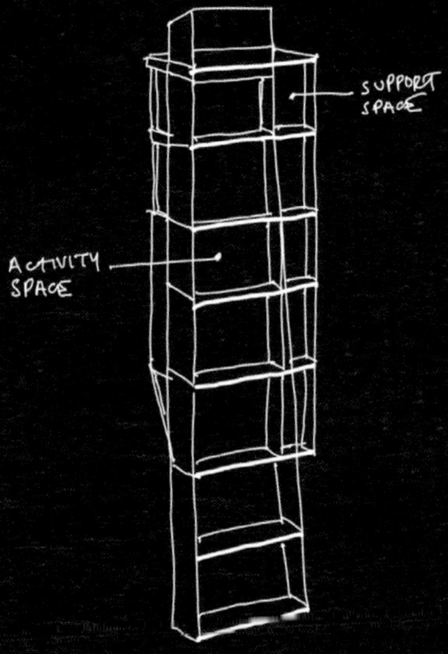

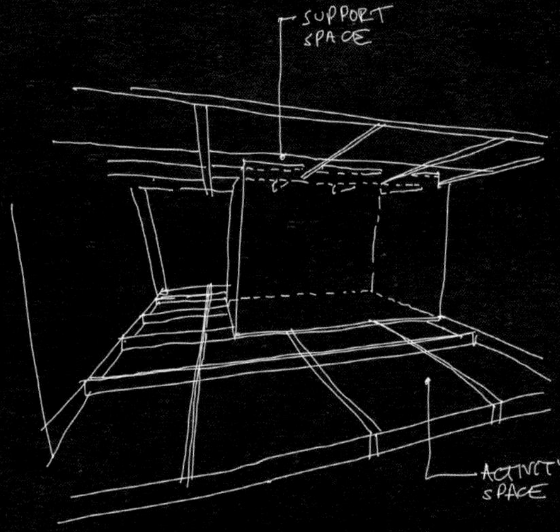

Assembly sequence and on-site fabrication

This project makes use of current technologies for structures and facades, as used in traditionally constructed buildings, combined with emerging technologies to create a mass-customised, complex geometry building. Assemblies and their components are simplified to generate off-site prefabricated construction systems which are more economic than their equivalent of site-based systems of construction. Rather than maximising the off-site prefabrication part of the construction, as is commonly the case in the construction of complex geometry buildings, this project moves the emphasis of fabrication and installation toward locally based, and on-site, fabrication; reducing the impact of carbon emissions during construction as a result of a reduced need to transport finished assemblies to the construction site.

This project incorporates geometries which are inclined from the vertical whose connections cannot be easily described by drawings of plans and sections; 3D modelling is required to both document the geometry and to communicate the sequence of installing components and assemblies on the job site. In terms of environmental design, these geometries require a 3D modelling approach to allow the connections of the environmental system to be understood and documented with accuracy. This approach of 3D modelling and 2D drawing allows the design to consider accurately the interaction between the system elements and their difference in relative orientation, which is common in complex geometry forms.

The building is environmentally design-led, with an external envelope that requires high levels of thermal insulation, such that the framing needs to have a high level of thermal insulation in this harsh winter climate. The glazing, for example, has a set of site-assembled framing into which double-glazed units are inserted and elements of window which are fixed to the outside for larger scale openings have a different orientation, are self-supporting and have even higher levels of thermal insulation required. The remainder of the building is opaque and accommodates some external equipment for air-handling and servicing of the building, all of which are enclosed externally to overcome the

Perspective view of exterior

4. Perspective view of exterior

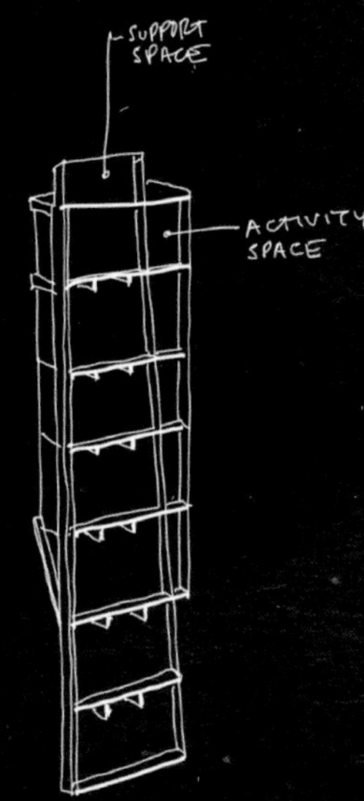

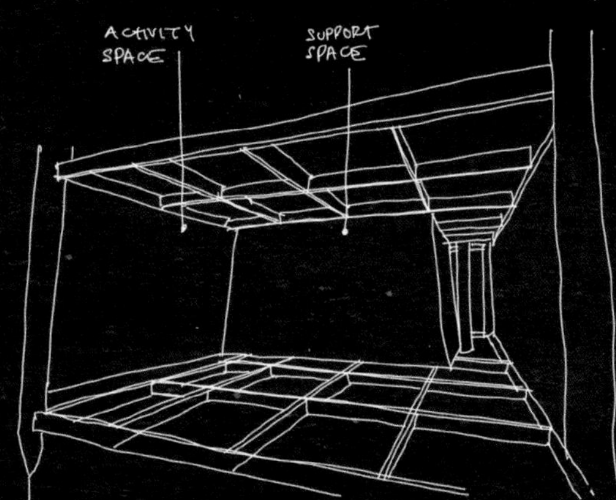

harsh winter conditions. The structure of the building is fully encapsulated in highly insulated facade panels. The structure is in steel in order to achieve the complex forms of the building, and additional electrical equipment is enclosed in a fully enclosed and thermally insulated rooftop box over this six-storey building. Each of the three bands comprising the building contains two floors within it. Each of the two floors is occupied by a single tenant in this hotel building adjacent to a port. It is envisaged that the building as a kit of parts will be deployed at different scales, and as a set of buildings which are juxtaposed and independent of each other, and are used to accommodate small groups in relatively remote locations.

The use of locally based contractors for on-site installation is that they are able to undertake construction work which would be more complex than would be the case if a larger contractor were used, with the standard systems and standard methods that would apply over a range of geographical locations and a wide range of projects. This project-specific advantage of a local contractor allows mass customisation methods to be deployed for construction. These methods are based around providing a 3D model of all connections internally and externally to allow the steelwork for the frame to be manufactured using smaller, shorter length and lighter steel member sizes that can be transported by easily by road. Facade assemblies can be fabricated and installed on site instead of being prefabricated at some distance away. Environmental control systems can be assembled and integrated into the internal walls to maximise the amount of free space.

This approach had the benefit of being able to have clear internal spaces that were uninterrupted by services and by structural members that could not have been integrated into the internal walls. This approach had additional benefits for the services installation of electrical lighting and natural ventilation in that the standard set of components could be brought together at the design stage instead of relying on a performance specification resulting in a reduced energy consumption in the building in use.

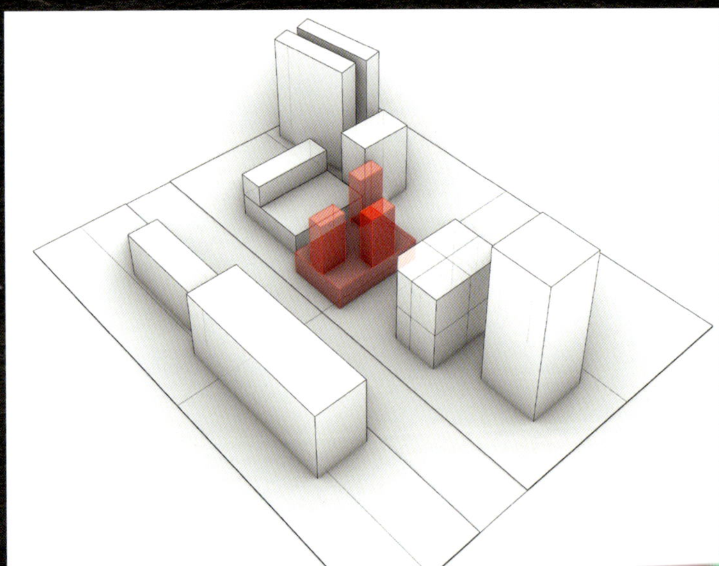

1. Project volume in site context

2. Project volume in site context

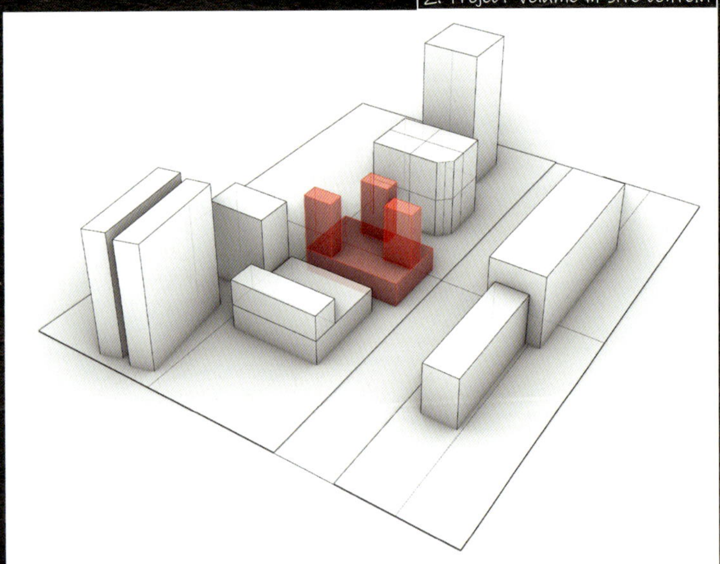

1. Site plan with surrounding context

Option 1 divides the building into two blocks, with the link block between them, in response to the geometry of the composition.

2. Site plan with surrounding context

Option 2 creates a link between the two buildings by narrowing down the point at which the buildings meet; this is the point of entry into the hotel.

3. Site plan with surrounding context

Option 3 creates a differentiation in the vertical section of the form rather than in horizontal plan.

Site context

The primary requirement for this hotel building for long-term residents, in relation to its context, is to have external spaces that are set away from the street; creating an external space for a café and bar where the building makes an immediate social connection to its neighbours and to its few neighbouring buildings; a specific visual link is made to its immediate neighbour in order to sit comfortably in this edge of town environment.

The design of the building is based on creating a set of juxtaposed forms, each of which is at the scale of neighbouring buildings of that size, which have visual connections created between each form; an alternative to a single building form which is differentiated visually only by variation in a common facade treatment.

The juxtaposed building forms have 'crevices', or deep slots, introduced into the facades to allow daylight to penetrate deep into the building and provide greater differentiation of the volumes within. Hotel apartment suites are highly differentiated from one another, resulting in the complex form of the building. The site context for this hotel project is of an urban centre where there is a mixture of taller office buildings and lower-rise residential buildings. The hotel sits at the mid-height between the taller buildings and the shorter buildings; creating a transition between them in stepping down from the height of taller commercial buildings to that of the lower-height residential buildings. The building is set on a rectangular site; adjoining a building which is currently separate and which has a mixture of residential and commercial space.

Option 1 creates a smaller-scale intervention which forms a continuation of the arrangement of the form of the adjacent building; a block which is likely to remain, such that the two buildings create a connection between them. The division of Option 1 into two blocks, with the link block between them, is in response to the geometry of those two buildings. Option 2 creates a link between the two buildings by narrowing down the point at which the buildings meet; this is the point of entry into the hotel. Option 3 creates a differentiation in the vertical section of the form rather than in horizontal plan; the form steps, in and out, in

erspective view of environmental volumes

2. Perspective view of environmental volumes

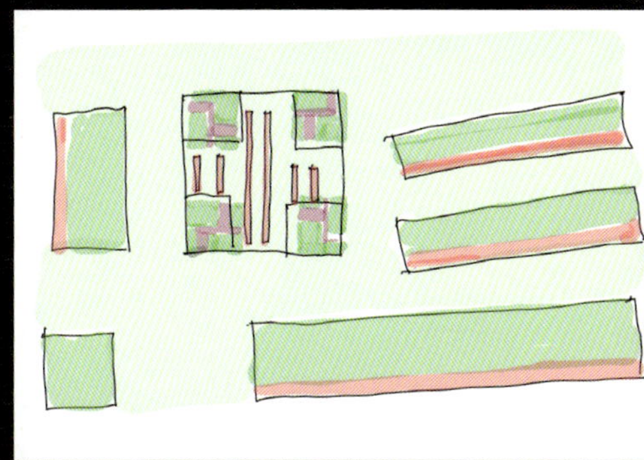

1. Figure-ground diagram of tempered environment

Option 1
Dark green spaces are highly tempered but are reduced to accommodation volumes only.

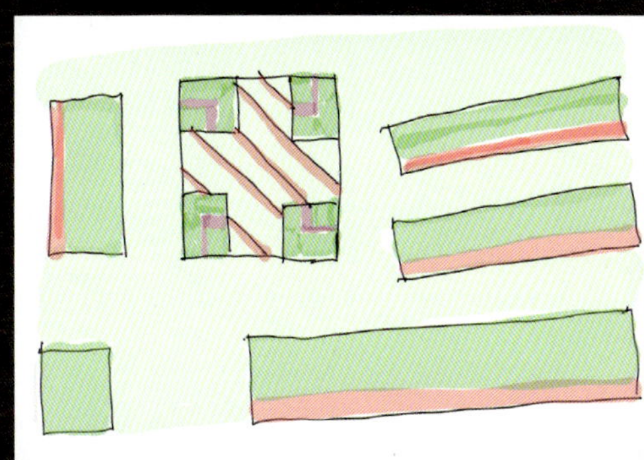

2. Figure-ground diagram of tempered environment

Option 2
Red spaces are less tempered than dark green spaces but are more tempered than light green circulation space.

3. Figure-ground diagram of tempered environment

Option 3
Lighter green spaces are the least tempered spaces, these spaces interface directly with external space.

vertical section in response to the brief/program and creates restaurant and bar spaces inside the hotel for a mixture of a public space and public facilities; all in addition to the hotel apartment suites. The form of the building occupies the site at the upper level, but narrows down at street level in order to accommodate the entrance and commercial spaces required; providing a visual transparency through the building and unifying the space around the hotel at street level. Functions within are oriented so as to have views down to the street below as well as to create views up to the spaces within the hotel.

The site context is one of unused land adjacent to a port for which the land has been abandoned and the building stands almost alone at the edge of the site. It is thought that these buildings will be built as isolated forms. Single versions of these buildings will be constructed in remote locations. The buildings have views out on three sides and can either be protected from the weather or can be opened up with views out to where the occupants are perhaps most concerned about when they can have clear visibility of adjacent spaces. This is not an urban building; instead it is a building which is set in partial isolation from that which surrounds it but requires high levels of thermal insulation with different glazing arrangements on different facades and protection from harsh weather.

The design of the building was intended to be used for a range of locations within the same country. This harsh, northern hemisphere climate is characterised by winter storms with high winds and snow that lasts for two to three months of the year. The summers are warm and dry but temperate. As a result, the design of the building for remote locations was orientated and optimised for remote locations with only an electricity supply to the building from an adjacent road. The form of the building is consequently optimised for having its inclined wall set against the prevailing wind in winter, as well as having surfaces which avoid ledges for the build-up of snow and ice during winter months. Doors and windows are shuttered for protection during storms, giving rise to the characteristic forms of the facades.

1. Sectional perspective view

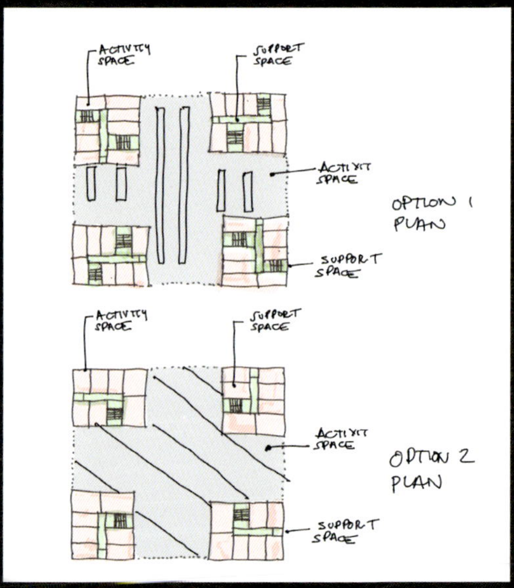

Spatial arrangement

Option 1 is one of two blocks set side by side with a central entrance area.

Option 2 has access at the side of the building between the existing building and the new building.

2. Sectional perspective view

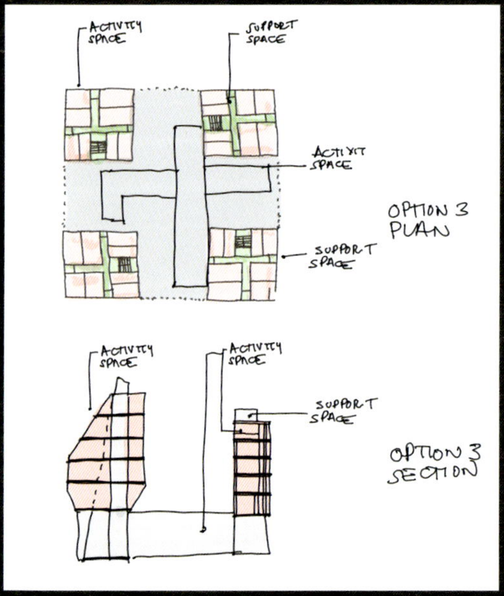

Option 3 develops the changes in vertical section rather than in horizontal plan.

Spatial arrangement

The spatial arrangement for Option 1 is one of two blocks set side by side with a central entrance area. The hotel rooms are arranged along two corridors down the centre of each block, with stairs and lifts/elevators set at each end that provide access to rooms on the upper floors. Option 2 has access at the side of the building between the existing building and the new building. Access to the ground floor lobby is in the middle of the long facades, with secured access to stairs and lifts/elevators. Rooms are arranged in a single block with a central corridor and stairs at each end. Option 3 has a similar layout to Option 2 but begins to develop the changes in vertical section rather than in horizontal plan. The building is accessed from each end, with a central lobby from which lifts/elevators and stairs take residents up to the upper floors. Stairs and lifts/elevators are set at each end of the building, and there is a central corridor with rooms arranged on both sides on the upper levels. The general spatial arrangement is of two floors for each of the three blocks. The building comprises three blocks; each block is divided into two floors and is occupied by a single group or family. The ground floor area is for the storage of equipment, with an ease of access to snowmobiles and road vehicles that can be stored either in this ground floor area or outside. The residential accommodation is arranged over two floors with a mezzanine floors for two groups or a family. The spatial arrangement was subject to the juxtaposition of these modular housing units. The three options show 12 units juxtaposed in different combinations; each dwelling has a clear open space on each habitable floor. The units are set adjacent to one another, with high levels of thermal insulation between dwellings in order that unoccupied dwellings do not draw heat energy from the occupied dwelling. This was a key consideration given the harsh climates in which these buildings are located. The arrangement allows for a module which is fitted out entirely with circulation provisions for the staircase and lift/elevator. This module also contains storage equipment for common use during winter months, including emergency provisions and spare parts for the snow-based land vehicles at ground level.

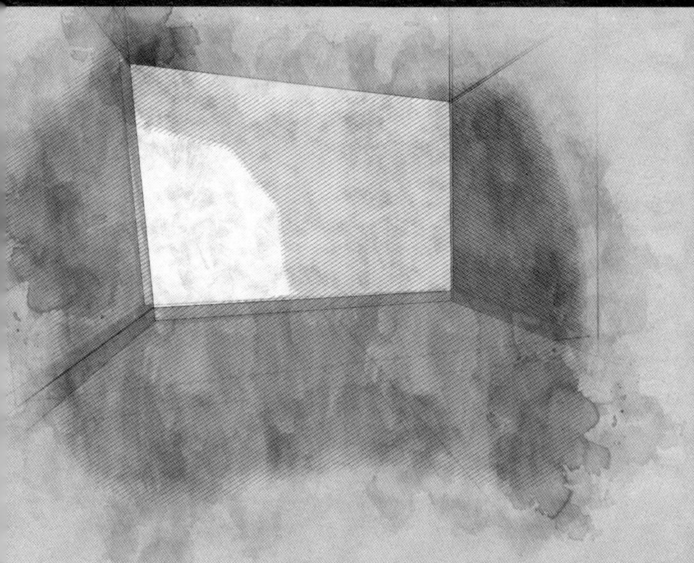

Perspective view of interior

2. Perspective view of interior

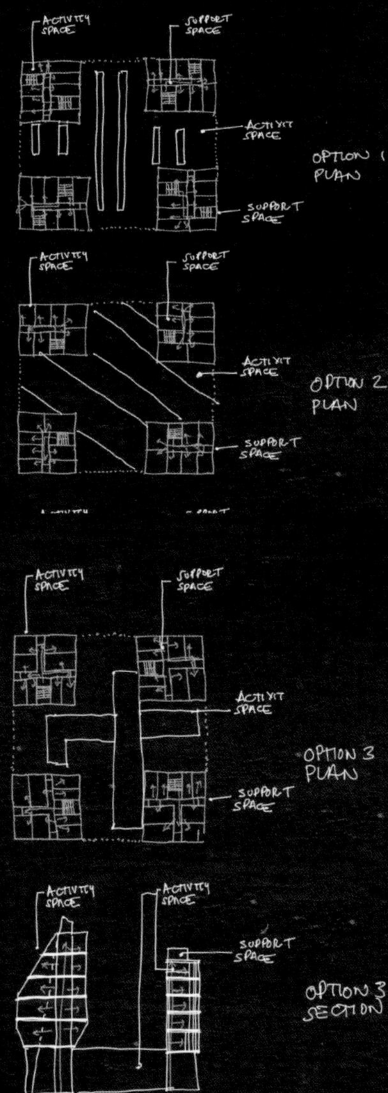

Internal circulation

Option 1 is based on distribution from a central space which is accessed at both ends into the lift/elevator lobby.

Option 2 has the hotel entrance positioned in a recessed slot between the existing building and the new building.

Option 3 has access provided by way of separate lobbies positioned at each end of the building.

Residential units are designed to be arranged in groups, with a ground floor setting of an external storage unit and enclosing walls. Units are set out parallel to one another but offset by a full unit width in order to ensure that each unit has similar levels of daylight and sunlight. Units are set slightly apart in order to ensure natural ventilation to all rooms and maintain the group as a linked building rather than as separate housing units, while avoiding the need for a central light well.

Internal circulation

The internal circulation for Option 1 is based on distribution from a central space which is accessed at both ends into the lift/elevator lobby. From the lobby, lifts/elevators take residents up to the upper floors; each level accommodates a modest number of rooms. Two of the lifts/elevators are used as service lifts/elevators. Option 2 has the hotel entrance positioned in a recessed slot between the existing building and the new building; the lobby extends under the main block, providing a point of access to two lifts/elevators and two sets of stairs. At upper levels, a central corridor on each floor links stairs positioned at each end, providing access to all apartments. Option 3 has a similar layout, but access is provided by way of separate lobbies positioned at each end of the building, such that hotel apartments can be divided into two independent groups of rooms, with potentially a separate lobby serving each hotel. This arrangement provides access to lift/elevator lobbies at each end of the building, with corridor access at upper levels.

The internal circulation comprises staircases on the inclined side of the building, which has glazed windows set vertically in order to provide views out in that direction as well as to observe weather conditions. The upper floor apartments are accessed from the circulation core; the lower duplex units are accessed directly from the workshop unit on the ground floor. The lower units suit occupants for whom the workshops are seen as an extension of their home. The form of one side of the building reflects the need for accommodating staircases that project outwards from the building and then turn and come back into the building above the level of the podium.

1A. Isometric view of environmental volumes

2A. Isometric view of environmental volumes

1B. Isometric view of environmental volumes

2B. Isometric view of environmental volum

Environmental strategy

The environmental strategy for all three options is based on a single environmental zone for each apartment; a mixture of mechanical and natural ventilation to all habitable rooms. A second set of environmental zones exists for circulation spaces for corridors, stairs and the ground floor lobby. In Option 1 the stairs and corridor in both blocks are linked, providing straightforward access for mechanical ventilation to those parts with stairs having additional natural ventilation. A similar principle applies in Option 2 where stairs and corridor are linked into a single system; but in this option, there is a separate lift/elevator lobby entrance area which is also considered to be part of the circulation zone, with its associated lower levels of ventilation. These principles apply to Option 3, where all rooms share a single environmental zone, but because of the varying levels of occupation of apartment suites, systems activate in response to their occupation status.

The environmental strategy is one of a highly insulated building with relatively small amounts of glazing, but the glazing is sufficiently tall in order to provide views both up and down such that the windows are of a different shape. This is in order to provide different views out while protecting the windows on the facades from effects of harsh weather as well as to minimise the percentage of glazing area in relation to the opaque facade. The opaque panels are highly insulated. In summer months, the building can be naturally ventilated by opening vents in the corners of the building which are closed during the remainder of the year. The thermally insulated equipment to service the building is roof mounted. The building is operated in passive mode as much as possible by ensuring that the interior is kept warm through the winter months, with heating generated by an electrical supply that comes to the building from the road nearby. The electricity supply is used as sparingly as possible to maintain a temperature level when occupied, but with as much recirculation of heat energy as is possible.

The environmental strategy is based on providing the highest level of thermal insulation that can practically be achieved, while balanced against the need for air to be refreshed inside each dwelling. The num-

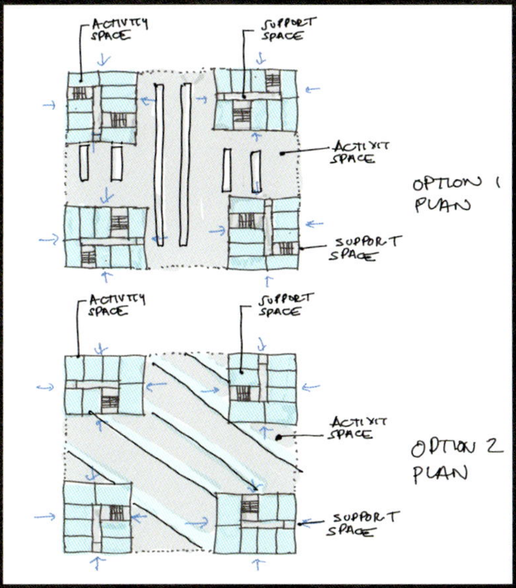

Daylight strategy for direct sunlight and cross ventilation.
Option 1 arranges the building as four blocks separated by an external space.
Option 2 widens the central circulation space in order to add the main entrance floor.

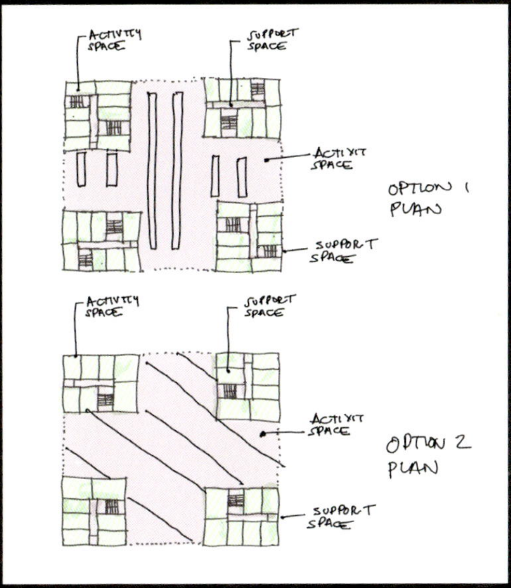

Environmental zones
Option 1 provides three environmental zones in each block and a semi-tempered circulation zone.
Option 2 provides two environmental zones in each block and a semi-tempered circulation zone.

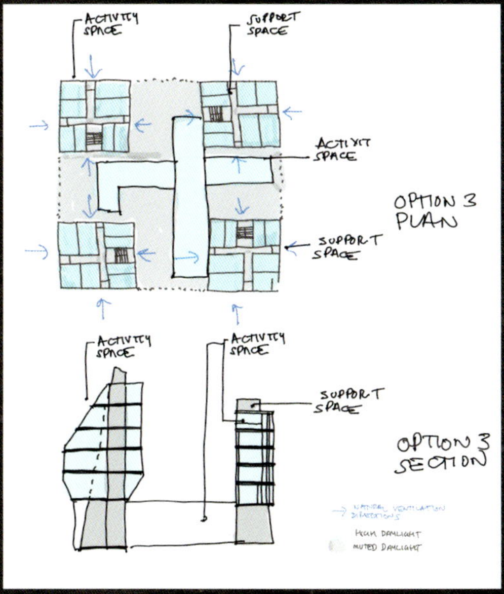

Daylight strategy for direct sunlight and cross ventilation.
Option 3 arranges the building as two larger blocks with communal spaces on the ground floor and accommodation above.

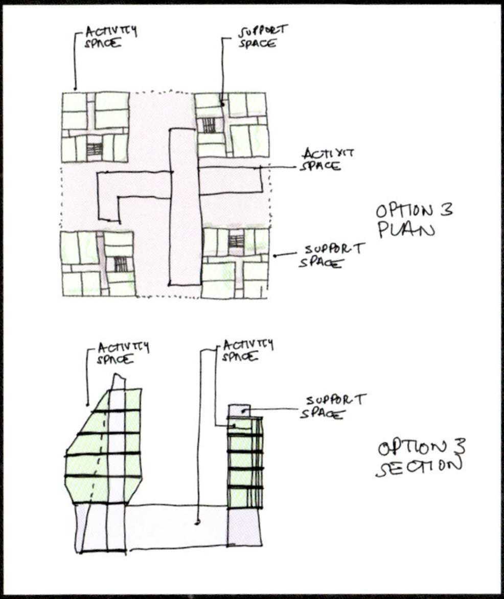

Environmental zones
Option 3 provides three environmental zones in each block and two semi-tempered circulation zones.

ber of air changes per hour is higher than that of an average dwelling due to the work activities being carried out in the dwellings which also serve as a winter workplace. Each dwelling is considered to be a single environmental zone with warmed air being circulated through ducts in floors, as is typical in this climate. Warm air is recirculated through a heat exchanger. The level of thermal insulation is balanced against that provision in order that the building does not become overly insulated in relation to the amount of heat energy that is required inside in order to avoid condensation occurring on internal faces.

Part of the strategy of daylight and sunlight control is to arrange the units as a group in order to benefit from a common energy supply and environmental control system. Equipment is set at ground floor level, with shared workshop facilities and repair space.

The environmental strategy makes use of modular elements of construction which are assembled as rectilinear and triangular forms. Each provides a specific solution to the needs of workrooms which are well illuminated, bedrooms which are more enclosed, kitchens which are well ventilated, bathrooms which are compact and living rooms which have both small spaces and larger areas. The kit of parts can be assembled in different combinations based on the needs of each group of occupiers; moving the units can be done with regular lifting equipment mounted on a road vehicle.

The internal arrangements include spaces for balconies, winter gardens and living spaces, with downward-facing inclined glazing that provides views out while providing protection from solar gain. Other living spaces are cantilevered out, providing sheltered external spaces beneath.

Units can be arranged to be continuous in a row, or can be juxtaposed in different combinations to suit occupiers. Some units can be turned through 180 degrees and returned to their same position in the structure, or can be inverted to create a different geometry within each space. The kit of parts provides independence to the group of occupiers; this suits the needs of occupiers who are remote from other communities for parts of the year.

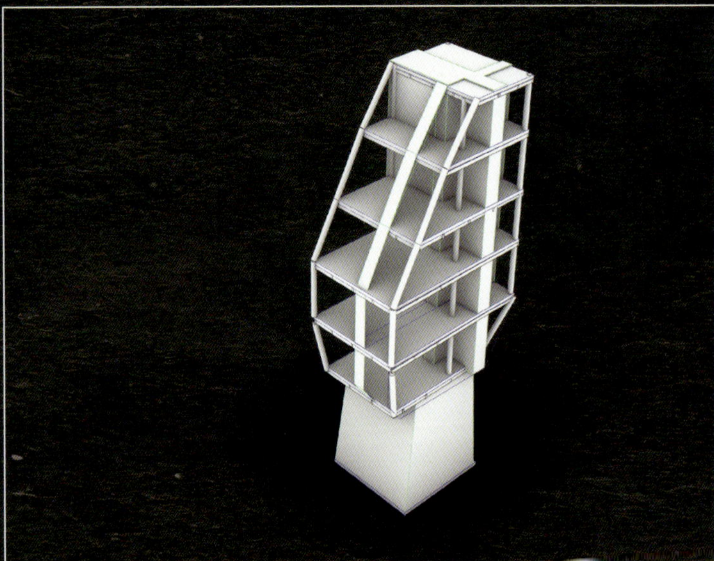

1A. Isometric view of structure

2A. Isometric view of structure

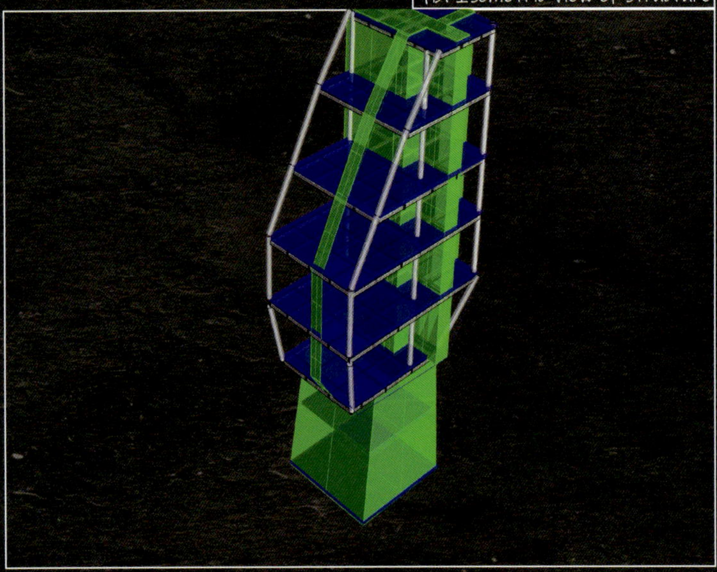

1B. Isometric view of structure

2B. Isometric view of structu

Structural strategy

The primary structure is one of a frame which is light in weight with load-bearing facades; the internal finish of the facades is exposed within the building. The structural strategy for Option 1 is based on a regular structural grid. Stairs are formed as enclosures which are light in weight. Option 2 uses a similar strategy in a rotated form and becomes a single building form. In Option 3, the use of lightweight construction provides the varying geometry in the load-bearing facades.

The structural strategy is one of using light-gauge steel framing to form prefabricated wall panels and floor cassette panels which arrive by roads and which are installed on site. The windows, glazing and doors and the outer cladding are added afterwards in order to create a completely weather-tight and highly insulated envelope. Cut-outs in the cassette floors are formed for staircases and are also strengthened with additional framing where elements are required to be added, such as for wall radiators and stairs which are inserted into the voids between floor cassettes. The building is assembled together as a prefabricated kit of parts. The external envelope is then added to it to ensure complete weathertightness and high levels of thermal insulation. The ground floor of the building is also thermally insulated with an insulated lifting door and regular door for vehicle and pedestrian access. These openings are accommodated with a steel frame that is integrated with the light-gauge steel framing at ground floor level. The building is raised above ground on a reinforced concrete set of pads linked by ground beams such that the building sits above ground on its own pedestals, which are above the harsh winter climate where these buildings will be deployed.

The structural strategy is based on using prefabricated components which are transported by road to the site. This approach precluded the use of long trailers as local roads do not suit trailers. The prefabricated nature of wall panels and floor panels, combined with a requirement for them to be light in weight, led to a structural frame of pressed steel sections for both walls and floors which are clad in a sheathing board which is also light in weight, without the weight that makes them dif-

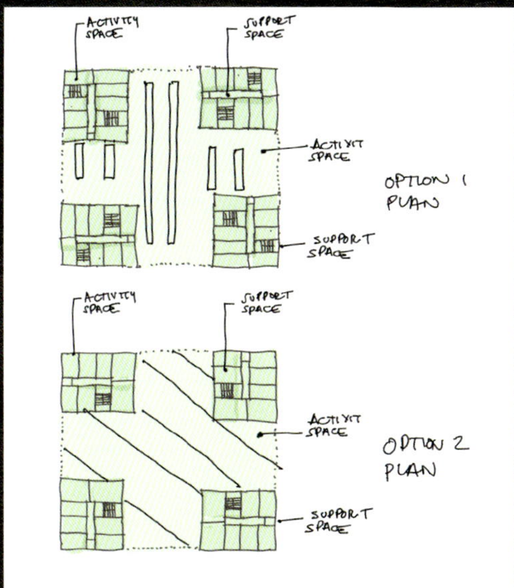

Structural strategy: Zones

Option 1 is based on a regular structural grid.

Option 2 uses a similar strategy to Option 1 in a rotated form and becomes a single building form.

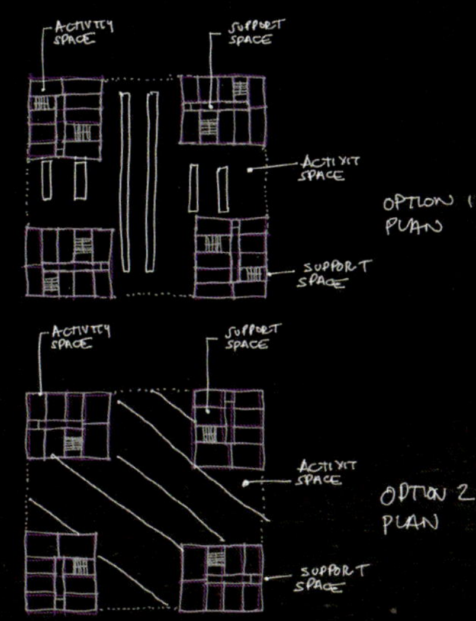

Structural strategy: Framing

Option 1 encloses the core spaces and dividing space into sets of apartments.

Option 2 is largely a steel frame.

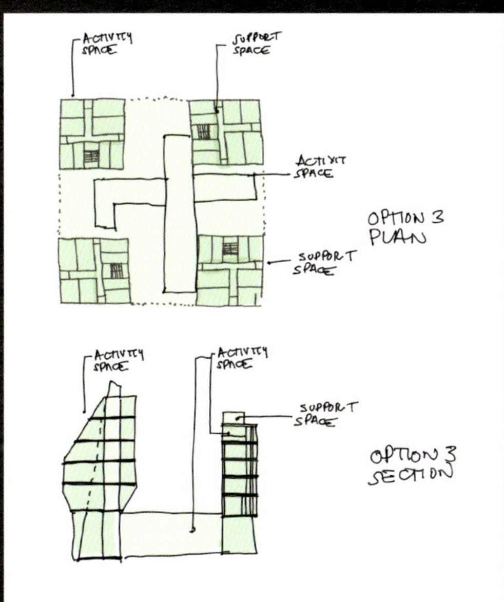

Structural strategy: Zones

Option 3 uses lightweight construction to provide the varying geometry in the load-bearing facades.

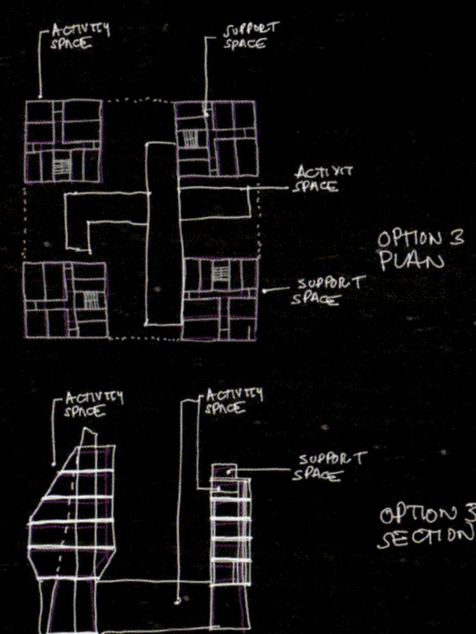

Structural strategy: Zones

Option 3 is a mixed solution of reinforced concrete and steel.

ficult to position into place on site. Acoustic insulation between floors was solved by adding multiple layers of a thin deck onto the structural floor members. This method of construction provides freedom in the distribution of windows and in the form, allowing the design to respond closely to the need to have views out and for services to pass through different areas of the external walls, which gave rise to the characteristic geometry of the facades.

The structural strategy is of creating each module as a structure which can be added to others as part of a dimensionally coordinated group. Modular units can be arranged around a central core which is set in one corner of the apartment unit. Each module is constructed as a steel frame which is clad in highly thermally insulated lightweight cladding panels. Inclined roofs have similar panels, adapted for roof configurations. Glazed panels often occupy a complete wall; solar protection is added where needed to suit the needs of the orientation in relation to sun path. Structures are not restricted to a single-sized module; some are twice the width in order to create a set of spaces that vary in geometry as well as size, avoiding the sense of being in a space created from two single rooms fitted together.

Not all structures interlock; some cantilever outwards in order to form balconies at the sides of buildings. Some combinations allow apartment units to join at points, should a link be needed. Other modular units are larger, suiting a simpler arrangement of spaces but with an irregular geometry in the way they are fitted together.

Groups of apartments can be interlocked in groups to create rectangular ring-shape of dwellings. Each apartment is assembled independently, in different combinations of module. The space at the centre is used as workshop space which is shared by all houses. Cantilevered modules are used only where a balcony is created; the module above the block is sometimes cantilevered outwards to form both a shelter for the terrace as well as an inclined glazed living room. The grouping of apartments reduces the surface area of their external envelope; reducing their energy expenditure when all dwellings are occupied. It is anticipated that some units will eventually be used as workplaces only.

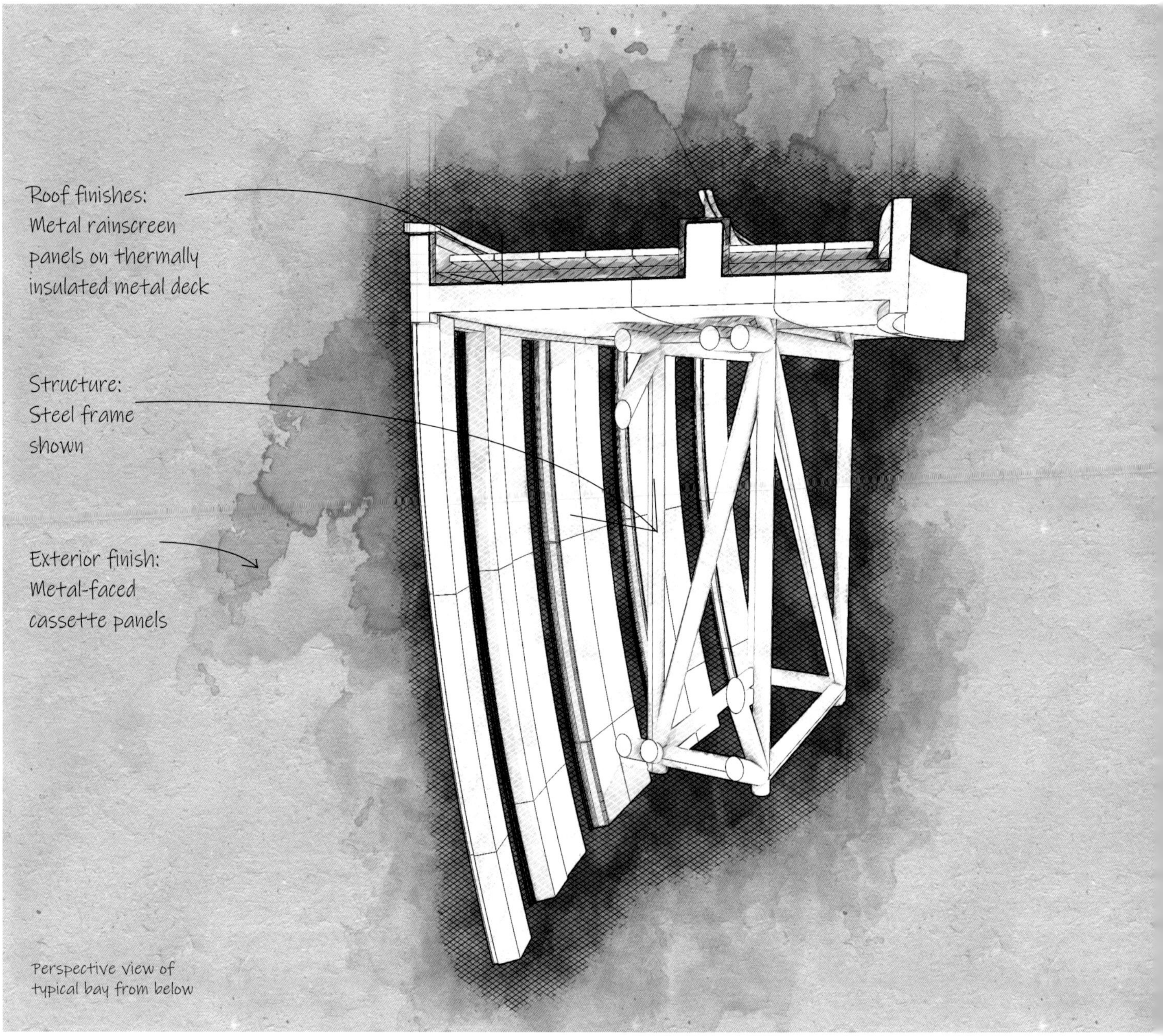

Perspective view of typical bay from below

Typical bay adjacent to facade

In this project, the typical bay is a single dwelling. During construction, the first task is to build the ground-level workshop which is also used as temporary living accommodation. The second step is to cut the components for the first dwelling which becomes a prototype; a quality check on all the components that have been fabricated in the workshop. Plumbing, lighting and environmental control equipment for the first unit arrive prefabricated and prepackaged; stored in the workshop until the first dwelling is constructed. This approach allows only materials to be delivered to site, to be transformed into wall panels and floor panels; avoiding the need to transport by road finished components which are high in volume.

The envelope of the building is based on using rectilinear assemblies which are put together to provide the characteristic forms of the building. Buildings are clad in a timber-look panel cladding; the advantage of the timber-look cladding being that it is not required to be modular and can be cut and adjusted to suit changing layouts. The material can be reused in different geometric arrangements or facade without the need to replace it. The cut joints for different size units when reused, are reassembled, with connections having a stagger from joint to joint; there is no requirement to align joints vertically. The cladding material can be used and reused in different configurations and can be re-cut to length to suit the changing requirements of the changing combinations of the different prefabricated volumes of the building.

The load-bearing structure of the facades is thermally insulated externally; the walls are enclosed in large-scale cladding panels, faced in timber-look boards. Glazed elements are introduced into openings set within the light-gauge steel frame. The framing that forms part of the glazing is also clad in board to provide a continuous material across the opaque areas of the facade.

The external envelope comprises a set of panels which are fire resistant and which reduce the thermal transmission from out-

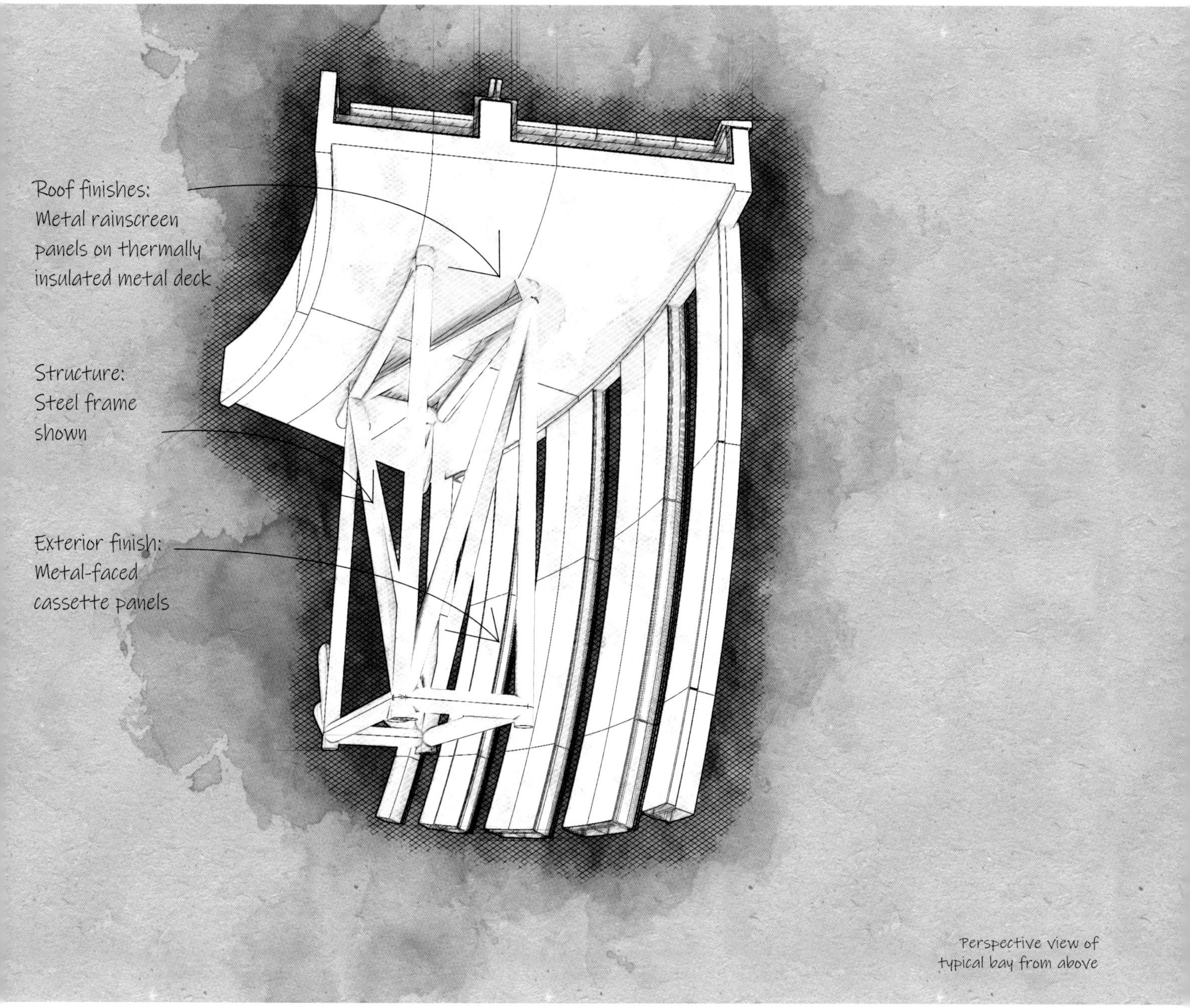

Perspective view of
typical bay from above

side to inside. Highly insulated window surrounds form part of the light-gauge framing. Glazed windows are set between the framing members. Where the glazing depth is greater than the width of the framing, the window is encapsulated in a steel frame which is set within the light-gauge steel framing. The envelope is highly thermally insulated in order to require as little heat energy as possible to temper the interior spaces.

The wall panels are integrated within the light-gauge steel wall panels. Panel assemblies arrive by road as prefabricated wall panels which are then installed in place. The floor cassettes and the glazing are inserted afterwards. Corners of the frame are rounded in order to minimise the buildup of snow and ice in winter.

In this project the typical bay is the complete single dwelling. As a result of the structure being a single form, stability is achieved through the construction of the complete form over three floors. The disposition of windows is such that it was optimised around the needs of a braced frame that provides both walls and floors. The same level of electrical lighting and glazing was provided at each floor level in order to provide a flexibility of use.

The external envelope makes use of both vertical and horizontal baffles which either reflect or block sunlight around window openings. These devices are used in conjunction with continuous vertical slots, which admit fresh air for cross ventilation within spaces. All glazing that faces outwards is sealed; ventilation is provided by slots in the sides of spaces that are indented in relation to each other.

The ground floor workshop space becomes a building in its own right when construction of the dwellings is complete. Circulation routes connect the housing units; routes are identified by rooflights which vary in width to suit the need for daylight within areas of the workshop. Rooflights are lined with vertically set baffles which can be lowered in winter to provide greater water tightness against heavy snowfall.

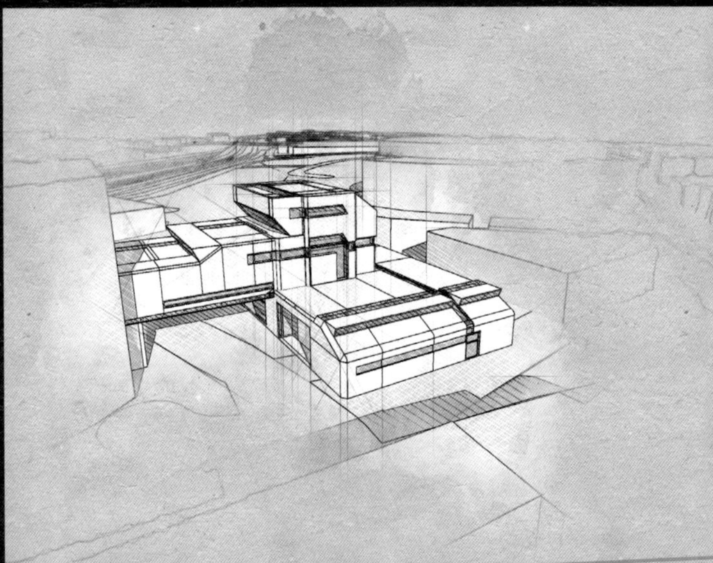

1. Perspective view of exterior

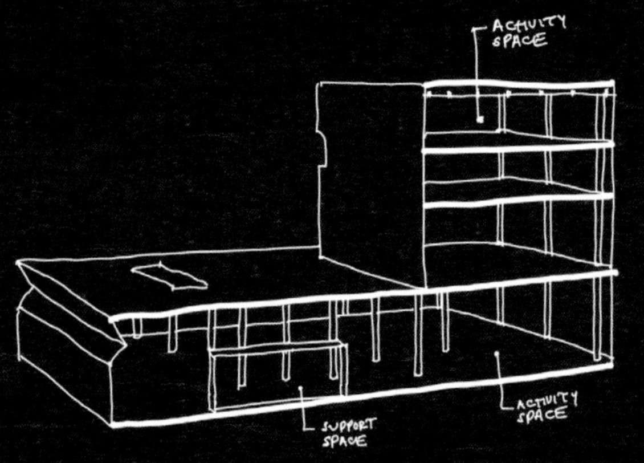

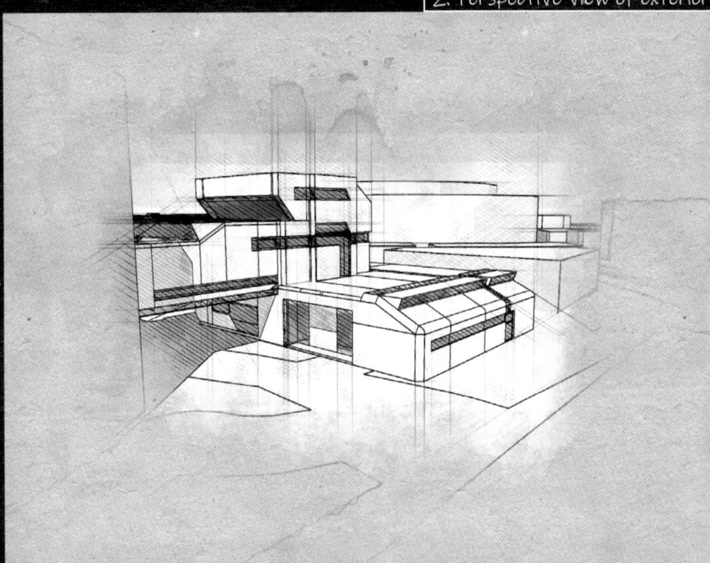

2. Perspective view of exterior

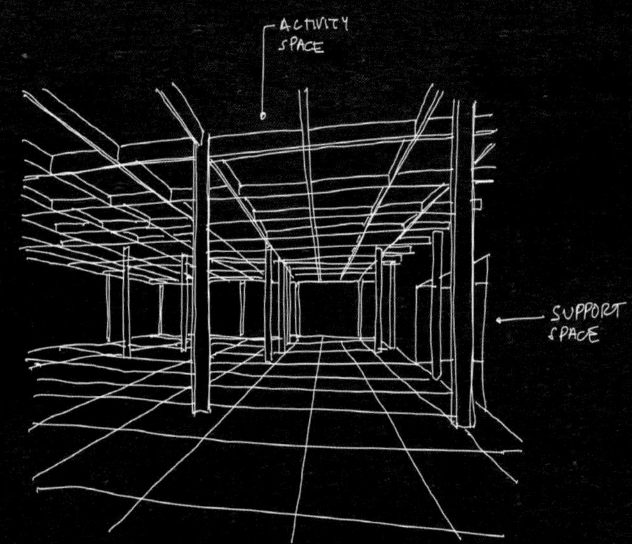

Assembly, disassembly and user manual

An aim of the project is to create a 'user manual' for the building, showing how components and assemblies can be disassembled, reused and recycled. A key aim in this project was to be able to show what materials and assemblies had been used in the construction of the building, and how they might be recycled and reused when the building undergoes change in the future. The aim is to recycle what we have already cycled; to use again what has already been fabricated. What can we use from the building that may need to be replaced or added to? What can we reuse from the materials used to construct the building?

A key requirement of this project is an environmental requirement for the eventual recycling and reuse of as many of the products used in the building as possible. This requirement assumes that parts of the building will be either refurbished or replaced in the near future. As a result, a highly 'componentised' building has been designed. The aim of recycling and reusing building systems is achieved practically, by designing the building as a set of connected small-scale buildings where each of the smaller constructions can be removed, replaced with relative ease, and maintained to a higher standard than might otherwise have been possible. A primary aim is to have as long a lifespan as possible for the components and assemblies of 'active' environmental systems in the building, without the need to remove and replace complete assemblies; a strategy of replacing individual components based on a maintenance cycle. This goal is achieved by providing much higher amounts of access to equipment that can be maintained easily; positioning mechanical devices more locally to where they are needed. This approach has the benefit of not requiring a single large-scale mechanical and electrical equipment installation; increasing efficiency by reducing the size of each assembly and the distance between the point of supply and the point of use. This approach creates a set of localised environmental zones which have the benefit of being largely self-contained and which can be maintained easily. Maintenance is a key part of this design such that a 'user manual' for the building is provided; a detailed guide to maintaining the building as a 'crafted product', with assemblies inside

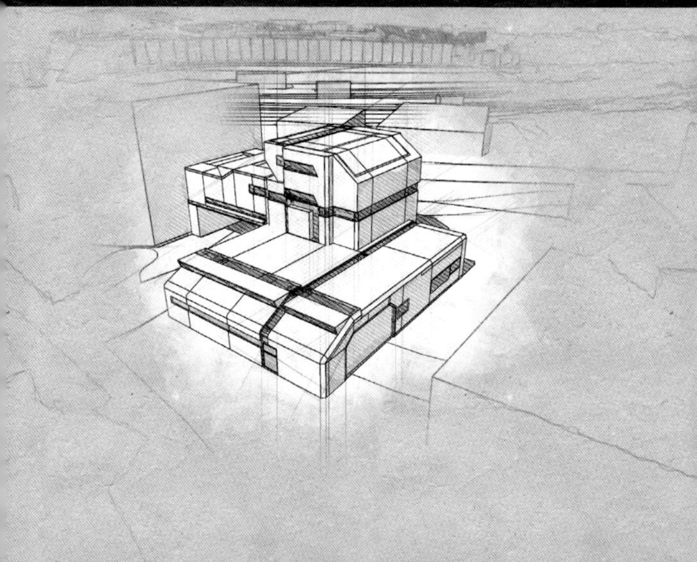

Perspective view of exterior

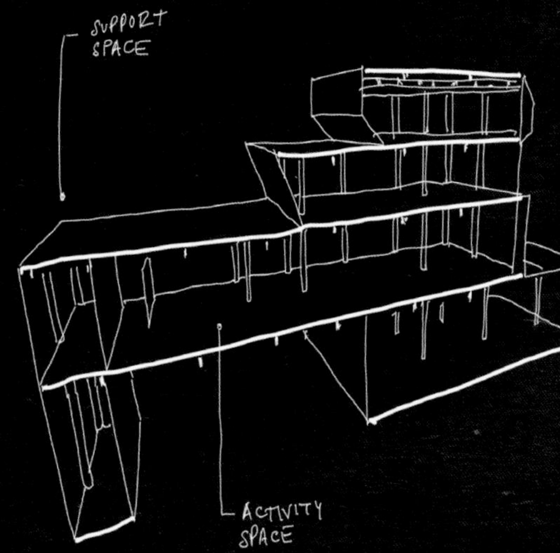

4. Perspective view of exterior

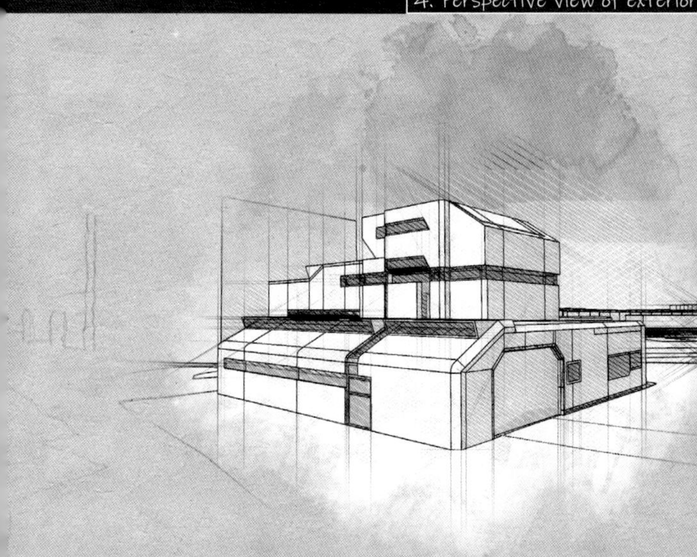

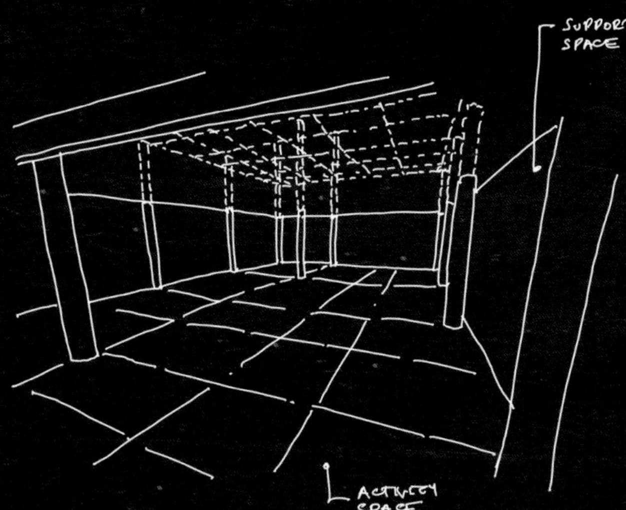

the building having their own manual and with their specific provisions for maintenance. This approach allows the building to be understood by the user as a series of small environmental zones rather than as a single set of spatial enclosures supported by a single environmental control system.

This building comprises a set of prefabricated building units which are pre-assembled in the manner of shipping containers arriving by road. The units, all of which are approximately 2.5 metres wide, are delivered to site by road. They are then assembled in bays in order to provide the complete building form. Most of the building is assembled as self-contained units with its external wall included. Other parts are set onto a steel frame, in order for the space beneath to be used for the passage of road vehicles through to other parts of the site. The assembly of units demonstrate the ability of a system to be not only single-storey elements in a non-urban location, but capable of being constructed in an industrial area; responding to the reqiorements typical of industrial buildings of being able to form a bridge over roads for the free passage of vehicles around the site and to accommodate large-scale openings in opaque walls, rooflights and rooftop machinery. These are all packaged and form a set of juxtaposed elements. When an element is required to be refurbished, it is then partly disassembled in the usual way in situ with items on the roof, for example, being replaced on a small-scale, flexible basis. Complete units can be swapped out and this involves the elements being taken off site for disassembly and for reintegration into other components. Alternatively, it is imagined that the unit will be disengaged from the building, will be removed for repair and upgrading, then returned to the site where it is reinstalled with its service equipment already in place. This approach aims to reduce disruption in refurbishment and replacement as much as possible, and to take the task away to another facility that is remote from the site and most suited for repair and replacement activities to be carried out typically at the edge of the city. This building is in the industrial part at the edge of the city centre, where disruption due to building work would potentially disrupt activities within the building.

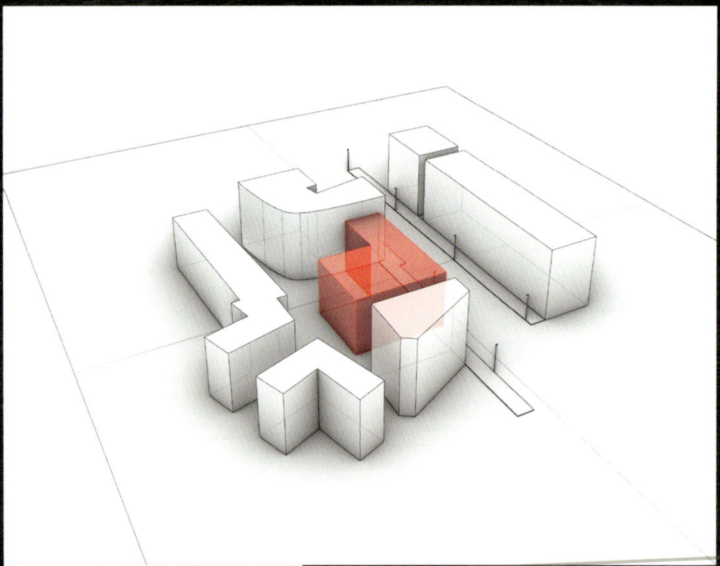
1. Project volume in site context

1. Site plan with surrounding context

Option 1 is a standalone building with a profile that is stepped in section.

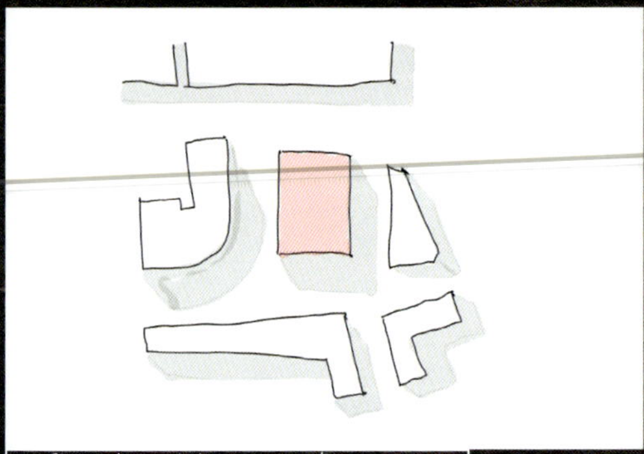
2. Site plan with surrounding context

Option 2 groups everything together over two floors with a single floor plate.

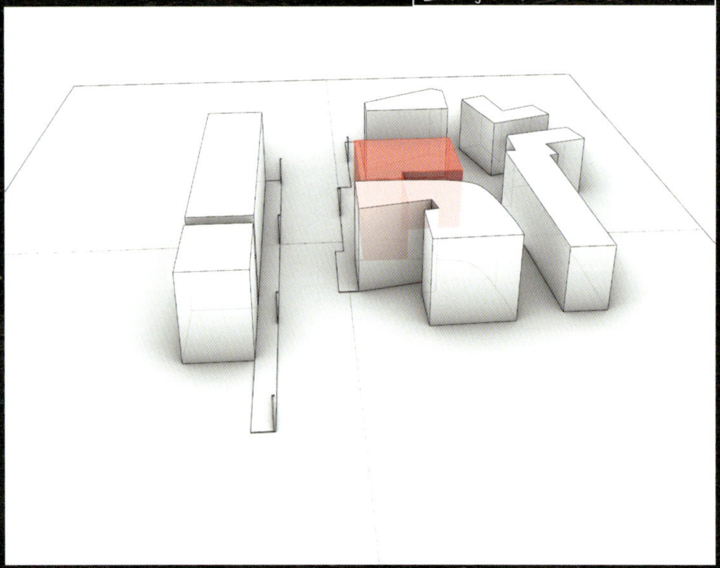
2. Project volume in site context

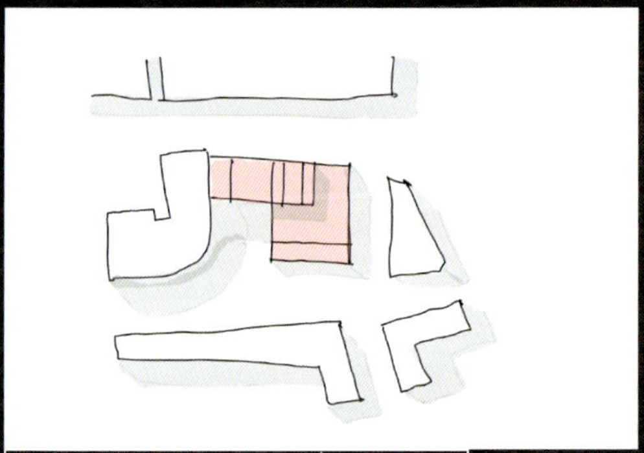
3. Site plan with surrounding context

Option 3 provides vehicle access to the rear of the site; to the other industrial buildings that surround this building.

Site context

This project is for a manufacturing start-up facility for small companies that have found a market for products that require a shorter supply chain for supply to a local region. The brief/program requires a suite of buildings arranged across two sites, with this building being a set of single-storey volumes arranged to facilitate commercial vehicle access. Spaces are conceived as highly flexible workspaces for assembly of components manufactured elsewhere. The essential concept is of a 'kit of parts' of prefabricated assemblies that can be used from building to building and which could be installed easily.

The single 'kit of parts' approach that was taken on this project allows parts of buildings, including electrical and mechanical equipment and facade panels, to be exchanged in order to meet the key requirement of the brief/program for flexibility. The building occupies a vacant site with empty buildings and space for new-build additions. The buildings are a mixture of reused structures and new structures. An essential part of the approach is to work with both existing buildings and new buildings by creating new forms between existing forms. The approach is the opposite of that often put forward: The removal and replacement of buildings is often the norm; a 'lightweight' intervention was the approach adopted here. This approach allows new buildings, or part-buildings, to be easily integrated into what is already there. The design included a kit of parts for complete building modules, facade panels, lift/elevator, stairs, washrooms and services equipment.

All assemblies are modular and are secured together in a straightforward way. The design ensures that the height and mass of each building steps down from taller adjacent buildings in order to ensure that they appear to be a 'natural' fit into their surroundings, and are geometrically aligned with the immediate environment and with the alignment of adjacent buildings. Fitting into, and appearing to complete, the current massing is a key component of the approach-to-site context. This is achieved by use of the modular construction, where spaces can be interlinked and stacked in different sizes adjacent to one another. Option 1 is a standalone building with a profile that is stepped in section,

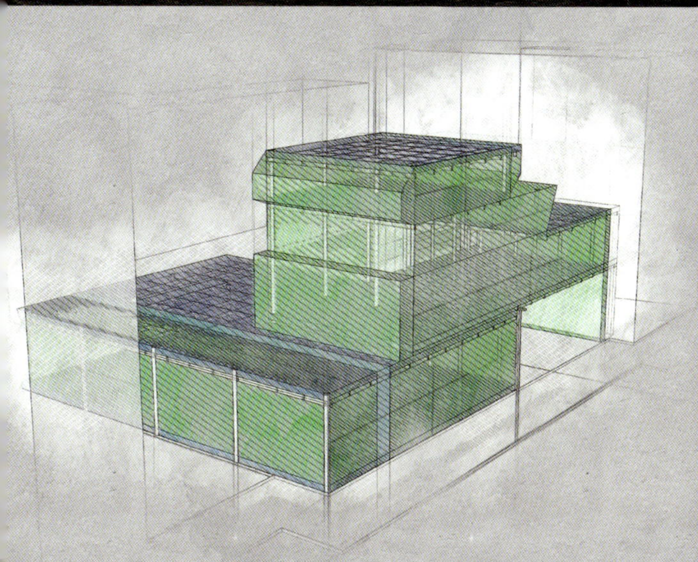

Perspective view of environmental volumes

1. Figure-ground diagram of tempered environment

Option 1
Dark green spaces are highly tempered but are reduced to accommodation volumes only.

2. Perspective view of environmental volumes

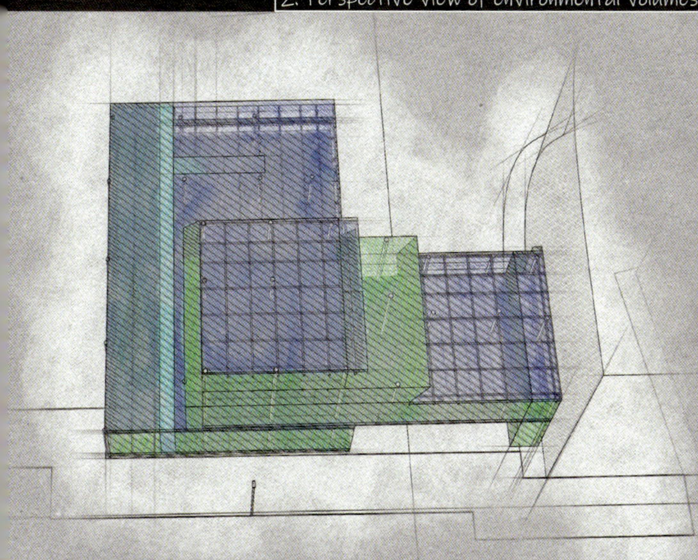

2. Figure-ground diagram of tempered environment

Option 2
Red spaces are less tempered than dark green spaces but are more tempered than violet circulation space.

3. Figure-ground diagram of tempered environment

Option 3
Violet spaces are the least tempered spaces, these spaces interface directly with external space.

such that part of the building is arranged over two floors; another part is arranged over an additional single floor. Option 2 groups everything together over two floors with a single floor plate, such that the two floors correspond to the height of the adjacent building with a curved facade.

Option 3 continues the Option 2 provision of vehicle access to the rear of the site; to the other industrial buildings immediately behind a part of the facility while linking the building to its neighbour, with a future possibility of breaking through the wall into the adjacent building itself. This provides an urban-scale form as a gateway through to the site; enclosing the site and providing an urban design that contributes to the fabric of the buildings and the massing of buildings as they exist already.

The site context of this project is one where prefabrication is a requirement; a site-based approach to construction for this building would not be a practical solution as there are high value activities being carried out in neighbouring buildings. Owners of adjacent buildings would only agree to this site being developed with a minimum of disruption to their activities. This requirement resulted in the approach of prefabricated building modules being delivered and installed within a short timescale. The response to site context is one of using a series of elements of the building which are forms in their own right; individual volumes with their own role of providing manufacturing space, office space and storage space. The building fits into its context as a result of being optimised for juxtaposed functions, which are fitted together in an economical manner. This approach allows the building to respond to its context by having forms which are differentiated into urban scale forms and which fit with some purpose into their site.

The alternative approach of moving walls and floors in order to fit into the immediate site context would have created a form that was unable to differentiate its volumes into elements that would fit harmoniously with the cityscape. The design creates a coherent set of spatial volumes which allows the building to fit geometrically into its surroundings; bringing some expression of the clarity of functions being carried out within the building – a way of being able to fit into its site context.

1. Sectional perspective view

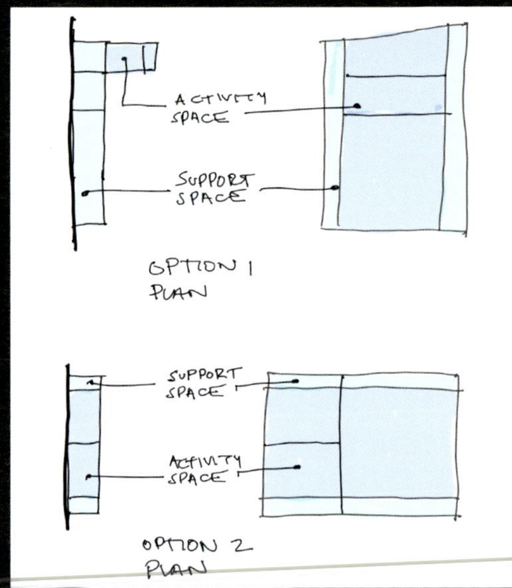

Spatial arrangement

Option 1 arranges the support spaces, or service spaces, along the sides of the building.

Option 2 has the service space of lift/elevator stairs, washrooms and storage areas set at the sides of the building.

2. Sectional perspective view

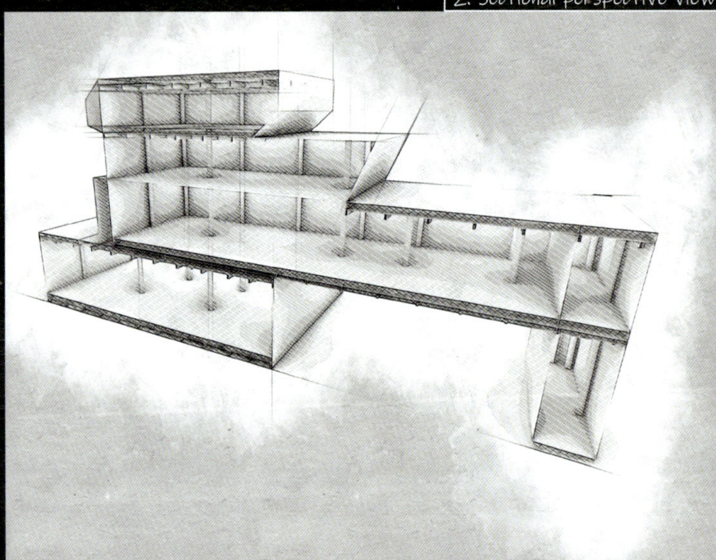

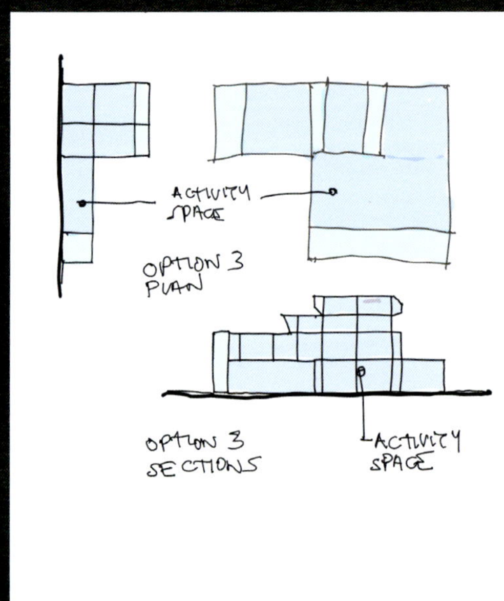

Option 3 creates the urban design nature of this project, arranges the same spaces over two floors with a ground floor that extends the width of the site.

Spatial arrangement

The building comprises a set of small-scale, stackable and interlocking components for mechanical ventilation, electrical lighting and emergency power generation. The spatial concept is to accommodate a set of spaces lit naturally with bands of clear glazing, with sliding external solar shading panels in order to admit greater or lesser amounts of daylight. The resulting facade is one of a series of interlocking volumes reflecting the requirements of the brief/program.

The spatial arrangement of Option 1 is to arrange the support spaces, or service spaces, along the sides of the building, creating clear floor space for manufacturing activities in the centre of the building. This occurs over the ground floor, while the upper floor has service space on one side and open office space adjacent to it. For Option 2, which exists over two floors, the central space is completely clear, as are the service space of lift/elevator stairs, washrooms and storage areas which are set at the sides of the building. Option 3 creates the urban design nature of this project, arranges the same spaces over two floors with a ground floor that extends the width of the site, and additional space on top that projects out to meet its neighbour. The service spaces for each of these volumes is distributed, as shown in the diagram, with three small service spaces in the smaller volumes and a slightly larger service space provided in the main manufacturing facility. The general concept for the spatial arrangement of this building is that internal spaces are defined by each of the 2.5-metre-wide modules that are delivered to site such that the minimum size space that is enclosed is 2.5 metres and the next adjacent size is typically 5.0 metres, having two modules joined together.

This approach suits the personalization of these buildings, which have sufficient variety in them to be able to respond to the spatial organisation required within the building. It is assumed that large numbers of rooms will be joined together, but the system is essentially a set of modules 2.5 metres wide, which can be widened or alternatively joined to make larger-scale spaces. The module is able to create forms such as those used in this project, where there are intersecting overlap-

Perspective view of interior

2. Perspective view of interior

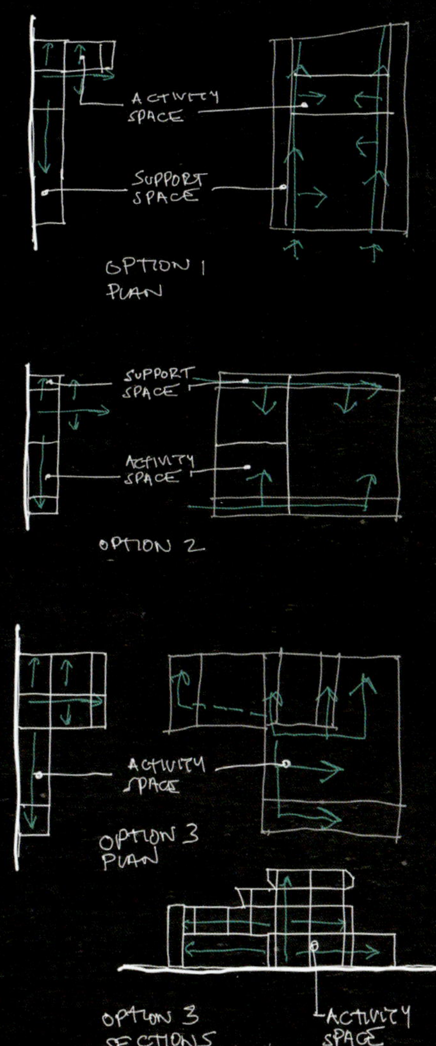

Internal circulation Option 1 follows routes that link the service cores, from where access into the building is provided at each end of the building. Option 2 uses a similar principle; rotating the entrances through 90 degrees, allowing access from the vehicle roadside. Option 3 provides circulation routes to a highly differentiated set of workshop spaces.

ping and overlaid forms which are mounted one above the other. This construction system suits light industrial buildings; able to respond to the needs of mass customisation for different size modules for related projects that use the same system for fabrication and installation. This project used a 2.5-metre-wide module for ease of transport by road that uses an economical method of loading vehicles.

The preferred Option 3 for spatial arrangement was selected on the basis of its ability to respond to the geometry of the site, with the benefit of being able to have daylight admitted to all manufacturing spaces and all office spaces. The production space on the ground floor was subdivided into three parts to make use of the L-shaped plan that resulted from the disposition of volumes, which consider the need for a raised set of volumes above the access road into the rear of the site.

Meeting rooms are set adjacent to the circulation spaces, projecting above roof level; accessed from the adjacent support space that accommodates stairs and a lift/elevator. These volumes project upwards to a similar height to light reflectors, set in circulation spaces.

Internal circulation

The internal circulation for Option 1 follows routes that link the service cores, from where access into the building is provided at each end of the plan. Access to workshops and service spaces is provided from these two corridors. Option 2 uses a similar principle; rotating the entrances through 90 degrees, allowing access from the vehicle roadside as well as from the other side of the building where there is no vehicle access; as shown on the left-hand side of the diagram of Option 2. In Option 3 the main entrance is at the internal corner of the L-shape, allowing distribution to the upper floors by way of a lift/elevator and stairs to smaller workshops, as well as forward to the cores and main workshop spaces. Option 3 provides circulation routes to a highly differentiated set of workshop spaces.

The light reflectors which project above roof level direct light down into the circulation spaces in the ground floor spaces. The arrangement is similar to that used on facades, where the blades serve as solar shading devices in both vertical and horizontal planes.

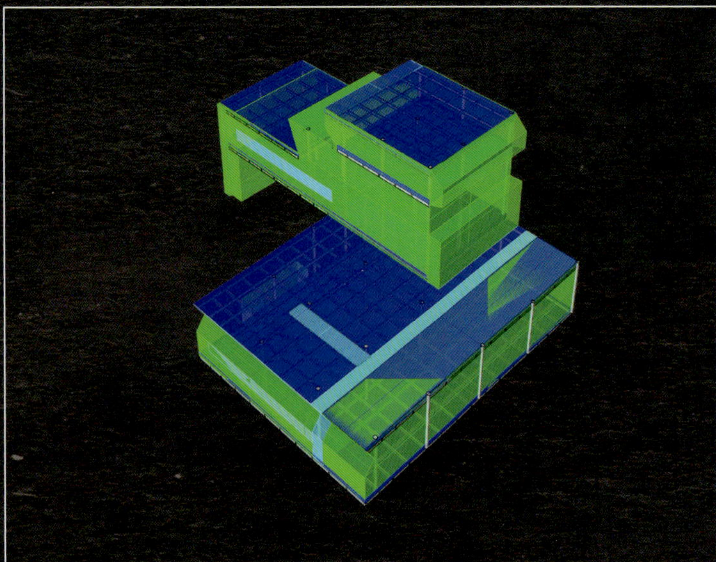

1A. Isometric view of environmental volumes

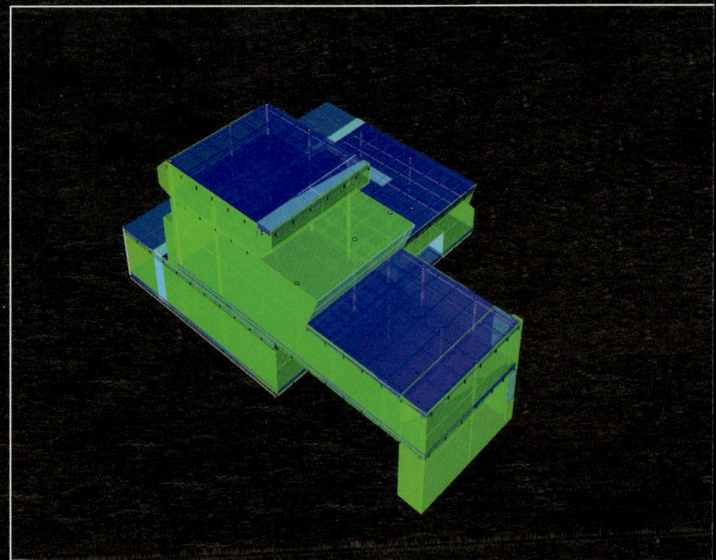

2A. Isometric view of environmental volumes

1B. Isometric view of environmental volumes

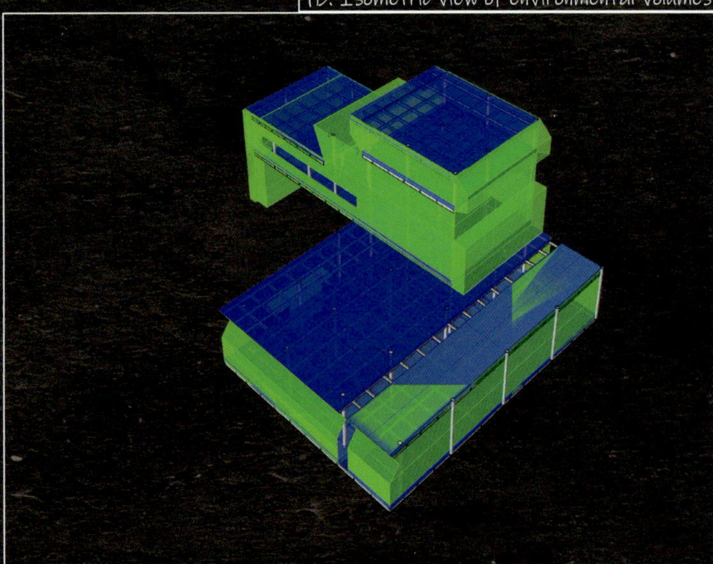

2B. Isometric view of environmental volum

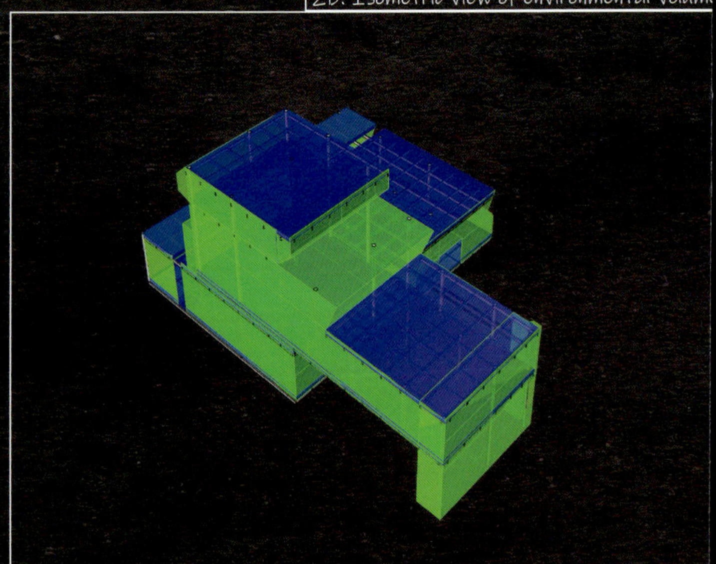

Environmental strategy

The environmental concept is to create three different environmental zones; a large ground floor space; an upper floor arranged above that space and a third volume extending out from the upper floor, supported on one side by a service module. The overall building form has two spine cores extending down the middle of each of the two parts of the L-shape on plan. There are stairs at each end of the spine core; where they intersect is the lift/elevator. The spine core occupies most of the length of the building, occupied by workshops and storage spaces. The edges of these spaces have top-lit glazing. The inner face of the external walls provide space for storage racks as well as an inner surface for the fixing of equipment used in the facility. The outer wall is highly thermally insulated; formed from metal-faced composite panels.

The approach to the separation of support space and activity space has led to the building comprising three environmental zones which intersect, but which have very different environmental requirements; the ground floor space, where most of the manufacturing takes place, is shown in green in the diagram. Storage is in the higher racks on the upper floor. The environmental strategy is to provide environmental zones for a manufacturing environment; a secondary environmental zone is the support space of stairs, lift/elevator and washrooms, which are integrated with the storage spaces at the sides of the building. There are different environmental conditions in the workshop where there are open doors, in the office space which is enclosed and in the service spaces which need less ventilation due to its lower level of occupancy.

The overall environmental strategy is to consider each of the 2.5-metre-wide modules as separate packages with their own thermal insulation on the sides which are exposed to the outside of the building. The framing allows for future insulation to be put in to one side of the manufacturing spaces. Should that module be required to be relocated on the site, the 2.5-metre-wide module when joined to its neighbour has a 200mm zone created for the width, and a 100mm zone on the side of each panel, creating a 200mm x 200mm-wide zone between two

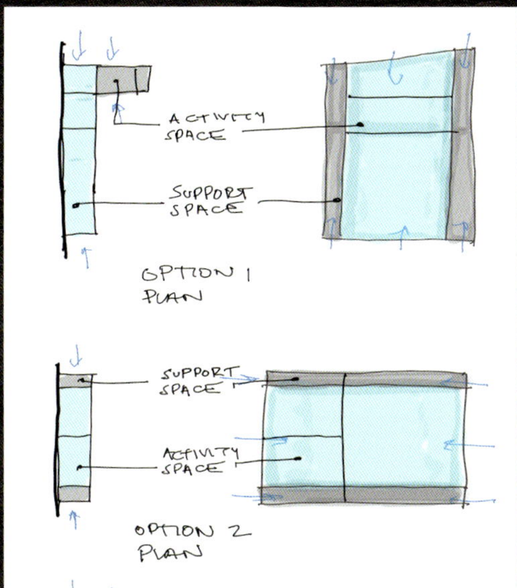

Daylight strategy for direct sunlight and cross ventilation.

Option 1
Daylight and air is introduced through two opposite facing facades.

Option 2
Daylight and air is introduced through two opposite facing facades.

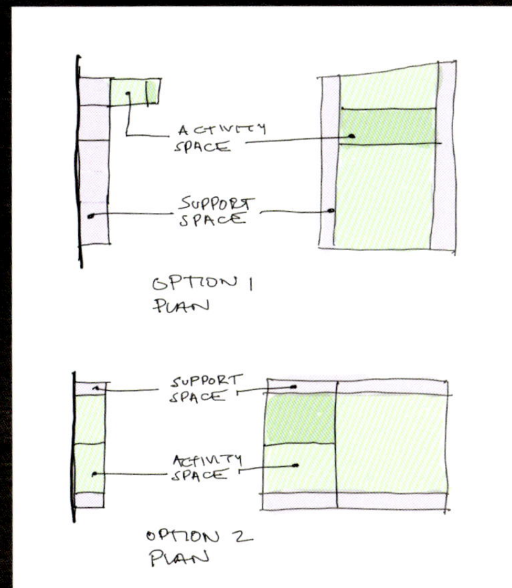

Environmental zones

Option 1
The building is divided into three environmental zones.

Option 2
The building is divided into two environmental zones.

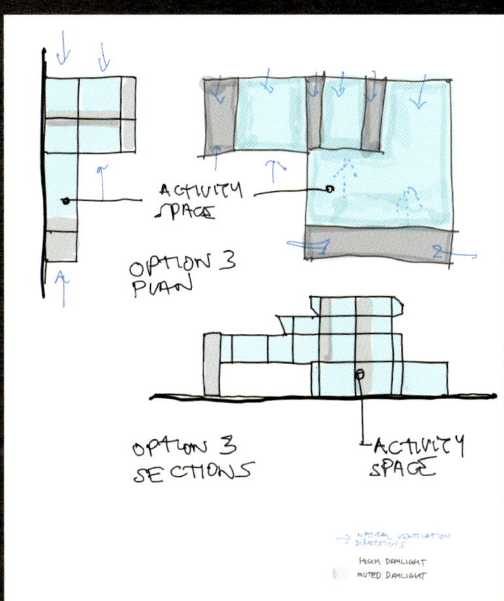

Daylight strategy for direct sunlight and cross ventilation.

Option 3
Daylight and air is introduced through all facades and all support spaces.

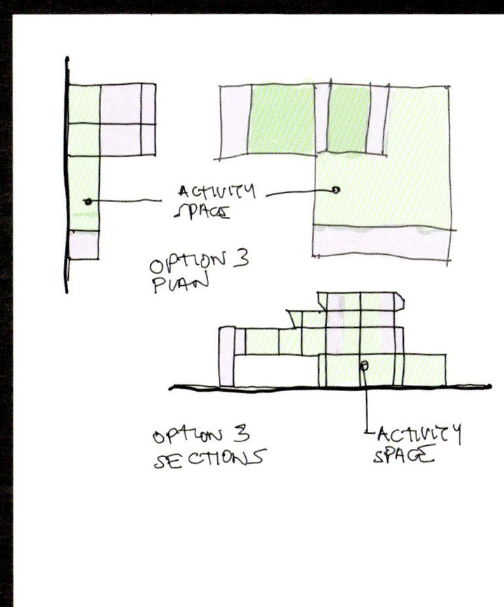

Environmental zones

Option 3
The building is divided into three environmental zones; the associated support zones, providing an additional three zones.

panels for the introduction of thermally insulated walls and for them to be used in all configurations, such that the grid of the building is an environmental grid of lines of thermal insulation that can be inserted into panels as needed. This system is driven by the need for thermal insulation in these largely opaque manufacturing buildings, which have a kit of parts of rooflights that are generally inclined into the building and allow light to enter deep into the floor plan. The inclined rooflights are hooded and inclined inwards in order to provide passive solar control. The inclined rooflights are angled away from their vertical covers; the rectilinear grid of panels with their lines of thermal insulation create a thermal or environmental grid and plan and a strategy for rooflights in vertical section.

The environmental strategy for the distribution of ducted air and associated natural ventilation through the building was complemented by the approach to bringing natural daylight into the building. Air is supplied in ducts from roof level down the height of the taller parts of the project and distributed horizontally into the manufacturing space. Daylight is admitted in a direction perpendicular to the distribution of ducted air and electrical lighting. Natural daylight is provided by rooflights and high-level glazing on walls at the sides of the building. This approach provides daylighting to the edges of the manufacturing space whilst providing separation from the noises of the adjacent street, and provides the privacy required for tasks being carried out in the manufacturing areas. Daylight is directed into the ground-level spaces from baffles which either reduce solar gain or direct daylight downwards into circulation spaces. Similar devices are fixed to the facades in order to provide solar shading for horizontally oriented areas of glazing. Both rooflights and facade glazing are recessed into bands of opaque panels in order to provide passive shading. The overall width of each rooflight band corresponds to the enclosed workspace beneath; each corridor is enclosed at roof level partly by a rooflight and partly by opaque panels. On facades, a similar principle is followed; corridor walls are created partly in glass. The arrangement of corridors is expressed as indents in the panels to form the characteristic low-relief panels.

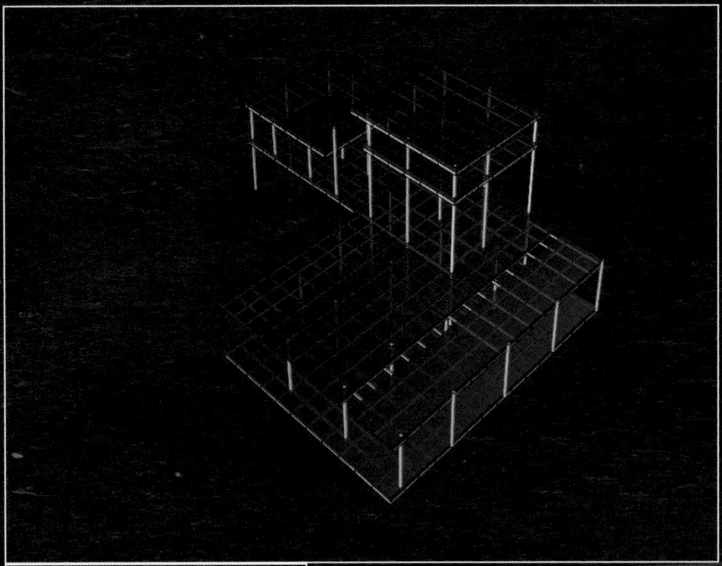

1A. Isometric view of structure

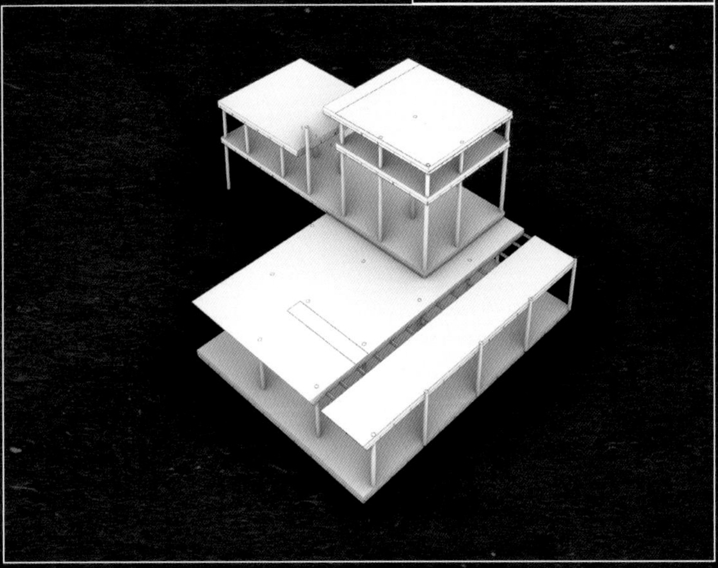

1B. Isometric view of structure

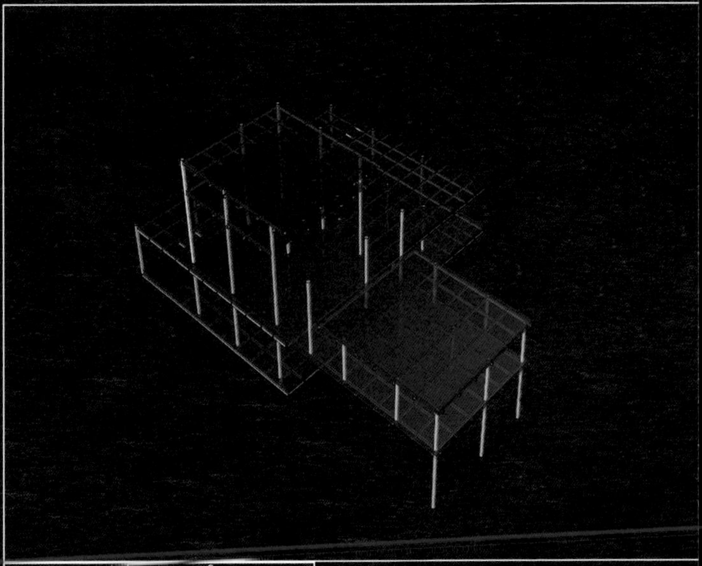

2A. Isometric view of structure

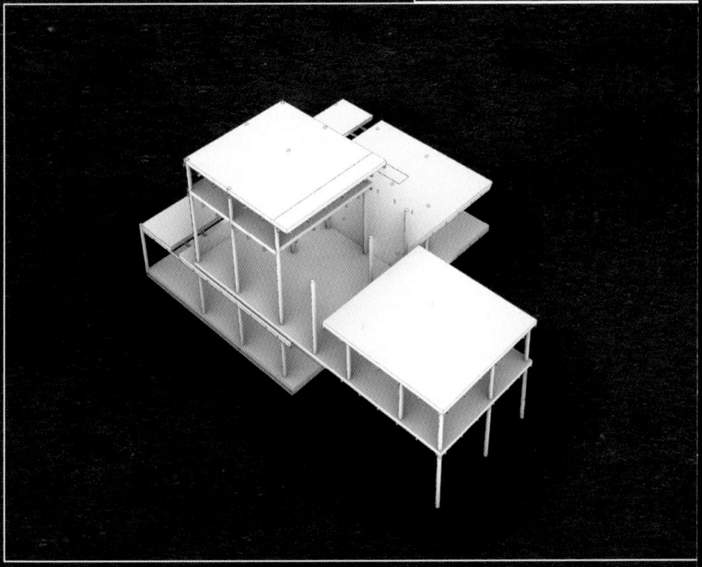

2B. Isometric view of structu

Structural strategy

A key requirement for the structural design is for column-free, open spaces where possible. The structural design is based on a partly prefabricated primary structure; this includes pre-assembled floor units which are bolted together on site to form continuous prefabricated floor plates. When the changes are made to the building, those floor deck units can be moved and reconfigured to suit changes. The brief/program requires this flexibility; parts of the building may require modification in the near future.

Doors may need to be created very quickly; an essential part of the structural design has been the ability to include bays that can have vertical framing that can be removed in order to create new door openings. At the roof level, the structural strategy for all three options is of a steel frame; trusses span across the width of the floor plates to create a set of column-free spaces. In Option 3, columns are avoided by the use of long-span trusses, which avoid the need for columns in the space below.

The flexibility and the small-scale nature of the steel framing allow the three spatial forms that comprise the design to be integrated as three different structural volumes, as shown in the diagrams. The small-scale framing and omission of secondary steelwork allows for very close coordination with the external envelope to create a highly thermally insulated envelope.

The section of space at upper floor level that forms a road over an access road allows assemblies to be lifted and lowered directly to and from a flat-bed truck. The projecting space also serves as a canopy, forming a semi-outdoor transition space for manoeuvring equipment without the need to enclose the space; the volume can be enclosed with roller shutter doors if needed in the near future. The sides of the open space underneath the bridge are enclosed by the building itself on one side, and by a neighbouring building on the other side; the bridge form accommodates a fabrication workshop. The structural design is continuous with that of the facades; the use of prefabrication reduces environmental impact during construction; the use of scaffolding to

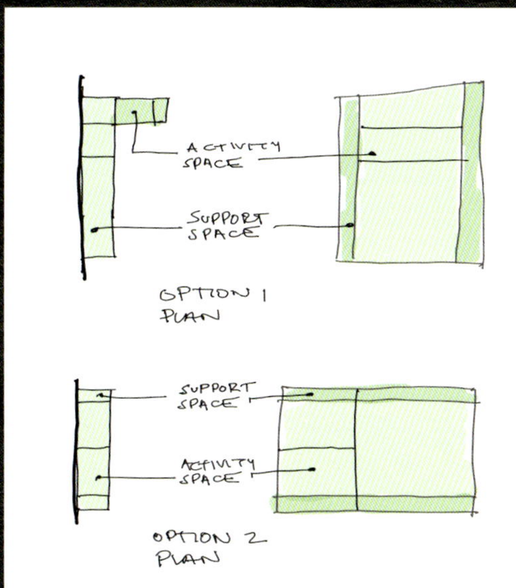

Structural strategy: Zones

Option 1 has structural walls which traverse the width of the building.

Option 2 cores provide structural stability to the frame.

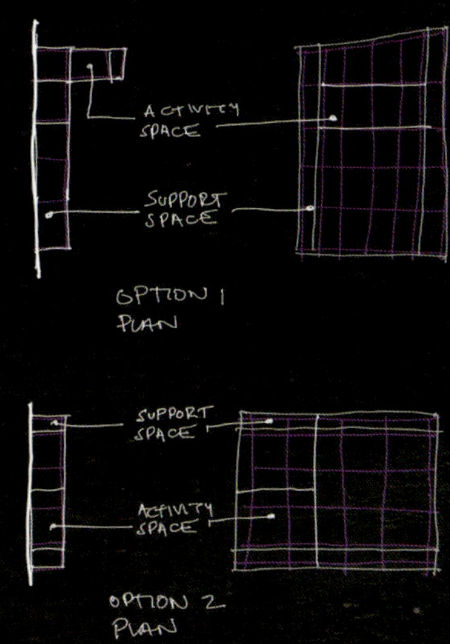

Structural strategy: Framing

Option 1 is a concrete-based frame.

Option 2 is largely a steel frame.

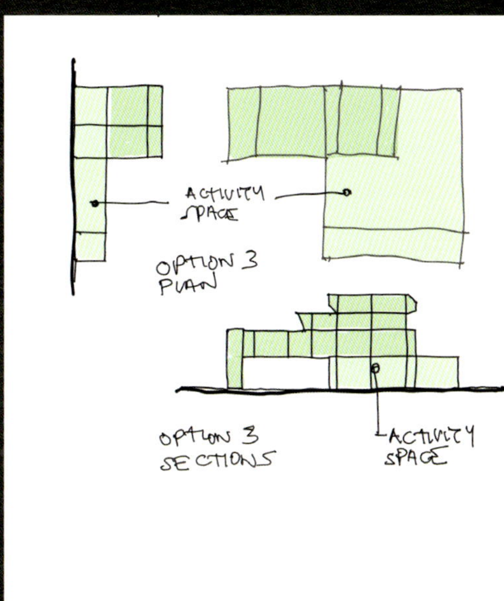

Structural strategy: Zones Option 3 has structural walls formed as cores as well as columns in the activity spaces.

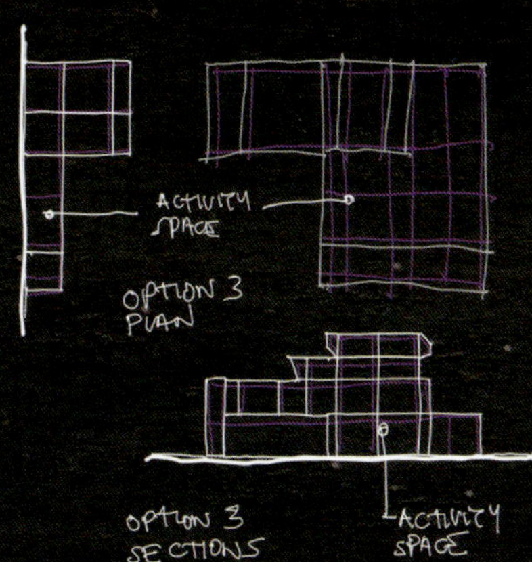

Structural strategy: Zones Option 3 is a mixed solution of reinforced concrete and steel.

install the facades has been avoided, with more time needed to fix all the panels back and adjust on site. The chosen prefabricated approach has steel frames arriving in pre-assembled 'ladders' which are ready to be put in place and bolted together in a shorter period of time than would otherwise have been the case.

The structural strategy is one of following the environmental grid of thermally insulated panels which are created on all four sides of each of the prefabricated modules. Each module has a 100mm or 200mm zone, such that when two panels are set next to each other along their length, they form a 200mm wide zone for the future introduction of thermal insulation if panels are relocated to an external wall.

The structural grid follows the environmental grid of lines of thermal insulation. Modules as seen in plan are 2.5 metres wide and storey-height. Panels are stacked one above the other to create multi-storey assemblies, extending over three storeys in one part of the site and a single storey elsewhere. Part of the second storey volume forms a bridge over a road that is required to maintain the passage of road vehicles as well as provide a canopy for ground-level access at the building entrance. All panels are designed to be able to be strengthened in the near future. Rooflights are generally in the inclined plane, supported on part of the structural steel and light-gauge steel structure that is an integral part of the structural design of the building.

Overall, the structural strategy is based on using a single structural grid across the building while allowing the floor slabs to be highly differentiated in their geometry. The bridge portion of the building is supported by a service space that is constructed at ground level. This propped cantilever principle was used as columns could not extend down to the ground floor at those points due to restrictions applied to access of the adjacent building.

The profiles for both roof and facade are part of a set of indented facade panels that follow the lines of facade glazing and rooflight. The primary structure of columns has secondary infill framing added to provide the framing to support the facade and roof panels. This approach reduces the need for secondary supports; the columns can be exposed visually.

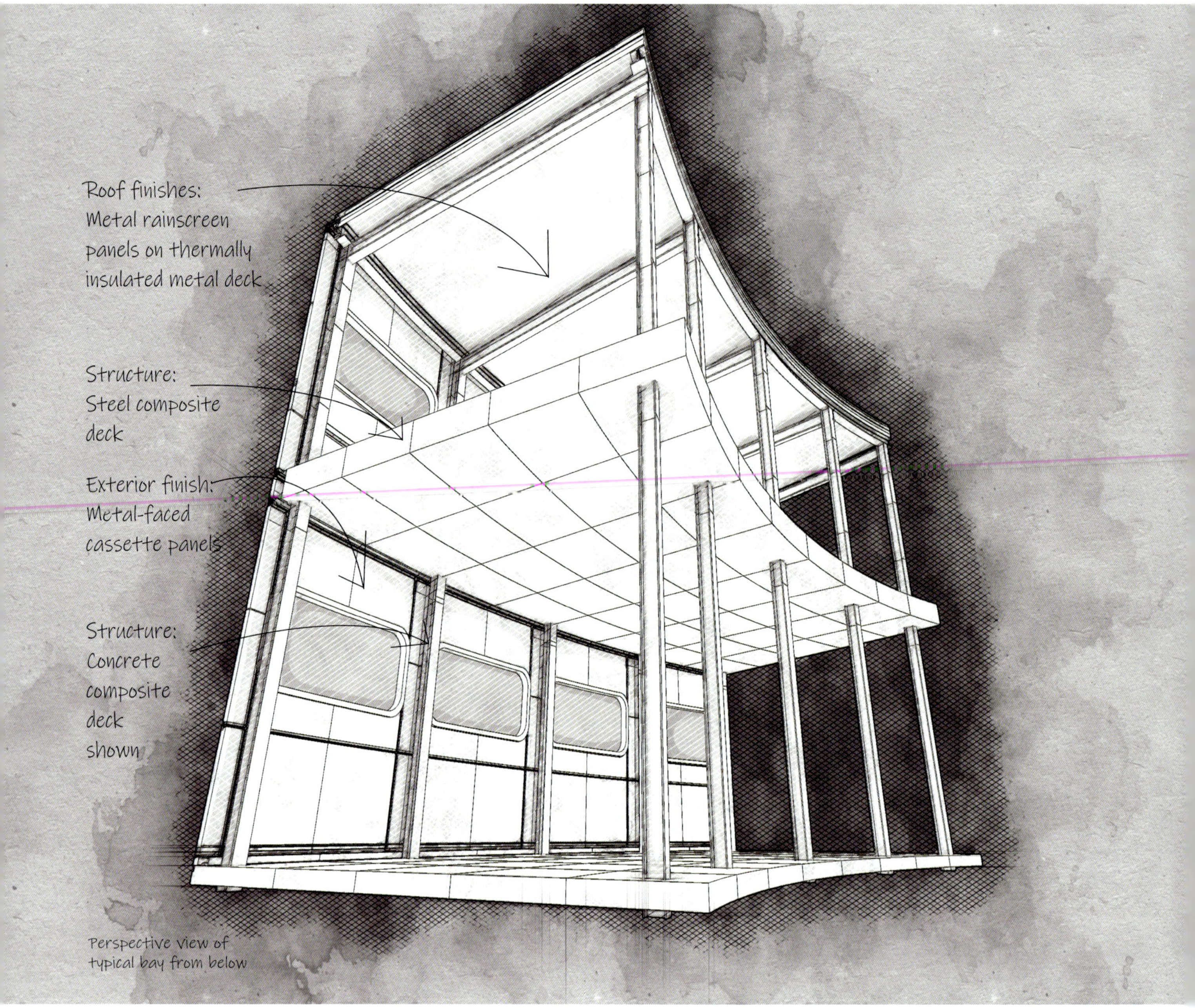

Typical bay adjacent to facade

The concept for the external envelopes is to have a small-scale frame that follows the shapes of the panels, such that the panels are fixed directly to this structure; there is no secondary structure, as panels span from floor to floor or from floor to roof. Cladding panels are fixed directly to the steel frame at their corners and along their horizontal edges. All panels are point fixed for speed of installation; there are no continuous fixings along the edges of panels. This allows panels to be installed rapidly and ensures that loads are transferred evenly from steel frame to cladding panel. It is unusual to have point fixings supporting outer panels, but the advantage here is speed of installation; a prefabricated kit of parts that can be installed within a few days, allowing the building to become operational as quickly as possible. As a result, interfaces between the spatial volumes that comprise the building are reduced and simplified.

The modular nature of the structural bays provides a high degree of flexibility, including bays for windows and tall door openings. Every panel is effectively a 'knockout' panel, where parts of the structure can be removed to create a mixture of window and door openings to suit the evolution of the building. This requirement can be achieved by removing structural components from parts of the openings of the panel, and inserting window panels in their place. Glazing is inwardly angled to assist weather tightness when the windows are open during periods of rain; avoiding a buildup of snow and ice on units that need to be opened and closed during winter months. The kit-of-parts approach extends to smaller-scale elements such as the lighting track and rails for cleaning equipment. Stairs are steel framed with perforated metal treads and balustrades that can be changed and replaced as part of the evolving functionality of the building. The design considers the need for near-future changes which are expected to take place; a changing arrangement of spaces which will be optimised again to provide a well-lit and well-ventilated flexible workplace.

Typical bays are created from each of the modules that are delivered by road which are 2.5 metres wide and 7.5 metres long. These modules

Perspective view of typical bay from above

are joined together to create larger volumes. Envelopes are prefabricated and are either attached or fixed in the factory or alternatively a complete set of facade units is fixed to the structure. In this project the panels of both units are fully prefabricated as a result of the restrictions on construction time, which is short as a result of the requirements of neighbouring owners. The same material is used for the walls and roofs which are metal panels and transparent glass. The transparent glass is used for thin bands of windows which are set deep into the facade in order to create passive external shading. Panels are generally fixed in rainscreen configuration such that the waterproofing layer on both roofs as applied before the panels are inserted together. The weatherproofing of the roof is formed on site and is achieved by having some external wall and roof panels fixed after the seal has been made between adjacent panels or adjacent prefabricated units.

The typical bay makes use of rooflights which are inclined from the vertical plane in order to protect them from the harsh winter environment. These rooflights are 2.5 metres wide and form a typical bay in their own right, extending the full width of the building both in the upper levels of the office and design studios as well as the ground floor manufacturing space. The purpose of using a common system for inclined glazing used as a rooflight was to provide an even level of daylighting across both office and manufacturing functions. The primary tasks being carried out in both spaces make use of computer screens in order to control manufacturing equipment and as a primary tool for work in the office and studio spaces.

Facade panels are formed in a moulded material that takes up the indentations and depressions of both facades and roofs, which share a common visual language of both panel arrangements and joint lines. The facade panels have closed vertical joints in the manner of rainscreen cladding; the roof panels have semi-open joints with a roof membrane set behind them. Both facade glazing and rooflights are silicone sealed between the double-glazed units, supported on steel frames to which they are fixed directly. This glazing type is also used on inclined areas of glazing which have solar shading devices fixed to them.

1. Perspective view of exterior

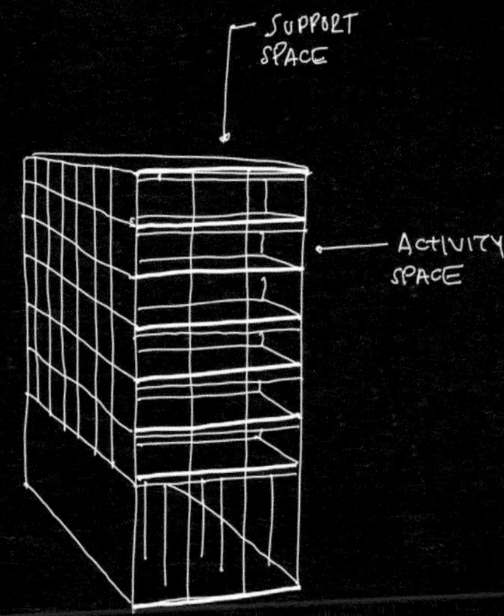

2. Perspective view of exterior

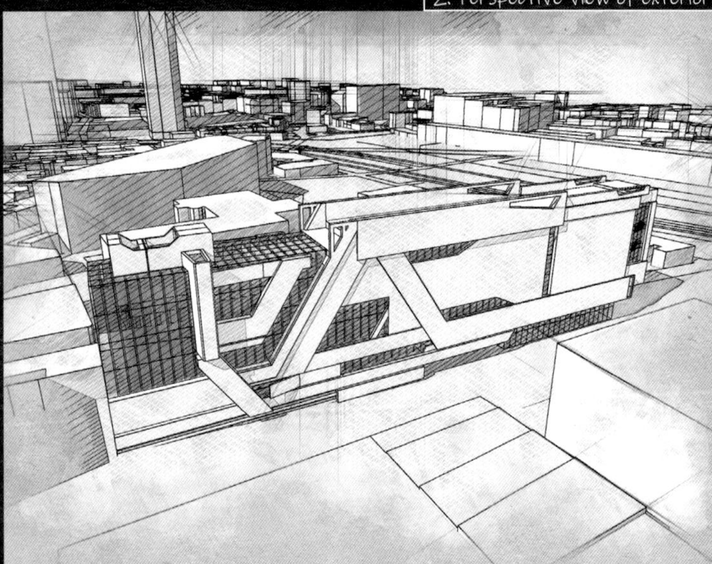

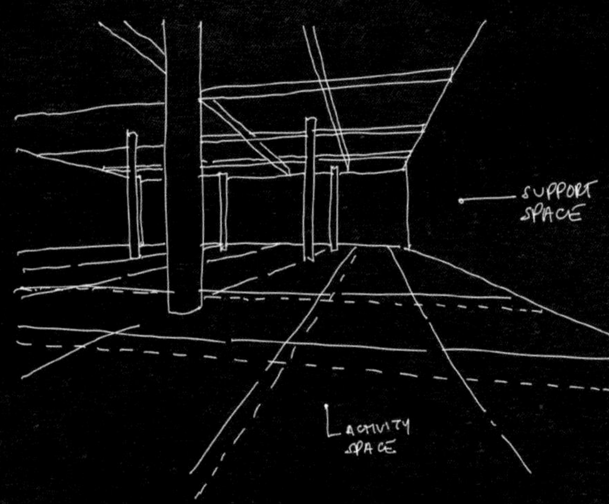

Loose-fit construction for environmental design

The loose-fit nature of building construction is a theme that was developed in this project in order to allow the environmental control systems to be installed and partially replaced without the need to involve other assemblies in the building. Buildings are often constructed using a loose-fit approach between different assemblies so that they can be installed and maintained independently of one another. For example, facades are usually installed to function independently of their supporting structure; internal finishes are usually installed independently of the facades. Environmental control systems are installed independently of structure, facade and interior finishes, but are also required to interface with the interior finishes; typically in the ceiling zone. Suspended ceilings in commercial buildings allow for ceiling tiles to be demounted in order to gain access to the services installation in the void between the ceiling and the soffit of the structural floor above. This approach provides some flexibility between the systems to allow services to be partially replaced and maintained during their lifespan. Some recent installations in buildings have removed the need for suspended ceilings by arranging the services equipment of air-handling ducts, diffusers and electrical supplies in an arrangement such that they can be seen as a visible part of the construction. Electrical lighting forms a part of this arrangement by allowing all components of the services installation and environmental control systems to be made visible within the building. The interface between environmental control systems and facades usually results in a diffuser or a louvre being required, usually forming a part of the facade system where ducts for air handling are fixed to the facade system; the facade system provides a diffuser for air to be drawn in or to be extracted from the building. This interface can be modified or upgraded at a later date, but any changes or modifications require the participation of both a facade contractor and a services contractor working together. Where ducts and pipes pass through fire-protected walls, fire-resisting collars are required in order to make the link between the two adjacent spaces. These interfaces make the environmental control systems less flexible and

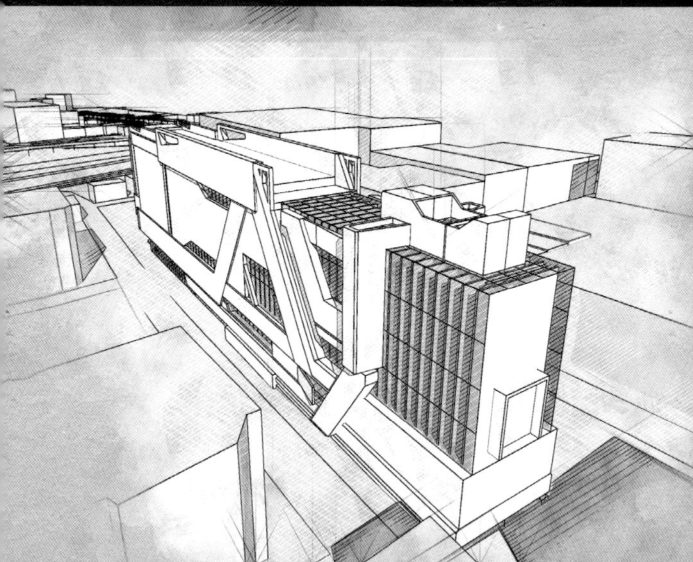

Perspective view of exterior

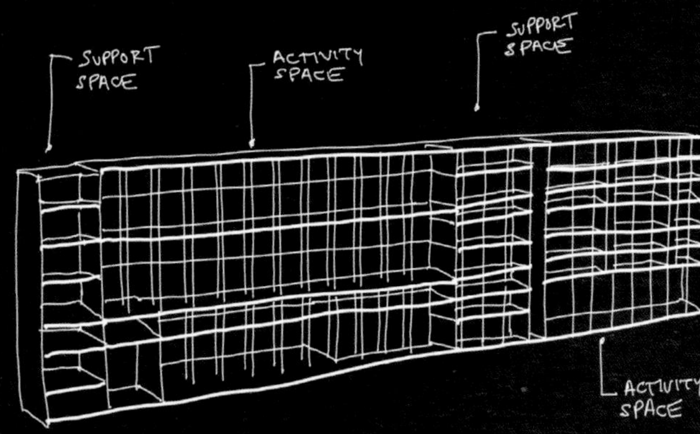

4. Perspective view of exterior

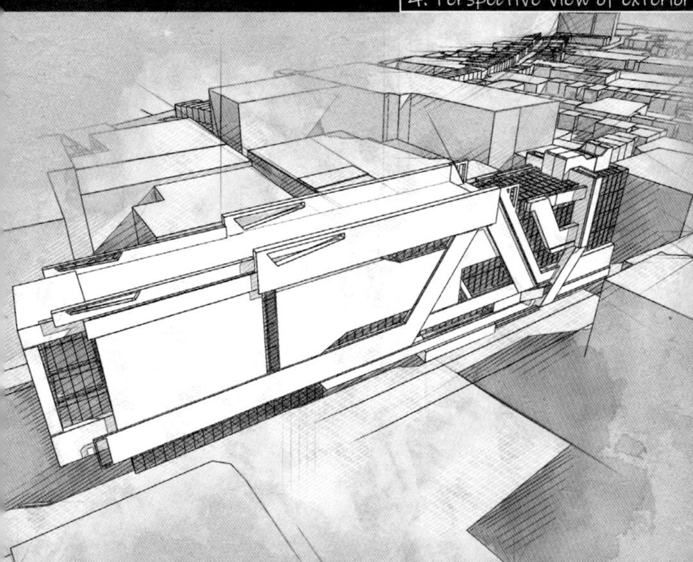

less loose-fit in their ability to be updated in response to changing performance requirements. As a result of these interfaces, it can be difficult to replace parts of the services installation in order to increase energy efficiencies within the building. However, interfaces are often 'shared' components between systems, which provides an efficiency in their use. This efficiency can be lost elsewhere, in the support systems and fixings used to support air-handling ducts and suspended ceilings. These fixing systems are usually separate, allowing modifications to be made independently of other systems, except at interfaces. Likewise, the fixing systems for other packages are also independent of one another, which can lead to providing more fixings then would be required if fixings were shared across systems. A disadvantage of sharing fixings is that if one system is replaced, then it will either have to provide its own new fixing or will necessitate an attempt to use the existing fixing, which may not be suitable for the modifications required. This approach of installing independent fixings provides long-term flexibility, but creates a short-term issue of having more material used to construct the building then would be the case if fixings could be combined.

The approach adopted for this project was to develop a set of fixings which suited both services installations and interior finishes. This was achieved in part by introducing an arrangement of cast-in sockets which were installed on a grid of 1.5 metres by 1.5 metres across the underside of floor slabs, in order for services to be changed independently of one another without the need to create a secondary system of new fixings. The structure could accommodate new fixings to it directly rather than introducing a third intermediary system between a support for an air-handling duct for example, and floor slabs. This preparation of the underside of floor slabs for future adaptation avoids the need to use intermediary systems of clamps and secondary supports within the ceiling zone at a later date.

The relationship between the facades and the structure was enhanced for long-term flexibility by adding cost in sockets to the vertical face of floor slabs for future solar-shading devices.

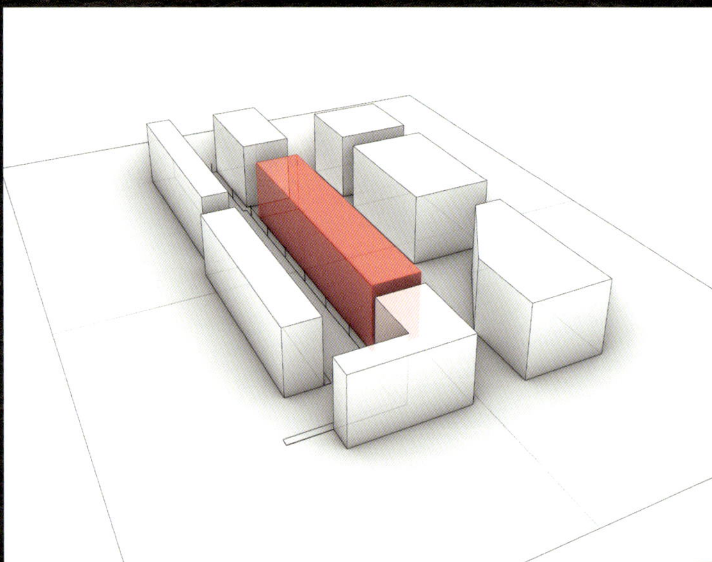

1. Project volume in site context

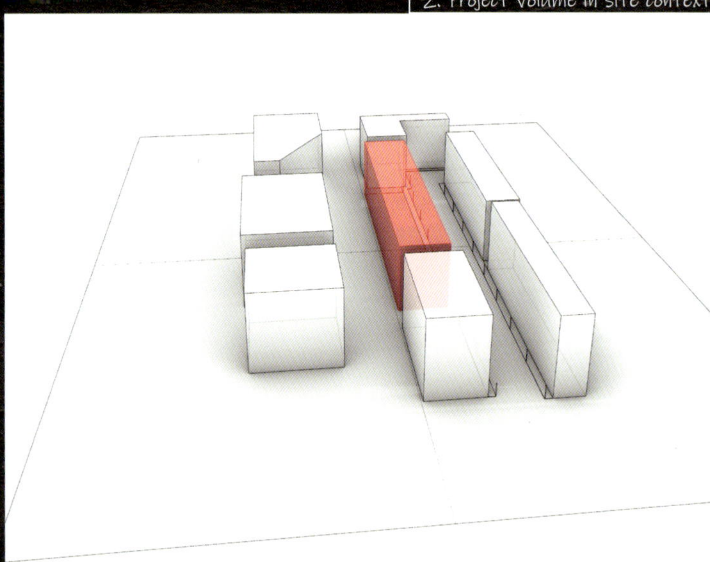

2. Project volume in site context

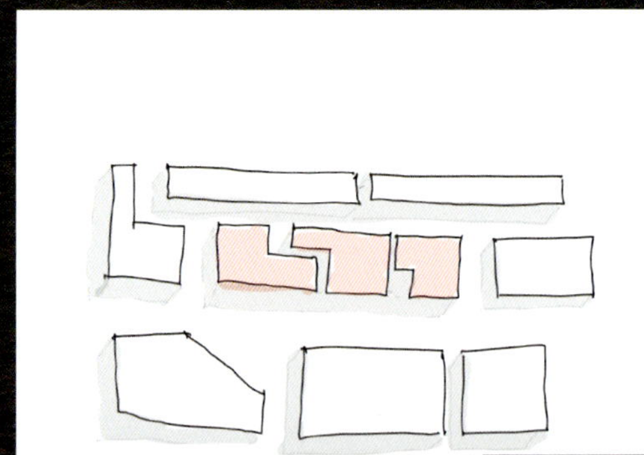

1. Site plan with surrounding context

Option 1 has three blocks, set side by side, in order to fit the urban scale of the surrounding buildings.

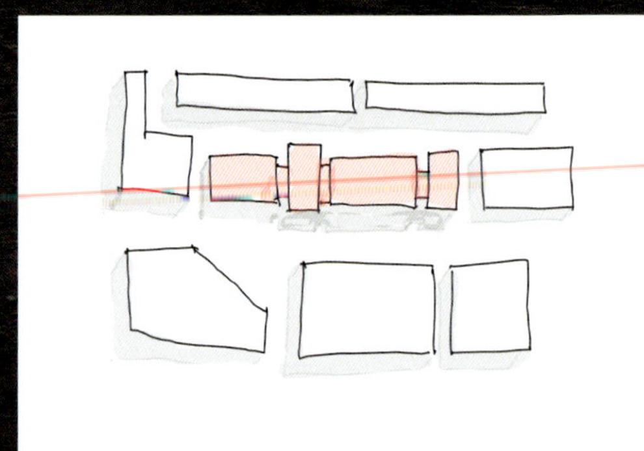

2. Site plan with surrounding context

Option 2 divides those three blocks further into four separate forms by dividing the three activities into two smaller blocks.

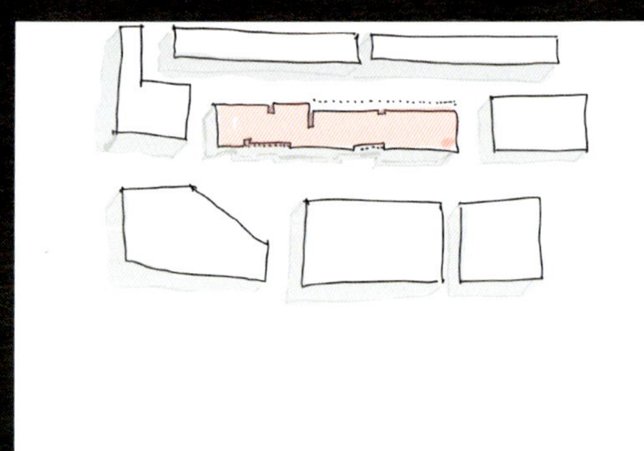

3. Site plan with surrounding context

Option 3 creates greater differentiation between the external forms of the facility, each of which is still at the scale of nearby blocks.

Site context

The site context is an inner-city area where this research and development facility is not part of the business district but is set in the context of a mixed set of building types; it is self-contained but reaches out to its neighbours. The brief/program required the building to be divided into three parts: a light manufacturing hall, research and development studios and cellular offices. The facility is divided into three sets of spaces that reflect the functions within the building. A large reception space for visitors is set at ground level, with the light manufacturing hall set above this space which interlocks with an adjacent exhibition space. A primary aim of the facility is to create public areas in the building for large numbers of visitors through an interaction between the three component functions accommodated within the building.

Option 1 has three blocks, set side by side, in order to fit the urban scale of the surrounding buildings in both height and in massing, with gaps between the blocks that provide points of entry to the facility; presenting also a distinct identity to each of the blocks within the overall identity of the building. Option 2 divides those three blocks further into four separate forms by dividing the three activities into two smaller blocks that are of similar size to those of the immediate urban neighbourhood. Overlaps between facilities are addressed with the introduction of 'link' blocks between each of the four forms. The link blocks can be accessed at street level on both sides of the building, as is the case with Option 1. The massing remains the same height as in Option 1, as do the two adjacent buildings at each end of the site.

Option 3 creates greater differentiation between the external forms of the facility, each of which is still at the scale of nearby blocks; creating a single identity for this R&D facility. This approach suggests a greater interaction between the functions in the facility rather than their 'separation', which is expressed in Options 1 and 2. A differentiation between parts of the building is expressed with 'notches' cut into the facades; the notches create a differentiation between the spaces within, as well as creating views along the facade on two sides within the facility.

Research and development studios and cellular offices are accessed

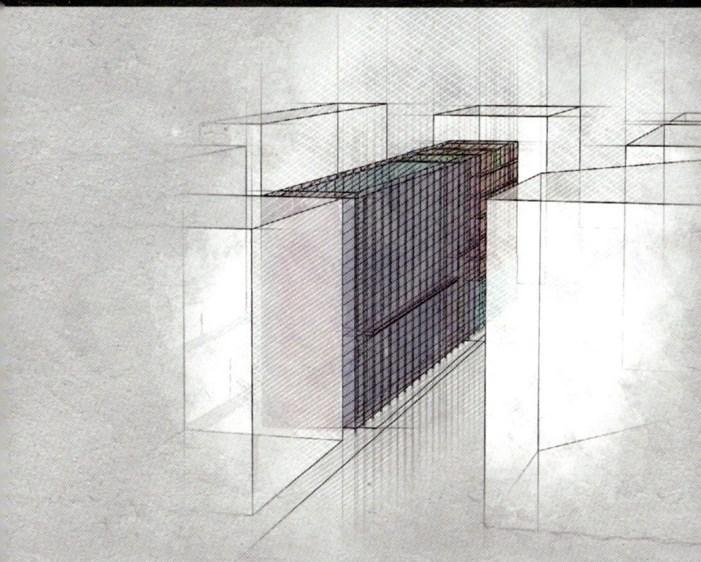

Perspective view of environmental volumes

2. Perspective view of environmental volumes

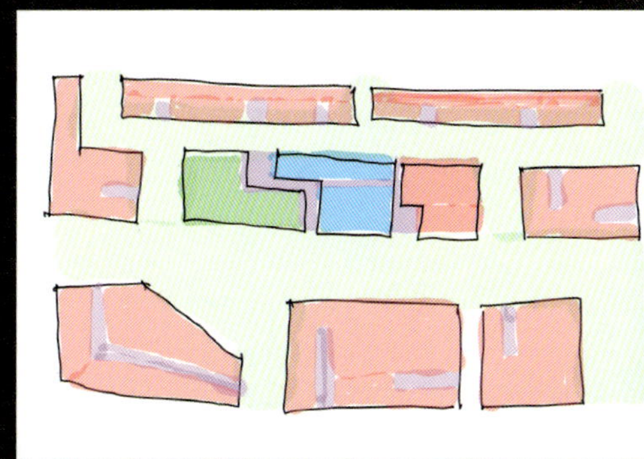

1. Figure-ground diagram of tempered environment

Option 1
Dark green spaces are highly tempered but are reduced to specific volumes only.

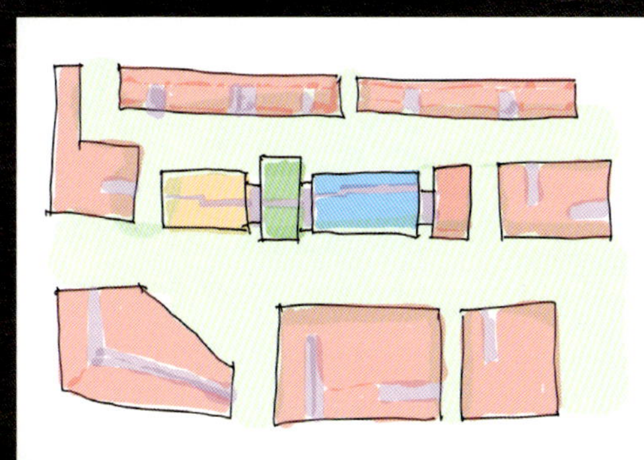

2. Figure-ground diagram of tempered environment

Option 2
Dark blue spaces are less tempered than dark green spaces but are more tempered than blue spaces.

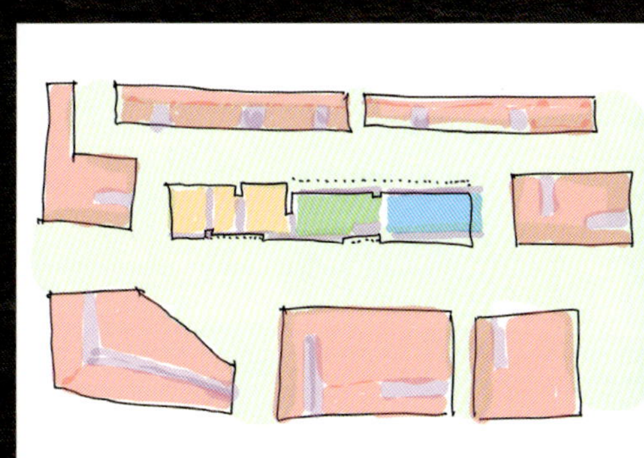

3. Figure-ground diagram of tempered environment

Option 3
Violet spaces are the least tempered spaces. These spaces interface directly with external space.

from one side from long galleries. The opposite side has glazed walls which look out over the city centre from its edge, so that these spaces are not set out about a central corridor but instead expand in extent from side to side of the building, with access on one side of the floor plan.

The facility is part of a set of large-scale building developments and is of a height similar to its neighbours, presenting itself as an inviting environment where visitors from the public enjoy dramatic views as they climb escalators on the sides of the building to reach presentation facilities at the top of the building. Research and development studios are glazed from floor to ceiling, with narrow glazing bands that are assembled with vertical framing set at 1.0-metre centres in order to create a more intimate scale to the spaces within. These research and development spaces address the need to conceal parts of the research work from the public gaze by having circulation spaces cloak the R&D spaces; providing public access to upper floors with views up and down the building. The facades are essentially inhabited by the circulation spaces; the research work is carried on behind those inhabited walls, which have the level of privacy required. This approach avoids the need for this facility to be located away from the city centre, either at an edge-of-city site or at a rural site away from the public gaze. Instead this facility engages with its city centre location, not by turning its back on that location, and not by having a series of highly opaque walls, but instead to wrap the R&D facilities within a set of inhabited facades.

Two wedge-shaped voids are set in the building to provide natural ventilation and daylight to adjacent interior spaces. This void has the benefit of reducing the overall visual massing of the building. An alternative solution was to divide the building into two halves along its length and provide link bridges across the external void that is formed. The void creates a zone for natural ventilation and daylighting; the bridges provide additional meeting spaces, while others provide routes for internal circulation. The division of the building provides views through the building as a result of the visual 'slice' through floor plates.

1. Sectional perspective view

2. Sectional perspective view

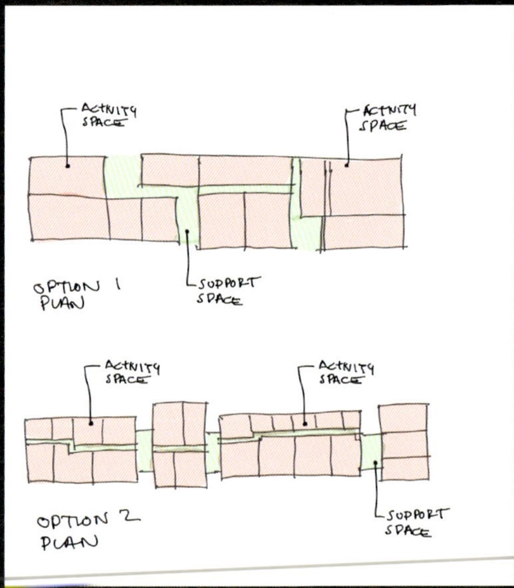

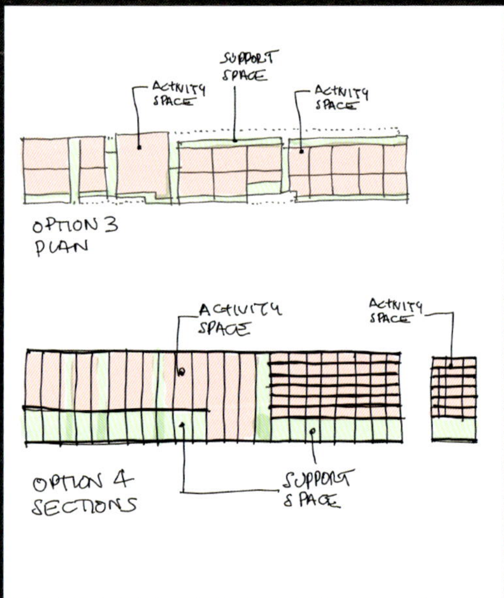

Spatial arrangement

Option 1 has prototyping spaces that occupy volumes expressed in the outside form of the building.

Option 2 sets three link spaces between four volumes and has corridors that wind through the length of the building.

Option 3 sets the circulation space on both facades and allows deep slots that traverse the width of the building.

Spatial arrangement

The general form of this building is a rectangular-shaped 'slab' with a high level of differentiation in the external and internal elements that result from the complex spatial arrangement within. The spatial arrangement reflects the interlinked relationships between the spaces that are a fundamental part of the brief/program. The R&D centre accommodates a set of linked external terraces which are protected by wind breaks formed by tall glass screens that deter the strongest effects of winds. The terraces provide a space for changing exhibitions and associated pavilions that are put onto the roof for display. The space is 50% external, 50% internal and is essentially an external room formed by the continuity of the spaces on either side.

Floor plates have a spine core extending along their centre, creating a continuous service space down the full length of the building. The spine core contains stairs, lifts/elevators, washrooms for public areas, meeting rooms and storage. The prototyping facility has a more complex arrangement of functions with an amphitheatre, exhibition space and meeting rooms. Circulation routes are required to link quickly, with large numbers of people moving up and down the building. The spatial arrangement of Option 1 is of prototyping spaces that occupy volumes expressed in the outside form of the building, with passages through from outside to inside and across with a corridor in the centre of one of the blocks. The facility has areas arranged as volumes in their own right, linked together to form the overall volume of the building with slightly different floor layouts of spaces on each floor, but the entrance slots shown in green on the plan of Option 1 are consistent through all floor levels.

Option 2 sets three link spaces between four volumes and has corridors that wind through the length of the building. Spaces are arranged on both sides of the winding corridor. This arrangement allows for future changes in the use of spaces. Option 3 sets the circulation space on both facades and allows deep slots that traverse the width of the building to provide both the identity of each volume as well as a unity of the composition. The inclined part of the exoskeleton supports

Perspective view of interior

2. Perspective view of interior

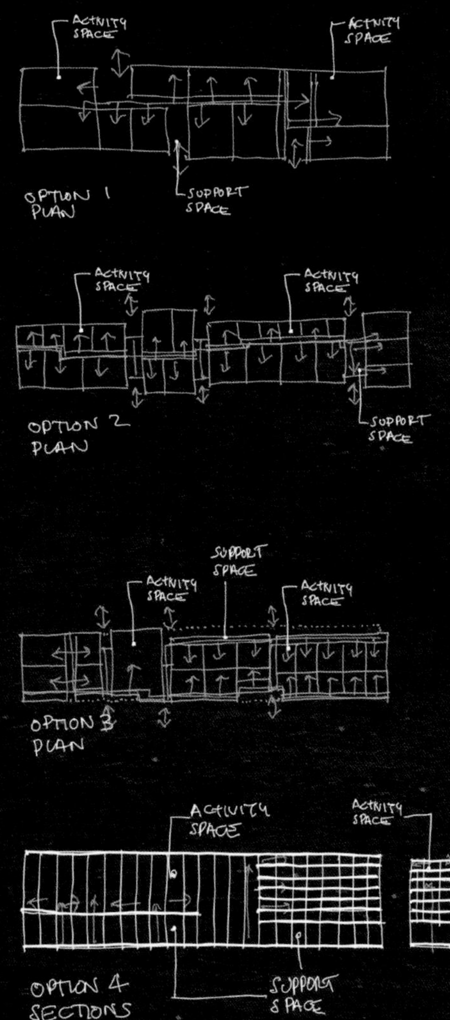

Internal circulation

Option 1 has a corridor that passes through the link within the central 'block' that is reached from the outside.

Option 2 requires the circulation to follow a route where it changes direction in order to respond to the needs of the facility functions.

Option 3 sets the circulation routes along the edges of the building where they extend down one side of the building to its full extent.

a set of terraced work spaces which look out into an inclined external void between the two constituent parts of the building. The void has enclosed bridges which cross the building. The external void provides a zone for natural ventilation on both sides of this space.

Internal circulation

The internal circulation of Option 1 is of a corridor that passes through the link within the central 'block' that is reached from the outside, through a large entrance 'slot' on each side of the long facades. There is a large external slot in the centre of the spine corridor, as well as one at each end, which are set on opposing sides of the facades. Access into each of the facility functions is straightforward from this linear core circulation route. Option 2 develops this concept further with greater differentiation in each of the blocks, but requires the circulation to follow a route where it changes direction in order to respond to the needs of the facility functions. This condition occurs on the upper floors where there is a greater number of smaller work spaces. Vertical access is provided by the cores, which serve as 'hubs' between each of the four blocks that comprise the building. In Option 3 the circulation routes are set along the edges of the building where they extend down one side of the building to its full extent, but extend only half the length of the building on the other side. The internal circulation areas are located within the zone of the external walls in order that activities within the building are essentially hidden from public view. A distribution and movement of people provides a pedestrian flow where the numbers of people in any point avoids concentration spots where corridors become too narrow for the numbers of people passing through them. This situation is typically a result of staircases being introduced into that zone. Instead, staircases are positioned on the outside of those circulation spaces in order to provide a continuous pedestrian route on both sides of the building which is uninterrupted by additional elements. The circulation zones can be widened beyond the perimeter of the building while still being within the confines of the site to meet potential changes in patterns of circulation in the pedestrian flow.

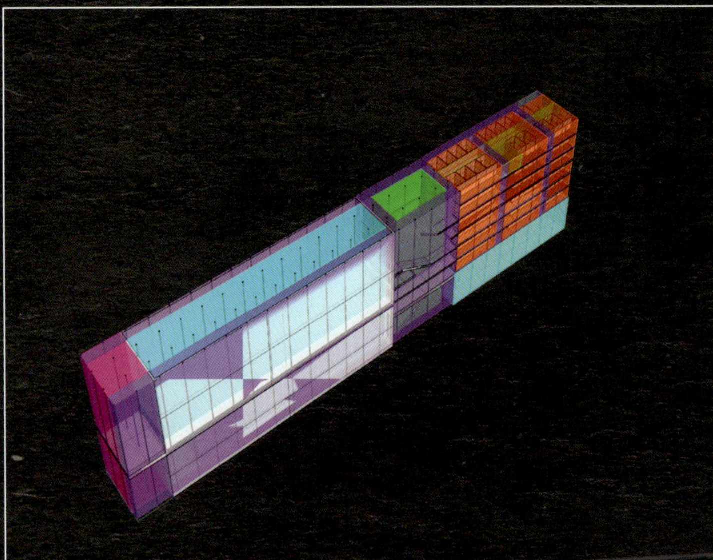

1A. Isometric view of environmental volumes

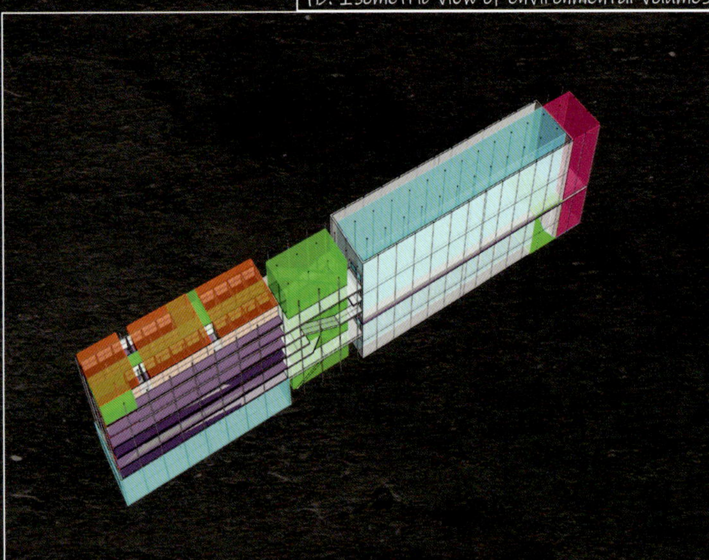

1B. Isometric view of environmental volumes

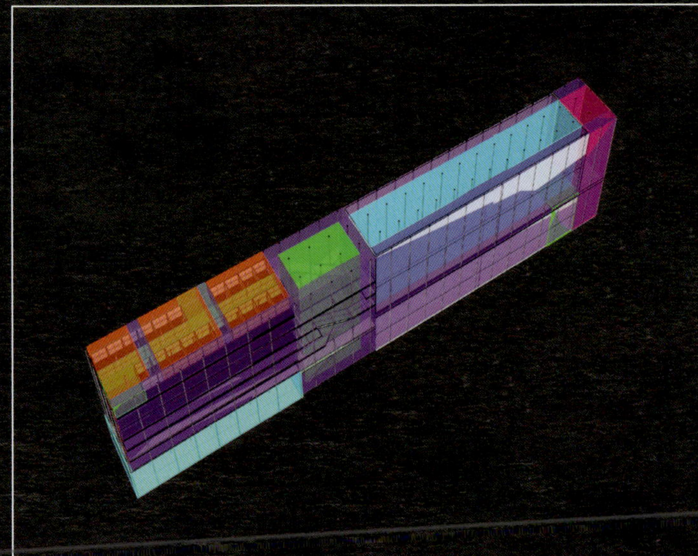

2A. Isometric view of environmental volumes

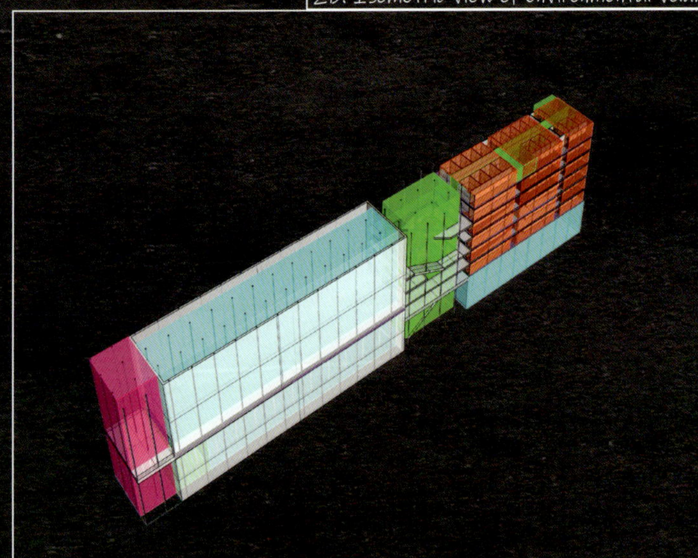

2B. Isometric view of environmental volum

Environmental strategy

The building has two large 'blade' forms set on one side of the building. The function of the blades is to provide support for externally mounted air-handling ducts that supply air on one side of the building; air is returned on the other side for the major floors in the building. Air-handling units and chillers are mounted on the outside of the building with fresh air supplied by air ducts on the lower side, giving them a characteristic appearance. This is a method of providing air handling to the whole building from the centre without using floor area, allowing the units to be accessed externally from maintenance access decks that are positioned inside the two 'blades' on each side of the building. Access ladders and walkways are set between the ducts to provide access for maintenance. The complete assembly of vertical ducts enclosed as 'blades', together with the air-handling units and chillers, provides a cyclical use of energy with as much energy recovery as possible as the air is refreshed. Circulation spaces provide buffer zones between inside and outside spaces.

The environmental strategy of Option 1 is to create a single environmental zone for each of the three blocks. The entrance spaces that divide those three blocks are environmental buffer zones between inside and outside; benefitting from the recovered heating or cooling energy.

Option 2 makes the differentiation between blocks greater; in this option the link blocks serve as environmental buffer zones, as shown in violet. The blocks in red, blue, green, and orange are independently controlled zones for air circulation, and for natural ventilation. Option 3 takes this concept one step further, using the facade zones as the environmental buffer with the users walking along the edges of the building in an interstitial zone between the external walls and the internal walls of the facility. The slots that cross the entire width of the building are used to provide natural ventilation in the mid-season, circulated with fans that distribute and recycle fresh air internally.

TThe environmental strategy is one of locating air-handling ducts and services equipment on the public side of the building; the other side of

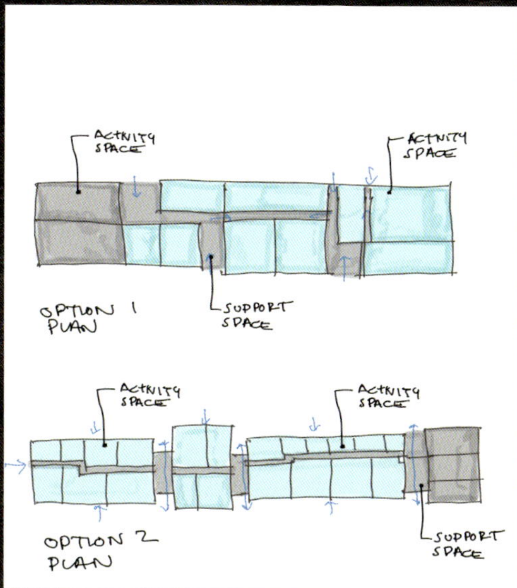

Daylight strategy for direct sunlight and cross ventilation.

Option 1 arranges the building as two blocks separated by an open void.

Option 2 widens the central circulation space in order to add the main entrance floor.

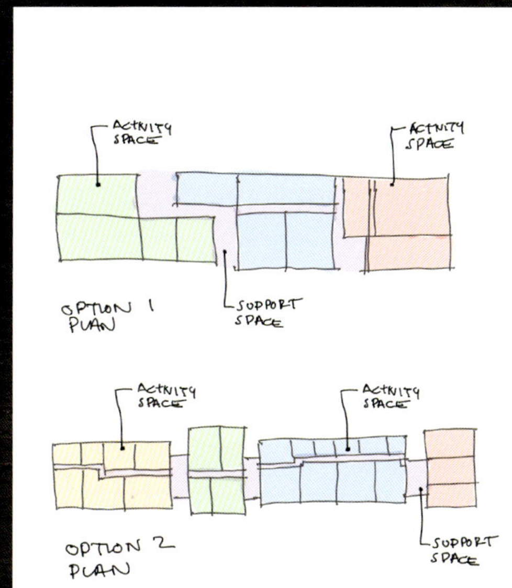

Environmental zones

Option 1 creates a single environmental zone for each of the three blocks.

Option 2 has link blocks serving as environmental buffer zones.

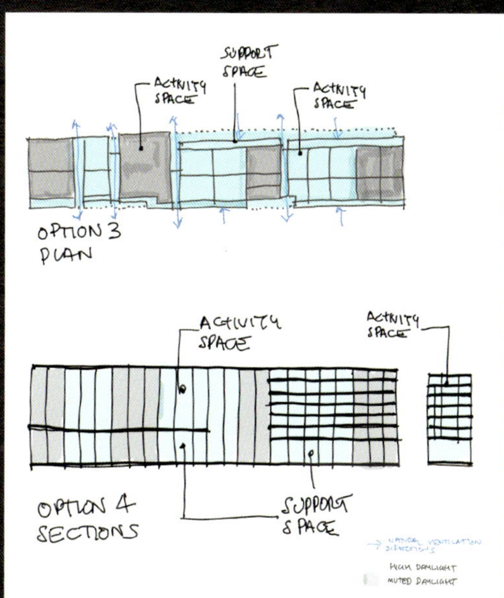

Daylight strategy for direct sunlight and cross ventilation.

Option 3 arranges the building as two larger blocks with communal spaces on the ground floor and accommodation above.

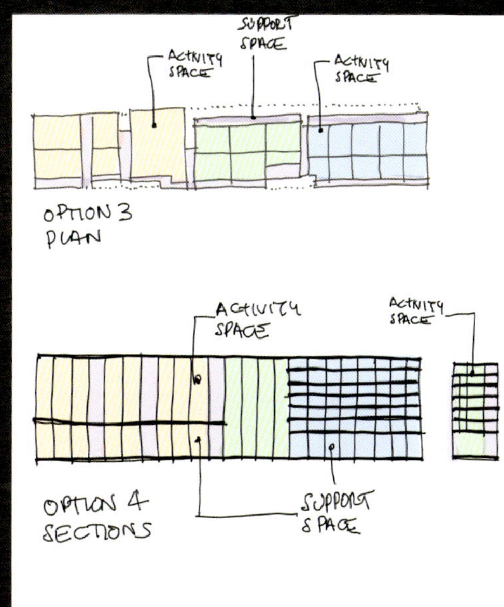

Environmental zones

Option 3 uses the facade zones as an interstitial buffer zone between the external walls and the internal walls.

the building circulation space is set adjacent to the facades. Services are distributed in the corridor space at ceiling level; passing into each of the studios and offices within concealed ducts. Services are accessible from the terrace space that also forms a corridor linking workspaces to staircases. Each group of studios and offices is divided into three with a service core in order to reduce the length of corridor.

The environmental zones set adjacent to one another are all enclosed by a buffer zone between the environmental zones and the outside of the building, where buffer zones are formed, but within the circulation space that forms the inhabited facade that extends the length of the long facades on both sides of the building.

The environmental buffer zones allow tempered air from each of the zones to be distributed into the circulation zones when not required to redirect air from other areas; recirculated and mixed with fresh air for the different activities in the building. Air which is to be expelled from the building is first distributed into the circulation spaces which have low levels of occupancy over the course of a working day. Heat exchangers retain most of the heating or cooling energy from air that is being expelled from the building after it has been recirculated through secondary zones and circulation zones following its passage through the main spaces of the building.

The environmental strategy focused on an evolving need to integrate natural ventilation and solar control and enhance the effective introduction of daylight in the coming years. The systems required for these passive systems of energy control have been designed, but their installation was not required in the building during the first construction period.

This approach is about allowing the performance of the building to evolve during its lifespan without adding significant cost to the construction in the first phase of the assembly of the building. This approach allows the environmental control systems and the facades to be effectively upgraded in the near future as part of an aim to reduce energy consumption through the introduction of passive controls for light and solar gain.

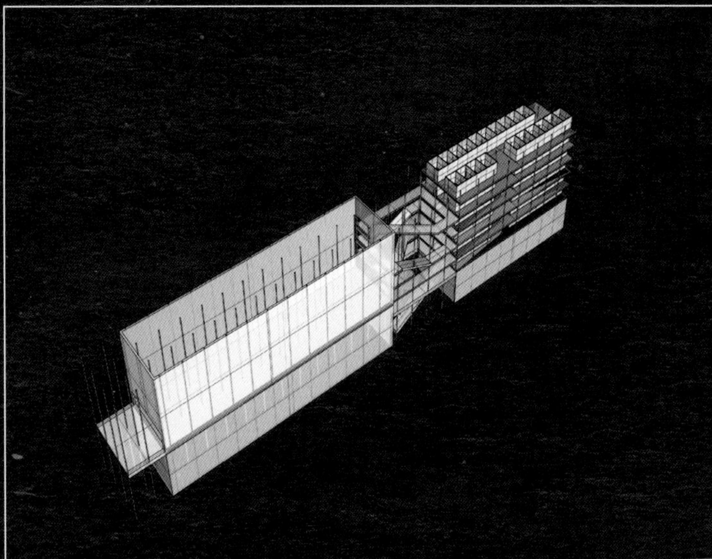

1A. Isometric view of structure

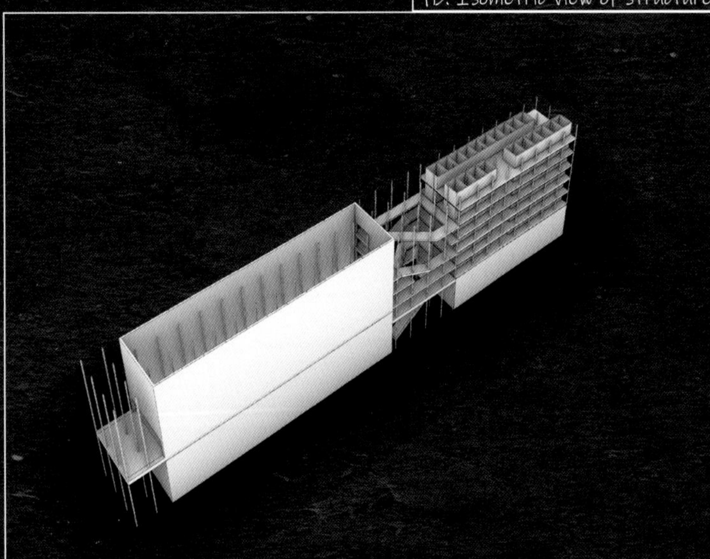

1B. Isometric view of structure

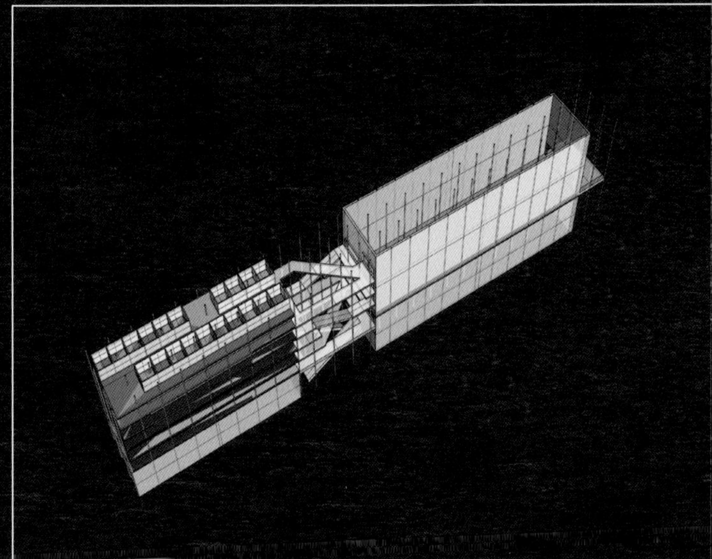

2A. Isometric view of structure

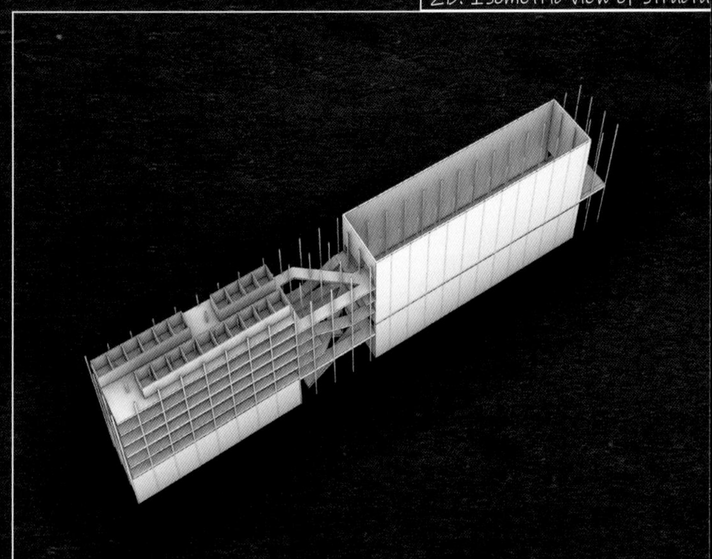

2B. Isometric view of structu

Structural strategy

The structural strategy is one of a regular reinforced concrete frame with additional elements created by the inclined enclosures for circulation and for services distribution down the building from roof level. The structure is one of columns without structural walls between workspaces. The outer walls form part of the structural frame in which there are structural walls that support the services equipment and ducts which distribute air down the length of the building. This is essentially a 'building within a building' structurally, with a double row of columns at the edges of the two long elevations.

The structural strategy is based on the introduction of steel frames at different scales in order to create the characteristic geometry of the building, which is driven by the need to support services externally as they are distributed from the roof downwards through a series of inclined and horizontally oriented ducts. A steel frame structure was chosen over a reinforced concrete structure, as the need for encasing the steelwork with a fire-protective layer was considered to be more cost effective as a result of the need to construct the building quickly. The use of steel a frame allowed the ductwork to be fixed more easily to the steel structure, as well as introducing secondary framing to create points of support for the external panel system and areas of glazing. Although the visual expression of the building is one of concrete-based facade panels, cladding is fixed back with stainless steel fixings at points which requires them to be fixed directly to the primary structure rather than to rails, which would have been required if the panels were of a more lightweight construction.

The overall structural design is one of a steel frame with beams and columns at floor levels only. The structure is an 'interpretation' of a reinforced concrete structure fabricated from steel in order to reduce construction time, allowing the facades to be fixed quickly as well as the floor slabs to be set into the depth of the steel beams for rapid construction and to reduce the overall height of the of the building. The downstand beams forming part the structure is encased in protective boards which form part of the internal partitioning between

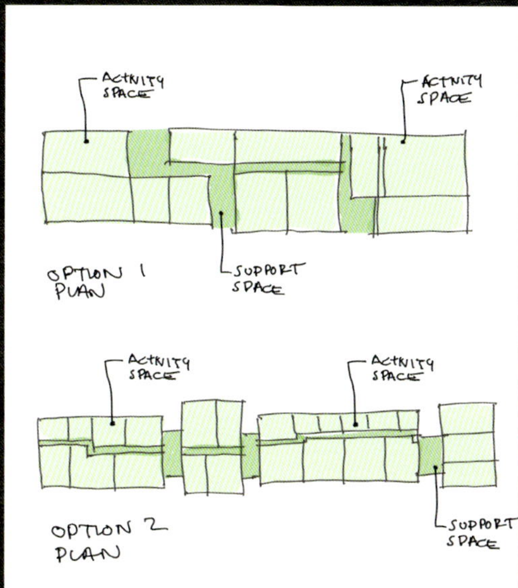

Structural strategy: Zones
Option 1 has structural walls which traverse the narrow width of the building.
Option 2 a frame that provides structural stability to the concrete cores.

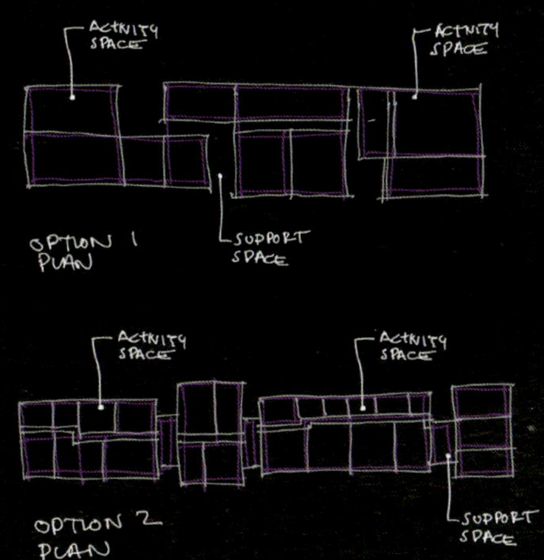

Structural strategy: Framing
Option 1 encloses the core spaces and dividing space into sets of apartments.
Option 2 is largely a steel frame.

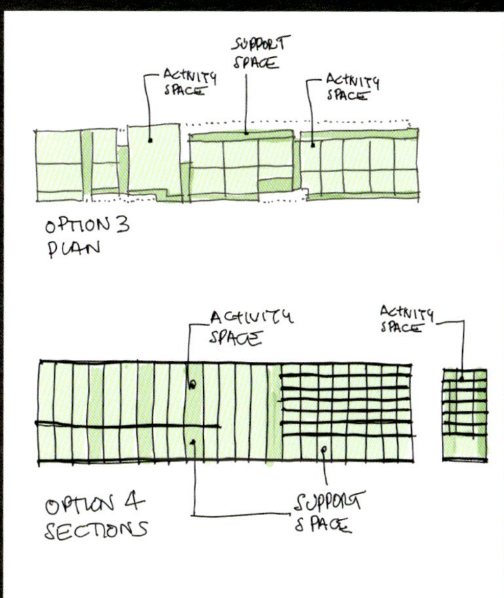

Structural strategy: Zones
Option 3 has structural walls formed as cores and mixes those with columns in the activity spaces.

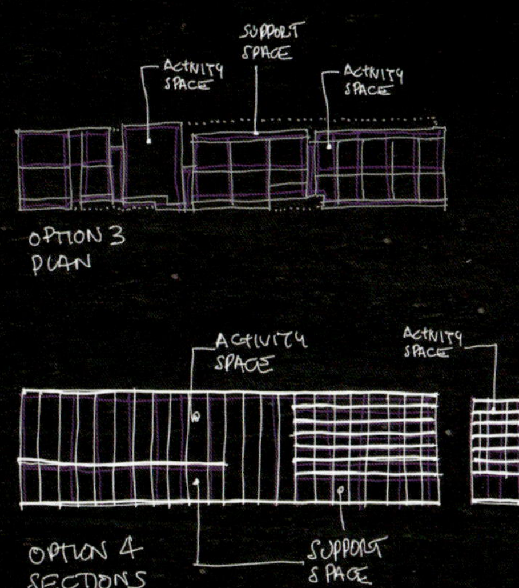

Structural strategy: Zones
Option 3 is a mixed solution of reinforced concrete and steel.

spaces, allowing for those zones to also carry services – which would be difficult if reinforced concrete beams and columns were used. The primary structure makes use of framing members which are closer together than would be required to span economically between floor slabs. This increased number of columns is used on the external walls, as the panels which enclose it have vertical joints with a lightweight cladding system that requires supports at 3.0-metre centres. This increases the number of columns on the external walls, but as elsewhere columns are set out at 7.5-metre centres. The greater amount of structure on the perimeter avoids the need for framing to support the facades, as well as the internal walls and associated services zone within the external walls.

Columns are also increased in number in the central corridors to allow a non-loadbearing panel system to be used as internal partitions between corridors and R&D spaces, to provide the levels of thermal insulation and acoustic insulation between zones of circulation and working or activity zones. This approach allows prefabricated partitions to be fixed directly to the floor and ceiling in some places. In most locations the partitions span from column to column, which provides a zone between the underside of the slab and the top of the partition into which a glazed screen can be added.

This admits a consistent level of borrowed light to the circulation space, without the need to have framing in a regular partitioning system that would be required to span from floor to ceiling as a result of the light-gauge framing used within the internal partitions. In the arrangement used in this project, partitions are supported at floor level and are restrained along their vertical edges in order to provide a continuous slot at ceiling level, interrupted only by the primary steels. This larger scale approach to internal installations provides greater flexibility in being able to remove elements as large-scale panels rather than the site-based method of using framing with a dry lining attached to each side. This allows the elements of the partition to be reused around the building in response to change; moving assemblies around the building were found to be less disruptive than their replacement.

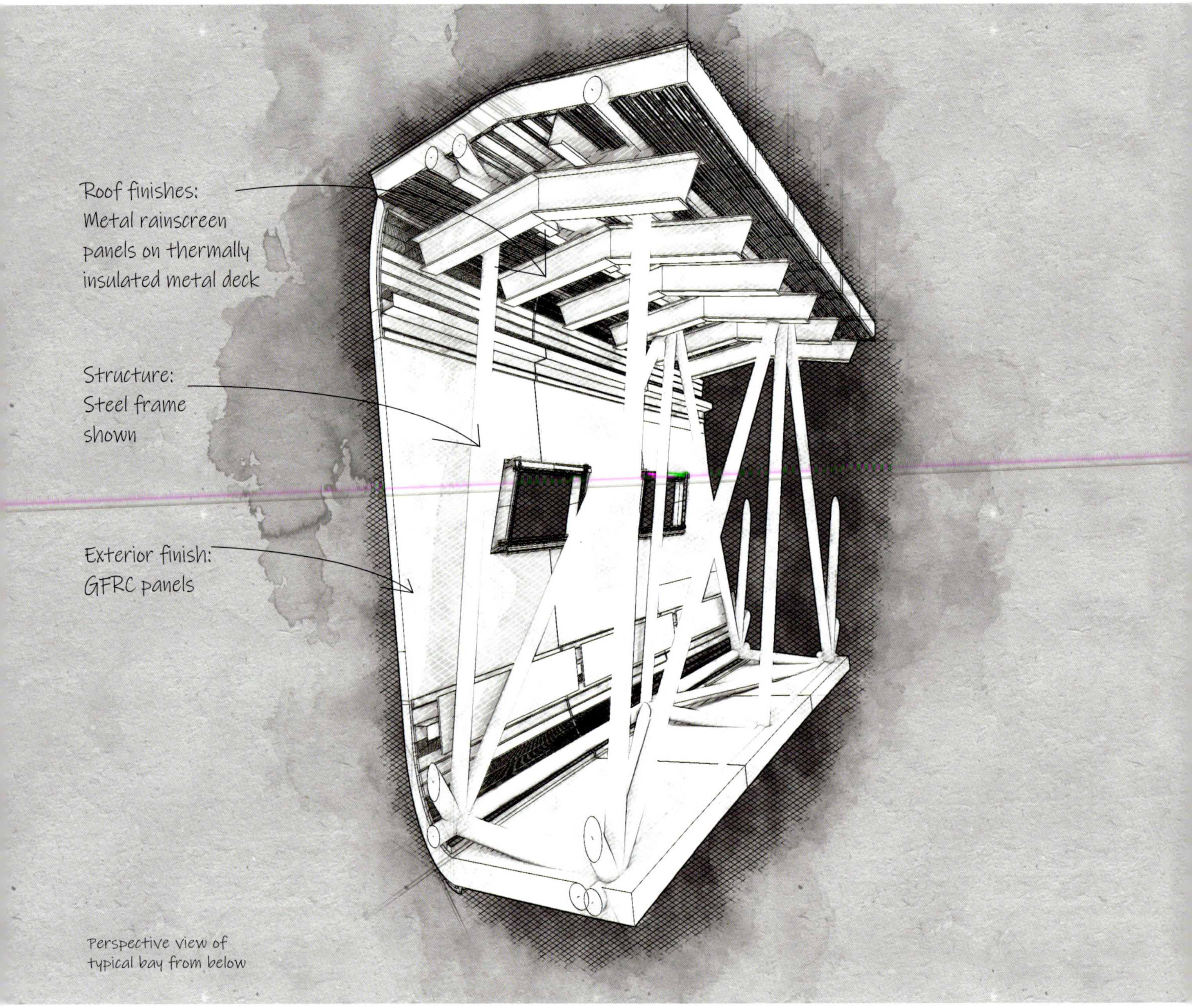

Perspective view of typical bay from below

Typical bay adjacent to facade

The external envelope comprises a set of concrete-based panels which follow the lines of the large-scale framing elements which are both inclined and horizontal to enclose elements of circulation. Glazing elements are considered to be 'infill' assemblies within this large scale structure. The modular vertical panels are supported on a corresponding grid of vertical framing in order to provide modular research and development studios and offices. Facilities at each end of the building include a light-manufacturing space with translucent glazing supported by thin steel frames; the glazing extends over several floors in some cases. R&D spaces are arranged on adjacent floors which are stepped in section; the void between floors aims to create a sense of individual teams being part of a larger enetrprise; extending over three adjacent floors of studios and offices.

The external envelope is first constructed from its exoskeleton form, which not only contributes to the structural stability of the building but also provides support for mechanical and electrical equipment; mainly ducted air that moves around the building. This approach of the distribution of services provides an enclosure between the outside of the building and the lightweight enclosures within; creating a contrast between the heavyweight structure that provides stability and the internal structure which is lighter in weight, allowing the functions of research and development and design studios to change in their proportion as an internal refurbishment exercise that does not require changes to the facades. The structure and services create the primary expression of the building; they are not required to be a 'visual map' of spatial functions behind, which gives a greater flexibility for internal changes that do not require replacement.

A typical bay comprises a steel frame of structural steels, used for both columns and beams. Floor slabs are formed as composite steel and concrete decks. This rapid form of construction allows for the structure to be prepared for the facades to be fixed to them, with the external facades fixed directly to the primary structure and thermal breaks that pass through the backing wall for the facades. The backing wall of

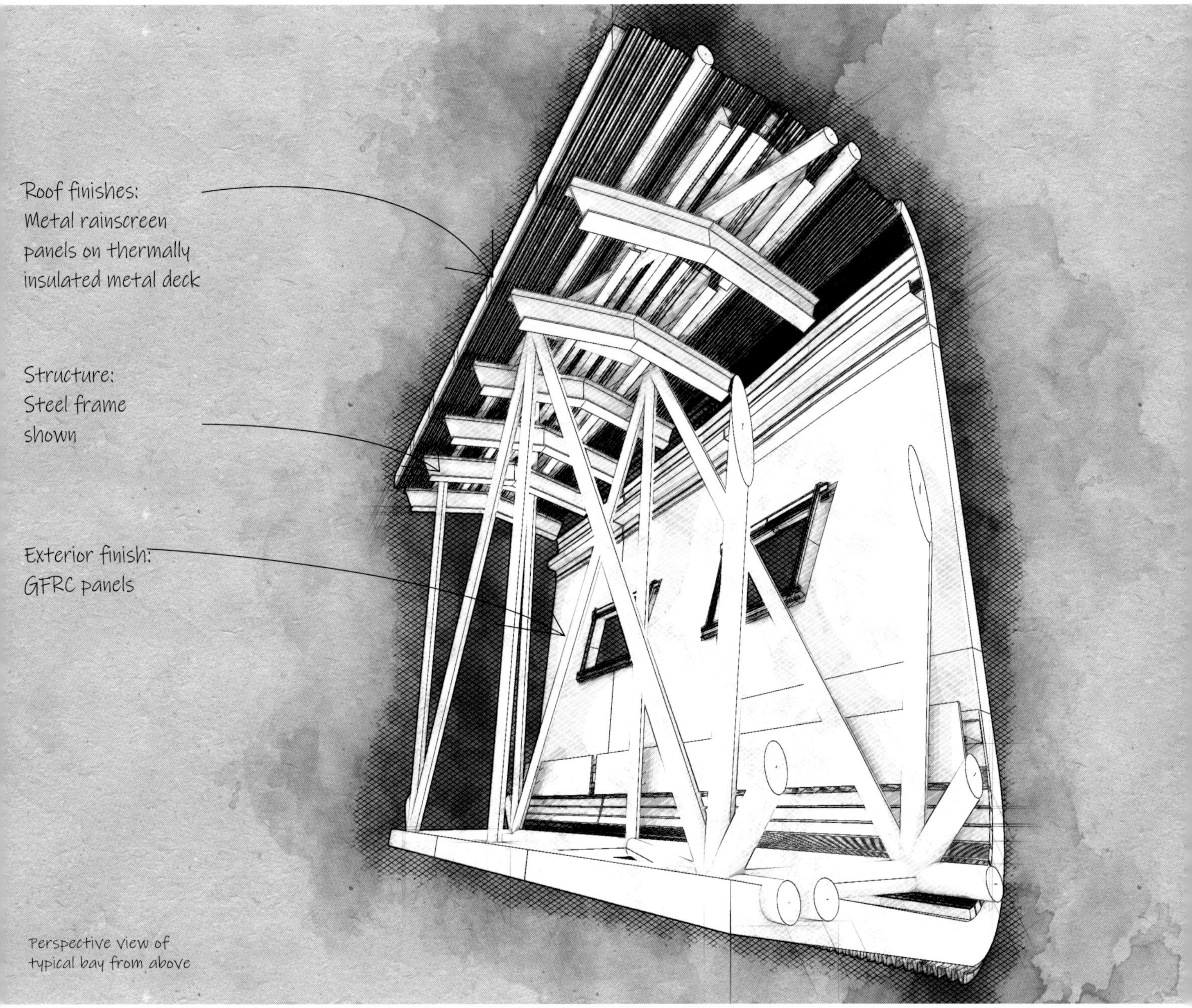

Perspective view of
typical bay from above

the facades is also prefabricated and is fixed to the primary structure within the depth of the structural zone. Ceilings are exposed within the building, with services fixed directly to the underside of the composite decks and short hangers to allow air conditioning ducts, electrical and water supply to be fixed directly. This avoids the need for suspended ceilings. The use of prefabricated backing walls is repeated in the main partitions inside the building in dividing the service spaces from the activity spaces, comprising the walls that surround the cores.

The typical bay integrates the environmental grid of the building which is generated by the electrical lighting installation, and the passage of ducted air which is projected into the space from the core areas. This is done in preference to using a structural grid to organise the design. The environmental grid is then applied to the structural grid such that distances between columns are established from the need to reduce electrical lighting and support ducts, rather than to optimise for the depth of structural beams. In this project, the primary purpose of the design of the typical bay is to create a clear space within the building which is uninterrupted by the need for ceiling-supplied services. The cores distribute air vertically and then project air horizontally across floor plates. This creates two types of typical bay; one with clear space and the other which is entirely services-oriented in distributing vertically from the roof level down and introduced externally through voids in the facade panels. This approach allows services that may need ducted air to enter the building as a result of already being within the external envelope which projects from the building. This approach also avoids the need for interfaces between services and facades, as each projecting core in the building creates its own external wall area protected externally by metal rainscreen panels. Ducted services are thermally insulated around the assemblies themselves rather than requiring the use of an external envelope to create that thermally insulated zone. This approach avoids the risk of interstitial condensation occurring within the walk-in services area inside the envelope zone; the services area is naturally ventilated to the outside of the building.

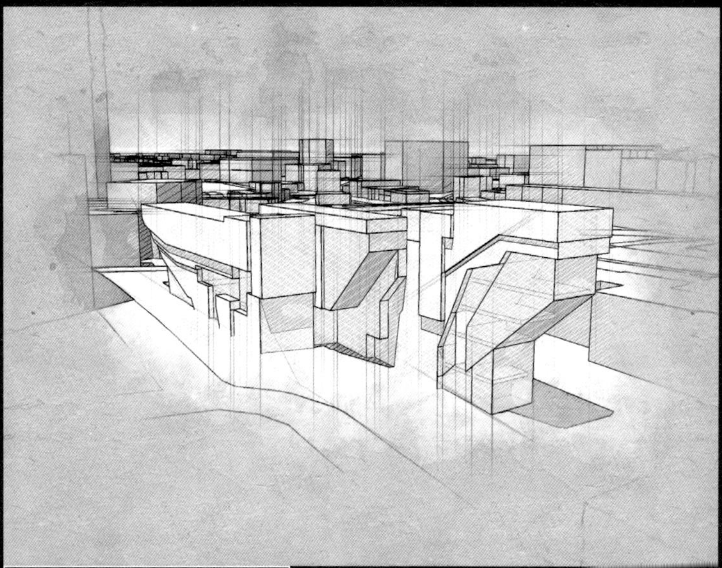

1. Perspective view of exterior

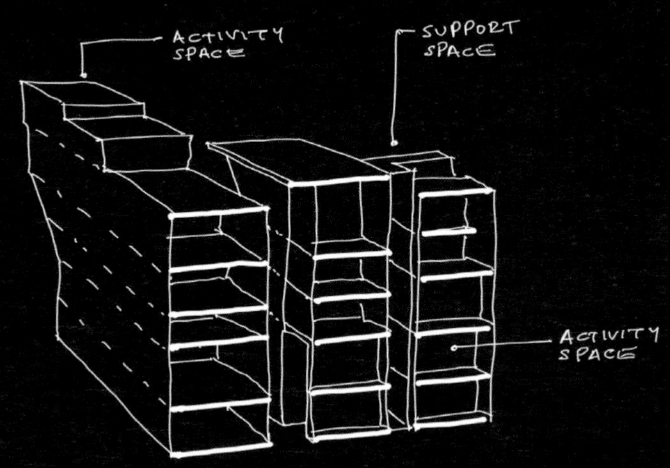

2. Perspective view of exterior

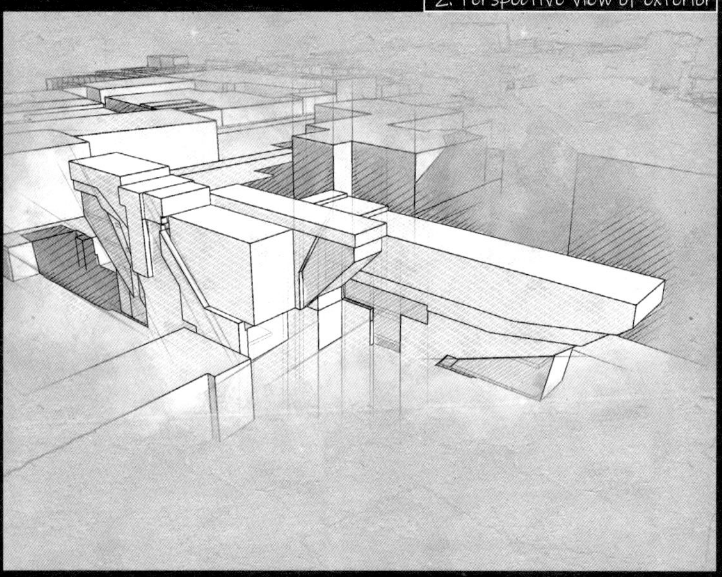

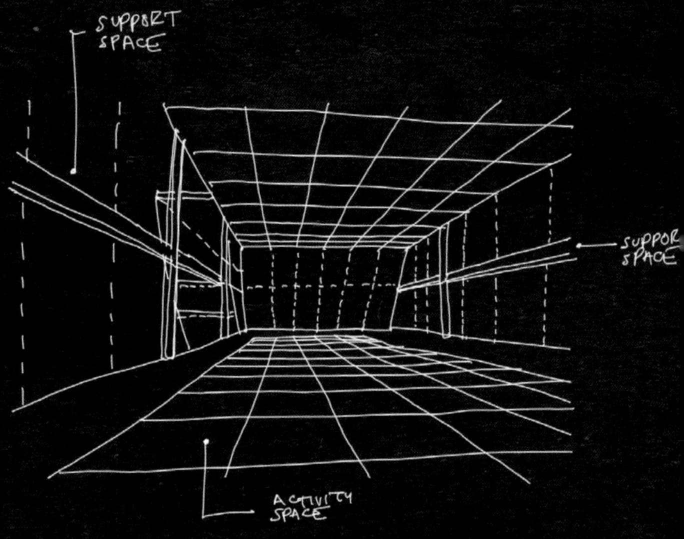

Environmental design for public space

The provision of public space was a key requirement for this space in order to replace an open grassed area that was lost as a result of the construction of the building. This new public space extends beyond the ground level; parts of the building are also accessible to students and staff. Space for seating and repose extends beyond the ground floor reception and its associated facilities. A large public space extends up through the height of the building to form a vertically arranged sculpture court in each of the two outer blocks. These internal sculpture courts are set within a circulation route in each of the two inclined building forms. The public space continues beyond the external walls of each block, beneath the overhanging soffits of the upper floors and into the grassed space surrounding the three constituent volumes of the building. The inclined forms provide a canopy for sculptures which are also arranged outside the building. Students are encouraged to move among these sculpted forms beneath the canopy; an active participation is intended between sculptures, people, walls and canopy. Seating forms part of the sculpture court, which offers participation where people might sit among the sculpture, both 'groups' of participants being set against the visual 'backdrop' of the external walls and canopy. The projecting form above the sculptures, together with the end wall of the building beneath the canopy, form an 'outdoor room' offering active participation for visitors. This is not residual space, but forms part of a set of ground-level sculpture courts linked to vertically arranged spaces for the display of sculpture in order to create a public domain for interaction with sculpture that is arranged both 'vertically' within the building and horizontally outside the building. Canopies are set within a seating arrangement around the sculpture displayed externally; these outdoor spaces marking the perimeter of the site.

The public space surrounding the building is formed without the need for enclosed courtyards, nor is there a single focus within the external space, such as a lawn in front of a single entrance to the building, for example. Instead, this building has a less formal arrangement of linked 'blocks', each with their own entrance. Each block has an associated

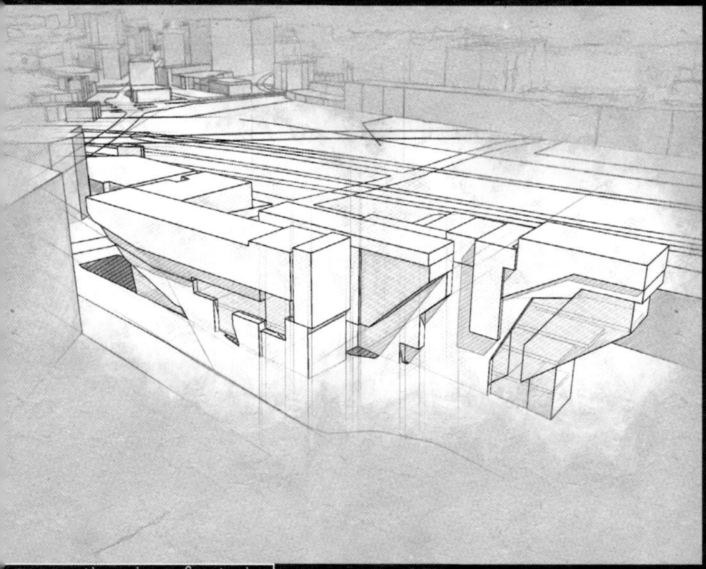

Perspective view of exterior

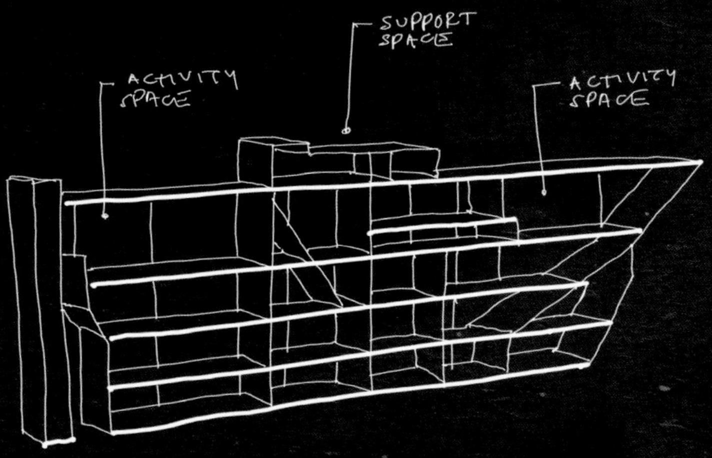

4. Perspective view of exterior

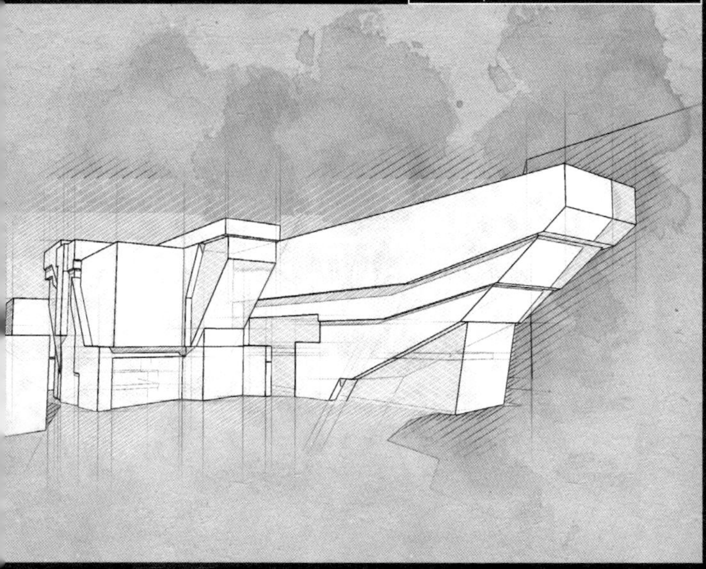

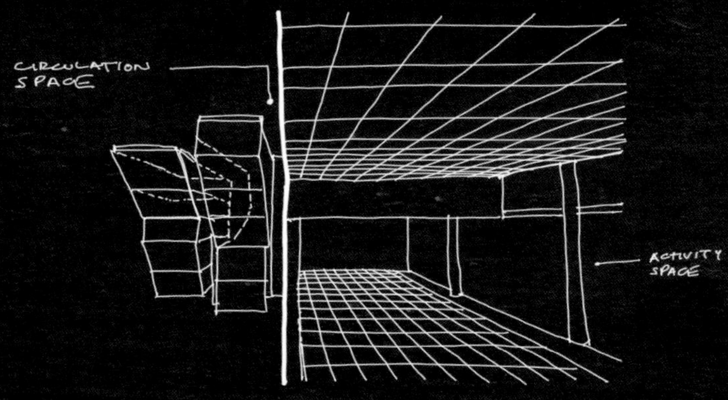

open space surrounding it, creating a set of public spaces by establishing pockets of rectilinear space which extend out from the multiple building entrances. Spaces extend out to the corners of the open site; corners are marked by and inhabited by sculptures which create a visual frame around the building.

The sculptures set around the building are arranged with either 'backdrop' walls, low level walls or screens which create a sense of place; a sense of partial enclosure that goes beyond the 'outdoor room' concept by creating an outside domain which can be inhabited and which can be framed by the building's external walls. Both building users and passers-by can enter a set of small public spaces; interacting with the sculptures. People within these spaces can be seen by other visitors or passers-by as interacting with the sculpture. Visitors can be seen sitting next to, standing alongside, or walking past sculptures which bring a dynamism to each public space, almost as if the sculptures are moving among the temporary inhabitants of the space. This sense of dynamism creates a set of small-scale public spaces which surround the building; a contrast with the expectation on campus of public space being mainly open-grassed areas. The public domain both outside and inside this building forms an extension or a continuation of the architectural language of the building; enclosing both the building and its public spaces with a single language of materials and form. This single architectural language frames activities within the building and within this external domain by removing barriers between public space and the volumes that comprise the three constituent parts of the building.

The public space forms an extension of the building by positioning sculptures to inhabit the external areas as well as to continue them within as a vertically arranged sculpture court, continuing the experience of public space into the building. Sculptures continue to be framed by the same visual language of 'backdrop' walls as those used in the external walls of the building. The outside domain of this project is created by replacing a previously open grass space, providing protection from wind and sun at different times of year through the provision of screens and canopies which are inhabited by sculpture.

1. Project volume in site context

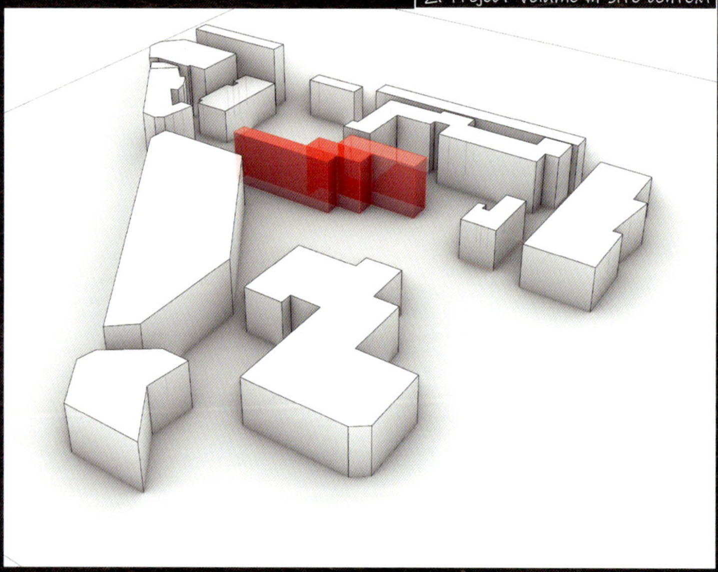

2. Project volume in site context

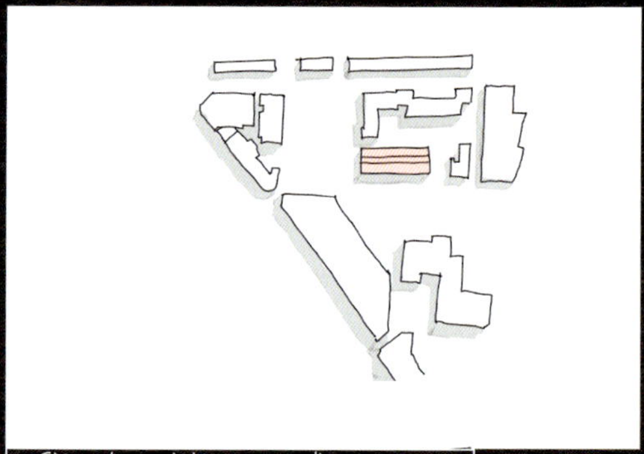

1. Site plan with surrounding context

Option 1 creates a box-like form with an external space within its perimeter.

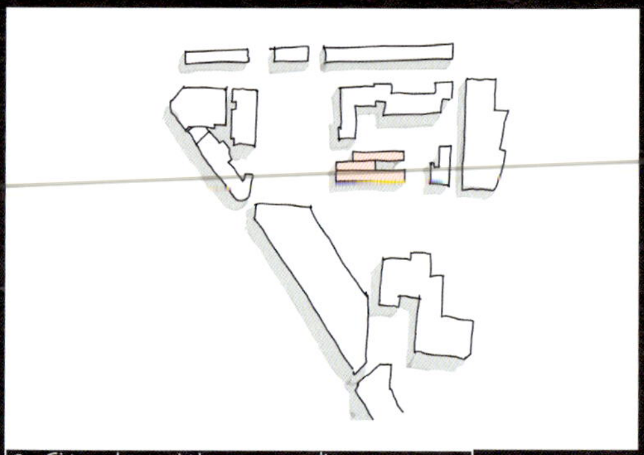

2. Site plan with surrounding context

Option 2 forms two separate wings with a central space aligned with one of the wings.

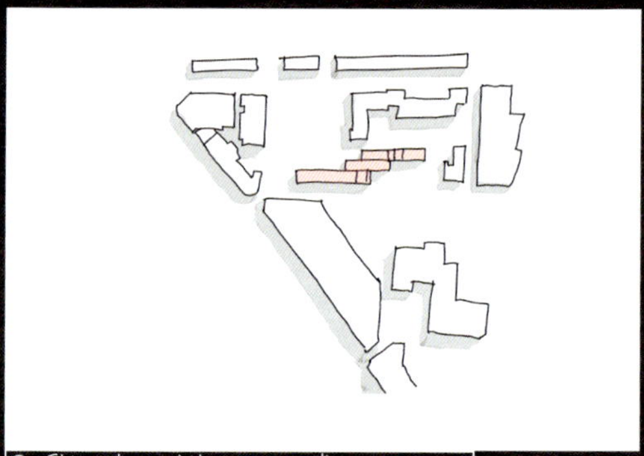

3. Site plan with surrounding context

Option 3 offsets, from each other, all three of the primary volumes.

Site context

The context of the building is a university teaching campus where adjacent buildings are of similar volume and height. Surrounding buildings fit well together visually, but communicate little of the spaces enclosed within their walls. This project responds to its site context by revealing the volumes within the building as external forms which are largely opaque, and which could be observed and recognised by those walking past the building.

The 'differentiated' forms that comprise the building can also allow its occupants to form an intuitive understanding of the organisation of spaces without the need for an internal central volume that would provide a sense of spatial orientation. The approach of differentiating internal volumes with external forms helps to communicate some of what is taking place inside without the need for highly glazed facades. The design also aims to avoid the need for large areas of undifferentiated opaque facades, which would not interact with the site context of the surrounding academic buildings and facilities. The sculpture courts, set at each end of the building, create a strong link between the forms that comprise the building and its neighbours. This building expresses form through some of the spatial volumes within; lecture theatres with their classic seating arrangement are expressed as wedge-shaped volumes, for example. Positions of staircases can be seen through partially glazed facades which are set between projecting forms of adjacent teaching spaces. Research spaces, arranged in open tiers, are identified by glazed openings which are set on each side of the building; these spaces are juxtaposed with the forms of opaque-walled lecture theatres and their associated spaces for access.

Circulation occurs between the three blocks that serve the lecture theatres, research spaces and offices within each of the two outer blocks. The form with the longest of the cantilevered lecture theatres has office spaces arranged on one of the side elevations, some of which are opaque in order to accommodate workshops and are arranged as individual forms within the overall facade compositions. Other areas of opaque wall and roof accommodate services equipment which is dis-

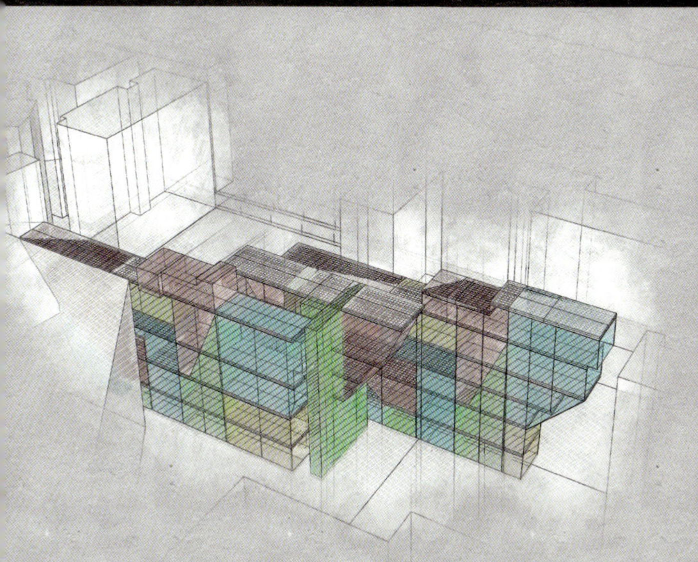

Perspective view of environmental volumes

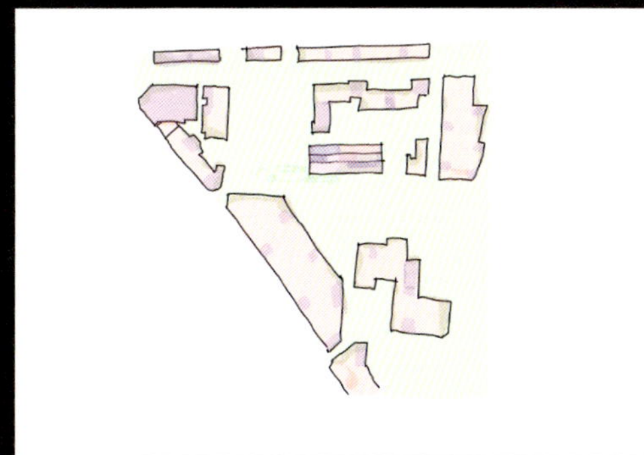

1. Figure-ground diagram of tempered environment

Option 1
Dark violet spaces are highly tempered.

2. Perspective view of environmental volumes

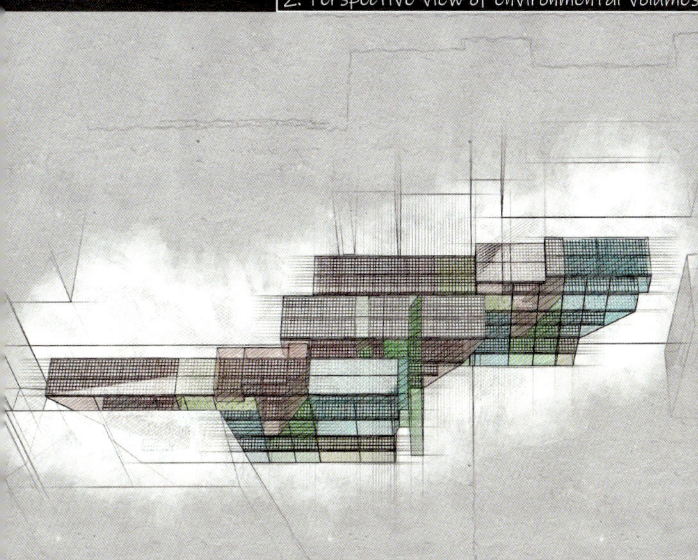

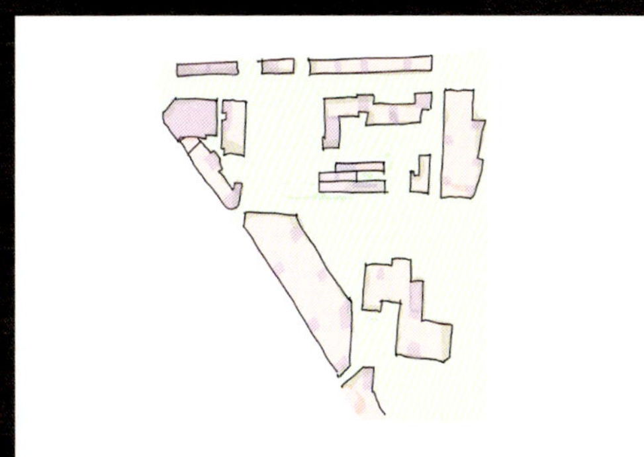

2. Figure-ground diagram of tempered environment

Option 2
Light violet spaces are less tempered than dark violet spaces spaces.

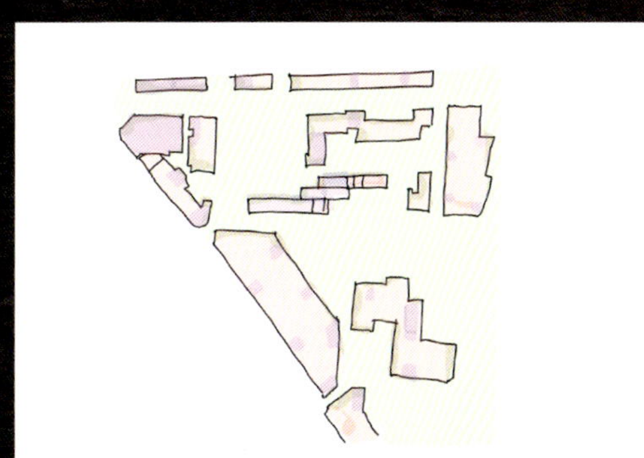

3. Figure-ground diagram of tempered environment

Option 3
Red spaces are the least tempered spaces. these spaces interface directly with external space.

tributed from roof level in each of the three blocks down, to the spaces beneath. The building occupies a site which was previously used as a diagonal pedestrian route across the site, on which no buildings had previously been constructed. The site has been used as an open-grassed area within the campus. The new building replaced that amenity with pockets of public space that form part of the set of forms that comprise the building. These courts create points of interaction between buildings, sculpture and people with four seating areas set around the building. These four focal points have artworks arranged among the seating within the same space; some of the sculptures occupy part of the seating itself. The exhibit spaces draw people into focused spaces that are created for their use. This arrangement reflects the use of the existing open-grassed space, where small groups would gather separately from other groups around them. Those informal areas of focus for people to sit together has been replaced with a more structured set of spaces that bring the advantages of greater social interaction within the sculpture courts, framed by the external walls of the new building. The newly formed site context allows people to walk past the buildings and interact with these semi-formal public spaces; bringing people closer to the new building with its seating areas and art exhibits. The site context of the set of materials used for the facades of adjacent buildings is continued in this project; the external forms making use of the key materials used in adjacent academic buildings. This approach of continuity of the use of materials allows the design to reflect the changes and developments in the technology of each of those construction materials in the years since the campus was first developed. The way that materials are fabricated, prepared and fixed are in constant development, both in terms of their workmanship and towards the more economical use of energy in their fabrication and installation. This technical development is applied to this building, which uses smaller components and panels than was the case in some earlier buildings in order to reduce the energy requrement for their manufacture, delivery to site and installation; smaller wall panels reflect that change to smaller-scale components with associated energy savings.

1. Sectional perspective view

2. Sectional perspective view

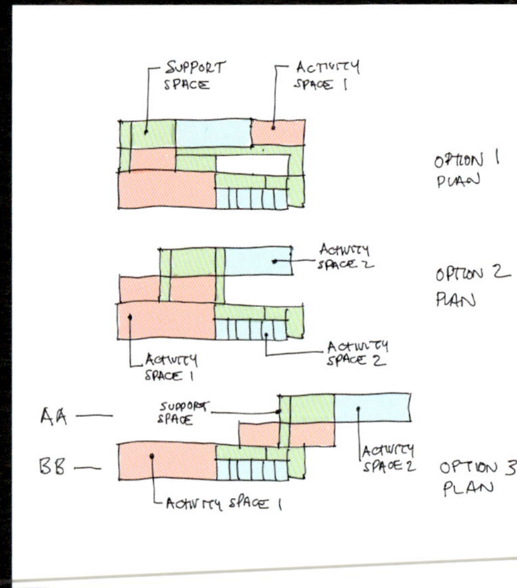

Option 1 organises space around the open courtyard, with activity spaces separated from one another.

Option 2 has two separate wings that provide more daylight and natural ventilation.

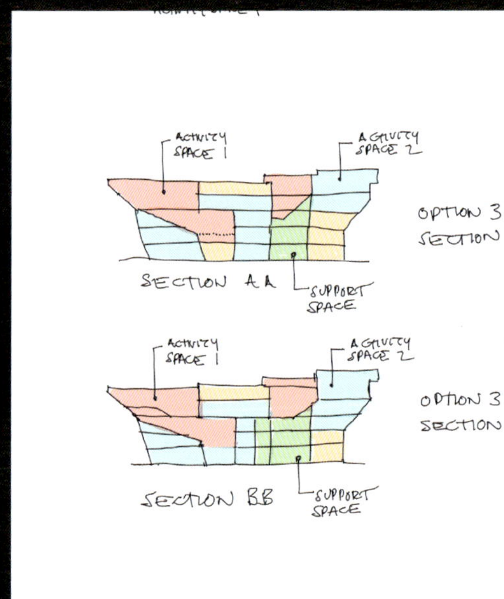

Option 3 offsets, from each other, all activity spaces.

Spatial arrangement

The spatial arrangement is driven by lecture theatres such that these volumes, which are expressed on the outside of the building, occupy the inclined parts of each block. The approach of reflecting the shape of internal forms on the outside of the building creates an opportunity for a canopied external space to be provided at each end of the building; space which is occupied by sculpture courts. This approach of modelling the external forms of the building allows both the form of the lecture theatre and the external space it creates to be clearly visible from outside the building. The overall organisation of spaces within the building is visible to both occupants and visitors; the external forms are arranged in order to allow the general spatial arrangement of internal spaces to be as clear as possible from outside of the building. This approach provides the opportunity for the spatial arrangement to drive the visual expression of the forms of the building; providing the opportunity for a clear differentiation between spaces seen as opaque volumes externally and spaces which are seen as glazed open spaces within the building. This arrangement forms the basis of the environmental strategy; the blocks are arranged as three intersecting volumes which are then linked together in order to reduce the amount of external envelope. In this disposition of volumes, internal circulation spaces are integrated within the overall form of the building rather than being expressed on the facades. The forms which are expressed on the outside of the building are the main spaces, not areas of circulation. This spatial arrangement within the building avoids an ambiguity in the relationship between what is expressed as a spatial arrangement on the outside of the building, and what is experienced within the building; external forms and internal spaces correspond with each other. The building comprises five lecture theatres of different size, with teaching rooms arranged between them; research spaces occupy the other volumes which are expressed in the external envelope of the building. The lecture theatres are accommodated in the opaque volumes; the research spaces have partially glazed walls which are arranged in tiers to reflect the internal arrangement of these spaces.

Perspective view of interior

2. Perspective view of interior

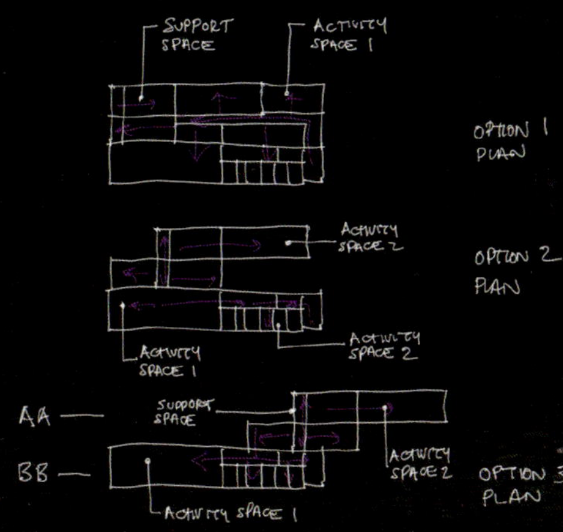

Internal circulation

Option 1 has circulation spaces extending throughout the building.

Option 2 has two separate wings in order to reduce circulation space.

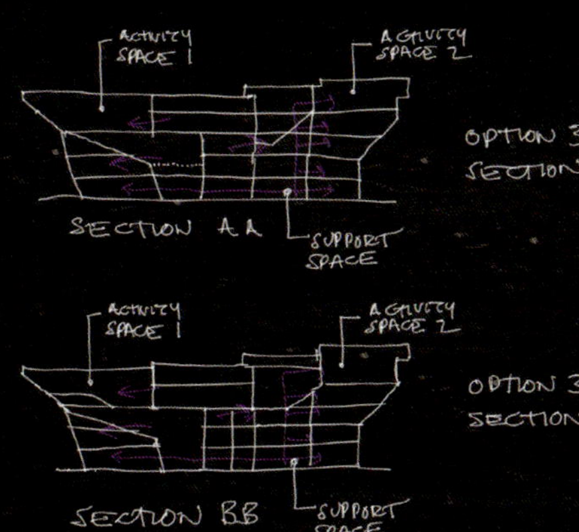

Option 3 reduces circulation spaces when compared with the other options.

Internal circulation

Circulation spaces traverse the width of the building and are linked by by corridors extending the length of the spatial arrangement. Circulation areas use their enclosing walls to accommodate showcases for displays related to the teaching and research activities being carried out in the department. This building expresses the activities within through the geometry of the form and through a mixture of glazed and opaque spaces; movement of people within the building is not expressed visually on the facades, as circulation spaces occupy interstitial spaces between them. The widths of the three blocks comprising the building are too narrow for a circulation route to be added to the sides of spaces. Instead, most of the larger spaces occupy the full width of the building. The spatial organisation results in circulation routes crossing the width of the building; movement around the building being distributed to adjacent spaces with only a short distance to be travelled down each corridor. Staircases, lifts/elevators and washrooms are arranged in support 'blocks' that extend the width of the building and which are divided by the circulation routes, which extend the length of each part of the building. Internal circulation routes are daylit from borrowed light taken from adjacent teaching spaces, as they are all internal routes; only at the highest floor is daylight fully admitted, allowing it to be drawn down into the circulation spaces on lower levels. This approach avoids glazed walls in circulation spaces with their associated energy cost in tempering these environments; some electrical lighting is needed during daylight hours in circulation spaces. The energy cost of electrical lighting to supplement daylight is lower than the equivalent cost of heating and cooling energy that would have been needed if glazed facades and a glazed roof were used in an arrangement of internal circulation set adjacent to external walls. The borrowed daylight from adjacent classrooms provides a continuity and relatively even levels of daylight throughout the circulation spaces. The daylight within circulation spaces allows some of the geometry of the internal spaces to be revealed through their enclosing walls. Circulation routes form space between lecture theatres rather than being residual spaces.

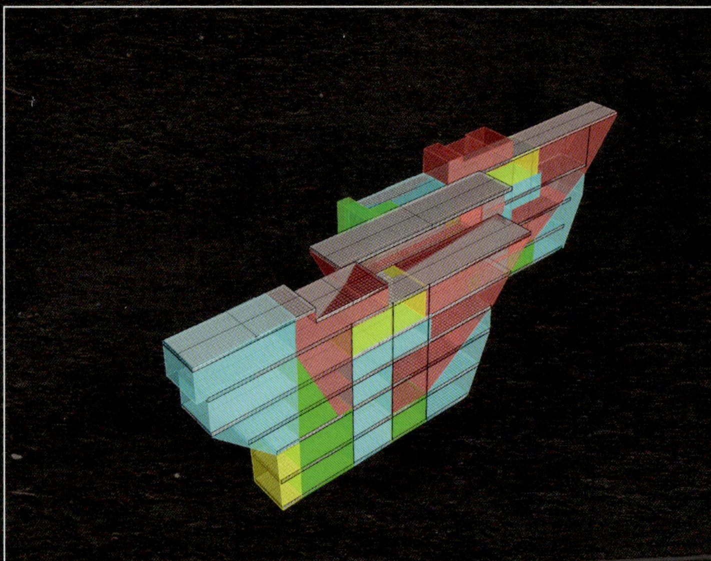

1A. Isometric view of environmental volumes

1B. Isometric view of environmental volumes

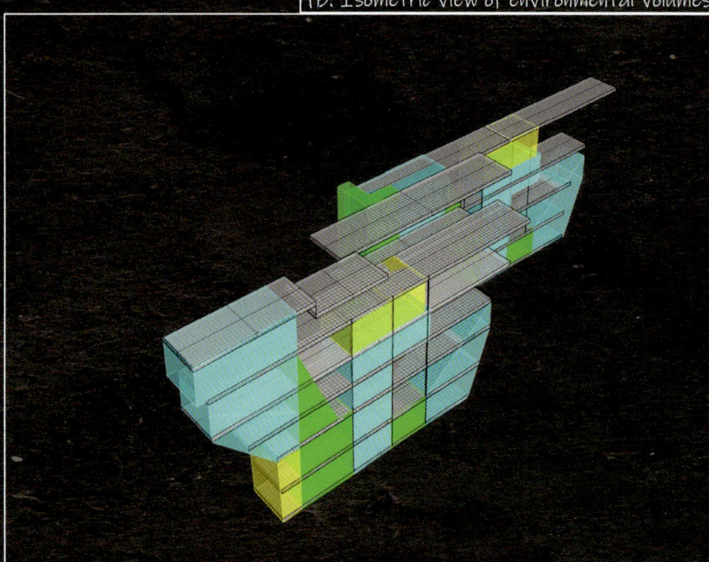

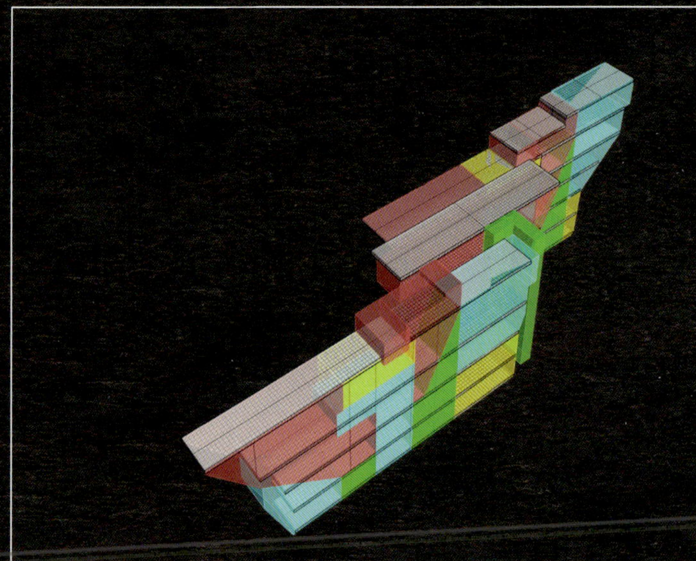

2A. Isometric view of environmental volumes

2B. Isometric view of environmental volum

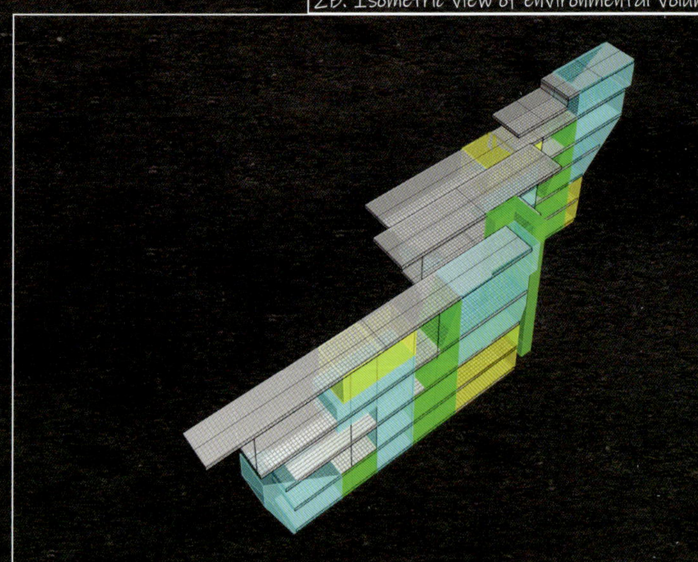

Environmental strategy

The environmental strategy is one of considering each of the three blocks as an independent building, such that the heating, cooling and ventilation requirements between the lecture theatres and the adjacent research spaces are shared. When the lecture spaces are not in use the system does not supply air to those volumes, instead distributing to adjacent areas occupied by students and staff, such as work rooms. This approach is based on the distribution of ducted air to spaces based on occupancy requirements at different times, in order for the building to be operated efficiently from the point of view of energy consumption. Spaces outside the lecture theatres, including the open space research areas, are naturally ventilated where possible from the sides through glazing which has electrically operated opening windows. The projecting blocks of lecture and meeting space at each end of the building have both opaque and glazed panels in the external walls to admit fresh air into those spaces. Opaque panels open into a void from which air is drawn through ducts into each of the lecture theatres.; their use changing with the seasons. Mechanical services are roof-mounted and are distributed down opaque external walls within ducts and behind the facade panels, which are part of these structures and partly enclosures for the distribution of services around the building. The environmental strategy is one of creating more thermally insulated spaces to the opaque volumes than behind the glazed areas. This approach allows the distribution of opaque walls and glazed walls to be brought into a balance that ensures less energy is used to operate the building for heating and cooling than would be the case if a more glazed approach were taken to the external envelope. The environmental strategy is driven by the forms of the external envelope, which ensure high levels of thermal insulation in spaces which are only periodically used: primarily lecture theatres, which are fully enclosed in the classic manner in order to provide a closed space for audio-visual and slide presentations for teaching. The enclosed nature of lecture theatres results in ducted air being required in these spaces, but which can be redirected to internal circulation spaces as well as to the research

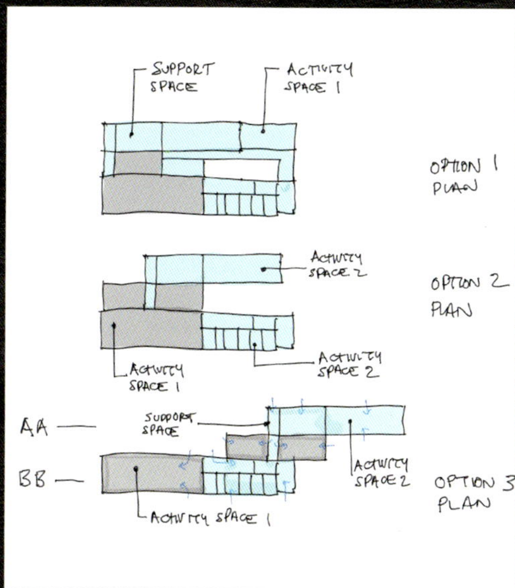

Daylight strategy for direct sunlight and cross ventilation.
Option 1 admits daylight and air on only one side of each internal space.
Option 2 admits daylight and air on only one side of almost all internal spaces.

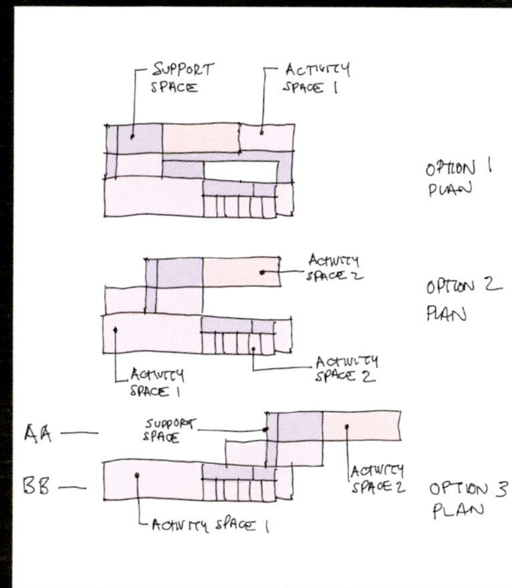

Environmental zones
Option 1 creates eight environmental zones.
Option 2 creates seven environmental zones.

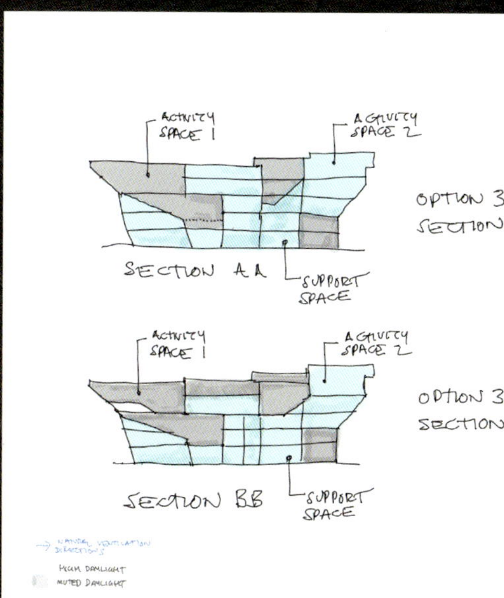

Daylight strategy for direct sunlight and cross ventilation.
Option 3 admits daylight and air on two sides of almost all internal spaces.

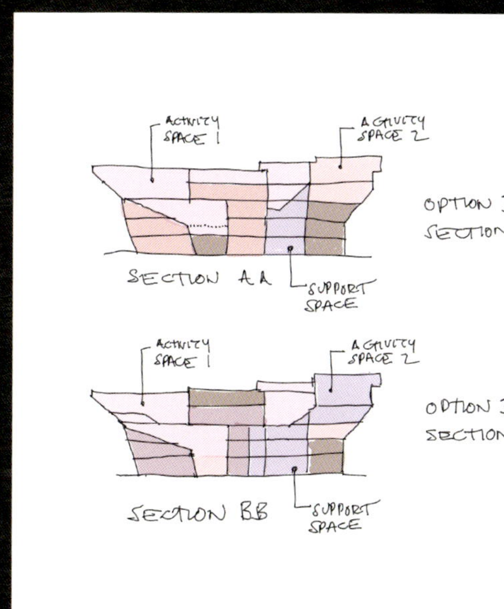

Environmental zones
Option 3 is formed as six environmental zones, the lowest number of all options.

spaces which form open terraces of work areas. This approach allows ducted air to be recirculated with a heat recovery system in order to reduce the energy requirement. Option 3 considers the building as a set of small-scale environmental zones in order to accommodate the different activities within each environmental zone, all of which have different functions, occupancy levels and frequencies of use. The flexibility of distributing air and services between the different environmental zones encourages a reduction of energy consumption as a result of each zone functioning separately, and independently of its of its neighbours.

Daylight is admitted to the research spaces, offices and workshops with relatively small amounts of glazing in order to create an intimate working atmosphere within each of the environmental zones which correspond to the volumes as seen from outside the building. The environmental strategy embraces natural daylight within the building as well as having a priority of reducing the energy required for heating and cooling. Daylight provision to working spaces for research and for office and administration is such that electrical lighting is not generally required during hours of daylight as a result of the use of light shelves and clear glazing. The areas of opening window and fixed glazed slots are smaller than would otherwise be the case because of the use of clear glass, protected by solar shading, which is provided by a light shelf set on the top edge of glazed openings in order to provide protection from the effects of the sun while still admitting levels of daylight required in those spaces.

The outside faces of these opaque walls have services fixed to the outside which, in part, form the low-relief language of these indented opaque facades. Other opaque facades accommodate large-sized teaching rooms within the building. The external sculpture courts are continued inside the building adjacent to research spaces. These public spaces are semi-external, forming an environmental buffer zone between the main spaces of activity and the outside of the building. The glazed areas of facade do not achieve the levels of thermal insulation of the opaque facades, so are designed as a semi-external environment.

1A. Isometric view of structure

1B. Isometric view of structure

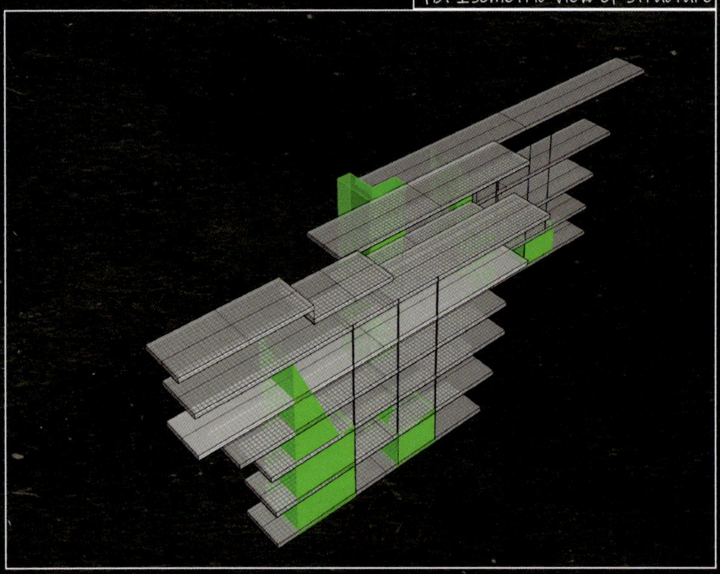

2A. Isometric view of structure

2B. Isometric view of structur

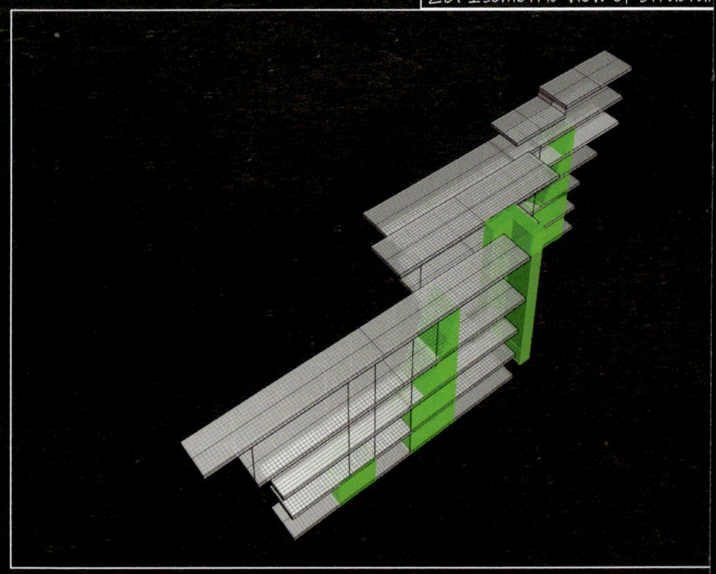

Structural strategy

The structural strategy is based on a steel-framed skeleton which makes use of triangulated framing behind opaque envelope panels, with framing within glazed facades following the joint lines between panels. The panelisation of the glazing is not rectilinear; the framing that supports the glazing supports the edges of glazed panels which are often not vertical. Inside the building, columns are vertical. In some areas the primary structural steel follows that same arrangement of joints such that the framing for the all three buildings forms a single frame with triangulated members which is neither visible on the outside of the building nor from the inside.

Steel members are so arranged in order to form a continuous steel frame which integrates primary and secondary steelwork to create the characteristic shapes of the building, as seen both from the outside and inside the main interior spaces. Steel was considered to be more economical than an equivalent reinforced concrete frame as opaque walls were not required to have exposed concrete surfaces that would have allowed the use of concrete to be economical. Instead, the facades are faced in GFRC (glass fibre reinforced concrete) panels which are fixed directly to the primary steel structure. The steel frame is clad in thermally insulated lightweight backing panels. The internal walls are dry lined. The primary structure provides support for the glazed areas along primary lines of structure in order to avoid the need for secondary steelwork to that would support the glass only. This approach allowed a visual differentiation to be created between primary glazed areas and secondary glazed areas where the framing for the glass is set within bays of glazing. These components form large-scale windows rather than the small-scale type more commonly used. This allows the arrangement of glazing to be economical as a result of using structural members which form a part of the primary structural frame.

Cores set within the building are formed within a grid of steel columns with non-loadbearing, light-gauge steel framing set between them to provide wall enclosures. Openings in the reinforced concrete floors are framed by steel columns and beams to support staircases and open-

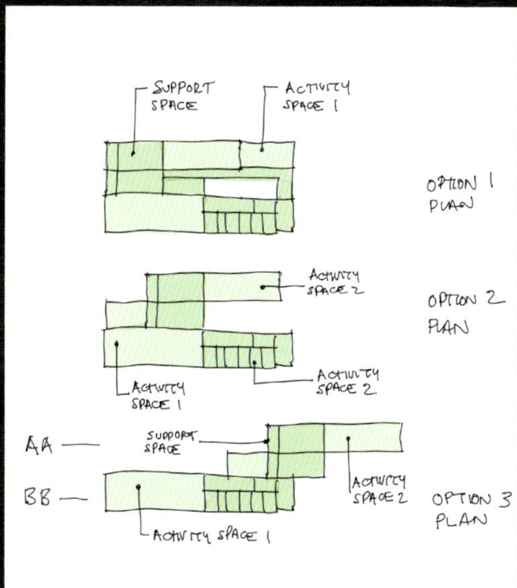

Structural strategy: Zones

Option 1 has a rectilinear structural frame.

Structural strategy: Zones

Option 2 has frames divided to suit the geometry.

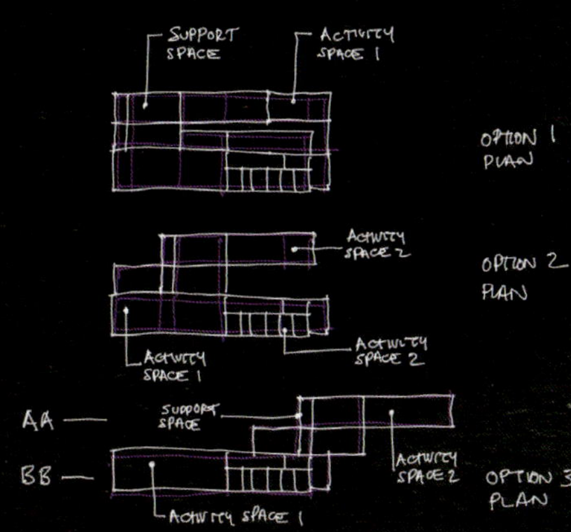

Structural strategy: Framing

Option 1 encloses the core spaces and dividing space into sets of spaces.

Option 2 is largely a steel frame.

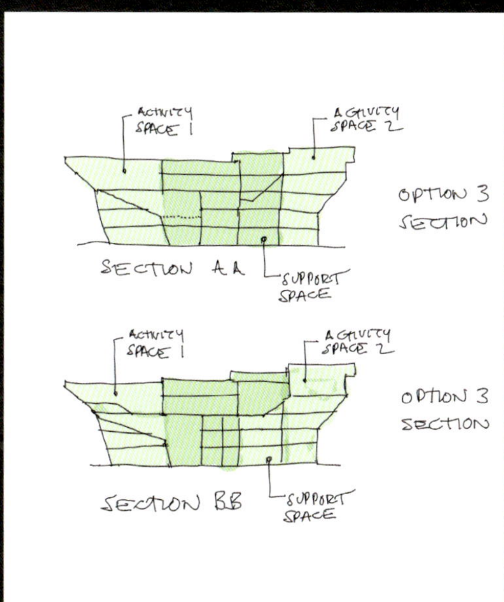

Structural strategy: Zones

Option 3 has frames divided to suit the geometry.

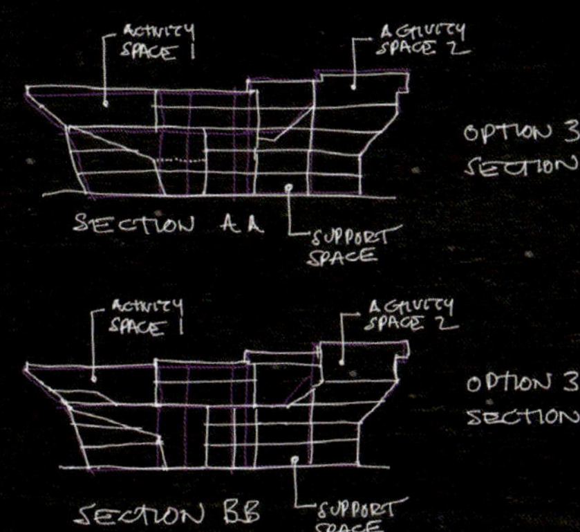

Structural strategy: Zones

Option 3 is a mixed solution of reinforced concrete and steel.

ings in slabs for the passage of services. Ducts for air handling are fixed to the steel structural members that support facade panels. Ducts are distributed across the outside of the building, passing through the lightweight backing walls which are formed to allow services to pass through into the building. The use of non-structural backing wall panels provides an economical solution to the passage of ducts through the external wall. The structure is an economical frame that economically supports both backing walls and cladding panels. The steel frame has more steelwork in areas that support the facades and in areas around the cores in order to provide a structural system that allows the facades and the cores to be enclosed economically. Consequently, there is no regular structural grid as the steelwork responds to the needs of forming support for the enclosures of the building.

The structure is not revealed within the building except as framing to the glazed areas of facade; these areas of exposed steelwork have a mixture of intumescent paint protection and fire-resistant board. The structure is conceived to frame the volumes which enclose the building both externally and internally. This strategy is followed in order to ensure that the structure provides an efficient support for external walls and internal finishes, with a minimum of secondary framework for the facades and for the internal walls.

This approach results in a hybrid solution of primary structural members and pressed steel sections used to reduce the quantity of materials required for the construction of the structural frame. This approach requires close dimensional coordination at an early stage of the project in order for fixing requirements of those systems to be integrated, while still ensuring a flexibility in the final arrangement of both facades and internal walls.

The structural strategy benefits from the use of smaller-scale framing members to create a large-scale frame that describes the geometry of the building. This avoids the need for different scales of construction of having large-scale equipment for the primary frame and then scaffolding for the secondary assemblies; installation for the facades and roof proceeds from temporary platforms as installation progresses.

Perspective view of typical bay from below

Typical bay adjacent to facade

The external envelope comprises non-rectilinear double-glazed units forming areas of glazed wall which are enclosed in triangular volumes. Some are semi-transparent; others are fully clear-glazed with solar shading canopies attached externally. Other parts of the glazing are fixed back to framing that follows the non-rectilinear shape of the glazing, fixed back to the primary structure, forming a dense frame of triangulated members to create the characteristic forms of the building. Opaque panels are made from lightweight concrete panels which provide both the required durability and which follow the facade language of adjacent parts of the university campus.

At an early stage of the project, the use of a steel frame with a mix of primary structural members and secondary light-gauge steel members ensured that a high degree of efficiency was introduced in the use of material. The resulting design is one where the joints between panels on both the facade and on the interior wall finishes are closely coordinated with one another in order to share the fixing points of both external and internal systems. The structural system which combines primary and secondary steelwork supports both the glazing and the externally positioned air handling ducts and electrical supplies to most internal spaces. This approach to the external envelope which forms a typical bay is used throughout the building; the approach with the external envelope in relation to a typical bay is to have the different scales of steelwork within a single depth of structure, which allows the light-gauge steelwork to be integrated within the depth of the primary steelwork, reducing the facade zone to a practical minimum; the facade zone is optimised for depth in order to optimise costs. The projecting part of the facades as seen from outside of the building is both a visual expression of the distribution of services behind the opaque facade panels, while also revealing the framing supporting the glazing. The two parts of the steelwork are integrated so that the services can all be set on the outside of the building.

The narrow width of the building does not allow for circulation zones to be added to the sides of the building, resulting in a single circulation

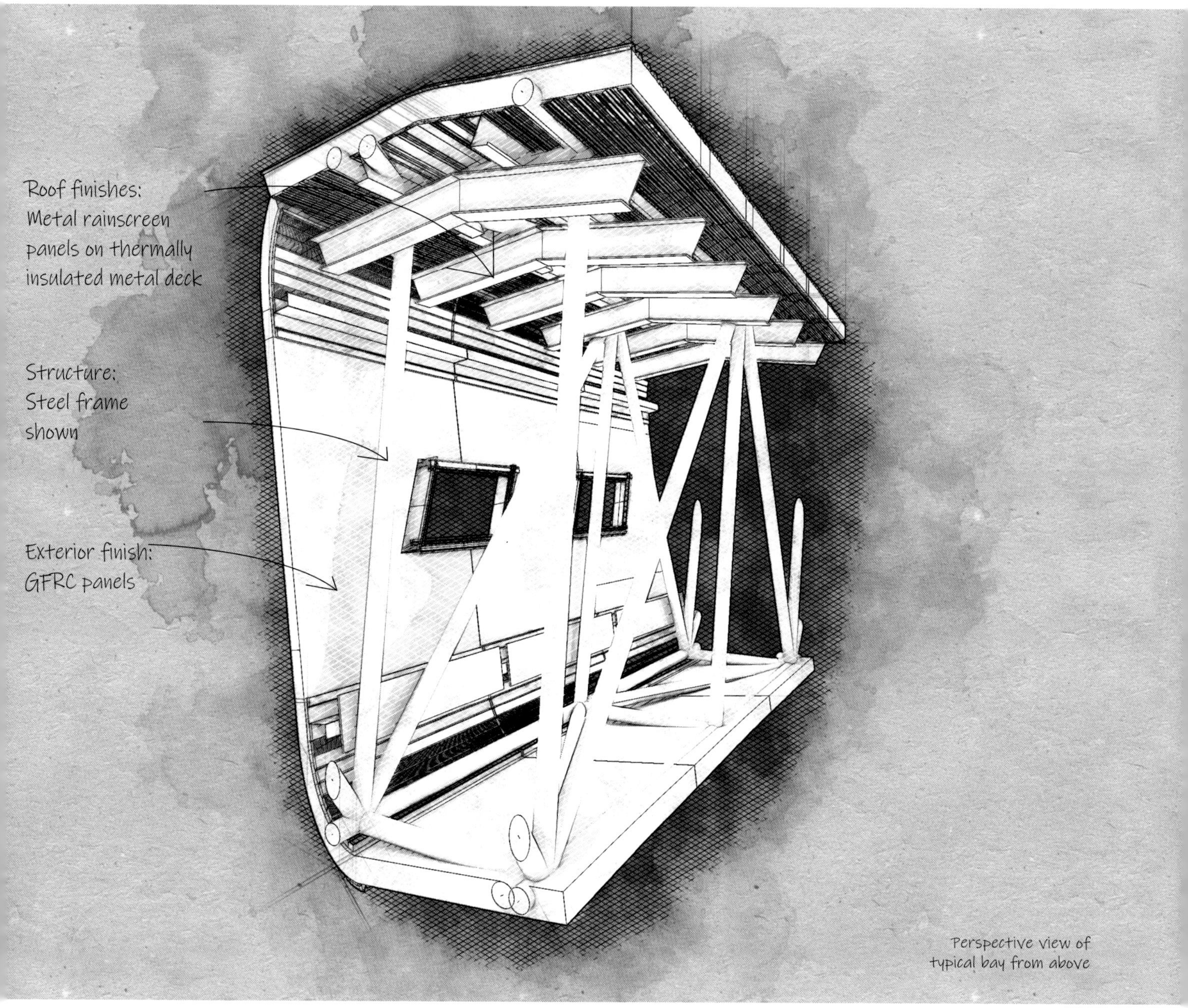

Perspective view of typical bay from above

zone extending down the centre of the building. The layout of the building is such that there are no circulation zones set between each of the three blocks; they are not needed as a result of the circulation traversing the width of the building rather than primarily running through its length. This arrangement follows from the need to have a closely formed set of linked spaces and volumes which reduce the area of the external walls, which are highly thermally insulated.

This approach reduces the energy required both to construct and to operate the building by bringing the volumes of space closer together without intermediary service spaces or more generous zones for internal circulation. The design does not require circulation spaces with glazed end walls that would require tempered air to heat or cool those transition spaces. The building is an expression of a tightly arranged set of volumes where the extensive opaque facades are modelled through the use of varying facade depths that are necessary for the passage of air-handling ducts and services on the outside of the building. The approach of a mixed structural frame and secondary light-gauge steel members allows for internal built-in furniture such as shelving to be fixed directly to that framing on the inside face of the external wall. This approach allows external walls to integrate storage space, services equipment, shelving and drop-down desks within the inside face of the walls in offices.

This approach to the external envelope allows the building to have its external surfaces 'shrink-wrapped' to reduce the surface of the building, for the purposes of energy efficiency. While this strategy may increase the costs of the external envelope when compared to a rectilinear building form with flat facades, the environmental installation requires little space within the building for the vertical distribution of services, nor is space required for equipment within the support spaces of the services cores. Support spaces are reduced in scope to enclose stairs, lifts/ elevators and washrooms. Few openings are required in floor slabs, allowing teaching spaces and research rooms to be free of services equipment, with the corresponding benefit of spatial clarity provided by spaces which are closely matched by their external form.

Newtecnic have produced a number of volumes on contemporary building technology which provide reference material for engineering and architecture students and professionals around the world. The Modern Construction Series is published by Birkhäuser Verlag GmbH. In addition, the Facades Technical Review, from RIBA Publications was published in spring 2007.

The text and drawings are by Andrew Watts. The designs and renders are by Andrew Watts and Howard Tee. The book is designed by Yasmin Watts.

David Marold is Acquisitions Editor at Birkhäuser Verlag GmbH in Vienna. He has driven this book from a set of basic layouts to a completed book. He has a passion for books and their design, ranging from their wider content to the quality of print paper, to the overall reader experience.

Andrew Watts an architect and engineer and the author of the Modern Construction series of textbooks. He specialises in the architectural and engineering design of large-scale buildings of complex form. Andrew is a founding director of Newtecnic. He is a Fellow of three UK engineering institutions in recognition of his engineering-based designs; the Institution of Civil Engineers; the Institution of Engineering Designers; the Institution of Engineering and Technology. Andrew holds charterships in the UK for architecture and engineering from the Royal Institute of British Architects and the Institution of Engineering Designers. In the US, he holds an ASCE membership.

Yasmin Watts is a sculptor, architect and creative director of Newtecnic, leading the exploration of links between sculpture, architecture and public art. She is a founding director of the company. Yasmin is focused on creating sculptures in public spaces in the built environment; the fusion of architecture and sculpture has been a key driver in the work behind all the projects shown in this book. She is a registered architect in the UK and is a Fellow of the Royal Society of Arts. Yasmin is continuing her research with the Royal College of Art.

The author would like thank Bettina Algieri for the content and production editing of this book. The author would also like to thank Alun Brown for the task of proofreading the text.

Newtecnic is a world-leading firm of engineering designers and architects led by Andrew Watts, Howard Tee and Yasmin Watts. The Modern Construction series forms an essential part of their research work which informs the design of projects. The Newtecnic approach, based on research from first principles, allows the company to achieve architectural and engineering design solutions for the complete building, from concept to production information, including engineering and architectural design for structure, facades and the internal environment. With 3D BIM, Newtecnic designs models that become highly evolved during the design process. Components of these BIM models, with accompanying text and images to illustrate design processes, form the basis of the Modern Construction Series. The engineering and architectural design skills of Newtecnic allow the firm to communicate, through the Modern Construction series, the key issues of 21st century building engineering and design. Newtecnic are holders of *The Queen's Award for Enterprise* and is ranked in the top three of *New Civil Engineer 100 Companies of the Year 2019.*

Glossary of terms devised for this book

The following expressions used in this book are defined below as working definitions only, and are defined for the purposes of this book only. These terms have been used by the author on projects shown in this book at the early stages of projects among architectural and engineering team designed at Newtecnic. They are not industry-standard terms.

'Activity' space and 'support' space

A key aim of this project is to use the separation between 'activity space', which comprises the main spaces within the building, and 'support' space, which accommodates the technical and vertical circulation spaces. This approach creates zones within a building; typically for 'activity' spaces, or useable spaces, and spaces for the movement of people around a floor plate. 'Support' spaces, or service spaces, are considered here to accommodate stairs, lifts/elevators, washrooms, mechanical and electrical equipment rooms and associated storage space. The spatial arrangements of activity space, support space or circulation space should not reduce their mutual effectiveness.

A **'backpack'** is a set of environmental control equipment, mechanical and electrical installations and associated service equipment which is fixed to the sides of the building, supplied from the roof level. This arrangement is used in preference to locating these installations within dedicated floors of a building or on its roof.

A **'building within a building'** is an architectural concept of having two layers of enclosure which provide a deep facade zone. This zone can be used to accommodate service equipment or internal circulation for example, and provides the opportunity to free internal space from these support functions while also providing opportunities for natural ventilation, controlled daylight and solar shading.

A **'differentiated form'** is one where there is a close interaction between the geometry of the internal space and the external facade or envelope which encloses it. Differentiated forms are those which are differentiated visually on the outside as a result of each volume whose geometry follows closely that of the internal space. An **'integrated form'** is one where interior spaces are independent of the external envelope, such that internal spaces are arranged within a single external envelope. An integrated form combines internal spaces in a way which is not reflected in the visual perception of the volumes from outside the building.

An **'environmental zone'** comprises a space or a group of spaces where a single set of environmental controls are provided. The facade zone, which is considered to be part of the external envelope, can also be considered as an environmental zone or a buffer zone.

An 'environmental buffer zone' is an area or volume within a building which is positioned between the inner spaces and the outside of the building, or alternatively between environmental zones, in order to create an area which is semi-external or semi-internal and may be partially ventilated and partially tempered. A buffer zone reduces the need to provide full air conditioning for example, or full mechanical ventilation or full heating for cooling in an area adjacent to a facade This approach can support the idea of a 'building within a building' from the environmental design point of view.

A **'floor plate'** is the usable area of the floor slabs or floor construction, which excludes the openings created by staircases and services and typically constitutes an 'activity zone'.

A **'kit of parts'** is a set of possibly prefabricated components that may be individual parts of the building as assemblies or as individual components. In the projects shown in this book, building assemblies across structure, envelope and internal environment are coordinated as part of an interlinked set of assemblies.

An **'outdoor room'** is an external space which is defined by the floor and the walls surrounding it. The walls are usually external walls rather than internal walls to form something resembling a courtyard, but which may not be recognised as a specific space other than to provide a continuity from internal spaces to external space; but without a ceiling or roof.

A **'shrink wrap'** describes the tendency for the external volumes of a building to follow closely the internal forms and shapes of the internal spaces, such that they appear to visually shrink-wrap the volumes inside the building, instead of adopting a rectilinear form that is independent of those spaces.

Solar gain is defined here as being the heat energy absorbed, transferred or transmitted into the building. The projects, as described here, control this effect through the use of external shading devices combined with a specific glass type. The types of glass used may be different in each of the individual forms that comprise a single project.

Thermal comfort is defined here as being a range of temperatures and associated relative humidity which is comfortable, as experienced by occupants in going about their normal tasks or routines in the specific internal environment for which thermal comfort is provided. Thermal comfort will be considered to be different in conditions in a gym from those of a desk-based office space, for example.

A **'visual map of spatial functions'** is a visualisation of the spatial arrangement within a building, as experienced visually either from outside the building or within the interior spaces. A set of facades, or alternatively views across open spaces within a building, may provide a visual diagram of where the 'main' spaces are in a building and where the circulation spaces are positioned, such that the building can be understood intuitively by visitors arriving at the building without the need for specific guidance, allowing them to visually take in the overall functions undertaken within the building.

The following bibliography is suggested for further reading, based on the design methods used for the projects in this book.

Construction technologies in architecture

Modern Construction Handbook, 5th edition
Birkhäuser, 2019

Modern Construction Envelopes, 3rd edition
Birkhäuser, 2019

Modern Construction Case Studies, 2nd edition
Birkhäuser, 2019

Environmental design in architecture

Environmental Design Sourcebook: Innovative Ideas for a Sustainable Built Environment
McLean, W., Silver, P.
RIBA Publishing, 2021

Environmental Design: An Introduction for Architects and Engineers
Thomas, R. (editor)
Taylor and Francis, 2005

The Environments of Architecture: Environmental Design in Context
Thomas, R., Garnham, T.
Taylor and Francis, 2007

Energy and Environment in Architecture
Baker, N., Steemers, K.
Taylor and Francis, 2005

The Environmental Design Pocketbook
Pelsmakers, S.
RIBA Publishing, 2015

Sustainable Environmental Design
Rassia, S., Pardalos, P. (editors)
Springer, 2012

Author
Andrew Watts
London, England

Acquisitions Editor: David Marold, Birkhäuser Verlag, Vienna, Austria
Content & Production Editor: Bettina R. Algieri, Birkhäuser Verlag, Vienna, Austria

Layout: Yasmin Watts, London, England
Cover design: Floyd Schulze

Proofreading: Alun Brown, Vienna, Austria
Printing and binding: Holzhausen, die Buchmarke der Gerin Druck GmbH, Wolkersdorf, Austria

Library of Congress Control Number: 2021936964

Bibliographic information published by the German National Library
The German National Library lists this publication in the Deutsche Nationalbibliografie; detailed bibliographic data are available on the Internet at http://dnb.dnb.de

ISBN 978-3-0356-2143-3 Hardcover edition
ISBN 978-3-0356-2144-0 Softcover edition
e-ISBN (PDF) 978-3-0356-2147-1

P.O. Box 44, 4009 Basel, Switzerland
Part of Walter de Gruyter GmbH, Berlin/Boston

987654321 www.birkhauser.com

景观设计学（中英文）
LANDSCAPE ARCHITECTURE FRONTIERS

中国科学引文数据库核心库来源期刊
A CSCD (Chinese Science Citation Database) Core Collection Journal

2015美国景观设计师协会交流类荣誉奖
2015 ASLA Honor Award of Communication Category

046 VOLUME 8 ISSUE 4
2020. 08
CN 10-1467/TU ISSN 2096-336X
NATIONAL CIRCULATION CODE 80-985

主管 中华人民共和国教育部
主办 高等教育出版社有限公司 北京大学
承办 北京大学建筑与景观设计学院
出版 高等教育出版社有限公司

SUPERVISOR Ministry of Education of the People's Republic of China
ADMINISTRATORS Higher Education Press Limited Company Peking University
ORGANIZER College of Architecture and Landscape, Peking University
PUBLISHER Higher Education Press Limited Company

目录

主编寄语

论文

观点与评论

主题实践

探索与过程

出版社 / **责任编辑** 张雪丽 / **地址** 北京市朝阳区惠新东街4号富盛大厦15层（100029）/ **网址** journal.hep.com.cn / **电话** 0086-10-5855 6534 / **编辑部** / **编辑部主任** 佘依爽 / **责任编辑** 田乐 / **编辑** 王颖、田晓劼（兼本期内容编辑）、王胤瑜、冉玲于、张健（兼）/ **探索与过程专栏编辑** 陆小璇 / **美术指导** 王江 / **美术编辑** 陈丽丽 / **海外编辑** 姜斌 / **地址** 北京市海淀区中关村北大街127-1号北大科技园303-3室（100080）/ **电话** 0086-10-6274 7821 / **电子邮箱** lafrontiers@foxmail.com / **网站** www. lafrontiers.com @景观设计学LAFrontiers / **支持机构** 中国城市科学研究会景观学与美丽中国建设专业委员会 景观中国网站 www.landscape.cn @景观中国网 / **运营** 佘依爽、王秀丽 / **运营咨询** 0086-10-6274 5785 / **订阅咨询** 0086-10-6274 7841 / **广告经营许可证号** 京西工商广字第0430号 / **印刷** 北京雅昌艺术印刷有限公司 / **国内发行** 北京怡然置业装饰设计书店 / **国际发行** 中国国际图书贸易总公司 / **邮发代号** 80-985 / **定价** RMB 58.00 HKD 100.00 TWD 450.00 USD 40.00 EUR 35.00

目标与范围

《景观设计学》定位于景观设计的学术研究与设计实践的交叉领域，探讨如何通过景观设计学途径，探索解决中国和世界生态与环境问题的新观念、新理论和新方法；通过介绍和推广前沿景观设计实践，倡导有助于实现美丽中国与美丽地球的新美学和新文化；架设研究与社会需求之间的桥梁、科学与艺术之间的桥梁，引领当代景观设计学科的发展。读者群为相关领域的科研人员和专业实践群体、院校师生、决策者和广大城乡环境的建设者。

Aims and Scope

Landscape Architecture Frontiers puts its focus on the intersecting spheres of academic research and design practice in landscape architecture, discussing new opinions, theories, and approaches to address environmental and ecological issues through landscape architecture; advocating new aesthetics and new culture which benefit the beauty of China and the world by introducing and promoting most recent practice of landscape architecture. It acts as a bridge connecting research and social needs, science and art, leading the development of the discipline. Our audience includes researchers and professional architects, faculties and students, policy makers in related fields, and people who work on the environmental constructions in both urban and rural areas.

CONTENTS

EDITORIAL

PAPERS

VIEWS & CRITICISMS

THEMATIC PRACTICES

EXPERIMENTS & PROCESSES

PUBLISHER | EXECUTIVE EDITOR ZHANG Xueli **ADD** 4 Huixin Dongjie, Beijing 100029, China **WEBSITE** journal.hep.com.cn **TEL** 0086-10-5855 6534 **EDITORIAL OFFICE** | EDITORIAL DIRECTOR SHE Yishuang EXECUTIVE EDITOR Tina TIAN EDITORS WANG Ying, TIAN Xiaojie (Editor-in-charge of this issue), WANG Yinyu, RAN Lingyu, Angus ZHANG **COLUMN HOST OF EXPERIMENTS AND PROCESSES** LU Xiaoxuan **ART DIRECTOR** WANG Jiang **GRAPHIC DESIGNER** Lily CHEN OVERSEAS EDITOR JIANG Bin **ADD** Rm. 303-3, Peking University Science Park, 127-1 Zhongguancun North Street, Haidian District, Beijing (100080) **TEL** 0086-10-6274 7821 **EMAIL** lafrontiers@foxmail.com **WEBSITE** www.lafrontiers.com **SUPPORTING ORGANIZATIONS** | The Committee of Landscape Architecture, Chinese Society for Urban Studies (CLA) www.landscape.cn **OPERATION TEAM** | SHE Yishuang, WANG Xiuli **BUSINESS INQUIRIES** | 0086-10-6274 5785 **SUBSCRIPTION INQUIRIES** | 0086-10-6274 7841 **PRINTED BY** | Beijing Artron Colour Printing Co., Ltd. **GENERAL AGENCY IN CHINA** | Beijing Yiran Bookshop **GENERAL AGENCY ABROAD** | China International Book Trading Corporation **PRICE** | RMB 58.00 HKD 100.00 TWD 450.00 USD 40.00 EUR 35.00